Lecture Notes in Artificial Intelligence 2837
Edited by J. G. Carbonell and J. Siekmann

Subseries of Lecture Notes in Computer Science

Springer
*Berlin
Heidelberg
New York
Hong Kong
London
Milan
Paris
Tokyo*

Nada Lavrač Dragan Gamberger
Hendrik Blockeel Ljupčo Todorovski (Eds.)

Machine Learning: ECML 2003

14th European Conference on Machine Learning
Cavtat-Dubrovnik, Croatia, September 22-26, 2003
Proceedings

 Springer

Series Editors

Jaime G. Carbonell, Carnegie Mellon University, Pittsburgh, PA, USA
Jörg Siekmann, University of Saarland, Saarbrücken, Germany

Volume Editors

Nada Lavrač
Ljupčo Todorovski
Jožef Stefan Institute, Dept. of Intelligent Systems
Jamova 39, 1000 Ljubljana, Slovenia
E-mail:{Nada.Lavrac/Ljupco.Todorovski}@ijs.si

Dragan Gamberger
Rudjer Bošković Institute
Bijenička 54, 10000 Zagreb, Croatia
E-mail: Dragan.Gamberger@irb.hr

Hendrik Blockeel
Katholieke Universiteit Leuven, Dept. of Computer Science
Celestijnenlaan 200A, 3001 Leuven, Belgium
E-mail: Hendrik.Blockeel@cs.kuleuven.ac.be

Cataloging-in-Publication Data applied for

A catalog record for this book is available from the Library of Congress

Bibliographic information published by Die Deutsche Bibliothek
Die Deutsche Bibliothek lists this publication in the Deutsche Nationalbibliographie;
detailed bibliographic data is available in the Internet at <http://dnb.ddb.de>.

CR Subject Classification (1998): I.2, F.2.2, F.4.1

ISSN 0302-9743
ISBN 3-540-20121-1 Springer-Verlag Berlin Heidelberg New York

This work is subject to copyright. All rights are reserved, whether the whole or part of the material is
concerned, specifically the rights of translation, reprinting, re-use of illustrations, recitation, broadcasting,
reproduction on microfilms or in any other way, and storage in data banks. Duplication of this publication
or parts thereof is permitted only under the provisions of the German Copyright Law of September 9, 1965,
in its current version, and permission for use must always be obtained from Springer-Verlag. Violations are
liable for prosecution under the German Copyright Law.

Springer-Verlag Berlin Heidelberg New York,
a member of BertelsmannSpringer Science+Business Media GmbH

http://www.springer.de

© Springer-Verlag Berlin Heidelberg 2003
Printed in Germany

Typesetting: Camera-ready by author, data conversion by Olgun Computergrafik
Printed on acid-free paper   SPIN: 10955628   06/3142   5 4 3 2 1 0

Preface

The proceedings of ECML/PKDD 2003 are published in two volumes: the *Proceedings of the 14th European Conference on Machine Learning* (LNAI 2837) and the *Proceedings of the 7th European Conference on Principles and Practice of Knowledge Discovery in Databases* (LNAI 2838). The two conferences were held on September 22–26, 2003 in Cavtat, a small tourist town in the vicinity of Dubrovnik, Croatia.

As machine learning and knowledge discovery are two highly related fields, the co-location of both conferences is beneficial for both research communities. In Cavtat, ECML and PKDD were co-located for the third time in a row, following the successful co-location of the two European conferences in Freiburg (2001) and Helsinki (2002). The co-location of ECML 2003 and PKDD 2003 resulted in a joint program for the two conferences, including paper presentations, invited talks, tutorials, and workshops.

Out of 332 submitted papers, 40 were accepted for publication in the ECML 2003 proceedings, and 40 were accepted for publication in the PKDD 2003 proceedings. All the submitted papers were reviewed by three referees. In addition to submitted papers, the conference program consisted of four invited talks, four tutorials, seven workshops, two tutorials combined with a workshop, and a discovery challenge.

We wish to express our gratitude to

- the authors of submitted papers,
- the program committee members, for thorough and timely paper evaluation,
- invited speakers Pieter Adriaans, Leo Breiman, Christos Faloutsos, and Donald B. Rubin,
- tutorial and workshop chairs Stefan Kramer, Luis Torgo, and Luc Dehaspe,
- local and technical organization committee members,
- advisory board members Luc De Raedt, Tapio Elomaa, Peter Flach, Heikki Mannila, Arno Siebes, and Hannu Toivonen,
- awards and grants committee members Dunja Mladenić, Rob Holte, and Michael May,
- Richard van der Stadt for the development of CyberChair which was used to support the paper submission and evaluation process,
- Alfred Hofmann of Springer-Verlag for co-operation in publishing the proceedings, and finally
- we gratefully acknowledge the financial support of the Croatian Ministry of Science and Technology, Slovenian Ministry of Education, Science, and Sports, and the Knowledge Discovery Network of Excellence (KDNet). KDNet also sponsored the student grants and best paper awards, while Kluwer Academic Publishers (the Machine Learning Journal) awarded a prize for the best student paper.

We hope and trust that the week in Cavtat in late September 2003 will be remembered as a fruitful, challenging, and enjoyable scientific and social event.

June 2003

Nada Lavrač
Dragan Gamberger
Hendrik Blockeel
Ljupčo Todorovski

ECML/PKDD 2003 Organization

Executive Committee

Program Chairs:	Nada Lavrač (Jožef Stefan Institute, Slovenia) ECML and PKDD chair
	Dragan Gamberger (Rudjer Bošković Institute, Croatia) ECML and PKDD co-chair
	Hendrik Blockeel (Katholieke Universiteit Leuven, Belgium) ECML co-chair
	Ljupčo Todorovski (Jožef Stefan Institute, Slovenia) PKDD co-chair
Tutorial and Workshop Chair:	Stefan Kramer (Technische Universität München, Germany)
Workshop Co-chair:	Luis Torgo (University of Porto, Portugal)
Tutorial Co-chair:	Luc Dehaspe (PharmaDM, Belgium)
Challenge Chair:	Petr Berka (University of Economics, Prague, Czech Republic)
Advisory Board:	Luc De Raedt (Albert-Ludwigs University Freiburg, Germany)
	Tapio Elomaa (University of Helsinki, Finland)
	Peter Flach (University of Bristol, UK)
	Heikki Mannila (Helsinki Institute for Information Technology, Finland)
	Arno Siebes (Utrecht University, The Netherlands)
	Hannu Toivonen (University of Helsinki, Finland)
Awards and Grants Committee:	Dunja Mladenić (Jožef Stefan Institute, Slovenia)
	Rob Holte (University of Alberta, Canada)
	Michael May (Fraunhofer AIS, Germany)
	Hendrik Blockeel (Katholieke Universiteit Leuven, Belgium)
Local Chairs:	Dragan Gamberger, Tomislav Šmuc (Rudjer Bošković Institute)
Organization Committee:	Darek Krzywania, Celine Vens, Jan Struyf (Katholieke Universiteit Leuven, Belgium), Damjan Demšar, Branko Kavšek, Milica Bauer, Bernard Ženko, Peter Ljubič (Jožef Stefan Institute, Slovenia), Mirna Benat (Rudjer Bošković Institute), Dalibor Ivušić (The Polytechnic of Dubrovnik, Croatia), Zdenko Sonicki (University of Zagreb, Croatia)

ECML 2003 Program Committee

H. Blockeel, Belgium
A. van den Bosch, The Netherlands
H. Boström, Sweden
I. Bratko, Slovenia
P. Brazdil, Portugal
W. Buntine, Finland
M. Craven, USA
N. Cristianini, USA
J. Cussens, UK
W. Daelemans, Belgium
L. Dehaspe, Belgium
L. De Raedt, Germany
S. Džeroski, Slovenia
T. Elomaa, Finland
F. Esposito, Italy
B. Filipič, Slovenia
P. Flach, UK
J. Fürnkranz, Austria
J. Gama, Portugal
D. Gamberger, Croatia
J.-G. Ganascia, France
L. Getoor, USA
H. Hirsh, USA
T. Hofmann, USA
T. Horvath, Germany
T. Joachims, USA
D. Kazakov, UK
R. Khardon, USA
Y. Kodratoff, France
I. Kononenko, Slovenia
S. Kramer, Germany
M. Kubat, USA
S. Kwek, USA
N. Lavrač, Slovenia
C. Ling, Canada
R. López de Màntaras, Spain
D. Malerba, Italy
H. Mannila, Finland
S. Matwin, Canada
J. del R. Millán, Switzerland
D. Mladenić, Slovenia
K. Morik, Germany
H. Motoda, Japan
R. Nock, France
D. Page, USA
G. Paliouras, Greece
B. Pfahringer, New Zealand
E. Plaza, Spain
J. Rousu, Finland
C. Rouveirol, France
L. Saitta, Italy
T. Scheffer, Germany
M. Sebag, France
J. Shawe-Taylor, UK
A. Siebes, The Netherlands
D. Sleeman, UK
R.H. Sloan, USA
M. van Someren, The Netherlands
P. Stone, USA
J. Suykens, Belgium
H. Tirri, Finland
L. Todorovski, Slovenia
L. Torgo, Portugal
P. Turney, Canada
P. Vitanyi, The Netherlands
S.M. Weiss, USA
G. Widmer, Austria
M. Wiering, The Netherlands
R. Wirth, Germany
S. Wrobel, Germany
T. Zeugmann, Germany
B. Zupan, Slovenia

PKDD 2003 Program Committee

H. Ahonen-Myka, Finland
E. Baralis, Italy
R. Bellazzi, Italy
M.R. Berthold, USA
H. Blockeel, Belgium
M. Bohanec, Slovenia
J.F. Boulicaut, France
B. Crémilleux, France
L. Dehaspe, Belgium
L. De Raedt, Germany
S. Džeroski, Slovenia
T. Elomaa, Finland
M. Ester, Canada
A. Feelders, The Netherlands
R. Feldman, Israel
P. Flach, UK
E. Frank, New Zealand
A. Freitas, UK
J. Fürnkranz, Austria
D. Gamberger, Croatia
F. Giannotti, Italy
C. Giraud-Carrier, Switzerland
M. Grobelnik, Slovenia
H.J. Hamilton, Canada
J. Han, USA
R. Hilderman, Canada
H. Hirsh, USA
S.J. Hong, USA
F. Höppner, Germany
S. Kaski, Finland
J.-U. Kietz, Switzerland
R.D. King, UK
W. Kloesgen, Germany
Y. Kodratoff, France
J.N. Kok, The Netherlands
S. Kramer, Germany
N. Lavrač, Slovenia
G. Manco, Italy

H. Mannila, Finland
S. Matwin, Canada
M. May, Germany
D. Mladenić, Slovenia
S. Morishita, Japan
H. Motoda, Japan
G. Nakhaeizadeh, Germany
C. Nédellec, France
D. Page, USA
Z.W. Ras, USA
J. Rauch, Czech Republic
G. Ritschard, Switzerland
M. Sebag, France
F. Sebastiani, Italy
M. Sebban, France
A. Siebes, The Netherlands
A. Skowron, Poland
M. van Someren, The Netherlands
M. Spiliopoulou, Germany
N. Spyratos, France
R. Stolle, USA
E. Suzuki, Japan
A. Tan, Singapore
L. Todorovski, Slovenia
H. Toivonen, Finland
L. Torgo, Portugal
S. Tsumoto, Japan
A. Unwin, Germany
K. Wang, Canada
L. Wehenkel, Belgium
D. Wettschereck, Germany
G. Widmer, Austria
R. Wirth, Germany
S. Wrobel, Germany
M.J. Zaki, USA
D.A. Zighed, France
B. Zupan, Slovenia

ECML/PKDD 2003 Additional Reviewers

F. Aiolli
A. Amrani
A. Appice
E. Armengol
I. Autio
J. Azé
I. Azzini
M. Baglioni
A. Banerjee
T.M.A. Basile
M. Bendou
M. Berardi
G. Beslon
M. Bevk
A. Blumenstock
D. Bojadžiev
M. Borth
J. Brank
P. Brockhausen
M. Ceci
E. Cesario
S. Chiusano
J. Clech
A. Cornuéjols
J. Costa
T. Curk
M. Degemmis
D. Demšar
J. Demšar
M. Denecker
N. Di Mauro
K. Driessens
T. Erjavec
T. Euler
N. Fanizzi
S. Ferilli
M. Fernandes
D. Finton
S. Flesca
J. Franke
F. Furfaro
T. Gärtner
P. Garza

L. Geng
A. Giacometti
T. Giorgino
B. Goethals
M. Grabert
E. Gyftodimos
W. Hämäläinen
A. Habrard
M. Hall
S. Hoche
E. Hüllermeier
L. Jacobs
A. Jakulin
T.Y. Jen
B. Jeudy
A. Jorge
R.J. Jun
P. Juvan
M. Kääriäinen
K. Karimi
K. Kersting
J. Kindermann
S. Kiritchenko
W. Kosters
I. Koychev
M. Kukar
S. Lallich
C. Larizza
D. Laurent
G. Leban
S.D. Lee
G. Legrand
E. Leopold
J. Leskovec
O. Licchelli
J.T. Lindgren
F.A. Lisi
T. Malinen
O. Matte-Tailliez
A. Mazzanti
P. Medas
R. Meo
T. Mielikäinen

H.S. Nguyen
S. Nijssen
A. Nowé
M. Ohtani
S. Ontañón
R. Ortale
M. Ould Abdel Vetah
G. Paaß
I. Palmisano
J. Peltonen
L. Peña
D. Pedreschi
G. Petasis
J. Petrak
V. Phan Luong
D. Pierrakos
U. Rückert
S. Rüping
J. Ramon
S. Ray
C. Rigotti
F. Rioult
M. Robnik-Šikonja
M. Roche
B. Rosenfeld
A. Sadikov
T. Saito
E. Savia
C. Savu-Krohn
G. Schmidberger
M. Scholz
A.K. Seewald
J. Sese
G. Sigletos
T. Silander
D. Slezak
C. Soares
D. Sonntag
H.-M. Suchier
B. Sudha
P. Synak
A. Tagarelli
Y. Tzitzikas

R. Vilalta   M. Wurst   I. Zogalis
D. Vladušič   R.J. Yan   W. Zou
X. Wang   X. Yan   M. Žnidaršič
A. Wojna   H. Yao   B. Ženko
J. Wróblewski   X. Yin

ECML/PKDD 2003 Tutorials

KD Standards
Sarabjot S. Anand, Marko Grobelnik, and Dietrich Wettschereck

Data Mining and Machine Learning in Time Series Databases
Eamonn Keogh

Exploratory Analysis of Spatial Data and Decision Making Using Interactive Maps and Linked Dynamic Displays
Natalia Andrienko and Gennady Andrienko

Music Data Mining
Darrell Conklin

ECML/PKDD 2003 Workshops

First European Web Mining Forum
Bettina Berendt, Andreas Hotho, Dunja Mladenić, Maarten van Someren, Myra Spiliopoulou, and Gerd Stumme

Multimedia Discovery and Mining
Dunja Mladenić and Gerhard Paaß

Data Mining and Text Mining in Bioinformatics
Tobias Scheffer and Ulf Leser

Knowledge Discovery in Inductive Databases
Jean-François Boulicaut, Sašo Džeroski, Mika Klemettinen, Rosa Meo, and Luc De Raedt

Graph, Tree, and Sequence Mining
Luc De Raedt and Takashi Washio

Probabilistic Graphical Models for Classification
Pedro Larrañaga, Jose A. Lozano, Jose M. Peña, and Iñaki Inza

Parallel and Distributed Computing for Machine Learning
Rui Camacho and Ashwin Srinivasan

Discovery Challenge: A Collaborative Effort in Knowledge Discovery from Databases
Petr Berka, Jan Rauch, and Shusaku Tsumoto

ECML/PKDD 2003 Joint Tutorials-Workshops

Learning Context-Free Grammars
Colin de la Higuera, Jose Oncina, Pieter Adriaans, Menno van Zaanen

Adaptive Text Extraction and Mining
Fabio Ciravegna, Nicholas Kushmerick

Table of Contents

Invited Papers

From Knowledge-Based to Skill-Based Systems:
Sailing as a Machine Learning Challenge 1
   Pieter Adriaans

Two-Eyed Algorithms and Problems.................................. 9
   Leo Breiman

Next Generation Data Mining Tools: Power Laws and Self-similarity
for Graphs, Streams and Traditional Data........................... 10
   Christos Faloutsos

Taking Causality Seriously: Propensity Score Methodology Applied
to Estimate the Effects of Marketing Interventions 16
   Donald B. Rubin

Contributed Papers

Support Vector Machines with Example Dependent Costs 23
   Ulf Brefeld, Peter Geibel, and Fritz Wysotzki

Abalearn: A Risk-Sensitive Approach to Self-play Learning in Abalone.... 35
   Pedro Campos and Thibault Langlois

Life Cycle Modeling of News Events Using Aging Theory 47
   Chien Chin Chen, Yao-Tsung Chen, Yeali Sun, and Meng Chang Chen

Unambiguous Automata Inference by Means of State-Merging Methods ... 60
   François Coste and Daniel Fredouille

Could Active Perception Aid Navigation
of Partially Observable Grid Worlds? 72
   Paul A. Crook and Gillian Hayes

Combined Optimization of Feature Selection and Algorithm Parameters
in Machine Learning of Language 84
   *Walter Daelemans, Véronique Hoste, Fien De Meulder,
   and Bart Naudts*

Iteratively Extending Time Horizon Reinforcement Learning............. 96
   Damien Ernst, Pierre Geurts, and Louis Wehenkel

Volume under the ROC Surface for Multi-class Problems 108
  César Ferri, José Hernández-Orallo, and Miguel Angel Salido

Improving the AUC of Probabilistic Estimation Trees 121
  César Ferri, Peter A. Flach, and José Hernández-Orallo

Scaled CGEM: A Fast Accelerated EM 133
  Jörg Fischer and Kristian Kersting

Pairwise Preference Learning and Ranking 145
  Johannes Fürnkranz and Eyke Hüllermeier

A New Way to Introduce Knowledge into Reinforcement Learning 157
  Pascal Garcia

Improvement of the State Merging Rule on Noisy Data
in Probabilistic Grammatical Inference 169
  Amaury Habrard, Marc Bernard, and Marc Sebban

COllective INtelligence with Sequences of Actions –
Coordinating Actions in Multi-agent Systems 181
  Pieter Jan 't Hoen and Sander M. Bohte

Rademacher Penalization over Decision Tree Prunings 193
  Matti Kääriäinen and Tapio Elomaa

Learning Rules to Improve a Machine Translation System 205
  David Kauchak and Charles Elkan

Optimising Performance of Competing Search Engines
in Heterogeneous Web Environments 217
  Rinat Khoussainov and Nicholas Kushmerick

Robust k-DNF Learning via Inductive Belief Merging 229
  Frédéric Koriche and Joël Quinqueton

Logistic Model Trees 241
  Niels Landwehr, Mark Hall, and Eibe Frank

Color Image Segmentation: Kernel Do the Feature Space 253
  Jianguo Lee, Jingdong Wang, and Changshui Zhang

Evaluation of Topographic Clustering and Its Kernelization 265
  Marie-Jeanne Lesot, Florence d'Alché-Buc, and Georges Siolas

A New Pairwise Ensemble Approach for Text Classification 277
  Yan Liu, Jaime Carbonell, and Rong Jin

Self-evaluated Learning Agent in Multiple State Games 289
  Koichi Moriyama and Masayuki Numao

Classification Approach towards Ranking and Sorting Problems 301
   *Shyamsundar Rajaram, Ashutosh Garg, Xiang Sean Zhou,
   and Thomas S. Huang*

Using MDP Characteristics to Guide Exploration
in Reinforcement Learning 313
   Bohdana Ratitch and Doina Precup

Experiments with Cost-Sensitive Feature Evaluation 325
   Marko Robnik-Šikonja

A Markov Network Based Factorized Distribution Algorithm
for Optimization 337
   Roberto Santana

On Boosting Improvement: Error Reduction and Convergence Speed-Up .. 349
   Marc Sebban and Henri-Maxime Suchier

Improving SVM Text Classification Performance
through Threshold Adjustment 361
   James G. Shanahan and Norbert Roma

Backoff Parameter Estimation for the DOP Model 373
   Khalil Sima'an and Luciano Buratto

Improving Numerical Prediction with Qualitative Constraints 385
   Dorian Šuc and Ivan Bratko

A Generative Model for Semantic Role Labeling 397
   Cynthia A. Thompson, Roger Levy, and Christopher D. Manning

Optimizing Local Probability Models for Statistical Parsing 409
   Kristina Toutanova, Mark Mitchell, and Christopher D. Manning

Extended Replicator Dynamics as a Key to Reinforcement Learning
in Multi-agent Systems 421
   Karl Tuyls, Dries Heytens, Ann Nowe, and Bernard Manderick

Visualizations for Assessing Convergence and Mixing of MCMC 432
   Jarkko Venna, Samuel Kaski, and Jaakko Peltonen

A Decomposition of Classes via Clustering to Explain
and Improve Naive Bayes 444
   Ricardo Vilalta and Irina Rish

Improving Rocchio with Weakly Supervised Clustering 456
   Romain Vinot and François Yvon

A Two-Level Learning Method for Generalized Multi-instance Problems .. 468
   Nils Weidmann, Eibe Frank, and Bernhard Pfahringer

Clustering in Knowledge Embedded Space 480
    Yungang Zhang, Changshui Zhang, and Shijun Wang

Ensembles of Multi-instance Learners.............................. 492
    Zhi-Hua Zhou and Min-Ling Zhang

Author Index 503

From Knowledge-Based to Skill-Based Systems: Sailing as a Machine Learning Challenge

Pieter Adriaans

FNWI / ILLC
University of Amsterdam
Plantage Muidergracht 24
1018 TV Amsterdam
The Netherlands
pietera@science.uva.nl
http://turing.wins.uva.nl/~pietera/ALS/

Abstract. This paper describes the Robosail project. It started in 1997 with the aim to build a self-learning auto pilot for a single handed sailing yacht. The goal was to make an adaptive system that would help a single handed sailor to go faster on average in a race. Presently, after five years of development and a number of sea trials, we have a commercial system available (www.robosail.com). It is a hybrid system using agent technology, machine learning, data mining and rule-based reasoning. Apart from describing the system we try to generalize our findings, and argue that sailing is an interesting paradigm for a class of hybrid systems that one could call Skill-based Systems.

1 Introduction

Sailing is a difficult sport that requires a lot of training and expert knowledge [1],[9],[6]. Recently the co-operation of crews on a boat has been studied in the domain of cognitive psychology [4]. In this paper we describe the Robosail system that aims at the development of self-learning steering systems for racing yachts [8]. We defend the view that this task is an example of what one could call skill-based systems. The connection between verbal reports of experts performing a certain task and the implementation of ML for those task is an interesting emerging research domain [3],[2], [7]. The system was tested in several real-life race events and is currently commercially available.

2 The Task

Modern single-handed sailing started its history with the organization of the first Observer Single-Handed Transatlantic Race (OSTAR) in 1960. Since that time the sport has known a tremendous development and is the source of many innovations in sailing. A single-handed skipper can only attend the helm for about 20% of his time. The rest is divided between boat-handling, navigation, preparing meals, doing repairs and sleeping. All single-handed races allow the skippers to use some kind of autopilot. In its simplest form such an autopilot is attached to a flux-gate compass and it can only maintain a compass course. More sophisticated autopilots use a variety of sensors (wind, heel, global positioning system etc.) to steer the boat optimally. In all races the use of engines to propel the boat and of electrical winches to operate the sails is forbidden. All boat-handling except steering is to be done with manual power only.

It is clear that a single-handed sailor will be less efficient than a full crew. Given the fact that a single-handed yacht operates on autopilot for more than 80 % of the time a slightly more efficient autopilot would already make a yacht more competitive. In a transatlantic crossing a skipper will alter course maybe once or twice a day based on meteorological data and information and from various other sources like the positions of the competitors. From an economic point of view the automatization of this task has no top priority. It is the optimization of the handling of the helm from second to second that offers the biggest opportunity for improvement. The task to be optimized is then: *steer the ship as fast as possible in a certain direction and give the skipper optimal support in terms of advice on boat-handling, early warnings, alerts etc.*

3 Introduction

Our initial approach to the limited task of maintaining the course of a vessel was to conceive it as a *pure machine learning task*. At any given moment the boat would be in a certain region of a complex state-space defined by the array of sensor inputs. There was a limited set of actions defined in terms of a force exercised on the rudder, and there was a reward defined in terms of the overall speed of the boat. Fairly soon it became clear that it was not possible to solve the problem in terms of simple optimization of a system in a state-space:

- There is no neutral theory-free description of the system. A sailing yacht is a system that exists on the border between two media with strong non-linear behavior, wind and water. The interaction between these media and the boat should ideally be modelled in terms of complex differential equations. A finite set of sensors will never be able to give enough information to analyze the system in all of its relevant aspects. A careful selection of sensors given economical, energy management and other practical constraint is necessary. In order to make this selection one needs a theory about what to measure.
- Furthermore, given the complexity of the mathematical description, there is no guarantee that the system will know regions of relative stability in which it can be controlled efficiently. The only indication we have that efficient control is possible is the fact that human experts do the task well, and the best guess as to select which sensors is the informal judgement of experts on the sort of information they need to perform the task. The array of sensors that 'describes' the system is in essence already anthropomorphic.
- Establishing the correct granularity of the measurements is a problem. Wind and wave information typically comes with the frequency of at least 10 hz.

But hidden in these signals are other concepts that exist only on a different timescale eg. gusts (above 10 seconds), veering (10 minutes) and sea-state (hours). A careful analysis of sensor information involved in sailing shows that sensors and the concepts that can be measured with them cluster in different time-frames (hundreds of seconds, minutes, hours). This is a strong indication for a modular architecture. The fact that at each level decisions of a different nature have to be taken strongly suggest an architecture that consists of a hierarchy of agents that operate in different time-frames: lower agents have a higher measurement granularity, higher agents a lower one.
– Even when a careful selection of sensors is made and an adequate agent-architecture is in place the convergence of the learning algorithms is a problem. Tabula rasa learning is in the context of sailing impossible. One has to start with a rough rule-based system that operates the boat reasonably well and use ML techniques to optimize the system.

In the end we developed a hybrid agent based system. It merges traditional AI techniques like rule based reasoning with more recent methods developed in the ML community. Essential for this kind of systems is the link between expert concepts that have a fuzzy nature and learning algorithms. A simple example of an expert rule in the Robosail system is: *If you sail close-hauled then luff in a gust*. This rule contains the concepts 'close-hauled', 'gust' and 'luff'. The system contains agents that represent these concepts:

– Course agent: If the apparent wind angle is between A and B then you sail close hauled
– Gust agent: If the average apparent wind increases by a factor D more than E seconds then there is a gust
– Luff agent: Steer Z degrees windward.

The related learning methodology then is:

– Task: Learn optimal values for A,B,C,D,E,Z
– Start with expert estimates then
– Optimize using ML techniques

This form of *symbol grounding* is an emerging area of research interest that seems to be of vital importance to the kind of skill-based systems like Robosail [8], [2], [7], [5].

4 The System

The main systems contains four agents: Skipper, Navigator, Watchman and Helmsman. These roles are more or less modelled after the task division on a modern racing yacht [9]. Each agent lives in a different time frame. the agents are ordered in a subsumption hierarchy. The skipper is intended to take strategical decisions with a time interval of say 3 to 6 hours. He has to take into account weather patterns, currents, seastate, chart info etc. Currently this process is only partly automated. It results in the determination of a waypoint, i.e. a location on the map where we want to arrive as soon as possible. The navigator and the watchman have the responsibility to get to the waypoint. The navigator deals with the more tactic aspects of this process. He knows the so-called polar diagrams of the boat and its behavior in various sea states. He also has a number of agents at his disposal that help him to asses the state of the ship: do we carry too much sail, is there too much current, is our trim correct etc. The reasoning of the navigator results in a compass course. This course could change within minutes. The watchman is responsible for keeping this course with optimal velocity in the constantly changing environment (waves, wind shifts etc.). He gives commands to the helmsman, whose only responsibility it is to make and execute plans to get and keep the rudder in certain positions in time.

The AI solution: a hybrid agent based approach

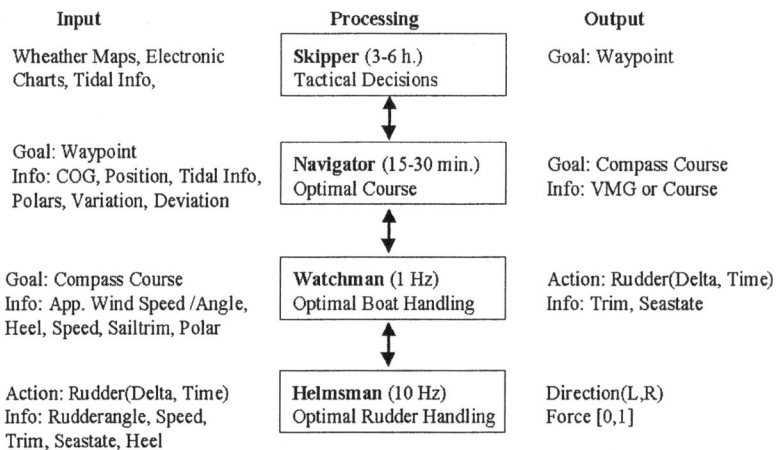

Fig. 1. The hierarchy of main agents

There are a number of core variables: log speed, apparent wind speed and angle, rudder angle, compass course, current position, course on ground and speed on ground. These are loaded into the kernel system. Apart from these core variables there are a number of other sensors that give information. Amongst others: canting angle mast, swivel angle keel, heel sideways, heel fore-aft, depth, sea state, wave direction, acceleration in various directions. Others will activate agents that warn for certain undesirable situations (i.e. depth, temperature of the water). Others are for the moment only used for human inspection (i.e. radar images). For each sensor we have to consider the balance between the contribution to speed and safety of the boat and the negative aspects like energy consumption, weight, increased complexity of the system.

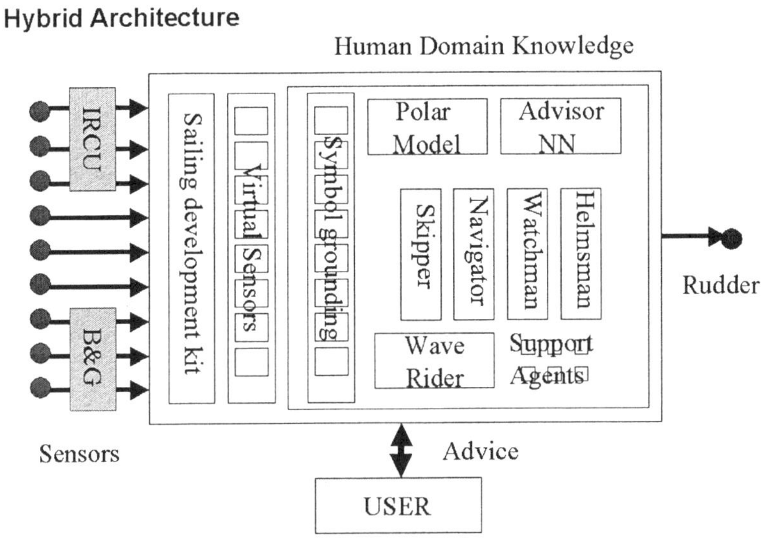

Hybrid Architecture

Fig. 2. The main architecture

The final system is a complex interplay between sensor-, agent- and network technology, machine learning and AI techniques brought together in a hybrid architecture. The hardware (CE radiation level requirements, water and shock proof, easy to mount and maintain) consists of:

- CAN bus architecture: Guaranteed delivery
- Odys Intelligent rudder control unit (IRCU): 20 kHz, max. 100 Amp (Extensive functions for self-diagnosis)
- Thetys Solid state digital motion sensor and compass
- Multifunction display
- Standard third party sensors with NMEA interface (e.g. B&G)

The software functionality involves:

- Agent based architecture
- Subsumption architecture
- Model builder: on line visual programming
- Real Time flow charting
- Relational database with third party datamining facility
- Web enabling
- Remote control and reporting

Machine Learning and AI techniques that are used:

- Watch man: Case Based Reasoning
- Helmsman: neural network on top of PID controller
- Advisor: nearest-neighbor search

- Agents and virtual sensors for symbol grounding
- Data-explorer with machine learning suite
- Waverider: 30 dimensional ARMA model
- Off line KDD effort: rule induction on the basis of fuzzy expert concepts

Several protypes of the Robsosail system have been tested over the years: the first version in the Single Handed Transatalantic in 2000, a second prototype was evaluated on board the Kingfisher during a trip from Brazil to the UK. A final evaluation was done on board of the Syllogic Sailing Lab during the Dual Round Britain and Ireland in 2002. In 2003 the first commercial version is available.

5 Lessons Learned

The Robosail application is a hybrid system that can be placed somewhere between pure rule-based systems and pure machine learning systems. The nature of these systems raises some interesting philosophical issues concerning the nature of rules and their linguistic representations. In the course of history people have *discovered* that certain systems can be built and controlled, without really understanding why this is the case. A sailing boat is such a system. It is what it is because of ill-understood hydro- and aerodynamical principles and has a certain form because the human body has to interact with it. It is thoroughly an anthropomorphic machine. Human beings can handle these systems, because they are the result of a long evolutionary process. Their senses are adapted to those regions of reality that are relatively stable and are sensitive to exactly those phase changes that give relevant information about the state of the systems. In a process of co-evolution the language to communicate about these concepts emerged. Specific concepts like 'wave', 'gust' and 'veering' exist because they mark relevant changes of the system. Their cognitive status however is complex, and it appears to be non-trivial to develop automated systems that discover these concepts on the basis of sensor data.

A deeper discussion of these issues would have to incorporate an analysis of the nature of rules that is beyond the scope of this paper. The rules of a game like chess exist independently of their verbal representation. We use the verbal representation to communicate with others about the game and to train young players. A useful distinction is the one between *constitutive rules* and *regulative rules*. The constitutive rules define the game. If they are broken the game stops. An example for chess would be: *You may not move a piece to a square already occupied by one of your own pieces.* Regulative rules define good strategies for the game. If you break them you diminish your chances of winning, but the game does not stop. An example of a regulative rule for chess would be: *When you are considering giving up some of your pieces for some of your opponent's, you should think about the values of the men, and not just how many each player possesses.* Regulative rules represent the experience of expert players. They have a certain fuzzyness and it is difficult to implement them in pure knowledge-based systems. The only way we can communicate about skills is in terms of regulative rules. The rule *If you sail clause hauled then luff in gust* is an example. Verbal reports of experts in terms of regulative rules can play an important role in the design of systems. From a formal point of view they reduce the complexity of the task. They tell us *where to look* in the state space of the system. From a cognitive point of view they play a similar role in teaching skills. They tell the student roughly what to do. The fine tuning of the skill is then a matter of training.

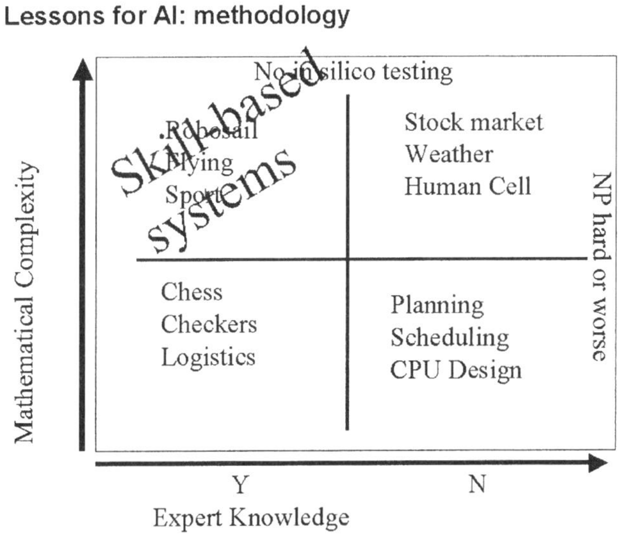

Lessons for AI: methodology

	No in silico testing	
Robosail Flying Sports	Stock market Weather Human Cell	
Chess Checkers Logistics	Planning Scheduling CPU Design	

Mathematical Complexity ↑ — NP hard or worse

Expert Knowledge: Y / N →

Fig. 3. A taxonomy of systems

This discussion suggests that we can classify tasks in two dimensions: 1) The expert dimension: Do human agents perform well on the task and can they report verbally on their actions and 2) The formal dimension: do we have adequate formal models of the task that allow us to perform tests in silico? For chess and a number of other tasks that were analyzed in the early stages of AI research the answer to both questions is yes. Operations research studies systems for which the first answer is no and the second answer is yes. For sailing the answer to the first question is positive, the answer to the second question negative. This is typical for skill-based systems. This situation has a number of interesting methodological consequences: we need to incorporate the knowledge of human experts into our system, but this knowledge in itself is fundamentally incomplete and needs to be embedded in an adaptive environment. Naturally this leads to issues concerning symbol grounding, modelling human judgements, hybrid architectures and many other fundamental questions relevant for the construction of ML applications in this domain.

A simple sketch of a methodology to develop skill-based systems would be:

– Select sensor type and range based on expert input
– Develop partial model based on expert terminology

- Create agents that emulate expert judgements
- Refine model using machine learning techniques
- Evaluate model with expert

6 Conclusion and Further Research

In this paper we have sketched our experiences creating an integrated system for steering a sailing yacht. The value of such practical projects can hardly be overestimated. Building real life systems is 80% engineering and 20% science. One of the insights we developed is the notion of the existence of a special class of skill-based systems. Issues in constructing these systems are: the need for a hybrid architecture, the interplay between discursive rules (expert system, rule induction)and senso-motoric skills (pid-controllers, neural networks), a learning approach, agent technology, the importance of semantics and symbol grounding and the importance of jargon. The nature of skill-based systems raises interesting philosophical issues concerning the nature of rules and their verbal representations.

In the near future we intend to develop more advanced systems. The current autopilot is optimized to sail as fast as possible from A to B. A next generation would also address tactical and strategic tasks, tactical: win the race (modelling your opponents), strategic: bring the crew safely to the other side of the ocean. Other interesting ambitions are: the construction of better autopilots for multihulls, the design an ultra-safe autonomous cruising yacht, establish an official speed record for autonomous sailing yachts and deploy the Robosail technology in other areas like the Automotive industry and aviation industry.

References

1. Frank Bethwaite. *High Performance Sailing*. Thomas Reed Publications, 1996.
2. Xia Chris Harris, Hong and Qiang Gan. *Adaptive Modelling, Estimation and Fusion from Data*. Springer, 2002.
3. Ross Garret. *The Symmetry of sailing*. Sheridan House, 1987.
4. Edwin Hutchins. *Cognition in the wild*. MIT Press, 1995.
5. N.K. Poulsen M. Nørgaard, O. Ravn and L.K. Hansen. *Neural Networks for Modelling and Control of Dynamic Systems*. Springer, 2000.
6. C.A. Marchaj. *Sail Performance, theory and practice*. Adlard Coles Nautical, 1996.
7. Tano Shun'Ichi Takeshi Furuhashi and Hans-Arno Jacobson. *Deep Fusion of Computational and Symbolic Processing*. Physica Verlag, 2001.
8. Martijn van Aartrijk, Claudio Tagliola, and Pieter Adriaans. Ai on the ocean: The robosail project. In Frank van Harmelen (Editor), editor, *Proceedings of the 15th European Conference on Artificial Intelligence*, pages 653–657. IOS Press, 2002.
9. Cornelis van Rietschoten and Barry Pickthall. *Blue Water Racing*. Dodd, Mead & Company, 1985.

Two-Eyed Algorithms and Problems

Leo Breiman

Department of Statistics, University of California, Berkeley
leo@stat.Berkeley.Edu

Two-eyed algorithms are complex prediction algorithms that give accurate predictions and also give important insights into the structure of the data the algorithm is processing. The main example I discuss is RF/tools, a collection of algorithms for classification, regression and multiple dependent outputs. The last algorithm is a preliminary version and further progress depends on solving some fascinating questions of the characterization of dependency between variables.

An important and intriguing aspect of the classification version of RF/tools is that it can be used to analyze unsupervised data–that is, data without class labels. This conversion leads to such by-products as clustering, outlier detection, and replacement of missing data for unsupervised data.

The talk will present numerous results on real data sets. The code (f77) and ample documentation for RFtools is available on the web site
www.stat.berkeley.edu/RFtools.

References

1. Leo Breiman. Random forests. *Machine Learning*, 45(1):5–32, 2001.

Next Generation Data Mining Tools: Power Laws and Self-similarity for Graphs, Streams and Traditional Data

Christos Faloutsos

School of Computer Science, Carnegie Mellon University, Pittsburgh, PA
christos@cs.cmu.edu

Abstract. What patterns can we find in a bursty web traffic? On the web or internet graph itself? How about the distributions of galaxies in the sky, or the distribution of a company's customers in geographical space? How long should we expect a nearest-neighbor search to take, when there are 100 attributes per patient or customer record? The traditional assumptions (uniformity, independence, Poisson arrivals, Gaussian distributions), often fail miserably. Should we give up trying to find patterns in such settings?
Self-similarity, fractals and power laws are extremely successful in describing real datasets (coast-lines, rivers basins, stock-prices, brain-surfaces, communication-line noise, to name a few). We show some old and new successes, involving modeling of graph topologies (internet, web and social networks); modeling galaxy and video data; dimensionality reduction; and more.

Introduction – Problem Definition

The goal of data mining is to find patterns; we typically look for the Gaussian patterns that appear often in practice and on which we have all been trained so well. However, here we show that these time-honored concepts (Gaussian, Poisson, uniformity, independence), often fail to model real distributions well. Further more, we show how to fill the gap with the lesser-known, but even more powerful tools of self-similarity and power laws.

We focus on the following applications:

- Given a cloud of points, what patterns can we find in it?
- Given a time sequence, what patterns can we find? How to characterize and anticipate its bursts?
- Given a graph (e.g., social, or computer network), how does it look like? Which is the most important node? Which nodes should we immunize first, to guard against biological or computer viruses?

All three settings appear extremely often, with vital applications. Clouds of points appear in traditional relational databases, where records with k-attributes become points in k-d spaces; e.g. a relation with patient data (age, blood pressure, etc.); in geographical information systems (GIS), where points can be, e.g., cities on a two-dimensional map; in medical image databases with, for example, three-dimensional brain scans, where we want to find patterns in the brain activation [ACF+93]; in multimedia databases, where objects can be represented as points in feature space [FRM94]. In all these settings, the distribution of k-d points is seldom (if ever) uniform [Chr84], [FK94]. Thus, it is important to characterize the deviation from uniformity in a succinct way (e.g. as a sum of Gaussians, or something even more suitable). Such a description is vital for data mining [AIS93],[AS94], for hypothesis testing and rule discovery. A succinct description of a k-d point-set could help reject quickly some false hypotheses, or could help provide hints about hidden rules.

A second, very popular class of applications is time sequences. Time sequences appear extremely often, with a huge literature on linear [BJR94], and non-linear forecasting [CE92], and the recent surge of interest on sensor data [OJW03] [PBF03] [GGR02]

Finally, graphs, networks and their surprising regularities/laws have been attracting significant interest recently. The applications are diverse, and the discoveries are striking. The World Wide Web is probably the most impressive graph, which motivated significant discoveries: the famous Kleinberg algorithm [Kle99] and its closely related PageRank algorithm of Google fame [BP98]; the fact that it obeys a "bow-tie" structure [BKM+00], while still having a surprising small diameter [AJB99]. Similar startling discoveries have been made in parallel for power laws in the Internet topology [FFF99], for Peer-to-Peer (gnutella/Kazaa) overlay graphs [RFI02], and for who-trusts-whom in the epinions.com network [RD02]. Finding patterns, laws and regularities in large real networks has numerous applications, exactly because graphs are so general and ubiquitous: Link analysis, for criminology and law enforcement [CSH+03]; analysis of virus propagation patterns, on both social/e-mail as well as physical-contact networks [WKE00]; networks of regulatory genes; networks of interacting proteins [Bar02]; food webs, to help us understand the importance of an endangered species.

We show that the theory of fractals provide powerful tools to solve the above problems.

Definitions

Intuitively, a set of points is a fractal if it exhibits self-similarity over all scales. This is illustrated by an example: Figure 1(a) shows the first few steps in constructing the so-called *Sierpinski triangle*. Figure 1(b) gives 5,000 points that belong to this triangle. Theoretically, the Sierpinski triangle is derived from an equilateral triangle ABC by excluding its middle (triangle A'B'C') and by recursively repeating this procedure for each of the resulting smaller triangles. The resulting set of points exhibits 'holes' in any scale; moreover, each smaller triangle is a *miniature replica* of the whole triangle. In general, the characteristic of fractals is this *self-similarity* property: parts of the fractal are similar (exactly or statistically) to the whole fractal. For our experiments we use 5,000 sample points from the Sierpinski triangle, using Barnsley's algorithm of Iterated Function Systems [BS88] to generated these points quickly.

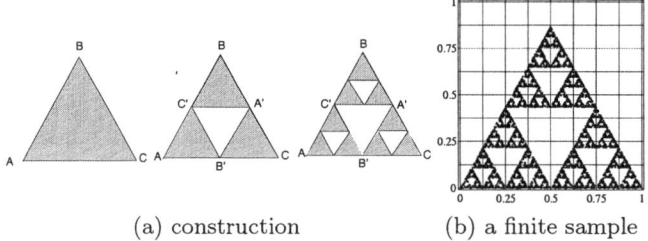

(a) construction   (b) a finite sample

Fig. 1. Theoretical fractals: the Sierpinski triangle (a) the first 3 steps of its recursive construction (b) a finite sample of it (5K points)

Notice that the resulting point set is neither a 1-dimensional Euclidean object (it has infinite length), nor 2-dimensional (it has zero area). The solution is to consider *fractional* dimensionalities, which are called *fractal dimensions*. Among the many definitions, we describe the *correlation* fractal dimension, D, because it is the easiest to describe and to use.

Let $nb(\epsilon)$ be the average number of neighbors of an arbitrary point, within distance ϵ or less. For a real, finite cloud of E-dimensional points, we follow [Sch91] and say that this data set is *self-similar in the range of scales* r_1, r_2 if

$$nb(\epsilon) \propto \epsilon^D \qquad r_1 \leq \epsilon \leq r_2 \qquad (1)$$

The *correlation integral* is defined as the plot of $nb(\epsilon)$ versus ϵ in log-log scales; for self-similar datasets, it is linear with slope D.

Notice that the above definition of fractal dimension D encompasses the traditional Euclidean objects: lines, line segments, circles, and all the standard curves have $D=1$; planes, disks and standard surfaces have $D=2$; Euclidean volumes in E-dimensional space have $D = E$.

Discussion – How Frequent Are Self-similar Datasets?

The reader might be wondering whether any real datasets behave like fractals, with linear correlation integrals. *Numerous* the real datasets give linear correlation integrals, including longitude-latitude coordinates of stars in the sky, population-versus-area of the countries of the world [FK94]; several geographic datasets [BF95] [FK94]; medical datasets [FG96]; automobile-part shape datasets [BBB+97,BBKK97].

There is overwhelming evidence from multiple disciplines that fractal datasets appear *surprisingly* often [Man77](p. 447),[Sch91]:

- coast lines and country borders ($D \approx 1.1$ - 1.3);
- the periphery of clouds and rainfall patches ($D \approx 1.35$)[Sch91](p.231);
- the distribution of galaxies in the universe ($D \approx 1.23$);
- stock prices and random walks ($D=1.5$)
- the brain surface of mammals ($D \approx 2.7$);
- the human vascular system ($D = 3$, because it has to reach every cell in the body!)
- even traditional Euclidean objects have linear box-counting plots, with integer slopes

Discussion – Power Laws

Self-similarity and power laws are closely related. A *power law* is a law of the form

$$y = f(x) = x^a \qquad (2)$$

Power laws are the only laws that have no characteristic scales, in the sense that they remain power laws, even if we change the scale: $f(c * x) = c^a * x^a$

Exactly for this reason, power laws and self-similarity appear often together: if a cloud of points is self similar, it has no characteristic scales; any law/pattern it obeys, should also have no characteristic scale, and it should thus be a power law.

Power laws also appear extremely often, in diverse settings: in text, with the famous Zipf law [Zip49]; in distributions of income (the Pareto law); in scientific citation analysis (Lotka law); in distribution of areas of lakes, islands and animal habitats (Korcak's law [Sch91,HS93,PF01]) in earthquake analysis (Gutenberg-Richter law [Bak96]; in LAN traffic [LTWW94]; in web click-streams [MF01]; and countless more settings.

Conclusions

Self-similarity and power laws can solve data mining problems that traditional methods can not. The two major tools that we cover in the talk are: (a) the "correlation integral" [Sch91] for a set of points and (b) the "rank-frequency" plot [Zip49] for categorical data. The former can estimate the intrinsic dimensionality of a cloud of points, and it can help with dimensionality reduction [TTWF00], axis scaling [WF02], and separability [TTPF01]. The rank-frequency plot can spot power laws, like the Zipf's law, and many more.

References

[ACF+93] Manish Arya, William Cody, Christos Faloutsos, Joel Richardson, and Arthur Toga. QBISM: A prototype 3-D medical image database system. *IEEE Data Engineering Bulletin*, 16(1):38–42, March 1993.

[AIS93] Rakesh Agrawal, Tomasz Imielinski, and Arun Swami. Mining association rules between sets of items in large databases. In *Proc. ACM SIGMOD*, pages 207–216, Washington, DC, May 26-28 1993.

[AJB99]   R. Albert, H. Jeong, and A.-L. Barabasi. Diameter of the world-wide web. *Nature*, 401:130–131, September 1999.
[AS94]   Rakesh Agrawal and Ramakrishnan Srikant. Fast algorithms for mining association rules in large databases. In *Proc. of VLDB Conf.*, pages 487–499, Santiago, Chile, Sept. 12-15 1994.
[Bak96]   Per Bak. How nature works : The science of self-organized criticality, September 1996.
[Bar02]   Albert-Laszlo Barabasi. *Linked: The New Science of Networks*. Perseus Publishing, first edition, May 2002.
[BBB+97]   Stefan Berchtold, Christian Boehm, Bernhard Braunmueller, Daniel A. Keim, and Hans-Peter Kriegel. Fast similarity search in multimedia databases. In *SIGMOD Conference*, pages 1–12, 1997.
[BBKK97]   Stefan Berchtold, Christian Boehm, Daniel A. Keim, and Hans-Peter Kriegel. A cost model for nearest neighbor search in high-dimensional data space. *PODS*, pages 78–86, 1997.
[BF95]   Alberto Belussi and Christos Faloutsos. Estimating the selectivity of spatial queries using the 'correlation' fractal dimension. In *Proc. of VLDB*, pages 299–310, Zurich, Switzerland, September 1995.
[BJR94]   George E.P. Box, Gwilym M. Jenkins, and Gregory C. Reinsel. *Time Series Analysis: Forecasting and Control*. Prentice Hall, Englewood Cliffs, NJ, 3rd edition, 1994.
[BKM+00]   Andrei Broder, Ravi Kumar, Farzin Maghoul1, Prabhakar Raghavan, Sridhar Rajagopalan, Raymie Stata, Andrew Tomkins, and Janet Wiener. Graph structure in the web: experiments and models. In *WWW Conf.*, 2000.
[BP98]   Sergey Brin and Lawrence Page. The anatomy of a large-scale hypertextual (web) search engine. *Computer Networks and ISDN Systems*, 30(1–7):107–117, 1998.
[BS88]   M.F. Barnsley and A.D. Sloan. A better way to compress images. *Byte*, pages 215–223, January 1988.
[CE92]   M. Castagli and S. Eubank. *Nonlinear Modeling and Forecasting*. Addison Wesley, 1992. Proc. Vol. XII.
[Chr84]   S. Christodoulakis. Implication of certain assumptions in data base performance evaluation. *ACM TODS*, June 1984.
[CSH+03]   H. Chen, J. Schroeder, R. Hauck, L. Ridgeway, H. Atabaksh, H. Gupta, C. Boarman, K. Rasmussen, and A. Clements. Coplink connect: Information and knowledge management for law enforcement. *CACM*, 46(1):28–34, January 2003.
[FFF99]   Michalis Faloutsos, Petros Faloutsos, and Christos Faloutsos. On power-law relationships of the internet topology. In *SIGCOMM*, pages 251–262, 1999.
[FG96]   Christos Faloutsos and Volker Gaede. Analysis of the z-ordering method using the hausdorff fractal dimension. *VLDB*, September 1996.
[FK94]   Christos Faloutsos and Ibrahim Kamel. Beyond uniformity and independence: Analysis of R-trees using the concept of fractal dimension. In *Proc. ACM SIGACT-SIGMOD-SIGART PODS*, pages 4–13, Minneapolis, MN, May 24-26 1994. Also available as CS-TR-3198, UMIACS-TR-93-130.
[FRM94]   Christos Faloutsos, M. Ranganathan, and Yannis Manolopoulos. Fast subsequence matching in time-series databases. In *Proc. ACM SIGMOD*, pages 419–429, Minneapolis, MN, May 25-27 1994. 'Best Paper' award; also available as CS-TR-3190, UMIACS-TR-93-131, ISR TR-93-86.

[GGR02] Minos N. Garofalakis, Johannes Gehrke, and Rajeev Rastogi. Querying and mining data streams: You only get one look. *ACM SIGMOD*, page 635, June 2002. (tutorial).
[HS93] Harold M. Hastings and George Sugihara. *Fractals: A User's Guide for the Natural Sciences*. Oxford University Press, 1993.
[Kle99] Jon M. Kleinberg. Authoritative sources in a hyperlinked environment. *Journal of the ACM*, 46(5):604–632, 1999.
[LTWW94] W.E. Leland, M.S. Taqqu, W. Willinger, and D.V. Wilson. On the self-similar nature of ethernet traffic. *IEEE Transactions on Networking*, 2(1):1–15, February 1994. (earlier version in SIGCOMM '93, pp 183-193).
[Man77] B. Mandelbrot. *Fractal Geometry of Nature*. W.H. Freeman, New York, 1977.
[MF01] Alan L. Montgomery and Christos Faloutsos. Identifying web browsing trends and patterns. *IEEE Computer*, 34(7):94–95, July 2001.
[OJW03] C. Olston, J. Jiang, and J. Widom. Adaptive filters for continuous queries over distributed data streams. *ACM SIGMOD*, 2003.
[PBF03] Spiros Papadimitriou, Anthony Brockwell, and Christos Faloutsos. Adaptive, hands-off stream mining. *VLDB*, September 2003.
[PF01] Guido Proietti and Christos Faloutsos. Accurate modeling of region data. *IEEE TKDE*, 13(6):874–883, November 2001.
[RD02] M. Richardson and P. Domingos. Mining knowledge-sharing sites for viral marketing. In *SIGKDD*, pages 61–70, Edmonton, Canada, 2002.
[RFI02] M. Ripeanu, I. Foster, and A. Iamnitchi. Mapping the gnutella network: Properties of large-scale peer-to-peer systems and implications for system design. *IEEE Internet Computing Journal*, 6(1), 2002.
[Sch91] Manfred Schroeder. *Fractals, Chaos, Power Laws: Minutes from an Infinite Paradise*. W.H. Freeman and Company, New York, 1991.
[TTPF01] Agma Traina, Caetano Traina, Spiros Papadimitriou, and Christos Faloutsos. Tri-plots: Scalable tools for multidimensional data mining. *KDD*, August 2001.
[TTWF00] Caetano Traina, Agma Traina, Leejay Wu, and Christos Faloutsos. Fast feature selection using the fractal dimension,. In *XV Brazilian Symposium on Databases (SBBD)*, Paraiba, Brazil, October 2000.
[WF02] Leejay Wu and Christos Faloutsos. Making every bit count: Fast nonlinear axis scaling. *KDD*, July 2002.
[WKE00] Chenxi Wang, J. C. Knight, and M. C. Elder. On computer viral infection and the effect of immunization. In *ACSAC*, pages 246–256, 2000.
[Zip49] G.K. Zipf. *Human Behavior and Principle of Least Effort: An Introduction to Human Ecology*. Addison Wesley, Cambridge, Massachusetts, 1949.

Taking Causality Seriously: Propensity Score Methodology Applied to Estimate the Effects of Marketing Interventions

Donald B. Rubin

Department of Statistics, Harvard University, Cambridge MA
rubin@stat.harvard.edu

Propensity score methods were proposed by Rosenbaum and Rubin (1983, Biometrika) as central tools to help assess the causal effects of interventions. Since their introduction two decades ago, they have found wide application in a variety of areas, including medical research, economics, epidemiology, and education, especially in those situations where randomized experiments are either difficult to perform, or raise ethical questions, or would require extensive delays before answers could be obtained. Rubin (1997, Annals of Internal Medicine) provides an introduction to some of the essential ideas. In the past few years, the number of published applications using propensity score methods to evaluate medical and epidemiological interventions has increased dramatically. Rubin (2003, Erlbaum) provides a summary, which is already out of date.

Nevertheless, thus far, there have been few applications of propensity score methods to evaluate marketing interventions (e.g., advertising, promotions), where the tradition is to use generallly inappropriate techniques, which focus on the prediction of an outcome from an indicator for the intervention and background characteristics (such as least-squares regression, data mining, etc.). With these techniques, an estimated parameter in the model is used to estimate some global "causal" effect. This practice can generate grossly incorrect answers that can be self-perpetuating: polishing the Ferraris rather than the Jeeps "causes" them to continue to win more races than the Jeeps ¡=¿ visiting the high-prescribing doctors rather than the low-prescribing doctors "causes" them to continue to write more prescriptions.

This presentation will take "causality" seriously, not just as a casual concept implying some predictive association in a data set, and will show why propensity score methods are superior in practice to the standard predictive approaches for estimating causal effects. The results of our approach are estimates of individual-level causal effects, which can be used as building blocks for more complex components, such as response curves. We will also show how the standard predictive approaches can have important supplemental roles to play, both for refining estimates of individual-level causal effect estimates and for assessing how these causal effects might vary as a function of background information, both important uses for situations when targeting an audience and/or allocating resources are critical objectives.

The first step in a propensity score analysis is to estimate the individual scores, and there are various ways to do this in practice, the most common being logisitic regression. However, other techniques, such as probit regression or discriminant analysis are also possible, as are the robust methods based on the t-family of long tailed distributions. Other possible methods include highly non-linear methods such as CART or neural nets. A critical feature of estimating propensity scores is that diagnosing the adequacy of the resulting fit is very straightforward, and in fact guides what the next steps in a full propensity score analysis should be. This diagnosing takes place without access to the outcome variables (e.g., sales, number of prescriptions) so that that objectivity of the analysis is maintained. In some cases, the conclusion of the diagnostic phase must be that inferring causality from the data set at hand is impossible without relying on heroic and implausible assumptions, and this can be very valuable information, information that is not directly available from traditional approaches.

Marketing applications from the practice of AnaBus, Inc. will also be presented. AnaBus currently has a Small Business Innovative Research Grant from the US NIH to implement essential software to allow the implementation of the full propensity score approach to estimating the effects of interventions. Other examples will also be presented if time permits, for instance, an application from the current litigation in the US on the effects of cigarette smoking (Rubin, 2002, Health Services Outcomes Research).

An extensive reference list from the author is included. These references are divided into five categories. First, general articles on inference for causal effects not having a focus on matching or propensity scores. Second, articles that focus on matching methods before the formulation of propensity score methods – some of these would now be characterized as examples of propensity score matching. Third, articles that address propensity score methods explicitly, either theoretically or through applications. Fourth, articles that document, by analysis and/or by simlulation, the superiority of propensity-based methods, especially when used in combination with model-based adjustments, over model-based methods alone. And fifth, introductions and reviews of propensity score methods. The easiest place for a reader to start is with the last collection of articles.

Such a reference list is obviously very idiosyncratic and is not meant to imply that only the author has done good work in this area. Paul Rosenbaum, for example, has been an extremely active and creative contributor for many years, and his text book "Observational Studies" is truly excellent. As another example, Rajeev Deheija and Sadek Wahba's 1999 article in the Journal of the American Statistical Association had been very influential, especially in economics.

References

General Causal Inference Papers

(1974). "Estimating Causal Effects of Treatments in Randomized and Nonrandomized Studies." Journal of Educational Psychology, 66, 5, pp. 688-701.

(1977). "Assignment to Treatment Group on the Basis of a Covariate." Journal of Educational Statistics, 2, 1, pp. 1-26. Printer's correction note 3, p. 384.

(1977). "Assignment to Treatment Group on the Basis of a Covariate." Journal of Educational Statistics, 2, 1, pp. 1-26. Printer's correction note 3, p. 384.

(1978). "Bayesian Inference for Causal Effects: The Role of Randomization." The Annals of Statistics, 7, 1, pp. 34-58.

(1983). "Assessing Sensitivity to an Unobserved Binary Covariate in an Observational Study with Binary Outcome." The Journal of the Royal Statistical Society, Series B, 45, 2, pp. 212-218. (With P.R. Rosenbaum).

(1983). "On Lord's Paradox." Principles of Modern Psychological Measurement: A Festschrift for Frederick Lord, Wainer and Messick (eds.). Erlbaum, pp. 3-25. (With P.W. Holland).

(1984). "Estimating the Effects Caused by Treatments." Discussion of "On the Nature and Discovery of Structure" by Pratt and Schlaifer. Journal of the American Statistical Association, 79, pp. 26-28. (With P.R. Rosenbaum).

(1984). "William G. Cochran's Contributions to the Design, Analysis, and Evaluation of Observational Studies." W.G. Cochran's Impact on Statistics, Rao and Sedransk (eds.). New York: Wiley, pp. 37-69.

(1986). "Which Ifs Have Causal Answers?" Discussion of Holland's "Statistics and Causal Inference." Journal of the American Statistical Association, 81, pp. 961-962.

(1988). "Causal Inference in Retrospective Studies." Evaluation Review, pp. 203-231. (With P.W. Holland).

(1990). "Formal Modes of Statistical Inference for Causal Effects." Journal of Statistical Planning and Inference, 25, pp. 279-292.

(1990). "Neyman (1923) and Causal Inference in Experiments and Observational Studies." Statistical Science, 5, 4, pp. 472-480.

(1991). "Dose-Response Estimands: A Comment on Efron and Feldman." Journal of the American Statistical Association, 86, 413, pp. 22-24.

(1994). "Intention-to-Treat Analysis and the Goals of Clinical Trials." Clinical Pharmacology and Therapeutics, 87, 1, pp. 6-15. (With L.B. Sheiner).

(1996). "Identification of Causal Effects Using Instrumental Variables." Journal of the American Statistical Association, 91, 434, as Applications Invited Discussion Article with discussion and rejoinder, pp. 444-472. (With J.D. Angrist and G.W. Imbens).

(1997). "Bayesian Inference for Causal Effects in Randomized Experiments with Noncompliance." The Annals of Statistics, 25, 1, pp. 305-327. (With G. Imbens).

(1997). "Estimating Outcome Distributions for Compliers in Instrumental Variables Models." Review of Economic Studies, 64, pp. 555-574. (With G. Imbens).

(1998). "More Powerful Randomization-Based p-values in Double-Blind Trials with Noncompliance." Statistics in Medicine, 17, pp. 371-385, with discussion by D.R. Cox, pp. 387-389.

(1999). "Addressing Complications of Intention-To-Treat Analysis in the Combined Presence of All-or-None Treatment-Noncompliance and Subsequent Missing Outcomes." Biometrika, 86, 2, pp. 366-379. (With C. Frangakis).

(1999). "Causal Inquiry in Longitudinal Observational Studies," Discussion of 'Estimation of the Causal Effect of a Time-varying Exposure on the Marginal Mean of a Repeated Binary Outcome' by J. Robins, S. Greenland and F-C. Hu. Journal of the American Statistical Association, 94, 447, pp. 702-703. (With C.E. Frangakis).

(1999). "Teaching Causal Inference in Experiments and Observational Studies." Proceedings of the Section on Statistical Education of the American Statistical Association, pp. 126-131.

(2000). "Statistical Issues in the Estimation of the Causal Effects of Smoking Due to the Conduct of the Tobacco Industry." Chapter 16 in Statistical Science in the Courtroom, J. Gastwirth (ed.). New York: Springer-Verlag, pp. 321-351.

(2000). "The Utility of Counterfactuals for Causal Inference." Comment on A.P. Dawid, "Causal Inference Without Counterfactuals". Journal of the American Statistical Association, 95, 450, pp. 435-438.

(2000). "Causal Inference in Clinical and Epidemiological Studies via Potential Outcomes: Concepts and Analytic Approaches." Annual Review of Public Health, 21, pp. 121-145. (With R.J.A. Little).

(2000). "Statistical Inference for Causal Effects in Epidemiological Studies Via Potential Outcomes." Proceedings of the XL Scientific Meeting of the Italian Statistical Society, Florence, Italy, April 26-28, 2000, pp. 419-430.

(2001). "Estimating The Causal Effects of Smoking." Statistics in Medicine, 20, pp. 1395-1414.

(2001). "Self-Experimentation for Causal Effects." Comment on 'Surprises From Self-Experimentation: Sleep, Mood, and Weight', by S. Roberts. Chance, 14, 2, pp. 16-17.

(2001). "Estimating the Effect of Unearned Income on Labor Supply, Earnings, Savings and Consumption: Evidence from a Survey of Lottery Players." American Economic Review, 19, pp. 778-794. (With G.W. Imbens and B. Sacerdote).

(2002). "Statistical Assumptions in the Estimation of the Causal Effects of Smoking Due to the Conduct of the Tobacco Industry." [CD-ROM] In Social Science Methodology in the New Millennium. Proceedings of the Fifth International Conference on Logic and Methodology (J. Blasius, J. Hox, E. de Leeuw and P. Schmidt, eds.), October 6, 2000, Cologne, Germany. Opladen, FRG: Leske + Budrich. P023003.

(2002). "School Choice in NY City: A Bayesian Analysis of an Imperfect Randomized Experiment", with discussion and rejoinder. Case Studies in Bayesian Statistics, Vol. V. New York: Springer-Verlag. C. Gatsonis, B. Carlin and A. Carriquiry (eds.), pp. 3-97. (With Barnard, J., Frangakis, C. and Hill, J.)

(2002). "Principal Stratification in Causal Inference." Biometrics, 58, 1. pp. 21-29. (With C. Frangakis).

(2002). "Clustered Encouragement Designs with Individual Noncompliance: Bayesian Inference with Randomization, and Application to Advance Directive Forms." With discussion and rejoinder, Biostatistics, 3, 2, pp. 147-177. (With C.E. Frangakis and X.-H. Zhou.)

(2002). "Discussion of 'Estimation of Intervention Effects with Noncompliance: Alternative Model Specification,' by Booil Jo". Journal of Educational and Behavioral Statistics, 27, 4, pp. 411-415. (With F. Mealli.)

(2003). "Assumptions Allowing the Estimation of Direct Causal Effects: Discussion of 'Healthy, Wealthy, and Wise? Tests for Direct Causal Paths Between Health and Socioeconomic Status' by Adams et al.'". Journal of Econometrics, 112, pp. 79-87. (With F. Mealli.)

(2003). "A Principal Stratification Approach to Broken Randomized Experiments: A Case Study of Vouchers in New York City." Journal of the American Statistical Association, 98, 462, with discussion and rejoinder. (With J. Barnard, C. Frangakis, and J. Hill.)

(2003). "Assumptions When Analyzing Randomized Experiments with Noncompliance and Missing Outcomes." To appear in Health Services Outcome Research Methodology. (With F. Mealli.)

(2003). "Hypothesis: A Single Clinical Trial Plus Causal Evidence of Effectiveness is Sufficient for Drug Approval." Clinical Pharmacology and Therapeutics, 73, pp. 481-490. (With C. Peck and L.B. Sheiner.)

(2003). "Teaching Statistical Inference for Causal Effects in Experiments and Observational Studies." To appear in The Journal of Educational and Behavioral Statistics.

Matching Methods, Pre-propensity Score Paper

(1973). "Matching to Remove Bias in Observational Studies." Biometrics, 29, 1, pp. 159-183. Printer's correction note 30, p. 728.

(1976). "Multivariate Matching Methods that are Equal Percent Bias Reducing, I: Some Examples." Biometrics, 32, 1, pp. 109-120. Printer's correction note p. 955.

(1976). "Multivariate Matching Methods that are Equal Percent Bias Reducing, II: Maximums on Bias Reduction for Fixed Sample Sizes." Biometrics, 32, 1, pp. 121-132. Printer's correction note p. 955.

(1980). "Bias Reduction Using Mahalanobis' Metric Matching." Biometrics, 36, 2, pp. 295-298. Printer's Correction p. 296 ((5,10) = 75%).

Propensity Score Techniques and Applications

(1983). "The Central Role of the Propensity Score in Observational Studies for Causal Effects." Biometrika, 70, pp. 41-55. (With P. Rosenbaum).

(1984). "Reducing Bias in Observational Studies Using Subclassification on the Propensity Score." Journal of the American Statistical Association, 79, pp. 516-524. (with P.R. Rosenbaum).

(1985). "The Use of Propensity Scores in Applied Bayesian Inference." Bayesian Statistics, 2, Bernardo, DeGroot, Lindley and Smith (eds.). North Holland, pp. 463-472.

(1985). "Constructing a Control Group Using Multivariate Matched Sampling Incorporating the Propensity Score." The American Statistician, 39, pp. 33-38. (With P.R. Rosenbaum).

(1985). "The Bias Due to Incomplete Matching." Biometrics, 41, pp. 103-116. (With P.R. Rosenbaum).

(1992). "Projecting from Advance Data Using Propensity Modelling". The Journal of Business and Economics Statistics, 10, 2, pp. 117-131. (With J.C. Czajka, S.M., Hirabayashi, and R.J.A. Little).

(1992). "Affinely Invariant Matching Methods with Ellipsoidal Distributions." The Annals of Statistics, 20, 2, pp. 1079-93. (With N. Thomas).

(1992). "Characterizing the Effect of Matching Using Linear Propensity Score Methods with Normal Covariates." Biometrika, 79, 4, pp. 797-809. (With N. Thomas).

(1995). "In Utero Exposure to Phenobarbital and Intelligence Deficits in Adult Men." The Journal of the American Medical Association, 274, 19, pp. 1518-1525. (With J. Reinisch, S. Sanders and E. Mortensen.)

(1996). "Matching Using Estimated Propensity Scores: Relating Theory to Practice." Biometrics, 52, pp. 249-264. (With N. Thomas).

(1999). "On Estimating the Causal Effects of Do Not Resuscitate Orders." Medical Care, 37, 8, pp. 722-726. (With M. McIntosh).

(1999). "The Design of the New York School Choice Scholarship Program Evaluation". Research Designs: Inspired by the Work of Donald Campbell, L. Bickman (ed.). Thousand Oaks, CA: Sage. Chapter 7, pp. 155-180. (With J. Hill and N. Thomas).

(2000). "Estimation and Use of Propensity Scores with Incomplete Data." Journal of the American Statistical Association, 95, 451, pp. 749-759. (With R. D'Agostino, Jr.).

(2002). "Using Propensity Scores to Help Design Observational Studies: Application to the Tobacco Litigation." Health Services & Outcomes Research Methodology, 2, pp. 169-188, 2001.

Matching & Regression Better than Regression Alone

(1973). "The Use of Matched Sampling and Regression Adjustment to Remove Bias in Observational Studies." Biometrics, 29, 1, pp. 184-203.

(1973). "Controlling Bias in Observational Studies: A Review." Sankhya - A, 35, 4, pp. 417-446. (With W.G. Cochran).

(1979). "Using Multivariate Matched Sampling and Regression Adjustment to Control Bias in Observational Studies." The Journal of the American Statistical Association, 74, 366, pp. 318-328.

(2000). "Combining Propensity Score Matching with Additional Adjustments for Prognostic Covariates." Journal of the American Statistical Association, 95, 450, pp. 573-585. (With N. Thomas.)

Propensity Score Reviews

(1997). "Estimating Causal Effects From Large Data Sets Using Propensity Scores." Annals of Internal Medicine, 127, 8(II), pp. 757-763.

(1998). "Estimation from Nonrandomized Treatment Comparisons Using Subclassification on Propensity Scores." Nonrandomized Comparative Clinical Studies, U. Abel and A. Koch (eds.) Dusseldorf: Symposion Publishing, pp. 85-100.

(2003). "Estimating Treatment Effects From Nonrandomized Studies Using Subclassification on Propensity Scores." To appear in Festschrift for Ralph Rosnow. Erlbaum publishers.

Support Vector Machines with Example Dependent Costs

Ulf Brefeld, Peter Geibel, and Fritz Wysotzki

TU Berlin, Fak. IV, ISTI, AI Group, Sekr. FR5-8
Franklinstr. 28/29, D-10587 Berlin, Germany
{geibel,wysotzki}@cs.tu-berlin.de

Abstract. Classical learning algorithms from the fields of artificial neural networks and machine learning, typically, do not take any costs into account or allow only costs depending on the classes of the examples that are used for learning. As an extension of class dependent costs, we consider costs that are example, i.e. feature and class dependent. We present a natural cost-sensitive extension of the support vector machine (SVM) and discuss its relation to the Bayes rule. We also derive an approach for including example dependent costs into an arbitrary cost-insensitive learning algorithm by sampling according to modified probability distributions.

1 Introduction

The consideration of cost-sensitive learning has received growing attention in the past years ([9,4,5,8]). As it is stated in the Technological Roadmap of the MLnetII project (European Network of Excellence in Machine Learning, [10]), the inclusion of costs into learning and classification is one of the most relevant topics of future machine learning research.

The aim of the inductive construction of classifiers from training sets is to find a hypothesis that minimizes the mean predictive error. If costs are considered, each example not correctly classified by the learned hypothesis may contribute differently to the error function. One way to incorporate such costs is the use of a cost matrix, which specifies the misclassification costs in a class dependent manner (e.g. [9,4]). Using a cost matrix implies that the misclassification costs are the same for each example of the respective class.

The idea we discuss in this paper is to let the cost depend on the single example and not only on the class of the example. This leads to the notion of example dependent costs, which was to our knowledge first formulated in [6]. Besides costs for misclassification, we consider costs for correct classification (gains are expressed as negative costs).

One application for example dependent costs is the classification of credit applicants to a bank as either being a "good customer" (the person will pay back the credit) or a "bad customer" (the person will not pay back parts of the credit loan).

The gain or the loss in a single case forms the (mis-) classification cost for that example in a natural way. For a good customer the cost for correct classification is the negative gain of the bank. I.e. the cost for correct classification is not the same for all customers but depends on the amount of money borrowed. Generally there are no costs to be expected (or a small loss related to the handling expenses), if the customer is rejected, since he or she is incorrectly classified as a bad customer. For a bad customer, the cost for misclassification corresponds to the actual loss that has been occured. The gain of correct classification is zero (or small positive, if one considers handling expenses of the bank).

As opposed to the construction of a cost matrix, we claim that using the example costs directly is more natural and will lead to the production of more accurate classifiers. If the real costs are example dependent as in the credit risk problem, learning with a cost matrix means that in general only an approximation of the real costs is used. When using the classifier based on the cost matrix e.g. in the real bank, the real costs as given by the example dependent costs will occur and not the costs specified by the cost matrix. Therefore using example dependent costs is better than using a cost matrix for theoretical reasons, provided that the learning algorithm used is able to use the example dependent costs in an appropriate manner.

In this paper, we consider the extension of support vector machines (SVMs, [11, 2, 3]) by example dependent costs, and discuss its relationship to the cost-sensitive Bayes rule. In addition we provide an approach for including example-dependent costs into an arbitrary learning algorithm by using modified example distributions.

This article is structured as follows. In section 2 the Bayes rule in the case of example dependent costs is discussed. In section 3, the cost-sensitive SVM for non-separable classes is described. Experiments on some artificial domains can be found in section 5. In section 4, we discuss the inclusion of costs by resampling the dataset. The conclusion is presented in Section 6.

2 Example Dependent Costs

In the following we consider binary classification problems with classes -1 (negative class) and $+1$ (positive class). For an example $\mathbf{x} \in \mathbf{R}^d$ of class $+1$, let

- $c_{+1}(\mathbf{x})$ denote the cost of misclassifying $\mathbf{x}$
- and $g_{+1}(\mathbf{x})$ the cost of classifying $\mathbf{x}$ correctly.

The functions c_{-1} and g_{-1} are equivalently given for examples of class -1. In our framework, gains are expressed as negative costs. I.e. $g_y(\mathbf{x}) < 0$, if there is a gain for classifying $\mathbf{x}$ correctly into class y. $\mathbf{R}$ denotes the set of real numbers. d is the dimension of the input vector.

Let $r : \mathbf{R}^d \longrightarrow \{+1, -1\}$ be a classifier (decision rule) that assigns $\mathbf{x}$ to a class. According to [11] the risk of r with respect to the distribution function P of $(\mathbf{x}, y)$ is given by

$$R(r) = \int Q(\mathbf{x}, y, r) dP(\mathbf{x}, y). \tag{1}$$

The loss function Q is defined by

$$Q(\mathbf{x}, y, r) = \begin{cases} g_y(\mathbf{x}) & \text{if } y = r(\mathbf{x}) \\ c_y(\mathbf{x}) & \text{else.} \end{cases} \qquad (2)$$

We assume that the density $p(\mathbf{x}, y)$ exists. Let $X_y = \{\mathbf{x} \mid r(\mathbf{x}) = y\}$ the region of decision for class y. Then the risk can be rewritten with $p(\mathbf{x}, y) = p(\mathbf{x}|y)P(y)$ as

$$R(r) = \int_{X_{+1}} g_{+1}(\mathbf{x})p(\mathbf{x}|+1)P(+1)d\mathbf{x} + \int_{X_{+1}} c_{-1}(\mathbf{x})p(\mathbf{x}|-1)P(-1)d\mathbf{x} \qquad (3)$$
$$+ \int_{X_{-1}} g_{-1}(\mathbf{x})p(\mathbf{x}|-1)P(-1)d\mathbf{x} + \int_{X_{-1}} c_{+1}(\mathbf{x})p(\mathbf{x}|+1)P(+1)d\mathbf{x}.$$

$P(y)$ is the prior probability of class y, and $p(\mathbf{x}|y)$ is the class conditional probability density of class y. The first and the third integral express the costs for correct classification, whereas the second and the fourth integral express the costs for misclassification. We assume, that the integrals defining R exist. This is the case, if the cost functions are integrable and bounded.

The risk $R(r)$ is minimized, if $\mathbf{x}$ is assigned to class $+1$, if

$$g_{+1}(\mathbf{x})p(\mathbf{x}|+1)P(+1) + c_{-1}(\mathbf{x})p(\mathbf{x}|-1)P(-1)$$
$$\leq g_{-1}(\mathbf{x})p(\mathbf{x}|-1)P(-1) + c_{+1}(\mathbf{x})p(\mathbf{x}|+1)P(+1)$$

holds, and to class -1 otherwise. From this, the following proposition is derived.

Proposition 1 (Bayes Classifier). *The function*

$$r^*(\mathbf{x}) = \text{sign}[(c_{+1}(\mathbf{x}) - g_{+1}(\mathbf{x}))p(\mathbf{x}|+1)P(+1) \qquad (4)$$
$$- (c_{-1}(\mathbf{x}) - g_{-1}(\mathbf{x}))p(\mathbf{x}|-1)P(-1)]$$

minimizes R.

r^* is called the Bayes classifier (see e.g. [1]). As usual, we define $\text{sign}(0) = +1$. We assume $c_y(\mathbf{x}) - g_y(\mathbf{x}) > 0$ for every example $\mathbf{x}$, i.e. there is a real benefit for classifying $\mathbf{x}$ correctly.

From (4) it follows that the classification of examples depends on the *difference* of the costs for misclassification and correct classification, not on their actual values. Therefore we will assume $g_y(\mathbf{x}) = 0$ and $c_y(\mathbf{x}) > 0$ without loss of generality.

Given a training sample $(\mathbf{x}^{(1)}, y^{(1)}, c^{(1)}), \ldots, (\mathbf{x}^{(l)}, y^{(l)}, c^{(l)})$ with $c^{(i)} = c_{y^{(i)}}(x^{(i)})$, the empirical risk is defined by

$$R_{\text{emp}}(r) = \frac{1}{l}\sum Q(\mathbf{x}^{(i)}, y^{(i)}, r).$$

It holds $Q(\mathbf{x}^{(i)}, y^{(i)}, r) = c^{(i)}$, if the example is misclassified and $Q(\mathbf{x}^{(i)}, y^{(i)}, r) = 0$ otherwise. In our case, R_{emp} corresponds to the mean misclassification costs defined using the example dependent costs.

Proposition 2 ([11]). *If both cost functions are bounded by a constant B, then it holds with a probability of at least $1 - \eta$*

$$R(r) \leq R_{emp}(r) + B\sqrt{\frac{h(\ln\frac{2l}{h}+1) - \ln\frac{\eta}{4}}{l}},$$

where h is the VC-dimension of the hypothesis space of r.

Vapnik's result from [11] (p. 80) holds in our case, since the only assumption he made on the loss function is its non-negativity and boundedness.

Let $\bar{c}_{+1}$ and $\bar{c}_{-1}$ be the *mean* misclassification costs for the given distributions. Let r^+ be the Bayes optimal decision rule with respect to these class dependent costs. Then it is easy to see that $R(r^*) \leq R(r^+)$, where $R(r^*)$ (see above) and $R(r^+)$ are evaluated with respect to the example dependent costs. I.e. because the example dependent costs can be considered to be the real costs occuring, their usage can lead to decreased misclassification costs. Of course this is only possible if the learning algorithm is able to incorporate example dependent costs.

In the following, we will discuss the cost-sensitive construction of an r using the SVM approach. In the presentation we assume that the reader is familiar with SVM learning.

3 Support Vector Machines

If the class distributions have no overlap there is a decision rule r^* with zero error. It holds $R(r^*) = 0$, independent of the cost model used. Since the cost model does not influence the optimal hypothesis, we will not consider hard margin SVMs in this paper. For soft margin SVMs the learning problem can be stated as follows.

Let $S = \{(\mathbf{x}^{(i)}, y^{(i)}) | i = 1, \ldots, l\} \subset \mathbf{R}^d \times \{+1, -1\}$ be a training sample and $c_{y^{(i)}}(\mathbf{x}^{(i)}) = c^{(i)}$ the misclassification costs defined above. For learning from a finite sample, only the sampled values of the cost functions need to be known, not their definition. We divide S into subsets $S_{\pm 1}$ which contain the indices of all positive and negative examples respectively. By means of $\phi : \mathbf{R}^d \to \mathcal{H}$ we map the input data into a feature space $\mathcal{H}$ and denote the corresponding kernel by $K(\cdot, \cdot)$. The optimization problem can now be formulated as

$$\min_{\mathbf{w},b,\xi} \tfrac{1}{2}\|\mathbf{w}\|_{\mathcal{H}}^2 + C \sum_{i \in S_{+1}} c_{+1}(\mathbf{x}^{(i)}) \xi_i^k \\ + C \sum_{i \in S_{-1}} c_{-1}(\mathbf{x}^{(i)}) \xi_i^k \tag{5}$$

$$\text{s.t.} \quad y^{(i)}\left(\mathbf{w} \cdot \phi(\mathbf{x}^{(i)}) + b\right) \geq 1 - \xi_i \tag{6}$$

$$\xi_i \geq 0, \tag{7}$$

where the regularization constant $C > 0$ determines the trade-off between the weighted empirical risk and the complexity term.

w is the weight vector that together with the threshold b defines the classification function $f(\mathbf{x}) = \text{sign}(h(\mathbf{x}) + b)$ with $h(\mathbf{x}) = \mathbf{w} \cdot \phi(x)$. The slack variable ξ_i is zero for objects, that have a functional margin of more than 1. For objects with a margin of less than 1, ξ_i expresses how much the object fails to have the required margin, and is weighted with the cost value of the respective example. ξ is the margin slack vector containing all ξ_i. $\|\mathbf{w}\|_{\mathcal{H}}$ can be interpreted as the norm of h.

With $k = 1, 2$ we obtain the soft margin algorithms including individual costs (1-norm SVM and 2-norm SVM). Both cases can be extended to example dependent costs.

1-Norm SVM. Introducing non-negative Lagrange multipliers $\alpha_i, \mu_i \geq 0$, $i = 1, \ldots, l$, we can rewrite the optimization problem with $k = 1$ and resolve the following primal Lagrangian

$$L_P(\mathbf{w}, b, \xi, \alpha, \mu) = \frac{1}{2} \|\mathbf{w}\|_{\mathcal{H}}^2$$
$$+ C \sum_{i \in S_{+1}} c_{+1}(\mathbf{x}^{(i)}) \xi_i + C \sum_{i \in S_{-1}} c_{-1}(\mathbf{x}^{(i)}) \xi_i$$
$$- \sum_{i=1}^{l} \alpha_i \left[y^{(i)} \left(\mathbf{w} \cdot \phi(\mathbf{x}^{(i)}) + b \right) - 1 + \xi_i \right] - \sum_{i=1}^{l} \mu_i \xi_i.$$

Taking the derivative with respect to $\mathbf{w}$, b and ξ leads to

$$\frac{\partial L_P}{\partial \mathbf{w}} = \mathbf{w} - \sum_{i=1}^{l} \alpha_i y^{(i)} \phi(\mathbf{x}^{(i)}) = \mathbf{0} \tag{8}$$

$$\frac{\partial L_P}{\partial b} = - \sum_{i=1}^{l} \alpha_i y^{(i)} = 0 \tag{9}$$

$$\frac{\partial L_P}{\partial \xi_i} = C\, c_{+1}(\mathbf{x}^{(i)}) - \alpha_i - \mu_i = 0, \forall i \in S_{+1} \tag{10}$$

$$\frac{\partial L_P}{\partial \xi_i} = C\, c_{-1}(\mathbf{x}^{(i)}) - \alpha_i - \mu_i = 0, \forall i \in S_{-1} \tag{11}$$

Substituting (8)-(11) into the primal, we obtain the dual Lagragian that has to be maximized with respect to the α_i

$$L_D(\alpha) = \sum_{i=1}^{l} \alpha_i - \frac{1}{2} \sum_{i,j=1}^{l} \alpha_i \alpha_j y^{(i)} y^{(j)} K(\mathbf{x}^{(i)}, \mathbf{x}^{(j)}). \tag{12}$$

Equation (12) is called the 1-norm soft margin SVM. Note that the values of the cost function c_y do not occur in L_D.

The Karush-Kuhn-Tucker conditions hold, and the corresponding complementary conditions are

$$\xi_i \left(C\, c_{+1}(\mathbf{x}^{(i)}) - \alpha_i \right) = 0, \ \forall i \in S_{+1} \tag{13}$$
$$\xi_i \left(C\, c_{-1}(\mathbf{x}^{(i)}) - \alpha_i \right) = 0, \ \forall i \in S_{-1}. \tag{14}$$

Thus the α_i are bounded within the so called box constraints

$$0 \leq \alpha_i \leq C\, c_{+1}(\mathbf{x}^{(i)}), \forall i \in S_{+1} \qquad (15)$$
$$0 \leq \alpha_i \leq C\, c_{-1}(\mathbf{x}^{(i)}), \forall i \in S_{-1}. \qquad (16)$$

I.e. in the case of example dependent costs, the box constraints depend on the cost value for the respective example.

2-Norm SVM. The optimization problem in (7) leads with $k = 2$ to the minimization of the primal Lagrangian

$$\begin{aligned}L_P(\mathbf{w}, b, \xi, \alpha) &= \frac{1}{2}\|\mathbf{w}\|_{\mathcal{H}}^2 \\&+ \frac{C}{2}\sum_{i \in S_{+1}} c_{+1}(\mathbf{x}^{(i)})\,\xi_i^2 + \frac{C}{2}\sum_{i \in S_{-1}} c_{-1}(\mathbf{x}^{(i)})\,\xi_i^2 \\&- \sum_{i=1}^{l} \alpha_i \left[y^{(i)}\left(\mathbf{w}\cdot\phi(\mathbf{x}^{(i)}) + b\right) - 1 + \xi_i\right].\end{aligned}$$

Analogous to the 1-norm case, the minimization of the primal is equivalent to maximizing the dual Lagrangian given by

$$\begin{aligned}L_D(\alpha) &= \sum_{i=1}^{l}\alpha_i - \frac{1}{2}\sum_{i,j=1}^{l}\alpha_i\alpha_j y_i y_j K(\mathbf{x}^{(i)}, \mathbf{x}^{(j)}) \\&- \frac{1}{2}\sum_{i \in S_{+1}} \frac{\alpha_i^2}{C\, c_{+1}(\mathbf{x}^{(i)})} - \frac{1}{2}\sum_{i \in S_{-1}} \frac{\alpha_i^2}{C\, c_{-1}(\mathbf{x}^{(i)})}.\end{aligned}$$

In contrast to the 1-norm SVM, L_D depends on the values of the costs functions c_y. The quadratic optimization problem can be solved with slightly modified standard techniques, e.g. [3].

3.1 Convergence to the Bayes Rule

In [7] the cost free SVM learning problem is treated as a regularization problem in a reproducing kernel Hilbert space (RKHS) $\mathcal{H}_K$

$$\min_{h,b,\xi} \frac{1}{l}\sum_{i=1}^{l} \xi_i^k + \lambda\|h\|_{\mathcal{H}_K}^2, \qquad (17)$$

with $f(\mathbf{x}) = h(\mathbf{x}) + b$ subject to (6),(7). Lin showed in [7] that the solution to (17) approximates the Bayes rule for large training sets, if $\lambda = \frac{1}{2lC}$ is chosen in an optimal manner, and the kernel is rich enough (e.g. spline kernels).

Analogous to Lin we can rewrite the optimization problem in (5) to get

$$\min_{h,b,\xi} \frac{1}{l}\sum_{i=1}^{l} c_{y^{(i)}}(\mathbf{x}^{(i)})\,\xi_i^k + \lambda\|h\|_{\mathcal{H}_K}^2, \qquad (18)$$

subject to (6),(7), where (6),(7) can be rewritten to

$$1 - y^{(i)} f(\mathbf{x}^{(i)}) \leq \xi_i \tag{19}$$
$$\xi_i \geq 0. \tag{20}$$

We define the function $(z)_+ = 0$, if $z < 0$, and $(z)_+ = z$, else. Then (19) and (20) can be integrated into the single inequality

$$(1 - y^{(i)} f(\mathbf{x}^{(i)}))_+ \leq \xi_i. \tag{21}$$

With this inequality, the minimization problem can be rewritten to

$$\min_{h,b,\xi} \frac{1}{l} \sum_{i=1}^{l} c_{y^{(i)}}(\mathbf{x}^{(i)})((1 - y^{(i)} f(\mathbf{x}^{(i)}))_+)^k + \lambda \|h\|_{\mathcal{H}_K}^2. \tag{22}$$

For $l \to \infty$, the data driven term converges to

$$E_{\mathbf{X},Y}[c_Y(\mathbf{X})((1 - Yf(\mathbf{X}))_+)^k] \tag{23}$$

with random variables Y and $\mathbf{X}$. Equation (23) is equivalent to

$$E_{\mathbf{X}}[E_Y[c_Y(\mathbf{X})((1 - Yf(\mathbf{X}))_+)^k | \mathbf{X}]]. \tag{24}$$

(24) can be minimized, by minimizing $E_Y[.]$ for every fixed $\mathbf{X} = \mathbf{x}$ giving the expression to be minimized

$$c_{-1}(\mathbf{x})((1 + f(\mathbf{x}))_+)^k (1 - p(\mathbf{x})) + c_{+1}(\mathbf{x})((1 - f(\mathbf{x}))_+)^k p(\mathbf{x}), \tag{25}$$

where $p(\mathbf{x}) := p(+1|\mathbf{x})$.

According to the proof in [7] it can be shown that the function f that minimizes (25) minimizes the modified expression

$$g = c_{-1}(\mathbf{x})(1 + f(\mathbf{x}))^k (1 - p(\mathbf{x})) + c_{+1}(\mathbf{x})(1 - f(\mathbf{x}))^k p(\mathbf{x}). \tag{26}$$

By setting $z := f(\mathbf{x})$ and solving $\frac{\partial g}{\partial z} = 0$, we derive the decision function

$$f^*(\mathbf{x}) = \frac{[c_{+1}(\mathbf{x})p(\mathbf{x})]^{\frac{1}{k-1}} - [c_{-1}(\mathbf{x})(1 - p(\mathbf{x}))]^{\frac{1}{k-1}}}{[c_{+1}(\mathbf{x})p(\mathbf{x})]^{\frac{1}{k-1}} + [c_{-1}(\mathbf{x})(1 - p(\mathbf{x}))]^{\frac{1}{k-1}}}.$$

A random pattern is assigned to class $+1$ if $f^*(\mathbf{x}) \geq 0$ and to class -1 otherwise. The above proves the following proposition.

Proposition 3. *In the case $k = 2$, $sign(f^*(\mathbf{x}))$ is a minimizer of R, and it minimizes (23). It holds*

$$sign(f^*(\mathbf{x})) = r^*(\mathbf{x}).$$

$sign(f^*(\mathbf{x}))$ can be shown to be equivalent to (4) in the case $k = 2$ by using the definition of the conditional density and by simple algebraic transformations.

It can be conjectured from proposition 3 that SVM learning approximates the Bayes rule for large training sets. For $k = 1$ the corresponding cannot be shown.

4 Re-sampling

Example dependent costs can be included into a cost-insensitive learning algorithm by re-sampling the given training set. First we define the mean costs for each class by

$$B_y = \int_{\mathbf{R}^d} c_y(x) p(x|y) dx. \qquad (27)$$

We define the global mean cost $b = B_{+1}P(+1) + B_{-1}P(-1)$. From the cost-sensitive definition of the risk in (3) it follows that

$$\frac{R(r)}{b} = \int_{X_{+1}} \frac{c_{-1}(\mathbf{x})p(\mathbf{x}|-1)}{B_{-1}} \frac{B_{-1}P(-1)}{b} d\mathbf{x} + \int_{X_{-1}} \frac{c_{+1}(\mathbf{x})p(\mathbf{x}|+1)}{B_{+1}} \frac{B_{+1}P(+1)}{b} d\mathbf{x}.$$

I.e. we now consider the new class conditional densities

$$p'(\mathbf{x}|y) = \frac{1}{B_y} c_y(\mathbf{x}) p(\mathbf{x}|y)$$

and new priors

$$P'(y) = P(y) \frac{B_y}{B_{+1}P(+1) + B_{-1}P(-1)}.$$

It is easy to see that $\int p'(\mathbf{x}|y) d\mathbf{x} = 1$ holds, as well as $P'(+1) + P'(-1) = 1$.

Because b is a constant, minimizing the cost-sensitive risk $R(r)$ is equivalent to minimizing the cost-free risk

$$\frac{R(r)}{b} = R'(r) = \int_{X_{+1}} p'(\mathbf{x}|-1) P'(-1) d\mathbf{x} + \int_{X_{-1}} p'(\mathbf{x}|+1) P'(+1) d\mathbf{x}.$$

The following proposition holds.

Proposition 4. *A decision rule r minimizes R' if it minimizes R.*

The proposition follows from $R(r) = bR'(r)$.

In order to minimize R', we have to draw a new training sample from the given training sample. Assume that a training sample $(\mathbf{x}^{(1)}, y^{(1)}, c^{(1)})$, ..., $(\mathbf{x}^{(l)}, y^{(l)}, c^{(l)})$ of size l is given. Let C_y the total cost for class y in the sample. Based on the given sample, we form a second sample of size lN by random sampling from the given training set, where $N > 0$ is a fixed real number.

It holds for the compound density

$$p'(\mathbf{x}, y) = p'(\mathbf{x}|y) P'(y) = \frac{c_y(\mathbf{x})}{b} p(\mathbf{x}, y). \qquad (28)$$

Therefore, in each of the $\lfloor Nl \rfloor$ independent sampling steps, the probability of including example i in this step into the new sample should be determined by

$$\frac{c^{(i)}}{C_{+1} + C_{-1}}$$

i.e. an example is chosen according to its contribution to the total cost of the fixed training set. Note that $\frac{C_{+1}+C_{-1}}{l} \approx b$ holds. Because of $R(r) = bR'(r)$, it holds $R_{\text{emp}}(r) \approx b \cdot R'_{\text{emp}}(r)$, where $R_{\text{emp}}(r)$ is evaluated with respect to the given sample, and $R'_{\text{emp}}(r)$ is evaluated with respect to the generated cost-free sample. I.e. a learning algorithm that tries to minimize the expected cost-free risk by minimizing the mean cost-free risk will minimize the expected cost for the original problem. From the new training set, a classifier for the cost-sensitive problem can be learned with a cost-insensitive learning algorithm.

Re-Sampling from a fixed sample is only sensible, if the original sample is large enough. Especially a multiple inclusion of the same example into the new training set can cause problems, e.g. when estimating the accuracy using cross validation, where the example may occur in one of the training sets *and* in the respective test set. We assume that the re-sampling method is inferior to using the example dependent costs directly. Thorough experiments on this point have to be conducted in the future.

5 Experiments

We have shown in section 2 that the usage of example dependent costs will in general lead to decreased costs for classifier application. In section 3 we showed that the inclusion of example dependent costs into the SVM is possible and sound. To demonstrate the effects of the example dependent costs and the convergence to the Bayes classifier, we have conducted experiments on two artificial domains. The two classes of the first data set where defined by Gaussian distributions having means $\mu_{\pm 1} = (0, \pm 1)^T$ and equal covariance matrices $\Sigma_{\pm 1} = 1$ respectively. The cost functions $c_{\pm 1}$ are defined as follows

$$c_y(\mathbf{x}) = \frac{2}{1 + \exp(-yx_1)}, \quad y \in \{+1, -1\}, \tag{29}$$

see figure 1.a. We used radial basis function kernels for learning. The result of learning is also displayed in fig. 1.b-d for different number of training examples ($l = 128, 256, 512$).

For the given distributions, and the given cost functions, the expected risk is given by

$$R = \frac{1}{2} \int_{X_{-1}} \frac{2}{2\pi(1 + e^{-x_1})} e^{-\frac{1}{2}(x_1^2 + (x_2-1)^2)} d\mathbf{x}$$
$$+ \frac{1}{2} \int_{X_{+1}} \frac{2}{2\pi(1 + e^{x_1})} e^{-\frac{1}{2}(x_1^2 + (x_2+1)^2)} d\mathbf{x}.$$

The decision boundary is determined by the equality of the two integrands. After simple transformations it can be seen that the class boundary is defined by the hyperplane $x_1 + 2x_2 = 0$ and the optimal Bayes classifier decides in favour of class $+1$ if $x_1 + 2x_2 \geq 0$ and -1 otherwise. Figure 1 shows the approximation of the Bayes classifier for data sets containing 128, 256 and 512 examples with

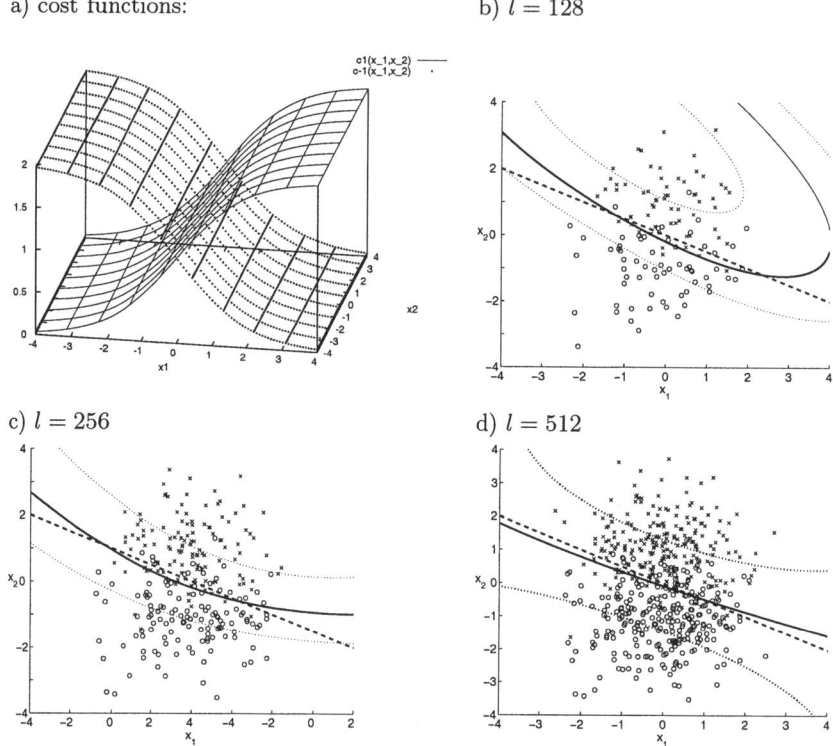

Fig. 1. Cost functions and approximation of the Bayes optimal classifier (drawn through and dashed line) with $l = 128, 256, 512$. The projections of the points on the dotted lines lie on the margin hyperplanes.

individual costs given in (29). The optimal parameter settings were determined by cross validation. We do not present the parameter settings, because they are not interesting for the purpose of this article.

The Bayes classifier *without* costs is defined by the line $x_2 = 0$. Using class dependent instead of example dependent costs results in lines $x_2 = -\frac{1}{2}ln(\frac{\bar{c}_{+1}}{\bar{c}_{-1}})$, where $\bar{c}_{\pm 1}$ denote the costs for positive and negative examples respectively. In contrast to example dependent costs, a rotation of the line is not possible for class dependent costs.

The decision based on class dependent costs is suboptimal for points between the lines $x_1 + 2x_2 \geq 0$ and $x_2 = -\frac{1}{2}ln(\frac{\bar{c}_{+1}}{\bar{c}_{-1}})$. For the cost functions in (29), the theoretical mean costs are given by $\bar{c}_{+1} = \bar{c}_{-1} = 1.0$. I.e. the decision based on class dependent costs is suboptimal with respect to the example dependent costs for points between the lines $x_1 + 2x_2 \geq 0$ and $x_2 = 0$.

An example for using class dependent costs computed as mean costs is shown in fig. 2.a. Here the individual costs in (29) were averaged for both classes and the resulting means interpreted as class dependent costs $\bar{c}_{+1} = 0.989$ and $\bar{c}_{-1} = 0.984$

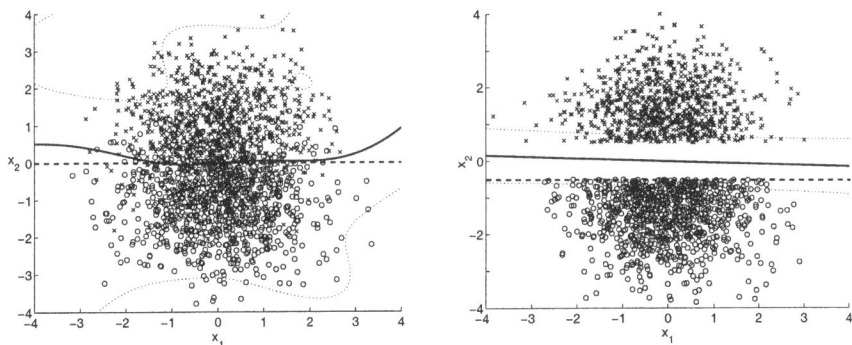

Fig. 2. a) Using class dependent, i.e. mean costs (left figure). b) Result for separable dataset with the example costs in (29) (right figure).

respectively. The learned classifier therefore coincides approximately with the cost-free Bayes classifier, see fig. 2.a. I.e. the information about the costs is lost by using class dependent costs.

An example of a separable data set with example dependent costs given in (29) is shown in fig. 2.b. As expected the resulting classifier is not influenced by using the cost functions (29). Note that due to prop. 1 the Bayes classifier r^* in (4) is defined by the class boundary $x_2 = -0.5$. Since we defined sign$(0) = +1$ and decide in favour of class $+1$ if $r^* \geq 0$, all points within the tube $-0.5 \leq x_2 \leq 0.5$ are assigned to class $+1$ by r^*. Allowing an arbitrary choice of the class, if the argument of sign in (4) equals to zero, yields a whole set of Bayes decision rules. From this set, the SVM has constructed one with maximum margin.

6 Conclusion

In this article, we discussed a natural cost-sensitive extension of SVMs by example dependent classification and misclassification costs. The cost-insensitive SVM can be obtained as a special case of the SVM with example dependent costs.

We showed, that the Bayes rule only depends on differences between costs for correct classification and for misclassification. This allows us to define a simplified learning problem where the costs for correct classification are assumed to be zero. For the simplified problem, we stated a bound for the cost-sensitive risk. A bound for the original problem with costs for correct classification can be obtained in a similar manner.

We have stated the optimization problems for the soft margin support vector machine with example dependent costs and derived the dual Lagrangians. For the case $k = 2$, we discussed the approximation of the Bayes rule using SVM learning. However a formal proof of convergence is still missing.

We suspect that the inclusion of example dependent costs may be sensible in the hard margin case too, i.e. for separable classes (fig. 2). It may lead to more robust classifiers and will perhaps allow the derivation of better error bounds.

Independently from the SVM framework, we have discussed the inclusion of example dependent costs into a cost-insensitive learning algorithm by resampling the original examples in the training set according to their costs. This way example dependent costs can be incorporated into an arbitrary cost-insensitive learning algorithm.

The usage of example dependent costs instead of class dependent costs will lead to a decreased misclassification cost in practical applications, e.g. credit risk assignment.

References

1. Ch. M. Bishop. *Neural Networks for Pattern Recognition*. Oxford University Press, Oxford, 1995.
2. C. J. C. Burges. A Tutorial on Support Vector Machines for Pattern Recognition. *Knowledge Discovery and Data Mining*, 2(2), 1998.
3. N. Cristianini and J. Shawe-Taylor. *An Introduction to Support Vector Machines (and Other Kernel-Based Learning Methods)*. Cambridge University Press, 2000.
4. Charles Elkan. The foundations of Cost-Sensitive learning. In Bernhard Nebel, editor, *Proceedings of the seventeenth International Conference on Artificial Intelligence (IJCAI-01)*, pages 973–978, San Francisco, CA, August 4–10 2001. Morgan Kaufmann Publishers, Inc.
5. M. Kukar and I. Kononenko. Cost-sensitive learning with neural networks. In Henri Prade, editor, *Proceedings of the 13th European Conference on Artificial Intelligence (ECAI-98)*, pages 445–449, Chichester, 1998. John Wiley & Sons.
6. A. Lenarcik and Z. Piasta. Rough classifiers sensitive to costs varying from object to object. In Lech Polkowski and Andrzej Skowron, editors, *Proceedings of the 1st International Conference on Rough Sets and Current Trends in Computing (RSCTC-98)*, volume 1424 of *LNAI*, pages 222–230, Berlin, June 22–26 1998. Springer.
7. Yi Lin. Support vector machines and the bayes rule in classification. *Data Mining and Knowledge Discovery*, 6(3):259–275, 2002.
8. Yi Lin, Yoonkyung Lee, and Grace Wahba. Support vector machines for classification in nonstandard situations. *Machine Learning*, 46(1-3):191–202, 2002.
9. Dragos D. Margineantu and Thomas G. Dietterich. Bootstrap methods for the cost-sensitive evaluation of classifiers. In *Proc. 17th International Conf. on Machine Learning*, pages 583–590. Morgan Kaufmann, San Francisco, CA, 2000.
10. Lorenza Saitta, editor. *Machine Learning – A Technological Roadmap*. University of Amsterdam, 2000. ISBN: 90-5470-096-3.
11. V. N. Vapnik. *The Nature of Statistical Learning Theory*. Springer, New York, 1995.

Abalearn: A Risk-Sensitive Approach to Self-play Learning in Abalone

Pedro Campos[1] and Thibault Langlois[1,2]

[1] INESC-ID, Neural Networks and Signal Processing Group, Lisbon, Portugal
pfpc@mega.ist.utl.pt
[2] Faculdade de Ciências da Universidade de Lisboa, Departamento de Informática
Lisbon, Portugal
tl@di.fc.ul.pt

Abstract. This paper presents Abalearn, a self-teaching Abalone program capable of automatically reaching an intermediate level of play without needing expert-labeled training examples, deep searches or exposure to competent play.
Our approach is based on a reinforcement learning algorithm that is risk-seeking, since defensive players in Abalone tend to never end a game.
We show that it is the risk-sensitivity that allows a successful self-play training. We also propose a set of features that seem relevant for achieving a good level of play.
We evaluate our approach using a fixed heuristic opponent as a benchmark, pitting our agents against human players online and comparing samples of our agents at different times of training.

1 Introduction

This paper presents Abalearn, a self-teaching Abalone program directly inspired by Tesauro's famous TD-Gammon [14], which used Reinforcement Learning (RL) methods to learn by self-play a Backgammon evaluation function. We chose Abalone because the game's dynamics represent a difficult challenge for RL methods, particularly for methods of self-play training. It has been shown [8] that Backgammon's dynamics are crucial to the success of TD-Gammon, because of its stochastic nature and the smoothness of its evaluation function. Abalone, on the other hand, is a deterministic game that has a very weak reinforcement signal: in fact, players can easily repeat the same kind of moves and the game may never end if one doesn't take chances.

Exploration is vital for RL to work well. Previous attempts to build an agent capable of learning how to play games through reinforcement either use expert-labeled training examples [5] or exposure to competent play (online play against humans [3] or learning by playing against a heuristic player [5]). We propose a method capable of efficient self-play learning for the game Abalone that is based on risk-sensitive RL [7]. We also provide a set of features and state representations for learning to play Abalone, using only the outcome of the game as a training signal.

Table 1. Complexity of several games.

Game	Branch	States	Source
Chess	30–40	10^{50}	[4]
Checkers	8–10	10^{17}	[10]
Backgammon	±420	10^{20}	[18]
Othello	±5	$< 10^{30}$	[20]
Go 19×19	±360	10^{160}	[11]
Abalone	±80	$< 3^{61}$	[1]

The rest of the paper is organized as follows: section 2 briefly analyses the game's complexity. Section 3 refers and explains the most significant previous RL efforts in games. Section 4 details the training method behind Abalearn and section 5 describes the state representations used. Finally, section 6 presents the results obtained using a heuristic player as benchmark, as well as results of games against other programs and human expert players. Section 7 draws some conclusions about our work.

2 Complexity in the Game Abalone

The rules of Abalone are simple to understand: to win, one has to push off the board 6 out of the 14 opponent's stones by outnumbering him/her[1]. Despite this apparent simplicity, the game is very popular and challenging [1]. Table 1 compares the branching factor and the state space dimension of some zero-sum games. The data was gathered from a selection of papers that analyzed those games.

These are all estimated values, since it is very difficult to determine rigorously the true values of these variables. Abalone has a branching factor higher than Chess, Checkers and Othello, but does not match the complexity of Go. The branching factor in backgammon is due to the dice rolls and is the main reason why other search techniques have to be used for this game.

The problem in Abalone is that when the two players are defensive enough, the game can easily go on forever, making the training more difficult (since it weakens the reinforcement signal).

3 Related Work

In this section we present a small survey on programs that learn to play games using RL. The most used method is Temporal Difference Learning, or TD-Learning. Samuel's checkers player [9] already used a form of temporal difference learning, as well as Michie's Tic-tac-toe player [6]. They both pre-date reinforcement learning as a field, but both basically use the same ideas.

---

[1] For further information about the games rules and strategies, please refer to the Official Abalone Web-site: www.abalonegames.com.

3.1 The Success of TD-Gammon

Tesauro's TD-Gammon [16] caused a small revolution in the field of RL. TD-Gammon was a Backgammon player that needed very few domain knowledge, but still was able to reach master-level play [15]. The learning algorithm, a combination of TD(λ) with a non-linear function approximator based on a neural network, became quite popular.

Besides predicting the expected return of the board position, the neural network also selected both agent and opponent's moves throughout the game. The move selected was the one for which the function approximator gave the higher value.

Modeling the value function with a neural network poses a number of difficulties, including what the best network topology is and what the input encoding should look like. Tesauro used a number of backgammon-specific features in addition to the other information representing the board to increase the information immediately available to the neural network. He found that this additional information gave another performance improvement.

TD-Gammon's surprising results were never repeated to other complex board games, such as Go, Chess and Othello. Many authors [11, 2, 8] have discussed Backgammon's characteristics that make it perfectly suitable for TD-learning through self-play. Among others, they emphasize: the speed of the game (TD-Gammon was trained by playing 1.5 million games), the smoothness of the game's evaluation function which facilitates the approximation via neural networks, and the stochastic nature of the game: the dice rolls force exploration, which is vital in RL.

Pollack and Blair show that a method initially considered weak – training a neural network using a simple hill-climbing algorithm – leads to a level of play close to the TD-Gammon level [8], which sustains that there is a bias in the dynamics of Backgammon that inclines it in favor of TD-learning techniques. Although Tesauro does not entirely agree with Pollack and Blair [17], it is quite surprising that such a simple procedure works at all.

3.2 Exposure to Competent Play

Learning from self-play is difficult as the network must bootstrap itself out of ignorance without the benefit of exposure to skilled opponents. As a consequence, a number of reported successes are not based on the networks' own predictions, but instead they learn by playing against commercial programs, heuristic players, human opponents or even by simply observing recorded games between human players. This approach helps to focus on the state space fraction that is really relevant for good play, but places the need of an expert player, which is what we want to obtain in the first place.

The Chess program KnightCap was trained by playing against human opponents on an internet chess server [3]. As its rate improved, it attracted stronger and diverse opponents, since humans tend to choose partners of the same level of play. This was crucial to KnightCap's success, since the opponents guided

KnightCap throughout its training (similar to the dice rolls in backgammon, which facilitated exploration of the state space). Thrun's program, NeuroChess [19], was trained by playing against GNUChess, a heuristic player, using TD(0).

Dahl [5] proposes an hybrid approach for Go: a neural network is trained to imitate local game shapes made by an expert database via supervised learning. A second net is trained to estimate the safety of groups of stones using TD(λ), and a third net is trained, also by TD(λ)-Learning to estimate the potential of non-occupied points of the board.

4 Abalearn's Training Methodology

Temporal difference learning (TD-learning) is an unsupervised RL algorithm [12]. In TD-learning, the evaluation of a given position is adjusted by using the differences between its evaluation and the evaluations of successive positions.

Sutton defined a whole class of TD algorithms which look at predictions of positions which are further ahead in the game and weight them exponentially less according to their temporal distance by the parameter λ.

Given a series of predictions, $V_0, ..., V_t, V_{t+1}$, then the weights in the evaluation function can be modified according to:

$$\Delta w_t = \alpha \left(V_{t+1} - V_t \right) \sum_{k=1}^{t} \lambda^{t-k} \nabla_w V_k \qquad (1)$$

TD(0) is the case in which only the one state preceding the current one is changed by the TD error ($\lambda = 0$). For larger values of λ, but still $\lambda < 1$, more of the preceding states are changed, but each more temporally distant state is changed less. We say that earlier states are given less credit for the TD error [13].

Thus, the λ parameter determines whether the algorithm is applying short range or long range prediction. The α parameter determines how quickly this learning takes place.

A standard feed-forward two-layer neural network represents the agent's evaluation function over the state space and is trained by combining TD(λ) with the Backpropagation procedure. We used the standard sigmoid as the activation function for the hidden and output layers' units. Weights are initialized to small random values between -0.01 and 0.01.

Rewards of $+1$ are given whenever the agent pushes an opponent's stone off the board or whenever it wins the game. When the agent loses the game or when the opponent pushes an agent's stone the reward is -1, otherwise it is 0 [2].

---

[2] Another option would be to give a positive reward only at the end of the game (when six stones have been pushed off the board). The agent would be able to learn to "sacrify" stones in order to improve its position. This option has not been used in the present paper, in part because we believe that a value function that take into account sacrifices must be much more difficult to approximate. This may be an interesting direction for future work.

One of the problems we encountered was that self-play was not effective because the agent repeatedly kept playing the same kind of moves, never ending a game. When training is based on self-play, the problem of exploration is very important because the agent may restrict itself to a small portion of the state space and become weaker and weaker, because the opponent is itself. This characteristic is not specific to the Abalone but applies to any agent that learns by self-play.

One way to favor exploration of the state space is to use an ϵ-greedy policy. During training, the agent follows an ϵ-greedy policy, selecting a random action with probability ϵ and selecting the action judged by the current evaluation function as having the highest value with probability $1-\epsilon$. The drawback of this solution is that it introduces noise in the policy "blindly" i.e. without taking into account the value of the current state.

The solution was to provide the agent with a sensitivity to risk during learning. Mihatsch and Neuneier [7] recently proposed a method that can help accomplish this. Their risk–sensitive RL algorithm transforms the temporal differences. In this approach, $\kappa \in (-1, 1)$ is a scalar parameter which specifies the desired risk–sensitivity. The function

$$\chi^\kappa : x \mapsto \begin{cases} (1-\kappa)x \text{ if } x > 0, \\ (1+\kappa)x \text{ otherwise} \end{cases} \quad (2)$$

is called the transformation function, since it is used to transform the temporal differences according to the risk sensitivity. The risk sensitive TD algorithm updates the estimated value function V according to

$$V_t(s_t) = V_{t-1}(s_t) + \alpha \chi^\kappa [R(s_t, a_t) + \gamma V_{t-1}(s_{t+1}) - V_{t-1}(s_t)] \quad (3)$$

When $\kappa = 0$ we are in the risk–neutral case. If we choose κ to be positive then we overweight negative temporal differences

$$R(s_t, a_t) + \gamma V(s_{t+1}) - V(s_t) < 0 \quad (4)$$

with respect to positive ones. That is, we overweight transitions to states where the immediate return $R(s, a)$ happened to be smaller than in the average. On the other hand, we underweight transitions to states that promise a higher return than in the average. In other words, the agent is risk-avoiding when $\kappa > 0$ and risk-seeking when $\kappa < 0$. We discovered that negative values for κ lead to an efficient self-play learning (see section 6).

When a neural network function approximator is used with Risk-Sensitive Reinforcement Learning, the TD(λ) update rule for parameters becomes:

$$w_{t+1} = w_t + \alpha \chi^\kappa(d_t) \sum_{k=1}^{t} \lambda^{t-k} \nabla_w V(s_k; w) \quad (5)$$

with

$$d_t = R(s_t, a_t) + \gamma V(s_t; w) - V(s_{t-1}; w)$$

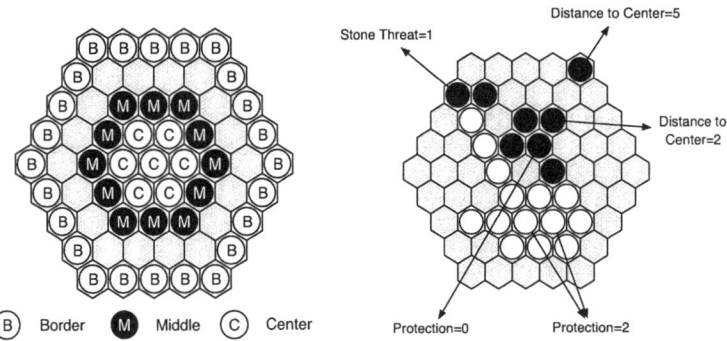

Fig. 1. The architecture used for Abalearn 2 encodes: the number of stones in the center, in the middle, in the border and pushed off the board (left) and the same for the opponent's stones. Abalearn 3 adds some basic features of the game (right).

5 Efficient State Representation

The state representation is crucial to a learning system, since it defines everything the agent might ever learn. In this section, we describe the neural network architectures we implemented and studied.

Let us first consider a typical architecture that is trained to evaluate board positions using a direct representation of the board. We call the agent using this architecture Abalearn 1. It is a basic and straightforward state representation, since it merely describes the contents of the board: it maps each position in the board to -1 if the position contains an opponent's stone, +1 if it contains an agent's stone and 0 if it is empty. It also encodes the number of stones pushed off the board (for both players).

We wish the network to achieve a good level of play. Clearly, this task can be better accomplished by exploiting some characteristics of the game that are relevant for good play. We used a simple architecture that encodes the number of stones in the center, in the middle, in the border and pushed off the board (see Figure 1); and the same for the opponent's stones. The state is thus represented by a vector of 8 features, plus a bias input unit set to 1. We called this agent Abalearn 2. This network is quite a simple feature map, but it is capable of learning to play Abalone, as we will see in the next section.

We then incorporated into a new architecture (Abalearn 3) some extra handcrafted features, illustrated in Figure 1. Abalearn 3 adds some relevant (although basic) features of the game to the previous architecture. We added: *protection* (number of stones totally surrounded by stones of the same color), the average distance of the stones to the center of the board and the number of stones threatened (see Figure 1).

6 Results

In this section we present the results of two training methods. Common parameter values in both methods are: $\alpha = 0.1, \gamma = 0.9$. Unless specified, the value of the λ parameter was 0.7.

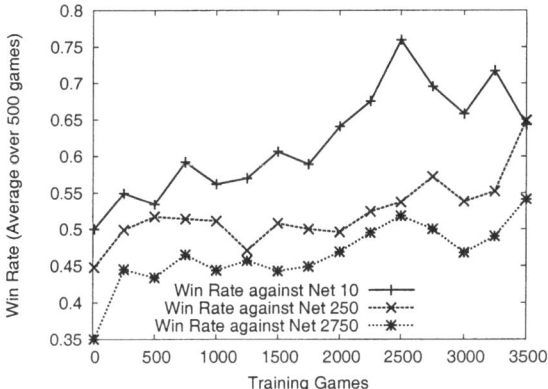

Fig. 2. Comparison between some reference networks, sampled after 10, 250 and 2750 training games (average of 500 games) shows that learning is succeeding.

Method I. This method applies standard TD(λ) using Abalearn 2, described in the previous section. In method I, the agent plays 1000 games against a random opponent in order to extract some basic knowledge (mainly learning to push the opponent's stones off the board). After that phase, we train the agent using self-play. This method never succeeds when using self-play training from the beginning.

Method I(a). This method is the same as Method I. Only the state representation changes to Abalearn 3. This method is necessary to prove the benefit of the added features in Abalearn 3 with respect to Abalearn 2.

Method II. We wished to obtain an agent capable of efficient and automatic self-play learning. Method II accomplishes this. It applies the risk-sensitive version of TD(λ) using self-play and Abalearn 3, also described in the previous section. Exploration is important especially at the beginning of the train, so we used a decreasing ϵ: after each game t, $\epsilon_{t+1} = 0.99 \times \epsilon_t$, with $\epsilon_0 = 0.9$.

Testing Methods. The most straightforward method for testing our agents is by averaging their win rate against a good heuristic[3] player. The heuristic function sums the distance to the center of the board of each stone (subtracts if it's an opponent stone). We also tested our agents by playing some games against the best Abalone program and by making them play at the Abalone Website against human experts.

6.1 Method I: Standard TD(λ)

We tested our networks against three networks sampled during previous training. Figure 2 shows the results. Each curve represents an average over 500 games. Each network on the X-Axis plays against Net 10, Net 250 and Net 2750 (networks sampled after 10, 250 and 2750 training games respectively). As we can

---
[3] We use a simple Minimax search algorithm.

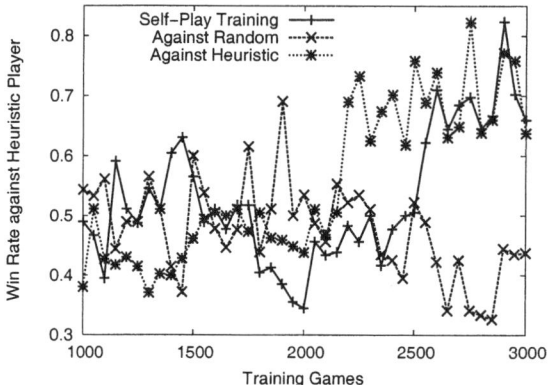

Fig. 3. Performance of the agents when trained against different kinds of opponents.

Table 2. Comparison between the two methods (Win Rate against Heuristic Player).

Training Games	Method I	Method I(a)
500	48%	68%
1000	52%	72%
2000	54%	76%
3000	71%	79%

see, it is easy for the networks to win Net 10. On the other hand, Net 2750 is far superior to all the others.

Exposure to Competent Play. A good playing partner offers knowledge to the learning agent, because it easily leads the agent through the relevant fractions of the state space.

In this experiment, we compare agents that are trained by playing against a random opponent, a strong minimax player and by self-play. Figure 3 summarizes the results. Each point corresponds to an average over 500 games against the heuristic opponent. We can see that a skilled opponent is more useful than a random opponent, as expected.

The Benefit of the Features. Table 2 compares the two state representations: it presents the win percentage against a heuristic player over 100 testing games, using method I and I(a). The agent trained with method I(a) uses the state representation with added features (see section 5) and after only 1000 games of training, presents a better performance than the agent trained with method I. This proves the features added were relevant to learning the game and yielded better performances.

6.2 Method II: Self-play with Risk-Seeking TD(λ)

Figure 4 shows the results of training for four different risk sensitivities: $\kappa = -1$ (the most risk-seeking agent), $\kappa = -0.8$, $\kappa = -0.3$ and $\kappa = 0$ (the classical risk-neutral case). We trained and tested 10 agents. We can see that performance is

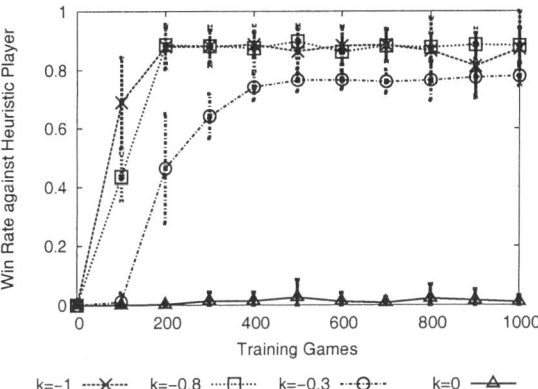

Fig. 4. Performance of the risk-sensitive RL agents when trained by self-play for various values of risk-sensitivity. Self-play is efficient for negative values of risk-sensitivity.

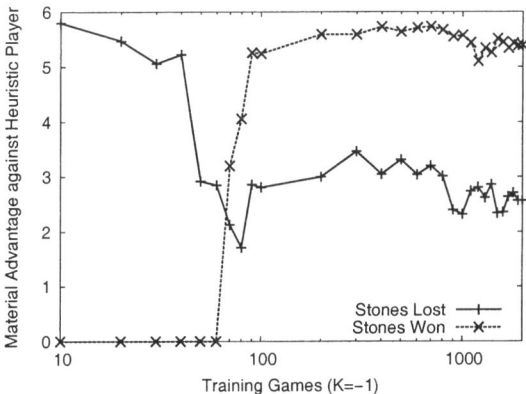

Fig. 5. Improvement in performance of the risk-seeking self-playing agent ($\kappa = -1$).

best when $\kappa = -0.8$ and $\kappa = -1$. We verified that after 10000 games of self-play training with $\kappa = -1$ performance kept the same (see Figure 5, which plots the results for the first 2000 games). By assuming that losses are inevitable, the agent ignores most of the negative temporal differences and the weights associated to the material advantage are positively rewarded.

We trained the agent with $\kappa = 0$ and it didn't learn to push the opponent's stones, thereby losing most games agianst the heuristic player, except for 1 out of 10 runs of the experiment. This is because the lack of risk-sensitivity leads to highly conservative policies where the agent learns to maintain its stones in the center of the board and avoids to push opponent's stones. This experiment illustrates the importance of risk-sensitivity in self-play learning: in method I(a), performance is worse (see Table 2).

Performance against the best program. We wanted to evaluate how TD-learning fares competitively against other methods. ABA-PRO, a commercial

Table 3. Abalearn using method I with fixed 1-ply search depth only loses when the opponent's search depth is 6-ply. Method II performs better.

Method I Depth=1 vs.:	Stones Won	Stones Lost	Moves	First Move
ABA-PRO Depth=4	0	0	31	ABA-PRO
ABA-PRO Depth=5	0	0	23	ABA-PRO
ABA-PRO Depth=6	0	2	61	ABA-PRO
Method II Depth=1 vs.:	Stones Won	Stones Lost	Moves	First Move
ABA-PRO Depth=4	0	0	29	ABA-PRO
ABA-PRO Depth=5	0	0	21	ABA-PRO
ABA-PRO Depth=6	0	0	42	ABA-PRO

Table 4. Abalearn playing online managed to win intermediate players.

Abalearn Method I vs.:	Stones Won	Stones Lost	First Move
ELO 1448 (weak intermediate)	6	1	Human Player
ELO 1590 (strong intermediate)	3	6	Human Player
ELO 1778 (expert)	0	6	Human Player
Abalearn Method II vs.:	Stones Won	Stones Lost	First Move
ELO 1501 (intermediate)	2	0	Human Player
ELO 1500 (intermediate)	6	1	Human Player
ELO 1590 (strong intermediate)	6	1	Human Player
ELO 1590 (strong intermediate)	6	3	Human Player
ELO 1590 (strong intermediate)	6	4	Human Player
ELO 1590 (strong intermediate)	6	4	Human Player

application, that is one of the best Abalone computer players built so far [1] relies on sophisticated search methods and hand-tuned heuristics that are hard to discover. It also uses deep, highly selective searches (ranging from 2 to 9-ply). Therefore, we pitted Abalearn trained as described before against ABA-PRO.

Table 3 shows some results obtained varying the search depth of ABA-PRO and maintaining our agent performing a fast 1-ply search[4]. The free-version is limited to 6-ply search.

As we can see, Abalearn only loses 2 stones when its' opponent search depth is 6. This shows that it is possible to achieve a good level of play using our training methodology. Once again, method II performs better (never loses).

Performance against Human Experts. To better assess Abalearn's level of play, we made it play online at the Abalone Official Server. As in all other games, players are ranked by their ELO.

Table 4 shows the results of some games played by Abalearn online against players of different ELOs. Method I won a player with ELO 1448 by 6 to 1 and managed to lose by 3 to 6 against an experienced 1590 ELO player. When

---

[4] When the game reaches a stage where both players repeat the same moves for 20 consecutive times, we end the game (tie by repetition). We carried out this experiment manually because we didn't implement an interface between the two programs.

playing against a former Abalone champion, Abalearn using method I lost by 6 to 0, but it took more than two hours for the champion to beat Abalearn, mainly because Abalearn defends very well and one has to try to ungroup its stones slowly towards a victory.

Method II is more promising because of its incorporated extra features[5]. We have tested it against players of ELO 1501, 1500 and 1590 (see Table 4).

7 Conclusions

This paper describes a program, Abalearn, that learns how to play the game of Abalone using the TD(λ) algorithm and a neural network to model the value function. The relevant information given to the learning agent is limited to the reinforcement signal and a set of features that define the agent's state. The programs learns by playing against itself.

We showed that the use of a Risk-Sensitive version of the TD(λ) algorithm allows the agent to learn by self-play. The performance level of Abalearn is evaluated against a heuristic player, a commercial application and human players. In all cases Abalearn shows a promising performance. The best agent wins about 90% of the games against the heuristic player and ties against strong opponents. Our agent only uses a single-step lookahead. One possible direction for further work is to integrate search with RL as Baxter et al. have shown [2].

Acknowledgements

The authors wish to thank the anonymous reviewers of this paper, who provided valuable advice and interesting suggestions.

References

1. O. Aichholzer, F. Aurenhammer, and T. Werner. Algorithmic fun: Abalone. Technical report, Institut for Theoretical Computer Science, Graz University of Technology, 2002.
2. J. Baxter, A. Tridgell, and L. Weaver. Knightcap: a chess program that learns by combining TD(λ) with game-tree search. In *Proc. 15th International Conf. on Machine Learning*, pages 28–36. Morgan Kaufmann, San Francisco, CA, 1998.
3. J. Baxter, A. Tridgell, and L. Weaver. Learning to play chess using temporal differences. *Machine Learning*, 40(3):243–263, 2000.
4. D. F. Beal and M. C. Smith. Temporal difference learning for heuristic search and game playing. *Information Sciences*, 122(1):3–21, 2000.
5. F. A. Dahl. Honte, a go-playing program using neural nets. 1999.
6. D. Michie. Experiments on the mechanization of game-learning – part i. characterization of the model and its parameters. *The Computer Journal*, 6:232–236, 1963.

---

[5] To play against the latest version of Abalearn online, please visit the following URL: http://neural.inesc.pt/Abalearn/index.html.

7. O. Mihatsch and R. Neuneier. Risk-sensitive reinforcement learning. *Machine Learning*, 49:267–290, 2002.
8. J. B. Pollack and A. D. Blair. Co-evolution in the successful learning of backgammon strategy. *Machine Learning*, 32(1):225–240, 1998.
9. A. Samuel. Some studies in machine learning using the game of checkers. *IBM Journal of Research and Development*, 3(3):211–229, 1959.
10. J. Schaeffer, M. Hlynka, and V. Jussila. Temporal difference learning applied to a high-performance game-playing program. In *Proceedings of the International Joint Conference on Artificial Intelligence (IJCAI)*, pages 529–534, 2001.
11. N. Schraudolph, P. Dayan, and T. J. Sejnowski. Temporal difference learning of position evaluation in the game of go. In *Advances in Neural Information Processing Systems*, volume 6. Morgan Kaufmann Publishers, Inc., 1994.
12. R. S. Sutton. Learning to predict by the methods of temporal differences. *Machine Learning*, 3:9–44, 1988.
13. R. S. Sutton and A. G. Barto. *Reinforcement Learning: An Introduction Reinforcement Reinforcement Learning: an Introduction*. The MIT Press, 1st edition, 1998.
14. G. Tesauro. Practical issues in temporal difference learning. In John E. Moody, Steve J. Hanson, and Richard P. Lippmann, editors, *Advances in Neural Information Processing Systems*, volume 4, 1992.
15. G. Tesauro. Td-gammon, a self-teaching backgammon program, achieves master-level play. In *Proceedings of the AAAI Fall Symposium on Intelligent Games: Planning and Learning*, pages 19–23, Menlo Park, CA, 1993. The AAAI Press.
16. G. Tesauro. Temporal difference learning and td-gammon. *Communications of the ACM*, 38(3):58–68, 1995.
17. G. Tesauro. Comments on "co-evolution in the successful learning of backgammon strategy". *Machine Learning*, 32(3):41–243, 1998.
18. G. Tesauro. Programming backgammon using self-teaching neural nets. *Artificial Intelligence*, 134:181–199, 2002.
19. S. Thrun. Learning to play the game of chess. In G. Tesauro, D. Touretzky, and T. Leen, editors, *Advances in Neural Information Processing Systems 7*, pages 1069–1076. The MIT Press, Cambridge, MA, 1995.
20. T. Yoshioka, S. Ishii, and M. Ito. Strategy acquisition for the game othello based on reinforcement learning. *IEICE Transactions on Inf. and Syst.*, 12(E82 D), December 1999.

Life Cycle Modeling of News Events Using Aging Theory*

Chien Chin Chen[1], Yao-Tsung Chen[1], Yeali Sun[2], and Meng Chang Chen[1]

[1] Institute of Information Science, Academia Sinica, Taiwan
{paton,ytchen,mcc}@iis.sinica.edu.tw
[2] Dept. of Information Management, National Taiwan University, Taiwan
sunny@im.ntu.edu.tw

Abstract. In this paper, an adaptive news event detection method is proposed. We consider a news event as a life form and propose an aging theory to model its life span. A news event becomes popular with a burst of news reports, and it fades away with time. We incorporate the proposed aging theory into the traditional single-pass clustering algorithm to model life spans of news events. Experiment results show that the proposed method has fairly good performance for both long-running and short-term events compared to other approaches.

1 Introduction

Nowadays, the Web has become a huge information treasure. Via the simple Hyper Text Markup Language (HTML) [1], people can publish and share valuable knowledge conveniently and easily. However, as the number of Web documents increases, obtaining desired information from the Web becomes time-consuming and sometimes requires specific knowledge to make best use of search engines and returned results. On-line news reflects such an information explosion problem. It is difficult to access and assimilate desired information from the hundreds of news documents from different agencies generated per day. Techniques such as classification [7][9] and personalization [5][6], were invented to facilitate news reading. However, the classification method is not totally effective in that readers generally follow news by interesting threads, not categories. Moreover, unexpected events, such as accidents, awards and sport championships, are out of the learned user profile. Therefore, to reduce search time and search results a precise event detection method, which discovers news events automatically, is necessary.

Event detection is part of Topic Detection and Tracking (TDT) [2] in which a news event is defined as incidents that occur at some place and time associated with some specific actions. In contrast with a category in the traditional text classification, events are localized in space and time. The job of event detection is to find out new events in several news streams. Besides discussing the TDT techniques of on-line news, in this paper we also discuss one interesting issue about news events — the

---

* This research was partly supported by NSC under grant NSC 91-2213-E-001-019.

life cycle. Usually, new news events appear in a news burst and gradually die out as time goes on [8]. Ignoring temporal relations of news events will degrade the performance of a TDT system. Previous works [3][14] were aware of the importance of the temporal information of news events to TDT. Their experimental results showed that modeling temporal information of news events could discriminate between similar but distinct events efficiently. In this paper, we propose the concept of aging theory to model life cycles of news events. Experiments show that our approach can improve the deficiencies of other methods.

The rest of the paper is organized as follows. In Section 2, we give a review of related works. In Section 3, we propose the concept of aging theory. Section 4 describes the algorithms that apply the aging theory to a news reading system. We evaluate the system performance in Section 5. Finally, conclusions and future work are given in Section 6.

2 Related Works

The project Topic Detection and Tracking (TDT) [2] is a DARPA-sponsored activity to detect and track news events from streams of broadcast news stories. It consists of three major tasks: segmentation, detection and tracking. Our focus, retrospective detection task [3][14], is unsupervised learning oriented [11]. Without giving any labeled training examples, the job of retrospective detection is to identify events from a news corpus. The traditional hierarchical agglomerative clustering (HAC) algorithm [13] is suitable for retrospective detection. However, the computation cost of HAC, which is quadratic to the number of input documents when using group average clustering [14], makes it infeasible when the number of news documents per day is high. Yang, et al. [14] used the technique of bucketing and re-clustering to speed up HAC. However, there is a chance that information from a long running event would be spread over too many buckets and thus divide the event into several events [14].

Another popular approach to retrospective detection is single-pass clustering (or incremental clustering) [4]. The single-pass clustering method processes the input documents iteratively and chronologically. A news document is merged with the most similar detected-cluster if the similarity between them is above a pre-defined threshold; otherwise, the document is treated as the seed of a new cluster. However, by only considering the similarity between clusters and documents will lead context-similar, but event-different, stories to be merged together. In order to obtain better clusters, temporal relations between news documents (or clusters) must be incorporated into the clustering algorithm. Allan, et al. [3] proposed a time-based threshold approach to model the temporal relation. By increasingly raising the detection threshold, distant documents are difficult to align with existing clusters. Therefore, different events could be discerned. Yang, et al. [14] modeled the temporal relation in a time window and a decaying function. The size of a time window specifies the number of prior documents (or events) to be considered when clustering. The decaying function weights the influence of a document in the window based on the gap between it and the examined document. Similar to the time-based threshold approach, distant documents in the time window make less impact on clustering than those nearby.

Even though the above methods enhance the result of the single-pass clustering algorithm, they are not adaptable for all types of event detections. The increasing threshold of time-based threshold method keeps distant stories of long-running events from tracking while the large window size of the time window method may mix up many expired, context-similar, short-term events. In order to balance the tradeoff, and tackle both long-running and short-term events, a self-adaptive event life cycle management mechanism is necessary. We present an aging theory for event cycle in Section 3. For more information about TDT, [4] gives a detailed survey of existing systems and approaches in recent years.

3 Aging Theory

A news event is considered a life form with stages of birth, growth, decay and death. To track life cycles of events, we use the concept of energy function. Like the endogenous fitness of an artificial life agent [10], the value of energy function indicates the liveliness of a news event in its life span. The energy of an event increases when the event becomes popular, and it diminishes with time. Therefore, a function of the number of news documents can be used to model the growing stage of events. On the other hand, to model the process of diminishing or aging stages, a decay factor is required.

3.1 Notations and Definitions

The news documents to an event is analogous to *foods* to a life form, As various foods do not contribute the same *nutrition* to a life form, different news documents make different contributions to an event's liveliness (i.e. popularity). The degree of the similarity between a news document and an event is used to represent the nutrition contribution. The accumulated similarity between news documents and event V in a time slot t is denoted by x_t. The time slot t can be any time interval. In the implementation, we use one day as a time slot.

We then define α as the *nutrition transferred factor* and β as the *nutrition decayed factor*, $0<\alpha<1$, $0<\beta<1$, and $y_t = g(x_1,...,x_t, \alpha, \beta)$. α decides the increase of nutrition from an input news document and β decides the nutrition loss in a period. The net nutrition y_t is a compound variable consisting of the nutrition of each time slot $x_1,...,x_t$, α and β. Different $g()$s mean different efficiencies of nutrition for different events. A function $F(y)$ has the following properties and is called the energy function of V:

$$0 \leq F(y) \leq 1 \tag{1}$$

$F(y)$ is a strictly increasing function of y

$$F(\infty) = 1 \text{ and } F(0) = 0 \tag{2}$$

The problem of event life cycle management is to find the optimal combination of α and β such that the energy value is 1 when all news documents of the event V appear. However, by Equation (2), the energy value would never be 1. Therefore, we loosen the equation and redefine the optimal condition as

$$F(r \cdot y_T) = s \quad (3)$$

where
- r is a proportion of $\Sigma_{i=1,...T}(\alpha x_i)$;
- s is a constant;
- T is the number of time slots.
- Both r and s are selected by the users.

3.2 Growth Only

One extreme case of the event life cycle is *no decay*, which means the energy of the event will be accumulated with the clustering of related news documents. In this case, y_t is simply the count of related news documents. Formally, we let $y_t = \Sigma_{i=1,...,t}(\alpha x_i)$. We want Equation (3) to hold, so

$$F(r \cdot \sum_{i=1,...,T}(\alpha x_i)) = s \quad (4)$$

Since the F is a strictly increasing function of y, we can take the inverse function F^{-1} for both sides of Equation (4):

$$r\sum_{i=1,...,T}(\alpha x_i) = F^{-1}(s)$$

We then divide both sides by $r\Sigma_{i=1,...,T}(\alpha x_i)$ to solve α,

$$\alpha^* = F^{-1}(s) / r\sum_{i=1,...,T}(\alpha x_i) \quad (5)$$

3.3 Constant Decay

The extreme case described above is not very likely in real world systems because the energy of an event should not only grow but also eventually diminish with age. Hence, we present the constant decay method which subtracts a constant value for each time slot in this section.

Formally, the domain of the energy function of constant decay is defined as follows:

$$y_t = \sum_{i=1,...,t}(\alpha x_i - \beta) = \alpha \sum_{i=1,...,t}(x_i) - \beta t \quad (6)$$

There are two parameters in Equation (6); hence we need two equations to solve them. Let r_1, r_2 denote two proportions of $\Sigma_{i=1,...,T}(\alpha x_i)$. Then

$$y_{t_1} = \alpha r_1 \sum_{i=1,...,T}(x_i) - \beta t_1 \quad (7)$$

and

$$y_{t_2} = \alpha r_2 \sum_{i=1,...,T}(x_i) - \beta t_2 \quad (8)$$

As in the previous section, we substitute Equations (7) and (8) into the optimal condition (3), take the inverse function F^{-1} of both sides and get

$$\alpha r_1 \sum_{i=1,\dots,T}(x_i) - \beta t_1 = F^{-1}(s_1) \tag{9}$$

and

$$\alpha r_2 \sum_{i=1,\dots,T}(x_i) - \beta t_2 = F^{-1}(s_2) \tag{10}$$

Solve α and β by (9) and (10):

$$\alpha^* = [t_2 F^{-1}(s_1) - t_1 F^{-1}(s_2)]/[(r_1 t_2 - r_2 t_1)\sum_{i=1,\dots,T}(x_i)] \tag{11}$$

and

$$\beta^* = \{r_1[t_2 F^{-1}(s_1) - t_1 F^{-1}(s_2)]/(r_1 t_2 - r_2 t_1) - F^{-1}(s_1)\}/t_1 \tag{12}$$

4 Representations and Algorithms

4.1 News Document Representation

Both news documents and events were represented as vectors in the conventional vector space model (VSM) [13], but each has a different scheme to determine term weights. For news documents, we use the traditional TF-IDF [13] scheme for term weighting, which is defined as

$$w_{t,d} = tf_{t,d} \cdot \log \frac{N}{df_t} \tag{13}$$

where

$w_{t,d}$ is the weight of term t in document d;

$tf_{t,d}$ is the within-document term frequency (TF);

$log(N/df_t)$ is the inverted document frequency (IDF),

N is the number of documents in the system corpus,

df_t is the number of documents in the corpus which t occurs.

The term weights of a news event are obtained from a set of detected documents. However, due to the temporal relation of news documents, the event's weights must be updated progressively to reflect event evolution. We adopt the classic Rocchio method [12] to update the term weights of events incrementally.

$$w_{t,e} = (1-\gamma) \cdot w_{t,e} + \gamma \cdot w_{t,d} \tag{14}$$

where

$w_{t,e}$ is the weight of term t in the detected event e;

$w_{t,d}$ is the weight of term t in the inserted document d;

γ is a parameter between 0 and 1.

Simply, the term weight of an event is a weighted combination of its original term weight and the term weights of newly detected news documents. Besides the term vector, we also assign each event a real number *eng*, called *energy value*, to indicate its vitality. The energy of an event increases when the event is popular, and it decreases with a constant value for each period of time. Therefore, events that receive little interest will gradually fade out.

4.2 Event Detection Algorithm

Based on the aging theory described in Section 3, the energy-based event detection algorithm is as in Figure 1. E is a set of candidate news events which are detected by the algorithm. Initially, E is set as empty. For each incoming news document d, the similarity between d and the most similar detected event in E is examined against a predefined threshold, called $threshold_{detect}$. The similarity is the cosine function between the vectors of news document and news event.

Energy-based Event Detection Algorithm:
$E = null$;
For each news document d from on-line news stream
    $e = \text{ARGMAX}_{e \in E}(sim(e,d))$;
    If $sim(e,d) >= threshold_{detect}$ then
        $e.EnergyUpdate(d)$;
        $e.VectorUpdate(d)$;
    else
        $e_{new} = CreateNewsEvent(d)$;
        add e_{new} into E;
    end if
end for

Fig. 1. The energy-based event detection algorithm.

If the similarity is greater than the threshold, we classify the news into the event and update the event's term vector and energy value. *EnergyUpdate()* increases the energy value of the corresponding event. Intuitively, the similarity values between the event and its documents can be summed as the energy value. However, this unbounded value will cause hot event, consisting of a burst of news documents, to have huge energy values and a longer life span than the event actually has. To overcome this pitfall, the energy function defined in Section 3 is used to constrain the energy value. The formula of *e.EnergyUpdate(d)* is defined as

$$eng_e = F(F^{-1}(eng_e) + \alpha \cdot sim(e,d)) \tag{15}$$

where
    eng_e is the energy value of the event e;
    $F()$ is the energy function;
    $F^{-1}()$ is the inverse energy function;
    $sim(e,d)$ is the cosine value between the event e and the document d;
    α is the energy transferred factor.

In this study, we adopt a sigmoid function as the energy function which converts the sum of similarities into a bounded extent. The sigmoid function is defined as:

$$F(y) = \frac{10y}{1+10y}, y>0 \qquad (16)$$

=0, otherwise.

One of the distinguishing features of the sigmoid function is that it maps a very large input domain into a small output domain. As shown in Figure 2, the output ranges between 0 and 1. Therefore, by using the sigmoid function, energy values can be limited between 0 and 1, which is consistent to the definition of the energy function described in Section 3. Another interesting feature of the sigmoid function is that it is a nonlinear function. The curve is much steeper around the origin than the extremities. This kind of growth often reflects the development of an event. It is usually accompanied by a burst of news documents in the beginning, and then gradually fades away. Since the energy value is constrained, we can interpret the status of the event by partitioning the range of the output of the sigmoid function. In practice, we can divide the output of the sigmoid function into three parts, each part representing a different situation of an event. High sigmoid values indicate hot events, and low sigmoid values indicate that events are out of date.

After increasing the energy value, the function *VectorUpdate()* is called to capture up-to-date event status. We use the above Rocchio formula [12] to update the term vector of the detected event. That is, we assume the inserted document d is positive feedback and use it to adjust the term weights of the event.

In case the similarity between the incoming document d and the most similar event is smaller than $threshold_{detect}$ or the set of E is empty, the detection algorithm will create a new event. The function *CreateNewsEvent()* forms the term vector of the newly created event by copying it from the input news document.

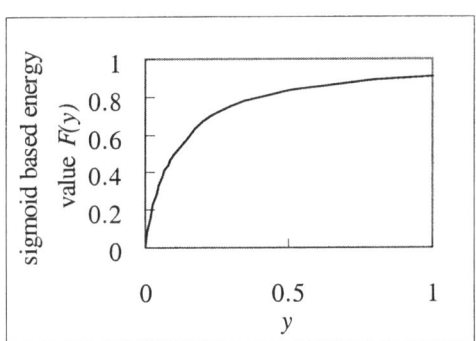

Fig. 2. The graph of the sigmoid function.

4.3 Energy Decay Algorithm

In contrast to the energy-based event detection algorithm which generates new events, the energy decay algorithm shown in Figure 3 is used to remove antiquated events.

Since events are time dependent, an event detection system is defective unless it can remove expired events. The energy decay algorithm periodically (e.g., every midnight) checks the energy values of events and removes antiquated events to keep all events in a news reading system up to date.

The energy value of every detected event is periodically reduced with a decay factor β, and the value of β is calculated by the aging theory. When no or few documents are added to an event, its energy value will gradually decline. Moreover, if an event's energy value is lower than a predefined threshold, called $threshold_{remove}$, we suppose the event is out of date and remove it from the validated set E. With the energy-based event detection algorithm and the energy decay algorithm, the lifespan of a news event can be determined by the liveliness of the event. The more related news documents it has, the longer its lifespan. This makes life cycle management of news events self-adaptive.

```
Energy Decay Algorithm:
For each event e in E
        eng_e = eng_e - β;
        if eng_e <= threshold_remove then
                Remove e from E;
        End if
End for
```

Fig. 3. The energy decay algorithm.

5 Empirical Evaluations

Two experiments were designed to evaluate and verify the proposed theory. In the first experiment, the training part of our data corpus is used to acquire the optimal aging parameters. We use the learned parameters to plot the variation of energy values of events in the testing part of the corpus. Some interesting observations from this experiment are discussed below. Then, we evaluate the performance of our method against three other methods in terms of traditional TDT metrics. The experimental results show that our method is more adaptive than others in both long-running and short-term events.

5.1 Data Corpus

Table 1 details the corpus we made by collecting news documents from several online news agencies for evaluations. We forgo the TDT pilot study corpus [4] for evaluations because it does not offer us a set of training data to obtain the aging parameters. Moreover, we believe that the aging parameters are category-derived. Each category will have its own best aging parameters in relation to its events. Therefore, we compile a corpus that comprises events of all sorts of categories to conclude our purpose. In this study, 18 events in politics are used for evaluations. In the future, events of other categories will be used as well. Besides, we have categorized types of events based on the event period. Events were identified as short-term events if they vanished within three days. In contrast, if the life of an event lasted over a week, we call the event a long-running event. Categorizing the type of events could help us in discussing the strength of each of the comparing methods in different situations.

Table 1. Statistics of data corpus.

	Training Data	Testing Data
Start-end date	2002/10/1 – 2002/10/31	2002/11/1 – 2002/12/31
Number of news documents	13,267	30,256
Number of labeled events	8	10
Event period <= 3	2	1
7 >= event period > 3	2	3
Event period > 7	4	6

5.2 Experiment 1: Growth of Energy Values of News Events

This experiment inspects the effect of aging parameters on the life cycle of news events. According to formulas (11) and (12), the values of α and β are determined by the points (r_1, s_1) and (r_2, s_2). We set r_1 and s_1 as 0.20 and r_2 and s_2 as 0.85 and the corresponding t_1 and t_2 are replaced by the times where the sum of similarity exceeds the r_1 and r_2 portion of the sum of similarities between the event and all its documents. The final values of α and β, 0.118659 and 0.145198 respectively, are the averages of the results of all training events.

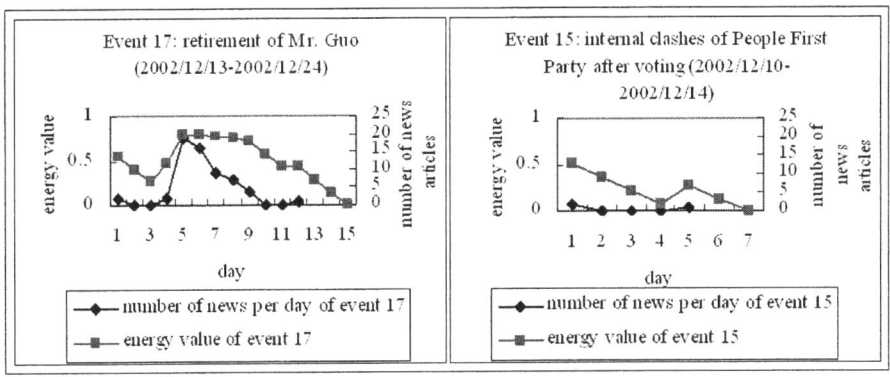

Fig. 4. The growth of the energy value.

Figure 4 shows the energy values and numbers of news documents per day of some of the testing events. We chose these events because they are difficult tasks in event detection. The event in the left began with very few related news documents, and it immediately quieted for a while until some follow-up news occurred. During the quiet period, it is hard for an event detection system to identify whether the event has ended, especially if it had a weak beginning. An early death announcement will cause serious errors since there were plenty of follow-ups. However, holding all weak beginning events will overly emphasize the importance of weak events, which may cause false alarms. Fortunately, our aging theory could tackle this kind of dilemma. Since the sigmoid function is a nonlinear function, the steeper slope near the origin point gives an event a higher vitality even if that event is inactive at an early stage. As a result, the high initial energy value helps the event survive the quiet period to track the follow-ups. What if the event is indeed a weak event, as Event 15 in figure 4? In this case, our decay mechanism could eliminate this event after a short period of time. As shown in figure 4, this event only lasted for two more days. Observing the contrast between events in Figure 4, we found that our aging theory could ascertain the rise and fall of an event progress.

5.3 Experiment 2: Event Detection Comparisons

In this experiment, our aging method (A) is compared to three proposed methods. The baseline method (B) [4] is a basic single-pass clustering algorithm. The time-based threshold method (T) [3] and the time window method (W) [14] enhanced the single-pass clustering algorithm with temporal information. Each of the above methods groups the testing part of the corpus into several clusters. The top ten best-matched clusters generated from each method were chosen for performance comparisons. The degree of match between a testing event and a generated cluster is determined by the number of news documents belonging to both the testing event and the cluster. As a result, 10 generated clusters from each method are evaluated using six official TDT measures [4] including: precision (p), recall (r), miss (m), false alarm (f), F1-measure ($F1$) and cost (c).

Table 2 shows the results of the experiments in which, *T0.02*, *T0.05*, and *T0.1* are time-based threshold methods with 0.02, 0.05 and 0.1 time penalty [3] respectively. *W2000*, *W2000d*, and *W3000d* are the time window methods with window sizes [14] of 2000 and 3000 respectively. The lowercase letter *d* indicates that the window is decaying-based [14].

Table 2. Experiment results on testing events.

	P	r	m	f	F1	c
B	0.68	0.75	0.25	0.0007	0.63	0.006
A	0.73	0.75	0.24	0.0002	**0.72**	0.005
T0.02	0.88	0.58	0.41	0.00008	0.67	0.008
T0.05	0.87	0.57	0.42	0.00008	0.67	0.008
T0.1	**0.93**	0.47	0.52	**0.00003**	0.61	0.01
W2000	0.56	**0.89**	**0.1**	0.002	0.62	**0.004**
W2000d	0.76	0.67	0.32	0.0002	0.65	0.006
W3000d	0.65	0.8	0.19	0.0006	0.66	**0.004**

In table 2, approximately all temporal-based methods out-perform the baseline method. Our aging method achieves both reasonable precision and recall which results in the best *F1* score, while the time-based threshold method achieves good precision but loses recall. The time window method has good recall but decreased precision. Even though the lowest cost comes from the time window method, we believe that is due to the fact that the majority of testing events are long-running. If we separately compare the time window method with our aging method on a short-term event, as shown in table 3, we find that the time window method is not suitable for short-term events. During the detection process on a short-term event, the fixed window size will overly emphasize the influence of the short-term event so that many context-similar but event-different news stories are merged into the event, which therefore results in low precision scores. As indicated in Figure 5, the last peak of the curve of the *window2000* method is a mis-merged event. Our aging method, on the other hand, lets the event control its own lifespan; consequently it outperforms the time window method for short-term events.

Table 3. Experiment results on short-term event.

	P	*r*	*m*	*F*	*F1*	*c*
A	0.61	0.79	0.2	0.0003	0.69	0.004
W2000	0.12	0.91	0.08	0.005	0.21	0.006
W2000d	0.37	0.83	0.16	0.001	0.51	0.004
W3000d	0.22	0.83	0.16	0.002	0.34	0.005

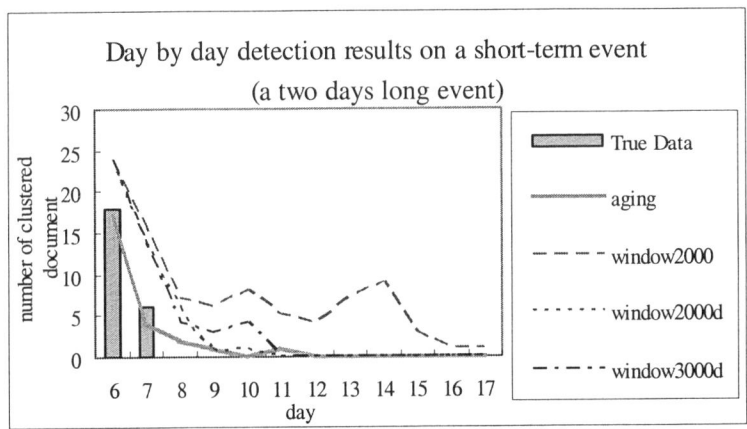

Fig. 5. Event detection results on a short-term event.

The time-based threshold method sacrifices its recall to achieve high precision, especially in long-running events (as shown in table 4). The growing threshold could keep somewhat context-similar, but event-different, news stories from being included in a detected event. Thus it results in a substantial amount of clusters. However, continuingly increasing the threshold may break the storylines of a long-running event into pieces, which consequently results in a high miss rate. As we can see from Figure 6, the long-running event was fragmented into twelve clusters when using the time-based threshold method, while our aging method merely broke the event into one major and three trivial parts.

Table 4. Experiment results on 6 long-running events.

	p	r	m	f	F1	c
A	0.72	**0.68**	**0.31**	0.0002	**0.67**	**0.006**
T0.02	0.88	0.46	0.53	0.00005	0.60	0.01
T0.05	0.87	0.51	0.49	0.00007	0.61	0.009
T0.1	**0.94**	0.37	0.62	**0.00002**	0.52	0.012

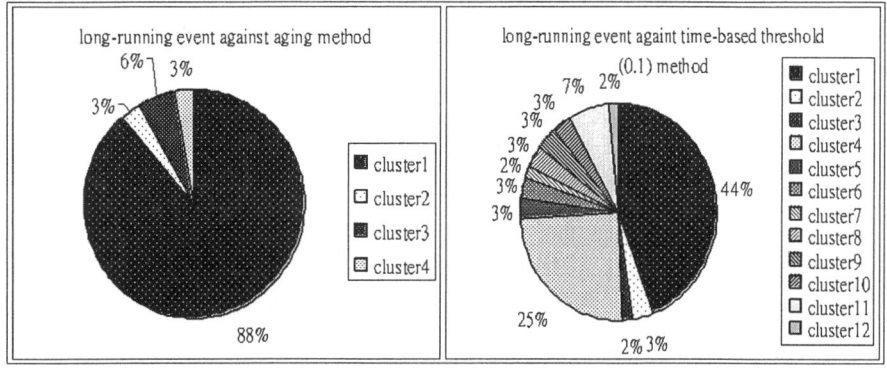

Fig. 6. Aging method on a long-running event.

Experiment results show that the time window method scores high on long running events but perform poorly for short-term events. The time-based threshold has a high precision rate as well as a high miss rate on long-running events. Our aging method has fairly good performance in both long-running and short-term events.

6 Conclusions

In this study, the aging theory is incorporated into the traditional single-pass clustering algorithm to detect and track news events. The growth of energy value synchronizes well with the event progress. Moreover, experiment results show that the proposed method performs well for both long-running and short-term events in comparison to other approaches. We are now applying our method to other categories, such as finance, sports and entertainment. We believe that using category-specific aging parameters achieves the best results for event detection in all possible categories.

References

1. http://www.w3.org/MarkUp/
2. http://morph.ldc.upenn.edu/TDT/
3. James Allan, Ron Papka and Victor Lavrenko, "On-Line New Event Detection and Tracking," in proceedings of the 21st annual international ACM SIGIR conference on research and development in information retrieval, pp. 37-45, 1998.
4. James Allan, Jaime Carbonell, George Doddington, Jonathan Yamron and Yiming Yang, "Topic Detection and Tracking Pilot Study: Final Report," in proceedings of the DARPA Broadcast News Transcription and Understanding Workshop, pp. 194-218, 1998.
5. Daniel Billsus, Michael J. Pazzani, "A Personal News Agent that Talks, Learns and Explains," Third International Conference on Autonomous Agents, 1999.
6. Chien Chin Chen, Meng Chang Chen and Yeali Sun, "PVA : A Self-Adaptive Personal View Agent," Journal of Intelligent Information Systems, 18:2/3, 173-194, 2002.
7. Wen-Lin Hsu, Sheau-Dong Lang, "Classificaiton Algorithms for NETNEWS Articles," in proceedings of 8th ACM international conference on information and knowledge management, pp. 114-121, 1999.
8. Jon Kleinberg, "Bursty and Hierarchical Structure in Streams," in proceedings of the eighth ACM SIGKDD international conference on knowledge discovery and data mining, pp. 91-101, 2002.
9. Shian-Hua Lin, Meng Chang Chen, Jan-Ming Ho and Yueh-Mn Huang, "ACIRD : Intelligent Internet Documents Organization and Retrieval," IEEE Transactions on Knowledge and Data Engineering, Vol. 14, No. 3, May/Jun, 2002.
10. Filippo Menczer, Richard K. Belew and Wolfram Willuhn, "Artificial Life Applied to Adaptive Information Agents," In Spring Symposium on Information Gathering from Distributed, Heterogeneous Database, AAAI Press, 1995.
11. Tom Mitchell, "Machine Learning," McGraw Hill, 1997.
12. Joseph John Rocchio, "Relevance Feedback in Information Retrieval," In the SMART Retrieval System, pp. 313-323. Prentice Hall, 1971
13. Gerard Salton, "Automatic Text Processing: The Transformation, Analysis, and Retrieval of Information by Computer," Addison-Wesley, 1989.
14. Yiming Yang, Tom Pierce and Jaime Carbonell, "A Study on Retrospective and On-Line Event Detection," in proceedings of the 21st annual international ACM SIGIR conference on research and development in information retrieval, pp. 28-36, 1998.

Unambiguous Automata Inference by Means of State-Merging Methods

François Coste and Daniel Fredouille

IRISA-INRIA,
Campus Universitaire de Beaulieu
35042 Rennes Cedex
{francois.coste,daniel.fredouille}@irisa.fr
http://www.irisa.fr/

Abstract. We consider inference of automata from given data. A classical problem is to find the smallest compatible automaton, i.e. the smallest automaton accepting all examples and rejecting all counter-examples. We study unambiguous automata (UFA) inference, an intermediate framework between the hard nondeterministic automata (NFA) inference and the well known deterministic automata (DFA) inference. The search space for UFA inference is described and original theoretical results on both the DFA and the UFA inference search space are given. An algorithm for UFA inference is proposed and experimental results on a benchmark with both deterministic and nondeterministic targets are provided showing that UFA inference outperforms DFA inference.

Introduction

Motivations: We consider inference of *nondeterministic automata* (NFA) from given data. A classical problem is to find the smallest compatible automaton, i.e. the smallest automaton accepting all examples and rejecting all counter-examples. When automata are *deterministic* (DFA), the problem has been extensively studied and is NP-complete [Gol78,PW89]. However, if enough examples and counter-examples are provided, polynomial inference algorithms using *state-merging method* perform well [OG92,Lan92,LPP98].

NFA inference is known to be harder than DFA inference [Hig97]. But, in the Occam's razor paradigm, it is worth noticing that NFA may be exponentially smaller than DFA. NFA also represent some structures - like "gaps" in genomic - more explicitly than DFA, and therefore are better suited to be interpreted by an expert of the application domain. Experimental results of [CF00,DLT01] show that inferring regular languages using classes of automata containing nondeterministic representations is a promising approach.

Nevertheless, all the complexity of NFA is not necessary to take advantage of nondeterminism. We propose to study the inference of an intermediate class of automata, the *unambiguous automata* (UFA). As we will show in this article, inferring UFA enables to introduce a reasonable amount of nondeterminism while keeping some advantages of the DFA representation.

To tackle UFA inference, we consider this problem as a search of a particular UFA in a space of NFA. We propose to adapt states-merging methods - which have been proven successful for DFA inference - to realize UFA inference. We first describe the search space for NFA inference in the state-merging framework by revisiting results of [DMV94] (section 1). Then, we propose operators allowing to explore this search space by considering only unambiguous automata (section 2). Thanks to operators defined in section 2, different strategies for exploring the search space can be applied. We have implemented a greedy strategy together with a heuristic inspired from classical DFA inference algorithms. This algorithm is shown to perform better on a benchmark of the domain than the original DFA algorithm. A comparison with the DeLeTe2 algorithm which infer residual finite state automata (RFSA) [DLT01] showing that each algorithm is more adapted to different subparts of the benchmark is also given.

Definitions and Notations: We denote by $|E|$ the cardinality of a set E. A *partition* of a set E is a set of subsets of E such that the intersection of each pair of subsets is empty and the union of all subsets is E. An element of a partition is called a *block*. Let Σ be a finite alphabet, we denote by Σ^* the set of words on Σ, by ϵ the empty word and by $|u|$ the length of a word u of Σ^*.

Definition 1. *A* nondeterministic automaton, *or NFA, is a 5-tuple $\langle \Sigma, Q, I, \delta, F \rangle$ where Σ is the input alphabet, Q is a finite set of states, $I \subseteq Q$ is the set of initial states, δ is the transition mapping defined from $Q \times \Sigma$ to 2^Q, F is the set of final states. The δ function is classically extended to words by: $\forall q \in Q,\ \forall a \in \Sigma,\ \forall w \in \Sigma^*,\ \delta(q, \epsilon) = \{q\},\ \delta(q, aw) = \bigcup_{q' \in \delta(q,a)} \delta(q', w)$. A tuple $\langle q, a, q' \rangle$ with $q' \in \delta(q, a)$ is called a* transition

The regular language recognized by an automaton A is $L(A) = \{w \in \Sigma^* \mid \exists q_i \in I,\ \delta(q_i, w) \cap F \neq \emptyset\}$. We associate two languages to each state q of an automaton, its *prefix language* which is the set of words w such that $q \in \delta(I, w)$; and its *suffix language* which is the set of words w such that $\delta(q, w) \cap F \neq \emptyset$. NFA are considered *trimmed* (i.e. no state has an empty prefix or suffix language). The size of a NFA A is defined as its number of states.

A *deterministic finite automaton*, or DFA is a NFA $\langle \Sigma, Q, I, \delta, F \rangle$ such that: $|I| = 1$ and $\forall q \in Q, \forall a \in \Sigma, |\delta(q,a)| \leq 1$. Some particular DFA can be defined. The *canonical automaton* of the regular language L, denoted by $A(L)$, is the unique minimal DFA accepting L. The *universal automaton*, $UA(\Sigma)$ or more simple UA, is the canonical automaton $A(\Sigma^*)$ accepting all words on Σ (figure 2).

An *acceptance* for a word $w \in \Sigma^*$ - with $w = a_1 \ldots a_{|w|}$ - in an automaton $A = \langle \Sigma, Q, I, \delta, F \rangle$ is a sequence $(q_0, \ldots, q_{|w|})_w$ of $|w|+1$ states such that $q_0 \in I$, $\forall i \in [1, |w|],\ q_i \in \delta(q_{i-1}, a_i),\ q_{|w|} \in F$. Transitions $\langle q_{i-1}, a_i, q_i \rangle$ are said *reached* by the acceptance. The *ambiguity degree* of an automaton A is the maximum number of acceptances that exist in A for a word of Σ^*. An *unambiguous finite automaton*, or UFA, is a NFA with an ambiguity degree inferior or equal to one (figure 1). When a NFA is not a UFA, we say it is ambiguous.

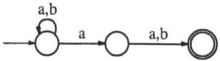

Fig. 1. An example of UFA, representing the language $\Sigma^* a \Sigma$

Notice that the class of DFA is included in the class of UFA. DFA and UFA are obviously included in the class of NFA. NFA, UFA and DFA can represent any regular language.

This document includes theorems for which only hints of proofs are provided; for complete proofs the reader can consult [CF03].

1 Search Space for Automata Inference

The search space we want to explore is the restriction to UFA of the search space for NFA inference by means of state-merging methods. This first section presents and revisits the NFA search space described by [DMV94,Dup96]. Next section will study its restriction to UFA.

In the framework of inference from given data [Gol78], we try to infer languages from a *training sample*. In this paper, we define a training sample of a language L to be a couple of finite sets $\langle S_+, S_- \rangle$, where $S_+ \subseteq L$ is called the *positive training sample* and $S_- \subseteq \Sigma^* \setminus L$ is called the *negative training sample*. For the sake of clarity we consider only the positive training sample in sections 1 and 2. However, results of these sections can be easily extended to consider *unbiased inference* [AS95,Cos99], i.e. to consider symmetrically the two parts of the sample.

An underlying assumption for inference of an automaton is that the positive training sample is "representative enough" of the language to learn. This can be formalized by the notion of *structural completeness* which intuitively means that all constituents of target automaton are useful for the sample recognition. More formally:

Definition 2. *A positive training sample S_+ is said to be* structurally complete *with respect to an automaton A iff there exists an acceptance set $\mathcal{A}$ containing exactly one acceptance for each word of S_+ such that:*

- *every transition of A is reached by an acceptance of $\mathcal{A}$,*
- *every initial state of A is the first state of an acceptance of $\mathcal{A}$,*
- *every final state of A is the last state of an acceptance of $\mathcal{A}$.*

Structural completeness hypothesis enables one to restrict the search space to a finite ordered set[1] of automata with a top and a bottom element. The top element of this set is the universal automaton and the bottom element is the *Maximal Canonical Automaton* (figure 2).

---

[1] Vocabulary of this paper concerning ordered sets is taken from [DP90].

Definition 3. *The* maximal canonical automaton *with respect to a positive sample* $S_+ = \{w_1, \ldots, w_{|S_+|}\}$, *denoted by* $MCA(S_+)$ *or more simply* MCA, *is the union of canonical automata* $A(\{w_i\})$ *for each word of the sample* ($i \in [1, |S_+|]$).

The MCA realizes a learning by rote of the positive sample. Inference in the state-merging framework consists in generalizing the language recognized by the MCA by *merging* its states (or unifying them, see [DMV94] for a constructive definition). Given an automaton A, and a partition π on states of A, we can construct an automaton A/π. A/π is constructed by merging the states of A being in a same block of the partition. We say that A/π *is derived* from A with respect to partition π.

We denote the set of partitions on the states of MCA by $\boldsymbol{P}(MCA)$. An order on the partitions of $\boldsymbol{P}(MCA)$ can be defined as follows: we say that a partition π_2 *directly derives* from partition π_1, denoted by $\pi_1 \prec \pi_2$, if π_2 can be constructed from π_1 as follows: $\exists b_1, b_2, \in \pi_1, b_1 \neq b_2, \pi_2 = (\pi_1 \setminus \{b_1, b_2\}) \cup \{b_1 \cup b_2\}$. The transitive closure of $\prec$ is denoted by $\prec^*$. $\boldsymbol{P}(MCA)$ is a complete lattice of partitions under the $\prec^*$ order relation.

The relation $\prec^*$ between partitions is extended to the relation $\prec_A^*$ between automata as follows: $A_1 \prec_A A_2 \Leftrightarrow \exists \pi_1, \pi_2 \in \boldsymbol{P}(MCA), \pi_1 \prec \pi_2, A_1 = MCA/\pi_1, A_2 = MCA/\pi_2$. The transitive closure of $\prec_A$, denoted by $\prec_A^*$, defines an order relation on automata. An automaton A inferior in the sense of $\prec_A^*$ to an automaton A' is said to be *derivable* from A'.

Let $\boldsymbol{A}_{\mathrm{NFA}}(MCA)$, or more simply $\boldsymbol{A}(MCA)$, denote the set of NFA derivable from MCA. In the following sections, we extend this notation to any classes of automata and any automata, for example $\boldsymbol{A}_{\mathrm{DFA}}(A)$ will denote the set of deterministic automata derived from automaton A. The following theorem holds (illustrated by figure 2).

Theorem 11 *The search space for NFA under the hypothesis of structural completeness of a positive training sample* S_+ *is* $\boldsymbol{A}(MCA(S_+))$.
Hint of the proof: *The proof is an extension of the proof provided by [DMV94] taking into account our more precise definition of structural completeness and NFA having more than one initial state.*□

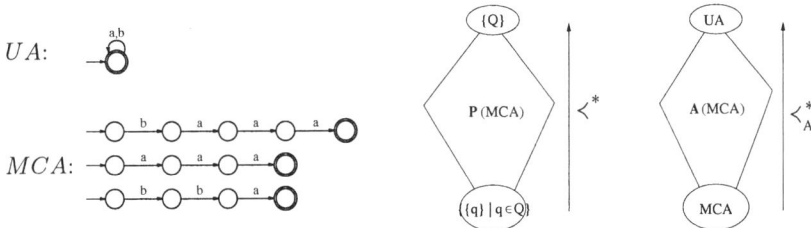

Fig. 2. Universal automaton (UA), Maximal canonical automaton (MCA) for $S_+ = \{aaa, bba, baaa\}$, $\boldsymbol{P}(MCA)$ and $\boldsymbol{A}(MCA)$.

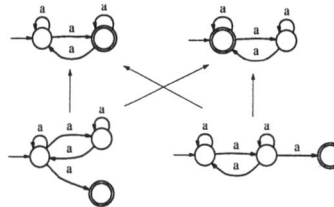

Fig. 3. We cannot deduce that $P(MCA)$ being a lattice, $A(MCA)$ is also a lattice because an automaton of $A(MCA)$ can be derived from more than one partition of $P(MCA)$. The figure illustrates this point by exhibiting a couple of automata - the two on top - without greatest lower bound under $\prec_A^*$ order relation (relation is represented by arrows).

Let us remark that, as illustrated by figure 3, even if $P(MCA)$ is a lattice of partitions, $A(MCA)$ is not a lattice of automata under $\prec_A^*$ order relation. This shows clearly a misuse of terms used in the regular grammatical inference community.

2 Search Space for UFA Inference

2.1 From DFA to UFA

The inference search space has often been restricted to DFA, and NFA inference can be considered to be harder than DFA inference (indeed, NFA do not have a canonical form and are not polynomially learnable from given data whereas DFA are [Hig97]). We show, in this section, that properties known for the restriction of the search space to DFA are also valid for the restriction of the search space to UFA.

The bottom element of the search space of DFA is the prefix tree acceptor denoted by $PTA(S_+)$ or more simply PTA [DMV94] and is obtained by determinisation of MCA. For UFA, MCA being unambiguous, the bottom element stays MCA like for the search space of NFA.

A first link between DFA and UFA search space is given by theorem 21:

Theorem 21 *Let A be a UFA and S_+ a positive training sample structurally complete with respect to A. There exists one and only one partition π in $P(MCA)$ such that $A = MCA/\pi$.*
Hint of the proof: *There exists a partition π such that $A = MCA/\pi$ (entailed by UFA $\subset$ NFA and theorem 11). We have to show that this partition is unique.*

For each word $w \in S_+$, A being a UFA, there exists only one acceptance acc_1 for this word in A. The acceptance acc_2 for w in MCA defines a mapping function from states of MCA to states of A, every ith state of acc_2 being mapped to ith state of acc_1. This mapping defines for every state of MCA the unique block of partition it can be in, and therefore the unique possible partition. □

This property was known for DFA and theorem 21 replaces it in the more general framework of UFA. From theorem 21 and as illustrated by figure 4, UFA have the advantage over NFA of being represented by only one partition. DFA have the advantage over NFA and UFA of having a canonical form.

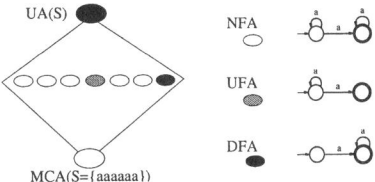

Fig. 4. The figure shows partitions of minimum size 2 representing the same language $L = a^+$ in $P(MCA)$ with $S_+ = \langle\{aaaaaa\}\rangle$. When looking at derived automata from these partitions, we count a unique DFA, two UFA and 7 NFA, 5 being isomorphic.

To explore the search space of UFA, we could consider only state-merging from the MCA leading to other UFA. Indeed, we show in [CF03] - extending a theorem of [Dup96] for DFA - that all UFA of the search space can be reached from the MCA by a sequence of merge considering only UFA.

Nevertheless, we focus in this paper on another state-merging operator for UFA inference called *unambiguous merging*. This operator can be considered as the counterpart of the *deterministic merging* operator which has been extensively used in DFA inference algorithms (e.g. [OG92,LPP98]).

2.2 From Deterministic Merging to Unambiguous Merging

The deterministic merging operator is based on a procedure called *merging for determinisation*. After introducing a few definitions and a property, we present the dual *merging for disambiguisation* procedure and then the unambiguous merging operator[2].

Two states q_1 and q_2 are said to be in *common prefix relation* (resp. in *common suffix relation*) if the intersection of their prefix languages (resp. their suffix languages) is not empty. Two states q_1 and q_2 simultaneously in common prefix relation and in common suffix relation are said in *parallel acceptance relation*, denoted by $q_1 \parallel q_2$.

Property 21 *An automaton $A = \langle \Sigma, Q, I, \delta, F \rangle$ is ambiguous iff it has two different states in parallel acceptance relation.*
Hint of the proof: *For every couple of different states $\langle q_1, q_2 \rangle$ in parallel acceptance relation, there exists a word u common to their prefix languages and a word v common to their suffix languages. This is equivalent to the existence of two acceptances for the word uv, the first reaching q_1 and the second q_2 by the word u.* □

The sets of common prefix and common suffix relations can be computed and incrementally maintained after each merge [CF00]. Common suffix relation is presented here for the first time but can be maintained exactly like incompatibility relation presented in [CF00]. Parallel acceptance relation is directly deduced from the previous.

By using these relations, we can now define the *merging for disambiguisation* procedure (algorithm 1). This procedure consists in merging pair of states in

---
[2] Formal properties of the deterministic merging operator have never been formalized, this section provides both its extension to the unambiguous case and a formalization of this operator properties.

Algorithm 1 Merging for disambiguisation of $A = \langle \Sigma, Q, I, \delta, F \rangle$
1: **while** $\exists q_1, q_2 \in Q, q_1 \parallel q_2,\ q_1 \neq q_2$ **do**
2: $\quad A \leftarrow merge(A, q_1, q_2)$

parallel acceptance relation. Each merge possibly entailing new relations, the procedure stops merging when no more couple of states are in parallel acceptance relation.

Compared to merging for determinisation, which can be defined as merging of all states in common prefix relation, merging for disambiguisation merges all states both in common prefix relation and common suffix relation. Therefore merging for disambiguisation realizes only a subset of the merging needed by merging for determinisation and allows a finer exploration of the search space.

Merging for disambiguisation (resp. merging for determinisation) does all necessary and sufficient merging to reach the "closest" UFA (resp. DFA) derived from a NFA. We formalize this fact for UFA by property 22:

Property 22 *Let A be a NFA, and A' the UFA obtained by merging for disambiguisation of A. Then every UFA of $\boldsymbol{A}_{UFA}(A)$ is in $\boldsymbol{A}_{UFA}(A')$.*
Hint of the proof: *Let $A = A_1, A_2, \ldots, A_n = A'$ be the sequence of automata created by the merging for disambiguisation procedure. From property 21 we can show that there is no UFA in $\boldsymbol{A}_{UFA}(A_i) - \boldsymbol{A}_{UFA}(A_{i+1})$. The theorem can then be proven by induction on $i \in [1, n[$.* □

Let us remark that property 22 entails that whatever the order of merging realized by merging for disambiguisation (or merging for determinisation), these merging always lead to the same automaton.

We now introduce the operator of *unambiguous merging* (resp. *deterministic merging*. Unambiguous (resp. deterministic) merging consists in merging two states of an automaton and applying merging for disambiguisation (resp. determinisation) to the resulting automaton.

We will denote by $A_1 \prec_{dis} A_2$ (resp. $A_1 \prec_{det} A_2$) if automaton A_2 can be obtained by applying one unambiguous (resp. deterministic) merging on A_1. Relations $\prec_{dis}^*$ and $\prec_{det}^*$ will denote respectively the transitive closure of $\prec_{dis}$ and $\prec_{det}$.

As shown by theorem 22, every UFA derived from a given UFA A - i.e. automata of $\boldsymbol{A}_{UFA}(A)$ - can be reached by a sequence of unambiguous merging from A. More formally: $\forall A_1, A_2 \in \text{UFA},\ A_1 \in \boldsymbol{A}(A_2) \Rightarrow A_2 \prec_{dis}^* A_1$.

Theorem 22 *Let A be a UFA, for all UFA A' of $\boldsymbol{A}_{UFA}(A)$, there exists a sequence of automata $A_0, \ldots, A_n$ such that $A_0 \prec_{dis} A_1 \prec_{dis} \ldots \prec_{dis} A_n$ and $A = A_0,\ A' = A_n$.*
Hint of the proof: *This can be proven as a consequence of property 22.*□

The counterpart of this theorem for DFA and deterministic merging is also true, i.e.: $\forall A_1, A_2 \in \text{DFA},\ A_1 \in \boldsymbol{A}(A_2) \Rightarrow A_2 \prec_{det}^* A_1$.

Section 3 presents the use of the operator of unambiguous merging to explore the space of UFA.

3 Experimental Comparison

3.1 Algorithms and Benchmarks

Section 2 detailed both the search space for UFA and operators available to explore it. Different strategies can be applied when using these operators. Our experimental results are based on a greedy search - presented by algorithm 2 - which is the classical approach applied for DFA inference (e.g. [OG92,LPP98]). The choose-two-states method of this algorithm represents the heuristic, i.e.

Algorithm 2 Principle of greedy state-merging algorithms.

Function greedy-state-merging-algorithm$(S = \langle S_+, S_- \rangle)$
$A \leftarrow MCA(S_+)$ (or $A \leftarrow PTA(S_+)$ for DFA inference)
while choose-two-states(A, q_1, q_2) do
    $A' \leftarrow$ state-merging(A, q_1, q_2)
    if A' is compatible with S_- then $A \leftarrow A'$
return A

---

the order used to try state-mergings. The state-merging method depends on which class of automata is inferred: we use deterministic merging and unambiguous merging for respectively DFA and UFA inference.

We compared the best heuristic known for DFA inference, called EDSM [LPP98], a hill-climbing strategy for UFA (detailed in subsection 3.2) and inference of RFSA (Residual Finite State Automata) with the DeLeTe2 algorithm [DLT01]. The experimental comparison of DFA, UFA and RFSA inference is based on benchmarks provided in [DLT00,DLT01]. These benchmarks contain training and testing sets for languages generated using different methods: construction of random DFA, random NFA and random regular expressions. We added to this benchmark languages generated by a UFA generator.

The UFA generator takes five parameters: a number of states N, a probability p_i for a state to be initial, a probability p_f to be final, an alphabet Σ and a number of transition t. After constructing the N states of the generated automaton A, each state is set initial with probability p_i; then each state is set final with probability p_f, except if this entails that A became ambiguous; and then, we try t times to insert a new transition $\langle q_1, a, q_2 \rangle$ between states of A (q_1, q_2 and a being chosen uniformly in $Q \times \Sigma \times Q$), this transition insertion is rejected if it entails A to be ambiguous. UFA of the benchmark have been generated with parameters: $N = 20$, $p_i = 0.3$, $p_f = 0.3$, $t = 60$ and $\Sigma = \{0, 1\}$.

Training and testing samples are generated with the method used in [DLT01]: for each word w of the sample, its length is chosen uniformly in $[0, 29]$ and w is chosen uniformly between words of this length. w is labeled by '+' if it is in the generated language and by '-' otherwise. 30 languages are generated for each size of training sample (50, 100, 150 or 200). The generated language is kept only if the corresponding training sample contains at most 80%, and at least 20%, of words labeled by '+'. Testing sample of each language contains 1000 examples and counter-examples.

3.2 Heuristics for UFA and DFA Inference

Heuristic: For UFA inference, we use a hill-climbing heuristic, i.e. we choose the unambiguous merging leading to the smallest automaton (which is equivalent to the unambiguous merging entailing the most state-mergings). For DFA inference we used the EDSM heuristic (for Evidence Driven State-Merging). This heuristic has been proposed by [LPP98] and won the grammatical inference competition Abbadingo [Abb98]. EDSM chooses the deterministic merging that entails the most number of merge between final states by merging for determinisation.

In practice, these two heuristics need the computation respectively of each possible deterministic mergings and unambiguous mergings of two states. A score is given to each state pair (consisting in the number of merged states for UFA, and of the number of merged final states for DFA), and the states pair with the best score is choosen.

Even if *a priori* different, these two heuristics may be seen as closely related to each other with respect to the notion of acceptance.

Indeed, the choice of counting merge between final states instead of merge between every states in EDSM can be seen as a measure of the "size" of the intersection of suffixes languages of the two scored states. The prefix languages of states of a DFA being disjoint, this measure can also be seen as a measure of the number of acceptances being unified by the state-merging.

This idea is also present in the hill-climbing heuristic for UFAs. Each state-merging computed by the merging for disambiguisation procedure is due to the existence of two acceptances for a word. These state-mergings therefore enable to unify acceptances, and the number of merged states can can be considered as a measure of the number of unified acceptances.

Use of counter-examples: Counter-examples may be used in different ways. We can consider biased inference which consists in generalizing examples and stopping the generalization with the counter-examples [DMV94]. We can also consider unbiased inference [AS95,Cos99], which consider that the couple S_+ and S_- are examples respectively of the target language L and of $L_- = \Sigma^* \setminus L$. In this context, the two languages L and L_- are inferred by generalizing simultaneously S_+ and S_- using a *classifier automaton*. Generalization is stopped with the constraint $L \cap L_- = \emptyset$ (instead of $L \cap S_- = \emptyset$).

The DeLeTe2 algorithm works in the biased inference paradigm. The EDSM heuristic has been presented in [LPP98] in the unbiased inference paradigm but can also be applied to biased inference (as presented in the previous paragraph). In this paper we compare the use of the EDSM heuristic for DFA inference both in the unbiased and biased paradigm, hill-climbing for UFA inference both in the unbiased and biased paradigm and DeLeTe2. Corresponding algorithms will be denoted respectively D_{edsm}, Db_{edsm}, U_{hc}, Ub_{hc}, and DLT2. We will also consider the majority vote denoted by MAJ.

Generator	NFA				Regular Expressions			
Sample size	50	100	150	200	50	100	150	200
MAJ	69.0	66.2	65.7	67.8	64.7	66.7	62.3	62.8
Db_{edsm}	67.1	70.0	73.1	73.3	**83.7**	85.5	91.8	92.1
D_{edsm}	67.0	67.6	70.7	71.0	79.5	81.7	89.7	93.1
Ub_{hc}	**70.4**	70.8	74.0	73.1	75.8	82.9	91.7	91.2
U_{hc}	67.0	71.2	73.7	71.3	76.0	81.5	88.8	91.0
DLT2	69.8	**74.8**	**77.1**	**79.4**	81.7	**91.7**	**92.3**	**95.9**
Generator	UFA				DFA			
Sample size	50	100	150	200	50	100	150	200
MAJ	83.8	82.1	81.4	81.9	70.7	71.0	72.5	73.8
Db_{edsm}	89.2	91.1	**94.3**	93.2	69.1	**73.3**	74.8	76.3
D_{edsm}	79.1	81.0	89.6	90.2	65.7	68.3	70.4	74.7
Ub_{hc}	**90.7**	**91.9**	94.2	**93.8**	70.4	73.4	74.5	77.5
U_{hc}	89.7	89.8	92.5*	91.6	**71.1**	72.9	**75.9**	**77.8***
DLT2	88.6	90.4	91.9	92.7	61.9	65.1	68.3	70.7

Fig. 5. Average recognition level on test sets.

3.3 Inference Results

The evaluation consists in scoring each algorithm for each benchmark thanks to its average recognition level on the test sets (figure 5). Like [DLT01], we also compare algorithms thanks to matches (noted algo1-algo2 in figure 6). A match consists in counting the number of time an algorithm is better than another (in term of recognition rate), and we count a tie when the difference is not significant (using the Mac Nemar test [Die98]). Those matches are noted as tuple: wonByAlgo1,nbTie,wonByAlgo2. Since experiments have been made on different machines with different implementations, comparing running time is difficult. Nevertheless, in these experimentations, our algorithm Ub_{hc} seems to be 2 orders of magnitude slower than DLT2, which is slower than Db_{edsm}. The symbol * in the cell designates when some experiments have not finished due to the time limit of 100h on 750 Mhz cpu (more precisely, two runs on the 480 runs of the algorithm U_{hc} did not finished on time).

We remark that algorithms based on UFA inference have better recognition scores on the benchmark than the original DFA algorithm (Ub_{hc} won 170 times against 119 for Db_{edsm}). This result was hoped for NFA, regular expressions and UFA benchmarks. More surprisingly, UFA inference performs better than DFA inference on the DFA benchmark. We explain this by considering that choosing the wrong unambiguous merging at a step of the algorithm causes less constraints on future mergings than choosing a wrong deterministic merging. A wrong unambiguous merging can therefore be "partly corrected" by future mergings.

We can also remark that the biased versions of the algorithms are much better than the unbiased one on benchmarks for which L and $\Sigma^* \setminus L$ are not generated symmetrically (Ub_{hc} won 135 times against 63 for U_{hc}, and Db_{edsm} won 168 times against 56 for D_{edsm} on these benchmarks).

Generator	NFA				Regular Expressions			
Sample size	50	100	150	200	50	100	150	200
D_{edsm}-Db_{edsm}	10,8,12	5,13,12	5,10,15	6,12,12	7,12,11	5,13,12	5,16,9	3,23,4
Ub_{hc}-Db_{edsm}	16,9,5	11,12,7	12,10,8	12,10,8	5,12,13	11,6,13	10,14,6	6,10,14
U_{hc}-Ub_{hc}	4,11,15	4,20,6	5,18,7	6,11,13	9,13,8	9,5,16	5,13,12	6,13,11
DLT2-Ub_{hc}	9,6,15	12,13,5	14,10,6	16,11,3	15,8,7	17,8,5	10,10,10	18,9,3
Generator	UFA				DFA			
Sample size	50	100	150	200	50	100	150	200
D_{edsm}-Db_{edsm}	1,4,25	1,6,23	2,13,15	6,6,18	4,10,16	2,7,21	2,12,16	7,10,13
Ub_{hc}-Db_{edsm}	17,6,7	13,14,3	7,15,8	13,9,8	13,13,4	11,14,5	8,16,6	15,11,4
U_{hc}-Ub_{hc}	5,15,10	4,14,12	3,15,11*	3,12,15	8,16,6	4,21,5	10,18,2	10,16,3*
DLT2-Ub_{hc}	6,11,13	4,14,12	3,13,14	6,13,11	1,7,22	1,2,27	2,6,22	2,5,23

Fig. 6. Matches between algorithms.

When comparing UFA and RFSA inference, tables of figures 5 and 6 show that UFA inference and RFSA inference are each better suited to different subpart of the benchmark: Ub_{hc} performs better than DLT2 on UFA and DFA based benchmarks. However, DLT2 is the best algorithm on benchmarks based on NFA and regular expressions. Thus, we suppose that the class of UFA is "closer" to DFA than the class of RFSA is "close" to NFA and regular expressions.

Conclusion

We have revisited the search space for automata inference. We formalized properties known on the DFA search space, and extended them to the UFA search space. This work leaded to the extension of the well known deterministic merging operator to the unambiguous merging operator, which seems very promising for automata inference. Indeed, this new operator allows us to propose a heuristic closely related to EDSM [LPP98]. The use of the unambiguous merging operator together with this heuristic has been shown to perform well on benchmarks of the domain.

Deeper studies on the deterministic merging operator and on the unambiguous merging operator have shown that these operators give a lattice structure to the search space [CF03]. Therefore, practical results presented in this paper use only part of the available theoretical properties. Integrating these properties in inference algorithms is an open perspective to our research.

References

[Abb98] Abbadingo one, 1998. http://abbadingo.cs.unm.edu/.
[AS95] R. Alquézar and A. Sanfeliu. Incremental grammatical inference from positive and negative data using unbiased finite state automata. In Shape, Structure and Pattern Recognition, *Proc. Int. Workshop on Structural and Syntactic Pattern Recognition, SSPR'94, Nahariya (Israel)*, pages 291–300, 1995.

[CF00]   F. Coste and D. Fredouille. Efficient ambiguity detection in C-NFA, a step toward inference of non deterministic automata. *Grammatical Inference: Algorithms and Applications, ICGI'00*, pages 25–38, 2000.

[CF03]   F. Coste and D. Fredouille. What is the search space for the inference of nondeterministic, unambiguous and deterministic automata? Technical report, IRISA, to appear, download: http://www.irisa.fr/prive/dfredoui/down/report.ps.gz, 2003.

[Cos99]   F. Coste. State merging inference of finite state classifiers. Technical Report INRIA/RR-3695, IRISA, September 1999.

[Die98]   Thomas G. Dietterich. Approximate statistical test for comparing supervised classification learning algorithms. *Neural Computation*, 10(7):1895–1923, 1998.

[DLT00]   F. Denis, A. Lemay, and A. Terlutte. Learning regular languages using non deterministic finite automate. *Grammatical Inference: Algorithms and Applications, ICGI'00*, 2000.

[DLT01]   F. Denis, A. Lemay, and A. Terlutte. Learning regular languages using RFSA. In *Proceedings of the 12th International Conference on Algorithmic Learning Theory, ALT'01*, pages 348–363, 2001.

[DMV94]   P. Dupont, L. Miclet, and E. Vidal. What is the search space of the regular inference ? *Grammatical inference and Applications, ICGI'94*, pages 25–37, 1994. Springer Verlag.

[DP90]   B. Davey and A. Priesley. *Introduction to lattices and order*. Cambridge mathematical textbooks, 1990.

[Dup96]   P. Dupont. *Utilisation et apprentissage de modèles de langages pour la reconnaissance de la parole continue*. PhD thesis, Ecole Nationale Supérieure des Télécommunications, 1996.

[Gol78]   E. M. Gold. Complexity of automaton identification from given data. *Information and Control*, 37:302 – 320, 1978.

[Hig97]   C. Higuera (de la). Characteristic sets for polynomial grammatical inference. *Machine Learning*, 27:125–138, 1997.

[Lan92]   K. J. Lang. Random dfa's can be approximately learned from sparse uniform examples. *5th ACM workshop on Computation Learning Theorie*, pages 45 – 52, 1992.

[LPP98]   K. J. Lang, B. A. Pearlmutter, and R. A. Price. Results of the abbadingo one DFA learning competition and a new evidence-driven state merging algorithm. *Lecture Notes in Computer Science*, 1433:1–12, 1998.

[OG92]   J. Oncina and P. García. Inferring regular languages in polynomial update time. *Pattern Recognition and Image Analysis*, pages 49 – 61, 1992.

[PW89]   L. Pitt and M. Warmuth. The minimum consistent DFA problem cannot be approximated within any polynomial. In *21st ACM Symposium on Theory of Computing*, pages 421–444, 1989.

Could Active Perception Aid Navigation of Partially Observable Grid Worlds?

Paul A. Crook and Gillian Hayes

Institute of Perception, Action and Behaviour,
School of Informatics, University of Edinburgh,
5 Forrest Hill, Edinburgh. EH1 2QL, UK
{paulc,gmh}@dai.ed.ac.uk
http://www.dai.ed.ac.uk/homes/paulc/index.html

Abstract. Due to the unavoidable fact that a robot's sensors will be limited in some manner, it is entirely possible that it can find itself unable to distinguish between differing states of the world (the world is in effect partially observable). If reinforcement learning is used to train the robot, then this confounding of states can have a serious effect on its ability to learn optimal and stable policies. Good results have been achieved by enhancing reinforcement learning algorithms through the addition of memory or the use of internal models. In our work we take a different approach and consider whether active perception could be used instead. We test this using omniscient oracles, who play the role of a robot's active perceptual system, in a simple grid world navigation problem. Our results indicate that simple reinforcement learning algorithms can learn when to consult these oracles, and as a result learn optimal policies.

1 Introduction

Partially observable environments cause particular problems when reinforcement learning is used to learn the task. Reinforcement learning algorithms associate rewards and actions with states, but in partially observable environments the true state can be masked. This makes it virtually impossible (apart from some very simple worlds [1]) for basic 1-step reinforcement learning algorithms to converge to optimal policies [2, pp73–78]. Work in this area has shown that when learning algorithms are augmented with memory [3] or the ability to learn a model of their world [4,5], they can find optimal solutions to this type of problem. Our aim is to examine an alternative approach. Rather than equipping the learning algorithms with memory or the ability to model their environment, we propose to equip agents or robots with sensors which they can actively control, and hope to demonstrate that the learning algorithms can learn to use this active perception to find optimal solutions.

This paper considers the questions: (i) could an agent learn to use an active perceptual system?, (ii) is there any benefit for an agent in using such a system to disambiguate its current state? To study the fundamentals of the problem we consider simulated agents moving around deterministic grid worlds, for example

Sutton's Grid World (Fig. 1). In order to focus on the questions raised above we make the assumption that it is possible to give an agent an active perception system which it could use to disambiguate the current state. To this end we introduce oracles which the agent can consult. These play the role of active perception systems which can disambiguate the agent's current state perfectly, see section 2.4. Thus the hypotheses that we attempt to test are:

(i) Reinforcement learning algorithms can learn when to use additional resources in order to determine an agent's true state in a partially observable grid world.
(ii) Resolving the agent's true state in a partially observable world allows reinforcement learning algorithms to learn optimal policies.

2 Background

2.1 Reinforcement Learning & Partially Observable Worlds

Whitehead [2, p72] identifies two distinct problems which occur when using reinforcement learning with robotic systems in partially observable environments: local and global impairment.

As an example of local impairment consider a robot standing at one of two similar looking T-junctions. It is unable to distinguish between the two junctions and hence regards them as the same state. We use the phrase *aliased state* to refer to such states which appear to be identical but in the underlying model are distinct. The robot's policy when learnt using reinforcement learning can only link a single action to the perceived single state, thus it will execute the same action at both of the T-junctions. If at one T-junction the optimal action is to turn left and at the other it is to turn right then the single action learnt by the policy will be wrong in one of the two cases[1]. More generally, when learning a state-action policy where there exist aliased states, the policy will sometimes select actions which are inconsistent with the actual underlying state.

Global impairment occurs where inconsistent state values produced by aliased states are used to update the state values of otherwise consistent states. This occurs independently of whether the action selected in the aliased states is inconsistent. As an example, consider again the robot standing at one of the two T-junctions. If the optimal action at both T-junctions is the same, *e.g.* turn left, then action selection is not a problem as the policy can link this single action with the single perceived state, however there is still a problem with representing the value of the aliased states. In reinforcement learning the policy is generally represented by storing a value for each state or each state-action pair. These values indicate the utility of being in that state (or selecting a given action from that state). Given that the two T-junctions are perceived as one and the same location, a single state value or single set of state-action values will be stored. The stored value(s) will be updated to represent the value of being at both of the T-junctions and hence over time become a weighted[2] average of the true value

---
[1] Assuming the only possible actions are turn left or right.
[2] Weighted by the number of times each state is visited.

of each of the underlying states. Now, if one junction is far from the goal and the other is very close to the goal, their averaged value will make the junction that is far from the goal appear more attractive than it should, while the junction near the goal will appear to be a less valuable state than it should. If 1-step backup of state values is employed, such as in SARSA or Q-learning [6, p146, p149], then these averaged state values will be used to update those states around the T-junctions causing errors in their state values and possibly also in the selection of actions. These errors in the state values can propagate from state to state affecting the whole of the robot's policy.

2.2 Satisficing & Optimal Memoryless Policies

Littman [7] considered learning state-action policies in partially observable environments and introduced the useful concepts of *satisficing* and *optimal memoryless policies*. A policy is said to be satisficing if independent of its initial state an agent following this policy is guaranteed to reach the goal. A memoryless policy is a policy which selects an action based solely on the current sensation. SARSA and Q-learning are examples of reinforcement learning algorithms which work on exactly this basis. If the performance of a policy is measured by the number of steps taken to reach the goal summed over all possible initial states of the agent (*total steps*), then an optimal policy is one that achieves the minimum total steps to the goal and an optimal memoryless policy is a policy that achieves the minimum number of total steps which can be achieved by a memoryless policy.

Singh et al.[8] proved that an optimal memoryless policy is arbitrarily worse than the optimal policy which can be achieved in the absence of aliased states. Despite this result, Littman [7] used branch and bound techniques to demonstrate that it is possible to find optimal memoryless solutions for various grid world navigation problems, and for the range of grid worlds examined, the optimal memoryless policies did not take an unreasonable number of extra steps.

2.3 Eligibility Traces

Whitehead [2] indicates that global impairment prevents 1-step backup reinforcement learning algorithms from being able to learn stable and optimal policies for partially observable environments. However Loch and Singh [9] showed that the simple addition of eligibility traces to reinforcement learning allows it to find optimal memoryless policies in grid world navigation problems. Eligibility traces appear to avoid the problem posed by global impairment by updating a chain of previously visited states.

2.4 Active Perception

By active perception we mean a perceptual system which an agent can direct in order to vary the input it receives from the world. An obvious example is a video camera mounted on a robotic arm. An agent equipped with such a camera can direct the movement of the arm and thus obtain different views of its surroundings. In the context of grid worlds, active perception would involve the agent being able to choose which grid squares make up its input state. At this stage however we are interested in simplifying the problem in order to understand the underlying dynamics. Therefore rather than equip the grid world agents with active perception systems which they would have to learn to coordinate, we have instead provided them with oracles.

Introducing oracles which the agents can consult is a useful test. If an agent can learn when to make appropriate use of an oracle, then it should be able to learn when to use an active perceptual system. On the other hand, if it fails to make use of an oracle, it seems unlikely that it could learn to use an active perception system, especially as the latter may require the coordination of many more actions. In the experiments presented below we have used two types of oracle. These correspond to two possible questions "where am I?" or "where should I go?". The first, the *State Oracle*, can on request provide the agent with an unambiguous state representation of its current location. The second, the *Action Oracle*, explicitly directs the agent based on a known optimal solution (the solution used is that indicated by the arrows in Fig. 1).

Our hypothesis, that agents using active perception (or in this case oracles) together with eligibility traces should be able to learn optimal solutions, stems from the observation that oracles resolve the problem of local action selection, and eligibility traces address the issue of global impairment.

We do not currently envisage using oracles when implementing this technique on real robots. They are introduced as a useful simplification to aid understanding of the underlying problems. However, it is possible to imagine scenarios where resource constraints might make the use of oracles worthwhile, *e.g.* mass produced military robots with limited computational power and sensors, which have access to a central computer to aid their exploration. To avoid overloading the central computer or to minimise the number of transmissions they make, these robots might only call on the central computer (their oracle) when unable to determine their location independently.

3 Experiments

The experiments presented here use Sutton's Grid World (Fig. 1) which consists of a 9×6 grid containing various obstacles and a goal in the top right hand corner (indicated by an asterisk). An agent in this world can choose between four *physical actions*; move north, south, east and west. The agent receives a reward of -1 for each action which does not move it directly to the goal state and a reward of 0 for moving directly to the goal state. State transitions are deterministic and each action moves it one square in the appropriate direction. If an agent selects a physical action whose execution is obstructed by an obstacle or wall, then the agent's location remains unaltered but it receives the same -1 reward as above. When the agent reaches the goal state it is relocated to a uniformly random start state.

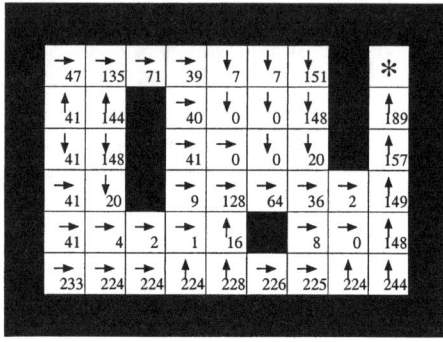

Fig. 1. Sutton's grid world. Values indicate the observations obtained by an agent observing the eight squares surrounding its current location (Eight Adjacent Squares Agent). Arrows shows an example optimal policy

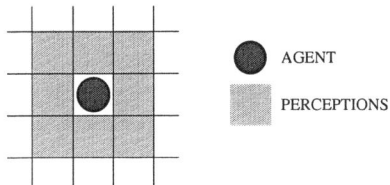

Fig. 2. Eight Adjacent Squares Agent has a state representation formed by observing the eight squares surrounding its current location

Littman [7] modified Sutton's original problem by introducing an agent whose state representation is formed by observing the eight squares adjacent to its current location (Fig. 2), an *Eight Adjacent Squares Agent*. This is opposed to an agent whose state representation is its location in the world given in Cartesian coordinates and is more representative of the problem faced by a robot in a building. For an Eight Adjacent Squares Agent there are multiple locations that are aliased; Fig. 1 shows indicative values which represent the perception of such an agent. Some of the aliased states cause the agent to learn inconsistent actions, *e.g.* perception 148 occurs in three locations: (i) four squares directly below the goal, (ii) near the middle of the obstacle which is to the left of the goal and (iii) near the middle of the far obstacle. As can be seen from Fig. 1 the optimal solution (indicated by the arrows) requires a different action in one of the three occurrences of this perceptual state. Other aliased states cause only global impairment, *e.g.* perception 2 which occurs just below the obstacle near the goal and just below the far obstacle. In this case the optimal action is always the same, *i.e.* move east, but the aliased state values cause problems as one location is very near the goal and the other is quite a distance away.

We used three types of agent:

(i) *Eight Adjacent Squares Agent.* An agent whose state representation is formed by observing the 8 squares adjacent to its current location, as shown in Fig. 2.

(ii) *Action Oracle Agent.* An agent who has the same state representation as the Eight Adjacent Squares Agent but has an additional action allowing it to ask the Action Oracle in which direction it should go. The agent then immediately executes the action specified by the oracle.
(iii) *State Oracle Agent.* An agent whose normal state representation is the same as the Eight Adjacent Squares Agent, but who can ask the State Oracle where it is. On asking the oracle the agent receives a state representation that corresponds to its absolute location in the world given in Cartesian coordinates.

The latter two agents receive a reward of −1 for selecting the action to ask their respective oracles a question. This reward is in addition to the reward for executing any subsequent actions. The way this works in practice is that the Action Oracle Agent, on asking its oracle where to go, transitions to an adjacent location in the grid world based on the optimal action from its current location, and receives a reward of −2 (−1 for asking the oracle and −1 for the action executed). The State Oracle Agent, on asking its oracle where it is, sees a state transition from its normal representation of its current location to an absolute coordinate system representation of the same location, receiving a penalty of −1 for asking the oracle. It then has to learn the optimal action to execute from this new state representation. Once it selects a physical action, its state representation reverts back to normal, *i.e.* it is formed by observing the 8 squares adjacent to its new location. This dual representation of the State Oracle Agent's location in the world more than doubles the state space which it needs to explore.

A range of reinforcement learning algorithms were used: SARSA, Q-learning, SARSA(λ) with replacement traces, Watkins's Q(λ) with accumulating traces. For details of the learning algorithms see [6, p146, p149, p181, p184] respectively. All of the learning algorithms continuously updated their policies. Actions are selected greedily using the current policy with a probability of $(1-\epsilon)$. In cases where actions have the same value, ties were broken at random. In the remaining ϵ cases the action executed was selected randomly between all the available actions. In all cases above, random selection is uniform across all possibilities. State-action values for all the learning algorithms were initiated at zero.

The following values were used for all learning algorithms: (i) learning rates (α) of 0.1 and 0.01, (ii) discount rate $\gamma = 0.9$, (iii) probability of random action (ϵ) started at 20% and decayed linearly reaching zero at the $200,000^{th}$ action-learning step, thereafter it remained at zero. For the learning algorithms SARSA(λ) and Watkins's Q(λ) a range of values were tried for the eligibility trace decay rate (λ); from 0.01 to 0.9. Results are shown for $\lambda = 0.9$ which was in general found to perform the best.

4 Evaluation

To test the first hypothesis we ran the agents for 400,000 action-learning steps and looked at example policies learnt by individual agents to examine if they were making appropriate use of the oracles.

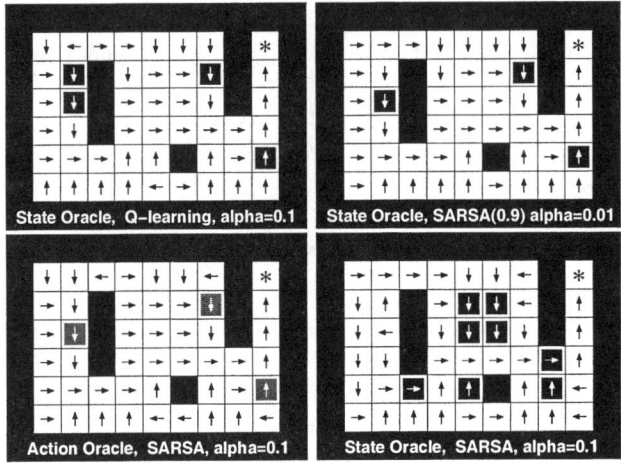

Fig. 3. Example policies learnt after 400,000 action-learning steps. Arrows indicate the physical action selected by the policy. Squares containing filled blocks indicate where the policy is to consult the oracle in order to select the shown physical action

To evaluate the second hypothesis we again ran the agents for 400,000 action-learning steps but evaluated the current policy after every 1000 action-learning steps. The policy is evaluated by executing it greedily and determining the total steps required to reach the goal from every possible starting position. Separate counts were kept of physical actions and requests to the oracle. The agent is limited to a maximum of 1000 steps (total of both physical actions and requests to oracles) to reach the goal from each starting position. There are 46 non-goal starting states in Sutton's Grid World, so a policy that fails to reach the goal from all of them would have a maximum total number of steps of 46,000. Each combination of agent, world, learning algorithm and values of α and λ was repeated 100 times giving 100 samples per data point.

5 Results

Fig. 3 shows examples of the policies learnt for both Action and State Oracle Agents, using SARSA, Q-learning and SARSA(λ). Grid squares containing filled blocks indicate where the policy is to consult the oracle. Of the examples shown three have learnt that they achieve a better solution if they consult their respective oracle when they are in the three squares labelled 148 in Fig. 1. As was discussed in section 3, the squares labelled 148 are perceived to be identical but the action required for an optimal solution is not the same in each location. In the fourth example in Fig. 3 the agent consults the State Oracle when in the squares labelled 0, 2 and 16 in Fig. 1. The grid squares labelled 0 require different actions to be executed in different locations. The squares labelled 2 are aliased but require the same action to be executed in both locations. Square 16 is not aliased. Of the examples shown, the top right (State Oracle, SARSA(λ) with $\lambda = 0.9$ and $\alpha = 0.01$) is an optimal solution in terms of physical actions.

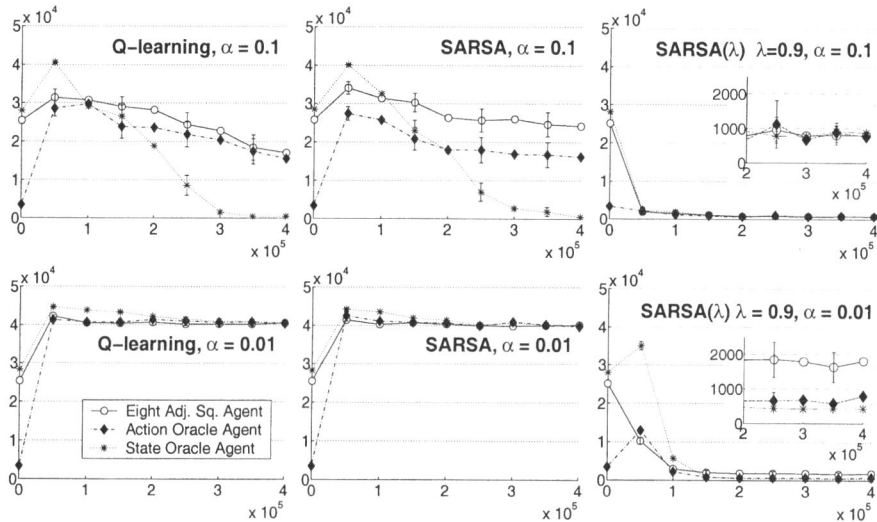

Fig. 4. Plot of mean total steps (sum of physical actions and requests to oracles) found when policies were evaluated, versus action-learning steps. To simplify plots data points are only shown for every 50,000 action-learning steps. Bars indicate 95% confidence intervals. The two inserts show enlargements of the tail of their respective plots

Fig. 4 allows comparison of the mean total steps (sum of physical actions and requests to the oracles) of the three agents. Plots are shown for each of the learning algorithms with the exception of Watkins's $Q(\lambda)$. Plots for Watkins's $Q(\lambda)$, which are not shown due to space constraints, are very similar to those for SARSA(λ). The top three plots show results for $\alpha = 0.1$, the lower three plots show results for $\alpha = 0.01$.

For $\alpha = 0.01$ the two 1-step backup algorithms (SARSA and Q-learning) fail to learn reasonable policies using any of the agents. The mean total steps in these six cases remains just below the maximum of 46,000 steps. Results for SARSA and Q-learning are better when $\alpha = 0.1$, with the mean total steps for all three agents falling as learning progresses. Even so, the Eight Adjacent Squares Agent struggles to learn reasonable solutions. This is expected as 1-step backup of state values will cause global impairment of the learnt policies. The curve for the Action Oracle Agent is better in the case of SARSA but almost identical to the Eight Adjacent Squares Agent for Q-learning. The most significant difference is shown by the State Oracle Agent. It is slower to learn initially, due to the increase in the state space caused by the State Oracle (see section 3), but in the longer term it achieves much better results than either of the other two agents. In the two plots for SARSA(λ), the total mean steps of all three agents reduce rapidly, convergence occurring more quickly with $\alpha = 0.1$ than $\alpha = 0.01$, as would be expected. Inserts, which show the tail of both of these plots, indicate that for $\alpha = 0.1$ there is no distinction between the mean total steps for the three types of agent. However, for $\alpha = 0.01$ the average policy learnt by the eight adjacent squares agent is worse than that for the two agents which can use oracles.

To get a clearer picture of what is occurring we classify the policies that have been learnt into five categories: optimal, better than memoryless optimal, memoryless optimal, other satisficing and non-satisficing. We define these terms specifically for Sutton's grid world in terms of the total physical actions taken when the policy is evaluated. The optimal policy for Sutton's grid world is 404 physical actions. Littman [7] showed that the optimal memoryless solution for Sutton's grid world is 416 physical actions. Note that these terms are defined in terms of physical actions and exclude requests to oracles. This is in order to make a level comparison between agents with oracles and those without. Littman's [7] definition of a satisficing policy is one that reaches the goal from all possible start states. Our measure of satisficing is stricter than this requirement as the agent is limited to 1,000 actions from each start state, after which the run is truncated and the policy deemed to be non-satisficing. Note that this measure includes requests to oracles as it is possible for an agent to select no physical actions and spend all its time talking to the oracle. The other satisficing class contains those policies that are satisficing but exceed the number of physical action steps required by the other categories. The five categories are summarised in table 1.

Fig. 5 shows the categorisation of policies from 100 trials over the course of 400,000 action-learning steps. Top left shows the policies learnt by the State Oracle Agent using Q-learning with $\alpha = 0.1$. By the end of the trials the majority of policies are classified as other satisficing (72 policies), with 4 that are memoryless optimal, 20 that are better than memoryless optimal and 4 non-satisficing. No optimal policies have been learnt. These results are better than expected as the State Oracle only addresses the issue of local action selection, not that of global impairment. The success of this agent with 1-step backup learning algorithms is, however, heavily dependent on the value of α as no satisficing policies are learnt for $\alpha = 0.01$. The categorisation of policies learnt by the State Oracle Agent using SARSA (not shown) is very similar with final results of 79 other satisficing, 6 memoryless optimal, 14 better than memoryless optimal, and 1 non-satisficing.

Fig. 5 also shows the categorisation of policies for SARSA(λ) for each of the three agents. Separate plots are shown for $\alpha = 0.1$ and 0.01 for the Action Oracle and State Oracle Agents. For the Eight Adjacent Squares Agent, which has no access to an oracle, with $\alpha = 0.1$ the majority of solutions are memoryless optimal, 83 at the end of the 100 trials, with 4 other satisficing policies and 13 non-satisficing. The results are similar for this agent with $\alpha = 0.01$ (not shown), 68 memoryless optimal, 11 other satisficing and 21 non-satisficing. This is in line with our expectations, as Loch and Singh [9] showed that the use of eligibility traces allowed agents to find optimal memoryless solutions.

With $\alpha = 0.1$ the Action Oracle Agent initially generates a small number of optimal policies, however these quickly disappear indicating that they are not stable and by the end the majority of policies (65) are memoryless optimal, 19 are better than memoryless optimal, 1 other satisficing, and 15 non-satisficing. The State Oracle Agent learns a large number (73) of better than memoryless

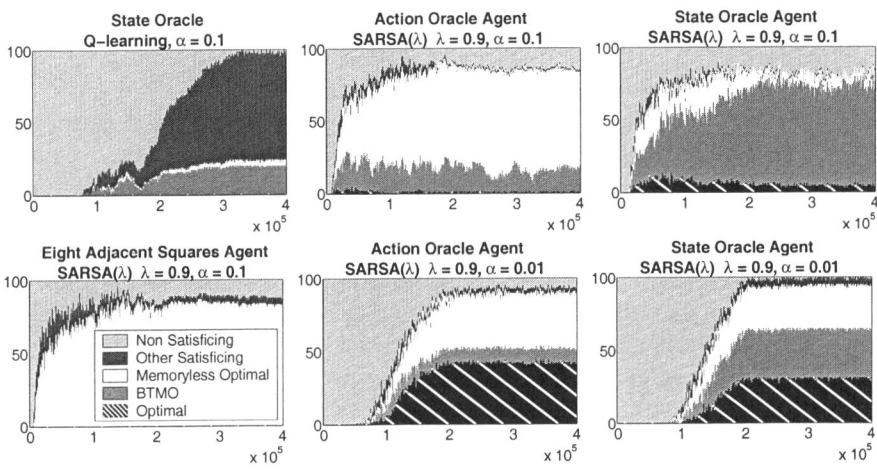

Fig. 5. Plots show categorisation of policies versus action-learning steps. Height of shaded areas indicate numbers of policies out of a total of one hundred that fall into each classification

Table 1. Policy categories for Sutton's Grid World

Goal Reached From All Start States	Total Physical Actions	Policy Category
yes	404	Optimal
yes	405 – 415	Better Than Memoryless Optimal (BTMO)
yes	416	Memoryless Optimal
yes	> 416	Other Satisficing
no	-	Non-Satisficing

optimal policies, 7 memoryless optimal, 4 optimal, and 1 other satisficing policy, the remaining 15 being non-satisficing. With $\alpha = 0.01$ both oracle agents learn significantly more optimal policies. The Action Oracle Agent learns 41 optimal policies, 10 better than memoryless optimal, 39 memoryless optimal, 3 other satisficing, and 7 non-satisficing. The State Oracle learns 31 optimal policies, 33 better than memoryless optimal, 30 memoryless optimal, 5 other satisficing, and 1 non-satisficing.

Over all, the plots for SARSA(λ) indicate that although the mean total steps for the three types of agent are close (Fig. 4), the actually policies that each learns varies significantly. Unlike the Eight Adjacent Squares Agent, both of the oracle agents learn optimal and better than memoryless optimal policies, especially when a lower value of α is used.

6 Discussion & Conclusion

The locations where the oracles are consulted in Fig. 3 generally correspond to places where we would expect difficulties due to state aliasing. Thus it appears that our first hypothesis is confirmed, in that reinforcement learning algorithms can learn to make good use of external resources in order to clarify the agent's current state. This indicates that agents should be able to make use of active perception systems when solving partially observable navigation problems.

Our second hypothesis is also not falsified as either oracle agent when combined with SARSA(λ) and Watkins's Q(λ) can learn optimal policies. Plots for Watkins's Q(λ) are not shown; they are similar to SARSA(λ), although significantly fewer optimal policies are learnt.

The State Oracle Agent generates more optimal policies than the Action Oracle Agent for $\alpha = 0.1$. For $\alpha = 0.01$ it has a lower mean total steps than the Action Oracle Agent whilst almost matching the number of optimal solutions learnt by the Action Oracle Agent. The success of the State Oracle Agent is encouraging since compared to the Action Oracle, which has access to a known optimal policy, the State Oracle has no extra information about the task. The results indicate that in order to aid an agent dealing with a partially observable task, an active perception system only has to provide non-ambiguous representations (within the context of the task) for the current state, *i.e.* it does not have to provide any additional knowledge or reasoning about the problem.

The frequency with which optimal policies are learnt appears to be limited and dependent on the value of α. Possible causes of this limit could be: (i) the cost of perceptual actions is too high; (ii) that the advice given by the Action Oracle to its agent may be of little value unless the agent's own policy has converged to closely match that used by the Action Oracle; (iii) there is some step change in complexity between better than memoryless optimal and optimal policies for Sutton's Grid World.

We briefly looked at varying the cost of perceptual actions. As the perceptual action cost decreases, the number of optimum policies learnt by the Action Oracle Agent increases. However, as the perceptual cost tends to zero, the individual agents tend towards the rather uninteresting policy of always asking the Action Oracle what to do. Also, for the range of perceptual action rewards tried, the State Oracle Agent failed to learn any satisficing policies. There is no constraint preventing the State Oracle Agent from continuously requesting information from the State Oracle, and with the perceptual action cost reduced to -0.5, and a discount factor (γ) of 0.9, it is less costly to talk to the oracle forever, than to attempt to reach the goal from some of the more distant locations in the grid world. There is a limited cost range within which the State Oracle Agent should learn satisficing policies, however this range is task specific and identifying it requires prior knowledge of the problem. This we would prefer to avoid.

In conclusion, the oracles were introduced as an idealised active perception system, and their success suggests that the use of active perception should provide a feasible approach to solving partially observable navigation problems.

7 Future Work

Future work flowing from this paper includes: (i) examining what prevents the combination of oracles and eligibility traces from generating a greater number of optimal solutions; (ii) generating comparative results for agents that use memory or internal models; (iii) extending these results to other grid world and also non-minimum time problems, *e.g.* McCallum's New York driving problem [10]; (iv) testing the performance of agents using actual active perception systems.

Acknowledgements

Paul Crook would like to thank EPSRC without whose funding this work would not be possible. We would also like to thank Alison Pease for proof reading drafts of this paper and the reviewers for their useful comments.

References

1. Paul A. Crook and Gillian Hayes. Learning in a state of confusion: Perceptual aliasing in grid world navigation. In *Towards Intelligent Mobile Robots 2003 (TIMR 2003), 4th British Conference on (Mobile) Robotics*, UWE, Bristol, 2003 *(in press)*.
2. Steven D. Whitehead. *Reinforcement Learning for the Adaptive Control of Perception and Action*. PhD thesis, University of Rochester, Department of Computer Science, Rochester, New York, 1992.
3. Pier Luca Lanzi. Adaptive agents with reinforcement learning and internal memory. In Jean-Arcady Meyer et al., editor, *From Animals to Animats 6: Proceedings of the Sixth International Conference on the Simulation of Adaptive Behavior (SAB'2000)*, pages 333–342. The MIT Press, Cambridge, MA, 2000.
4. Lonnie Chrisman. Reinforcement learning with perceptual aliasing: The perceptual distinctions approach. In *Tenth National Conference on Artificial Intelligence*, pages 183–188. AAAI/MIT Press, 1992.
5. Andrew Kachites McCallum. Overcoming incomplete perception with utile distinction memory. In *Tenth International Machine Learning Conference (ML'93)*, pages 190–196, Amherst, MA, 1993.
6. Richard S. Sutton and Andrew G. Barto. *Reinforcement Learning: An Introduction*. The MIT Press, Cambridge, MA, 1998.
7. Michael L. Littman. Memoryless policies: Theoretical limitations and practical results. In Dave Cliff et al., editor, *From Animals to Animats 3: Proceedings of the Third International Conference on Simulation of Adaptive Behavior (SAB'94)*, pages 238–245. The MIT Press, Cambridge, MA, 1994.
8. Satinder P. Singh, Tommi Jaakkola, and Michael I. Jordan. Learning without state-estimation in partially observable Markovian decision processes. In *International Conference on Machine Learning*, pages 284–292, 1994.
9. John Loch and Satinder Singh. Using eligibility traces to find the best memoryless policy in partially observable Markov decision processes. In *Proc. 15th International Conf. on Machine Learning*, pages 323–331. Morgan Kaufmann, San Francisco, CA, 1998.
10. Andrew Kachites McCallum. Learning to use selective attention and short-term memory in sequential tasks. In P. Maes et al., editor, *From Animals to Animats 4: Proceedings of the Fourth International Conference on Simulation of Adaptive Behavior (SAB'96)*, pages 315–324. The MIT Press, Cambridge, MA, 1996.

Combined Optimization of Feature Selection and Algorithm Parameters in Machine Learning of Language

Walter Daelemans[1], Véronique Hoste[1], Fien De Meulder[1], and Bart Naudts[2]

[1] CNTS Language Technology Group
University of Antwerp
Universiteitsplein 1, B-2610 Antwerpen
{daelem,hoste,dmeulder}@uia.ua.ac.be
[2] Postdoctoral researcher of the Fund for Scientific Research, Flanders, Belgium
ISLAB, University of Antwerp
bart.naudts@ua.ac.be

Abstract. Comparative machine learning experiments have become an important methodology in empirical approaches to natural language processing (i) to investigate which machine learning algorithms have the 'right bias' to solve specific natural language processing tasks, and (ii) to investigate which sources of information add to accuracy in a learning approach. Using automatic word sense disambiguation as an example task, we show that with the methodology currently used in comparative machine learning experiments, the results may often not be reliable because of the role of and interaction between feature selection and algorithm parameter optimization. We propose genetic algorithms as a practical approach to achieve both higher accuracy within a single approach, and more reliable comparisons.

1 Introduction

Supervised machine learning methods are investigated intensively in empirical computational linguistics because they potentially have a number of advantages compared to standard statistical approaches. For example, Inductive Logic Programming (ILP) systems allow easy integration of linguistic background knowledge in the learning system, induced rule systems are often more interpretable, memory-based learning methods incorporate smoothing of sparse data by similarity-based learning, etc.

Frequently, research in machine learning (ML) of natural language takes the form of *comparative ML experiments*, either to investigate the role of different information sources in learning a task, or to investigate whether the bias of some learning algorithm fits the properties of natural language processing tasks better than alternative learning algorithms.

For the former goal, results of experiments with and without a certain information source are compared, to measure whether it is responsible for a statistically significant increase or decrease in accuracy. An example is text categorization: we may be interested in investigating whether part-of-speech tagging (adding the contextually correct morphosyntactic classes to the words in a document) improves the accuracy of a Bayesian text classification system or not. This can be achieved by comparing the accuracy of the classifier with and without the information source.

In the latter goal, investigating the applicability of an algorithm for a type of task, the *bias* of an algorithm refers to the representational constraints and specific search heuristics it uses. Some examples of bias are the fact that decision tree learners favor compact decision trees, and that ILP systems can represent hypotheses in terms of first order logic in contrast to most other learning methods which can only represent propositional hypotheses. In such experiments, two or more ML algorithms are compared for their accuracy on the same data. One example is a comparison between eager and lazy learning algorithms for language tasks: we may want to show that abstracting from infrequent examples, as done in eager learning, is harmful to generalization accuracy [5].

Apart from their inherent interest, the comparative machine learning approach has also gained importance because of the influence of competitive research evaluations such as SENSEVAL[1] and the CoNLL shared tasks[2], in which ML and other systems are compared on the same train and test data. SENSEVAL concerns research on *word sense disambiguation*, which we will use as a test case in this paper.

Word Sense Disambiguation (WSD) is a natural language processing task in which a word with more than one sense has to be disambiguated by using information from the context in which the word occurs. E.g. *knight* can (among others) refer to a chess piece or a medieval character. WSD is an essential subcomponent in applications such as machine translation (depending on the sense, *knight* will be translated into French as either *cavalier* or *chevalier*), language understanding, question answering, information retrieval, and so on. Over the last five years, two SENSEVAL competitions have been run to test the strengths and weaknesses of WSD systems with respect to different words, different aspects of language, and different languages in carefully controlled contexts [10, 8]. Machine learning methods such as decision list learning and memory-based learning have been shown to outperform hand-crafting approaches in these comparisons, leading to a large body of comparative work of the two types discussed earlier.

A seminal paper by Mooney on the comparison of the accuracy of different machine learning methods [16] on the task of WSD is a good example of this classifier comparison approach. He tested seven ML algorithms on their ability to disambiguate the word *line*, and made several conclusions in terms of algorithm bias to explain the results. Many more examples can be found in the recent NLP literature of similar studies and interpretations [17, 9, 15], often with contradictory results and interpretations.

In the remainder of this paper, we will first describe standard methodology in Section 2 and show empirically that this methodology leads to conclusions

---

[1] http://www.senseval.org.
[2] http://www.aclweb.org/signll.

that are not reliable for our WSD problem and for other machine learning tasks inside and outside computational linguistics (Section 3). In Section 4 we show that the joint optimization of feature selection and algorithm parameters using a genetic algorithm is computationally feasible, leads in general to good results, and could therefore be used both to achieve higher accuracy and more reliable comparisons. Section 5 discusses our results in the light of related research.

2 Limitations of Standard Methodology

Crucial for objectively comparing algorithm bias and relevance of information sources is a methodology to reliably measure differences and compute their statistical significance. A detailed methodology has been developed for this [21] involving approaches like k-fold cross-validation [11, 1, 7] to estimate classifier quality (in terms of accuracy or derived measures like precision, recall, and F-score), as well as statistical techniques like McNemar [7] and paired cross-validation t-tests for determining the statistical significance of differences between algorithms or between presence or absence of information sources. Although this methodology is not without its problems [18], it is generally accepted and used both in machine learning and in most work in statistical NLP.

Many factors potentially play a role in the outcome of a (comparative) machine learning experiment: the data used (the sample selection and the sample size), the information sources used (the features selected) and their representation (e.g. as nominal or binary features), and the algorithm parameter settings (most ML algorithms have various parameters that can be tuned).

In a typical comparative machine learning experiment, two or more algorithms are compared for a fixed sample selection, feature selection, feature representation, and (default) algorithm parameter setting over a number of trials (cross-validation), and if the measured differences are statistically significant, conclusions are drawn about which algorithm is better suited to the problem being studied and why (mostly in terms of algorithm bias)[3]. Sometimes different sample sizes are used to provide a learning curve, and sometimes parameters of (some of the) algorithms are optimized on training data, or heuristic feature selection is attempted, but this is exceptional rather than common practice in comparative experiments. Interactions between different factors, like the effect of interleaved feature selection and algorithm parameter optimization, have to the best of our knowledge not yet been investigated systematically in comparative machine learning experiments for language processing problems.

In the remainder of this paper, we test the hypotheses that (i) feature selection, algorithm parameter optimization, and their joint optimization cause larger differences in accuracy within a single algorithm than differences observed between different algorithms using default parameter settings and feature input, and (ii) that the effect of adding and removing an information source when using default parameters can be reversed when re-optimizing the algorithm parameters. The implication of evidence for these hypotheses is that a large part of

---

[3] A similar approach is taken for the comparison of information sources.

the comparative machine learning of language literature may not be reliable. Another implication is that joint optimization can lead to significantly higher generalization accuracies, but this issue is not the focus of this paper.

3 Feature Selection, Parameter Optimization, and Their Interaction

In this Section, we analyze the impact of algorithm parameter optimization, feature selection, and the interaction between both on classifier accuracy in comparative experiments on WSD data and on the UCI benchmark datasets.

Feature (subset) selection is the process in which a subset of the available predictor features defining the input of the classification task are removed if they cannot be shown to be relevant in solving the learning task [11]. For computational reasons we used a *backward selection* algorithm. We start with all available features and look at the effect on accuracy of deleting one of the features, and continue deleting until no more accuracy increase is reported. Algorithm parameter optimization is the process in which parameters of a learning system (e.g. learning rate for neural networks, or the number of nearest neighbors in memory-based learning), are tuned for a particular problem. Although most machine learning systems provide sensible default settings, it is by no means certain that they will be *optimal* parameter settings for some particular task. In both cases (feature selection and parameter optimization), we are performing a *model selection* task which is well-known in machine learning. But as we mentioned earlier, whereas some published work in computational linguistics discusses either feature selection for some task, or algorithm parameter optimization for others, the effects of their interaction have, as far as we know, never been studied systematically.

The general set-up of our experiments is the following. Each experiment is done using a 10-fold cross-validation on the available data. This means that the data is split in 10 partitions, and each of these is used once as test set, with the other nine as corresponding train set. For each dataset, we provide information about the accuracy of two different machine learning systems under four conditions:

1. Using their respective default settings.
2. After optimizing the feature subset selection (backward selection) using default parameter settings, for each algorithm separately. (Optimization step 1).
3. After optimizing the algorithm parameters for each algorithm individually. Each "reasonable" parameter setting is tested with a 10-fold cross-validation experiment. (Optimization step 2).
4. After performing feature selection interleaved with optimization of the parameters for each algorithm in turn. (Optimization step 3).

We expect from our first hypothesis that each optimization step can increase the accuracy of the best result (as measured by the average result over the 10 experiments) considerably. In general, we expect the differences we record for the same algorithm over the four conditions to be much larger than the difference between the two learning algorithms when using default settings. As we are primarily interested in showing the variability of results due to the different optimizations, all results reported will be cross-validation results, and not results on an *additional* held-out dataset (this would imply an additional cross-validation loop within the cross-validation loop, which is computationally infeasible). For the WSD data we will report results on test datasets used by SENSEVAL which give an indication of the usefulness of the approach for improving accuracy.

3.1 Machine Learning Methods and Data

We chose two machine learning techniques for our experiments: the memory-based learning package TIMBL [6][4], and the rule induction package RIPPER [3]. These two approaches provide extremes of the *eagerness* dimension in ML (the degree in which a learning algorithm abstracts from the training data in forming a hypothesis). TIMBL is an example of lazy learning, RIPPER of eager learning.

For TIMBL the following algorithm parameters were optimized: similarity metrics, feature weighting metrics, class voting weighting, and number of nearest neighbors (varied between 1 and 45). For RIPPER the following parameter settings were varied: class ordering, negative tests in the rule conditions, hypothesis simplification magnitude, and example coverage. See [6, 3] for explanation of these parameters.

The "line" data set has become a benchmark dataset for work on word sense disambiguation. It was first produced and described by Leecock, Towell, and Voorhees [14]. It consists of instances of the word *line*, taken from the 1987-89 Wall Street Journal and a 25 million word corpus from the American Printing House for the Blind. 4,149 examples of occurrences of *line* were each tagged with one of six WordNet senses: text, formation, division, phone, cord, product. Because the "product" sense is 5 times more common than any of the other senses, a sampled dataset was also used in which all senses are represented equally. For each sense, 349 instances were selected at random, producing a total of 2094 examples with each sense having an equal share. This kind of sampling has been done before, and has also been reported in the literature [16]. However, we made our own sample as the other samples were not readily available. This means that our sampled data results cannot be compared directly to those of other systems.

Here is an example of an instance representing one occurrence of the word *line* in the corpus:

line-n.w9_15:17036:,pen,NN,writing,VBG,those,DT,lines,line,NNS,was,
VBD,that,IN,of,IN,0,0,0,0,0,0,0,0,0,0,0,0,0,0,0,0,0,0,0,0,0,0,0,0,0,0,
0,0,0,0,0,0,0,0,0,0,0,0,0,0,0,0,0,0,0,0,0,0,0,0,0,0,0,0,0,0,0,0,0,0,0,
0,0,0,0,0,0,0,0,0,0,0,0,0,0,0,0,0,0,0,0,0,0,1,0,0,0,0,0,0,0,0,0,0,0,0,
0,0,0,0,0,0,0,0,0,0,0,0,0,0,0,0,0,1,0,0,1,0,0,0,0,0,0,0,0,0,0,0,0,0,0,
0,0,0,1,0,0,0,0,0,0,0,0,0,0,0,1,0,0,0,0,0,0,0,0,0,1,0,0,0,0,0,0,0,0,0,
0,0,0,0,0,0,0,0,0,0,0,text.

---

[4] Available from http://ilk.kub.nl.

Table 1. Results of TIMBL and RIPPER on different WSD data sets when using (i) default settings, (ii) backward selection, (iii) parameter optimization, and (iv) interleaved backward selection and parameter optimization.

"line" (complete)		TIMBL	RIPPER
WORDS	(default)	60.2	63.9
	(feat. sel.)	62.7	63.9
	(param. opt.)	63.4	70.2
	(interleaved opt.)	64.5	91.3
WORDS+POS	(default)	57.8	63.8
	(feat. sel.)	62.7	64.7
	(param. opt.)	64.3	71.6
	(interleaved opt.)	64.9	76.4

"line" (sampled)		TIMBL	RIPPER
WORDS	(default)	59.1	40.4
	(feat. sel.)	60.3	40.9
	(param. opt.)	66.4	61.2
	(interleaved opt.)	66.7	63.3
WORDS+POS	(default)	56.9	41.4
	(feat. sel.)	61.5	41.6
	(param. opt.)	67.3	60.5
	(interleaved opt.)	68.1	61.1

The first entry (*line-n.w9_15:17036:*) is an ID tag for the instance, and is ignored in the learning process. Next are the three context words occurring before the focus word, together with their parts of speech. Then follows the form of the word *line*, in this case the plural, together with its base form (*line*), and its part of speech (*NNS*). Then we can see the right context of the focus words, also with parts of speech. The next 200 features are binary features, each indicating the presence or absence of the 200 most salient context words of *line*.

3.2 Results on the WSD Datasets

In Table 1, if we focus on the variation for a single algorithm over the four conditions, we can see that parameter optimization, feature selection, and combined feature selection with parameter optimization lead to major accuracy improvements compared to the results obtained with default parameter settings. These 'vertical' accuracy differences are much larger than the 'horizontal' algorithm-comparing accuracy differences.

The fact that we could observe large standard deviations in the optimization experiments, also confirms the necessity of parameter optimization (only the best result is represented in Table 1 for each optimization step).

With respect to the selected parameter settings and feature combinations, we found that parameter settings which are optimal when using all features are not necessarily optimal when performing feature selection. Furthermore, we could observe that the feature selection considered to be optimal for TIMBL was often different from the one optimal for RIPPER.

Table 2. Results of TIMBL and RIPPER on different UCI data sets when using (i) default settings, (ii) backward selection, (iii) parameter optimization, and (iv) interleaved backward selection and parameter optimization.

Dataset		TIMBL	RIPPER
database for fitting contact lenses	(default)	75.0	79.2
	(feat. sel.)	**87.5**	**87.5**
	(param. opt.)	**87.5**	**87.5**
	(interleaved opt.)	**87.5**	**87.5**
contraceptive method choice	(default)	48.5	46.8
	(feat. sel.)	52.2	48.2
	(param. opt.)	54.2	**49.8**
	(interleaved opt.)	**54.8**	**49.8**
breast-cancer-wisconsin	(default)	95.7	93.7
	(feat. sel.)	96.3	95.3
	(param. opt.)	97.4	**95.7**
	(interleaved opt.)	**97.6**	**95.7**
car evaluation database	(default)	94.0	87.0
	(feat. sel.)	94.0	87.0
	(param. opt.)	**96.9**	**98.4**
	(interleaved opt.)	**96.9**	**98.4**
postoperative patient data	(default)	55.6	**71.1**
	(feat. sel.)	**71.1**	**71.1**
	(param. opt.)	**71.1**	**71.1**
	(interleaved opt.)	**71.1**	**71.1**

We conclude that we have found evidence for our hypothesis (i) that the accuracy differences between different machine learning algorithms using standard comparative methodology will in general be lower than the differences in accuracy resulting from interactions between algorithm parameter settings and information source selection, at least for this task (see [4] for similar results on other language datasets).

3.3 Results on the UCI Benchmarks

We investigated whether the effect is limited to natural language processing datasets by applying the same optimalization to 5 UCI benchmark datasets[5]: "database for fitting contact lenses" (24 instances), "contraceptive method choice" (1473 instances), "breast-cancer-wisconsin" (699 instances), "car evaluation database" (1728 instances) and "postoperative patient data" (90 instances). Compared to our language processing datasets, these datasets are small. From the results in Table 2, we nevertheless see the same effects: the default settings for the algorithms are not optimal; the difference in accuracy for a single algorithm in the four conditions generally overwhelms accuracy differences found between the algorithms, and in cases like the "car evaluation database", we see

---
[5] http://www.ics.uci.edu/ mlearn/MLRepository.html.

that the initial result (TIMBL outperforms RIPPER) is reversed after optimization. Similar effects explain why in the ML of natural language literature, so many results and interpretations about superiority of one algorithm over the other are contradictory.

4 Genetic Algorithms for Optimization

Our results of the previous Section show that a proper comparative experiment requires extensive optimization of a combinatorially explosive nature, and that the obtainable accuracy increase by going to this trouble are considerable. Optimization and model selection problems of the type described in this paper are of course not unique to machine learning of language. Solutions like *genetic algorithms* (GAs) have been used for a long time as domain-independent techniques suitable for exploring optimization in large search spaces such as those described in this paper. We applied this optimization technique to our datasets.

The evolutionary algorithm used to optimize the feature selection and parameter optimization employs an algorithmic scheme similar to that of *evolution strategies*: a population of μ individuals forms the genetic material from which λ new individuals are created using crossover and mutation. The μ best individuals of this bigger temporary population are selected to become the next generation of the algorithm.

An individual contains particular values for all algorithm parameters and for the selection of the features. E.g., for TIMBL, the large majority of these parameters control the use of a feature (ignore, weighted overlap, modified value difference), and are encoded in the chromosome as ternary alleles. At the end of the chromosome the 5-valued weighting parameter w and the 4-valued neighbor weighting parameter d are encoded, together with the k parameter which controls the number of neighbors. The latter is encoded as a real value which represents the logarithm of the number of neighbors. The quality or fitness of an individual is the classification result returned by TIMBL with these particular parameter settings. A similar approach is followed for encoding the RIPPER parameters into an individual.

The initial population is filled with individuals consisting of uniformly sampled values. The mutation operator replaces, independently for each position and with a small probability, the current value with an arbitrary other value. The mutation rates of the features are set independently of that of w and d. In the case of the k parameter, Gaussian noise is added to the current value. The crossover operators used are the traditional 1-point, 2-point and uniform crossovers. They operate on the whole chromosome. The selection strength can be controlled by tuning the proportion μ/λ; an alternative strategy chooses the μ best individuals from the combination of μ parents and λ children. The GA parameters were set using limited explorative experimentation. We are aware that the algorithm parameter optimization problem we try to solve with GAs also applies to the GAs themselves.

Table 3. Validation results for TIMBL on five word experts, for datasets with and without keyword information. For the smaller datasets, interleaved backward keyword selection and parameter optimization results are included and are shown to be worse than those of the GA. For the larger dataset, only the GA could be used to perform interleaved optimization because the other method had become too computationally expensive. SENSEVAL test set results are between brackets for default vs. GA with keywords.

WE	Words+POS		
	Def.	Opt.	GA
bar	48.1	55.3	*66.3*
channel	60.9	70.5	*73.9*
develop	19.3	**29.6**	**29.6**
natural	42.8	52.7	*58.9*
post	60.2	66.5	*75.6*

WE	Words + POS + Keywords	
	Def.	GA
bar	44.8 (47.0)	**66.9 (59.6)**
channel	63.3 (50.7)	**75.4 (53.4)**
develop	17.0 (37.7)	**29.6 (29.0)**
natural	40.3 (31.1)	**61.3 (43.7)**
post	57.4 (51.9)	**77.8 (58.2)**

4.1 Results

The WSD data sets discussed in Table 3 were selected from the SENSEVAL-2 data, which provided training and test material for different ambiguous words. Each word was given a separate training and test set. We chose five of these words randomly, taking into account the following restrictions: at least 150 training items should be available, and the word should have at least 5 senses, each sense being represented by at least 10 training items. This process came up with the words *bar, channel, develop, natural, post*. Instances were made for each occurrence of each word in the same way as for the *line* data.

We see that the GA succeeds in finding solutions that are significantly better than the default solutions and the best solutions obtained by a heuristic combined feature selection and algorithm parameter optimization approach. The main advantage of the GA is that it allows us to explore much larger search spaces, for this problem e.g., also the use of context keywords, which would be computationally impossible with the heuristic methods in Section 3.

For the words with POS and keywords results we added between brackets for the default and GA results the results on the SENSEVAL test sets, showing that the optimization can indeed be used not only for showing the variability of the results, but also for obtaining higher predictive accuracy (although this should ideally be shown using two embedded cross-validation loops which turned out to be computationally infeasible for our data).

Table 4. Results of TIMBL with default settings and after interleaved feature selection and parameter optimization with a GA on the different WSD data sets for different information sources.

	Default			GA		
			words+POS			words+POS
dataset	words	words+POS	+keywords	words	words+POS	+keywords
"bar"	**50.0**	48.1	44.8	56.4	66.3	**66.9**
"channel"	62.3	60.9	**63.3**	72.0	73.9	**75.4**
"develop"	16.3	**19.3**	17.0	**34.8**	29.6	29.6
"natural"	41.6	**42.8**	40.3	55.6	58.9	**61.3**
"post"	**62.5**	60.2	57.4	71.0	75.6	**77.8**
"line" (sampled)	**59.1**	56.9	57.0	**66.9**	**66.9**	**66.9**

4.2 Results on the Comparison of Information Sources

In Table 4, we find evidence for our second hypothesis (the effect of adding an information source can switch between positive and negative depending on the optimization). E.g. where results with the default settings would lead to a conclusion that keyword features don't help for most WSD problems except "channel", the GA optimization shows that combinations of parameter settings and feature selection can be found for all WSD problems except "develop" which show exactly the opposite.

5 Related Research and Conclusion

Most comparative ML experiments, at least in computational linguistics, explore only one or a few points in the space of possible experiments for each algorithm to be compared. We have shown that regardless of the methodological accuracy with which the comparison is made, there is a high risk that other areas in the experimental space may lead to radically different results and conclusions. In general, the more effort is put in optimization (in this paper by exploring the interaction between feature selection and algorithm parameter optimization), the better the results will be, and the more reliable the comparison will be. Given the combinatorially explosive character of this type of optimization, we have chosen for GAs as a computationally feasible way to achieve this; no other heuristic optimization techniques allow the complex interactions we want to optimize. As a test case we used WSD datasets. In previous work [4] we showed that the same effects also occur in other tasks, like part of speech tagging and morphological synthesis.

The current paper builds on results obtained earlier on WSD [19, 20] in which we found that independent optimization of algorithm parameters for each word to be disambiguated led to higher accuracy, which at one point we thought to be a limitation of the method used (memory-based learning). In this paper, we show that the problem is much more general than for a single algorithm (e.g. RIPPER behaves similarly). We also showed in this paper that feature selection and algorithm parameter optimization interact highly, and should be jointly optimized. We also build on earlier, less successful attempts to use GAs for optimization in memory-based learning [12, 13]. GAs have been used for parameter optimization in ML a great deal, including for memory-based learning. A different discussion point concerns the lessons we have to draw from the relativity of comparative machine learning results. In an influential recent paper, Banko and Brill [2] conclude that "We have no reason to believe that any comparative conclusions drawn on one million words will hold when we finally scale up to larger training corpora". They base this point of view on experiments comparing several machine learning algorithms on one typical NLP task (confusable word disambiguation in context) with data selection sizes varying from 1 million to 1 billion. We have shown in this paper that data sample size is only one aspect influencing comparative results, and that accuracy differences due to algorithm parameter optimization, feature selection, and especially the interaction between both easily overwhelm the accuracy differences reported between algorithms (or information sources) in comparative experiments. Like the Banko and Brill study, this suggests that published results of comparative machine learning experiments (and their interpretation) may often be unreliable.

The good news is that optimization of as many factors as possible (sample selection and size, feature selection and representation, algorithm parameters), when possible, will offer important accuracy increases and (more) reliable comparative results. We believe that, in the long term, a GA approach offers a computationally feasible approach to this huge optimization problem.

References

1. Ethem Alpaydin. Combined 5×2 cv F test for comparing supervised classification learning algorithms. *Neural Computation*, 11(8):1885–1892, 1999.
2. Michele Banko and Eric Brill. Scaling to very very large corpora for natural language disambiguation. In *Proceedings of the 39th Annual Meeting of the Association for Computational Linguistics*, pages 26–33. Association for Computational Linguistics, 2001.
3. William W. Cohen. Fast effective rule induction. In *Proc. 12th International Conference on Machine Learning*, pages 115–123. Morgan Kaufmann, 1995.
4. Walter Daelemans and Véronique Hoste. Evaluation of machine learning methods for natural language processing tasks. In *Proceedings of the Third International Conference on Language Resources and Evaluation (LREC 2002)*, pages 755–760, 2002.
5. Walter Daelemans, Antal van den Bosch, and Jakub Zavrel. Forgetting exceptions is harmful in language learning. *Machine Learning*, 34:11–41, 1999.
6. Walter Daelemans, Jakub Zavrel, Ko van der Sloot, and Antal van den Bosch. Timbl: Tilburg memory based learner, version 4.0, reference guide. Technical report, ILK Technical Report 01-04, 2001.
7. Thomas G. Dietterich. Approximate statistical tests for comparing supervised classification learning algorithms. *Neural Computation*, 10(7):1895–1923, 1998.
8. Phil Edmonds and Adam Kilgarriff, editors. *Journal of Natural Language Engineering special issue based on Senseval-2*, volume 9. Cambridge University Press, 2003.

9. Gerard Escudero, Lluis Marquez, and German Rigau. Boosting applied to word sense disambiguation. In *European Conference on Machine Learning*, pages 129–141, 2000.
10. Adam Kilgarriff and Martha Palmer, editors. *Computers and the Humanities special issue based on Senseval-1*, volume 34. 1999.
11. Ron Kohavi and George H. John. Wrappers for feature subset selection. *Artificial Intelligence*, 97(1–2):273–323, 1997.
12. Anne Kool, Walter Daelemans, and Jakub Zavrel. Genetic algorithms for feature relevance assignment in memory-based language processing. In Claire Cardie, Walter Daelemans, Claire Nédellec, and Erik Tjong Kim Sang, editors, *Proceedings of the Fourth Conference on Computational Natural Language Learning and of the Second Learning Language in Logic Workshop, Lisbon, 2000*, pages 103–106. Association for Computational Linguistics, Somerset, New Jersey, 2000.
13. Anne Kool, Jakub Zavrel, and Walter Daelemans. Simultaneous feature selection and parameter optimization for memory-based natural language processing. In Ad Feelders, editor, *Proceedings of the 10th BENELEARN meeting*, pages 93–100. Tilburg, The Netherlands, 2000.
14. Claudia Leacock, Geoffrey Towell, and Ellen Voorhees. Corpus-based statistical sense resolution. In *Proceedings of the ARPA Workshop on Human Language Technology*, pages 260–265, March 1993.
15. Yoong Keok Lee and Hwee Tou Ng. An empirical evaluation of knowledge sources and learning algorithms for word sense disambiguation. In *Proceedings of the 2002 Conference on Empirical Methods in Natural Language Processing (EMNLP-2002)*, pages 41–48, 2002.
16. Raymond J. Mooney. Comparative experiments on disambiguating word senses: An illustration of the role of bias in machine learning. In Eric Brill and Kenneth Church, editors, *Proceedings of the Conference on Empirical Methods in Natural Language Processing*, pages 82–91. Association for Computational Linguistics, Somerset, New Jersey, 1996.
17. Hwee Tou Ng and Hian Beng Lee. Integrating multiple knowledge sources to disambiguate word sense: An exemplar-based approach. In Arivind Joshi and Martha Palmer, editors, *Proceedings of the Thirty-Fourth Annual Meeting of the Association for Computational Linguistics*, pages 40–47, San Francisco, 1996. Morgan Kaufmann Publishers.
18. Steven L. Salzberg. On comparing classifiers: Pitfalls to avoid and a recommended approach. *Data Mining and Knowledge Discovery*, 1(3):317–327, 1997.
19. Jorn Veenstra, Antal Van den Bosch, Sabine Buchholz, Walter Daelemans, and Jakub Zavrel. Memory-based word sense disambiguation. *Computing and the Humanities*, 2000.
20. Walter Daelemans Véronique Hoste, Iris Hendrickx and Antal van den Bosch. Parameter optimization for machine-learning of word sense disambiguation. *Natural Language Engineering*, pages 311–325, 2002.
21. Sholom Weiss and Nitin Indurkhya. *Predictive Data Mining: A Practical Guide*. Morgan Kaufmann, San Francisco, 1998.

Iteratively Extending Time Horizon Reinforcement Learning

Damien Ernst*, Pierre Geurts**, and Louis Wehenkel

Department of Electrical Engineering and Computer Science
Institut Montefiore, University of Liège
Sart-Tilman B28, B4000 Liège, Belgium
{ernst,geurts,lwh}@montefiore.ulg.ac.be

Abstract. Reinforcement learning aims to determine an (infinite time horizon) optimal control policy from interaction with a system. It can be solved by approximating the so-called Q-function from a sample of four-tuples (x_t, u_t, r_t, x_{t+1}) where x_t denotes the system state at time t, u_t the control action taken, r_t the instantaneous reward obtained and x_{t+1} the successor state of the system, and by determining the optimal control from the Q-function. Classical reinforcement learning algorithms use an ad hoc version of stochastic approximation which iterates over the Q-function approximations on a four-tuple by four-tuple basis. In this paper, we reformulate this problem as a sequence of *batch mode* supervised learning problems which in the limit converges to (an approximation of) the Q-function. Each step of this algorithm uses the full sample of four-tuples gathered from interaction with the system and extends by one step the horizon of the optimality criterion. An advantage of this approach is to allow the use of standard batch mode supervised learning algorithms, instead of the incremental versions used up to now. In addition to a theoretical justification the paper provides empirical tests in the context of the "Car on the Hill" control problem based on the use of ensembles of regression trees. The resulting algorithm is in principle able to handle efficiently large scale reinforcement learning problems.

1 Introduction

Many interesting problems in many fields can be formulated as closed-loop control problems, i.e. problems whose solution is provided by a mapping (or a control policy) $u_t = \mu(x_t)$ where x_t denotes the state at time t of a system and u_t an action taken by a controlling agent so as to influence the instantaneous and future behavior of the system. In many cases these problems can be formulated as *infinite horizon discounted reward discrete-time optimal control problems*, i.e. problems where the objective is to find a (stationary) control policy $\mu^*(\cdot)$ which maximizes the expected return over an infinite time horizon defined as follows:

---

* Research Fellow FNRS
** Postdoctoral Researcher FNRS

$$J_\infty^\mu = \lim_{N \to \infty} E\left\{\sum_{t=0}^{N-1} \gamma^t r_t\right\}, \qquad (1)$$

where $\gamma \in [0,1[$ is the discount factor, r_t is an instantaneous reward signal which depends only on the state x_t and action u_t at time t, and where the expectation is taken over all possible system trajectories induced by the control policy $\mu(\cdot)$.

Optimal control theory, and in particular dynamic programming, aims to solve this problem "exactly" when the explicit knowledge of system dynamics and reward function are given a priori. In this paper we focus on *reinforcement learning (RL)*, i.e. the use of automatic learning algorithms in order to solve the optimal control problem "approximately" when the sole information available is the one we obtain from system transitions from t to $t+1$. Each system transition provides the knowledge of a new four-tuple (x_t, u_t, r_t, x_{t+1}) of information and we aim here to compute $\mu^*(.)$ from a sample $\mathcal{F} = (x_t^k, u_t^k, r_t^k, x_{t+1}^k), k = 1, \ldots, \ell$ of such four-tuples.

It is important to contrast the RL protocol with the standard batch mode supervised learning protocol, which aims at determining, from the sole information of a sample S of input-output pairs (i, o), a function $h^* \in \mathcal{H}$ ($\mathcal{H}$ is called the hypothesis space of the learning algorithm) which minimizes the expected approximation error, e.g. defined in the case of least squares regression by the following functional:

$$\text{Err}^h = \sum_{(i,o) \in S} |h(i) - o|^2. \qquad (2)$$

Notice that the use of supervised learning in the context of optimal control problems would be straightforward if, instead of the sample $\mathcal{F}$ of four-tuples, we could provide the learning algorithm with a sample of input-output pairs $(x, \mu^*(x))$ (see for example [9] for a discussion on the combination of such a scheme with reinforcement learning). Unfortunately, in many interesting control problems this type of information can not be acquired directly, and the specific difficulty in reinforcement learning is to infer a good approximation of the optimal control policy only from the information given in the sample $\mathcal{F}$ of four-tuples. Existing reinforcement learning algorithms can be classified into two categories:

- *Model based RL methods:* they use (batch mode or incremental mode) supervised learning to determine from the sample $\mathcal{F}$ of four-tuples on the one hand an approximation of the system dynamics:

$$f_1(x, u, x') \approx P(x_{t+1} = x' | x_t = x, u_t = u) \qquad (3)$$

and on the other hand an approximation of the expected reward function:

$$f_2(x, u) \approx E\{r_t | x_t = x, u_t = u\}. \qquad (4)$$

Once these two functions have been obtained, model based algorithms derive the optimal control policy by dynamic programming [5, 8].

– *Non-model based RL methods:* they use incremental mode supervised learning in order to determine an approximation of the Q-function associated to the control problem. This function is (implicitly) defined by the following equation (known as the Bellman equation):

$$Q(x, u) = E\left\{r_t + \gamma \max_{u'} Q(x_{t+1}, u') \Big| x_t = x, u_t = u\right\}. \quad (5)$$

The optimal control policy can be directly determined from this (unique) Q-function by the following relation

$$\mu^*(x) = \arg\max_u Q(x, u). \quad (6)$$

The most well-known algorithm falling into the latter category is the so-called Q-learning method [11].

Our proposal is based on the observation that neither of these two approaches are able to fully exploit the power of modern supervised learning methods. Indeed, model based approaches are essentially linked to so-called state space discretization which aims at building a finite Markov Decision Problem (MDP) and are strongly limited by the curse of dimensionality: in order to use the dynamic programming algorithms, the state and control spaces need to be discretized and the number of cells of any discretization scheme increases exponentially with the number of dimensions of the state space. Non-model based approaches have, to our best knowledge, been combined only with *incremental* (on-line) learning algorithms (see e.g. [10]).

With respect to these approaches, we propose a novel non-model based RL framework which is able to exploit any *generic batch mode* supervised learning algorithm to model the Q-function. The resulting algorithm is illustrated on a simple problem where it is combined with three supervised learning algorithms based on regression trees. The rest of the paper is organized as follows: Section 2 introduces the underlying idea of our approach and gives a precise description of the proposed algorithm; Section 3 provides a validation in the context of the "Car on the Hill" control problem; Section 4 provides discussions, directions for future research and conclusions.

2 Iteratively Extending Time Horizon in Optimal Control

The approach that we present is based on the fact that the optimal (stationary) control policy of an *infinite* horizon problem can be formalized as the limit of a sequence of *finite* horizon control problems, which can be solved in an iterative fashion by using any standard supervised learning algorithm.

2.1 Iteratively Extending time Horizon in Dynamic Programming

We consider a discrete-time stationary stochastic system defined by its dynamics, i.e. a transition function defined over the Cartesian product $X \times U \times W$ of the state space X, the control space U, and the disturbance space W:

$$x_{t+1} = f(x_t, u_t, w_t), \quad (7)$$

a reward signal also defined over $X \times U \times W$:

$$r_t = r(x_t, u_t, w_t), \qquad (8)$$

a noise process defined by a conditional probability distribution:

$$w_t \sim P_w(w = w_t | x = x_t, u = u_t), \qquad (9)$$

and a probability distribution over the initial conditions:

$$x_0 \sim P_x(x = x_0). \qquad (10)$$

For a given (finite) horizon N, let us denote by

$$\pi_N(t, x) \in U, t \in \{0, \ldots, N-1\}; x \in X \qquad (11)$$

a (possibly time varying) N-step control policy (i.e. $u_t = \pi_N(t, x_t)$), and by

$$J_N^{\pi_N} = E\{\sum_{t=0}^{N-1} \gamma^t r_t\} \qquad (12)$$

the N-step reward of the closed-loop system using this policy. An N-step optimal policy is a policy which among all possible such policies maximizes $J_N^{\pi_N}$ for any P_x on the initial conditions. Notice that (under mild conditions) such a policy always does indeed exist although it is not necessarily unique.

Our algorithm exploits the following properties of N-step optimal policies (these are classical results of dynamic programming theory [1]):

1. The sequence of policies obtained by considering the sequence of Q_i-functions iteratively defined by

$$Q_1(x, u) = E\{r_t | x_t = x, u_t = u\} \qquad (13)$$

and

$$Q_N(x, u) = E\left\{r_t + \gamma \max_{u'} Q_{N-1}(x_{t+1}, u') \middle| x_t = x, u_t = u\right\}, \forall N > 1, \qquad (14)$$

and the following two conditions[1]

$$\pi_N^*(0, x) = \arg\max_u Q_N(x, u), \forall N \geq 0 \qquad (15)$$

and

$$\pi_N^*(t+1, x) = \pi_{N-1}^*(t, x), \forall N > 1, t \in \{0, \ldots, N-2\} \qquad (16)$$

is optimal.
2. The sequence of stationary policies defined by $\mu_N^*(x) = \pi_N^*(0, x)$ converges (globally, and for any P_x on the initial conditions) to $\mu^*(x)$ in the sense that

$$\lim_{N \to \infty} J_\infty^{\mu_N^*} = J_\infty^{\mu^*}. \qquad (17)$$

3. The sequence of functions Q_N converges to the (unique) solution of the Bellman equation (eqn. (5)).

---
[1] Actually this definition does not necessarily yield a unique policy, but any policy which satisfies this condition is appropriate, and it is straightforward to define a procedure constructing such a policy from the sequence of Q_i-functions.

2.2 Iteratively Extending Time Horizon in Reinforcement Learning

The proposed algorithm is based on the use of supervised learning in order to produce a sequence $\hat{Q}_i$ of approximations of the Q_i-functions defined above, by exploiting at each step the full sample of four-tuples $\mathcal{F} = (x_t^k, u_t^k, r_t^k, x_{t+1}^k), k = 1, \ldots, \ell$ in batch mode together with the function produced at the preceding step.

Initialization. The algorithm starts by using the sample $\mathcal{F}$ of four-tuples in order to construct an approximation of $Q_1(x, u)$. This can be achieved using the x_t, u_t components of each four-tuple as inputs, and the r_t component as output and by using a supervised regression algorithm in order to find in its hypothesis space $\mathcal{H}$ a function satisfying

$$\hat{Q}_1 = \arg\min_{h \in \mathcal{H}} \sum_{k=1}^{\ell} |h(x_t^k, u_t^k) - r_t^k|^2. \tag{18}$$

Iteration. Step i ($i > 1$) of the algorithm uses the function produced at step $i-1$ to modify the output of each input-output pair associated to each four-tuple by

$$o_i^k = r_t^k + \gamma \max_{u'} \hat{Q}_{i-1}(x_{t+1}^k, u') \tag{19}$$

and then applies the supervised learning algorithm to build

$$\hat{Q}_i = \arg\min_{h \in \mathcal{H}} \sum_{k=1}^{\ell} |h(x_t^k, u_t^k) - o_i^k|^2. \tag{20}$$

Stopping Conditions. For the theoretical sequence of policies an error bound on the sub-optimality in terms of the number of iterations is given by the following equation

$$|J_\infty^{\mu_N^*} - J_\infty^{\mu^*}| < \frac{\gamma^N B_r}{1 - \gamma}, \tag{21}$$

where $B_r > \sup r(x, u, w)$. This equation can be used to fix an upper bound on the number of iterations for a given a priori fixed optimality gap.

Another possibility is to exploit the convergence property of the sequence of Q_i-functions in order to decide when to stop the iteration, e.g. when

$$|\hat{Q}_N - \hat{Q}_{N-1}| < \epsilon. \tag{22}$$

Control Policy Derivation. The final control policy seen as an approximation of the optimal stationary closed-loop policy is in principle derived by

$$\hat{\mu}^*(x) = \hat{\mu}_N^*(x) = \arg\max_u \hat{Q}_N(x, u). \tag{23}$$

If the control space is finite, this can be done using exhaustive search. Otherwise, the algorithm to achieve this will depend on the type of approximation architecture used.

Consistency. It is interesting to question under which conditions this algorithm provides consistency, i.e. under which conditions the sequence of policies generated by our algorithm and using a sample of increasing size would converge to the optimal control policy within a pre-specified optimality gap. Without any assumption on the used supervised learning algorithm and on the sampling mechanism nothing can be said about consistency. On the other hand, if each one of the true Q_i-functions can be arbitrarily well approximated by a function of the hypothesis space and if the sample (in asymptotic regime) contains an infinite number of times each possible state-action pair (x, u), then consistency is ensured trivially. Further research is necessary in order to determine less ideal assumptions both on the hypothesis space and on the sampling mechanism which would still guarantee consistency.

Solution Characterization. Another way to state the reinforcement learning problem would consist of defining the approximate Q-function as the solution of the following equation

$$\hat{Q} = \arg\min_{h \in \mathcal{H}} \sum_{k=1}^{l} \left| h(x_t^k, u_t^k) - \left(r_t^k + \gamma \max_{u'} h(x_{t+1}^k, u') \right) \right|^2. \tag{24}$$

Our algorithm can be viewed as an iterative algorithm to solve this minimization problem starting with an initial guess $Q_0(x, u) \equiv 0$ and at each iteration $i > 0$ updating the function according to

$$\hat{Q}_i = \arg\min_{h \in \mathcal{H}} \sum_{k=1}^{l} \left| h(x_t^k, u_t^k) - \left(r_t^k + \gamma \max_{u'} \hat{Q}_{i-1}(x_{t+1}^k, u') \right) \right|^2. \tag{25}$$

2.3 Supervised Regression Algorithm

In principle, the proposed framework can be combined with any available supervised learning method designed for regression problems. In order to be practical, the desirable features of the used algorithm are as follows:

- *Computational efficiency and scalability of the learning algorithm.* Specially with respect to sample size and dimensionality of the state space X and the control space U.
- *Modeling flexibility.* The Q_i-functions to be modeled by the algorithm are unpredictable in shape; hence no prior assumption can be made on the parametric shape of the approximation architecture, and the automatic learning algorithm should be able to adapt its model by itself to the problem data.
- *Reduced variance,* in order to work efficiently in small sample regimes.
- *Fully automatic operation.* The algorithm may be called several hundred times and it is therefore not possible to ask for a human operator to tune some meta-parameters at each step of the iterative procedure.
- *Efficient use of the model,* in order to derive the control from the Q-function.

In the simulation results given in the next section, we have compared three learning algorithms based on regression trees which we think offer a good compromise in terms of the criteria established above. We give a very brief description of each variant below.

Regression Trees. Classification and regression trees are among the most popular supervised learning algorithms. They combine several characteristics such as interpretability of the models, efficiency, flexibility, and fully automatic operation which make them particularly attractive for this application. To build such trees, we have implemented the CART algorithm as described in [4].

Tree Bagging. One drawback of regression trees is that they suffer from a high variance. Bagging [2] is an ensemble method proposed by Breiman that often improves very dramatically the accuracy of trees by reducing their variance. With bagging, several regression trees are built, each from a different bootstrap sample drawn from the original learning sample. To make a prediction with this set of M trees, we simply take the average predictions of these M trees. Note that, while bagging inherits several advantages of regression trees, it increases their computing times significantly.

Extremely Randomized Trees (Extra-trees). Besides bagging, several other methods to build tree ensembles have been proposed that often improve the accuracy with respect to tree bagging (e.g. random forests [3]). In this paper, we propose to evaluate our own recent proposal which is called "Extra-trees". Like bagging, this algorithm works by taking the average predictions of several trees. Each of these trees is built from the the original learning sample by selecting its tests fully at random. The main advantages of this algorithm with respect to bagging is that it is computationally much faster (because of the extreme randomization) and also often more accurate. For more details about this algorithm, we refer the interested reader to [6, 7].

3 Illustration: "Car on the Hill" Control Problem

The precise definition of the test problem is given in the appendix. It is a version of a quite classical test problem used in the reinforcement learning literature.

A car is traveling on a hill (the shape of which is given by the function $H(p)$ of Figure 3b). The objective is to bring the car in minimal time to the top of the hill ($p = 1$ in Figure 3b). The problem is studied in discrete-time, which means here that the control variable can be changed only every $0.1\,s$. The control variable acts directly on the acceleration of the car (eqn. (27), appendix) but can only assume two extreme values (full acceleration or full deceleration). The reward signal is defined in such a way that the infinite horizon optimal control policy is a minimum time control strategy (eqn. (29), appendix).

Our test protocol uses an "off-line" learning strategy. First, samples of four-tuples are generated from fixed initial conditions and random walk in the control space. Then these samples are used to infer control strategies according to the proposed method. Finally these control strategies are assessed.

3.1 Four-Tuples Generation

To collect the samples of four-tuples, we observed a number of episodes of the system. All episodes start from the same initial state corresponding to the car stopped at the bottom of the valley (i.e. $(p, s) = (-0.5, 0)$) and stop when the car leaves the region of the state space depicted in Figure 3a. In each episode, the action u_t at each time step is chosen at random with equal probability among its two possible values $u = -4$ and $u = 4$. We will consider hereafter three different samples of four-tuples denoted by $\mathcal{F}_1$, $\mathcal{F}_2$ and $\mathcal{F}_3$ containing respectively the four-tuples obtained after 1000, 300, and 100 episodes. These samples are such that $\#\mathcal{F}_1 = 58089$, $\#\mathcal{F}_2 = 18010$, and $\#\mathcal{F}_3 = 5930$. Note also that after 100 episodes the reward $r(x_t, u_t, w_t) = 1$ (corresponding to the goal state at the top of the hill) has been observed only 1 time, 5 times after 300 episodes, and 18 times after 1000 episodes.

3.2 Experiments

To illustrate the behavior of the algorithm, we first use the sample $\mathcal{F}_1$ with Extra-trees[2] As the action space is binary, we choose to separately model the functions $\hat{Q}_N(x, -4)$ and $\hat{Q}_N(x, 4)$ by two ensembles of 50 Extra-trees. The policy $\hat{\mu}_1^*$ obtained is represented in Figure 1a. Black bullets represent states for which $\hat{Q}_1(x, -4) > \hat{Q}_1(x, 4)$, white bullets states for which $\hat{Q}_1(x, -4) < \hat{Q}_1(x, 4)$, and grey bullets states for which $\hat{Q}_1(x, -4) = \hat{Q}_1(x, 4)$. Successive policies $\hat{\mu}_N^*$ for increasing N are given on Figures 1b-1f. After 50 iterations $\hat{\mu}_N^*$ has almost stabilized.

To associate a score to each policy $\hat{\mu}_N^*$, we define a set $X' : X' = \{(p, s) \in X | \exists i, j \in \mathbb{Z} | (s, p) = (0.125 * i, 0.375j)\}$ and estimate the value of $J_\infty^{\hat{\mu}_N}$ when $P_x(x_0) = \frac{1}{\#X'}$ if $x_0 \in X'$ and 0 otherwise. The evolution of the score for increasing N is represented in Figure 2a for the three learning algorithms. With Bagging and Extra-trees, we average 50 trees. After about 20 episodes, the score does not improve anymore. Comparing the three supervised learning algorithms, it is clear that bagging and Extra-trees are superior to single regression trees. Bagging and Extra-trees are very close to each other but the score of Extra-trees grows faster and is also slightly more stable.

On Figure 2b, we compare score curves corresponding to the three different sample sizes (with Extra-trees). As expected, we observe that a decrease of the number of four-tuples decreases the score.

To give a better idea of the quality of the control strategy induced by our algorithm, it would be interesting to compare it with the optimal one. Although it is difficult to determine analytically the optimal control policy for this problem, it is however possible to determine $J_\infty^{\mu^*}$ when the probability distribution on the initial states is such that $P_x(x_0 = x) = 1$ if x corresponds to the state

---
[2] The results with regression trees and tree bagging are discussed afterwards.

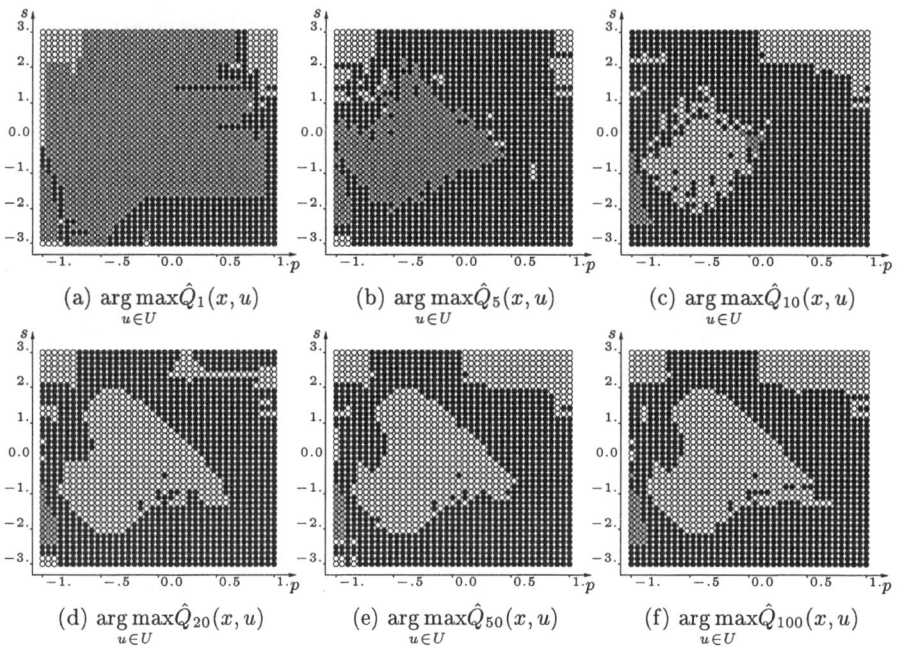

Fig. 1. Representation of $\hat{\mu}_N^*$ for different values of N. Sample $\mathcal{F}_1$

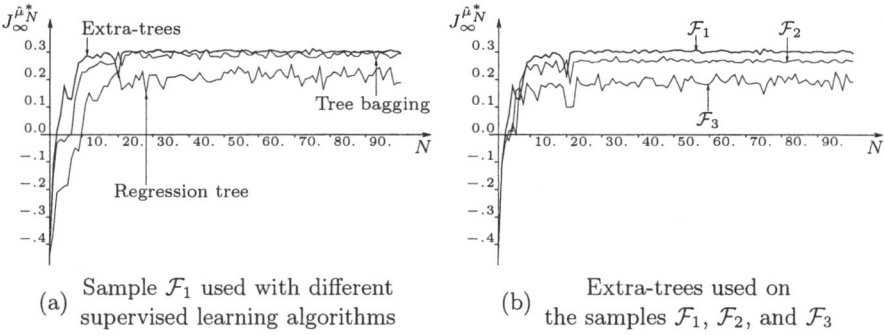

Fig. 2. Evaluation of the policy $\hat{\mu}_N^*$

$(p, s) = (-0.5, 0)$ and 0 otherwise. This is achieved by exhaustive search, trying out all possible control sequences of length k when the system initial state is $(p, s) = (-0.5, 0)$ and determining the smallest value of k for which there is a control sequence that leads the car on the top of the hill. From this procedure, we find a minimum value of $k = 19$ and then $J_\infty^{\mu^*} = 0.397214$ $(= \gamma^{k-1})$. If we use from the same initial state the policy learned by our algorithm (with Extra-trees), we get:

- from $\mathcal{F}_1$, $J_\infty^{\hat{\mu}^*_{100}} = 0.397214 = \gamma^{18}$
- from $\mathcal{F}_2$, $J_\infty^{\hat{\mu}^*_{100}} = 0.397214 = \gamma^{18}$
- from $\mathcal{F}_3$, $J_\infty^{\hat{\mu}^*_{100}} = 0.358486 = \gamma^{20}$

For the two largest samples, $J_\infty^{\hat{\mu}^*_{100}}$ is equal to the optimum value $J_\infty^{\mu^*}$ while it is only slightly inferior in the case of the smallest one.

3.3 Comparison with a Non-model Based Incremental Algorithm

It is interesting to question whether our proposed algorithm is more efficient in terms of learning speed than non-model based iterative reinforcement learning algorithms. In an attempt to give an answer to this question we have considered the standard Q-learning algorithm with a regular grid as approximation architecture[3].

We have used this algorithm during 1000 episodes (the same as the ones used to generate $\mathcal{F}_1$) and then we have extracted from the resulting approximate Q-function the policy $\hat{\mu}^*$ and computed $J_\infty^{\hat{\mu}^*}$ when considering the same probability distribution on the initial states as the one used to compute the values of $J_\infty^{\hat{\mu}^*_N}$ represented on Figures 2a-b. The highest value of $J_\infty^{\hat{\mu}^*}$ so obtained by repeating the process for different grid sizes (a 10×10, a 11×11, $\cdots$ and a 100×100 grid) is 0.039 (which occurs for a 13×13 grid). This value is quite small compared to $J_\infty^{\hat{\mu}^*_{100}} = 0.295$ obtained when using $\mathcal{F}_1$ as sample and the Extra-trees as regression method (Figure 2a). Even when using ten times more (i.e. 10,000) episodes with the Q-learning algorithm, the highest value of $J_\infty^{\hat{\mu}^*}$ obtained over the different grids is still inferior (it is equal to 0.232 and occurs for a 24×24 grid).

4 Discussion and Conclusions

We have presented a novel way of using batch mode supervised learning algorithms efficiently in the context of non-model based reinforcement learning. The resulting algorithm is fully autonomous and has been applied to an illustrative problem where it worked very well.

Probably the most important feature of this algorithm is that it can scale very easily to high dimensional problems (e.g. problems with a large number of input variables and continuous control spaces) by taking advantage of recent advances of supervised learning techniques in this direction. This feature can for example be exploited to handle more easily partially observable problems, where it is necessary to use as inputs a history of observations rather than just the current state. It could also be exploited to carry out reinforcement learning based on perceptual input information (tactile sensors, images, sounds) without requiring complex pre-processing.

---

[3] The degree of correction α used in the algorithm has been chosen equal to 0.1 and the Q-function has been initialized to zero everywhere at the beginning of the learning.

Although we believe that our approach to reinforcement learning is very promising, there are still many open questions. In the formulation of our algorithm, we have not made any assumption about the way the four-tuples are generated. However, the quality of the induced control policy depends obviously on the sampling mechanism. So, an interesting future research direction is the determination for a given problem of the smallest possible (for computational efficiency reasons) sample of four-tuples that gives a near optimal control policy. This will raise the related question of how to interact at best with a system so as to generate a good sample of four-tuples. One very interesting property of our algorithm is that these questions are decoupled from the question of the determination of the optimal control policy from a given sample of four-tuples.

Appendix: Precise Definition of the "Car on the Hill" Control Problem

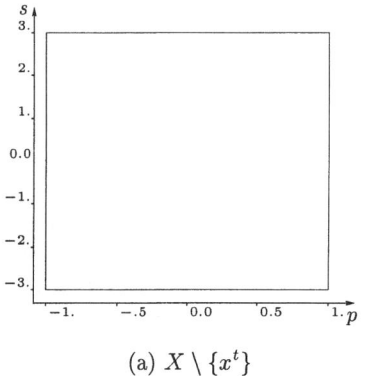

(a) $X \setminus \{x^t\}$

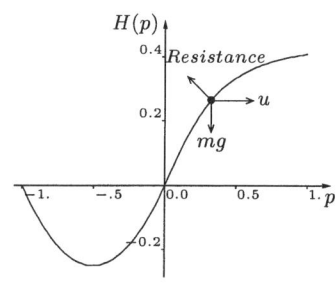

(b) Representation of $H(p)$ (shape of the hill) and of the different forces applied to the car

Fig. 3. The "Car on the Hill" control problem

System dynamics: The system has a continuous-time dynamics described by these two differential equations:

$$\dot{p} = s \tag{26}$$

$$\dot{s} = \frac{u}{m(1 + H'(p)^2)} - \frac{gH'(p)}{1 + H'(p)^2} - \frac{s^2 H'(p) H''(p)}{1 + H'(p)^2} \tag{27}$$

where m and g are parameters equal respectively to 1 and 9.81 and where $H(p)$ is a function of p defined by the following expression:

$$H(p) = \begin{cases} p^2 + p & \text{if } p < 0 \\ \frac{p}{\sqrt{1+5p^2}} & \text{if } p \geq 0 \end{cases} \tag{28}$$

The discrete-time dynamics is obtained by discretizing the time with the time between t and $t+1$ chosen equal to $0.100\,s$.

If p_{t+1} and s_{t+1} are such that $|p_{t+1}| > 1$ or $|s_{t+1}| > 3$ then a terminal state x^t is reached.

State space: The state space X is composed of $\{(p,s) \in \mathbb{R}^2 | |s| \leq 1 \text{ and } |p| \leq 3\}$ and of a terminal state x^t. $X \setminus \{x^t\}$ is represented on Figure 3a.

Action space: The action space $U = \{-4, 4\}$

Reward function: The reward function $r(x, u, w)$ is defined through the following expression:

$$r(x_t, w_t, u_t) = \begin{cases} -1 & \text{if } p_{t+1} < -1 \text{ or } |s_{t+1}| > 3 \\ 1 & \text{if } p_{t+1} > 1 \text{ and } |s_{t+1}| \leq 3 \\ 0 & \text{otherwise} \end{cases} \quad (29)$$

Decay factor: The decay factor γ has been chosen equal to 0.95. Notice that in this particular problem the value of γ actually does not influence the optimal control policy.

References

1. D. Bertsekas. *Dynamic Programming and Optimal Control*, volume I. Athena Scientific, Belmont, MA, 2nd edition, 2000.
2. L. Breiman. Bagging predictors. *Machine Learning*, 24(2):123–140, 1996.
3. L. Breiman. Random forests. *Machine Learning*, 45:5–32, 2001.
4. L. Breiman, J. Friedman, R. Olsen, and C. Stone. *Classification and Regression Trees*. Wadsworth International (California), 1984.
5. D. Ernst. *Near optimal closed-loop control. Application to electric power systems*. PhD thesis, University of Liège, Belgium, March 2003.
6. P. Geurts. *Contributions to decision tree induction: bias/variance tradeoff and time series classification*. PhD thesis, University of Liège, Belgium, May 2002.
7. P. Geurts. Extremely randomized trees. Technical report, University of Liège, 2003.
8. A. Moore and C. Atkeson. Prioritized Sweeping: Reinforcement Learning with Less Data and Less Real Time. *Machine Learning*, 13:103–130, 1993.
9. M. T. Rosenstein and A. G. Barto. Supervised learning combined with an actor-critic architecture. Technical report, University of Massachusetts, Department of Computer Science, 2002.
10. W. Smart and L. Kaelbling. Practical Reinforcement Learning in Continuous Spaces. In *Proceedings of the Sixteenth International Conference on Machine Learning*, 2000.
11. C. Watkins and P. Dayan. Q-learning. *Machine learning*, 8:279–292, 1992.

Volume under the ROC Surface for Multi-class Problems

César Ferri, José Hernández-Orallo, and Miguel Angel Salido

Dep. Sistemes Informàtics i Computació, Univ. Politècnica de València (Spain)
{cferri,jorallo,msalido}@dsic.upv.es

Abstract. Receiver Operating Characteristic (ROC) analysis has been successfully applied to classifier problems with two classes. The Area Under the ROC Curve (AUC) has been elected as a better way to evaluate classifiers than predictive accuracy or error and has also recently used for evaluating probability estimators. However, the extension of the Area Under the ROC Curve for more than two classes has not been addressed to date, because of the complexity and elusiveness of its precise definition. Some approximations to the real AUC are used without an exact appraisal of their quality. In this paper, we present the real extension to the Area Under the ROC Curve in the form of the Volume Under the ROC Surface (VUS), showing how to compute the polytope that corresponds to the absence of classifiers (given only by the trivial classifiers), to the best classifier and to whatever set of classifiers. We compare the real VUS with "approximations" or "extensions" of the AUC for more than two classes.

1 Introduction

In general, classifiers are used to make predictions for decision support. Since predictions can be wrong, it is important to know what the effect is when the predictions are incorrect. In many situations not every error has the same consequences. Some errors have greater cost than others, especially in diagnosis. For instance, a wrong diagnosis or treatment can have different cost and dangers depending on which kind of mistake has been done. In fact, it is usually the case that misclassifications of minority classes into majority classes (e.g. predicting that a system is safe when it is not) have greater costs than misclassifications of majority classes into minority classes (e.g. predicting that a system is not safe when it actually is). Obviously, the costs of each misclassification are problem dependent, but it is almost never the case that they would be uniform for a single problem. Consequently, accuracy is not generally the best way to evaluate the quality of a classifier or a learning algorithm.

Cost-sensitive learning [14] is a more realistic generalisation of predictive learning, and cost-sensitive models allow for a better and wiser decision making. The quality of a model is measured in terms of cost minimisation rather than error minimisation. When cost matrices are provided a priori, i.e. before learning takes place, the matrices have to be fully exploited to obtain models that minimise cost.

However, in many circumstances, costs are not known a priori or the models are just there to be evaluated or chosen. Receiver Operating Characteristic (ROC) analysis [5][9][13] has been proven to be very useful for evaluating given classifiers in these cases, when the cost matrix was not known at the moment the classifiers were constructed. ROC analysis provides tools to select a set of classifiers that will behave optimally and reject some other useless classifiers. In order to do this, the convex hull of all the classifiers is constructed, giving a "curve" (a convex polygon).

In the simplest case, a single 2-class classifier forms a 4-segment ROC curve (a polygon in a strict sense) with the point given by the classifier, two trivial classifiers (the classifier that always predicts class 0 and the classifier that always predicts class 1) and the origin, whose area can be computed. This area is called the Area Under the ROC Curve (AUC) and has become a better alternative than accuracy (or error), for evaluating classifiers. AUC is also used for probabilistic estimators, where these estimations are used where ranking prediction is important [10].

ROC analysis and the AUC measure have been extensively used in the area of medical decision making [7][15], in the field of knowledge discovery, data mining, pattern recognition [1] and science in general [13]. However, the applicability of ROC analysis and the AUC has only been shown for problems with two classes. Although ROC analysis can be extended in theory for multi-dimensional problems [12], practical issues (computational complexity and representational comprehensibility, especially) preclude its use in practice. The major hindrance is the high dimensionality. A confusion matrix obtained from a problem of c classes has c^2 positions, and ($c \cdot (c-1)$) dimensions (d), i.e. all possible misclassification combinations are needed.

Nonetheless, although difficult, it is possible to perform ROC analysis for more than two classes and to compute the AUC (more precisely, the Volume Under the ROC Surface, VUS). However, the trivial classifiers for more than two classes, the minimum and maximum volume have not been identified to date in the literature.

In this paper, we present the trivial classifiers, the equations, the maximum and minimum VUS, for classifiers of more than 2 classes. We use this to compute the real VUS for any classifier by the use of a Hyperpolyhedron Search Algorithm (HSA) [11]. We then compare experimentally the real VUS with several other (and new) approximations, showing which approximation is best.

2 ROC Analysis

The Receiver Operating Characteristic (ROC) analysis [5][9][13] allows the evaluation of classifier performance in a more independent and complete way than just using accuracy. ROC analysis has usually been presented for two classes, because it is easy to define, to interpret and it is computationally feasible.

ROC analysis for two classes is based on plotting the true-positive rate (TPR) on the y-axis and the false-positive rate (FPR) on the x-axis, giving a point for each classifier. A "curve" is obtained because we can obtain infinitely many derived classifiers along the segment that connects two classifiers just by voting them with different weights. Hence, any point *below* that segment will have greater cost for any class distribution and cost matrix, because it has lower TPR and/or higher FPR. According to this, given several classifiers, one can discard the classifiers that fall under the convex hull formed by the points representing the classifiers and the points (0,0) and (1,1), which represent the default classifiers always predicting negative and positive, respectively. A detailed description of ROC analysis can be found in [5][9].

The usual way to represent the ROC space is not, in our opinion, a very coherent way, since the true class is represented incrementally for correct predictions and the false class is represented incrementally for incorrect predictions. Moreover this choice is not easily extensible for more than two classes. Instead, we propose to represent the false-negative-rate (FNR) and the FPR. Now, the points (0,1) and (1,0) represent, respectively, the classifier that classifies anything as negative and the classifier that classifies anything as positive. The curve is now computed with points (0,1), (1,0) and (1,1).

Obviously, with this new diagram, instead of looking for the maximisation of the Area Under the ROC Curve (AUC) we have to look for its minimisation. A better option is to compute the Area Above the ROC Curve (AAC). In order to maintain accordance with classical terminology, we will refer to the AAC also as AUC.

3 Multi-class ROC Analysis

Srinivasan has shown in [12] that, theoretically, the ROC analysis extends to more than two classes "directly". For c classes, and assuming a normalised cost matrix, we have to construct a vector of $d = c(c-1)$ dimensions for each classifier. In general the cost of a classifier for c classes is:

$$Cost = \sum_{i,j,i \neq j} p(i) \cdot C(i,j) R(i,j)$$

where R is the confusion ratio matrix (each column normalised to sum 1), C is the cost matrix, and $p(i)$ is the absolute frequency of class i. From the previous formula, two classifiers 1 and 2 will have the same cost when they are on the same iso-performance hyperplane. However, the $d-1$ values of the hyperplane are not so straightforward and easy to obtain and understand as the slope value of the bi-dimensional case.

In the same way as the bi-dimensional case, the convex hull can be constructed, forming a polytope. To know whether a classifier can be rejected, it has to be seen whether the intersection of the current polytope with the polytope of the new classifier gives the new polytope, i.e., the new polytope is included in the first polytope [8].

Provided this direct theoretical extension, there are some problems.

– In two dimensions, doubling the probability of one class has a direct counterpart in costs. This is not so for $d > 2$, because there are many more degrees of freedom.
– The best algorithm for the convex hull of N points is $O(N \log N + N^{d/2})$ [8][3].
– In the 2-d case, it is relatively straightforward how to detect the trivial classifiers and the points for the minimum and maximum cases.

However, not only there are computational limitations but also representational ones. ROC analysis in two dimensions has a very nice and understandable representation, but it cannot be directly extended to more than two classes, because even for 3 classes we have a 6D space, quite difficult to be represented. In what follows, we illustrate the extension for 3 classes, although the expressions can be generalised easily.

3.1 Extending ROC Analysis for 3 Classes

In this part we consider the extension of ROC analysis for 3-class problems. In this context we consider the following cost ratio matrix for three-class classifiers:

		Actual		
		a	b	c
Predicted	a	h_a	x_1	x_2
	b	x_3	h_b	x_4
	c	x_5	x_6	h_c

This gives a 6-dimensional point $(x_1, x_2, x_3, x_4, x_5, x_6)$. The values h_a, h_b and h_c are dependent and do not need to be represented, because:

$$h_a + x_3 + x_5 = 1, \quad h_b + x_1 + x_6 = 1, \quad h_c + x_2 + x_4 = 1$$

3.1.1 Maximum VUS for 3 Classes

Let us begin by considering the maximum volume. The maximum volume should represent the volume containing all the possible classifiers. A point in the 1-long hypercube is a classifier if and only if:

$$x_3 + x_5 \leq 1, \quad x_1 + x_6 \leq 1, \quad x_2 + x_4 \leq 1$$

It is easy to obtain the volume of the space determined by these equations, just by using the probability that 6 random numbers under a uniform distribution $U(0,1)$ would follow the previous conditions. More precisely:

$$VUS_3^{max} = P(U(0,1) + U(0,1) \leq 1) \cdot P(U(0,1) + U(0,1) \leq 1) \cdot P(U(0,1) + U(0,1) \leq 1)$$
$$= [P(U(0,1) + U(0,1) \leq 1)]^3.$$

It is easy to see that the probability that the sum of two random numbers under the distribution $U(0,1)$ is less than 1 is exactly ½, i.e:

$$P(U(0,1) + U(0,1) \leq 1) = \tfrac{1}{2}, \quad \text{consequently} \quad VUS_3^{max} = (\tfrac{1}{2})^3 = 1/8$$

We have also considered the maximum VUS for c classes. It is easy to see that the volume of the space determined by valid equations for c classes is:

$$VUS^{max} = \prod_c [\, P(\Sigma_{c-1} U(0,1) \leq 1) \,] = [P(\Sigma_{c-1} U(0,1) \leq 1)]^c.$$

However, the probability that the sum of $c-1$ random numbers under the distribution $U(0,1)$ is less than 1 is difficult to be obtained. In particular, the probability density function of the sum of n uniform variables on the interval $[0,1]$ can be obtained using the characteristic function of the uniform distribution.

$$d_n(x) = F^{-1}\left[\left(\frac{i - \cos t + \sin t}{t}\right)^n\right] = \frac{1}{2(n-1)!}\sum_{k=0}^{n}(-1)^k\binom{n}{k}(x-k)^{n-1}\operatorname{sgn}(x-k)$$

Using the cumulative distribution function $D_n(x)$, we have that the probability that the sum of n random numbers with $U(0,1)$ is less than 1 is:

$$D_n(1) = \lim_{x \to 1}\int_{-\infty}^{x} d_n(x)dx = \frac{1}{2(n-1)!}\int_{-\infty}^{1^-}\sum_{k=0}^{n}(-1)^k\binom{n}{k}(x-k)^{n-1}\operatorname{sgn}(x-k)dx$$

For $n=1$ we have $D_1(1)=1$, for $n=2$ we have $D_2(1)=½$, for $n=3$, $D_3(1)=1/6$ and:
$$VUS_c^{max} = (D_{c-1}(1))^c$$
And hence we have, $VUS_2^{max}=1$, $VUS_3^{max}=1/8$ and $VUS_4^{max}=1/1296$. However, for $n>3$, D_n is complex. For such cases, we can approximate the sum of n random numbers under the distribution $U(0,1)$ with a single variable (Y) under the normal distribution with $\mu=n/2$ and $\sigma=n/12$ using the central limit theorem. Then:

$$P(Y \le 1) \approx P\left(\frac{Y-\frac{n}{2}}{\sqrt{\frac{n}{12}}} \le \frac{1-\frac{n}{2}}{\sqrt{\frac{n}{12}}}\right) = P\left(Z \le \frac{1-\frac{n}{2}}{\sqrt{\frac{n}{12}}}\right) = \Phi\left(\frac{1-\frac{n}{2}}{\sqrt{\frac{n}{12}}}\right)$$

Where Z is a standard normal distribution variable. Therefore, when $c>3$:

$$VUS_c^{max} \approx \left[\Phi\left(\frac{1-\frac{c-1}{2}}{\sqrt{\frac{c-1}{12}}}\right)\right]^c$$

3.1.2 Minimum VUS for 3 Classes

Now let us try to derive the minimum VUS. Without any knowledge we can construct trivial classifiers by giving more or less probability to each class, as follows:

		Actual		
		a	B	c
	a	h_a	h_a	h_a
Predicted	b	h_b	h_b	h_b
	c	h_c	h_c	h_c

where $h_a + h_b + h_c = 1$. These obviously include the three extreme trivial classifiers "everything is a", "everything is b" and "everything is c". Given a classifier:

		Actual		
		A	B	C
	a	v_{aa}	v_{ba}	v_{ca}
Predicted	b	v_{ab}	v_{bb}	v_{cb}
	c	v_{ac}	v_{bc}	v_{cc}

we can discard this classifier if and only if it is above a trivial classifier, formally:

$$\exists h_a, h_b, h_c \in \mathbb{R}^+ \text{ where } (h_a + h_b + h_c = 1) \text{ such that:}$$
$$v_{ba} \ge h_a, v_{ca} \ge h_a, v_{ab} \ge h_b, v_{cb} \ge h_b, v_{ac} \ge h_c, v_{bc} \ge h_c$$

From here, we can derive the following theorem (see [4] for the proof):

Theorem 1: Without any knowledge, a classifier $(x_1, x_2, x_3, x_4, x_5, x_6)$ can be discarded iff: $r_1 + r_2 + r_3 \ge 1$ where $r_1 = \min(x_1, x_2)$, $r_2 = \min(x_3, x_4)$ and $r_3 = \min(x_5, x_6)$.

Given the previous property, we only have to compute the space of classifiers that follow the condition that $r_1 + r_2 + r_3 \ge 1$ where $r_1 = \min(x_1, x_2)$, $r_2 = \min(x_3, x_4)$ and $r_3 = \min(x_5, x_6)$ to obtain the minimum volume corresponding to total absence of information. More precisely, we have to compute the volume formed by this condition jointly with the valid classifier conditions, i.e.:

$$x_3 + x_5 \le 1, \ x_1 + x_6 \le 1, \ x_2 + x_4 \le 1 \text{ and } r_1 + r_2 + r_3 \ge 1$$
where $r_1 = \min(x_1, x_2)$, $r_2 = \min(x_3, x_4)$ and $r_3 = \min(x_5, x_6)$

This volume is more difficult to be obtained by a probability estimation, due to the min function and especially because the first conditions and the last one are dependent. Let us compute this volume using a Monte Carlo method.

3.1.3 Monte Carlo Method for Obtaining Max and Min VUS

Monte Carlo methods are used to randomly generate a subset of cases from a problem space and estimate the probability that a random case follows a set of conditions. These methods are particularly interesting to approximate volumes, such as the volume under the ROC curve we are dealing with.

For this purpose, we generate an increasing number of points in the 6D hypercube of length 1 (i.e., we generate six variables $x_1, x_2, x_3, x_4, x_5, x_6$ using a uniform distribution between 0 and 1) and then check whether or not they follow the previous maximum or minimum conditions. Since we are working with a 1-length hypercube, the proportion of cases following the conditions is exactly the volume we are looking for.

In particular, we have obtained the following results:

- Maximum: 0.12483 for 1,000,000 cases, matching our theoretical $VUS_3^{max} = 1/8$.
- Minimum: 0.00555523 for 1,000,000 cases, which is approximately 1/180.

However, although we have obtained the exact maximum, we have not obtained the exact minimum (although 1/180 is conjectured). In the next section we introduce a method to compute the real VUS^{min}, and, more importantly, to obtain the ROC polytopes that form these volumes.

4 A Constraint Satisfaction Algorithm for the ROC Polytopes

In the previous section we have developed the conditions for the maximum and minimum VUS, given, respectively, when the best classifier is known (0, 0, 0, 0, 0, 0) and when no classifier is given (absence of information). However, we are interested in a way to obtain the border points of each space, i.e., the polytopes that represent both cases. What we need is a way to compute these polytopes given the set of conditions. A general system able to do this is HSA.

4.1 Hyperpolyhedron Search Algorithm (HSA)

In the constraint satisfaction literature, researchers have focussed on discrete and binary Constraint Satisfaction Problems (CSPs). However, many real problems (as the ROC surface problem) can be naturally modelled using non-binary constraints over continuous variables. Hyperpolyhedron Search Algorithm (HSA) [11] is a CSP solver that manages non-binary and continuous problems. HSA carries out the search through a hyperpolyhedron that maintains in its vertices those solutions that satisfy all non-binary constraints. The handling of the non-binary constraints (linear inequations) can be seen as the handling of global hyperpolyhedron constraints. Initially, the hyperpolyhedron is created by the Cartesian product of the variable domain bounds.

For each constraint, HSA checks the consistency, updating the hyperpolyhedron through linear programming techniques. Each constraint is a hyperplane that is intersected to obtain the new hyperpolyhedron vertices. The resulting hyperpolyhedron is a convex set of solutions to the CSP. A solution is an assignment of a value from its domain to every variable where all constraints are satisfied. HSA can determine: whether a solution exists (consistency), several solutions or the extreme solutions.

In the ROC surface problem, we will use HSA to determine the extreme solutions in order to calculate the convex hull of the resulting hyperpolyhedron. HSA does not compute the volume of the hyperpolyhedron. For this purpose, we are using QHull [2]. QHull is, among other things, an algorithm that implements a quick method for computing the convex hull of a set of points and the volume of the hull.

4.2 Maximum VUS Points for 3 Classes

Let us recover the equations for the maximum volume (valid classifier conditions):
$$x_3 + x_5 \leq 1, x_1 + x_6 \leq 1, x_2 + x_4 \leq 1$$
We introduce these equations to HSA and look for solutions for these six variables. We obtain 41 points (which can be simplified into just 27 points, see [4]) whose volume is, as expected, 0.125 (1/8).

4.3 Minimum VUS for 3 Classes

From Theorem 1, in order to compute the minimum VUS, we only have to compute the space of classifiers following that $r_1 + r_2 + r_3 \geq 1$ where $r_1 = \min(x_1, x_2)$, $r_2 = \min(x_3, x_4)$ and $r_3 = \min(x_5, x_6)$ to obtain the minimum volume corresponding to total absence of information. Using this condition and the hyper-cube conditions, we have:
$$x_3 + x_5 \leq 1, \quad x_1 + x_6 \leq 1, x_2 + x_4 \leq 1, \quad r_1 + r_2 + r_3 \geq 1$$
where $r_1 = \min(x_1, x_2)$, $r_2 = \min(x_3, x_4)$ and $r_3 = \min(x_5, x_6)$. Since the min function is not handled by HSA, we convert the last condition into eight equivalent inequations:
$$x_1 + x_3 + x_5 \geq 1, x_1 + x_3 + x_6 \geq 1, x_1 + x_4 + x_5 \geq 1, x_1 + x_4 + x_6 \geq 1,$$
$$x_2 + x_3 + x_5 \geq 1, x_2 + x_3 + x_6 \geq 1, x_2 + x_4 + x_5 \geq 1, x_2 + x_4 + x_6 \geq 1$$
and now we obtain a set of 25 points whose volume is 0.0055, which is approximately 1/180 and matches the volume obtained by the Monte Carlo method.

Some of these points are exactly on the surface of the volume and can be removed without modifying the volume in a simplified set of 9 points (see [4]).

4.4 Computing the VUS of Any Classifier

Now it seems that we can obtain the VUS of any classifier just be adding the coordinates of the point it represents and adding them as a new point to the minimum and then computing the convex hull. However, this would be a hasty step. The surprise would come up if we take the minimum (9 points, 1/180) and add the origin (the best classifier with no error at all). In this case, we obtain 10 points and 1/120 volume, which is a greater volume but it is not the maximum. This seems contradictory, because if we have the best classifier, we should obtain the maximum volume. The reason is the following. When we have the perfect classifier, represented by the point (0, 0, 0, 0, 0, 0), any classifier that has a value equal or greater than 0 in any coordinate is discardable and, logically, this should give 1/8, not 1/120. The issue is that whenever we add a new classifier we have to consider the conditions it produces, which are polytopes, not just points.

In other words, the perfect classifier generates the following discard equations:
$$x_1 \geq 0, x_2 \geq 0, x_3 \geq 0, x_4 \geq 0, x_5 \geq 0, x_6 \geq 0$$
These inequations are null, because all the values should be positive, and, hence, we only have the valid classifier conditions, and then we have the maximum volume 1/8.

Now let us consider the same thing for any arbitrary classifier C1:

		Actual		
		a	b	c
Predicted	a	z_{aa}	z_{ba}	z_{ca}
	b	z_{ab}	z_{bb}	z_{cb}
	c	z_{ac}	z_{bc}	z_{cc}

What can be discarded? The answer is that any classifier such that is worse than the classifier C1 (combined with the trivial classifiers), i.e., any classifier that would have greater values for the 6 dimensions. Consequently, given a new classifier C2:

		Actual		
		a	b	c
Predicted	a	v_{aa}	v_{ba}	v_{ca}
	b	v_{ab}	v_{bb}	v_{cb}
	c	v_{ac}	v_{bc}	v_{cc}

We have to look at all the classifiers constructed as a linear combination of the three trivial classifiers and the classifier C1, and see whether C2 is worse than any of the constructed classifiers. Formally, the linear combination is defined as:
$$h_a \cdot (1, 1, 0, 0, 0, 0) + h_b \cdot (0, 0, 1, 1, 0, 0) + h_c \cdot (0, 0, 0, 0, 1, 1) + h_d \cdot (z_{ba}, z_{ca}, z_{ab}, z_{cb}, z_{ac}, z_{bc})$$
And we can discard C2 when
$$\exists h_a, h_b, h_c, h_d \in \mathbb{R}^+ \text{ where } (h_a + h_b + h_c + h_d = 1) \text{ such that:}$$
$$v_{ba} \geq h_a + 0 + 0 + h_d \cdot z_{ba}, \quad v_{ca} \geq h_a + 0 + 0 + h_d \cdot z_{ca}, \quad v_{ab} \geq 0 + h_b + 0 + h_d \cdot z_{ab},$$
$$v_{cb} \geq 0 + h_b + 0 + h_d \cdot z_{cb}, \quad v_{ac} \geq 0 + 0 + h_c + h_d \cdot z_{ac}, \quad v_{bc} \geq 0 + 0 + h_c + h_d \cdot z_{bc}$$
This gives a system of inequations with 10 variables (z_{ij} are constants given by C1), that can be input to HSA, and then we obtain the edge six dimensions points from v_{ij}.

4.5 Real VUS for More than One Classifier

In the same way as before, given a set of classifiers, we can compute the true VUS of the set, just generalising the previous formula. Let us illustrate it for 4 classifiers Z, W, Y and X. In fact, what we have to do is to consider the linear combination of the three trivial classifiers with the four given classifiers, i.e.:
$$h_a \cdot (1, 1, 0, 0, 0, 0) + h_b \cdot (0, 0, 1, 1, 0, 0) + h_c \cdot (0, 0, 0, 0, 1, 1) + h_1 \cdot (z_{ba}, z_{ca}, z_{ab}, z_{cb}, z_{ac}, z_{bc})$$
$$+ h_2 \cdot (w_{ba}, w_{ca}, w_{ab}, w_{cb}, w_{ac}, w_{bc}) + h_3 \cdot (x_{ba}, x_{ca}, x_{ab}, x_{cb}, x_{ac}, x_{bc}) + h_4 \cdot (y_{ba}, y_{ca}, y_{ab}, y_{cb}, y_{ac}, y_{bc})$$

And now we can discard when:

$\exists h_a, h_b, h_c, h_d \in R^+$ where $(h_a + h_b + h_c + h_1 + h_2 + h_3 + h_4 = 1)$ such that:
$$v_{ba} \geq h_a + 0 + 0 + h_1 \cdot z_{ba} + h_2 \cdot w_{ba} + h_3 \cdot x_{ba} + h_4 \cdot y_{ba}$$
$$v_{ca} \geq h_a + 0 + 0 + h_1 \cdot z_{ca} + h_2 \cdot w_{ca} + h_3 \cdot x_{ca} + h_4 \cdot y_{ca}$$
$$v_{ab} \geq 0 + h_b + 0 + h_1 \cdot z_{ab} + h_2 \cdot w_{ab} + h_3 \cdot x_{ab} + h_4 \cdot y_{ab}$$
$$v_{cb} \geq 0 + h_b + 0 + h_1 \cdot z_{cb} + h_2 \cdot w_{cb} + h_3 \cdot x_{cb} + h_4 \cdot y_{cb}$$
$$v_{ac} \geq 0 + 0 + h_c + h_1 \cdot z_{ac} + h_2 \cdot w_{ac} + h_3 \cdot x_{ac} + h_4 \cdot y_{ac}$$
$$v_{bc} \geq 0 + 0 + h_c + h_1 \cdot z_{bc} + h_2 \cdot w_{bc} + h_3 \cdot x_{bc} + h_4 \cdot y_{bc}$$

This gives a system with 9+4 variables that can be solved by HSA, from which we again retain just 6 (v_{ij}) variables to obtain the polytope.

5 Evaluation of Multi-class Approximations to the VUS

In the previous section we have developed a method (conditions + HSA) to obtain the real VUS of any classifier for an arbitrary number of classes (the extension for more than 3 classes is trivial). However, this exact computation, although quite efficient for 3 and 4 classes, must be impractical for a higher number of classes or classifiers.

In the literature, there have been several approximations for the extension of the AUC measure for multi-class problems, either based on the interpretation of the AUC as distribution separability [6] or the meaning of the equivalent (for two classes) Wilcoxon statistic or GINI coefficient. However, there is no appraisal or estimation, either theoretical or practical, of how good they are.

In this section we gather and remind the approximations for the AUC for more than two classes known to date: macro-average, 1-point trivial AUC extension and some Hand & Till [6] variants. We are going to make a comparison with the real measure we have presented in this work: the exact VUS (through the HSA method).

We will give the definitions for three classes, although this can be easily extended to more classes. For the following definitions consider a classifier C2 as before.

5.1 Macro-average

The macro-average is just defined as the average of the class accuracies, i.e.:
$$MAVG_3 = (v_{aa} + v_{bb} + v_{cc}) / 3$$
This measure has been used as a very simple way to handle more appropriately unbalanced datasets (without using ROC analysis).

5.2 Macro-average Modified

We modify the original definition of macro-average because this does not consider the standard deviation between the points. For instance, using two classes, the point (0.2, 0.2) has greater AUC than the point (0.1, 0.3) although both points have identical macro-average. Thereby, we will employ the generalised mean instead of average:

$$\text{MAVG}_3\text{-MOD} = \left(\frac{1}{n}\sum_{k=1}^{n} a_k^t\right)^{1/t}$$

The best value for t between the arithmetic mean ($t=1$) and the geometric mean ($t\bullet 0$) has been estimated experimentally. The value $t=0.76$ obtains the best performance.

5.3 1-Point Trivial AUC Extension

Going back to two classes, the area for one point (v_{ba}, v_{ab}) (in our representation) is:
$$\text{AUC}_2 = \max(1/2,\ 1 - v_{ba}/2 - v_{ab}/2)$$
Extending trivially the previous formula, we have this extension for 1-point:
$$\text{AUC-1PT}_3 = \max(1/3,\ 1 - (v_{ba} + v_{ca} + v_{ab} + v_{cb} + v_{ac} + v_{bc})/3$$
This extension turns to be equal to the macro-average since the columns of the matrix sum to 1. The only difference is that the 1PT_3 measure is never lower than 1/3.

5.4 1-Point Hand and Till Extension

Hand and Till have presented a generalisation of the AUC measure [6] for soft classifiers, i.e., classifiers that assign a different score, reliability or probability with each prediction. Although we will deal with soft classifiers later, let us adapt Hand and Till's formulation for crisp classifiers, i.e., classifiers that predict one of the possible classes, without giving any additional information about the reliability or probability of the predicted class, or the other classes.

Hand and Till's extension for more than two classes is based on the idea that if we can compute the AUC for two classes i,j (let us denote this by $A(i,j)$), then we can compute an extension of AUC for any arbitrary number of classes by choosing all the possible pairs (1 vs. 1). Since $A(i,j) = A(j,i)$, this can be simplified as shown in the following Hand and Till's M function:

$$M = \frac{1}{c(c-1)}\sum_{i\neq j}\hat{A}(i,j) = \frac{2}{c(c-1)}\sum_{i<j}\hat{A}(i,j)$$

Pursuing this idea we are going to introduce three variants. The first variant is given if we consider the macro-average extension. Then we have:

$$\text{HT1a} = (\max(1/2, (v_{aa} + v_{bb})/2) + \max(1/2, (v_{aa} + v_{cc})/2) + \max(1/2, (v_{bb} + v_{cc})/2))\ /\ 3$$

This is equal to the 1PT. But if we take failures into account instead of hits, we have:

$$\text{HT1b} = (\max(1/2,\ 1-(v_{ba}+v_{ab})/2) + \max(1/2,\ 1-(v_{ca}+v_{ac})/2) + \max(1/2,\ 1-(v_{cb}+v_{bc})/2))\ /\ 3$$

This measure is slightly different from the previous ones and we will use this one. Another different way is normalisation, e.g., if we normalise only for classes a and b:

		Actual A	b
Predicted	a	$v_{aa}/(v_{aa}+v_{ab})$	$x = v_{ba}/(v_{ba}+v_{bb})$
	b	$y = v_{ab}/(v_{aa}+v_{ab})$	$v_{bb}/(v_{ba}+v_{bb})$

We have $\max(1/2, (x+y)/2)$ and the same for the rest of combinations. Namely:

$$\text{HT2} = (\max(1/2,\ 1 - (v_{ba}/(v_{ba}+v_{bb}) + v_{ab}/(v_{aa}+v_{ab}))/2) + \max(1/2,\ 1 - (v_{ca}/(v_{ca}+v_{cc}) + v_{ac}/(v_{aa}+v_{ac}))/2) + \max(1/2,\ 1 - (v_{cb}/(v_{cb}+v_{cc}) + v_{bc}/(v_{bb}+v_{bc}))/2))\ /\ 3$$

Finally, we can define a third variant that instead of computing partial AUCs of pairs of classes, computes the AUC of each class against the rest (1 vs. rest) and then average the results. For instance, the AUC of class a and the rest (b and c joined) will be obtained from a condensed 2x2 matrix:

		Actual	
		A	rest
Predicted	A	$v_{aa} / (v_{aa} + v_{ab} + v_{ac})$	$(v_{ba} + v_{ca}) / (v_{ba} + v_{ca} + v_{bb} + v_{bc} + v_{cb} + v_{cc})$
	rest	$(v_{ab} + v_{ac}) / (v_{aa} + v_{ab} + v_{ac})$	$(v_{bb} + v_{bc} + v_{cb} + v_{cc}) / (v_{ba} + v_{ca} + v_{bb} + v_{bc} + v_{cb} + v_{cc})$

Using cells (a,rest) and (rest,a) we have:

$AUC_{a,rest} = \max(1/2, 1 - [(v_{ab} + v_{ac}) / (v_{aa} + v_{ab} + v_{ac})]/2 - [(v_{ba} + v_{ca}) / (v_{ba} + v_{ca} + v_{bb} + v_{bc} + v_{cb} + v_{cc})]/2$

In the same way we can obtain $AUC_{a,rest}$ and $AUC_{a,rest}$. This allows us to define HT3:

$HT3 = (AUC_{a,rest} + AUC_{a,rest} + AUC_{a,rest}) / 3$

5.5 Experimental Evaluation

Once the previous approximations are presented, we are ready to evaluate them in comparison to the exact computation given by the HSA method.

We are interested in how well the approximations "rank" the classifiers. To evaluate which approximation is best, we generate a set of 100 random classifiers (more precisely, we randomly generate 100 normalised confusion matrices).

Then, we compute the value of each classifier for each approximation a (exact VUS, accuracy, macro-avg, mod-avb, 1-p trivial, HT1B, HT2, HT3). Next, we make a one-to-one comparison (a ranking) for each approximation a and fill a matrix M_a, which tells whether i is ranked above j. Done all this (for a detailed description of the methodology of this process, see [4]), we ready to compare approximations.

For instance, given the matrices M_1 and M_2 of two different methods, we compare the discrepancy of the matrices in the following way:

$$disc = \frac{2\sum_{i=1}^{n}\sum_{j=1, i<j}^{n} |M_1(i,j) - M_2(i,j)|}{n(n-1)}$$

With this formula we can evaluate the discrepancy of the methods for 3 class problems with respect the real VUS computed with the HAS method. The results are:

Accuracy	Macro-avg	Mod-avg (0.76)	1-p trivial	HT1B	HT2	HT3
0.08707	0,087071	0.0587879	0.09131	0.10404	0.14081	0.09677

According to these results, the best approximation is the modified macro-average (generalised mean). Note that this is the only one that is better than accuracy. Note also that for 2 classes, AUC = geomean(TPR, TNR), while for 3 classes, the best result is obtained somehow in the middle between the arithmetic mean and the geometric mean. This modified mean obtains the lower discrepancy among the studied approximations and hence could be used as an alternative to accuracy and macro-avg.

6 Conclusions

In this paper we have addressed the extension of ROC analysis for multi-class problems. We have identified the trivial classifiers and then derived the discard conditions, identified the maximum and minimum VUS and their polytopes, as well as the VUS for any arbitrary set of crisp classifiers. This is computed through the HSA algorithm. We have then compared experimentally the real VUS with several other approximations for crisp classifiers, showing which approximation is best. The best approximation seems to be a modification of the macro-average for one classifier.

For soft classifiers (i.e., classifiers that accompany each prediction with the reliability or, even better, with the estimated probabilities of each class), we have performed some preliminary experiments (see [4]) which show that the best approximation for soft classifiers is HT3. It is precisely for soft classifiers where the results can be more directly applicable to real-world problems.

For the moment, the results of this work dissuade the use of Hand and Till's and related measures as an extension of AUC for more than two classes for one crisp classifier. We propose an alternative approximation (mod-average). Nonetheless, for the case of soft classifiers the preliminary results in [4] are good for Hand and Till's extension (1 vs. 1, i.e. HT2) but especially for Fawcett's extension (1 vs. rest, i.e. HT3) already used in [9][10] for sets of classifiers or soft classifiers. Pursuing the work initiated here will bring a more justified use of AUC extensions as evaluation measure for classifiers. As future work, we would like to work further on soft classifiers, deriving accurate approximations of the real VUS in a reasonable time.

Acknowledgements

We thank Peter Flach for introducing us in the area of ROC analysis, and Tom Fawcett for some discussions on the multi-class extension. This work has been partially supported by CICYT under grant TIC2001-2705-C03-01, by the project DPI2001-2094-C03-03 from the Spanish Government, and by Universitat Politècnica de València under grant ref. 20020651. M.A. Salido enjoyed a stay as visiting research fellow (PPI-02-03) also funded by Universitat Politècnica de València.

References

1. Adams, N.M., Hand, D.J. "Comparing classifiers when the misallocation costs are uncertain, Pattern Recognition, Vol. 32 (7) (1999) pp. 1139-1147.
2. Barber, C.B.; Huhdanpaa, H. "QHull", The Geometry Center, University of Minnesota, http://www.geom.umn.edu/software/qhull/.
3. Boissonat, J.D.; Yvinec, M. "Algorithmic Geometry" Cambridge University Press, 1998.

4. Ferri C., Hernández-Orallo J., Salido M. A., "Volume Under the ROC Surface for Multi-class Problems. Exact Computation and Evaluation of Approximations" Technical Report DSIC. Univ. Politèc. València. 2003. http://www.dsic.upv.es/users/elp/cferri/VUS.pdf.
5. Flach P., Blockeel H., Ferri C., Hernández-Orallo J., Struyf J. "Decision support for data mining; Introduction to ROC analysis and its applications". In Data Mining and Decision Support: Integration and Collaboration. Kluwer Publishers. To appear. 2003.
6. Hand, D.J.; Till, R.J. "A Simple Generalisation of the Area Under the ROC Curve for Multiple Class Classification Problems" Machine Learning, 45, 171-186, 2001.
7. Hanley, J.A.; McNeil, B.J. "The meaning and use of the area under a receiver operating characteristic (ROC) curve" Radiology. 1982: 143:29-36.
8. Lane, T. "Extensions of ROC Analysis to Multi-Class Domains", ICML-2000 Workshop on cost-sensitive learning, 2000.
9. Provost, F., Fawcett, T. "Analysis and visualization of classifier performance: Comparison under imprecise class and cost distribution" in Proc. of The Third International Conference on Knowledge Discovery and Data Mining (KDD-97), pp. 43-48, AAAI Press, 1997.
10. Provost, F., Domingos P. "Tree Induction for Probability-based Ranking" Machine Learning 52:3, 199-215 , 2003.
11. Salido, M.A.; Giret, A. Barber, F. "Constraint Satisfaction by means of Dynamic Polyhedra" in Operations Research Proceedings 2001. Springer Verlag, pp: 405-412, 2002.
12. Srinivasan, A. "Note on the Location of Optimal Classifiers in N-dimensional ROC Space" Technical Report PRG-TR-2-99, Oxford University Computing Laboratory,
13. Swets, J., Dawes, R., Monahan, J. "Better decisions through science" Scientific American, October 2000, 82-87.
14. Turney P. "Cost-sensitive classification: Empirical evaluation of a hybrid genetic decision tree induction algorithm", Journal of Artificial Intelligence Research, 2, 369-409, 1995.
15. Zweig, M.H.; Campbell, G. "Receiver-operating characteristic (ROC) plots: a fundamental evaluation tool in clinical medicine", Clin. Chem, 1993; 39: 561-77.

Improving the AUC of Probabilistic Estimation Trees

César Ferri[1], Peter A. Flach[2], and José Hernández-Orallo[1]

[1] Dep. Sistemes Informàtics i Computació, Univ. Politècnica de València, Spain
{cferri,jorallo}@dsic.upv.es
[2] Department of Computer Science, University of Bristol, United Kingdom
Peter.Flach@bristol.ac.uk

Abstract. In this work we investigate several issues in order to improve the performance of probabilistic estimation trees (PETs). First, we derive a new probability smoothing that takes into account the class distributions of all the nodes from the root to each leaf. Secondly, we introduce or adapt some new splitting criteria aimed at improving probability estimates rather than improving classification accuracy, and compare them with other accuracy-aimed splitting criteria. Thirdly, we analyse the effect of pruning methods and we choose a cardinality-based pruning, which is able to significantly reduce the size of the trees without degrading the quality of the estimates. The quality of probability estimates of these three issues is evaluated by the 1-vs-1 multi-class extension of the Area Under the ROC Curve (AUC) measure, which is becoming widespread for evaluating probability estimators, ranking of predictions in particular.

1 Introduction

Decision-tree learning has been extensively used in many application areas of machine learning, especially for classification, because the algorithms developed for learning decision trees [3,13] represent a good compromise between comprehensibility, accuracy and efficiency. In the common setting, a classifier is defined as a function from a set of m arguments or attributes (which can be either nominal or numeric) to a single nominal value, known as the class. We denote by C the set of c classes, usually simply referred by natural numbers 0, 1, 2, ... c-1. By E we denote the set of unlabelled examples. A classifier is a function $f: E \rightarrow C$. Traditionally, this setting was sufficient for most of the classification problems and applications. However, more and more applications require some kind of reliability, likelihood or numeric assessment of the quality of each classification. In other words, we do not only want that the model predicts a class value for each example but also that it can give an estimate of the reliability of each prediction. Such classifiers are usually called *soft classifiers*. Soft classifiers are useful in many scenarios, including combination of classifiers, cost-sensitive learning and safety-critical applications. The most general presentation of a soft classifier is a probability estimator, i.e. a model that estimates the probability $p_i(e)$ of membership of class $i \in C$ for every example $e \in E$.

A trained decision tree can be easily adapted to be a probability estimator by using the absolute class frequencies of each leaf of the tree. For instance, if a node has the following absolute frequencies $n_1, n_2, ..., n_c$ (obtained from the training dataset) the estimated probabilities for that node can be derived as $p_i = n_i / \Sigma n_i$. Every new example falling into that leaf will have these estimated class probabilities. Such trees are called *Probability Estimation Trees* (PETs). However, despite this simple conversion from a decision tree classifier into a PET, the probability estimates obtained by PETs are quite poor with respect to other probability estimators [14,2].

Some recent works have changed this situation. First, Provost and Domingos [12] improve the quality of PETs by reassessing some classical techniques in decision tree learning. In particular, they found that frequency smoothing of the leaf probability estimates, such as Laplace correction, significantly enhances the estimates, especially if they are used for ranking. On the other hand, pruning (or related techniques such as C4.5 collapsing) is shown to be unhelpful for increasing probability estimates. Unpruned trees usually give the best results. Independently, in an earlier paper [7] we also improve the quality of PETs by considering Laplace correction for the leaves. In addition, we showed that splitting criteria aimed at increasing accuracy (or reducing error), such as GainRatio, GINI or DKM [13,3,10] are not necessarily the best criteria for estimating good probabilities. Splitting criteria based on probability ranking, such as the new AUC-splitting criterion [7] can produce better results when the aim is to obtain good probability estimates. These two works are first steps that show that decision trees can be successfully used as probability estimators, provided we reassess and redefine some of the traditional techniques specifically devised for improving the accuracy of decision trees.

Provost and Domingos [12] "believe that a thorough study of what are the best methods for PETs would be a successful contribution to machine-learning research". In this spirit and as a sequel and natural continuation of the above-mentioned works, in this paper we present the following enhancements: (*i*) a new smoothing method (*m-branch smoothing*) for estimating probabilities, that not only considers the leaves, but all the frequencies from the root to the leaf; (*ii*) a new splitting criterion (*MSEEsplit*) defined in terms of the minimum squared error of the probability estimates; and (*iii*) a simple pruning criterion based on the cardinalities of nodes that is able to reduce the size of trees, without degrading the quality of the probability estimates.

The paper is organised as follows. In Section 2 we describe in more detail what a PET is and how it can be evaluated. Section 3 presents the new smoothing method. Section 4 introduces two new splitting criteria, MAUCsplit and MSEEsplit. Section 5 analyses the use of pruning and presents the influence of the degree of pruning of the best pruning method we have found so far for PETs. Finally, Section 6 discusses the results, and Section 7 closes the paper and proposes future work.

2 PETs, Features and Evaluation

In this section we present some necessary definitions, the evaluation framework, the experimental setting and some previous results in order to set the stage for the rest of the paper. The main contributions of this work are presented in subsequent sections.

Given the set of unlabelled examples E and the set C of c classes, we define a *probability estimator* as a set of c functions $p_{i \in C}: E \to \Re$ such that $\forall p_{i \in C}, e \in E : 0 \le p_i(e) \le 1$ and $\forall e \in E \sum p_{i \in C}(e) = 1$. Decision trees are formed of nodes, splits and conditions. A *condition* is any Boolean function $g: E \to \{true, false\}$. A *split* is a set of s conditions $\{g_k : 1 \le k \le s\}$. In this paper, we consider the conditions of a split to be exhaustive and exclusive, i.e., for a given example one and only one of the conditions of a split is true. A *decision tree* can be defined recursively as follows: (*i*) a node with no associated split is a decision tree, called a leaf; (*ii*) a node with an associated split $\{g_k : 1 \leq k \leq s\}$ and a set of s children $\{t_k\}$, such that each condition is associated with one and only one child, and each child t_k is a decision tree, is also a decision tree. Given a tree t there is just a single node r that is not child of any other node. This special node is called the *root* of the tree. The sequence of nodes $<v_1, v_2, ..., v_d>$ from the root to a leaf l, where $v_d = l$ and v_1 is the root, is called the *branch* leading to l.

In the most straightforward and classical scenario a decision tree is learned by using a training set T, which is a set of labelled examples, i.e., a set of pairs of the form $<e, i>$ where $e \in E$ and $i \in C$. After the training stage, the examples will have been distributed among all the nodes in the tree, where the root node contains all the examples and downward nodes contain the subset of examples that are consistent with the conditions of the specific branch. Therefore, every node has particular absolute frequencies $n_1, n_2, ..., n_c$ for each class. The cardinality of the node is given by Σn_i. A *decision tree classifier* (DTC) is defined as a decision tree with an associated labelling of the leaves with classes. Usually, the assigned class is the most frequent class in the leaf ($argmax_i\{n_i\}$). A *probability estimation tree* (PET) is a decision tree where each leaf is assigned a probability distribution over classes. These probability estimates can for instance be relative frequencies $p_i = n_i / \Sigma n_i$.

2.1 DTCs, PETs and Their Evaluation

One of the first questions that may arise is whether a good DTC is always a good PET and vice versa. Although there is a high correlation between quality of DTCs and quality of PETs, some recent works have shown that many heuristics used for improving classification accuracy "reduce the quality of probability estimates" [12]. Hence, it is worth investigating new heuristics and techniques which are specific to PETs and that may have been neglected by previous work in DTCs.

But first of all, a standard measure for evaluating the quality of PETs must be established. As justified and used by [12,7] and other previous work, the AUC (Area under the ROC Curve) measure has been chosen for evaluation. The measure can be interpreted as the probability that a randomly chosen example e of class 0 will have an estimated $p_0(e)$ greater than the estimated $p_1(e)$. Consequently, this is a measure particularly suitable for evaluating ranked two-class predictions. Recently, an extension of the AUC measure for more than two classes has been proposed by Hand and Till [9]. The idea is to simply average the AUC of each pair of classes (1-vs-1 multiclass). We call this measure *MAUC* for multi-class AUC (Hand and Till denote the function by M). Clearly, MAUC = AUC when $c=2$.

In [7] we introduced a new method for efficiently computing MAUC based on the ranking of leaves rather than a ranking of examples. Hence, the complexity of the new method depends on the number of leaves rather than on the number of examples, frequently entailing better performance. In what follows, we use this optimisation.

2.2 Datasets and Experimental Methodology

We evaluated the methods presented in this paper on 50 datasets from the UCI repository [1]. Half of them have two classes, either originally or by selecting one of the classes and joining all the other classes, and the rest have more than two classes (multi-class datasets). The datasets are described in Table 1 and Table 2. The first two columns show the dataset number and name, the size (number of examples), the numbers of nominal and numerical attributes and the size of the minority class.

Table 1. Two-class datasets used.

#	DATASET	SIZE	ATTRIBUTES NOM	ATTRIBUTES NUM	%MIN CLASS
1	MONKS1	566	6	0	50
2	MONKS2	601	6	0	34.28
3	MONKS3	554	6	0	48.01
4	TIC-TAC	958	8	0	34.66
5	HOUSE-VOTES	435	16	0	38.62
6	AGARICUS	8124	22	0	48.2
7	BREAST-WDBC	569	0	30	37.26
8	BREAST-CAN-WISC	699	0	9	34.48
9	BREAST-WPBC	194	0	33	23.71
10	IONOSPHERE	351	0	34	35.9
11	LIVER-BUPA	345	0	6	42.03
12	PIMA-ABALONE	768	0	8	34.9
13	CHESS-KR-VS-KP	3196	36	0	47.78
14	SONAR	208	0	60	46.63
15	HEPATITIS	83	14	5	18.07
16	THYROID-HYPO	2012	19	6	6.06
17	THYROID-SICK-EU	2012	19	6	11.83
18	YEAST2C	1484	0	8	31.20
19	SPECT	267	22	0	20.60
20	HABERMN-BRST	306	0	3	26.47
21	SPAM	4601	0	57	39.40
22	CYL-BANDS	365	19	17	36.99
23	PIMA-DIABETES	768	0	8	34.90
24	SICK	2751	21	6	7.92
25	LYMPH_2C	142	15	3	42.96

Table 2. Multi-class datasets used.

#	DATASET	#CLASSES	SIZE	ATTRIBUTES NOM	ATTRIBUTES NUM	%MIN CLASS
26	HYPOTHYROID_3C	3	2750	21	6	3.24
27	BALANCE-SCALE	3	625	0	4	7.84
28	CARS	4	1728	6	0	3.76
29	DERMATOLOGY	6	366	33	1	5.46
30	NEW-THYROID	3	215	0	5	13.95
31	NURSERY4C	4	12957	8	0	2.53
32	PAGE-BLOCKS	5	5473	0	10	0.51
33	PENDIGITS	10	10992	0	16	9.60
34	TAE	3	151	2	3	32.45
35	IRIS	3	150	0	4	33.33
36	OPTDIGITS	10	5620	0	64	9.86
37	SEGMENTATION	7	2310	0	19	14.29
38	WINE	3	178	0	13	26.97
39	HEART-DIS-ALL	5	920	8	5	3.04
40	ANNEAL	5	898	32	6	0.89
41	HAYES-ROTH	3	160	4	0	19.38
42	WAVEFORM	3	5000	0	21	32.94
43	CMC	3	1473	7	2	22.61
44	ECOLI4C	4	336	0	7	7.44
45	AUTOS-DRVWHLS	3	205	9	16	4.39
46	SOLAR FLAREC	3	323	10	0	2.17
47	HORSECOLICOUTC	3	366	13	8	14.21
48	ANN-THYROID	3	7200	15	6	2.31
49	SPLICE	3	3190	60	0	24.04
50	SAT	6	6435	0	36	9.73

All experiments have been done within the SMILES system (http://www.dsic.upv.es/~flip/smiles/). The use of the same system for all the methods makes comparisons more impartial because all other things remain equal. We used the basic configuration of the system, which is a decision-tree learner quite similar to C4.5, but without pruning (unless stated), without node "collapsing" [13], and the GainRatio splitting criterion used by default (this configuration is sometimes called C4.4).

We performed a 20 times 5-fold cross-validation, thus making a total of 50 x 100 = 5,000 runs of SMILES for each method. We have used 5-fold cross-validation instead of 10-fold cross-validation because for computing the AUC we need examples of all the classes and some datasets have a small proportion of examples for the minority class. In what follows, for each dataset we show the arithmetic mean and the standard deviation of the 100 runs. Accuracy and AUC are shown as a percentage.

2.3 Results with Laplace and *m*-Estimate Smoothing

Previously, we have stated that, given any node with absolute frequencies $n_1, n_2, ..., n_c$ for each class (hence overall cardinality Σn_i), we can obtain a probability estimation tree by obtaining the probabilities as $p_i = n_i / \Sigma n_i$. One problem is that pure nodes with small cardinality will have the same probability as pure nodes with much higher cardinality. This is especially problematic for ranking predictions of unpruned trees, because most or all nodes tend to be pure and there are many ties between the rankings. A common solution to this problem is the use of *probability smoothing* such as Laplace correction and *m*-estimate, defined as follows:

$$\text{Laplace smoothing} \quad p_i = \frac{n_i + 1}{\left(\sum_{i \in C} n_i\right) + c} \qquad \text{m-estimate smoothing} \quad p_i = \frac{n_i + m \cdot p}{\left(\sum_{i \in C} n_i\right) + m}$$

where c is the number of classes. The probability p in the m-estimate is the expected probability without any additional knowledge, and it is either assumed to be uniform ($p = 1/c$) or estimated from the training distribution. In the uniform case, which we used in our experiments, it is easy to see that Laplace correction is a special case of the m-estimate with $m=c$.

Table 3. Effect of smoothing on AUC for two-class datasets ($m=4$).

#	WITHOUT SMOOTHING		LAPLACE SMOOTHING		M-ESTIMATE SMOOTHING	
	AUC	SD	AUC	SD	AUC	SD
1	96.8	3.7	97.9	2.7	97.9	2.7
2	71.2	4.3	70.2	4.8	70.2	4.8
3	97.7	1.3	99.1	0.9	99.1	0.9
4	76.2	3.6	87.2	2.8	87.2	2.8
5	93.6	2.5	98.2	1.4	98.2	1.4
6	100.0	0.0	100.0	0.0	100.0	0.0
7	91.9	2.9	96.8	1.8	96.8	1.8
8	93.3	2.1	97.9	1.1	97.9	1.1
9	59.6	8.9	64.2	9.5	64.2	9.5
10	90.8	4.2	94.6	3.7	94.6	3.7
11	61.1	6.1	67.0	6.8	67.0	6.8
12	67.2	1.7	79.0	1.4	79.0	1.4
13	99.5	0.3	100.0	0.1	100.0	0.1
14	66.0	7.6	73.5	7.2	73.5	7.2
15	65.5	11.6	75.7	9.1	75.7	9.1
16	90.5	3.9	97.9	1.0	97.9	1.0
17	80.7	3.1	85.1	2.6	84.6	2.7
18	64.8	2.9	74.3	2.8	74.3	2.8
19	67.4	7.1	74.3	7.1	75.0	7.2
20	56.3	6.6	64.3	7.5	64.3	7.5
21	91.7	0.9	96.9	0.5	96.9	0.5
22	66.6	5.4	68.5	5.1	68.5	5.1
23	65.9	4.2	75.3	3.8	75.3	3.8
24	89.3	3.1	98.7	0.8	98.7	0.8
25	78.7	7.8	87.3	6.9	87.3	6.9
ARITM	79.3		85.0		85.0	
GEOM	78.0		83.9		84.0	

Table 4. Effect of smoothing on AUC for multi-class datasets ($m=4$).

#	WITHOUT SMOOTHING		LAPLACE SMOOTHING		M-ESTIMATE SMOOTHING	
	AUC	SD	AUC	SD	AUC	SD
26	97.9	1.4	99.8	0.3	99.8	0.3
27	75.0	1.8	82.9	2.7	82.9	2.7
28	94.7	2.1	95.4	1.6	95.4	1.6
29	98.4	0.8	99.0	0.6	99.0	0.6
30	94.3	3.5	97.1	2.7	97.1	2.7
31	99.4	0.3	99.7	0.1	99.7	0.1
32	94.4	1.8	97.8	1.0	97.8	1.0
33	99.3	0.1	99.7	0.0	99.7	0.0
34	75.0	7.9	74.7	8.5	74.7	8.5
35	97.3	2.2	98.5	1.8	98.5	1.8
36	98.2	0.2	99.0	0.1	99.0	0.1
37	99.3	0.2	99.7	0.1	99.7	0.1
38	96.6	2.7	97.8	1.9	97.8	1.9
39	63.7	3.7	65.6	3.6	65.6	3.6
40	98.6	2.0	99.2	1.1	99.2	1.1
41	89.8	4.2	90.5	4.3	90.5	4.3
42	83.4	1.0	88.8	0.9	88.8	0.9
43	62.0	2.6	65.5	2.7	65.5	2.7
44	93.0	2.9	95.3	2.5	95.3	2.5
45	88.1	8.4	93.0	5.8	93.0	5.8
46	57.5	8.1	58.6	10.4	58.6	10.4
47	66.3	5.4	70.5	4.9	70.5	4.9
48	98.1	1.0	99.8	0.2	99.8	0.2
49	95.6	0.6	98.1	0.4	98.1	0.4
50	95.1	0.3	96.9	0.3	96.9	0.3
ARITM	88.4		90.5		90.5	
GEOM	87.3		89.5		89.5	

Tables 3 and 4 show the results (mean and standard deviation for the 5 × 20 iterations) without smoothing, with Laplace smoothing and with the *m*-estimate with uniform prior (the best experimental value for *m*, *m*=4 is used). These results are similar to those of [12,7] and they are shown here to serve as a reference from which we will illustrate our own improvements. The improvement of Laplace and *m*-estimate smoothing over no smoothing is obvious — especially for two-class datasets — and there is no need to perform a significance test. On the other hand, there is virtually no difference between Laplace smoothing and the best *m*-estimate.

3 *m*-Branch Smoothing

We continue to investigate whether the previous results can be further improved. In this section we propose a more sophisticated smoothing method called *m-branch smoothing*. In the next section we consider alternative splitting criteria that are designed specifically for probability estimation trees.

First of all, the previous *m*-estimate and Laplace smoothing methods consider a uniform class distribution of the sample. That is, they consider the global population uniform whereas in many cases the class probabilities are unbalanced. However, just taking this into account does not improve the measures significantly, since each node takes a subsample from the upper node, and this, once again, makes a subsample of the upper node, until the root is reached. Usually, this means that the sample used to obtain the probability estimate in a leaf is the result of many sampling steps, as many as the depth of the leaf. It makes sense, then, to consider this *history* of samples when estimating the class probabilities in a leaf. The idea is to assign more weight to nodes that are closer to the leaf.

Definition 1 (*m*-Branch Smoothing). Given a leaf node l and its associated branch $<v_1, v_2, ..., v_d>$ where $v_d = l$ and v_1 is the root, denote with n_i^j the cardinality of class i at node v_j. Define $p_i^0 = 1/c$. We recursively compute the probabilities of the nodes from 1 to d as follows:

$$p_i^j = \frac{n_i^j + m \cdot p_i^{j-1}}{\left(\sum_{i \in C} n_i^j\right) + m}$$

The *m*-branch smoothed probabilities of leaf l are given by p_i^d.

We note that *m*-branch smoothing is a recursive root-to-leaf extension of the *m-probability estimate* used by Bratko and Cestnik for decision tree pruning [5].

Since this is an iteration of the *m*-estimate, we could use a fixed value of *m*. However, if we use a small *m* the smoothing would almost be irrelevant for upper nodes, which have high cardinality. On the other hand, if we use a large *m* the small cardinalities at the bottom of the branch would have low relevance. In order to solve this we use a variable value, which depends on the size of the dataset and the depth. Define the *height* of a node as $h = d+1-j$ where d is the depth of the branch and j the depth of the node. The normalised height of a node is defined as $\Delta = 1 - 1/h$ in order to increase the correction closer to the root. We then parametrise the *m* value as follows:

$$m = M \cdot \left(1 + \Delta \cdot \sqrt{N}\right)$$

where M is a constant and N is the global cardinality of the dataset. The use of the square root of N is inspired by "the square root law", which connects the error and the sample size. The previous expression means that *m*-branch smoothing is performed with a value of M at the leaves, the next node up is done with $M + \frac{1}{2} \cdot M \cdot \sqrt{N}$, the next $M + \frac{2}{3} \cdot M \cdot \sqrt{N}$ until the root with $M + \frac{(d-1)}{d} \cdot M \cdot \sqrt{N}$.

In Tables 5 and 6 we compare *m*-branch smoothing (with the best experimental value for $M=4$) compared with the best previous results (*m*-estimate). We also perform a paired *t*-test to test the significance of the results. The 'Better?' column indicates whether *m*-branch smoothing performs significantly better (✓) or worse (✗) than

m-estimate smoothing, according to t-test with level of confidence 0.1. A tie (-) indicates the difference is not significant at this level.

Table 5. Comparison of m-estimate and m-branch smoothing on two-class datasets.

#	M-ESTIMATE SMOOTHING		M-BRANCH SMOOTHING		BETTER?
	AUC	SD	AUC	SD	
1	97.9	2.7	97.2	3.4	×
2	70.2	4.8	67.4	5.0	×
3	99.1	0.9	99.1	1.0	-
4	87.2	2.8	86.9	2.7	-
5	98.2	1.4	98.5	1.4	-
6	100.0	0.0	100.0	0.0	-
7	96.8	1.8	96.9	1.6	-
8	97.9	1.1	98.0	1.1	-
9	64.2	9.5	65.9	10.0	-
10	94.6	3.7	94.4	3.7	-
11	67.0	6.8	70.0	7.1	✓
12	79.0	1.4	82.2	1.4	✓
13	100.0	0.1	99.9	0.1	×
14	73.5	7.2	75.7	6.3	✓
15	75.7	9.1	77.5	9.4	-
16	97.9	1.0	98.1	1.0	-
17	84.6	2.7	86.1	2.7	✓
18	74.3	2.8	75.7	2.6	✓
19	75.0	7.2	77.9	7.0	✓
20	64.3	7.5	67.3	7.0	✓
21	96.9	0.5	97.0	0.5	-
22	68.5	5.1	68.5	5.2	-
23	75.3	3.8	78.8	3.3	✓
24	98.7	0.8	98.7	0.8	-
25	87.3	6.9	87.4	6.9	-
ARITMEAN	85.0		85.8		8 wins, 14 ties,
GEOMEAN	84.0		84.9		3 losses

Table 6. Comparison of m-estimate and m-branch smoothing on multi-class datasets.

#	4-ESTIMATE SMOOTHING		4-BRANCH SMOOTHING		BETTER?
	AUC	SD	AUC	SD	
26	99.8	0.3	99.8	0.2	✓
27	82.9	2.7	81.3	2.9	×
28	95.4	1.6	95.3	1.5	-
29	99.0	0.6	99.2	0.5	✓
30	97.1	2.7	97.4	2.7	-
31	99.7	0.1	99.7	0.1	×
32	97.8	1.0	98.8	0.7	✓
33	99.7	0.0	99.8	0.0	✓
34	74.7	8.5	75.0	8.7	-
35	98.5	1.8	98.5	1.8	-
36	99.0	0.1	99.3	0.1	✓
37	99.7	0.1	99.7	0.1	✓
38	97.8	1.9	97.8	1.8	-
39	65.6	3.6	69.1	3.6	✓
40	99.2	1.1	98.6	2.2	×
41	90.5	4.3	91.7	4.2	✓
42	88.8	0.9	95.0	0.5	✓
43	65.5	2.7	71.1	2.4	✓
44	95.3	2.5	95.6	2.6	-
45	93.0	5.8	91.7	7.1	-
46	58.6	10.4	59.3	12.0	-
47	70.5	4.9	76.2	5.2	✓
48	99.8	0.2	99.8	0.3	-
49	98.1	0.4	98.7	0.3	✓
50	96.9	0.3	98.3	0.2	✓
ARITMEAN	90.5		91.5		13 wins, 9 ties,
GEOMEAN	89.5		90.6		3 losses

The results (21 wins, 23 ties, 6 losses) show that there are many cases where the difference is not significant (especially when the AUC was close to 100) but there are many more cases where the results are improved than degraded. In overall geometric means, m-branch smoothing improves AUC with 1% from 86.7% to 87.7%.

4 Splitting Criteria for PETs

A crucial factor for the quality of a decision tree learner is its splitting criterion. A variety of splitting criteria, including Gini [3], Gain, Gain Ratio and C4.5 criterion [13], and DKM [10] have been presented to date. However, all these were designed and evaluated for classifiers, not for probability estimators. In this section we propose and investigate two splitting criteria specifically designed for PETs.

4.1 MAUC Splitting Criterion

In [7] we introduced a novel splitting criterion, which was aimed at maximising the AUC of the resulting tree rather than its accuracy. It simply computes the quality of each split as the AUC of the nodes resulting from that split, assuming a two-class problem. This can be generalised to more than two classes using Hand and Till's 1-vs-1 average [9].

Definition 2 (MAUCsplit). Given a split s, the quality of the split is defined as:

$$MAUCsplit(s) = MAUC(t_s)$$

where t_s indicates the tree with the node being split as root.

The idea of using the same measure for splitting that is used as well for evaluation seems straightforward. Nonetheless, in the same way that accuracy (expected error) is not necessarily the best splitting criterion for accuracy, MAUCsplit may not the best splitting criterion for MAUC.

4.2 MSEE Splitting Criterion

A different approach is to consider that the tree really *predicts probabilities*. It thus makes sense to minimise the quadratic error committed when guessing these probabilities. Consider a split where each of the children has estimated probabilities p_i for each class. Assume that nodes assign classes according to p_i. Consequently, p_i means the probability of examples of class i falling into the node but also means the probability of being classified as i. Assuming these two interpretations of p_i are independent, the probability that an example of class i is misclassified, denoted by $p_{e,i}$, can be estimated as follows:

$$p_{e,i} = p_i \cdot \sum_{j \neq i} p_j = p_i \cdot (1 - p_i)$$

In words, this combines the probability that an example is of class p_i and the probability that it is not classified accordingly (the sum of the rest of probabilities, which is $1 - p_i$). This is similar to the Gini index. However, we want to measure the quadratic error of the *prediction*, which in our case is not a class but a probability. Hence, given a misclassification:

- p_i should have been 1 but is p_i. Thus, the error can be estimated as $(1 - p_i)^2$.
- p_j ($j \neq i$) should have been 0 and is p_j. The error can be estimated as $(0 - p_j)^2$.

Consequently, we have a total quadratic error of:

$$Error_i = p_i \cdot (1 - p_i) \left((1 - p_i)^2 + \sum_{j \neq i} (0 - p_j)^2 \right) = p_i \cdot (1 - p_i) \left((1 - p_i)^2 + \sum_{j \neq i} p_j^2 \right)$$

Therefore, if we consider a split of n nodes, then we can compute the quality of the split as the negative value of the total error for all the nodes:

Definition 3 (MSEEsplit). Given a split s, the quality of the split is defined as:

$$MSEEsplit(s) = \sum_{k=1..n} q_k \cdot \left(-\sum_{i=1..c} Error_i \right)$$

where q_k indicates the relative cardinality of the k-th child in the split.

The way in which the error is obtained gives the name for the criterion: *Minimum Squared Expected Error* (MSEE). Note that this expression is similar to the Brier score [4], which has also been used recently as a measure for predictive models in similar applications as where AUC is used.

Both MAUCsplit and MSEEsplit are modified in order to penalise splits with a high number of children, in a similar way as GainRatio is a modification of the Gain criterion. The precise correction we have used in the experiments can be found in [8].

4.3 Splitting Criteria Comparison

We have compared several splitting criteria: GainRatio (as implemented in C4.5, i.e., considering only the splits with Gain greater than the mean [13]), MGINI (as implemented in CART [3]), DKM (as presented in [10]), MAUCsplit with children correction and MSEEsplit with children correction. We will show the results with the split smoothing that gives better results for each criterion. This smoothing has not to be confused with the smoothing used for computing the AUC for evaluating the PETs, which will always be m-branch smoothing. Table 7 summarises the results (the complete results can be found in [8]).

Table 7. Summary of Accuracy and AUC for several splitting criteria (geometric means).

		C4.5SPLIT	GAIN	MGINI	DKM	MAUCSPLIT	MSEE SPLIT	BETTER? MSEE vs C4.5
2-CLASS	ACCURACY	81.4	81.6	81.4	81.7	81.8	82.0	11 wins, 9 ties, 5 losses
	AUC	84.9	84.8	84.6	84.8	85.0	85.3	7 wins, 13 ties, 5 losses
>2-CLASS	ACCURACY	82.8	83.0	83.1	83.1	82.4	83.0	10 wins, 11 ties, 4 losses
	AUC	90.6	90.9	90.8	91.1	90.8	90.9	7 wins, 13 ties, 5 losses
ALL	ACCURACY	82.1	82.3	82.2	82.4	82.1	82.5	21 wins, 20 ties, 9 losses
	AUC	87.7	87.8	87.7	87.9	87.8	88.1	14 wins, 26 ties, 10 losses

According to these and previous results, the best DTC splitting criterion is DKM, but the difference is not significant with the rest of DTC criteria (MGINI, C4.5). The new criterion MAUCsplit is slightly better than C4.5 and MGINI, although differences are small and not significant. Finally, MSEEsplit appears to be the best, although differences are smaller with respect to C4.5 and even smaller with respect to DKM. The good behaviour of both MSEE and DKM may be explained because both methods use quadratic terms.

5 Pruning and PETs

As we have discussed in the introduction, in [12] it is argued that pruning is counterproductive for obtaining good PETs and, consequently, pruning (and related techniques) should be disabled. However, it is not clear whether the reason is that pruning is intrinsically detrimental for probability estimation, or that existing pruning methods are devised for accuracy and not for increasing AUC.

Independently, we have evaluated some classical pre-pruning and post-pruning methods, such as Expected Error Pruning and Pessimistic Error Pruning (see e.g. [6] for a comparison). Our results match those of [12]; even slight pruning degrades the quality (measured in terms of AUC) of the probability estimates. It seems that smoothing has a relevant effect here: if we disable smoothing, pruning is beneficial in some cases. Consequently, it looks as though the better the smoothing at the leaves is, the worse pruning will be. It appears that this will be especially true for our m-branch smoothing, since it takes into account all the branch nodes probabilities. Pruning will reduce the available information for estimating the probabilities. As a result, we do not expect to obtain new pruning methods that will increase the AUC of a PET, but we might be interested in designing pruning methods that reduce the size of the tree without degrading too much the quality of the PET.

One of the most important issues for estimating good probabilities is the size of the sample. Consequently, the poorest estimates of a PET will be obtained by the smallest nodes. If we have to decide to prune some nodes it makes sense to prune the smallest ones first. This would suggest a very simple pre-pruning method: nodes will not be expanded when their cardinality is lower than a certain constant. However, datasets with a large number of classes can have poor probability estimates with medium-large nodes if there are many small classes. Hence, we can refine cardinality-based pruning, by using the following definition:

Definition 4 (CardPerClass Pruning). Given a node l, it will be pruned when:

$$Card(l) < 2\frac{K}{c}$$

where $Card(l)$ is the cardinality of node l, K is a constant ($K=0$ means no pruning) and c is the number of classes.

In the following graph, we show the effect of CardPerClass pruning (with K-values ranging from 16 to 0). The results are shown for MSEEsplit with m-branch smoothing.

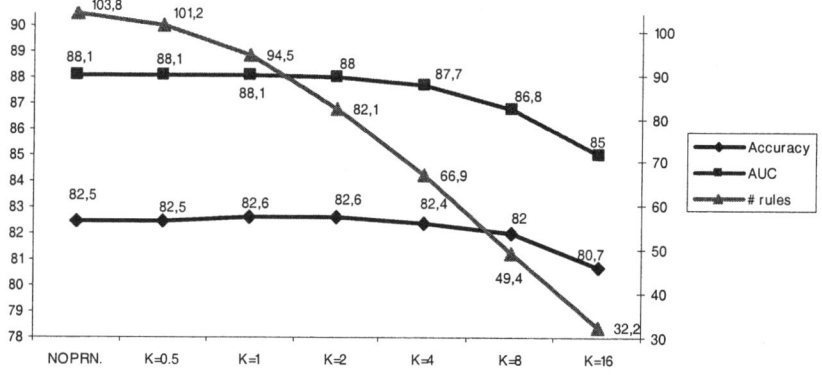

Fig. 1. Accuracy, AUC and number of rules for several pruning degrees (geometric mean).

As can be seen in Figure 1, only strong pruning is counterproductive for accuracy (and even behaves worse than other pruning methods). It is more interesting to observe the evolution of the AUC curve. The graph suggests that the quality of a PET is not significantly decreased until $K=4$, which, on the other hand, leads to a considerable decrease in the complexity of the trees.

6 Summary

In previous sections we have presented several enhancements in order to improve the AUC of PETs. In order to see the whole picture, we show below the accumulated progress of the techniques presented before.

Although there is a considerable improvement obtainable by using a simple smoothing such as Laplace smoothing (as shown previously [12,7]), there was still place for further improvement, as can be seen in Table 8. According to the nature and number of the datasets, and the quantity and quality of work developed for improving decision trees, we think that this is a significant result.

Table 8. Summary Table of AUC (only AUC and geomeans shown).

	C4.5SPLIT WITH-OUT SMOOTH		C4.5SPLIT WITH LAPLACE SMOOTH		C4.5SPLIT WITH MBRANCH SMOOTH		MSEESPLIT WITH MBRANCH SMOOTH		C4.5LAP VS MSEESPLIT MBRANCH + K=1 PRUNING
	ACC	AUC	ACC	AUC	ACC	AUC	ACC	AUC	BETTER IN AUC?
2-CLASS	81.4	78.0	81.4	83.9	81.4	84.9	82.1	85.4	11 wins, 9 ties, 5 losses
>2-CLASS	82.8	87.3	82.8	89.5	82.8	90.6	83.1	90.9	16 wins, 4 ties, 5 losses
ALL	82.1	82.5	82.1	86.7	82.1	87.7	82.6	88.1	27 wins, 13 ties, 10 losses

7 Conclusions and Future Work

In this work we have reassessed the construction of PETs, evaluating and introducing new methods for the three issues that are most important in PET construction: leaf smoothing, splitting criteria and pruning. We have introduced a new m-branch smoothing method that takes the whole branch of decisions into account, as well as a new MSEE splitting criterion aimed at reducing the squared error of the probability estimate.

Our new m-branch smoothing is significantly better than previous classical smoothings (Laplace or m-estimate). With respect to the splitting criteria, there are few works that compare existing splitting criteria for accuracy. Moreover, to our knowledge, this is the first work that compares the ranking of probability estimates of several splitting criteria for PETs. At this point, the conclusion is that all the good criteria presented so far are also good criteria for AUC and the differences between them are negligible. Nonetheless, pursuing new measures, we have found new splitting criteria such as AUCsplit and MSEEsplit comparable to the best known criterion (or even better, although this is not conclusive). Finally, we have shown that a simple cardinality pruning method can be applied (to a certain extent) to obtain simpler PETs without degrading their quality too much. Consequently, the idea that pruning is intrinsically bad for PETs is still in question, or, at least, we reiterate that a statement of its negative influence is "inconclusive" [12]. A very recent work has also suggested that a mild pruning could be beneficial [11].

As future work, other methods for improving the estimates (without modifying the structure of a single tree) such as the method presented in [11] (which uses the frequencies of all the leaves on the trees) could yield a method that takes into account all the information in the tree. Additionally, we think that better pruning methods for PETs could still be developed (considering the size of the dataset as an additional factor) — these might include the use of the *m-branch estimate* for pruning (as similar measures were originally introduced [5]).

Acknowledgments

This work has been partially supported by CICYT grant TIC2001-2705-C03-01. We would also like to thank the referees for their useful suggestions and references.

References

1. Blake, C., Merz, C. UCI repository of machine learning databases, University of California (http://www.ics.uci.edu/~mlearn/MLRepository.html), 1998.
2. Bradley, A.P. The use of the area under the ROC curve in the evaluation of machine learning algorithms. *Pattern Recognition*, 30(7): 1145-1159, 1997.
3. Breiman, L., Friedman, J.H., Olshen, R.A., Stone, C.J. *Classification and regression trees.* Belmont, CA, Wadsworth, 1984.
4. Brier, G.W. Verification of forecasts expressed in terms of probability. *Monthly Weather Rev.*, 78: 1-3, 1950.
5. Cestnik, B., Bratko, I. On estimating probabilities in tree pruning. In *Proc. European Working Sessions on Learning* (EWSL-91), Lecture Notes in Artificial Intelligence 482, pp.138-150, Springer-Verlag, 1991.
6. Esposito, F., Malerba, D., Semeraro, G. A Comparative Analysis of Methods for Pruning Decision Trees. *IEEE Trans. on Pattern Analysis and Machine Intelligence*, 19(5): 476-491, 1997.
7. Ferri, C., Flach, P., Hernández-Orallo, J. Learning Decision Trees using the Area Under the ROC Curve. In C. Sammut; A. Hoffman (eds.), *Proc. Int. Conf. on Machine Learning (ICML2002)*, pp. 139-146, Morgan Kaufmann, 2002.
8. Ferri, C., Flach, P., Hernández-Orallo, J.. *Decision Trees for Ranking: Effect of new smoothing methods, new splitting criteria and simple pruning methods.* Tech. Rep. Dep. de Sistemes Informàtics i Computació, Univ. Politècnica de València, 2003.
9. Hand, D.J., Till, R.J. A Simple Generalisation of the Area Under the ROC Curve for Multiple Class Classification Problems. *Machine Learning*, 45: 171-186, 2001.
10. Kearns, M., Mansour, Y. On the boosting ability of top-down decision tree learning algorithms. *Journal of Computer and Systems Sciences*, 58(1): 109-128, 1999.
11. Ling, C.X., Yan, R.J. Decision Tree with Better Ranking. In *Proc. Int. Conf. on Machine Learning (ICML2003)*, AAAI Press, 2003.
12. Provost, F., Domingos, P. Tree Induction for Probability-based Ranking. *Machine Learning* 52(3), 2003.
13. Quinlan, J.R. *C4.5. Programs for Machine Learning.* San Francisco, Morgan Kaufmann, 1993.
14. Smyth, P., Gray, A., Fayyad, U. Retrofitting decision tree classifiers using kernel density estimation. In *Proc. Int. Conf. on Machine Learning (ICML1995)*, pp. 506-514, Morgan Kaufmann, 1995.

Scaled CGEM: A Fast Accelerated EM

Jörg Fischer and Kristian Kersting

Institute for Computer Science, Machine Learning Lab
Albert-Ludwigs-University, Georges-Köhler-Allee, Gebäude 079,
D-79085 Freiburg i. Brg., Germany

Abstract. The EM algorithm is a popular method for maximum likelihood estimation of Bayesian networks in the presence of missing data. Its simplicity and general convergence properties make it very attractive. However, it sometimes converges slowly. Several accelerated EM methods based on gradient-based optimization techniques have been proposed. In principle, they all employ a line search involving several NP-hard likelihood evaluations. We propose a novel acceleration called SCGEM based on scaled conjugate gradients (SCGs) well-known from learning neural networks. SCGEM avoids the line search by adopting the scaling mechanism of SCGs applied to the expected information matrix. This guarantees a single likelihood evaluation per iteration. We empirically compare SCGEM with EM and conventional conjugate gradient accelerated EM. The experiments show that SCGEM can significantly accelerate both of them and is equal in quality.

1 Introduction

Bayesian networks [19] are one of the most important frameworks for representing and reasoning with probabilities. They specify joint probability distributions over finite sets of random variables, and have been applied to many real-world problems in diagnosis, forecasting, sensor fusion etc. Over the past years, there has been much interest in the problem of learning Bayesian networks from data. For learning Bayesian networks, parameter estimation is a fundamental task not only because of the inability of humans to reliably estimate the parameters, but also because it forms the basis for the overall learning problem [6].

It is often desired to find the parameters *maximizing the likelihood* (ML). The likelihood is the probability of the observed data as a function of the unknown parameters with respect to the current model. Unfortunately in many real-world domains, the data cases available are incomplete, i.e., some values may not be observed. For instance in medical domains, a patient rarely gets all of the possible tests. In presence of missing data, the maximum likelihood estimate typically cannot be written in closed form. It is a numerical optimization problem, and all known algorithms involve nonlinear, iterative optimization and multiple calls to a Bayesian network inference as subroutines. The latter ones have been proven to be NP-hard [4]. The most common technique for ML parameter estimation of Bayesian networks in the presence of missing data is the Expectation-Maximization (EM) algorithm.

Despite the success of the EM algorithm in practice due to its simplicity and fast initial progress, it has been argued (see e.g. [8, 13] and references in there) that the EM convergence can be extremely slow, and that more advanced second-order methods should in general be favored to EM. In the context of Bayesian networks, Thiesson [21], Bauer et al. [1], and Ortiz and Kaelbling [17] investigated acceleration of the EM algorithm. All approaches rely on conventional (gradient-based) optimization techniques viewing the change in values in the parameters at an EM iteration as generalized gradient (see [18] for a nice overview). Gradient ascent yields *parameterized EM*, and conjugate gradient yields *conjugate gradient EM* (CGEM). Although the accelerated EMs can significantly speed-up the EM, they all require more computational efforts than the basic EM. One reason is that they perform in each iteration a line search to choose an optimal step size. There are drawbacks of doing a line search. First, a line search introduces new problem-dependent parameters such as stopping criterion. Second, the line search involves several likelihood evaluations which are NP-hard for Bayesian networks. Thus, the line search dominates the computational costs resulting in a disadvantage of the accelerated EMs compared to the EM which does one likelihood evaluation per iteration. The computational extra costs have to be amortized over the long run to gain a speed-up.

The contribution of the present paper is a novel acceleration of EM called *scaled CGEM* (SCGEM) which overcomes the expensive line search. It evaluates the likelihood as often as the EM per iteration namely once. This also explains the title of the paper "A Fast Accelerated EM". SCGEM adopt the ideas underlying *scaled conjugate gradients* (SCGs) which are well-known from the field of learning neural networks [15]. SCGs employ an approximation of the Hessian of the scoring function to quadratically extrapolate the minimum instead of doing a line search. Then, a Levenberg-Marquardt approach [12] scales the step size. SCGEM adopts the scaling mechanism for maximization and applies it to the expected information matrix. This type of accelerated CGEM is novel. Other work for learning Bayesian networks investigated only approximated line searches [21, 17, 1], thus evaluates the likelihood at least twice per iteration. From the experimental results, we will argue that SCGEM can significantly accelerate both EM and CGEM, and is equal in quality.

We proceed as follows. After briefly introducing Bayesian networks in Section 2, we review maximum likelihood estimation via the EM and gradient ascent in Section 3. In Section 4, we motivate why accelerating EM is important and review basic acceleration techniques. Afterwards we introduce SCGEM in Section 5. In Section 6, we experimentally compare the SCGEM algorithm with the EM and CGEM algorithms. Before concluding, we discuss related work.

2 Bayesian Networks

Throughout the paper, we will use X to denote a random variable, x to denote a state and $\mathbf{X}$ (resp. $\mathbf{x}$) to denote a vector of variables (resp. states). We will use $\mathbf{P}$ to denote a probability distribution, e.g. $\mathbf{P}(X)$, and P to denote a probability value, e.g. $P(x)$.

A *Bayesian network* [19] represents the joint probability distribution $\mathbf{P}(\mathbf{X})$ over a set $\mathbf{X} = \{X_1, \ldots, X_n\}$ of random variables. In this paper, we restrict each X_i to have a finite set $x_i^1, \ldots, x_i^{j_i}$ of possible states. A Bayesian network is an augmented, acyclic graph, where each node corresponds to a variable X_i and each edge indicates a direct influence among the variables. We denote the parents of X_i in a graph-theoretical sense by $\mathbf{Pa}_i$. The family of X_i is $\mathbf{Fa}_i := \{X_i\} \cup \mathbf{Pa}_i$. With each node X_i, a conditional probability table is associated specifying the distribution $\mathbf{P}(X_i \mid \mathbf{Pa}_i)$. The table entries are $\theta_{ijk} = P(X_i = x_i^j \mid \mathbf{Pa}_i = \mathbf{pa}_i^k)$, where $\mathbf{pa}_i^k$ denotes the kth joint state of the X_i's parents. The network stipulates the assumption that each node X_i in the graph is conditionally independent of any subset $\mathbf{A}$ of nodes that are not descendants of X_i given a joint state of its parents. Thus, the joint distribution over $\mathbf{X}$ factors to $\mathbf{P}(X_1, \ldots, X_n) = \prod_{i=1}^n \mathbf{P}(X_i \mid \mathbf{Pa}_i)$. In the rest of the paper, we will represent a Bayesian network with given structure by the M-dimensional vector $\boldsymbol{\theta}$ consisting of all θ_{ijk}'s.

3 Basic ML Parameter Estimation

Our task is to learn the numerical parameters θ_{ijk} for a Bayesian network of a given structure. More formally, we have some initial model $\boldsymbol{\theta}$. We also have some set of data cases $\mathbf{D} = \{\mathbf{d}_1, \ldots, \mathbf{d}_N\}$. Each data case $\mathbf{d}_i$ is a (possibly) partial assignment of values to variables in the network. We assume that the data cases are independently sampled from identical distributions (iid. We seek those parameters $\boldsymbol{\theta}^*$ which maximize the likelihood $L(\mathbf{D}, \boldsymbol{\theta}) := P(\mathbf{D} \mid \boldsymbol{\theta})$ of the data. Due to the monotonicity of the logarithm, we can also seek the parameters maximizing the log-likelihood $LL(\mathbf{D}, \boldsymbol{\theta}) := \log P(\mathbf{D} \mid \boldsymbol{\theta})$. This simplifies because of the iid assumption to $\boldsymbol{\theta}^* = \mathrm{argmax}_{\boldsymbol{\theta} \in \mathcal{H}} \sum_{l=1}^N \log P(\mathbf{d}_l \mid \boldsymbol{\theta})$. Thus, the search space $\mathcal{H}$ to be explored is spanned by the space over the possible values of $\boldsymbol{\theta}$. In case of complete data $\mathbf{D}$, i.e., the values of all random variables are observed, Lauritzen [11] showed that maximum likelihood estimation simply corresponds to frequency counting. However, in the presence of missing data the maximum likelihood estimates typically cannot be written in closed form, and iterative optimization schemes like the EM or gradient-based algorithms are needed. We will now briefly review both approaches because SCGEM heavily builds on them.

The *EM algorithm* [5] is a classical approach to maximum likelihood estimation in the presence of missing values. The basic observation underlying the Expectation-Maximization algorithm is: learning would be easy if we knew the values for all the random variables. Therefore, it iteratively performs two steps to find the maximum likelihood parameters of a model: **(E-Step)** Based on the current parameters $\boldsymbol{\theta}$ and the observed data $\mathbf{D}$, the algorithm computes a distribution over all possible completions of each partially observed data case. **(M-Step)** Each completion is then treated as a fully-observed data case weighted by its probability. New parameters are then computed based on frequency counts.

More formally, the E-step consists of computing the expectation of the likelihood given the old parameters $\boldsymbol{\theta}^n$ and the observed data $\mathbf{D}$, i.e.,

$$Q(\boldsymbol{\theta} \mid \boldsymbol{\theta}^n, \mathbf{D}) = E\left[\log P(\mathbf{Z} \mid \boldsymbol{\theta}) \mid \boldsymbol{\theta}^n, \mathbf{D}\right] . \tag{1}$$

Here, $\mathbf{Z}$ is a random vector denoting the completion of the data cases $\mathbf{D}$. The current parameters $\boldsymbol{\theta}^n$ and the observed data $\mathbf{D}$ give us the conditional distribution governing the unobserved states. The expression $E[\cdot|\cdot]$ denotes the expectation over this conditional distribution. Q is sometimes called the *expected information matrix*. In the M-step, $Q(\boldsymbol{\theta} \mid \boldsymbol{\theta}^n, \mathbf{D})$ is maximized w.r.t. $\boldsymbol{\theta}$, i.e., $\boldsymbol{\theta}^{n+1} = \arg\max_{\boldsymbol{\theta}} Q(\boldsymbol{\theta} \mid \boldsymbol{\theta}^n, \mathbf{D})$. Lauritzen [11] showed that this leads to $\theta_{ijk}^* = \mathrm{ec}(\mathbf{fa}_i^{jk} \mid \mathbf{D}) / \mathrm{ec}(\mathbf{pa}_i^j \mid \mathbf{D})$ where $\mathbf{fa}_i^{jk}$ is the joint state consisting of the jth state of variable X_i and the kth joint state $\mathbf{pa}_i^k$ of $\mathbf{Pa}_i$. The term $\mathrm{ec}(\mathbf{a} \mid \mathbf{D})$ denotes the *expected counts* of the joint state $\mathbf{a}$ given the data. They are computed by $\mathrm{ec}(\mathbf{a} \mid \mathbf{D}) = \sum_{l=1}^{N} P(\mathbf{a} \mid \mathbf{d}_l, \boldsymbol{\theta}^n)$ where any Bayesian network inference engine can be used to compute $P(\mathbf{a} \mid \mathbf{d}_l, \boldsymbol{\theta}^n)$.

Gradient ascent, also known as *hill climbing*, is a classical method for finding a maximum of a (scoring) function. It iteratively performs two steps. First, it computes the *gradient* vector $\nabla_{\boldsymbol{\theta}}$ of partial derivatives of the log-likelihood with respect to the parameters of a Bayesian network at a given point $\boldsymbol{\theta} \in \mathcal{H}$. Then, it takes a small step in the direction of the gradient to the point $\boldsymbol{\theta} + \delta \nabla_{\boldsymbol{\theta}}$ where δ is the step-size parameter. The algorithm will converge to a local maximum for small enough δ, cf. [12]. Thus, we have to compute the partial derivatives of $LL(\mathbf{D}, \boldsymbol{\theta})$ with respect to θ_{ijk}. According to Binder *et al.* [3], they are given by

$$\frac{\partial LL(\mathbf{D}, \boldsymbol{\theta})}{\partial \theta_{ijk}} = \sum_{l=1}^{N} \frac{P(\mathbf{fa}_i^{jk} \mid \mathbf{d}_l, \boldsymbol{\theta})}{\theta_{ijk}} = \frac{\mathrm{ec}(\mathbf{fa}_i^{jk} \mid \mathbf{D})}{\theta_{ijk}} . \tag{2}$$

In contrast to EM, the described gradient-ascent method has to be modified to take into account the constraint that the parameter vector $\boldsymbol{\theta}$ consists of probability values, i.e., $\theta_{ijk} \in [0, 1]$ and $\sum_j \theta_{ijk} = 1$. A general solution is to reparameterize the problem so that the new parameters automatically respect the constraints on θ_{ijk} no matter what their values are. More precisely, we define the parameters $\beta_{ijk} \in \mathbb{R}$ such that $\theta_{ijk} = exp(\beta_{ijk}) / (\sum_l exp(\beta_{ilk}))$ where the β_{ijk} are indexed like θ_{ijk}. It can be shown using the chain rule of derivatives that

$$\frac{\partial LL(\mathbf{D}, \boldsymbol{\theta})}{\partial \beta_{ijk}} = \sum_{i'j'k'} \frac{\partial LL(\mathbf{D}, \boldsymbol{\theta})}{\partial \theta_{i'j'k'}} \cdot \frac{\partial \theta_{i'j'k'}}{\partial \beta_{ijk}} = \sum_{i'j'k'} \frac{\mathrm{ec}(\mathbf{fa}_{i'}^{j'k'} \mid \mathbf{D})}{\theta_{i'j'k'}} \cdot \frac{\partial \theta_{i'j'k'}}{\partial \beta_{ijk}}$$
$$= \mathrm{ec}(\mathbf{fa}_i^{jk} \mid \mathbf{D}) - \theta_{ijk} \sum_l \mathrm{ec}(\mathbf{fa}_i^{lk} \mid \mathbf{D}) .$$

An important view of the gradient for our purposes is the following. It highlights the close connection between gradient ascent and the EM:

$$\frac{\partial Q(\boldsymbol{\theta} \mid \boldsymbol{\theta}', \mathbf{D})}{\partial \beta_{ijk}} = \frac{\partial}{\partial \beta_{ijk}} E\left[\sum_{i'j'k'} c(\mathbf{fa}_{i'}^{j'k'} \mid \mathbf{D}) \cdot \log \theta_{i'j'k'} \,\Big|\, \boldsymbol{\theta}', \mathbf{D}\right]$$
$$= \frac{\partial}{\partial \beta_{ijk}} \sum_{i'j'k'} \mathrm{ec}(\mathbf{fa}_{i'}^{j'k'} \mid \mathbf{D}) \cdot \log \theta_{i'j'k'} = \sum_{i'j'k'} \mathrm{ec}(\mathbf{fa}_{i'}^{j'k'} \mid \mathbf{D}) \frac{\partial \log \theta_{i'j'k'}}{\partial \beta_{ijk}}$$
$$= \sum_{i'j'k'} \frac{\mathrm{ec}(\mathbf{fa}_{i'}^{j'k'} \mid \mathbf{D})}{\theta_{i'j'k'}} \cdot \frac{\partial \theta_{i'j'k'}}{\partial \beta_{ijk}} = \frac{\partial \log P(\mathbf{D} \mid \boldsymbol{\theta})}{\partial \beta_{ijk}} . \tag{3}$$

Thus, the gradient of the likelihood coincides with the gradient of the expected information matrix[1].

4 Accelerated ML Parameter Estimation

It has been argued that the EM convergence can be extremely slow, see e.g. [13, 8] and references in there. Assume that $\langle \boldsymbol{\theta}^n \rangle$ is a sequence of parameters computed by the EM algorithm. Furthermore, assume that $\langle \boldsymbol{\theta}^n \rangle$ converges to some $\boldsymbol{\theta}^*$. Then, in the neighbourhood of $\boldsymbol{\theta}^*$, the EM algorithm is essentially a linear iteration. However, as shown by Dempster et al. [5], the greater the proportion of missing information, the slower the rate of convergence (in the neighbourhood of $\boldsymbol{\theta}^*$). If the ratio approaches unity, EM will exhibit slow convergence. Therefore, more advanced second-order methods should in general be favored to EM.

In the context of Bayesian networks, Kersting and Landwehr [9] empirically compared second-order gradient techniques with the EM. They were able to show that the former ones can be competitive with EM, but EM remains the domain independent method of choice for ML estimation because of its simplicity and fast initial progress. Within the Bayesian network learning community several accelerated EM algorithms have been proposed and empirically compared with the EM algorithm [21, 17, 1]. We will now briefly review the basic acceleration techniques following [17] which are also the basic ingredients of SCGEM.

The most straightforward way to accelerate the EM is the *parameterized EM* (PEM). It is a gradient ascent where instead of following the gradient of the log-likelihood we follow the generalized[2] gradient $g_n := \boldsymbol{\theta}_{EM}^{n+1} - \boldsymbol{\theta}^n$, where $\boldsymbol{\theta}_{EM}^{n+1}$ denotes the EM update with respect to the parameters after the $n+1$-th iteration. The simple PEM uses a fixed step size δ when following the gradient, i.e., in every iteration the parameters are chosen according to $\boldsymbol{\theta}^{n+1} = \boldsymbol{\theta}^n + \delta \cdot g_n$. It is not a priori clear how to choose δ. Instead, it would be better to perform a series of *line searches* to choose δ in each iteration, i.e., to do a one dimensional iterative search for δ in the direction of the generalized gradient maximizing $LL(\mathbf{D}, \boldsymbol{\theta}^n + \delta \cdot g_n)$. One of the problems with the resulting algorithm is that a maximization in one direction could spoil past maximizations. This problem is solved by *conjugate gradient* EM.

Conjugate gradient EM (CGEM) computes so-called conjugate directions $h_0, h_1, \ldots$, which are orthogonal, and estimate the step size along these directions with line searches [7]. Following the scheme of PEM, it iteratively performs two steps starting with $\boldsymbol{\theta}^0 \in \mathcal{H}$ and $h_0 = g_0$:

1. (Conjugate directions) Set the next direction h_{n+1} according to $h_{n+1} = g_{\boldsymbol{\theta}^{n+1}} - \gamma_n \cdot h_n$ where

$$\gamma_n = \frac{(\nabla LL(\mathbf{D}, \boldsymbol{\theta}^{n+1})^T - \nabla LL(\mathbf{D}, \boldsymbol{\theta}^n)^T) \cdot g_{\boldsymbol{\theta}^{n+1}}}{(\nabla LL(\mathbf{D}, \boldsymbol{\theta}^{n+1})^T - \nabla LL(\mathbf{D}, \boldsymbol{\theta}^n)^T) \cdot h_n} . \quad (4)$$

---
[1] This means that gradient ascent is a so-called generalized EM.
[2] Generalized gradients perform regular gradient techniques in a transformed space.

2. (Line search) Compute θ^{n+1} by maximizing $LL(\mathbf{D},\theta^n +\delta \cdot h_{n+1})$ in the direction of h_{k+1}.

Usually, some initial EM steps are taken before switching to the CGEM. We refer to [7, 13] for more details on CGEM.

There are still drawbacks of doing a line search. First, it introduces new problem-dependent parameters such as a stopping criterion. Second, the line search involves several likelihood evaluations, i.e., network inferences which are known to be NP-hard [4]. Thus, the line search dominates the computational costs of CGEM resulting in a serious disadvantage compared to the EM which does one likelihood estimation per iteration. Therefore, it is not surprising that researchers in the Bayesian network learning community used inexact line search to reduce the complexity [21, 17, 1] when accelerating EM. Nevertheless, they require at least one additional likelihood evaluation per iteration compared to the EM. In the next section, we will show how to avoid the line search. We will adopt a variant of conjugate gradients called *scaled conjugate gradients* to accelerate EM. They are due to Møller [15] and led to significant speed up of learning neural networks while preserving accuracy.

5 Scaled Conjugate Gradient EM

Scaled conjugate gradient (SCG) substitutes the line search by employing an approximation of the Hessian of the error function to quadratically extrapolate the minimum using a Levenberg-Marquardt approach [12] to scale the step size. We will now apply this idea to CGEM in the context of maximum likelihood parameter estimation of Bayesian networks. Due to space restrictions, we will discuss the basic idea only. For more details about SCG, we refer to [15].

We quadratically approximate $LL(\mathbf{D},\theta^n)$ at $\mathbf{x}$, i.e., $LL(\mathbf{D},\theta^n)+\nabla LL(\mathbf{D},\theta^n)^T \cdot \mathbf{x} + \frac{1}{2}\mathbf{x}^T \cdot \nabla^2 LL(\mathbf{D},\theta^n) \cdot \mathbf{x}$. Then, the step size for CGEM is $(h_n^T \cdot \nabla LL(\mathbf{D},\theta^n))/(h_n^T \cdot \nabla^2 LL(\mathbf{D},\theta^n) \cdot h_n)$. However, one has to compute and store the Hessian matrix $\nabla^2 LL(\mathbf{D},\theta^n)$. To avoid this, Møller estimated $\nabla^2 LL(\mathbf{D},\theta^n) \cdot h_n$ with a Newton quotient. The approximation needs to be negative definite in order to obtain a maximum. Therefore, a scalar λ_n is introduced to assure the definiteness, i.e.,

$$s_n := \frac{\nabla LL(\mathbf{D},\theta^n +\sigma^n \cdot h_{k+1}) - \nabla LL(\mathbf{D},\theta^n)}{\sigma^n} + \lambda_n \cdot h_n, \ 0 < \sigma^n \ll 1. \quad (5)$$

The sign of $\delta_n := h_k^T \cdot s_n$ reveals if the adjusted Hessian approximation is negative definite. If $\delta_n \geq 0$ then the approximation is not negative definite, and λ_n is raised and s_n is estimated again. The new approximation s'_n can be derived from the old s_n via $s'_n = s_n + (\lambda_n - \lambda'_n) \cdot h_n$ where λ'_n is the raised λ_n. It is possible to determine in one step how much λ_n has to be risen to assure $\delta_n < 0$:

$$\delta_n < 0 \Leftrightarrow h_n^T \cdot s'_n < 0 \Leftrightarrow \delta_n + (\lambda_n - \lambda'_n) \cdot |h_n|^2 < 0 \Leftrightarrow \lambda'_n > \lambda_n + \delta_n/|h_n|^2 \ .$$

Following Møller, we chose $\lambda'_n = 2.0 \cdot (\lambda_n + \delta_n/|h_n|^2)$, i.e., $\delta'_n = -\delta_n - \lambda \cdot |h_n|^2$ as new estimate for δ_n.

This scaling mechanism combined with conjugate search directions as done in the CGEM (4) leads (in principle) to the SCGEM. For the sake of closeness to SCGs, we used in (5) the approximation of the second order information originally proposed by Møller. It requires one additional log-likelihood evaluation compared with the EM. Motivated by (1) and (3), we apply a different approximation in order to avoid the additional evaluation, namely $\nabla^2 LL(\mathbf{D}, \boldsymbol{\theta}^n) \approx E\left[\nabla^2 LL(\mathbf{Z} \mid \boldsymbol{\theta}) \mid \boldsymbol{\theta}^n, \mathbf{D}\right]$. It turns out that we approximate the Hessian of the log-likelihood $\nabla^2 LL(\mathbf{D}, \boldsymbol{\theta}^n)$ with the Hessian of the expected information score $\nabla^2 Q(\boldsymbol{\theta} \mid \boldsymbol{\theta}^n, \mathbf{D})$:

$$E\left[\frac{\partial^2 LL(\mathbf{Z} \mid \boldsymbol{\theta})}{\partial \beta_{i'j'k'} \partial \beta_{ijk}} \,\bigg|\, \boldsymbol{\theta}^n, \mathbf{D}\right]$$

$$= E\left[\frac{\partial}{\partial \beta_{i'j'k'}} \left(c(\mathbf{fa}_i^{jk} \mid \mathbf{D}) - \theta_{ijk} \sum_l c(\mathbf{fa}_i^{lk} \mid \mathbf{D})\right) \,\bigg|\, \boldsymbol{\theta}^n, \mathbf{D}\right]$$

$$= \left(-\sum_l \mathrm{ec}(\mathbf{fa}_i^{lk} \mid \mathbf{D})\right) \cdot \frac{\partial \theta_{ijk}}{\partial \beta_{i'j'k'}} \tag{6}$$

$$= \frac{\partial}{\partial \beta_{i'j'k'}} \left(\mathrm{ec}(\mathbf{fa}_i^{jk} \mid \mathbf{D}) - \theta_{ijk} \sum_l \mathrm{ec}(\mathbf{fa}_i^{lk} \mid \mathbf{D})\right) = \frac{\partial^2 Q(\boldsymbol{\theta} \mid \boldsymbol{\theta}^n, \mathbf{D})}{\partial \beta_{i'j'k'} \partial \beta_{ijk}}.$$

Now, recall that we are working in the reparameterized space, i.e., the β parameters are independent. The partial derivatives in (6) are zero when $i' \neq i$, $j' \neq j$, and $k' \neq k$. Thus, only the diagonal elements of $\nabla^2 Q(\boldsymbol{\theta} \mid \boldsymbol{\theta}^n, \mathbf{D})$ are non-zero. They are given by

$$\theta_{ijk} \cdot (\theta_{ijk} - 1) \cdot \sum_l \mathrm{ec}(\mathbf{fa}_i^{lk} \mid \mathbf{D}).$$

Moreover, the computation of s_n becomes linear in the number of parameters, namely

$$s_n = \mathrm{diag}(\nabla^2 Q(\boldsymbol{\theta} \mid \boldsymbol{\theta}^n, \mathbf{D}))^T \cdot h_n + \lambda_n \cdot h_n. \tag{7}$$

Because all involved quantities have been already computed for the gradient, the approximation does not cost any additional log-likelihood evaluations. Thus, SCGEM performs as many evaluations as the EM per iteration namely one.

6 Experiments

In the experiments described below, we implemented all three algorithms, i.e., EM, CGEM, and SCGEM using Netica API (http://www.norsys.com) for Bayesian network inference. We adapted the conjugate gradient described in [20] to fullfil the constraints described above and to become a CGEM. Based on this code, we adapted the scaled conjugate gradient as implemented in the Netlab library [16] to come up with the SCGEM. Two initial EM steps and a maximum of three consecutive scaling steps were set. To avoid zero entries in the associated conditional probability tables we used m-estimates ($m = 1$) [14].

Table 1. Description of the networks used in the experiments.

Name	Description
Alarm	Well-known benchmark network for the ICU ventilator management. It consists of 37 nodes and 752 parameters [2]. No latent variables.
Insurance	Well-known benchmark network for estimating the expected claim costs for a car insurance policyholder. It consists of 27 nodes (12 latent) and 1419 parameters [3].
3-1-3, 5-3-5	Two artificial networks with a feed-forward architecture known from neural networks [3]. There are three fully connected layers of $3 \times 1 \times 3$ (resp. $5 \times 3 \times 5$) nodes. Nodes of the first and third layers have 3 possible states, nodes of the second 2. In total, there are 81 (resp. 568) parameters.

Data were generated from four Bayesian networks whose main characteristics are described in Table 1. From each target network, we generated a test set of 10000 data cases, and (independently) training sets of 100, 200, 500 and 1000 data cases with a fraction of 0, 0.1, 0.2 and 0.3 of values missing at random of the observed nodes. The training sets were all subsets of the corresponding 1000 data sets. The values of latent nodes were never observed. For each training set, 10 different random initial sets of parameters were tried. We ran each algorithm on each data set starting from each of the initial sets of parameters. Each algorithm stopped when a limit of 200 iterations was exceeded or a change in log-likelihood at one iteration relative to the total change so far was smaller than $1 + 10^{-4}$. All learned models were evaluated on the test set using a standard measure, the *normalized-loss* $1/N \sum_{l=1}^{N} (\log P^*(\mathbf{d}_l) - \log P(\mathbf{d}_l))$, where P^* is the probability of the generating distribution. Normalized-loss measures the additional penalty for using an approximation instead of the true model, and is also a cross-entropy estimate. The closer the normalized-loss is to zero, the better.

To measure the computational costs, we counted the number of log-likelihood evaluations. This way we do not need to compare CPU times, which depend on implementation details. More over, the evaluations domininate all other costs for sufficiently large number N of data cases (assuming unit costs of arithmetic operations). All three algorithms require the computation of the expected counts, i.e., a likelihood evaluation. Computing (4) takes $O(M)$ extra work, and computing (7) takes $O(M \cdot d)$ extra work where d is the maximal number of possible states of a random variable in a given Bayesian network of M parameters. Thus, the work needed to be done in each (line search) iteration is approximately the same. This complies with our experience gained in the experiments.

The CGEM showed the expected behaviour. Considering only the normalized-loss, it reached similar normalized-losses than the EM. The 95% confidence (EM−CGEM) interval was $[-0.0175, -0.0099]$ favoring the EM. However, the CGEM had much higher computational costs than SCGEM. On average 19 line search iterations. To be fair, it has been argued that the CGEM does not need a very precise line search. For instance, Ortiz and Kaelbling [18] set a maximum of 10 line search iterations, and reported that this limit was often exceeded. To sim-

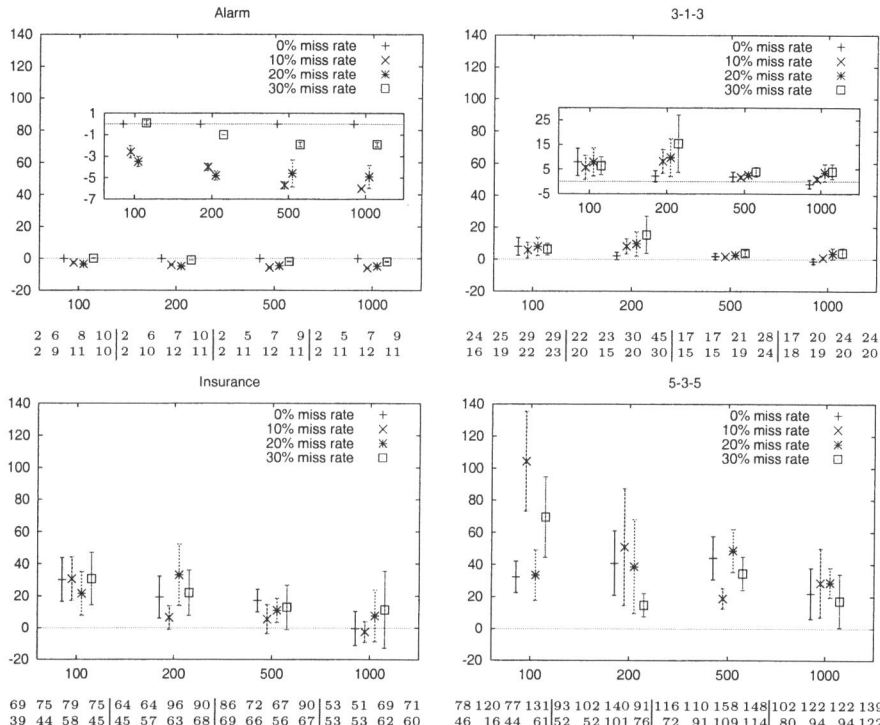

Fig. 1. The 95% confidence intervals for differences in number of iterations (EM−SCGEM). For each number of data cases (x axis) and each percentage of missing data (different line styles), the confidence intervals are shown. The figures within figures are close-ups of the corresponding areas. Each table below a figure shows the corresponding mean number of iterations for EM (upper row) and SCGEM (lower row) in order of appearance within the figure and rounded to the closest integer value.

ulate this, we fixed the log-likelihoods for CGEM originally reached, but varied the averaged number of line search iterations. It turned out that SCGEM would run significantly faster than the CGEM already with a limit of 3 line search inferences (95% confidence interval CGEM−SCGEM for a limit of 3 would be [22.42, 27.20], for a limit of 10 it would be [115.98, 128.86])[3]. Therefore, we omit CGEM from further discussion.

EM and SCGEM reached similar normalized-losses, i.e., were equal in quality. A *two-tailed, paired sampled t test* over all experiments showed that we cannot reject the null-hypothesis that EM and SCGEM differ on average performance ($p = 0.05$). There was a very small variation over the different networks. The confidence intervals (95%) for normalized-losses were: **Alarm** [−0.00116, −0.00025], **Insurance** [−0.00848, +0.00120], **3-1-3** [−0.00559, +0.00014] and **5-3-5** [+0.00591, +0.1620].

---

[3] Note that this analysis actually favors the CGEM. It is unlikely that the CGEM would reach the original log-likelihoods within one line search.

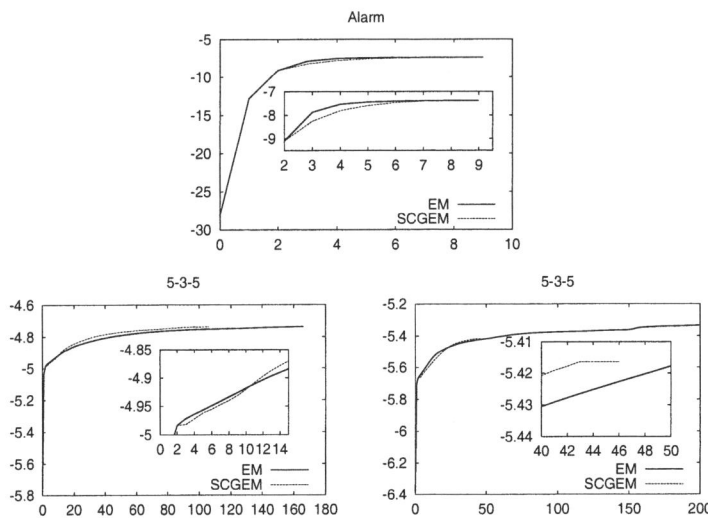

Fig. 2. Typical learning curves for EM and SCGEM on **Alarm** and **5-3-5**. The number of iterations, i.e., the number of log-likelihood evaluations is plotted against the log-likelihood achieved. The lower right plot shows the SCGEM getting trapped in scaling. The figures within figures are close-ups of the corresponding areas.

In total, SCGEM was faster then EM. Figure 1 summarizes the difference (EM−SCG) in number of iterations, i.e., number of likelihood iterations. The 95% confidence intervals are plotted. Readably, EM was faster than SCGEM on **Alarm**. However, there was only a difference of around 6 iterations. Moreover, this did not carry over to the other domains. SCGEM tended to be slightly faster on **3-1-3** ($\approx$ 5 iterations speed-up on average). On **Insurance** and **5-3-5**, the difference in average iterations increased to a $\approx$ 16 speed-up for **Insurance** and a $\approx$ 39 speed-up for **5-3-5**. However, this is averaged over different percentages of missing data. As Figure 1 shows, there can be speed-ups of more than 80 iterations depending on the percentage of missing informations. These results validate the theory as explained in Section 4: the more missing information, the higher the speed-up.

Compared with SCG, Kersting and Landwehr [9] reported that the EM had a faster initial progress. Compared to SCGEM, this does not hold any longer. Figure 2 shows some typical learning curves. For **Alarm**, the EM typically possessed a faster initial progress, but e.g. for **5-3-5**, the SCGEM typically overtook the EM after few iterations. However in contrast to the EM, the SCGEM got sometimes trapped in scaling. Surprisingly, this happened most of time for **Alarm** (54% of 136 cases) where SCGEM got no speed-up. The remaining trapped cases were distributed as follows: 6% on **3-1-3**, 16% on **Insurance**, and 24% on **5-3-5**. Interestingly, SCGEM reached better normalized-losses on **5-3-5** (taking the 'scaling traps' into account).

7 Related Work and Conclusions

Both, EM and gradients are well-known parameter estimation techniques. For a general introduction see [13, 12]. Møller [15] introduced SCG to estimate the parameters of neural networks. Lauritzen [11] introduced EM for Bayesian networks (see also Heckerman [6] for a nice tutorial). The original work on gradient-based approaches in the context of Bayesian networks was done by Binder et al. [3]. However, we are not aware of any application of SCG in order to accelerate the EM. Bauer et al. [1] reported on experiments with PEM for learning Bayesian networks. They did not report on results of CGEM. Thiesson [21] discussed conventional conjugate gradient accelerations of the EM, but did not report on experiments. Ortiz and Kaelbling [17] conducted experiments with PEM and CGEM for continuous models, namely density estimation with a mixture of Gaussian. Their results generally favor CGEM over PEM, although PEM can be superior for some domains. Finally, there are several acceleration techniques of the EM which do not apply conjugate gradients and have not reached much attention within Bayesian network learning. We refer to [8, 13] for a full account of them. Among this work, Lange [10] is closest to SCGEM. He proposed the expected information matrix as approximation of the Hessian together with a symmetric, rank-one update of the *complete* approximation matrix within a quasi-Newton technique. An interesting but orthogonal research discussed in [13] investigates criterions when to switch to CGEM. This is a promising research direction for SCGEM.

To conclude, we introduced *scaled conjugate gradient* EM for maximum likelihood parameter estimation of Bayesian networks. They overcome the expensive line search of traditional conjugate gradient EM. To the best of our knowledge, it is the first time that one reports on an accelerated EM for Bayesian networks which exhibits the same number of likelihood estimations per iteration then the EM. The experiments show that SCGEM is equal with EM and CGEM in quality but can significantly accelerate both. As predicted by theory, SCGEM seems especially well suited in the presence of many latent parameters, i.e., 'EM-hard' instances. The main future question seems to be the disarming of the scaling traps.

References

1. E. Bauer, D. Koller, and Y. Singer. Update Rules for Parameter Estimation in Bayesian Networks. In D. Geiger and P. P. Shenoy, editors, *Proceedings of the Thirteenth Annual Conference on Uncertainty in Artificial Intelligence (UAI-97)*, pages 3–13, Providence, Rhode Island, USA, 1997. Morgan Kaufmann.
2. I. Beinlich, H. Suermondt, R. Chavez, and G. Cooper. The ALARM monitoring system: A case study with two probabilistic inference techniques for belief networks. In J. Hunter, editor, *Proceedings of the Second European Conference on Artificial Intelligence and Medicine (AIME-89)*, volume 38 of *LNMI*, pages 247–256, City University, London, UK, 1989. Springer-Verlag.

3. J. Binder, D. Koller, S. Russell, and K. Kanazawa. Adaptive Probabilistic Networks with Hidden Variables. *Machine Learning*, 29(2/3):213–244, 1997.
4. G. F. Cooper. The computational complexity of probabilistic inference using Bayesian belief networks. *Artificial Intelligence*, 42:393–405, 1990.
5. A. Dempster, N. Larid, and D. Rubin. Maximum likelihood from incomplete data via the EM algorithm. *Journal of the Royal Statistical Society*, 39:1–38, 1977.
6. D. Heckerman. A tutorial on learning with Bayesian networks. Technical Report MSR-TR-95-06, Microsoft Research, 1995.
7. M. Jamshidian and R. I. Jennrich. Conjugate Gradient Accleration of the EM Algorithm. *Journal of the American Statistical Association*, 88(412):221–228, 1993.
8. M. Jamshidian and R. I. Jennrich. Accleration of the EM Algorithm by using Quasi-Newton Methods. *Jour. of the Royal Stat. Society B*, 59(3):569–587, 1997.
9. K. Kersting and N. Landwehr. Scaled Conjugate Gradients for Maximum likelihood: An Empirical Comparison with the EM Algorithm. In J. A. Gámez and A. Salmerón, editors, *Proceedings of the First European Workshop on Probabilistic Graphical Models (PGM-02)*, pages 89–98, Cuenca, Spain, 2002.
10. K. Lange. A quasi-Newton acceleration of the EM algorithm. *Statistica Sinica*, 5:1–18, 1995.
11. S. L. Lauritzen. The EM algorithm for graphical association models with missing data. *Computational Statistics and Data Analysis*, 19:191–201, 1995.
12. D. G. Luenberger. *Linear and Nonlinear Programming*. Addison-Wesley, 1984.
13. G. McLachlan and T. Krishnan. *The EM Algorithm and Extensions*. Wiley, 1997.
14. T. M. Mitchell. *Machine Learning*. The McGraw-Hill Companies, Inc., 1997.
15. M. Møller. A Scaled Conjugate Gradient Algoritm for Fast Supervised Learning. *Neural Networks*, 6:525–533, 1993.
16. I. Nabney. *NETLAB: Algorithms for Pattern Recognition*. Advances in Pattern Recognition. Springer-Verlag, 2001. http://www.ncrg.aston.ac.uk/netlab/.
17. L. E. Ortiz and L. P. Kaelbling. Accelerating EM: An Empirical Study. In K. B. Laskey and H. Prade, editors, *Proceedings of the Fifteenth Annual Conference on Uncertainty in Articial Intelligence (UAI-99)*, pages 512–521, Stockholm, Sweden, 1999. Morgan Kaufmann.
18. L. E. Ortiz and L. P. Kaelbling. Notes on methods based on maximum-likelihodd estimation for learning the parameters of the mixture-of-Gaussians model. Technical Report CS-99-03, Department of Computer Science, Brown University, 1999.
19. J. Pearl. *Reasoning in Intelligent Systems: Networks of Plausible Inference*. Morgan Kaufmann, 2. edition, 1991.
20. W. H. Press, S. A. Teukolsky, W. T. Vetterling, and B. P. Flannery. *Numerical Recipes in C: The Art of Scientific Computing*. Cambridge University Press, 2. edition, 1993. http://www.nr.com.
21. B. Thiesson. Accelerated quantification of Bayesian networks with incomplete data. In U. M. Fayyad and R. Uthurusamy, editors, *Proceedings of First International Conference on Knowledge Discovery and Data Mining*, pages 306–311, Montreol, Canada, 1995. AAAI Press.

Pairwise Preference Learning and Ranking

Johannes Fürnkranz[1] and Eyke Hüllermeier[2]

[1] Austrian Research Institute for Artificial Intelligence
Schottengasse 3, A-1010 Wien, Austria
juffi@oefai.at
[2] Informatics Institute, Marburg University
Hans-Meerwein-Str., Lahnberge, D-35032 Marburg, Germany
eyke@mathematik.uni-marburg.de

Abstract. We consider supervised learning of a ranking function, which is a mapping from instances to total orders over a set of labels (options). The training information consists of examples with partial (and possibly inconsistent) information about their associated rankings. From these, we induce a ranking function by reducing the original problem to a number of binary classification problems, one for each pair of labels. The main objective of this work is to investigate the trade-off between the quality of the induced ranking function and the computational complexity of the algorithm, both depending on the amount of preference information given for each example. To this end, we present theoretical results on the complexity of pairwise preference learning, and experimentally investigate the predictive performance of our method for different types of preference information, such as top-ranked labels and complete rankings. The domain of this study is the prediction of a rational agent's ranking of actions in an uncertain environment.

1 Introduction

The problem of learning with or from preferences has recently received a lot of attention within the machine learning literature[1]. The problem is particularly challenging because it involves the prediction of complex structures, such as weak or partial order relations, rather than single values. Moreover, training input will not, as it is usually the case, be offered in the form of complete examples but may comprise more general types of information, such as relative preferences or different kinds of indirect feedback.

More specifically, the learning scenario that we will consider in this paper consists of a collection of training examples which are associated with a finite set of decision alternatives. Following the common notation of supervised learning, we shall refer to the latter as *labels*. However, contrary to standard classification, a training example is not assigned a single label, but a set of *pairwise preferences* between labels, expressing that one label is preferred over another.

The goal is to use these pairwise preferences for predicting a total order, a *ranking*, of all possible labels for a new training example. More generally, we seek to induce a

---

[1] Space restrictions prevent a thorough review of related work in this paper, but we refer the reader to (Fürnkranz and Hüllermeier, 2003).

ranking function that maps instances (examples) to rankings over a fixed set of decision alternatives (labels), in analogy to a *classification function* that maps instances to single labels. To this end, we investigate the use of *round robin learning* or *pairwise classification*. As will be seen, round robin appears particularly appealing in this context since it can be extended from classification to preference learning in a quite natural manner.

The paper is organized as follows: In the next section, we introduce the learning problem in a formal way. The extension of pairwise classification to pairwise preference learning and its application to ranking are discussed in section 3. Section 4 provides some results on the computational complexity of pairwise preference learning. Results of several experimental studies investigating the predictive performance of our approach under various training conditions are presented in section 5. We conclude the paper with some final remarks in section 6.

2 Learning Problem

We consider the following learning problem:

Given:
- a set of *labels* $L = \{\lambda_i \,|\, i = 1 \ldots c\}$
- a set of *examples* $E = \{e_k \,|\, k = 1 \ldots n\}$
- for each training example e_k:
  - a set of *preferences* $P_k \subseteq L \times L$, where $(\lambda_i, \lambda_j) \in P_k$ indicates that label λ_i is preferred over label λ_j for example e_k (written as $\lambda_i \succ_k \lambda_j$)

Find: a function that orders the labels $\lambda_i, i = 1 \ldots c$ for any given example.

This setting has been previously introduced as *constraint classification* by Har-Peled et al. (2002). As has been pointed out in their work, the above framework is a generalization of several common learning settings, in particular (see ibidem for a formal derivation of these and other results)

- *ranking:* Each training example is associated with a total order of the labels, i.e., for each pair of labels (λ_i, λ_j) either $\lambda_i \succ_k \lambda_j$ or $\lambda_j \succ_k \lambda_i$ holds.
- *classification:* A single class label λ_i is assigned to each example. This implicitly defines the set of preferences $\{\lambda_i \succ_k \lambda_j \,|\, 1 \leq j \neq i \leq c\}$.
- *multi-label classification:* Each training example e_k is associated with a subset $S_k \subseteq L$ of possible labels. This implicitly defines the set of preferences $\{\lambda_i \succ_k \lambda_j \,|\, \lambda_i \in S_k, \lambda_j \in L \setminus S_k\}$.

As pointed out before, we will be interested in predicting a ranking (total order) of the labels. Thus, we assume that for each instance, there exists a total order of the labels, i.e., the pairwise preferences form a transitive and asymmetric relation. For many practical applications, this assumption appears to be acceptable at least for the *true* preferences. Still, more often than not the observed or *revealed* preferences will be incomplete or inconsistent. Therefore, we do not require the *data* to be consistent in the sense that transitivity and asymmetry applies to the P_k. We only assume that P_k is irreflexive ($\lambda_i \not\succ \lambda_i$) and anti-symmetric ($\lambda_i \succ \lambda_j \Rightarrow \lambda_j \not\succ \lambda_i$). (Note that $0 \leq |P_k| \leq c(c-1)/2$ as a consequence of the last two properties.)

3 Pairwise Preference Ranking

A key idea of our approach is to learn a separate theory for each of the $c(c-1)/2$ pairwise preferences between two labels. More formally, for each possible pair of labels (λ_i, λ_j), $1 \leq i < j \leq c$, we learn a model M_{ij} that decides for any given example whether $\lambda_i \succ \lambda_j$ or $\lambda_j \succ \lambda_i$ holds. The model is trained with all examples e_k for which either $\lambda_i \succ_k \lambda_j$ or $\lambda_j \succ_k \lambda_i$ is known. All examples for which nothing is known about the preference between λ_i and λ_j are ignored.

At classification time, an example is submitted to all $c(c-1)/2$ theories. If classifier M_{ij} predicts $\lambda_i \succ \lambda_j$, we count this as a vote for λ_i. Conversely, the prediction $\lambda_j \succ \lambda_i$ would be considered as a vote for λ_j. The labels are ranked according to the number of votes they receive from all models M_{ij}. Ties are first broken according to the frequency of the labels in the top rank (the class distribution in the classification setting) and then randomly.

We refer to the above technique as *pairwise preference ranking* or *round robin ranking*. It is a straight-forward generalization of pairwise or one-against-one classification, aka round robin learning, which solves multi-class problems by learning a separate theory for each pair of classes. In previous work, Fürnkranz (2002) showed that, for rule learning algorithms, this technique is preferable to the more commonly used one-against-all classification method, which learns one theory for each class, using the examples of this class as positive examples and all others as negative examples. Interestingly, despite its complexity being quadratic in the number of classes, the algorithm is no slower than the conventional one-against-all technique (Fürnkranz, 2002). We will generalize these results in the next section.

4 Complexity

Consider a learning problem with n training examples and c labels.

Theorem 1. *The total number of training examples over all $c(c-1)/2$ binary preference learning problems is*

$$\sum_{k=1}^{n} |P_k| \leq n \max_k |P_k| \leq n \binom{c}{2} = n \frac{c(c-1)}{2}$$

Proof. Each of the n training examples e_k will be added to all $|P_k|$ binary training sets that correspond to one of its preferences $\lambda_i \succ_k \lambda_j$. Thus, the total number of training examples is $\sum_{k=1}^{n} |P_k|$. As the number of preferences for each example is bounded from above by $\max_k |P_k|$, this number is no larger than $n \max_k |P_k|$, which in turn is bounded from above by the size of a complete set of preferences $nc(c-1)/2$. □

Corollary 1. (Fürnkranz, 2002) *For a classification problem, the total number of training examples is only linear in the number of classes.*

Proof. A class label expands to $c-1$ preferences, therefore $\sum_{k=1}^{n} |P_k| = (c-1)n$. □

Note that we only considered the number of training examples, but not the complexity of the learner that runs on these examples. For an algorithm with a linear run-time complexity $O(n)$ it follows immediately that the total run-time is $O(dn)$, where d is the maximum (or average) number of preferences given for each training example. For a learner with a super-linear complexity $O(n^a), a > 1$, the total run-time is much lower than $O((dn)^a)$ because the training effort is not spent on one large training set, but on many small training sets. In particular, for a complete preference set, the total complexity is $O(c^2 n^a)$, whereas the complexity for $d = c - 1$ (round robin classification) is only $O(cn^a)$ (Fürnkranz, 2002).

For comparison, the only other technique for learning in this setting that we know of (Har-Peled et al., 2002) constructs twice as many training examples (one positive and one negative for each preference of each example), and these examples are projected into a space that has c times as many attributes as the original space. Moreover, all examples are put into a single training set for which a separating hyper-plane has to be found. Thus, under the (reasonable) assumption that an increase in the number of features has approximately the same effect as a corresponding increase in the number of examples, the total complexity becomes $O((cdn)^a)$ if the algorithm for finding the separating hyper-plane has complexity $O(n^a)$ for a two-class training set of size n.

In summary, the overall complexity of pairwise constraint classification depends on the number of known preferences for each training example. While being quadratic in the number of labels if a complete ranking is given, it is only linear for the classification setting. In any case, it is more efficient than the technique proposed by Har-Peled et al. (2002). However, it should be noted that the price to pay is the large number of classifiers that have to be stored and tested at classification time.

5 Empirical Results

The previous sections have shown that round robin learning can be extended to induce a ranking function from a set of preferences instead of a single label. Yet, it turned out that computational complexity might become an issue. Especially, since a ranking induces a quadratic number of pairwise preferences, the complexity for round robin ranking becomes quadratic in the number of labels. In this context, one might ask whether it could be possible to improve efficiency at the cost of a tolerable decrease in performance: Could the learning process perhaps ignore some of the preferences without decreasing predictive accuracy too much? Apart from that, incomplete training data is clearly a point of practical relevance, since complete rankings will rarely be observable.

The experimental evaluation presented in this section is meant to investigate issues related to incomplete training data in more detail, especially to increase our understanding about the trade-off between the number of pairwise preferences available in the training data and the quality of the learned ranking function. For a systematic investigation of questions of such kind, we need data for which, in principle, a complete ranking is known for each example. This information allows a systematic variation of the amount of preference information in the training data, and a precise evaluation of the predicted rankings on the test data. Since we are not aware of any suitable real-world datasets, we have conducted our experiments with synthetic data.

5.1 Synthetic Data

We consider the problem of learning the ranking function of an expected utility maximizing agent. More specifically, we proceed from a standard setting of expected utility theory: $A = \{a_1, \ldots, a_c\}$ is a set of actions the agent can choose from and $\Omega = \{\omega_1, \ldots, \omega_m\}$ is a set of world states. The agent faces a problem of *decision under risk* where decision consequences are lotteries: Choosing act a_i in state ω_j yields a utility of $u_{ij} \in \mathbb{R}$, where the probability of state ω_j is p_j. Thus, the *expected utility* of act a_i is given by

$$\mathbb{E}(a_i) = \sum_{j=1}^{m} p_j \cdot u_{ij}. \tag{1}$$

Expected utility theory justifies (1) as a criterion for ranking actions and, hence, gives rise to the following preference relation:

$$a_i \succ a_j \Leftrightarrow \mathbb{E}(a_i) > \mathbb{E}(a_j). \tag{2}$$

Now, suppose the probability vector $p = (p_1, \ldots, p_m)$ to be a parameter of the decision problem (while A, Ω and the utility matrix matrix $U = (u_{ij})$ are fixed).

The above decision-theoretic setting can be used for generating synthetic data for preference learning. The set of instances corresponds to the set of probability vectors p, which are generated at random according to a uniform distribution over $\{p \in \mathbb{R}^m \,|\, p \geq 0,\, p_1 + \ldots + p_m = 1\}$. The ranking function associated with an example is given by the ranking defined in (2). Thus, an experiment is characterized by the following parameters: The number of actions/labels (c), the number of world states (m), the number of examples (n), and the utility matrix which is generated at random through independent and uniformly distributed entries $u_{ij} \in [0, 1]$.

5.2 Experimental Setup

In the following, we will report on results of experiments with ten different states ($m = 10$) and various numbers of labels ($c = 5, 10, 20$). For each of the three configurations we generated ten different data sets, each one originating from a different randomly chosen utility matrix U. The data sets consisted of 1000 training and 1000 test examples. For each example, the data sets provided the probability vector $p \in \mathbb{R}^m$ and a complete ranking of the c possible actions[2]. The training examples were labeled with a subset of the complete set of pairwise preferences as imposed by the ranking in the data set. The subsets that were selected for the experiments are described one by one for the experiments.

We used the decision tree learner C4.5 (Quinlan, 1993) in its default settings[3] to learn a model for each pairwise preference. For all examples in the test set we obtained a final ranking using simple voting and tie breaking as described in section 3.

---

[2] The occurrence of actions with equal expected utility has probability 0.
[3] Our choice of C4.5 as the learner was solely based on its versatility and wide availability. If we had aimed at maximizing performance on this particular problem, we would have chosen an algorithm that can directly represent the separating hyperplanes for each binary preference.

5.3 Ranking vs. Classification

Figure 1 shows experimental results for (a) using the full set of $c(c-1)/2$ pairwise preferences, (b) for the classification setting which uses only the $c-1$ preferences that involve the top label, and (c) for the complementary setting with the $(c-1)(c-2)/2$ preferences that do *not* involve the top label. There are several interesting things to note for these results. First, the difference between the error rates of the classification and the ranking setting is comparably small. Thus, if we are only interested in the top rank, it may often suffice to use the pairwise preferences that involve the top label. The advantage in this case is of course the reduced complexity which becomes linear in the number of labels. On the other hand, the results also show that the complete ranking information can be used to improve classification accuracy, at least if this information is available for each training example and if one is willing to pay the price of a quadratic complexity.

The results for the complementary setting show that the information of the top rank preferences is crucial: When dropping this information and using only those pairwise preferences that do not involve the top label, the error rate on the top rank increases considerably, and is much higher than the error rate for the classification setting. This is a bit surprising if we consider that in the classification setting, the average number of training examples for learning a model M_{ij} is much smaller than in the complementary setting. Interestingly, the effective number of training examples for the top labels might nevertheless decrease. In fact, in our learning scenario we will often have a few *dominating* actions whose utility degrees are systematically larger than those of other actions. In the worst case, the same action is optimal for all probability vectors p, and the complementary set will not contain any information about it. While this situation is of course rather extreme, the class distribution is indeed very unbalanced in our scenario. For example, we determined experimentally for $c = m = 10$ and $n = 1000$ that the probability of having the same optimal action for more than half of the examples is $\approx 2/3$, and that the expected Gini-index of the class distribution is $\approx 1/2$.

With respect to the prediction of complete rankings, the performance for learning from the complementary set of preferences is almost as good as the performance for learning from the complete set of preferences, whereas the performance of the ranking induced from the classification setting is considerably worse. This time, however, the result is hardly surprising and can easily be explained by the amount of information provided in the two cases. In fact, the complementary set determines the ranking of $c-1$ among the c labels, whereas the top label alone does hardly provide any information about the complete ranking.

As another interesting finding note that the classification accuracy decreases with an increasing number of labels, whereas the rank correlation increases (this is also revealed by the curves in Figure 3 below). In other words, the quality of the predicted rankings increases, even though the quality of the predictions for the individual ranks decreases. This effect can first of all be explained by the fact that the (classification)

c	prefs	error	rank corr.
5	ranking	13.380 ± 8.016	0.907 ± 0.038
	classification	14.400 ± 8.262	0.783 ± 0.145
	complement	32.650 ± 14.615	0.872 ± 0.051
10	ranking	15.820 ± 8.506	0.940 ± 0.018
	classification	16.670 ± 9.549	0.711 ± 0.108
	complement	24.310 ± 9.995	0.937 ± 0.018
20	ranking	24.030 ± 4.251	0.966 ± 0.004
	classification	26.370 ± 5.147	0.697 ± 0.066
	complement	32.300 ± 3.264	0.966 ± 0.004

Fig. 1. Comparison of ranking (a complete set of preferences is given) vs. classification (only the preferences for the top rank are given). Also shown are the results for the complementary setting (all preferences for the top rank are omitted).

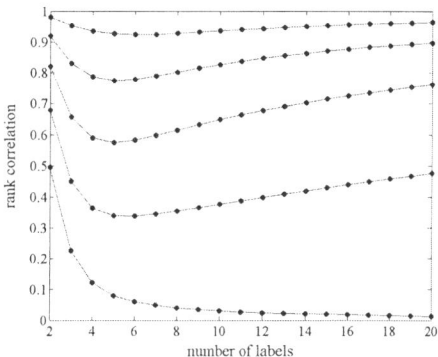

Fig. 2. Expected Spearman rank correlation as a function of the number of labels if all models M_{ij} have an error rate of ϵ (curves are shown for $\epsilon = 0.1, 0.2, 0.3, 0.4, 0.5$).

error is much more affected by an increase of the number of labels. As an illustration, consider random guessing: The chances of guessing the top label correctly are $1/m$, whereas the expected value of the rank correlation is 0 regardless of m. Moreover, one might speculate that the importance of a correct vote of each individual model M_{ij} decreases with an increasing number of labels. Roughly speaking, incorrect classifications of individual learners are better compensated on average. This conjecture is also supported by an independent experiment in which we simulated a set of homogeneous models M_{ij} through biased coin flipping with a prespecified error rate. It turned out that the quality measures for predicted rankings tend to increase if the number of labels becomes large (though the dependence of the measures on the number of labels is not necessarily monotone, see Fig. 2).

5.4 Missing Preferences

While the previous results shed some light on the trade-off between utility and costs for two special types of preference information, namely top-ranked labels and complete rankings, they do not give a satisfactory answer for the general case. The selected set of preferences in the classification setting is strongly focused on a particular label for each example, thus resulting in a very biased distribution. In the following, we will look at the quality of predicted rankings when selecting random subsets of pairwise preferences from the full sets with equal right.

Figure 3 shows the curves for the classification error in the top rank and the average Spearman rank correlation of the predicted and the true ranking over the number of preferences. To generate these curves, we started with the full set of preferences, and ignored increasingly larger fractions of it. This was implemented with a parameter p_i that caused any given preference in the training data to be ignored with probability p_i ($100 \times p_i$ is plotted on the x-axis).

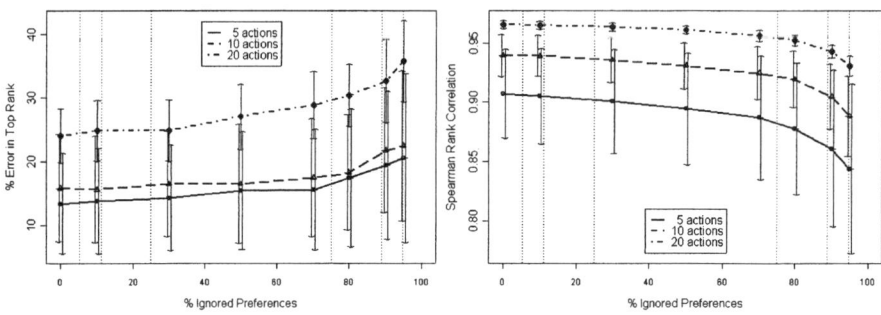

Fig. 3. Average error rate (left) and Spearman rank correlation (right) for various percentages of ignored preferences. The error bars indicate the standard deviations. The vertical dotted lines on the right indicate the number of preferences for classification problems (for 5, 10, and 20 classes), those on the left are the complementary sizes.

The similar shape of the three curves (for 5, 10, and 20 labels) suggests that the decrease in the ranking quality can be attributed solely to the missing preferences while it seems to be independent of the number of labels. In particular, one is inclined to conclude that—contrary to the case where we focused on the top rank—it is in general *not* possible to reduce the number of training preferences by an order of magnitude (i.e., from quadratic to linear in the number of labels) without severely decreasing the ranking quality. This can also be seen from the three dotted vertical lines in the right half of the graphs. These lines indicate the percentage of preferences that were present in the classification setting for 5, 10, and 20 labels (from inner-most to outer-most). A comparison of the error rates, given by the intersection of a line with the corresponding curve, to the respective error rates in Figure 1 shows an extreme difference between the coincidental selection of pairwise preferences and the systematic selection which is focused on the top rank.

Nevertheless, one can also see that about half of the preferences can be ignored while still maintaining a reasonable performance level. Even though it is quite common that learning curves are concave functions of the size of the training set, the descent in accuracy appears to be remarkably flat in our case. One might be tempted to attribute this to the redundancy of the pairwise preferences induced by a ranking: In principle, a ranking ρ could already be reconstructed from the $c - 1$ preferences $\rho_1 \succ \rho_2, \ldots, \rho_{c-1} \succ \rho_c$, which means that only a small fraction of the pairwise preferences are actually needed. Still, one should be careful with this explanation. First, we are not trying to reconstruct a single ranking but rather to solve a slightly different problem, namely to learn a ranking function. Second, our learning algorithm does actually not "reconstruct" a ranking as suggested above. In fact, our simple voting procedure does not take the dependencies between individual models M_{ij} into account, which means that these models do not really cooperate. On the contrary, what the voting procedure exploits is just the redundancy of preference information: The top rank is the winner only because it is preferred in $c - 1$ out of the $c(c-1)/2$ pairwise comparisons.

Finally, note that the shape of the curves probably also depends on the number of training examples. We have not yet investigated this issue because we were mainly

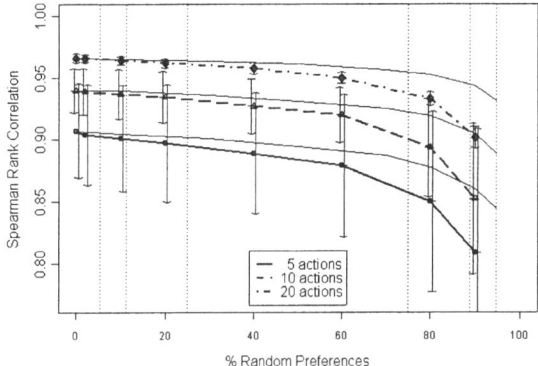

Fig. 4. Average Spearman rank correlation over various percentages of random preferences. The error bars indicate the standard deviations. The solid thin lines are the curves for ignored preferences (Figure 3).

interested in the possibility of reducing the complexity by more than a constant factor without losing too much of predictive accuracy. It would be interesting, for example, to compare (a) using $p\%$ of the training examples with full preferences and (b) using all training examples with $p\%$ of the pairwise preferences.

5.5 Mislabeled Preferences

Recall that our learning scenario assumes preference structures to be complete rankings of labels, that is transitive and asymmetric relations. As already pointed out, we do not make this assumption for *observed* preferences: First, we may not have access to complete sets of preferences (the case studied in the previous section). Second, the process generating the preferences might reproduce the underlying total order incorrectly and, hence, produce inconsistent preferences. The latter problem is quite common, for example, in the case of human judgments.

To simulate this behavior, we adopted the following model: Proceeding from the pairwise preferences induced by a given ranking, a preference $\lambda_i \succ \lambda_j$ was kept with probability $1 - p_s$, whereas with probability p_s, one of the preferences $\lambda_i \succ \lambda_j$ and $\lambda_j \succ \lambda_i$ was selected by a coin flip. Thus, in approximately $p_s/2$ cases, the preference will point into the wrong direction[4]. For $p_s = 0$, the data remain unchanged, whereas the preferences in the training data are completely random for $p_s = 1$.

Figure 4 shows the average Spearman rank correlations that were observed in this experiment. Note that the shape of the curve is almost the same as the shape of the curves for ignored preferences. It is possible to directly compare these two curves because in both graphs a level of $n\%$ means that $100 - n\%$ of the preferences are still intact. The main difference is that in Figure 3, the remaining $n\%$ of the preferences have been ignored, while in Figure 4 they have been re-assigned at random. To facili-

---

[4] In fact, we implemented the procedure by selecting $p_s/2$ preferences and reversing their sign.

tate this comparison, we plotted the curves for ignored preferences (the same ones as in Figure 3) into the graph (with solid, thin lines).

It is interesting to see that in both cases the performance degrades very slowly at the beginning, albeit somewhat steeper than if the examples are completely ignored. Roughly speaking, completely omitting a pairwise preference appears to be better than including a random preference. This could reasonably be explained by the learning behavior of a classifier M_{ij}: If M_{ij} does already perform well, an additional correct example will probably be classified correctly and thus improve M_{ij} only slightly (in decision tree induction, for example, M_{ij} will even remain completely unchanged if the new example is classified correctly). As opposed to this, an incorrect example will probably be classified incorrectly and thus produce a more far-reaching modification of M_{ij} (in decision tree induction, an erroneous example might produce a completely different tree). All in all, the "expected benefit" of M_{ij} caused by a random preference is negative, whereas it is 0 if the preference is simply ignored.

From this consideration one may conclude that a pairwise preference should better be ignored if it is no more confident than a coin flip. This can also be grasped intuitively, since the preference does not provide any information in this case. If it is more confident, however, it clearly carries some information and it might then be better to include it, even though the best way of action will still depend on the number and reliability of the preferences already available. Note that our experiments do not suggest any strategy for deciding whether or not to include an *individual* preference, given information about the uncertainty of that preference. In our case, each preference is equally uncertain. Thus, the only reasonable strategies are to include all of them or to ignore the complete sample. Of course, the first strategy will be better as soon as the probability of correctness exceeds $1/2$, and this is also confirmed by the experimental results. For example, the correlation coefficient remains visibly above 0.8 even if 80% of the preferences are assigned by chance and, hence, the probability of a particular preference to be correct is only 0.6. One may conjecture that pairwise preference ranking is particularly robust toward noise, since an erroneous example affects only a single classifier M_{ij} which in turn has a limited influence on the eventually predicted ranking.

6 Concluding Remarks

We have introduced pairwise preference learning as an extension of pairwise classification to constraint classification, a learning scenario where training examples are labeled with a preference relation over all possible labels instead of a single class label as in the conventional classification setting. From this information, we also learn one model for each pair of classes, but focus on learning a complete ranking of all labels instead of only predicting the most likely label. Our main interest was to investigate the trade-off between ranking quality and the amount of training information (in terms of the number of preferences that are available for each example). We experimentally investigated this trade-off by varying parameters of a synthetic domain that simulates a decision-theoretic agent which ranks its possible actions according to an unknown utility function. Roughly speaking, the results show that large parts of the information about pairwise preferences can be ignored in round robin ranking without losing too much predictive performance. In the classification setting, where one is only interested in predicting the top label, it also turned out that using the full ranking information rather than restricting to the pairwise preferences involving the top label does even improve the classification accuracy, suggesting that the lower ranks do contain valuable information. For reasons of efficiency, however, it might still be advisable to concentrate on the smaller set of preferences, thereby reducing the size of the training set by an order of magnitude.

The main limitation of our technique is probably the assumption of having enough training examples for learning each pairwise preference. For data with a very large number of labels and a rather small set of preferences per example, our technique will hardly be applicable. In particular, it is unlikely to be successful in collaborative filtering problems (Goldberg et al., 1992; Resnick and Varian, 1997; Breese et al., 1998), although these can be mapped onto the constraint classification framework in a straightforward way. A further limitation is the quadratic number of theories that has to be stored in memory and evaluated at classification time. However, the increase in memory requirements is balanced by an increase in computational efficiency in comparison to the technique of Har-Peled et al. (2002). In addition, pairwise preference learning inherits many advantages of pairwise classification, in particular its implementation can easily be parallelized because of its reduction to independent subproblems. Finally, we have assumed an underlying total order of the items which needs to be recovered from partial observations of preferences. However, partial orders (cases where several labels are equally preferred) may also occur in practical applications. We have not yet investigated the issue of how to generate (and evaluate) partial orders from learned pairwise predictions. Similarly, our current framework does not provide a facility for discriminating between cases where we know that a pair of labels is of equal preference and cases where we don't know anything about their relative preferences.

There are several directions for future work. First of all, it is likely that the prediction of rankings can be improved by combining the individual models' votes in a more sophisticated way. Several authors have looked at techniques for combining the predictions of pairwise theories into a final ranking of the available options. Proposals include weighting the predicted preferences with the classifiers' confidences (Fürnkranz, 2003) or using an iterative algorithm for combining pairwise probability estimates (Hastie and Tibshirani, 1998). However, none of the previous works have evaluated their techniques in a ranking context, and some more elaborate proposals, like error-correcting output decoding (Allwein et al., 2000), organizing the pairwise classifiers in a tree-like structure (Platt et al., 2000), or using a stacked classifier (Savicky and Fürnkranz, 2003) are specifically tailored to a classification setting. Taking into account the fact that we are explicitly seeking a ranking could lead to promising alternatives. For example, we are thinking about selecting the ranking which minimizes the number of predicted preferences that need to be reversed in order to make the predicted relation transitive. Departing from the counting of votes might also offer possibilities for extending our method to the prediction of preference structures more general than rankings (total orders), such as weak preference relations where some of the labels might not be comparable. Apart from theoretical considerations, an important aspect of future work concerns the practical application of our method and its evaluation using real-world problems. Unfortunately, real-world data sets that fit our framework seem to be quite rare. In fact, currently we are not aware of any data set of significant size that provides instances in attribute-value representation plus an associated complete ranking over a limited number of labels.

Acknowledgments

Johannes Fürnkranz is supported by an APART stipend (no. 10814) of the *Austrian Academy of Sciences*. The Austrian Research Institute for Artificial Intelligence is supported by the Austrian Federal Ministry of Education, Science and Culture.

References

E. L. Allwein, R. E. Schapire, and Y. Singer. Reducing multiclass to binary: A unifying approach for margin classifiers. *Journal of Machine Learning Research*, 1:113–141, 2000.

J. S. Breese, D. Heckerman, and C. Kadie. Empirical analysis of predictive algorithms for collaborative filtering. In G. F. Cooper and S. Moral (eds.), *Proceedings of the 14th Conference on Uncertainty in Artificial Intelligence (UAI-98)*, pp. 43–52, Madison, WI, 1998. Morgan Kaufmann.

J. Fürnkranz. Round robin classification. *Journal of Machine Learning Research*, 2:721–747, 2002.

J. Fürnkranz. Round robin ensembles. *Intelligent Data Analysis*, 7(5), 2003. To appear.

J. Fürnkranz and E. Hüllermeier. Pairwise preference learning and ranking. Technical Report OEFAI-TR-2003-14, Austrian Research Institute for Artificial Intelligence, Wien, Austria, 2003.

D. Goldberg, D. Nichols, B. M. Oki, and D. Terry. Using collaborative filtering to weave and information tapestry. *Communications of the ACM*, 35(12):61–70, 1992.

S. Har-Peled, D. Roth, and D. Zimak. Constraint classification: A new approach to multiclass classification. In N. Cesa-Bianchi, M. Numao, and R. Reischuk (eds.), *Proceedings of the 13th International Conference on Algorithmic Learning Theory (ALT-02)*, pp. 365–379, Lübeck, Germany, 2002. Springer-Verlag.

T. Hastie and R. Tibshirani. Classification by pairwise coupling. In M. Jordan, M. Kearns, and S. Solla (eds.), *Advances in Neural Information Processing Systems 10 (NIPS-97)*, pp. 507–513. MIT Press, 1998.

J. C. Platt, N. Cristianini, and J. Shawe-Taylor. Large margin DAGs for multiclass classification. In S. A. Solla, T. K. Leen, and K.-R. Müller (eds.), *Advances in Neural Information Processing Systems 12 (NIPS-99)*, pp. 547–553. MIT Press, 2000.

J. R. Quinlan. *C4.5: Programs for Machine Learning*. Morgan Kaufmann, San Mateo, CA, 1993.

P. Resnick and H. R. Varian. Special issue on recommender systems. *Communications of the ACM*, 40(3), 1997.

P. Savicky and J. Fürnkranz. Combining pairwise classifiers with stacking. In *Advances in Intelligent Data Analysis: Proceedings of the 5th International Symposium (IDA-03)*, Berlin, Germany, 2003. Springer-Verlag. To appear.

A New Way to Introduce Knowledge into Reinforcement Learning

Pascal Garcia

INSA de Rennes/IRISA, F-35043 Rennes Cedex, France
pascal.garcia@irisa.fr

Abstract. We present in this paper a method to introduce *a priori* knowledge into reinforcement learning using temporally extended actions. The aim of our work is to reduce the learning time of the Q-learning algorithm. This introduction of initial knowledge is done by constraining the set of available actions in some states. But at the same time, we can formulate that if the agent is in some particular states (called exception states), we have to relax those constraints. We define a mechanism called the propagation mechanism to get out of blocked situations induced by the initial knowledge constraints. We give some formal properties of our method and test it on a complex grid-world task. On this task, we compare our method with Q-learning and show that the learning time is drastically reduced for a very simple initial knowledge which would not be sufficient, by itself, to solve the task without the definition of exception situations and the propagation mechanism.

1 Introduction

Reinforcement Learning is a general framework in which an autonomous agent learns which actions to choose in particular situations (states) in order to optimize some reinforcements (rewards or punitions) in the long run [1]. A fundamental problem of its standard algorithms is that although many tasks can be formulated in this framework, in practice for large state space they are not solvable in reasonable time. There are two principal approaches for addressing these problems: The first approach is to apply generalization techniques (e.g., [2,3]). The second approach is to use temporally extended actions (e.g., [4,5,6,7,8,9]). A temporally extended action is a way of grouping actions to create a new one. For example, if the primitive actions of a problem are "make a step in a given direction", a temporally extended action could be "make ten steps to the north followed by two steps to the west". Temporally extended actions represent the problem at different levels of abstraction.

The aim of our work is to give a method to incorporate easily some *a priori* knowledge, about a task we try to solve by reinforcement learning, to speed-up the learning time. To introduce knowledge into reinforcement learning, we use some temporally extended actions for which the set of available actions can change during learning. We try to reduce the blind exploration of the agent by constraining the set of available actions. But because the *a priori* knowledge could be very simple, those constraints can make the agent unable to solve a task. So we define a way to relax those constraints (with what we call the exception conditions and the propagation mechanism). The structure of this paper is as follows. First we described our method in section 2. We give its two main properties in section 3. In section 4 and 5 we describe a complex grid-world task to compare our method with Q-learning [10]. We show that the learning time is drastically reduced for a very simple initial knowledge which is not sufficient by itself, to solve the task and so, must be updated.

2 Formalism

In this section we develop our method which we call *EBRL* for Exception-Based Reinforcement Learning. To make it easier for the reader we explain it with the help of the artificial problem presented in Figure 1. In this grid-world, the agent has to reach the cross; he can move in eight directions (north, north-east, ...) and some walls can be put in the grid (the agent is blocked by them).

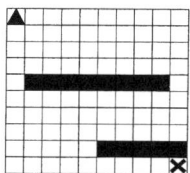

Fig. 1. The agent (triangle) has to reach the cross to solve the task.

2.1 Procedure, Rule and Exception

We define in this sub-section the syntax in which our temporally extended actions will be written. The semantic associated with this syntax is also explained. We represent a temporally extended action by a procedure:

```
Procedure_name(state,list_of_parameters) →
termination : termination condition
rule        : set of actions S₁
{exception  : ( exception condition, set of actions S₂)}^{0/1}
next        : continuation
```

The semantic associated with this syntax is:

- `state`: the state of the underlying Markov Decision Process (*MDP*);
- `list_of_parameters`: optional parameters, each parameter has a finite number of different possible values;
- `termination`: this is the condition of termination of the procedure. This condition only depends on the state and the parameters;

- **rule**: this rule produces a finite set of primitive or temporally extended actions (procedures). This rule is applied only if the exception condition is not fulfilled;
- **exception**:
  - exception condition: if this condition is fulfilled, we do not use the set of actions of the rule part, but instead, the set of actions produced by the exception part;
  - set of actions: a finite set of primitive or temporally extended actions (procedures). This rule is applied only if the exception condition is fulfilled. We have $S_1 \subseteq S_2$;
- **next**: continuation after the execution of an action of the rule or exception part. This part is a call to another procedure. If this procedure has parameters, they only depend on the state and the parameters of the current procedure.

When entering a procedure, we first test the termination condition; if it is not fulfilled, we test the exception condition; if this condition is true, we choose one of the exception actions and after its execution, we continue in the **next** part. If the exception condition is not fulfilled, we choose one of the action of the **rule** part and after its carrying out, we continue in the **next** part. In the remaining of the article, we call *program* a finite set of procedures and *main* the first procedure of the program to be executed.

2.2 Example

We illustrate, in this section, the syntax described above, to solve the artificial problem.

```
main(grid configuration) ⟶
termination : the agent is on the cross
rule        : { the set of actions which make the agent get closer to the cross }
exception   : (all the actions of the rule part lead to a wall, { all the primitive actions } )
next        : main()
```

The *a priori* knowledge is just to choose in each state of the underlying *MDP* the set of actions (amongst the eight possible ones) which gets the agent closer to the cross without taking the walls into account (there is between one and three such actions). The exception to this rule is when all those actions lead the agent to a wall; when this is the case, we relax the constraints and allow all actions.

2.3 Full State Representation

We use a program in interaction with an *MDP*. This program will help the learning agent to solve the problem represented by this *MDP*. We have seen that each procedure has the state of the underlying *MDP* as a parameter. We define the full state representation of a procedure as a 4-tuple (`procedure_name,state,` list_of_parameters, next_list) where procedure_name is the name of the procedure, state is the state of the underlying *MDP* when we enter this procedure, list_of_parameters is the possible parameters of the procedure and next_list is the list of procedures to be executed after the execution of procedure_name.

2.4 Induced Semi-Markov Decision Process

In this section we describe an algorithm called construct-SMDP which constructs a Semi-Markov Decision Process (*SMDP*) (see [11] and [5]), from a program $\mathcal{P}$ and an underlying *MDP* $\mathcal{M}$ (similar construction can be found in [4] and [5]). Note that this algorithm serves to demonstrate that the execution of a program on an *MDP* is an *SMDP*. We will never have to construct explicitly this *SMDP* when executing a program on an *MDP*. In the remaining of this article we note:

- $\mathcal{M} = (\mathcal{S}, \mathcal{A}, \mathcal{T}, \mathcal{R})$ the underlying *MDP* where $\mathcal{S}$ is a set of states, $\mathcal{A}$ is a set of actions, $\mathcal{T}$ is a Markovian transition model mapping $\mathcal{S} \times \mathcal{A} \times \mathcal{S}$ into probabilities in $[0,1]$, $\mathcal{R}$ is a reward function mapping $\mathcal{S} \times \mathcal{A} \times \mathcal{S}$ into real-valued rewards;
- $\mathcal{P}$ the program;
- $Main\_parameters$ the set of all possible lists of values for the parameter list of the main procedure;
- $\mathcal{A}'$ the set of all the actions of the rule and exception part of all the procedures of the program and, for the temporally extended actions, all possible instantiations of their parameters;
- $\mathcal{A}'(s')$, where $s' = (p, s, l, n)$ is a full state representation, is the set of all actions of the rule and exception part of the procedure p. If the terminal condition of p is fulfilled, $\mathcal{A}'(s') = \texttt{termination}$;
- $\mathcal{A}'_r(s')$, where $s' = (p, s, l, n)$ is the set of all actions of the rule part of the procedure p;
- $\mathcal{A}'_e(s')$ where $s' = (p, s, l, n)$ is the set of all actions of the exception part of the procedure p, if there is no exception part, $\mathcal{A}'_e(s') = \mathcal{A}'_r(s')$. We recall that $\mathcal{A}'_r(s') \subseteq \mathcal{A}'_e(s')$;
- $\texttt{next}(p, s, l)$, where p is a procedure, s a state of $\mathcal{M}$ and l a list of parameters, is the procedure of the next part of p, with its instantiated parameters.
- $\texttt{add}(e, l)$ returns the list with first element e and tail l. $\texttt{head}(l)$ returns the first element of l and $\texttt{tail}(l)$ returns the list l without its first element.

A state of the constructed *SMDP* is a full state representation of a procedure. The *SMDP* $(\mathcal{S}', \mathcal{A}', \mathcal{T}', \mathcal{R}', \beta)$ (where $\mathcal{S}'$, $\mathcal{A}'$, $\mathcal{T}'$, $\mathcal{R}'$ have the same meaning as $\mathcal{S}, \mathcal{A}, \mathcal{T}$ and $\mathcal{R}$ respectively and β is a mapping from $\mathcal{S}' \times \mathcal{A}' \times \mathcal{S}'$ into real value -see [5]-) is constructed as follows:

```
algorithm construct-SMDP(MDP : M, program : P,
discount factor : γ ∈]0, 1[)
begin
S' ← {main} × S × Main_parameters × {[]}
repeat
        forall t = (p, s, l, n) ∈ S', forall a ∈ A'(t)  do
                if a = p'(l')  then
                        t' ← (p', s, l', add(next(p, s, l), n))
                        S' ← S' ∪ {t'}
                        T'(t, a, t') ← 1
                        β(t, a, t') ← 1
                elseif a = termination and p ≠ main then
                        t' ← next-state(s, n)
                        S' ← S' ∪ {t'}
                        T'(t, a, t') ← 1
                        β(t, a, t') ← 1
                elseif a ∈ A  then
                        forall s' ∈ S  do
                                n' ← add(next(p, s, l), n)
                                t' ← next-state(s', n')
                                S' ← S' ∪ {t'}
                                T'(t, a, t') ← T(s, a, s')
                                R'(t, a, t') ← R(s, a, s')
                                β(t, a, t') ← γ
                        endforall
                endif
        endforall
until S' is stable (means that no new state
                has been added to S')
All unspecified value for T', R' and β are set to 0
return (S', A', T', R', β)
end

algorithm next-state(s : s ∈ S, n : next_list)
begin
if n ≠ []  then
        let p(l) = head(n)
        t ← (p, s, l, tail(n))
        return t
else
        in this case, the program is not correct,
        the program is not terminated and there is
        no next procedure to call
endif
end
```

We only consider program P and *MDP* M for which the `construct-SMDP` algorithm terminates. The `construct-SMDP` satisfies the definition of an *SMDP*. The Markov property is preserved because of the full state representation. This *SMDP* is what the agent faces when executing P in M. Note that we do not discount by 1 when calling a temporally extended action (procedure) and the immediate reward is zero. Moreover, we discount by γ and receive the immediate reward of the underlying *MDP* when executing a primitive action so, the solution of the constructed *SMDP* defines an optimal policy that maximizes the expected discounted sum of rewards (with discount factor γ) received by the agent executing P in M. Note that the optimal policy in the *SMDP* can be sub-optimal in the underlying *MDP*.

Proposition 1 *The* `construct-SMDP` *algorithm terminates if the* MDP M *is finite and the* `next_list` *of all possible full state representation is finite.*

Proof: By definition of a procedure, A' is finite and if M is finite and the `next_list` is finite for all full state representation, there is only a finite number of possible full state representation so, after a finite number of the repeat loop, no more new state will be added to S'. □

Definition 1 *A procedure p is said to create* next_list *cycle if and only if p can be reached by a temporally extended action of its rule or exception part.*

Proposition 2 *A sufficient condition to insure finite* `next_list` *is that there does not exist next_list cycle procedures.*

Proof: The `next_list` grows only when we choose in a procedure p a temporally extended action. If we do not have next_list cycle procedures, in the next part of p we cannot call a procedure already in `next_list` (else a temporally extended action of p has reached p) and because the program is composed of a finite number of procedures, the `next_list` cannot grow indefinitely. □

a) grid configuration b) exception states

Fig. 2. A wall is located between the agent and the cross.

a) grid configuration b) exception states

Fig. 3. Without propagation mechanism, the agent cannot escape of the dead-end.

2.5 Exception State and Propagation

We call direct exception state a state for which the exception condition is fulfilled. For example for the artificial problem and the program described in section 2.2, the state (main,(3,3),[],[]) (we represent the grid configuration only by the agent's position, see Figure 2 (a)) is said to be a direct exception state because the rule part prescribes to go in a wall and so the exception condition is fulfilled. We associate with a program and an underlying MDP a table $\mathcal{E}$ from full state representation to boolean. Let $s' = (p, s, l, n) \in \mathcal{S}'$. If $\mathcal{E}(s') = false$ then, in s', we only use the action of the rule part of procedure p. If $\mathcal{E}(s') = true$ then, in s', we only use the action of the exception part of procedure p. We call a state s for which $\mathcal{E}(s) = true$ an exception state. Initially all entries of this table are set to false. In the above exemple, when the agent, executing the program in the underlying MDP, encounters the state (main,(3,3),[],[]), we set $\mathcal{E}((\text{main},(3,3),[],[]))$ to true and now, in this state, the agent will rely only on the actions of the exception part.

After few iterations of the program we present in Figure 2 (b), in shaded cells, the exception states (a shaded cell with coordinates (x, y) as to be interpreted as a full state representation (main,(x,y),[],[]). In this case, it is sufficient to solve the task.

But this mechanism is very limited, for example, Figure 3 (a), the agent cannot escape of the dead-end because only states (main,$(6,4)$,[],[]), (main,$(6,5)$, [],[]) and (main,$(6,6)$,[],[]) of the induced SMDP will become exception states. We need a way to propagate this information back to the predecessor states. This way of propagating exception states is called the *propagation mechanism*.

Definition 2 *We say that $s_1 \to s_2 \to \cdots \to s_n$ is a rule part action path from s_1 to s_n in $\mathcal{M}'$ iff for all s_i where $1 \leq i < n$, there exists an action $a \in \mathcal{A}'_r(s_i)$ for which $\mathcal{T}'(s_i, a, s_{i+1}) > 0$.*

Definition 3 *We denote by $s \xrightarrow{a} s'$ that the action a has led to state s' starting from state s.*

We now define the property that must fulfill a propagation mechanism.

Definition 4 *Let s be a state of the induced SMDP where $\mathcal{E}(s) = false$. If for each action a of $\mathcal{A}'_r(s)$, there exists a rule part action path $s \xrightarrow{a} \cdots \to s_n$ where $\mathcal{E}(s_n) = true$ then, the propagation mechanism insures that after a finite number of time steps, $\mathcal{E}(s)$ will become true.*

For example, with any propagation mechanism, the program of the section 2.2, will now solve the dead-end example (see the properties section). An example of exception states with a propagation mechanism is given Figure 3 (b) for the dead-end example and after few iterations of the program.

Those propagation mechanisms can be designed by the user of our method but, we give here, a very simple and general propagation mechanism we will use in the result section. We call it the basic propagation mechanism:

Definition 5 *Let s_1 and s_2 be two states of $\mathcal{S}'$ where $\mathcal{E}(s_1) = false$ and $\mathcal{E}(s_2) = true$. If the agent makes a transition between s_1 and s_2 then, $\mathcal{E}(s_1)$ is set to true.*

The basic propagation mechanism fulfills the propagation mechanism property (note that the basic propagation propagates more than needed by the definition 4). Note that the basic propagation mechanism is cheap to compute, when executing an action a in s and ending up in state s', for example, we just have to look at the value of $\mathcal{E}(s')$ to know if we have to propagate. The size of the table $\mathcal{E}$ is always less than the size of the Q-table and each entry is just a boolean.

2.6 Learning

For a learning agent interacting with a Semi-Markov Descision Process, there exists a learning algorithm, called SMDP Q-learning which updates a state-action value function Q - which maps state-action pairs into real values (where actions can be primitive or temporally extended) - at every time period with the formula:

$$Q(s_t, a_t) \leftarrow Q(s_t, a_t) + \alpha(r_t + \beta_t \max_{a \in \mathcal{A}'(s_{t+1})} Q(s_{t+1}, a) - Q(s_t, a_t))$$

where a_t is the action (primitive or temporally extended) taken by the agent in s_t (a state of the $SMDP$), s_{t+1} is the new state after executing a_t in s_t, r_t is the reward and β_t the discount factor received by the agent and α is the learning rate. This learnt Q-function converges to the optimal Q-function under technical conditions similar to those for conventional Q-learning (see [5]).

3 Properties

We give in this section two properties of the *EBRL* method. We illustrate them with our artificial problem. We suppose in this section that every action gets executed in every state infinitely often.

Definition 6 *We say that $s_1 \to s_2 \to \cdots \to s_n$ is an exception part action path from s_1 to s_n in $\mathcal{M}'$ iff for all s_i, s_{i+1} where $1 \leq i < n$, there exists an action $a \in \mathcal{A}'_e(s_i)$ for which $\mathcal{T}'(s_i, a, s_{i+1}) > 0$.*

Definition 7 *For a procedure p, we note $\mathcal{S}'_p \subseteq \mathcal{S}'$ the set of states of the form (p, s, l, n).*

Definition 8 *For a procedure p, we note $\mathcal{B}_p \subseteq \mathcal{S}'_p$ the set of states of the form (p, s, l, n) for which there exists an exception part action path in $\mathcal{M}'$ leading to a state s' for which the termination condition of the procedure p is fulfilled.*

Theorem 1 *For a procedure p, if for each $s \in \mathcal{S}'_p$, for each action $a \in \mathcal{A}'_r(s)$, there exists a rule part action path $s \xrightarrow{a} \cdots \to s'$ leading to a state s' for which, either the termination condition of the procedure p is fulfilled or, s' is a direct exception state then, for each state of $\mathcal{B}_p$, the agent executing the procedure p can reach a state in $\mathcal{S}'_p$ for which the terminal condition of the procedure p is fulfilled.*

Proof:

a) For all $s \in \mathcal{S}'_p$, by hypothesis,
- Either there exists, for an action $a \in \mathcal{A}'_r(s)$, a rule part action path $s \xrightarrow{a} \cdots \to s'$ for which s' fulfills the termination condition of p. As $\mathcal{A}'_r(s) \subseteq \mathcal{A}'_e(s)$ using either set of actions ($\mathcal{A}'_r(s)$ or $\mathcal{A}'_e(s)$), depending of the value of $\mathcal{E}(s)$) we can reach the terminal condition of p.
- Or, for all $a \in \mathcal{A}'_r(s)$ there exists a rule part action path $s \xrightarrow{a} \cdots \to s'$ for which $\mathcal{E}(s') = true$ and so, by definition of the propagation mechanism, $\mathcal{E}(s)$ will become true after a finite number of iterations.

b) Let $s_1 \in \mathcal{B}_p$ then, by definition, there exists an exception part action path $s_1 \to s_2 \to \cdots \to s_n$ where s_n is a state for which the termination condition of the procedure p is fulfilled. For all s_i in this path where $1 \leq i < n$, If $\mathcal{E}(s_i) = false$ then by a), the agent can reach a state s' from s_i for which the terminal condition of the procedure p is fulfilled or $\mathcal{E}(s_i)$ will become true after a finite number of time steps. But, if $\mathcal{E}(s_i) = true$ then, there exists an exception part action which leads to s_{i+1}. □

For example we can prove with this theorem that the program defined in section 2.2, with a propagation mechanism, will get the agent to the cross, if it is possible to go to it in the underlying *MDP* using all the primitive actions. This is true even if the actions are stochastics ($p\%$ of the time, the action is executed correctly and $(1-p)\%$ of the time a randomly chosen action is executed instead).

A New Way to Introduce Knowledge into Reinforcement Learning   165

Definition 9 *We note $\mathcal{E}(\mathcal{M}')$ the SMDP obtained from $\mathcal{M}'$ in which for each state $s \in \mathcal{S}'$ if $\mathcal{E}(s) = true$, we only use the actions of $\mathcal{A}'_e(s)$ else, we only use the actions of $\mathcal{A}'_r(s)$.*

Proposition 3 *After a finite number of time steps, $\mathcal{E}$ does not change anymore. We then note the $\mathcal{E}$ table by $\mathcal{E}_f$.*

Proof: The table $\mathcal{E}$ has a finite number of entries and for a state s for which $\mathcal{E}(s) = false$ by the definition of the direct exception states and the propagation mechanism, either $\mathcal{E}(s)$ remains $false$ or after a finite number of time steps $\mathcal{E}(s)$ becomes $true$. □

Theorem 2 *SMDP Q-learning, applied to an agent executing $\mathcal{P}$ in $\mathcal{M}$ with exception table $\mathcal{E}$, will converge to the optimal policy in $\mathcal{E}_f$(construct-SMDP$(\mathcal{M}, \mathcal{P}, \gamma)$) w.p.1. if $\sum \alpha = \infty$ and $\sum \alpha^2 < \infty$.*

Proof: $\mathcal{E}_f$(construct-SMDP$(\mathcal{M}, \mathcal{P}, \gamma)$) is a finite $SMDP$ fulfilling the preconditions of the theorem 2 of Parr, R. [5]. □

This theorem tells us that we will obtain the best policy in the $SMDP$ obtained by the agent executing the program in the underlying MDP. This policy could be non optimal in the underlying MDP. Note that we can increase the search space and possibly the quality of the solution by relaxing the constraints in the states for which $\mathcal{E}(s) = false$. In doing so, for the problem of section 2.2 and for the problem of the following section, we are guaranteed to find the optimal solution in the underlying MDP.

4 Example

We will use a task very similar to the Sokoban game to illustrate our method because of its complexity.

We put an agent (who can move in 8 directions: north, north-east, east, ...) in a grid. A ball, a goal and walls are placed in the grid. The aim of the agent is to push the ball into the goal (see Figure 5 (a), where the agent, the ball, the goal and the walls are represented by a triangle, a filled circle, a cross and filled cells respectively). We assume the agent knows the ball and goal location. As the agent can only push the ball but not pull it, there are many situations in which the ball can become stuck or can have a limited set of cells in which it can be moved. The actions are stochastics: 90% of the time the action is executed correctly and 10% of the time another randomly chosen action is executed.

4.1 Task Program

We write in our formalism a program to help the agent solve a given grid configuration, this program is described in Figure 4.

The program is broken-down into two sub-tasks: firstly, go to the ball and secondly push the ball to the goal location. The {go to ball actions} set of the

```
main(state) ⟶
termination : the ball is in the goal location
rule        : Go_to_ball()
next        : Go_to_goal()

go_to_ball(state) ⟶
termination : the agent is next to the ball
rule        : {go to ball actions}
exception   : (all the actions in {go to ball actions} prescribe
              to go into a wall,{all the primitive actions})
next        : go_to_ball()

go_to_goal(state) ⟶
termination : the ball is in the goal location
rule        : if the agent is next to the ball then
              {go to goal actions} else go_to_ball()
exception   : (all the actions in {go to goal actions} prescribe
              to push the ball in a wall or the cell where the
              agent has to go to push the ball in this
              direction is a wall,
              {push_north([ball_location]),
              push_north_east([ball_location]), ...})
next        : go_to_goal()

push_north(state,[last_ball_location]) ⟶
termination : ball has been pushed
rule        : let (x,y) the cell to go, to push to
              the north.
              if can go to (x,y) then
              go_to([last_ball_location;x;y]) else
              learn_to_go_to([x;y])
next        : push([last_ball_location])

go_to(state,[last_ball_location;x;y]) ⟶
termination : ball has been pushed or agent on (x,y)
rule        : {go to actions}
next        : go_to([last_ball_location;x;y])

learn_to_go_to(state,[last_ball_location;x;y]) ⟶
termination : ball has been pushed or agent on (x,y)
rule        : {learn to go to actions}
exception   : (all the actions in {learn to go to actions}
              prescribe to go into a wall,
              {all the primitive actions})
next        : learn_to_go_to([last_ball_location;x;y])
```

Fig. 4. Program to help the agent to solve the task, see the text for details about the rule parts.

`go_to_ball` procedure is the set of actions which make the agent get closer to the ball without taking the walls into account (there is between one and three such actions for a given state). The {go to goal actions} set of the `go_to_goal` procedure is the set of procedures amongst `push_north`, `push_north_east`, ... which would make the ball get closer to the goal if there are no walls (there is between one and three such procedures). Note that in the rule part of the `go_to_goal` procedure, we test if the agent is next to the ball, this is because the actions could be stochastics. We only write the code for `push_north` because `push_north_east`, ..., are similar. In `push_north`, we test if we can go to the (x,y) cell. We just look at the 8 cells around the ball and test if there is a path using only those 8 cells; the {go to actions} set contains the action to take to go to (x,y) using those 8 cells when there is a path using only those 8 cells. The {learn to go to actions} set of the `learn_to_go_to` procedure is the set of actions which make the agent get closer to the ball without taking the walls into account. The **push** procedure terminates if the agent is not next to the ball and else pushes the ball. We can notice that the program gives explicitly only a very high level knowledge. It does not know how to avoid obstacles.

5 Results

In this section, we test our method on the grid configuration, presented in Figure 5 (a), which is quite difficult for the *a priori* knowledge given by the program. If we use the program without propagation mechanism, this task could not be solved. An epoch consists of 800 primitive actions, -0.01 reinforcement is given on each transition in the grid except when the ball is pushed into the goal location where a reinforcement of 10 is given. We use an ϵ-greedy policy of parameter 0.9, the discount factor γ is 0.999 and the learning rate α is 0.1. We plot two curves (Figure 5 (b)), one for the Q-learning algorithm and one for our method. Each 10 epochs we set the policy to the greedy one and plot the results which are averaged over ten runs and smoothed. The mean first time the greedy policy

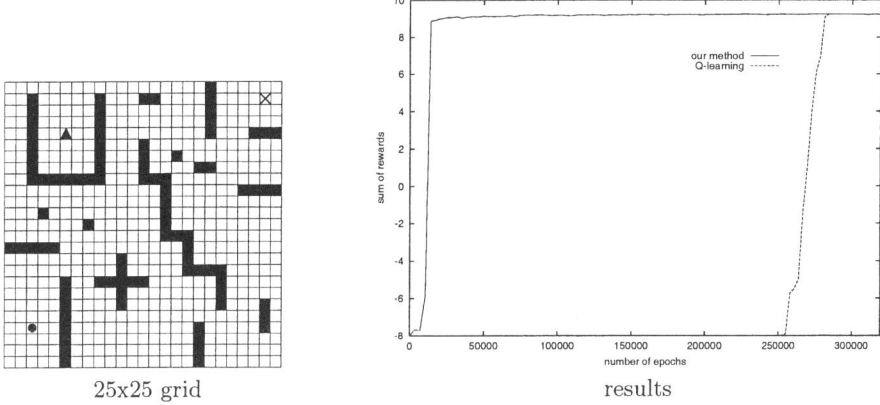

Fig. 5. Comparaison between Q-learning and our method.

solves the task is after 458 epochs with our method and after 248621 epochs for the Q-learning one. The number of states memorized at the end of this experimentation is 138214 for our method and 248948 for the Q-learning one. Note that the basic propagation is quite expansive in the number of memorized states but, explores a larger state space and so can find a better solution. Using various grid configurations, we noted that the learning time with our method depends more on the difficulty of the grid compare to the initial knowledge than on the state space size. Moreover, we also came to the conclusion that the larger the state space the better our method compared to Q-learning.

6 Conclusion

We have presented in this paper a method to introduce knowledge into reinforcement learning to speed-up learning using temporally extended actions. Our work can be related with the Parti-game algorithm of Moore [12] where a greedy controler helps the agent to reach a goal state. To deal with getting trapped, the Parti-game algorithm divides more and more thinly the state space to circumvent becoming trapped. Our method do not divide the state space, the resolution of the state space is given but the number of choices to be made in each state is variable. With variable resolution we can potentially store less states but note that if the *a priori* knowledge allows only one action in a given state, this state does not have to be stored (no choice has to be made in this state). We can formulate in our method that more than one action seems good *a priori* and so test different potentially good paths to the goal before increasing the search space. Moreover, we do not assume that the dynamic of the environment is deterministic, we can learn arbitrary reward functions and we do not need to learn a greedy controler. One of the main drawback of constraining the number of available actions is that it can be difficult to guarantee that with this *a priori* knowledge the agent can still solve the task. In this paper, we formulate and prove a theorem which can be used to guarantee that a given task can still be solved with our method. We tested our method on a complex grid-world task and showed that the learning time is drastically reduced compared to Q-learning. We currently test our method in a continuous state space.

References

1. Sutton, R.S. & Barto, A.G. (1998). *Introduction to Reinforcement Learning.* MIT Press/Bradford Books.
2. Singh, S.P., Jaakkola, T. & Jordan, M.I. (1995). *Reinforcement Learning with Soft State Aggregation* (pp. 361–368). NIPS 7. The MIT Press.
3. Tsitsiklis, J.N & Van Roy, B. (1997). *An analysis of temporal-difference learning with function approximation* (42(5):674–690). IEEE Transactions on Automatic Control.
4. Sutton, R.S., Precup, D. & Singh, S. (1999). *Between MDPs and Semi-MDPs: A Framework for Temporal Abstraction in Reinforcement Learning* (112:181-211). Artificial Intelligence.
5. Parr, R. (1998). *Hierarchical control and learning for Markov decision processes.* PhD thesis, University of California, Berkeley, California.
6. Dietterich, T.G. (2000). *An Overview of MAXQ Hierarchical Reinforcement Learning* (pp. 26–44). SARA.
7. Randlov, J. (1999). *Learning Macro-Actions in Reinforcement Learning.* NIPS 11, MIT Press.
8. Stone, P. & Sutton, R.S. (2001). *Scaling Reinforcement Learning Toward RoboCup Soccer.* Proceedings of the 18th International Conference on Machine Learning.
9. Menache, I., Mannor, S. & Shimki, N. (2002). *Q-Cut - Dynamic Discovery of Subgoals in Reinforcement Learning* (pp. 295–306). European Conference on Machine Learning. LNAI 2430.
10. Watkins, C.J.C.H. (1989). *Learning from Delayed Rewards.* PhD Thesis. University of Cambridge, England.
11. Puterman, M.L. (1994). *Markov Decision Processes.* Wiley, New York.
12. Moore, A.W. & Atkeson, C.G. (1995). *The Parti-game Algorithm for Variable Resolution Reinforcement Learning in Multidimensional State-spaces.* Advances in Neural Information Processing Systems.

Improvement of the State Merging Rule on Noisy Data in Probabilistic Grammatical Inference

Amaury Habrard, Marc Bernard, and Marc Sebban

EURISE – Université Jean Monnet de Saint-Etienne
23, rue du Dr Paul Michelon – 42023 Saint-Etienne cedex 2 – France
{amaury.habrard,marc.bernard,marc.sebban}@univ-st-etienne.fr

Abstract. In this paper we study the influence of noise in probabilistic grammatical inference. We paradoxically bring out the idea that specialized automata deal better with noisy data than more general ones. We propose then to replace the statistical test of the ALERGIA algorithm by a more restrictive merging rule based on a test of proportion comparison. We experimentally show that this way to proceed allows us to produce larger automata that better treat noisy data, according to two different performance criteria (perplexity and distance to the target model).

Keywords: probabilistic grammatical inference, noisy data, statistical approaches

1 Introduction

Nowadays the quantity of data stored in databases becomes more and more important. Beyond the fact that the amount of information is hard (in terms of complexity) to process by machine learning algorithms, these data often contain a high level of noise. To deal with this problem, many data reduction techniques aim at either removing irrelevant instances (prototype selection [1]) or deleting irrelevant features (feature selection [2]). These techniques always need positive examples and negative examples of the concept to learn. An outlier is seen as a positive (resp. negative) instance which should be negatively (resp. positively) labeled in absence of noise. However, in some real applications, it is difficult, even impossible, to have negative examples, that is for example the case in natural language processing. In such a context, learning algorithms exploit statistical information to infer a model allowing to define a probability distribution on positive data. Because of the absence of negative examples, standard data reduction techniques are not adapted for removing outliers, which require in fact specific processes. In the context of probabilistic models, an outlier can be seen as a weakly relevant instance, *i.e.* weakly probable because of noise. While such models are *a priori* known to be more efficient for dealing with noisy data, no study, as far as we know, has been devoted to analyze the impact of noise in the specific field of probabilistic grammatical inference.

Grammatical inference [3] is a subtopic of machine learning which aims at learning models from a set of sequences (or trees). Probabilistic grammatical inference allows to learn probabilistic automata defining a distribution on the language recognized by the automaton. In this framework, the data (always considered as positive) are supposed to be generated from a probability distribution, and the objective is to learn the automaton which generated the data. A successful learning task produces a probabilistic automaton which gives a good estimation of the initial distribution.

In this paper we are interested in probabilistic grammatical inference algorithms based on state merging techniques. In particular, we study the behavior of the ALERGIA algorithm [4, 5] in the context of noisy data. Our thought concerns the generalization process: we think that a generalization issued from the merging of noisy and correct data in the same state is particularly irrelevant. This can be dramatic, especially in cyclic automata, because this kind of generalization could increase the deviation from the initial distribution. Then we need to restrict the state merging rule for avoiding such situations. In ALERGIA, the generalization process consists in merging states that are considered statistically close according to a test based on the Hœffding bound [6]. However this bound is an asymptotic one and is then only relevant for large samples. To deal with small sets, [7] proposed a more general approach (called MALERGIA) using multinomial statistical tests in the merging decision. Despite its good performances with small dataset sizes, MALERGIA has a major disadvantage: a high complexity on very small datasets for which the calculation of a costly statistic is needed. In this paper we overcome both the ALERGIA and MALERGIA drawbacks. We replace the original test of ALERGIA by a more restrictive one based on a test of proportion comparison. This test can deal with both large and small datasets and we show experimentally that it better performs in the context of noisy data.

After a brief recall about probabilistic finite state automata and their learning algorithms, we describe in Section 2 the state merging rule of the algorithm ALERGIA and its extension with a multinomial approach in MALERGIA. In Section 3, we propose a new approach based on a test of proportion comparison. We theoretically prove that the bound of our test is always smaller than the Hœffding's one, expressing the fact that the merge will be always more difficult to be accepted in presence of noise. We also relate our work in comparison to the multinomial approach. Section 4 deals with experiments comparing the three approaches with different levels of noise.

2 Learning of Probabilistic Finite State Automata

Probabilistic Finite State Automata (PFSA) are a probabilistic extension of finite state automata and define a probability distribution on the strings recognized by the automata.

2.1 Definitions and Notations

Definition 1 *A PFSA A is a 6-tuple* $(Q, \Sigma, \delta, p, q_0, F)$. *Q is a finite set of states.* Σ *is the alphabet.* $\delta : Q \times \Sigma \to Q$ *is the transition function.* $p : Q \times \Sigma \to [0, 1]$ *is the probability of a transition.* q_0 *is the initial state.* $F : Q \to [0, 1]$ *is the probability for a state to be a final state.*

In this article, we only consider deterministic PFSA (called PDFA), *i.e.* where δ is injective. This means that given a state q and a symbol s, the state reached from the state q by the symbol s is unique if it exists. In order to define a probability distribution on Σ^* (the set of all strings built on Σ), p and F must satisfy the following consistency constraint: $\forall q \in Q, F(q) + \sum_{a \in \Sigma} p(q, a) = 1$.

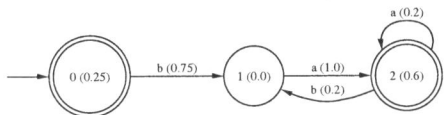

Fig. 1. A PDFA with $q_0 = 0$ and its probabilities

A string $s_0 \ldots s_{n-1}$ is recognized by an automaton A iff there exists a sequence of states $e_0 \ldots e_n$ such that: (i) $e_0 = q_0$, (ii) $\forall i \in [0, l-1], \delta(e_i, s_i) = e_{i+1}$, (iii) $F(e_n) \neq 0$. Then the automaton assigns to the string the following probability:

$$P_A(s_0 \ldots s_{n-1}) = \left(\Pi_{i=0}^{n-1} p(e_i, s_i)\right) * F(e_n)$$

For example the automaton represented in Figure 1 recognizes the string *baaa* with probability $0.75 \times 1.0 \times 0.2 \times 0.2 \times 0.6 = 0.018$.

2.2 Learning Algorithms

A lot of algorithms have been proposed to infer PDFA from examples [4, 5, 7–9]. Most of them follow the same scheme based on state merging and summarized in Algorithm 1. Given a set of positive examples S_+, the algorithm first builds the probabilistic prefix tree acceptor (PPTA). The PPTA is an automaton accepting all the examples of S_+ (see left part of Figure 2 for an example, λ corresponding to the empty string). It is constructed such that the states corresponding to common prefixes are merged and such that each state and each transition is associated with the number of times it is used while parsing the learning set. This number is then used to define the function p. If $C(q)$ is the number of times a state q is used while parsing S_+, and $C(q, a)$ is the number of times the transition (q, a) is used while parsing S_+, then $p(q, a) = \frac{C(q,a)}{C(q)}$. Similarly, if $C_f(q)$ is the number of times q is used as final state in S_+ for each state q, we have $F(q) = \frac{C_f(q)}{C(q)}$.

The second step of the algorithm consists in running through the *PPTA* (function *choose_states(A)*), and testing whether the considered states are statistically *compatible* (function *compatible*(q_i, q_j, α)). Several consecutive merging

Data: S_+ training examples (strings)
Result: A a PDFA
begin
$\quad A \leftarrow \text{build\_PPTA}(S_+);$
$\quad \textbf{while } (q_i, q_j) \leftarrow choose\_states(A) \textbf{ do}$
$\quad\quad \textbf{if } compatible(q_i, q_j, \alpha) \textbf{ then } merge(A, q_i, q_j);$
$\quad \textbf{end}$
$\quad \text{return } A;$
end

Algorithm 1. Generic algorithm for inferring PDFA

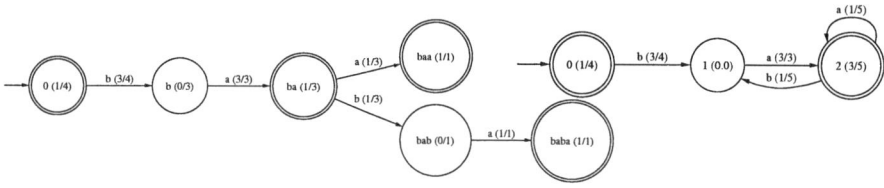

Fig. 2. PPTA of $S_+ = \{ba, baa, baba, \lambda\}$ on the left. On the right the PDFA obtained after two state mergings

operations are done in order to keep the automaton structurally deterministic. The algorithm stops when no more merging is possible. For example, the right part of Figure 2 represents the merging of the states labeled b and bab, and the merging of the three states labeled ba, baa, $baba$ from the PPTA on the left part of the figure.

2.3 Compatibility in the Algorithm ALERGIA

In ALERGIA [5], the compatibility of two states depends on: (i) the compatibility of their outgoing probabilities on the same letter, (ii) the compatibility of their probabilities to be final and (iii) the recursive compatibility of their successors.

Definition 2 *Two states q_1, q_2 are compatible iff: (i) $\forall a \in \Sigma \left| \frac{C(q1,a)}{C(q1)} - \frac{C(q2,a)}{C(q2)} \right|$ is not significantly higher than 0, (ii) $\left| \frac{C_f(q1)}{C(q1)} - \frac{C_f(q2)}{C(q2)} \right|$ is not significantly higher than 0, (iii) the two previous conditions are recursively satisfied for all the states reachable from $(q1, q2)$.*

The notion of significance is statistically assessed in ALERGIA. It consists in comparing the deviation between two proportions: $\left| \frac{x1}{n1} - \frac{x2}{n2} \right|$, where $n1 = C(q_1)$, $n2 = C(q_2)$, $x1$ equals either $C(q_1, a)$ or $C_f(q_1)$ and $x2$ either $C(q_2, a)$ or $C_f(q_2)$ ($a \in \Sigma$).

The test of compatibility is derived from the Hœffding bound [6]. This bound is used to define a probability on the estimation error of a Bernoulli variable p estimated by the quantity $\frac{x}{n}$, which is a frequency observed over n trials.

$$P\left(\left|p - \tfrac{x}{n}\right| < \left(\sqrt{\tfrac{1}{2}\ln\tfrac{2}{\alpha}}\right) * \tfrac{1}{\sqrt{n}}\right) > 1 - \alpha$$

Since ALERGIA takes into account two frequencies ($\tfrac{x1}{n1}$ and $\tfrac{x2}{n2}$), it must add two estimation errors that assesses, in a way, the worst possible case.

Definition 3 *Two proportions are compatible in* ALERGIA *iff:*

$$\left|\frac{x1}{n1} - \frac{x2}{n2}\right| < \sqrt{\frac{1}{2}\ln\frac{2}{\alpha}}\left(\frac{1}{\sqrt{n1}} + \frac{1}{\sqrt{n2}}\right) \quad (1)$$

Despite the fact that this upper-bound is statistically correct, we can note that by adding two estimation errors, the test tends to often accept a state merging. Consequently, the probability to wrongly accept a merging (risk of second type β) is under-estimated, that can have dramatic effects on the final automata, particularly in the presence of noise. Moreover, the asymptotic bound introduced in inequality (1) is only relevant for large samples. In order to overcome this drawback, Kermorvant and Dupont have proposed MALERGIA [7] for dealing with small datasets.

2.4 Compatibility in the Algorithm MALERGIA

In MALERGIA, each state of the automaton is associated with a multinomial distribution modeling the outgoing transition probabilities and the final probability. In other words, each state is associated with a multinomial random variable with parameters $\tau = \{\tau_1, \ldots, \tau_K\}$, each τ_i corresponding to the transition probability of the ith letter of the alphabet including a special final state symbol. In the PPTA each state is seen as a realization of the multinomial random variable τ (see [7] for more details). Two states are merged if they are both a realization of the same multinomial random variable. A statistical test following asymptotically a Khi-square distribution is used. When the constraints of approximation are not verified (*i.e.* for very small datasets), a Fisher exact test is used. However, in MALERGIA, this test requires the estimation of the probability of all contingency tables of size $2 \times K$ of the same marginal counts, that results in a very high complexity of the algorithm.

3 A New Compatibility Test Based on Proportions

In this section, we propose a new statistical approach overcoming the drawbacks of ALERGIA and MALERGIA and particularly relevant in presence of noise.

3.1 Statistical Framework

We use here a test of proportion comparison. It aims at comparing the proportions $\tfrac{x1}{n1}$ and $\tfrac{x2}{n2}$ (the same as those used in ALERGIA), estimators of the probabilities $p1$ and $p2$, and testing the hypothesis: $H_0 : p1 = p2$ versus $H_a : p1 \neq p2$. We compute the statistic:

$$Z = \frac{\frac{x1}{n1} - \frac{x2}{n2} - (p1 - p2)}{\sqrt{\hat{p}\hat{q}\frac{(n1+n2)}{n1n2}}} \quad \text{where } \hat{p} = 1 - \hat{q} = \frac{x1 + x2}{n1 + n2}$$

Z approximately follows the normal distribution when H_0 is true. We reject H_0 in favor of H_a whenever $|Z| > z_{\alpha/2}$ where $z_{\alpha/2}$ is the $(1 - \alpha/2)$-percentile of the normal distribution.

Then we consider that two proportions are not statistically different if:

$$\left| \frac{x1}{n1} - \frac{x2}{n2} \right| < z_{\frac{\alpha}{2}} * \sqrt{\hat{p}\hat{q}\frac{(n1+n2)}{n1*n2}}$$

Note that the constraints of approximation are satisfied when $n1 + n2 > 20$ or when $n1 + n2 > 40$ when either $x1$ or $x2$ is smaller than 5. When these conditions are not satisfied, we use a Fisher exact test, without the high calculation constraints of MALERGIA.

3.2 Theoretical Comparison

We have seen before that the risk β is under-estimated in ALERGIA. We prove now that our test results in a more restrictive merging rule.

Theorem 1 $\forall \alpha < 0.734, \forall 0 < \alpha' \leq 1$:

$$z_{\frac{\alpha}{2}} \sqrt{\hat{p}\hat{q}\frac{(n1+n2)}{n1*n2}} < \sqrt{\frac{1}{2}\ln(\frac{2}{\alpha'})} \left(\frac{1}{\sqrt{n1}} + \frac{1}{\sqrt{n2}} \right)$$

Proof. First we denote: $A = z_{\frac{\alpha}{2}} \sqrt{\hat{p}\hat{q}\frac{(n1+n2)}{n1*n2}}$ and $B = \sqrt{\frac{1}{2}\ln(\frac{2}{\alpha'})}(\frac{1}{\sqrt{n1}} + \frac{1}{\sqrt{n2}})$. Since $\hat{p} \leq 1$ and $\hat{q} \leq 1$ and so $\sqrt{\hat{p}\hat{q}} \leq 1$, then we can deduce that:

$$A < z_{\frac{\alpha}{2}} \sqrt{\frac{(n1+n2)}{n1*n2}} = z_{\frac{\alpha}{2}} \sqrt{\frac{1}{n2} + \frac{1}{n1}}$$

Then if we choose $\alpha < 0.734$, then the $(1 - \frac{\alpha}{2})$-percentile of the standard normal distribution is lower than 0.34, thus: $z_{\frac{\alpha}{2}} < 0.34 < \frac{1}{2}\ln(2) < \sqrt{\frac{1}{2}\ln(2)}$.

Moreover, for all $0 < \alpha' \leq 1$, $\ln(2) < \ln(\frac{2}{\alpha'})$, then

$$A \leq \sqrt{\frac{1}{2}\ln(\frac{2}{\alpha'})} \sqrt{(\frac{1}{n1} + \frac{1}{n2})}$$

and then since $\frac{1}{n2} + \frac{1}{n1} < \frac{1}{n1} + \frac{1}{n2} + \frac{2}{\sqrt{n1}\sqrt{n2}}$, for all $n1 > 0$ and $n2 > 0$, then $\sqrt{\frac{1}{n2} + \frac{1}{n1}} < \frac{1}{\sqrt{n1}} + \frac{1}{\sqrt{n2}}$ and we conclude that:

$$A \leq \sqrt{\frac{1}{2}\ln(\frac{2}{\alpha'})}(\frac{1}{\sqrt{n1}} + \frac{1}{\sqrt{n2}}) \qquad \square$$

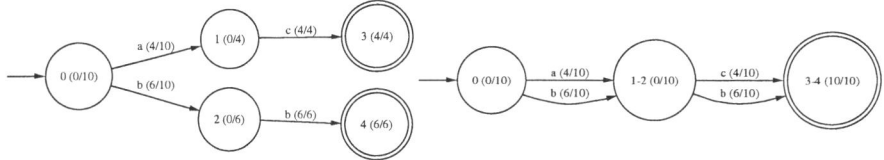

Fig. 3. Effect of a bad merging from a PPTA built with 4 strings ac and 6 strings bb

Assuming that we rarely build statistical tests with α higher than 0.5, the condition $\alpha < 0.734$ is not too constraining. The first direct consequence of this theorem is that our new merging rule is more restrictive, limiting the impact of potential noisy data. Secondly, such a rule tends to infer larger automata, both in the number of states and in the number of transitions. This situation can seem paradoxical. Actually, according to the theory of the learnable, and particularly in exact grammatical inference, too large automata tend to overfit the data resulting in a decrease of the generalization ability. This is true in exact grammatical inference, when we have both positive and negative examples, and when the goal consists in building a classifier which can predict, via a final state, the label of a new example. In this case, one must relax the merging constraint in the presence of noise, to allow a legitimate merging. Then we aim at inferring an automaton as small as possible to reduce the complexity of the model and then its VC-dimension. The problem seems to be different in probabilistic grammatical inference, where the inferred automaton is only able to provide a probability distribution. The error imputable to the automaton can come not only from an over-estimation but also from an under-estimation of the probability density. In this case, what is the consequence of a wrongly accepted merging due, for example, to the presence of noise? Figure 3 shows an explicit example. Before the merging, the probability of a string ac is $0.4 * 1 * 1 = 0.4$ and 0 for a string ab. Assume that a "bad" merging (of the states 1 and 2) is accepted, ac becomes under-estimated ($0.4 * 0.4 * 1 = 0.16$) and ab becomes more probable than ac ($0.4 * 0.6 * 1 = 0.24$). This example shows that, particularly in the presence of noise but also in noise-free situations, we must reduce the risk β, resulting in the rejection of some mergings, and then in the inference of larger automata.

Thus, we think that the use of a more specific and restrictive test is more relevant for dealing with noise. In MALERGIA, Kermorvant and Dupont empirically note that their merging rule is also more restrictive. However, we think that it is not sufficient. Actually in the multinomial approach, the frequencies of a noisy transition can be absorbed by the global aspect of the test. In our proportion-based test, the merging rule is applied on each transition allowing us to better detect differences between the two tested states. Our proportion test also works with small samples and thus has not the problem of the asymptotic Hœffding bound. For very small samples, a Fisher test is used. While, in the multinomial approach, the number of contingency tables to consider increases exponentially with the size of the alphabet (K), in our framework, we only consider tables of a constant size 2×2. We reduce then the complexity of the test.

4 Evaluation in the Context of Noisy Data

We compare, in this section, automata inferred with the test based on the Hœffding bound, those obtained with the multinomial approach and those obtained with the proportion-based test, in two types of situations. The first one deals with cases where the target automaton is *a priori* known. In this case we can measure the distance between the inferred automata and the target automaton. However we do not know always this one. In this case, we evaluate the merging rules in another series of experiments using a perplexity measure. This criterion assesses the relevance of the model on a test sample. In order to show the effectiveness of our approach, experiments were done on two types of data, strings and trees.

4.1 Evaluation Criteria

Distance from the target automaton: [10] defined distances between two hidden Markov models introducing the co-emission probability, that is the probability that two independent models generate the same string. The co-emission probability of two stochastic automata $M1$ and $M2$, is denoted $A(M1, M2)$ and defined as follows: $A(M1, M2) = \sum_{s \in \Sigma^*} P_{M1}(s) * P_{M2}(s)$. Where $P_{Mi}(s)$ is the probability of s given the model Mi. The co-emission probability allows us to define a distance D_a between two automata $M1$ et $M2$:

$$D_a(M1, M2) = \arccos\left(\frac{A(M1,M2)}{\sqrt{A(M1,M1)*A(M2,M2)}}\right)$$

$D_a(M1, M2)$ can be interpreted as the measure of the angle between two vectors representing the automata $M1, M2$ in a space where the base is the set of strings of Σ^*.

Perplexity measure: When the target automaton is not known, the quality of an inferred model M can be evaluated by the average likelihood on a set of strings S relatively to the distribution defined by M:

$$LL = \frac{1}{\|S\|} \sum_{j=1}^{|S|} \log P_M(s_j)$$

where $P_M(s_j)$ defines the probability of the jth string of S according to M. A perfect model can predict each element of the sample with a probability equal to one, and so $LL = 0$. In a general way we consider the perplexity of the test set which is defined by $PP = 2^{LL}$. A minimal perplexity ($PP = 1$) is reached when the model can predict each element of the test sample. Therefore we consider that a model is more predictive than another if its perplexity is lower.

4.2 Experimentations on Strings

Recall that our objective is to study the behavior of the three merging rules in the context of noisy data. To corrupt our training file, we replace a proportion γ (from 0.01 to 0.30) of letters of the training strings by a different letter randomly chosen in the alphabet. For each level of noise, we use several α parameters from

Base	Size	H	P	M	Sig
Reber D_a	3000	0.20 ± 0.153	0.16 ± 0.12	0.177± 0.13	yes
Reber P_e	3000	1.76± 0.14	1.74 ±0.13	1.75 ±0.13	yes
ATIS P_e	$\simeq 7000$	92.4± 11.58	62.7±6.25	64.4±9.49	yes
Agaricus + P_e	4208	2.23 ± 0.80	1.86±0.37	1.92±0.48	yes
Agaricus − P_e	3918	2.64±1.21	2.06±0.52	2.13±0.60	yes
Badges + P_e	210	24.6 ±2.51	22.3±2.19	20.0±2.95	yes
Badges − P_e	120	27.3±2.6	24.3±2.31	20.5±3.11	yes
Promoters + P_e	56	3.80±0.07	3.93±0.05	3.91±0.16	no for P vs M
Promoters − P_e	56	2.61±0.79	2.79±0.62	2.47±0.96	yes

Fig. 4. Results on databases of strings. Yes in the column **Sig** means that all the deviations between **H** and **P**, **H** and **M** and **P** and **M** are significant, otherwise we indicate which deviation is not significant

0.0001 to 0.1. The results presented in this section correspond for each approach to the optimal α, that is the one which provides the smaller evaluation measure. Since we use different levels of noise, the results are presented for each dataset by the mean ± the standard deviation. We test the significance of our results using a Student paired t-test with a first oder risk of 5%. In the presentation of our results, those concerning the Hœffding test end with **H**, those for the proportion one with **P**, and those for the multinomial approach end with **M**. We indicate results obtained with D_a for the distance and P_e for the perplexity. The column **Sig** indicates the significance of the results.

We use a first database for which the target automaton is *a priori* known. This one represents the Reber grammar [11]. When the target is unknown, we suppose to have a training set and a test set. Only the first one contains noisy data. We evaluate the perplexity measure on the test set. We use here eight databases: a sample generated from the Reber grammar; the ATIS database [12]; and three databases of the UCI repository [13]: Agaricus, Badges and Promoters. For these three bases, we consider positive and negative examples as two different concepts to learn. We use a 5-folds cross validation procedure for all the databases, except for the ATIS one which already contains a training and a test set, and for which we use different sizes of the training set (from 1000 to 13044).

The results of the experiments are synthesized on Figure 4. Globally, and independently on the complexity costs, which are highly in favor of our test, the merging rules based on our proportion test and on the multinomial test provide better results than ALERGIA, except for Promoters. This result can be explained by the relatively small size of the sample. Globally, the multinomial test works better than our approach on small datasets (Badges, Promoters), this fact confirms the original motivation of MALERGIA. However when the size of the training set grows, the proportion based-test is better (Reber, ATIS, Agaricus). Considering the level of noise, we noted that the results are highly in favor of our approach, particularly when the noise is higher than 8%. This behavior on the database Agaricus is shown on Figure 5. Note that the difference between the two approaches increases with the level of noise.

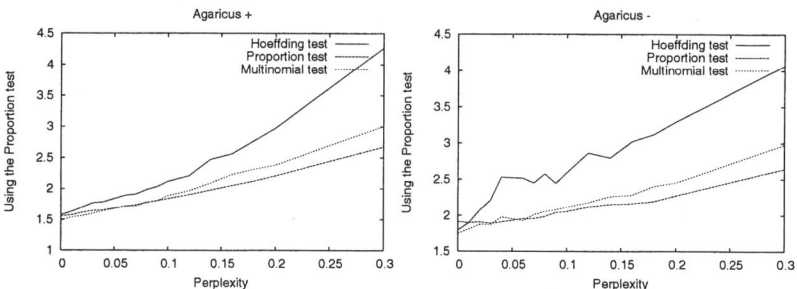

Fig. 5. Behavior of the merging rules on Agaricus *w.r.t.* different levels of noise

4.3 Experimentations on Trees

Since the interest about tree-structured data is increasing, notably because of their huge availability on the web, we also propose to evaluate our extension of ALERGIA to stochastic tree automata [14] (note that we consider bottom-up tree automata). The multinomial approach is not compared here because its adaption to bottom-up tree automata is not trivial.

Stochastic Tree Automata (STA): Tree automata [15] define a regular language on trees as a PDFA defines a regular language on strings. Stochastic tree automata are an extension of tree automata, defining a probability distribution on the tree language defined by the automaton. We use an extension of these automata taking into account the notion of type: stochastic many-sorted tree automata defined on a signature. We do not detail here these automata and their learning method. The interested reader can refer to [14,16]. We only precise that a learned stochastic tree automaton allows to define a probability distribution on trees recognized by the automaton. In the context of trees, we change a proportion γ of leaves in order to corrupt the learning set.

Experiments: We use three target grammars, one concerning stacks of objects, one on boolean expressions and another artificial dataset Art2. From each grammar we generate a sample of trees. We keep the same protocol as presented for experiments on strings. For cases where the target automaton is unknown, we use five datasets. We take a sample from each of the three previous tree grammars. Then we also use the database exploited for the PKDD'02 discovery challenge[1] (converted in trees as described in [17]). Finally, we treat the database **Student Loan** of the UCI repository, converting prolog facts in trees as describes in [18]. The results of the two series of experiments are presented on Figure 6. Experimentations on trees confirm the results observed on strings. Automata obtained using the proportion test are better with a lower standard deviation than those inferred with the test based on the Hœffding bound.

---

[1] http://lisp.vse.cz/challenge/ecmlpkdd2002/

Base	Size	D_a **H**	D_a **P**	Sig
Stacks D_a	3000	0.241 ± 0.164	0.225±0.17	yes
Art2 D_a	3000	0.555 ± 0.138	0.190±0.1	yes
Bool. D_a	5000	0.1 ± 0.049	0.096±0.046	yes
Stacks P_e	3000	1.85 ± 0.056	1.78±0.063	yes
Art2 P_e	3000	3.68 ± 0.45	3.21±0.21	yes
Bool. P_e	4000	2.60 ± 0.026	2.45±0.01	yes
PKDD'02 P_e	4178	6.90 ± 1.99	1.94 ±0.14	yes
Student Loan P_e	800	5.09± 1.48	2.88 ±0.26	yes

Fig. 6. Results for trees on the 8 databases

5 Conclusion

In this paper, we addressed the problem of dealing with noise in probabilistic grammatical inference. As far as we know, this problem has never been studied but seems very important because of the wide range of applications it is related to. Since the main objective in the probabilistic grammatical inference framework is to correctly estimate the probability distribution of the examples, we brought out the paradoxical fact that larger automata deal better with noise than more general (smaller) ones. We studied this behavior in the context of state merging algorithms and gave the intuitive idea that a bad merging, due to the presence of noise, could lead to a very bad estimation of the target distribution. Consequently we propose to use a restrictive statistical test during the inference process. Practically, we have proposed to replace the initial statistical test of the ALERGIA algorithm by a more restrictive one based on proportion comparison. We have proved its restrictiveness and shown its interest, in the context of noisy data both on artificial and real datasets.

While our approach deals better with noise, we have empirically noticed, in noise-free situations, that the results are quite similar with those of ALERGIA. We have also compared our test with the multinomial approach used in MALERGIA. Our proportion-based test is not only relevant, in terms of complexity and perplexity, on small and large datasets, but also provide better results for high level of noise.

We are currently working on theoretical aspects of our work. We aim at proving that the acceptance of a bad merging, especially in the context of noisy data, implies a larger deviation from the target distribution than its rejection.

Acknowledgements

The authors wish to thank Christopher Kermorvant for his help and for having allowed us to easily compare our work with MALERGIA. We also want to thank Thierry Murgue for his help and for his experience in the evaluation of PFSA.

References

1. Brodley, C., Friedl, M.: Identifying and eliminating mislabeled training instances. In: Thirteeth National Conference on Artificial Intelligence AAAI/IAAI, Vol. 1. (1996) 799–805
2. John, G., Kohavi, R., Pfleger, K.: Irrelevant features and the subset selection problem. In: 11th International Conference on Machine Learning. (1994) 121–129
3. Honavar, V., de la Higuera, C.: Introduction. Machine Learning Journal **44** (2001) 5–7
4. Carrasco, R., Oncina, J.: Learning stochastic regular grammars by means of a state merging method. In: Grammatical Inference and Applications, ICGI'94. Number 862 in LNAI, Springer Verlag (1994) 139–150
5. Carrasco, R., Oncina, J.: Learning deterministic regular grammars from stochastic samples in polynomial time. RAIRO (Theoretical Informatics and Applications) **33** (1999) 1–20
6. Hoeffding, W.: Probabilities inequalities for sums or bounded random variables. Journal of the American Association **58** (1963) 13–30
7. Kermorvant, C., Dupont, P.: Stochastic grammatical inference with multinomial tests. In: Proceedings of the Sixth International Colloquium on Grammatical Inference (ICGI). Volume 2484 of LNAI., Amsterdam, Springer (2002) 149–160
8. Ron, D., Singer, Y., Tishby, N.: On the learnability and usage of acyclic probabilistic automata. In: Computational Learning Theory, COLT'95. (1995) 31–40
9. Thollard, F., Dupont, P., de la Higuera, C.: Probabilistic dfa inference using kullback–leibler divergence and minimality. In Kauffman, M., ed.: Proceedings of the Seventeenth International Conference on Machine Learning. (2000) 975–982
10. Lyngsø, R., Pedersen, C., Nielsen, H.: Metrics and similarity measures for hidden Markov models. In: 7th International Conference on Intelligent Systems for Molecular Biology, ISMB '99 Proceedings, Heidelberg, Germany, AAAI Press, Menlo Park, CA94025, USA (1999) 178–186
11. Reber, A.: Implicit learning of artificial grammars. Journal of verbal learning and verbal behaviour **6** (1967) 855–863
12. Hirschman, L., Bates, M., Dahl, D., Fisher, W., Garofolo, J., Hunicke-Smith, K., Pallett, D., Pao, C., Price, P., Rudnicky, A.: Multi-site data collection for a spoken language corpus. In: Proc. DARPA Speech and Natural Language Workshop '92, Harriman, New York (1992) 7–14
13. Blake, C., Merz, C.: University of California Irvine repository of machine learning databases. http://www.ics.uci.edu/~mlearn/ (1998)
14. Habrard, A., Bernard, M., Jacquenet, F.: Generalized stochastic tree automata for multi-relational data mining. In: Proceedings of the Sixth International Colloquium on Grammatical Inference (ICGI). Volume 2484 of LNAI., Amsterdam, Springer (2002) 120–133
15. Comon, H., Dauchet, M., Gilleron, R., Jacquemard, F., Lugiez, D., Tison, S., Tommasi, M.: Tree Automata Techniques and Applications . Available on: http://www.grappa.univ-lille3.fr/tata (1997)
16. Carrasco, R., Oncina, J., Calera-Rubio, J.: Stochastic Inference of Regular Tree Languages. Machine Learning **44** (2001) 185–197
17. Habrard, A., Bernard, M., Jaquenet, F.: Mining probabilistic tree patterns in a medical database. Discovery Challenge of the 6th Conference PKDD'02 (2002)
18. Bernard, M., Habrard, A.: Learning stochastic logic programs. In Rouveirol, C., Sebag, M., eds.: Work-in-Progress Track at the 11th International Conference on Inductive Logic Programming. (2001) 19–26

COllective INtelligence with Sequences of Actions
Coordinating Actions in Multi-agent Systems

Pieter Jan 't Hoen and Sander M. Bohte

CWI, Centre for Mathematics and Computer Science
P.O. Box 94079, 1090 GB Amsterdam, The Netherlands
{hoen,sbohte}@cwi.nl

Abstract. The design of a Multi-Agent System (MAS) to perform well on a collective task is non-trivial. Straightforward application of learning in a MAS can lead to sub optimal solutions as agents compete or interfere. The COllective INtelligence (COIN) framework of Wolpert et al. proposes an engineering solution for MASs where agents learn to focus on actions which support a common task. As a case study, we investigate the performance of COIN for representative token retrieval problems found to be difficult for agents using classic Reinforcement Learning (RL). We further investigate several techniques from RL (model-based learning, Q(λ)) to scale application of the COIN framework. Lastly, the COIN framework is extended to improve performance for sequences of actions.

1 Introduction

As argued by Wellman [14, 15], a computational problem can be considered as a resource allocation problem. Borrowing from the insights of economics, it is however becoming increasingly clear that few concepts for resource allocation scale well with increasing complexity of the problem domain. In particular, centralized allocation planning can quickly reach a point where the design of satisfying solutions becomes complex and intractable. Conceptually, an attractive option is to devise a distributed system where different parts of the system each contribute to the solution for the problem. Embodied in a so-called distributed Multi-Agent System (MAS), the aim is thus to elicit "emergent" behavior from a collection of individual agents that each solve a part of the problem.

This emergent behavior relies implicitly on the notion that the usefulness of the system is expected to increase as the individual agents optimize their behavior. A weak point of such systems has however long been the typical bottom-up type of approach: researchers first build an intuitively reasonable system of agents and then use heuristics and tuned system parameters such that – hopefully – the desired type of behavior emerges from running the system. Only recently has there been work on more top-down type of approaches to establish the conditions for MASs such that they are most likely to exhibit good emergent behavior [1, 4, 2].

In typical problem settings, individual agents in the MAS contribute to some part of the collective through its private actions. The joint actions of all agents derive some reward from the outside world. To enable local learning, this reward has to be divided amongst the individual agents where each agent aims to increase its received reward by some form of learning. However, unless special care is taken as to how this reward is shared, there is a risk that agents in the collective work at cross-purposes. For example, agents can reach sub-optimal solutions by competing for scarce resources or by inefficient task distribution among the agents as they each only consider their own goals (e.g. a Tragedy of the Commons [3]).

The COllective INtelligence (COIN) framework, as introduced by Wolpert et al., suggests how to engineer (or *modify*) the rewards an agents receives for its actions (and to which it adapts to optimize) in *private utility functions*. Optimization of each agent's private utility here leads to increasingly effective emergent behavior of the collective, while discouraging agents from working at cross-purposes.

In particular, the work by Wolpert et al. explores the conditions sufficient for effective emergent behavior for a collective of independent agents, each employing "sufficiently powerful" Reinforcement Learning (RL) for optimizing their private utility. These conditions relate to (i) the learnability of the problem each agent faces, as obtained through each individual agent's private utility function, (ii) the relative "alignment" of the agents' private utility functions with the utility function of the collective (the *world utility*), and lastly (iii) the learnability of the problem. Whereas the latter factor depends on the considered problem, the first two in COIN are translated into conditions on how to shape the private utility functions of the agents such that the world utility is increased when the agents improve their private utility.

Wolpert et al. have derived private utility functions that perform well on the above first two conditions. The effectiveness of this top-down approach and their developed utilities are demonstrated by applying the COIN framework to a number of example problems: network routing [20], increasingly difficult versions of the Al Ferrol Bar problem [17], and Braess' paradox [11]. The COIN approach proved to be very effective for learning these problems in a distributed system. In particular, the systems exhibited excellent scaling properties. Compared to optimal solutions, it is observed that a system like COIN becomes relatively *better* as the problem is scaled up [17].

In recent work [10], the COIN framework has been applied to problems where different "single agent" RL algorithms are traditionally tested: grid-based world exploration games [10, 8]. In this problem-domain, agents move on a grid-like world where their aim is to collect tokens representing localized rewards as efficiently as possible (e.g. [8]). For a Multi-Agent System, the challenge is to find sequences of actions for each individual agent such that their *joint* sequences of actions optimize some predetermined utility of the collective. The main result of [10], in line with earlier work, is that the derived utility functions as advocated in the COIN framework significantly outperform standard solutions for using RL in collectives of agents.

We observe that in [10] the used RL algorithm, Q-learning, is the same as used in previous work on COIN. However, for learning sequences of actions with RL, there are substantially more powerful methods which we adapt for the COIN framework. We further report some modifications to these RL methods to address specific issues that arise in the COIN framework. We find that using these methods, our enhanced COIN approach yields more optimal exploration while converging more quickly.

We start from our replication efforts of the grid-world problem of [10]. We report an anomaly in that a collection of selfish, greedy agents proved to be performing similarly to the more elaborate and computationally intensive COIN approach. To find out whether this issue was isolated to the particular grid-world example chosen, we designed grid-worlds that require more coordination among the agents. We then found that in those cases COIN does provide significant improvements compared to simple, greedy agents.

This document is structured as follows. In Section 2, we describe the COIN framework. In Section 3 we report on our reproduction of [10]. In Section 4 we present problems that require more coordinated joint actions of a MAS. We also introduce an extension for COIN for sequences of actions. In Section 5, we adapt a number of more advanced RL methods for learning sequences of actions to the COIN framework, and report on the performance improvements. In Section 6 we discuss future work and conclude.

2 Background: COllective INtelligence

In this Section, we briefly outline the theory of COIN as developed by Wolpert et al. More elaborate details can be found in [21, 17, 18]. Broadly speaking, COIN defines the conditions that an agent's private utility function has to meet to increase the probability that learning to optimize this function leads to increased performance of the collective of agents. Thus, the challenge is to define a suitable private utility function for the individual agents, given the performance of the collective.

Formally, let ζ be the joint moves of all agents. A function $G(\zeta)$ provides the utility of the collective system, the *world utility*, for a given ζ. The goal is to find a ζ that maximizes $G(\zeta)$. Each individual agent η has a private utility function g_η that relates the reward obtained by the collective to the reward that the individual agent collects. Each agent will act such as to improve its own *payoff*. The challenge of designing the collective system is to find private utility functions such that when individual agents optimize their payoff, this leads to increasing world utility G, while the private function of each agent is at the same time also easily learnable (i.e. has a high *signal-to-noise* ratio, an issue usually not considered in traditional mechanism design).

Following a mathematical description of this issue, Wolpert et al. propose the **Wonderful Life Utility** (WLU) as a private utility function that is both *learnable* and *aligned* with G, and that can also be easily calculated. In a collective system consisting of multiple agents collectively collecting rewards (tokens) on a grid, as discussed in more detail in Section 3, the WLU for one agent η at time t with respect to the collective is ([10]):

$$WLT^0_{\eta,t}(\zeta) = GR_t(\zeta) - (T(L_{\hat{\eta},<t+1},\Theta) - T(L_{\hat{\eta},<t},\Theta)) \qquad (1)$$

where:

- ζ is the joint moves of all the agents.
- L is the location matrix of the agents over time. And
  - L_η is the location of agent η for all the time steps.
  - $L_{\eta,t}$ is the location of agent η at time step t.
  - $L_{\eta,<t}$ are the locations of agent η at earlier time steps.
  - $L_{\hat{\eta}}$ are the location of agents other than η.
- $T(L,\theta)$ returns the value of the tokens received from the location matrix[1].
  - θ is the location of the initial tokens.
  - $T(L,\theta) = \sum_{x,y} \theta_{x,y} min(1, L_{x,y})$, i.e. the tokens picked up are the visited tokens, but no more than once.
- $GR_t(\zeta) = T(L_{<t+1},\theta) - T(L_{<t},\theta)$, i.e. the value of all the tokens picked up at time step t.

Hence $WLT^0_{\eta,t}(\zeta)$ for agent η at time step t is equal to the value of all the tokens picked up by all the agents for that step minus the value of the tokens picked up by the other agents $\hat{\eta}$ at time step t. If agent η picks up a token τ at time step t, which is not picked up by the other agents, then η receives a reward of $T(\tau)$. If this token is however picked up by any of the other agents at time step t, then the first term GR_t of Equation 1 is unchanged while the second term drops with the value of τ. Agent η then receives a penalty $-T(\tau)$ for competing for a token targetted by one of the other agents $\hat{\eta}$.

Compared to the WLU function, other payoff functions have been considered in the literature for distributed Multi-Agent Systems: the Team Game utility function (TG), where the world-utility is equally divided over all participating agents, or the Selfish Utility (SU), where each agent only considers the reward that it itself collects through its actions. These two common alternatives are extreme examples. The TG utility can suffer from poor learnability, as for larger collectives it becomes very difficult for each agent to discern what contribution is made (low signal-to-noise ration), and the SU suffers from – potentially – poor alignment with the world-utility. The superiority of the use of private WLU functions with local reinforcement learning has been shown for a variety of problems [19, 17, 11]. In the terminology of the COIN framework, the WLU is *factored* and *aligned* with the world utility. The Aristocratic Utility (AU) is not treated in this work as [10] observes comparable performance for the AU and WLU while the former is significantly more difficult to implement.

---

[1] [10] uses V instead of T, which we use to not confuse the issue with the V as the valuation function in Q learning.

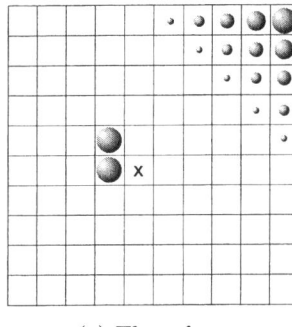

```
for(int x=0; x < n; x=x+1)
  for(int y=0; y < n; y=y+1) {
    tokens[x][y] = 1.2*(x+y-n)/(1.0*n);
    if(tokens[x][y] < 0.4)
      tokens[x][y] = 0; }
tokens[n/2][(n/2)-1] = 1.0;
tokens[(n/2)+1][(n/2)-1] = 1.0;
```

(a) The tokens   (b) The algorithm

Fig. 1. The original problem of [10]

We compute the WLU for an agent η by first letting all agents except η, i.e. $\hat{\eta}$, make their moves and only then moving η. For N moves, the agents $\hat{\eta}$ generate grids $grid_0$ to $grid_{N-1}$ where $grid_t$ documents the tokens picked up by agents $\hat{\eta}$ at time step t and the rewards which can be experienced by η for its moves. The agents $\hat{\eta}$ start from grid $grid_0$ filled with the initial tokens and with all grids $grid_{t>0}$ initially empty. At time t, agents $\hat{\eta}$ pick up tokens from $grid_t$ at their current locations. A penalty (that is: the negative of the value of the token) is then substituted for this token in $grid_t$. The grid $grid_{t+1}$ is then filled with (a copy of) the remaining tokens of $grid_t$ prior to the moves of agents $\hat{\eta}$ at timestep $t+1$. Agent η then starts at the modified grid $grid_0$ after the moves of the agents $\hat{\eta}$ are completed. Note that a token picked up by η at timestep t is removed from $grid_{t>}$; a token can only be picked up once.

3 Learning Joint Sequences of Actions

In this Section we present our findings when reproducing [10], with additional details from [6]. Agents in [10] jointly have to learn to explore a grid and efficiently retrieve the available tokens. The agents in one step move either up, down, right, or left. The order of movement for each of the agents is identical in each turn. The tokens on the grid are as defined in Algorithm 1 for a $n \times n$ grid where we consider the case from [10] where $n = 10$. A cluster of tokens increasing in value towards the edge of the grid is formed in a corner of the grid. Two extra tokens of value 1 are then added close to the center of the grid. This gives the grid of Figure 1(a) where **x** marks the initial location of the agents at $[n/2, n/2]$.

Each individual agent uses Q-learning [8] as its RL algorithm. A learner's input space consists of the location of the agent in the grid and the action space consists the four directions in which the agent can move. The policy π of an agent in [10] is stochastic according to a softmax function; in the policy, a random action a_i is chosen for state s and constant c (set at 50) with normalized chance in $[0,1]$ of $\frac{c^{Q(s,a_i)}}{\sum_j c^{Q(s,a_j)}}$. The discount factor γ is set to 0.95. The learning rate α_t at time step t for a state s is taken as $\alpha_t = \frac{1}{1+0.0002*visits(s)}$, where

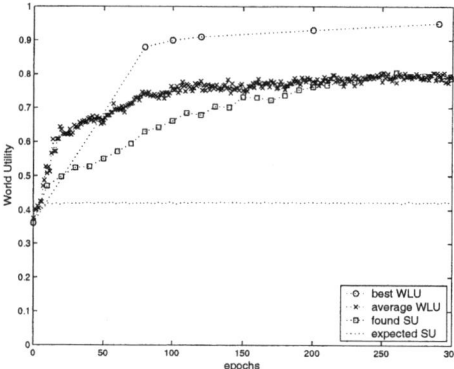

Fig. 2. Reproduced results

$visits(s)$ is the number of times the state s has been visited during a learning step ([6]). The decreasing value of α serves to induce agents to initially explore, and then gradually fine-tune their behavior to maximize their utility as α drops.

In Figure 2 we present the learning curves for the problem setting [10]. With the dynamic α of [10] we reproduced the low utility for the SU of ≈ 0.4. However, we found that for a fixed α of 0.1 using the SU, the MAS achieved a fitness of ≈ 0.8 in 300 epochs. For a small α, the selfish agents are able to focus gradually on collecting the tokens even though they directly compete. The large concentration of tokens in the corner of the grid acts as an attractor for these agents. In the further experiments we present results for a default value of α of 0.1 due to generally poor results for a dynamic α [2]. In Figure 2, we also show the results which correspond to findings in [10] for the WLU in a typical best case. Poorer solutions were however found when averaging over 100 runs.

Our finding suggests that the problem considered in [10] is not as well suited to present the additional distributed coordination capabilities of the COIN framework as was claimed. We therefore study more general token schemes where coordination of the joint actions is a prerequisite for high performance. In the further experiments we also each step randomize the order of movement for the agents to better simulate a realistic MAS.

4 Coordinated Grid-World Problems

Given the good performance of the SU in Section 3, we designed a number of token-retrieval problems that in particular play to the weaknesses of selfish

---

[2] This generally poor performance can be caused by the slow drop in the value of α with the number of visits to a state resulting in a high α for initial epochs which will cause a system to react strongly to rewards (α drops to 0.2, 0.1 and to 0.05 for respectively 20,000, 45,000 and 95,000 visits). Thus, a dynamic α allows for easy propagation of reward over regions with little feedback in reinforcement signal, but can also lead to strong fluctuations in behavior not suitable for difficult scenarios where delicate tuning of behavior is required.

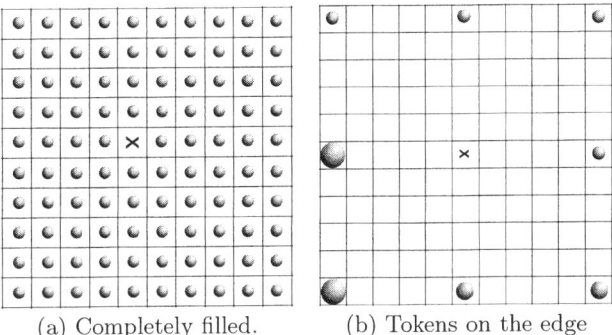

(a) Completely filled.　　(b) Tokens on the edge

Fig. 3. The two new grids

agents or have a low signal-to-noise ratio for learning. For both problems, a reasonable utility is achieved for a wide selection of parameters using the selfish utility or the team game, but the challenge is in achieving near to optimal performance. We present two interesting examples in Figures 3(a) and 3(b), where x marks the start locations of the agents.

In the problem of Figure 3(a), the whole grid (of size 10×10) is filled with tokens of value 1, except for the initial location of the agents. Each agent is allowed 10 moves. Thus, the agents have to disperse in order to maximize the number of visited nodes on the grid. The world utility is defined as the maximum number of tokens the agents can collectively pick up in their moves. Such a grid is representative of a situation where agents have little prior information of the world and have to devise a strategy for maximum exploration. This problem is difficult to solve due to the low signal-to-noise ratio with uniform reward for all visited locations. We increase the action-space by allowing the agents to move diagonally in order for them to better be able to disperse from their clustered initial position.

For the problem of Figure 3(b), differently valued tokens are placed on the edge of a 11×11 grid and agents take five steps. Diagonal moves are also possible. The agents are hence able to pick up all tokens if they cooperate perfectly by each focusing on a distinct token. This problem is representative of a complex set of tasks which must all be completed by one of the agents, but the different tasks have varying priorities. A solution is difficult to learn as agents may focus exclusively on the high priority tokens and neglect to collect the cheap tokens needed for high performance.

In the first coordination problem with eight agents, selfish agents using SU achieve a utility of close to 0.8 (Figure 4(a)). With a dynamic (high) α of Section 3, a high fitness is quickly reached but a higher eventual fitness is reached using a fixed α of 0.1. An absolute higher fitness was not found for a wide study of parameters. This problem is hence relatively simple for the SU to solve partially, but the challenge is in achieving (near to) full utility. The Team Game Utility (TG) achieved a comparable performance, but likewise suffers from a low signal-to-noise-ratio and is not able to improve performance beyond the presented level.

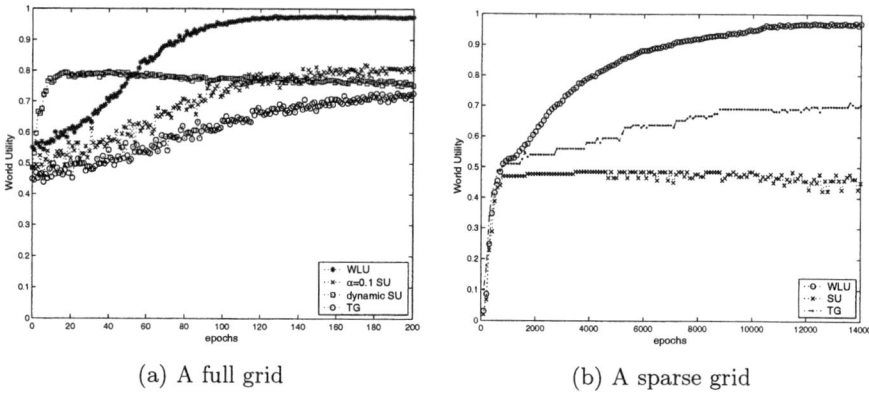

(a) A full grid   (b) A sparse grid

Fig. 4. Two new problems

Agents using the WLU showed slightly better performance with a final utility of 0.82. This low result was found to be caused by loops in the paths of the individual agents promoted by the COIN framework. Due to the softmax function for choice of action of Section 3, an agent is averse to actions with negative Q values. An agent η hence quickly learns to avoid penalties imposed by other agents $\hat{\eta}$. Agent η then tends to find a good partial path and revisit it as a 0 immediate reward[3] for an action is superior to receiving a penalty.

To alleviate this problem, we give an agent η a penalty for revisiting a state s which has been visited at an earlier time step in the same epoch. When agent η visits grid $grid_t$ during computation of the WLU as defined in Section 2, then instead of a token τ picked up being removed from grids $grid_{t>}$, a penalty $(-T(\tau))$ is set on these grids $grid_{t>}$ [4]. With this approach, an agent learns not to revisit an earlier part of its travels as this also results in a penalty. For the grid of Section 3(a), in Figure 4(a), the improved high performance with use of a penalty for revisiting states is given. In the rest of the paper, the agents using the WLU likewise pay a penalty for revisiting an earlier state as otherwise the performance of the COIN framework was found to be significantly lower.

In the second problem of Figure 3(b) agents using the Selfish Utility function are attracted to the high token values, making the collective perform poorly. As can be seen in Figure 4(b), a maximum fitness of close to 0.5 is temporarily achieved as the agents explore in search of good tokens. With increasing competition for the high value tokens, the positive reinforcement signal for these targets decreases and the agents become indecisive. For the TG, a maximum fitness (even after 50,000 epochs) of ≈ 0.7 is slowly reached as the agents are unable to effectively target a token due to the low signal-to-noise ratio. However, when using the WLU with a penalty for revisiting states, the agents are able to learn to pick up all the tokens (Figure 4(b)). A fitness of 0.5 is quickly reached and

---

[3] All tokens on this earlier part of the path have been retrieved.
[4] The penalty for revisiting a state may have to increase as the grid becomes more crowded and the agent needs an incentive to explore beyond an earlier successful route and across the negative penalties deposited by neighboring agents.

after an agent has chosen or won a token, the WLU issues sufficiently consistent penalties to convince the competing agents to look elsewhere on the grid.

Summarizing, in this section we have shown how the extended COIN framework outperforms the SU and TG for two illustrative problems. Agents in the COIN approach through the WLU are able to solve a general distribution problem where they overcome the low signal-to-noise ratio which limits the performance of the SU and TG. The agents using the WLU are also able to solve a difficult collaborative task where high priorities for a selection of task attracts naive learners at the expense of other tasks.

5 Scaling COIN

The RL algorithm used in [10] is plain Q-learning. Effectively, the update of the value-function after a move only considers the immediate reward and a valuation of the next state. It is well known that for agents optimizing grid-like world-exploration problems or learning sequences of actions, more effective RL algorithms have been developed (that take into account the expected future rewards of a sequence of moves). Wolpert et al. based their COIN framework on the presumption of individual agents using "sufficiently powerful" RL algorithms. In this Section, we explore several possibilities for using more powerful RL algorithms.

5.1 Enhanced RL Techniques

Watkins Q(λ): First, we applied Watkins' Q(λ) Learning [12, 8] in a COIN setting. Q(λ) learning has been reported to substantially improve on the results for learning for single agent applications. Through the use of eligibility traces [12, 8], a single agent can more efficiently propagate its experienced reinforcement signals through its Q-values. In the COIN framework, the propagation of a penalty produced by an agent η is expected to also more efficiently be propagated using Q(λ) over the paths of agents that interfere with the activities of η.

Within the WLU framework, we can devise an alternative to Q(λ) in the form of **Temporal Propagation of Penalties.** Temporal Penalty (TP) propagation works as follows: in the WLU, a penalty is incurred by the learner if it picks up a token at the same time step as one of the baseline agents would. Recall that the reward at time step t for agent η in Section 2 is defined as $WLT^0_{\eta,t}(\zeta)$. The reward (or penalty) for agent η is determined in an interwoven fashion with the moves made by the other agents in the *same* time step. A consequence of this definition is that an agent η is not penalized if it picks up a token at time t which one of the other agents $\hat{\eta}$ is *planning* to pick up at a later time step $t_n > t$. We can however *temporally propagate* a penalty for snatching any token by η from the other agents $\hat{\eta}$: let $S(L, \Theta)$ be the set of tokens picked up during movement. Then for $S_{\hat{\eta}} = S(L_{\hat{\eta}}, \Theta)$, our modified reward for agent η at time step t of $TPWLT^0_{\eta,t}(\zeta)$ is defined as:

$$GR_{\hat{\eta},t}(\zeta) + T(S(L_{\eta,t}, \Theta) \setminus S_{\hat{\eta}}) - T(S(L_{\eta,t}, \Theta) \cap S_{\hat{\eta}}). \tag{2}$$

The above modified utility function induces an agent η to consider all future actions of the other agents $\hat{\eta}$, and not just those that coincide for specific time steps. This can support a stronger cooperation between the agents.

Additionally, convergence of learning for an agent η can possibly be enhanced through multiple epochs of learning relative to the other agents $\hat{\eta}$ not only once, as defined in Section 2, but multiple times within one epoch: **Model Based Planning**. The potential expensive calculation of $WLT_{\eta,t}^0(\zeta)$ of Section 2 for each agent η is used several times by η to learn how to optimally behave relative to the other agents. Agent η traverses (copies of) the grids $grid_0$ to $grid_t$ not once, but n times during learning in one epoch. In [13], a similar model-based approach is used where agents learn according to a generalized DYNA-Q [8] architecture by interleaving of planning according to a learned world model and acting based on this model.

5.2 Results

As a case study for these more powerful RL algorithms within a COIN framework, we used the joint coordinated exploration problem of Figure 3(b). The tokens on the grid are however placed a distance of one from the edge, making the problem more illustrative by giving more opportunity for (discounted) feedback from the received rewards (as there are more successful paths for an agent to pick up a token from its initial position).

As shown in Figure 5(a), $Q(\lambda)$ aids the WLU in finding a solution to the problem. Convergence speed is improved significantly and full utility is reached. We found near identical performance gain relative to $Q(\lambda)$ for **Temporal Propagation of Penalties**. This similar gain is hypothesized to have roots in similar propagation of rewards. For $Q(\lambda)$, discounted penalties are carried over to bordering states in a traveled path, whereas for the temporal penalty propagation, penalties are carried over from states that will be visited near in the future.

Figure 5(b) shows the improved convergence when using model-based planning. Convergence is speeded up considerably as the number of learning iterations for one agent η relative to the other agents is increased from one (standard) to two to three. For larger problems, for example a larger grid, added iterations did further increase converge properties of the system. Preliminary results for more complex scenarios indicate that differentiating the frequency of model-based learning in accordance with the strength of the absolute experienced reward of η can further significantly speed up convergence (a strong reward is an indication of whether the agent is on the right track or should do something entirely else). By proportioning the learning of η relative to the experienced reward, η can benefit better from learning from the experienced rewards relative to the actions of $\hat{\eta}$.

6 Discussion and Conclusion

In this paper we studied the COllective INtelligence (COIN) framework of Wolpert et. al. We reproduced [10] as a case study where agents use standard

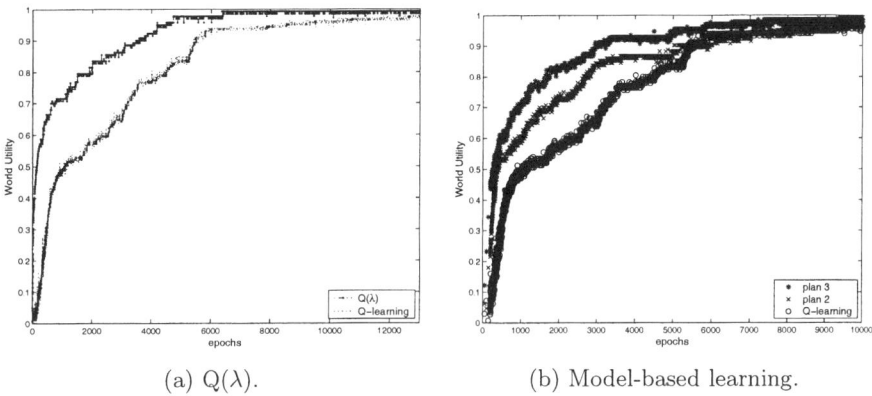

(a) Q(λ).   (b) Model-based learning.

Fig. 5. Extended RL applications

Reinforcement Learning (RL) techniques to collectively pick up tokens on a grid. We observed that for more complex problems the COIN framework is able to solve difficult MAS problems where fine-grained coordination between the agents is required, in contrast to multi-agent systems that use less advanced decentralized coordination.

We enhanced the COIN formalism to avoid pathological situations due to the nature of the WL utility-function. In particular we discounted actions looping back to earlier action sequences to promote a unique path traveled by an agent. This enhancement resulted in near optimal fitness for difficult token retrieval actions. Furthermore, we investigated the use of more powerful RL techniques within the (enhanced) COIN framework. We explored use of Watkins Q(λ) learning, model based learning, and the extended use of penalties in COIN over sequences of actions. All three extensions led to improved performance for the problems investigated and demonstrate methods for further improving the performance of the COIN framework in larger, more complex applications.

As future work we consider boot-strapping techniques for single agent RL to the COIN framework. RL in general can significantly benefit from directed exploration ([5, 9] and [16]). Sub-goal detection as in [7] can also greatly speed up the learning of complex tasks. For example, in [7] an agent learns to focus in learning on critical points in the task which form bottlenecks for good overall performance. An open question is how the above work can be integrated in the (extended) COIN Framework for task with bottlenecks occurring due to dynamic interactions in a MAS.

Acknowledgement We thank Stefan Blom for letting us use the STW cluster at CWI.

References

1. A. Barto and S. Mahadevan. Recent advances in hierarchical reinforcement learning. *Discrete-Event Systems journal*, 2003. to appear.

2. C. Guestrin, M. Lagoudakis, and R. Parr. Coordinated reinforcement learning. In *Proceedings of the ICML-2002 The Nineteenth International Conference on Machine Learning*, 2002.
3. G. Hardin. The tragedy of the commons. *Science*, 162:1243–1248, 1968.
4. M. Lauer and M. Riedmiller. An algorithm for distributed reinforcement learning in cooperative multi-agent systems. In *Proc. 17th International Conf. on Machine Learning*, pages 535–542. Morgan Kaufmann, San Francisco, CA, 2000.
5. T. Mitchell. *Machine Learning*. McGraw-Hill, 1997.
6. Personal communication with A. Agogino.
7. shai Menache, S. Mannor, and N. Shimkin. Q-cut - dynamic discovery of sub-goals in Reinforcement Learning. In T. Elomaa, H. Mannila, and H. Toivonen, editors, *Machine Learning: ECML 2002, 13th European Conference on Machine Learning*, volume 2430 of *LectureNotes in Computer Science*, pages 295–306. Springer, 2002.
8. R. Sutton and A. Barto. *Reinforcement learning: An introduction*. MIT-press, Cambridge, MA, 1998.
9. S. B. Thrun. Efficient exploration in reinforcement learning. Technical Report CMU-CS-92-102, Carnegie Mellon University, Pittsburgh, Pennsylvania, 1992.
10. K. Tumer, A. Agogino, and D. Wolpert. Learning sequences of actions in collectives of autonomous agents. In *Autonomous Agents & Multiagent Systems*, pages 378–385, part 1. ACM press, 2002.
11. K. Tumer and D. Wolpert. COllective INtelligence and Braess' paradox. In *Proceedings of the Sixteenth National Conference on Artificial Intelligence*, pages 104–109, Austin, Aug. 2000.
12. Watkins and Dayan. Q-learning. *Machine Learning*, 8:279–292, 1992.
13. G. Weiss. A multiagent framework for planning, reacting, and learning. Technical Report FKI-233-99, Institut für Informatik, Technische Universität München, 1999.
14. M. P. Wellman. The economic approach to artificial intelligence. *ACM Computing Surveys*, 28(4es):14–15, 1996.
15. M. P. Wellman. Market-oriented programming: Some early lessons. In S. Clearwater, editor, *Market-Based Control: A Paradigm for Distributed Resource Allocation*. World Scientific, River Edge, New Jersey, 1996.
16. M. Wiering. *Explorations in Efficient Reinforcement Learning*. PhD thesis, University of Amsterdam, 1999.
17. D. Wolpert and K. Tumer. An introduction to COllective INtelligence. Technical Report NASA-ARC-IC-99-63, NASA Ames Research Center, 1999. A shorter version of this paper is to appear in: Jeffrey M. Bradshaw, editor, Handbook of Agent Technology, AAAI Press/MIT Press, 1999.
18. D. Wolpert and K. Tumer. Optimal payoff functions for members of collectives. *Advances in Complex Systems*, 2001. in press.
19. D. H. Wolpert, K. Tumer, , and J. Frank. Using collective intelligence to route internet traffic. In *Advances in Neural Information Processing Systems-11*, pages 952–958, Denver, Dec. 1998.
20. D. H. Wolpert, K. Tumer, and J. Frank. Using collective intelligence to route internet traffic. In *Advances in Neural Information Processing Systems-11*, pages 952–958, Denver, 1998.
21. D. H. Wolpert, K. R. Wheeler, and K. Tumer. General principles of learning-based multi-agent systems. In O. Etzioni, J. P. Müller, and J. M. Bradshaw, editors, *Proceedings of the Third Annual Conference on Autonomous Agents (AGENTS-99)*, pages 77–83, New York, May 1–5 1999. ACM Press.

Rademacher Penalization
over Decision Tree Prunings

Matti Kääriäinen and Tapio Elomaa

Department of Computer Science, University of Helsinki, Finland
{matti.kaariainen,elomaa}@cs.helsinki.fi

Abstract. Rademacher penalization is a modern technique for obtaining data-dependent bounds on the generalization error of classifiers. It would appear to be limited to relatively simple hypothesis classes because of computational complexity issues. In this paper we, nevertheless, apply Rademacher penalization to the in practice important hypothesis class of unrestricted decision trees by considering the prunings of a given decision tree rather than the tree growing phase. Moreover, we generalize the error-bounding approach from binary classification to multi-class situations. Our empirical experiments indicate that the proposed new bounds clearly outperform earlier bounds for decision tree prunings and provide non-trivial error estimates on real-world data sets.

1 Introduction

Data-dependent bounds on generalization error of classifiers are bridging the gap that has existed between theoretical and empirical results since the introduction of computational learning theory. They allow to take situation specific information into account, whereas distribution independent results need to hold for all imaginable situations. Using *Rademacher complexity* [1, 2] to bound the generalization error of a training error minimizing classifier is a fairly new approach that has not yet been tested in practice extensively.

Rademacher penalization is in principle a general method applicable to any hypothesis class. However, in practice it does not seem amenable to complex hypothesis classes because the standard method for computing Rademacher penalties relies on the existence of an empirical risk minimization algorithm for the hypothesis class in question. The first practical experiments with Rademacher penalization used real intervals as the hypothesis class [3]. We have applied Rademacher penalization to two-level decision trees [4], which can be learned efficiently in the agnostic PAC model [5].

General decision tree growing algorithms are necessarily heuristic because of the computational complexity of finding optimal decision trees [6]. Moreover, the hypothesis class consisting of unrestricted decision trees is so vast that traditional generalization error analysis techniques cannot provide non-trivial bounds for it. Nevertheless, top-down induction of decision trees by, e.g., C4.5 [7] produces results that are very competitive in prediction accuracy with better motivated approaches. We consider the usual two-phase process of decision tree learning;

after growing a tree, it is pruned in order to reduce its dependency on the training data and to better reflect characteristics of future data. By the practical success of decision tree learning, prunings of an induced decision tree have to be considered an expressive class of hypotheses.

We apply Rademacher penalization to general decision trees by considering, not the tree growing phase, but rather the pruning phase. The idea is to view decision tree pruning as empirical risk minimization in the hypothesis class consisting of all prunings of an induced decision tree. First a heuristic tree growing procedure is applied to training data to produce a decision tree. Then a pruning algorithm, for example the *reduced error pruning* (REP) algorithm of Quinlan [8], is applied to the grown tree and a set of pruning data. As REP is known to be an efficient empirical risk minimization algorithm for the class of prunings of a decision tree, it can be used to compute the Rademacher penalty for this hypothesis class. Thus, by viewing decision tree pruning as empirical risk minimization in a data-dependent hypothesis class, we can bound the generalization error of prunings by Rademacher penalization. We also extend this generalization error analysis framework to the multi-class setting.

Our empirical experiments show that Rademacher penalization applied to prunings found by REP provides reasonable generalization error bounds on real-world data sets. Although the bounds still overestimate the test set error, they are much tighter than the earlier distribution independent bounds for prunings.

This paper is organized as follows. In Section 2 we recapitulate the main idea of data-dependent generalization error analysis. We concentrate on Rademacher penalization which we extend to cover the multi-class case. Section 3 concerns pruning of decision trees, reduced error pruning of decision trees being the main focus. Related pruning approaches are briefly reviewed in Section 4. Combining Rademacher complexity calculation and decision tree pruning is the topic of Section 5. Empirical evaluation of the proposed approach is presented in Section 6 and, finally, Section 7 presents the concluding remarks of this study.

2 Rademacher Penalties

Let $S = \{(x_i, y_i) \mid i = 1, \ldots, n\}$ be a sample of n examples $(x_i, y_i) \in \mathcal{X} \times \mathcal{Y}$ each of which is drawn independently from some unknown probability distribution on $\mathcal{X} \times \mathcal{Y}$. In the PAC and statistical learning settings one usually assumes that the learning algorithm chooses its hypothesis $h \colon \mathcal{X} \to \mathcal{Y}$ from some fixed hypothesis class $\mathcal{H}$. Under this assumption generalization error analysis provides theoretical results bounding the generalization error of hypotheses $h \in \mathcal{H}$ that may depend on the sample, the learning algorithm, and the properties of the hypothesis class. We consider the multi-class setting, where $\mathcal{Y}$ may contain more than two labels.

Let P be the unknown probability distribution according to which the examples are drawn. The *generalization error* of a hypothesis h is the probability that a randomly drawn example (x, y) is misclassified:

$$\epsilon_P(h) = P(h(x) \neq y).$$

The general goal of learning, of course, is to find a hypothesis with a small generalization error. However, since the generalization error depends on P, it cannot be computed directly based on the sample alone. We can try to approximate the generalization error of h by its *training error* on n examples:

$$\hat{\epsilon}_n(h) = \frac{1}{n} \sum_{i=1}^{n} \ell(h(x_i), y_i),$$

where ℓ is the 0/1 loss function for which $\ell(y, y') = 1$ if $y \neq y'$ and 0 otherwise.

Empirical Risk Minimization (ERM) [9] is a principle that suggest choosing the hypothesis $h \in \mathcal{H}$ with minimal training error. In relatively small and simple hypothesis classes finding a minimum training error hypothesis is computationally feasible. To guarantee that ERM yields hypotheses with small generalization error, one can try to bound $\sup_{h \in \mathcal{H}} |\epsilon_P(h) - \hat{\epsilon}_n(h)|$. Under the assumption that the examples are independent and identically distributed (i.i.d.), whenever $\mathcal{H}$ is not too complex, the difference of the training error of the hypothesis h on n examples and its true generalization error converges to 0 in probability as n tends to infinity.

The most common approach to deriving generalization error bounds is based on the VC dimension of the hypothesis class. The problem with this approach is that it provides optimal results only in the worst case — when the underlying probability distribution is as bad as it can be. Thus, the generalization error bounds based on VC dimension tend to be overly pessimistic. Moreover, the VC dimension bounds are hard to extend to the multi-class setting. Data-dependent generalization error bounds, on the other hand, can be provably almost optimal for any given domain [1]. In the following we review the foundations of a recent promising approach to bounding the generalization error.

A *Rademacher random variable* takes values $+1$ and -1 with probability $1/2$ each. Let $r_1, r_2, \ldots, r_n$ be a sequence of Rademacher random variables independent of each other and the data $(x_1, y_1), \ldots, (x_n, y_n)$. The *Rademacher penalty* of the hypothesis class $\mathcal{H}$ is defined as

$$R_n(\mathcal{H}) = \sup_{h \in \mathcal{H}} \left| \frac{1}{n} \sum_{i=1}^{n} r_i \ell(h(x_i), y_i) \right|.$$

The following symmetrization inequality [10], which covers also the multi-class setting, connects Rademacher penalties to generalization error analysis.

Theorem 1. *The inequality*

$$\mathbf{E}\left[\sup_{h \in \mathcal{H}} |\epsilon_P(h) - \hat{\epsilon}_n(h)|\right] \leq 2\mathbf{E}\left[R_n(\mathcal{H})\right]$$

holds for any distribution P, number of examples n, and hypothesis class $\mathcal{H}$.

The random variables $\sup_{h \in \mathcal{H}} |\epsilon_P(h) - \hat{\epsilon}_n(h)|$ and $R_n(\mathcal{H})$ are sharply concentrated around their expectations [1]. The concentration results are based on the following McDiarmid's bounded difference inequality [11].

Lemma 1 (McDiarmid's inequality). *Let $Z_1, \ldots, Z_n$ be independent random variables taking their values in a set A. Let $f: A^n \to \mathbb{R}$ be a function such that over all $z_1, \ldots, z_n, z_i' \in A$*

$$\sup |f(z_1, \ldots, z_i, \ldots, z_n) - f(z_1, \ldots, z_i', \ldots, z_n)| \leq c_i$$

for some constants $c_1, \ldots, c_n \in \mathbb{R}$. Then for all $\varepsilon > 0$

$$\mathbf{P}\left(f(Z_1, \ldots, Z_n) - \mathbf{E}[f(Z_1, \ldots, Z_n)] \geq \varepsilon\right) \text{ and}$$
$$\mathbf{P}\left(\mathbf{E}[f(Z_1, \ldots, Z_n)] - f(Z_1, \ldots, Z_n) \geq \varepsilon\right)$$

are upper bounded by $\exp(-2\varepsilon^2 / \sum_{i=1}^{n} c_i^2)$.

Using McDiarmid's inequality one can bound the generalization error of hypotheses using their training error and Rademacher penalty as follows.

Lemma 2. *Let $h \in \mathcal{H}$ be arbitrary. Then with probability at least $1 - \delta$*

$$\epsilon_P(h) \leq \hat{\epsilon}_n(h) + 2R_n(\mathcal{H}) + 5\eta(\delta, n), \tag{1}$$

where $\eta(\delta, n) = \sqrt{\ln(2/\delta)/(2n)}$ is a small error term that goes to zero as the number of examples increases.

Proof. Observe that replacing a pair $((x_i, y_i), r_i)$ consisting of an example (x_i, y_i) and a Rademacher random variable r_i by any other pair $((x_i', y_i'), r_i')$ may change the value of $R_n(\mathcal{H})$ by at most $2/n$. Thus, Lemma 1 applied to the i.i.d. random variables $((x_1, y_1), r_1), \ldots, ((x_n, y_n), r_n)$ and the function $R_n(\mathcal{H})$ yields

$$\mathbf{P}\left(R_n(\mathcal{H}) \leq \mathbf{E}[R_n(\mathcal{H})] - 2\eta(\delta, n)\right) \leq \frac{\delta}{2}. \tag{2}$$

Similarly, changing the value of any example (x_i, y_i) can change the value of $\sup_{h \in \mathcal{H}} |\epsilon_P(h) - \hat{\epsilon}_n(h)|$ by no more than $1/n$. Thus, applying Lemma 1 again to $(x_1, y_1), \ldots, (x_n, y_n)$ and $\sup_{h \in \mathcal{H}} |\epsilon_P(h) - \hat{\epsilon}_n(h)|$ gives

$$\mathbf{P}\left(\sup_{h \in \mathcal{H}} |\epsilon_P(h) - \hat{\epsilon}_n(h)| \geq \mathbf{E}\left[\sup_{h \in \mathcal{H}} |\epsilon_P(h) - \hat{\epsilon}_n(h)|\right] + \eta(\delta, n)\right) \leq \frac{\delta}{2}. \tag{3}$$

To bound the generalization error of a hypothesis $g \in \mathcal{H}$ observe that

$$\epsilon_P(g) \leq \hat{\epsilon}_n(g) + \sup_{h \in \mathcal{H}} |\epsilon_P(h) - \hat{\epsilon}_n(h)|.$$

Hence, by inequality (3), with probability at least $1 - \delta/2$

$$\epsilon_P(g) \leq \hat{\epsilon}_n(g) + \mathbf{E}\left[\sup_{h \in \mathcal{H}} |\epsilon_P(h) - \hat{\epsilon}_n(h)|\right] + \eta(\delta, n)$$
$$\leq \hat{\epsilon}_n(g) + 2\mathbf{E}[R_n(\mathcal{H})] + \eta(\delta, n),$$

where the second inequality follows from Theorem 1. Finally, applying inequality (2) yields that with probability at least $1 - \delta$

$$\epsilon_P(g) \leq \hat{\epsilon}_n(g) + 2R_n(\mathcal{H}) + 5\eta(\delta, n).$$

The usefulness of inequality (1) stems from the fact that its right-hand side depends only on the training sample and the Rademacher random variables but not on P directly. Hence, all the data that is needed to evaluate the generalization error bound is available to the learning algorithm. Furthermore, Koltchinskii [1] has shown that in the two-class situation the Rademacher penalty can be computed by an empirical risk minimization algorithm applied to relabeled training data. We now extend this method to the multi-class setting.

The expression for $R_n(\mathcal{H})$ is first written as the maximum of two suprema in order to remove the absolute value inside the original supremum:

$$R_n(\mathcal{H}) = \max \left(\sup_{h \in \mathcal{H}} \pm \frac{1}{n} \sum_{i=1}^{n} r_i \ell(h(x_i), y_i) \right).$$

The sum inside the supremum with positive sign is maximized by the hypothesis h_1 that tries to correctly classify those and only those training examples (x_i, y_i) for which $r_i = -1$. To formalize this, we associate each class $y \in \mathcal{Y}$ with a complement class label $\bar{y}$ that represents the set of all classes but y. We denote the set of these complement classes by $\overline{\mathcal{Y}}$ and extend the domain of the loss function ℓ to cover pairs $(y, z) \in \mathcal{Y} \times \overline{\mathcal{Y}}$ by setting $\ell(y, z) = 1$ if $z = \bar{y}$ and 0 otherwise. Using this notation, h_1 is the hypothesis that minimizes the empirical error with respect to a newly labeled training set $\{(x_i, z_i)\}_{i=1}^{n}$, where

$$z_i = \begin{cases} y_i, & \text{if } r_i = -1; \\ \bar{y}_i, & \text{otherwise.} \end{cases}$$

The case for the supremum with negative sign is similar.

Altogether, the computation of the Rademacher penalty entails the following steps.

- Toss a fair coin n times to obtain a realization of the Rademacher random variable sequence $r_1, \ldots, r_n$.
- Change the label y_i to $\bar{y}_i$ if and only if $r_i = +1$ to obtain a new sequence of labels $z_1, \ldots, z_n$.
- Find functions $h_1, h_2 \in \mathcal{H}$ that minimize the empirical error with respect to the set of labels z_i and $\bar{z}_i$, respectively. Here, we follow the convention that $\bar{\bar{z}} = z$ for all $z \in \mathcal{Y} \cup \overline{\mathcal{Y}}$.
- The Rademacher penalty is given by the maximum of $|\{i : r_i = +1\}|/n - \hat{e}(h_1)$ and $|\{i : r_i = -1\}|/n - \hat{e}(h_2)$, where the empirical errors $\hat{e}(h_1)$ and $\hat{e}(h_2)$ are with respect to the labels z_i and $\bar{z}_i$, respectively.

In the two-class setting, the set $\bar{y}$ of all classes but y, $\mathcal{Y} \setminus \{y\}$, is a singleton. Thus, changing class y to $\bar{y}$ amounts to flipping the class label. It follows that a normal ERM algorithm can be used to find the hypotheses h_1 and h_2 and hence the Rademacher penalty can be computed efficiently provided that there exists an efficient ERM algorithm for the hypothesis class in question.

In the multi-class setting, however, a little more is required, since the sample on which the empirical risk minimization is performed may contain labels from

$\mathcal{Y}$ and the loss function differs from the standard 0/1-loss. This, however, is not a problem with REP nor with T2, a decision tree learning algorithm used in our earlier study, since both empirical risk minimization algorithms can easily be adapted to handle this more general setting as explained in the next section for REP and argued by Auer et al. [5] for T2.

3 Growing and Pruning Decision Trees

A common approach in top-down induction of decision trees is to first grow a tree that fits the training data well and, then, prune it to reflect less the peculiarities of the training data — i.e., to generalize better. Many heuristic approaches [8, 12, 13] as well as more analytical ones [14, 15] to pruning have been proposed. A special class of pruning algorithms are the on-line ones [16, 17]. Even these algorithms work by the two-phase approach: An initial decision tree is fitted to the data and its prunings are then used as experts that collectively predict the class of observed instances.

Reduced error pruning was originally proposed by Quinlan [8]. It has been used rather rarely in practical learning algorithms mainly because it requires part of the available data to be reserved solely for pruning purposes. However, empirical evaluations of pruning algorithms indicate that the performance of REP is comparable to other more widely used pruning strategies [12, 13]. In analyses REP has often been considered a representative pruning algorithm [13, 18]. It produces an optimal pruning of a given tree — the smallest tree among those with minimal error (with respect to the set of pruning examples) [13, 19].

Table 1 presents the REP algorithm in pseudo code (for simplicity only for decision trees with binary splits). It works in two phases: First the set of pruning examples S is classified using the given tree T to be pruned. The node statistics are updated simultaneously. In the second phase — a bottom-up pruning phase — those parts of the tree that can be removed without increasing the error of the remaining hypothesis are pruned away. The pruning decisions are based on the node statistics calculated in the top-down classification phase.

The scarceness of (expensive) data used to be considered a major problem facing inductive algorithms. Therefore, REP's requirement of a separate pruning set of examples has been seen prohibitive. Nowadays the situation has turned around: In data mining abundance of data is considered to be a major problem for learning algorithms to cope with. Thus, it should not be a major obstacle to leave some part of the data aside from the decision tree building phase and to reserve it for pruning purposes.

REP is an ERM algorithm for the hypothesis class consisting of all prunings of a given decision tree (for a proof, see [19]). Thus, it can be used to efficiently compute Rademacher penalties and, hence, also generalization error bounds for the class of prunings of a decision tree. This leads us to the following strategy. First, we use a standard heuristic decision tree induction algorithm (C4.5) to grow a decision tree based on a set of training examples. The tree serves as a representation of the data-dependent hypothesis class that consists of its prun-

Table 1. The REP algorithm capable of handling complement labels also. The algorithm first classifies the pruning examples in a top-down pass using method classify and then, during a bottom-up pass, prunes the tree using method prune

```
decTree REP( decTree T, exArray S ) // Prune the tree
  for( i= 0 to S.length-1 ) classify( T, S[i] );
  prune( T ); return T;

void classify( decTree T, example e ) // Update node counters top-down
  T.total++; T.count[e.label]++;
  if( !leaf(T) )
    if( T.test(e)==0 ) classify( T.left, e );
    else classify( T.right, e );

int error( label y, cntArray count ) // Compute classification error
  int errors= 0;
  foreach( z in Y-{y} ) errors+= count[z];
  return errors + count[bar(y)];

int prune( decTree T ) // Output classification error after pruning
  int leafError= error( T.label, T.count );
  if( leaf(T) ) return leafError;
  int treeError= prune( T.left )+ prune( T.right );
  if( treeError < leafError ) return treeError;
  else replace T with a leaf labeled T.label;
    return leafError;
```

ings. As C4.5 usually performs quite well on real-world domains, it is reasonable to assume — even though it cannot be proved — that the class of prunings contains some good hypotheses.

Having grown a decision tree, we use a separate pruning data set to select one of the prunings of the grown tree as our final hypothesis. In this paper, we use REP as our pruning algorithm, but in principle any other pruning algorithm using the same basic pruning operation could be used as well. However, since REP is an empirical risk minimization algorithm, the derived error bounds will be the tightest when combined with it.

Our view on pruning is similar to that of Esposito et al. [20], who viewed many decision tree pruning algorithms as instantiations of search in the state space consisting of all prunings of a given decision tree, the state transition function being determined by the basic pruning operation. In this setting, REP can be seen as a search algorithm whose bias is determined by the ERM principle and the tendency to favor small hypotheses. Our goal, however, is not to analyze the search itself, but to evaluate the goodness of the final pruning produced by the search algorithm. We pursue this goal further in Section 5.

One shortcoming of the two-phase decision tree induction approach is that there does not exist any well-founded approach for deciding how much data to use for the training and pruning phases. Only heuristic data set partitioning schemes are available. However, the simple rule of using, e.g., two thirds of the data for training and the rest for pruning has been observed to work well in practice [13]. If the initial data set is very large, it may be computationally infeasible to use all the data for training or pruning. In that case one can use heuristic sequential sampling methods for selecting the size of the training set and determine the size of the pruning set, e.g., by using progressive Rademacher sampling [4]. Because REP is an efficient linear-time algorithm, it is not hit hard by overestimated pruning sample size.

4 Related Pruning Algorithms

REP produces the smallest of the most accurate prunings of a given decision tree, where accuracy is measured with respect to the pruning set. Other approaches for producing optimal prunings for different optimality criteria have also been proposed [21–24]. However, often optimality is measured over the training set. Then it is only possible to maintain the initial training set accuracy, assuming that no noise is present. Neither is it usually possible to reduce the size of the decision tree without sacrificing the classification accuracy. For example, Bohanec and Bratko [22] as well as Almuallim [24] have studied how to efficiently find the smallest pruning that satisfies a given minimum accuracy requirement.

The strategy of using one data set for growing a decision tree and another for pruning it closely resembles the on-line pruning setting [16, 17]. In it the prunings of the initial decision tree are viewed as a pool of experts. Thus, pruning is performed on-line, while giving predictions to new examples, rather than in a separate pruning phase. The main advantage of the on-line methods is that no statistical assumptions about the data generating process are needed and still the combined prediction and pruning strategy can be proven to be competitive with the best possible pruning of the initial tree. These approaches do not choose or maintain one pruning of the given decision tree, but rather a weighted combination of prunings which may be impossible to interpret by human experts. The loss bounds are meaningful only for very large data sets and there exists no empirical evaluation of the performance of the on-line pruning methods.

The pruning algorithms of Mansour [14] and Kearns and Mansour [15] are very similar to REP in spirit. The main difference with these pruning algorithms and REP is the fact that they do not require the sample S on which pruning is based to be independent of the tree T; i.e., T may well have been grown based on S. Moreover, the pruning criterion in both methods is a kind of a *cost-complexity* condition [21] that takes both the observed classification error and (sub)tree complexity into account. Both algorithms are *pessimistic*: They try to bound the true error of a (sub)tree by its training error. Since the training error is by nature optimistic, the pruning criterion has to compensate it by being pessimistic about the error approximation.

Both Mansour [14] and Kearns and Mansour [15] provide generalization error analyses for their algorithms. The bound presented in [14] measures the complexity of the class of prunings by the size of the unpruned tree. If this size or an upper bound for it is known in advance, the bound applies also when the pruning data is not independent of the tree to be pruned. Mansour's bound can be used in connection with REP, too, and we will use it as a point of comparison for our generalization error bounds in Section 6. Kearns and Mansour [15] prove that the generalization error of the pruning produced by their algorithm is bounded by that of the best pruning of the given tree plus a complexity penalty. However, the penalty term can grow intolerably large and cannot be evaluated because of its dependence on the unknown optimal pruning and hidden constants.

5 Combining Rademacher Penalization and Decision Tree Pruning

When using REP, the data sets used in growing the tree and pruning it are independent of each other. Therefore, any standard generalization error analysis technique can be applied to the pruning found by REP as if the hypothesis class from which REP selects a pruning was fixed in advance. A formal argument justifying this would be to carry out the generalization error analysis conditioned on the training data and then to argue that the bounds hold unconditionally by taking expectations over the selection of the training data set.

By the above argument, the theory of Rademacher penalization can be applied to the data-dependent class of prunings. Therefore, we can use the results presented in Section 2 to provide generalization error bounds for prunings found by REP (or any other pruning algorithm). Moreover, since REP is a linear-time ERM algorithm for the class of prunings, it can be used to evaluate the generalization error bounds efficiently.

To summarize, we propose the following decision tree learning strategy that provides a generalization error bound for the hypothesis it produces:

- Split the available data into a growing set and a pruning set.
- Use, e.g., C4.5 (without pruning) on the growing set to induce a decision tree.
- Find the smallest most accurate pruning of the tree built in the previous step using REP (or any other pruning algorithm) on the pruning set. This is the final hypothesis.
- Evaluate the error bound as explained in Section 2 by running REP two more times.

Even though the tree growing process is heuristic, the generalization error bounds for the prunings are provably true under the i.i.d. assumption. They are valid even if the tree growing heuristic fails, that is, when none of the prunings of the grown tree generalize well. In that case the bounds are, of course, unavoidably large. The situation is similar to, e.g., margin-based generalization error analysis, where the error bounds are good provided that the training data generating distribution is such that a hypothesis with a good margin distribution can be found. In our case the error bounds are tight whenever C4.5 works well for the data-generating distribution in question. The empirical evidence overwhelmingly demonstrates that C4.5 usually fares quite well.

Generalization error bounds can be roughly divided into two categories: Those based on a training set only and those requiring a separate test set [25]. Our generalization error bounds for prunings may be seen to lie somewhere between these two extremes. We use only part of the data in the tree growing phase. The rest — the set of pruning data — is used for selecting a pruning and evaluating the generalization error bound. Thus, some of the information contained in the pruning set may be lost as it cannot be used in the tree induction phase. However, the pruning set is still used for the non-trivial task of selecting a good pruning, so that some of the information contained in it can be exploited in the final hypothesis. The pruning set is thus used as a test set for the outcome of the tree growing phase and also as a proper learning set in the pruning phase.

6 Empirical Evaluation

The obvious performance reference for the approach of Rademacher penalization over decision tree prunings is to compare it to existing generalization error bounds such as the ones presented by Mansour [14] and Kearns and Mansour [15]. The bound in the latter is impossible to evaluate in practice because it requires knowing the depth and size of the pruning with the best generalization error. This leaves us with the bound of Mansour which only requires knowing the maximum size of prunings in advance. Bounds developed in the on-line pruning setting [16] are incomparable with the one presented in this paper because of the different learning model. Thus, they will not be considered here.

Mansour [14] derived, based on the Chernoff bound, the following bound for the generalization error of a decision tree h with k nodes:

$$\epsilon_P(h) < \hat{\epsilon}_n(h) + c\sqrt{\frac{k \log d + \log(2/\delta)}{n}},$$

where d is the arity of binary example vectors x_i and c is a constant. The bound applies only to binary decision trees in the two-class setting. When used for the class of unrestricted multi-class decision trees, the bound will give an overly optimistic estimate of what could be obtained with Mansour's proof technique in this more general setting. For the value of c we use a crude underestimate 0.5. Both these choices are in favor of Mansour's bound in the comparison.

The error bound based on Rademacher penalization depends on the data distribution so that its true performance can be evaluated only empirically. As benchmark data sets we use six large data sets from the UCI Machine Learning Repository, namely the Census income (2 classes), Connect (3 classes), Covertype (7 classes), and generated LED datasets (10 classes) with 5, 10, and 15 percent attribute noise and 300,000 instances. In each experiment we allocate 10 percent of the data for testing and split the rest to growing and pruning sets. As the split ratio we chose 2:1 as suggested by Esposito et al. [13].

Table 2. Averages and standard deviations of sizes of trees grown by C4.5 (left) and error bounds for REP (right) over 10 random splits of the data sets

Data set	Unpruned	Default	REP	Test set	R-bound	M-bound
Census	19732 ±732	1377 ±268	4749 ±397	4.9 ±0.1	8.7 ±0.2	49.9 ±0.9
Connect	10973 ±361	4253 ±104	4338 ±235	20.7 ±0.8	32.4 ±0.4	89.3 ±1.5
Cover	25356 ±221	22095 ±228	17404 ±179	6.9 ±0.1	12.7 ±0.1	44.0 ±0.2
LED24-5	27357 ±139	7042 ±74	3850 ±233	13.4 ±0.2	19.7 ±0.2	61.3 ±0.2
LED24-10	51790 ±204	13624 ±220	7671 ±323	26.4 ±0.1	36.8 ±0.2	91.7 ±0.2
LED24-15	71162 ±156	20273 ±259	11344 ±265	38.6 ±0.2	52.2 ±0.2	114.6 ±0.2

Table 2 summarizes the results of our experiments averaged over ten random splits of the data sets. Observe that the unpruned decision trees are very large, which means that the class of prunings may potentially be very complex. The results indicate that the default pruning of C4.5 and REP both manage to decrease the tree sizes considerably.

The right-hand side of Table 2 presents the test set accuracies and error bounds for REP prunings based on Rademacher penalization and Mansour's method. In both bounds, we set $\delta = 0.01$. Even though the bounds based on Rademacher penalization clearly overshoot the test set accuracies, they still provide reasonable estimates in many cases. Note that in the multi-class settings even error bounds above 50 percent are non-trivial. The Rademacher bounds are clearly superior to even the underestimates of the bounds by Mansour that we used as a benchmark. The amount by which the Rademacher bound overestimates the test set error is seen to be almost an order of magnitude smaller than the corresponding quantity related to Mansour's bound.

7 Conclusion

Modern generalization error bounding techniques that take the observed data distribution into account give far more realistic sample complexities and generalization error approximations than the distribution independent methods. We have shown how one of these techniques, namely Rademacher penalization, can be applied to bound the generalization error of decision tree prunings, also in the multi-class setting. According to our empirical experiments the proposed theoretical bounds are significantly tighter than previous generalization error bounds for decision tree prunings. However, the new bounds still appear unable to faithfully describe the performance attained in practice.

References

1. Koltchinskii, V.: Rademacher penalties and structural risk minimization. IEEE Trans. Inf. Theor. **47** (2001) 1902–1914
2. Bartlett, P.L., Mendelson, S.: Rademacher and Gaussian complexities: Risk bounds and structural results. JMLR **3** (2002) 463–482

3. Lozano, F.: Model selection using Rademacher penalization. In: Proc. 2nd ICSC Symposium on Neural Networks, NAISO Academic Press (2000)
4. Elomaa, T., Kääriäinen, M.: Progressive Rademacher sampling. In: Proc. 18th National Conference on Artificial Intelligence, MIT Press (2002) 140–145
5. Auer, P., Holte, R.C., Maass, W.: Theory and application of agnostic PAC-learning with small decision trees. In: Proc. 12th International Conference on Machine Learning, Morgan Kaufmann (1995) 21–29
6. Grigni, M., Mirelli, V., Papadimitriou, C.H.: On the difficulty of designing good classifiers. SIAM J. Comput. **30** (2000) 318–323
7. Quinlan, J.R.: C4.5: Programs for Machine Learning. Morgan Kaufmann (1993)
8. Quinlan, J.R.: Simplifying decision trees. Int. J. Man-Mach. Stud. **27** (1987) 221–248
9. Vapnik, V.N.: Estimation of Dependencies Based on Empirical Data. Springer (1982)
10. Van der Vaart, A.W., Wellner, J.A.: Weak Convergence and Empirical Processes. Springer (2000) Corrected second printing.
11. McDiarmid, C.: On the method of bounded differences. In: Surveys in Combinatorics. Volume 141 of London Mathematical Society Lecture Note Series. Cambridge University Press (1989) 148–188
12. Mingers, J.: An empirical comparison of pruning methods for decision tree induction. Mach. Learn. **4** (1989) 227–243
13. Esposito, F., Malerba, D., Semeraro, G.: A comparative analysis of methods for pruning decision trees. IEEE Trans. Pattern Anal. Mach. Intell. **19** (1997) 476–491
14. Mansour, Y.: Pessimistic decision tree pruning based on tree size. In: Proc. 14th International Conference on Machine Learning, Morgan Kaufmann (1997) 195–201
15. Kearns, M., Mansour, Y.: A fast, bottom-up decision tree pruning algorithm with near-optimal generalization. In: Proc. 15th International Conference on Machine Learning, Morgan Kaufmann (1998) 269–277
16. Helmbold, D.P., Schapire, R.E.: Predicting nearly as well as the best pruning of a decision tree. Mach. Learn. **27** (1997) 51–68
17. Pereira, F.C., Singer, Y.: An efficient extension to mixture techniques for prediction and decision trees. Mach. Learn. **36** (1999) 183–199
18. Oates, T., Jensen, D.: Toward a theoretical understanding of why and when decision tree pruning algorithms fail. In: Proc. 16th National Conference on Artificial Intelligence, MIT Press (1999) 372–378
19. Elomaa, T., Kääriäinen, M.: An analysis of reduced error pruning. J. Artif. Intell. Res. **15** (2001) 163–187
20. Esposito, F., Malerba, D., Semeraro, G.: Decision tree pruning as a search in the state space. In: Proc. 6th European Conference on Machine Learning. Volume 667 of Lecture Notes in Artificial Intelligence., Springer (1993) 165–184
21. Breiman, L., Friedman, J.H., Olshen, R.A., Stone, C.J.: Classification and Regression Trees. Wadsworth (1984)
22. Bohanec, M., Bratko, I.: Trading accuracy for simplicity in decision trees. Mach. Learn. **15** (1994) 223–250
23. Oliver, J.J., Hand, D.J.: On pruning and averaging decision trees. In: Proc. 12th International Conference on Machine Learning, Morgan Kaufmann (1995) 430–437
24. Almuallim, H.: An efficient algorithm for optimal pruning of decision trees. Artif. Intell. **83** (1996) 347–362
25. Langford, J.: Combining training set and test set bounds. In: Proc. 19th International Conference on Machine Learning, Morgan Kaufmann (2002) 331–338

Learning Rules to Improve
a Machine Translation System*

David Kauchak and Charles Elkan

Department of Computer Science
University of California, San Diego
La Jolla, CA 92037
{dkauchak,elkan}@cs.ucsd.edu

Abstract. In this paper we show how to learn rules to improve the performance of a machine translation system. Given a system consisting of two translation functions (one from language A to language B and one from B to A), training text is translated from A to B and back again to A. Using these two translations, differences in knowledge between the two translation functions are identified, and rules are learned to improve the functions. Context-independent rules are learned where the information suggests only a single possible translation for a word. When there are multiple alternate translations for a word, a likelihood ratio test is used to identify words that co-occur with each case significantly. These words are then used as context in context-dependent rules. Applied on the Pan American Health Organization corpus of 20,084 sentences, the learned rules improve the understandability of the translation produced by the SDL International engine on 78% of sentences, with high precision.

1 Introduction

Machine translation systems are now commonplace. For example, they can be found for free on a number of web sites. If we treat these systems as black box translation engines where text is input and the translation obtained, can we improve the translation performance automatically?

Most previous research in machine translation has focused on developing systems from the ground up. Modern systems generally employ statistical and/or learning methods ([Melamed, 2001] and [Yamada and Knight, 2001]). A number of translation systems are offered commercially not only to businesses, but also to anyone with web access ([FreeTranslation, 2002] and [Systran, 2002]). These systems are either stand-alone translation engines or integrated into a general information processing system ([Damianos et al., 2002]). Although these systems typically do not employ state of the art translation methods, they are widely used. In this paper, we examine these publicly available systems. The methods we describe work well on this type of system, but can also be employed on other machine translation systems.

---

* This material is based on work done for ORINCON Information Assurance sponsored by the United States Airforce and supported by the Air Force Research Laboratory under Contract F30602-02-C-0046.

The most common machine translation systems do word level translation. Although word level methods are the simplest, they have proved surprisingly successful. In an investigatory study in [Koehn and Knight, 2001], they show that 90% of the words in a corpus can be translated using a straightforward word for word translation. In this paper, we examine learning word level correction rules to improve machine translation systems. Rule learning approaches have proved successful in other natural language problems because they leverage statistical techniques and also tend to produce understandable and interpretable rules ([Brill, 1995]).

Most machine translation systems can translate in both directions between a language pair. Such a system can be thought of as two different functions, one that translates in one direction and a second that translates in the opposite direction. These functions are usually developed semi-independently and often the lexicon used by each is independent. This results in a difference in the knowledge built into each function. In this paper, we propose a method for automatically detecting this knowledge discrepancy and, using this information, for improving the translation functions. Given a word list in language A, we translate those words to language B and back again to language A. In some sense, the original word list defines a ground truth for the final set of translated words. Deviations from this ground truth point to cases where the system can be improved.

Using this setup, we describe how rules can be learned to improve these translation functions. Context-independent rules are learned where there is no ambiguity about the translation of a word. For words with multiple possible translations, a corpus is used to identify candidate context words and the likelihood ratio test is used to identify which of these context words co-occur significantly. Using these significant words, context-dependent rules are learned that disambiguate between ambiguous cases.

Using our method, 7,971 context-independent rules and 1,444 context-dependent rules are learned. These rules improve the understandability of the translation of 24,235 words and 78% of the sentences in the Pan American Health Organization corpus of over half a million words and 20,084 sentences.

2 Setup and Terminology

Before we explain the method for improving machine translation systems, we first define some terminology and assumptions. A machine translation system is a pair of translation functions (f, f') where L_1 and L_2 are natural languages and where f translates from L_1 to L_2 and vice versa for f'. We assume that we have unlimited access to the translation functions of a machine translation system, but not to the details of how the functions operate. We also assume that we have a large amount of text available in the languages that the machine translation system translates between. Finally, instead of trying to learn correction rules that change an entire sentence at once, we only learn rules that change a single word at a time.

In many situations, doing multiple single word changes leads to results similar to full sentence correction. Solving the single-word correction problem involves three different steps. The first step is to identify where a word is being translated incorrectly. Given this incorrectly translated word, the second step is to identify the correct translation for that word. Finally, given an incorrect translation and the appropriate correct translation, the third step is to generate rules capable of making corrections in new sentences.

The first two steps can be seen as data generation steps. These steps generate examples that can then be used to generate rules in the third step using some supervised learning method. The three steps can be written as follows:

1. Find mistakes: Find word s_i in sentence $\bar{s} \in L$ with input context $c_1(s_i)$ where s_i is translated incorrectly to t_i with output context $c_2(t_i)$.
2. Find corrections: Find the correct translation, r_i, for s_i in $\bar{s} \in L$ with input context $c_1(s_i)$, output context $c_2(t_i)$ and incorrect translation t_i.
3. Learn correction rules: Generate a correction function g such that $g(s_i, \bar{c}_1(s_i), t_i, \bar{c}_2(t_i)) = r_i$ for each data sample i. A rule fires when s_i is in the input sentence with context $c_1(s_i)$ and s_i is translated to t_i with context $c_2(t_i)$ by the original machine translation system. Firing changes t_i to r_i.

The contexts described above can be any representation of the context of a word in a corpus, but we will use the bag of words of the sentence containing the word. Although this loses positional information, it is a simple representation that minimizes the parameters required for learning. Our goal is to improve a machine translation system, given the assumptions stated above, by solving each of the three problems described. The key to our approach is that given a sentence $\bar{s}$ in a language, we can learn information from $f(\bar{s})$ and $f'(f(\bar{s}))$.

3 Analysis of Cases for an Example MT System

We examine one particular system and the application of the ideas above to improve this system. There are a number of commercial systems publicly available including [Systran, 2002] and [FreeTranslation, 2002]. Although Systran's system is more widely used, FreeTranslation offers more relaxed requirements on the length of the text to be translated. Also, initial comparison showed that results on AltaVista, which uses Systran's translation software, were comparable to the results obtained from FreeTranslation. Given a machine translation system, (f, f'), we calculate translations $f(w)$ and $f'(f(w))$ for a set of words w in L_1. In our case, we choose L_1 = English and L_2 = Spanish.

Table 1 shows a summary of the data generated using Freetanslation.com in February 2003 from 45,192 English words ([Red Hat, 2002]). A partition (i.e. non-overlapping, exhaustive set) of the possible outcomes is shown. We examine each of these cases and explain how each case provides information for improving the translation system (f, f'). For many machine translation systems, the default when the translation for w is unknown is to translate the word as w (i.e. $f(w) = w$). Throughout these examples, we will assume that equality implies that the system could not translate the word. A message or flag issued by the system could be used instead, if available.

$w = f'(f(w)) \neq f(w)$:
In this case, the word w is translated to a different string, $f(w)$, in the second language. When $f(w)$ is translated back to the original language, it is translated

back to the original word w. Generally, in this situation the machine translation system is translating these words correctly. Mistakes can still occur here if there are complementary mistakes in the lexicon in each direction. There is no information for the three problems described above in this case.

Table 1. The results from doing a three-way translation of approximately 45,192 English words to Spanish and back to English.

	Occurrences	Example $w, f(w), f'(f(w))$
$w = f'(f(w)) \neq f(w)$	9,330	dog, perro, dog
$w = f(w) \neq f'(f(w))$	278	metro, metro, meter
$w \neq f(w) = f'(f(w))$	8,785	scroll, rollo, rollo
$w = f(w) = f'(f(w))$	11,586	abstractness, abstractness, abstractness
$w \neq f(w) \neq f'(f(w))$	14,523	cupful, taza, cup

$w = f(w) \neq f'(f(w))$:
In this case, the word w is translated to the same string in the second language; however, it is then translated to a different string when it is translated back to the original language. This happens when w is a word in both languages (possibly with different meanings), which the translation system is unable to translate to the second language (for example, w = arena, $f(w)$ = arena, $f'(f(w))$ = sand). From these examples, we learn that the translation function f should translate $f'(f(w))$ to $f(w)$ (Problem 2). This information may or may not be useful. We can query f to see if this information is already known.

$w \neq f(w) = f'(f(w))$:
In this case, the word w is translated from the original language to the second language; however, it is then translated as the same word when translated back to the original language. There are two cases where this happens.
1. The most likely situation is that there is a problem with the translation system from the second language to the original language (i.e. in f') since the default behavior for translating an unknown word is to leave the word untranslated. In this case, two pieces of information are learned. First, if $f(w)$ is seen on the input and is translated to $f'(f(w))$ then a mistake has occurred (Problem 1). We can also suggest the correct translation. Given a sentence $\bar{s}$, if word s_i is translated to s_i and $s_i = f'(f(w))$, then s_i was incorrectly translated and the correct translation for s_i is w (Problem 2).
2. The second case, which is less likely, is that $f(w)$ is a word that, when translated back to the original language, is the same string (this is similar to case 2 below of $w = f(w) = f'(f(w))$). For example, w = abase, $f(w)$ = degrade (present subjunctive form of degradar, to degrade), $f'(f(w))$ = degrade. We can learn that $f(w)$ is an ambiguous word that can be translated as either w or $f'(f(w))$.

$w = f(w) = f'(f(w))$:

In this case, all the words are the same. There are two common situations.

1. If the word for w in the second language is actually w then the translation is correct. This is common with proper names (for example, w = Madrid, $f(w)$ = Madrid, $f'(f(w))$ = Madrid). In this case, no information is gained to solve the problems listed above.
2. If the system is unable to translate w, then $w = f(w)$. If this is the case, then it is unlikely that w will actually be a valid word in the second language (as shown above, this does happen 278 out of 45,192 times, where the $f(w)$ is translated to something different by f') and so the word again gets translated as w in the second translation step (for example, w = matriarchal, $f(w)$ = matriarchal, $f'(f(w))$ = matriarchal). In this case, the translation function f makes a mistake on word w (Problem 1).

$w \neq f(w) \neq f'(f(w)) \neq w$:

There are two situations that may cause this to happen. w may be a synonym for $f'(f(w))$ or there may be at least one error in the translation. If we assume that the knowledge in the translation systems is accurate, then both w and $f'(f(w))$ are appropriate translations for $f(w)$. These two cases can be disambiguated using contextual information.

One last piece of information can be obtained when $f(w) \neq f'(f(w))$. In these cases, some translation was done by f'. We can assume that if $f'(f(w))$ actually is a word in the original language. Using this, we can extend the word list in the original language.

4 Rule Learning

Using the framework described in Section 3, we can learn rules that improve the output of a translation system. We learn two different types of rules: context-independent and context-dependent. If there is no ambiguity about the translation of a word, then context is not required to disambiguate and a context-independent rule can be learned. If, on the other hand, there are multiple possible translations, then context is required to decide between the different possible translations. Figure 1 outlines the algorithm for generating the data and for learning both types of rules.

For preprocessing, the word lists is translated from the starting language to the alternate language and back to the original language. Table 2 summarizes the information that is used for generating rules from these translations. The input words are L_1 words. The current translations are the words expected to be seen in the output of the translation system. Finally, the correct translations indicate which word the output word should be changed to.

By examining the input words involved in the cases in Table 2, non-ambiguous words can be identified where an input word only has one learned correct translation. Notice that many of the entries in Table 2 are inherently ambiguous, such as when $w \neq f(w) \neq f'(f(w))$. Almost all non-ambiguous words are generated from the case when $w \neq f(w) = f'(f(w))$, where the system knows how to translate $f(w)$ from English but does not know how to translate it back to English.

Preprocessing steps
- Translate L_1 word list from L_1 to L_2 and back to L_1
- Translate L_2 word list from L_2 to L_1 and back to L_2
- Generate input word (L_2), current translation (L_1) and correct translation (L_2) triplets using rules in Table 2
- For all words, w, in corpus, generate frequency counts, $count(w)$
- Translate corpus from L_1 to L_2 to use for learning contexts

Generate context-independent rules for non-ambiguous words
- Identify non-ambiguous words by finding all "input words" with only a single suggested correct translation
- Generate context-independent rules of the form:
    g(input word,[ ],current translation,[ ]) → correct translation

Generate context-independent rules for k-dominant words
- Find sets of "input words" that have the same suggested correction translation. These words represent possible translation options. Identify k-dominant words where
    $count(option_i) > k$ and $count(option_j) = 0$ for all $j \neq i$
- Generate context-independent rules of the form:
    g(input word,[ ],current translation,[ ]) → $option_i$

Generate context-dependent rules for ambiguous words
- Get the possible context words t_j for each $option_i$ for the remaining ambiguous words
    - In the L_1 corpus, find sentences where $option_i$ appears and the corresponding ambiguous word is in the translated sentence in L_2
    - Get all possible context words t_j as the words surrounding $option_i$
- For each $option_i$, generate the context, $c(option_i)$, as all t_j that pass the significance level α threshold for the likelihood ratio test
- Learn context-dependent rules of the form:
    g(input word,[ ],current translation, $c(option_i)$) → $option_i$

Fig. 1. Outline of algorithm to learn rules to improve L_2 to L_1 translation. The preprocessing steps generate the initial data for use in learning the rules. The following three sets of steps describe the algorithms for learning the context-independent and context-dependent rules.

Table 2. Patterns for generating rules for Spanish to English improvement.

Case	Input word	Current translation	Correct translation
Eng Sp Eng $w \neq f(w) = f'(f(w))$ $f(w)$ is **not** an English word	$f(w)$	$f'(f(w))$	w
Eng Sp Eng $w \neq f(w) = f'(f(w))$ $f(w)$ **is** an English word	$f(w)$ $f(w)$	$f'(f(w))$ $f'(f(w))$	w $f'(f(w))$
Eng Sp Eng $w \neq f(w) \neq f'(f(w))$	$f(w)$ $f(w)$	$f'(f(w))$ $f'(f(w))$	w $f'(f(w))$
Sp Eng Sp $w = f(w) \neq f'(f(w))$ $f'(f(w)) = f(f'(f(w)))$	$f'(f(w))$	$f(f'(f(w)))$	$f(w)$
Sp Eng Sp $w = f(w) \neq f'(f(w))$ $f'(f(w)) \neq f(f'(f(w))) \neq f(w)$	$f'(f(w))$ $f'(f(w))$	$f(f'(f(w)))$ $f(f'(f(w)))$	$f(w)$ $f(f'(f(w)))$

For those words where there is only one known translation and therefore no ambiguity, a context-independent rule of the form $g(s,[],t,[]) = r$ can be learned, where s = input word, t = current translation and r = correct translation. Using this methodology, 7,155 context-independent rules are learned from the list of 45,192 words and the FreeTranslation engine.

4.1 Dealing with Ambiguous Words

For the remaining input word, current translation and correct translation triplets, there are at least two correct translations for the same input word. We must decide between these possible correct translations. We suggest two methods that both leverage a corpus in the target language, in this case English, to distinguish between translation options.

We would like to identify as many non-ambiguous words in the data as possible, since these rules are simpler. To do this, we can use the English corpus available. For our purposes, we use the Pan American Health Organization corpus ([PAHO, 2002]) that consists of over half a million words. Counting the occurrences of the possible translations (i.e. correct translation entries) can give some indication about which translation options are more likely. We define an input word as being k-dominant if one translation option occurs at least k times in the text and all other options do not appear at all. When a word is k-dominant, it is reasonable to assume that the input word should always be translated as the dominant option. We can learn a context-independent rule that states exactly this. Using this method, all of the k-dominant words with $k = 5$ are learned resulting in an additional 816 context-independent rules.

For all the input words where there are multiple possible translations and no one option is k-dominant, context can be used to disambiguate between the possible translations. The rules being learned have the possibility of both an input context and an output context. In practice only context in the input *or* output language is necessary. In our case, for Spanish to English improvement, English text is more readily available, so only the output contexts will be learned.

Given an ambiguous input word, a, that has *option$_1$,..., option$_n$* as possible correct translations, the goal is to learn a context for each possible translation, *option$_i$*, that disambiguates it from the other translations. We do this by gathering words from the English corpus that occur in the same sentences as each of the possible translation options *option$_1$,..., option$_n$*. We can use the machine translation system to verify that *option$_i$* actually gets translated to a (and correspondingly that a gets translated to *option$_i$*) in that context.

4.2 Determining Significant Context Words

The problem described above is the problem of collocation: finding words that are strongly associated. Many methods have been proposed for discovering collocations such as frequency counts, mean and variance tests, t-test, χ^2 test and likelihood ratio test ([Manning and Schütze, 1999]). The likelihood ratio test has been suggested as the most appropriate for this problem since it does not assume a normal distribution like the t-test nor does it make assumptions about the minimum frequency counts like the χ^2 test ([Dunning, 1993]).

For this problem, we have two different sets of sentences that we are interested in: the set S_i of sentences that contain the translation option t_i, and the set $\overline{S}_i$ of sentences that don't contain the translation option. The decision is for each context word w_j in the sentences belonging to S_i, whether or not that word is significantly associated with the translation option t_i or not.

The likelihood ratio test tests an alternate hypothesis against a null hypothesis. In this case, the null hypothesis is that the two groups of sentences (sentences with and without t_i) come from the same distribution with respect to the occurrence of w_j in the sentence. The alternate hypothesis is that the two groups of sentences are different with respect to the occurrence of w_j. We will also impose the further constraint that w_j must be *more* likely to occur in sentences of S_i.

For each set of sentences, the occurrence of w_j can be modeled using the binomial distribution. The assumption is that there is some probability that w_j occurs in a sentence. For both hypotheses, the likelihood equation is $\ell = p(S_i; \theta_1)p(\overline{S}_i; \theta_2)$. For the null hypothesis, the sentences come from the same distribution and therefore $\theta_1 = \theta_2 = \theta$. In all these situations, the maximum likelihood estimate of the parameter is used (the frequencies seen in the training data, in this case the English corpus). Using these parameter estimations, the likelihood ratio can be calculated in a similar fashion to [Dunning, 1993]. We compare this value with a significance level, α, to make a decision about whether the collocation is significant or not. We do this for all words in sentences that contain t_i, then construct context-dependent rules that contain all words that pass the significance test in the context. For our experiments, $\alpha = 0.001$ is an appropriate significance level. Intuitively, this means that there is a one in a thousand chance of a candidate word being misclassified as significant.

To improve the generality of the contexts learned, we perform the test on stemmed versions of the words and generate context-dependent rules using these stemmed words. The Porter stemmer ([Porter, 1980]) is used to stem the words. For the remainder of the paper, the results provided are for the stemmed versions.

5 Results

In this section, we examine the success of the learned rules in a real domain. We examine the Pan American Health Organization (PAHO) Conferences and General Services Division parallel texts. This data set consists of 180 pairs of documents in English and Spanish ([PAHO, 2002]).

The 180 Spanish documents consist of 20,084 sentences, identified by periods (minus a number of Spanish abbreviations), and 616,109 words, identified by surrounding white space. The sentences are translated using FreeTranslation.com to get the initial translation. Then, the rules learned using the algorithms in Section 4 are applied to change the sentences. For the context-independent rules, the rule fires anytime the appropriate words are seen in the original sentence and translated sentence. The context-dependent rules add the additional restriction that the translated sentence must also contain one of the words in the learned output context of the rule to fire.

Spanish:
El contenido de **alquitrán** en los cigarrillos de tabaco negro sin filtro es mayor que en los restantes tipos de cigarrillos y son aquellos precisamente los de mayor consumo en la población, lo que aumenta la potencialidad del tabaquismo como factor de riesgo.

Original translation:
The content of **alquitrán** in the black cigarettes of tobacco without filter is greater that in the remaining types of cigarettes and are those precise the of greater consumption in the population, what enlarges the potencialidad of the tabaquismo as factor of risk.

Improved translation:
The content of **tar** in the black cigarettes of tobacco without filter is greater that in the remaining types of cigarettes and are those precise the of greater consumption in the population, what enlarges the potencialidad of the tabaquismo as factor of risk.

Fig. 2. Example of an improvement in translation. The first sentence is the original Spanish sentence to be translated. The second sentence is the translation made by FreeTranslation.com. The final sentence is the translation after a learned improvement rule has been applied. The change is in bold.

Table 3. Summary of results for rules generated from a word list with 45,192 entries.

Rule type	Rules learned	Avg. # words in context	Rules used	Words changed
Context independent	6,783	NA	701	5,022
Context independent, dominant $k = 5$	809	NA	191	4,768
Context dependent, $\alpha = .001$	1,355	5	301	12,416

Over 9,000 rules are learned. Table 3 shows the results from applying these rules to the sentences. The rules change 22,206 words in the PAHO data set and 14,952 or 74% of the sentences. Figure 2 shows an example firing of a context-independent rule that changes "alquitrán" to "tar".

6 Using Extended Word Lists

The methods in this paper are based on having a word list in language L_1. In this section, we present two methods for extending this word list. One of the advantages of the rule learning method described above is that it is robust to erroneous words in the word list. If the system does not recognize a word in the word list then it will not get translated, as is the case where $w = f(w) = f'(f(w))$. No learning is done in this case, so erroneous words are filtered out by the machine translation system. Since a high quality word list is not required, the word lists can be constructed at least two different ways.

When translating w to $f(w)$ and back to the original language as $f'(f(w))$, if $f(w) \neq f'(f(w))$ then some translation was done between $f(w)$ and $f'(f(w))$. Given the robustness of the learning system, we can assume that if the machine translation system translates $f(w)$ to $f'(f(w))$, then $f'(f(w))$ is a word in the original language. Using this method, 419 additional words not in the original word list are learned.

In many circumstances, translation systems are to be used in a specific domain (for example medicine, politics, public health, etc.). The PAHO data set mentioned earlier contains documents in the public health domain. To improve the recall of the machine translation we can incorporate more rules that contain terminology that is relevant to this particular domain. We can do this by examining words in a corpus of a similar domain to add to the word list. In our case, since the PAHO data set contains the parallel text in English, we can use this text. The English version of the PAHO data set contains 5,215 new words that are not in the original word list.

Table 4 shows the results of learning rules with the original 45,192 words plus the 419 learned words and the 5,215 domain specific words. The additional words add 468 new rules. Although these new rules only constitute a small fraction of the total rules (~5%) they account for over 8% of the changes. In particular, the new, domain specific context-independent rules fire over four times more often than the rules learned from a generic word list. Because these additional rules are learned using domain specific words, they are much more likely to apply for translating text in that particular domain. With the addition of these new rules, 78% of the sentences are changed.

Table 4. Summary of results for rules generated using a general word list with 45,000 entries plus 419 learned words and 5,215 domain specific words.

Rule type	Rules learned	Avg. # words in context	Rules used	Words changed
Context independent	7,155	NA	903	6,526
Context independent, dominant $k = 5$	816	NA	200	5,038
Context dependent, $\alpha = .001$	1,444	5	327	12,671

7 Discussion

In this paper, we have examined a technique for improving a machine translation system using only plain text. One of the advantages of this approach is that the resources required to learn the rules are easier to obtain than traditional approaches that require aligned bitext ([Macklovitch and Hannan, 1996]). Also, our method makes no assumptions about the workings of the translation system.

By translating words from the original language to the second language and back to the original language, differences in information between the two translation functions are isolated. Using this information, we show how correction rules can be learned. Context-independent rules are learned when the system only suggests a single possible translation. When there is ambiguity about what the correct translation of a word is, the likelihood ratio is used to identify words that cooccur significantly which each translation option.

Using these rules, almost 25,000 words are changed on a corpus of over half a million words. On a sample of 600 changes, the context-independent rules have a precision of 99% and the context-dependent rules have a precision of 79%. One of the open questions for machine translation research is how to evaluate a translation. A few automated methods have been suggested such as BLEU ([Papineni et al., 2001]), which is based on n-gram occurrence in a reference text. Although these methods have merit, for the particular rules learned by our system, an n-gram metric would almost always see improvement since changing a Spanish word in English text to an English word will generally be better. For this reason, we instead chose to evaluate the results by hand.

A majority of the context-independent rules represent changes where the original system did not know any possible translation, so it is not surprising that the precision is high. The context-dependent rules have lower precision even though a significance level of 0.001 was used. The main reason for this lower precision is that the likelihood ratio can suggest collocations that are significant, but that are not useful for ambiguity resolution. This is attenuated when the counts are very small or when the ambiguous translation is common and the counts are therefore high. In these cases, common words such as "is", "that", "it", "have", etc. are identified as significant.

Another problem is the particular rule representation chosen. The context-dependent rules define the context as a bag of words. Unfortunately, a bag of words does not model many relationships, such as word order, syntax or semantics, which can be useful for discriminating significant collocations. For example, when deciding between "another" and "other" in the sentence fragment "Another important coordination type...", the location of "type" and the fact that it is singular suggests "another" as the correct translation.

One final problem is that stemming can cause undesired side effects in the contexts learned. As seen in the sentence fragment above, plurality is important, particularly when deciding between two translations that only differ by plurality. Unfortunately, stemming, in attempting to improve generality, removes the plurality of a word. The combination of these problems leads to a lower precision for the context-dependent rules. Future research should be directed towards employing alternate rule representations and alternate collocation techniques such as in [Krenn, 2000].

The techniques that we used in this paper are just the beginning of a wide range of improvements and applications that use existing machine translation systems as a resource. As new applications that use translation systems arise, particularly those in time and information critical fields, such as [Damianos et al., 2002], the importance of accurate automated translation systems becomes critical.

References

[Brill, 1995] Brill, E. 1995. Transformation-Based Error-Driven Learning and Natural Language Processing: A Case Study in Part-of-Speech Tagging. *Computational Linguistics* 21(4), p. 543-565.

[Damianos et al., 2002] Damianos, L., Ponte, J., Wohlever, S., Reeder, F., Day, D., Wilson, G. and Hirschman, L. 2002. MiTAP for Biosecurity: A Case Study. In *AI Magazine*, Winter 2002, p. 13-29.

[Dunning, 1993] Dunning, T. 1993. Accurate Methods for the Statistics of Surprise and Coincidence. Computational Linguistics 19(1), p. 61-74.
[FreeTranslation.com, 2002] http://www.freetranslation.com powered by SDL International's *Enterprise Translation Server.*
[Koehn and Knight, 2001] Koehn, P. and Knight, K. 2001. Knowledge Sources for Word-Level Translation Models. In *Empirical Methods in Natural Language Processing conference.*
[Krenn, 2000] Krenn, B. 2000. Collocation Mining: Exploiting Corpora for Collocation Identification and Representation. In *Proceedings of The Ninth EURALEX International Congress.*
[Melamed, 2001] Melamed, D. 2001. *Empirical Methods for Exploiting Parallel Texts.* The MIT Press.
[Macklovitch and Hannan, 1996] Macklovitch, E. and Hannan, M. 1996. Line'Em Up: Advances In Alignment Technology And Their Impact on Translation Support Tools. In *Proceedings of the Second Conference of the Association for Machine Translation in the Americas,* p. 41-57.
[Manning and Schütze , 1999] Manning, C. and Shütze, H. 1999. Foundations of Statistical Natural Language Processing. MIT Press.
[PAHO, 2002] Pan American Health Organization documents: http://crl.nmsu.edu/cgi-bin/Tools/CLR/clrcat#H8
[Papineni *et al.*, 2001] Papineni, K.A., Roukos, S., Ward, T. and Zhu, W.J. 2001. Bleu: A Method for Automatic Evaluation of Machine Translation. IBM Research Report, RC22176.
[Porter, 1998] Porter, M. 1980. An Algorithm for Suffix Stripping. Program (Automated Library and Information Systems), 14(3), p. 130-137.
[Red Hat, 2002] Linux, Red Hat 7.2, English word list /usr/dict/words.
[Systran, 2002] Systran Corporation (portals: Google, AOL, AltaVista, CompuServe, Lycos, OracleMobile.com).
[Yamada and Knight, 2001] Yamada, K. and Knight, K. 2001. A Syntax-based Statistical Translation Model. In *Proceedings of the Association for Computational Linguistics,* p. 523-530.
[Yarowsky, 1994] Yarowsky, D. 1994. Decision Lists for Lexical Ambiguity Resolution: Application to Accent Restoration in Spanish And French. In *Proceedings of the Association for Computational Linguistics,* p. 77-95.

Optimising Performance of Competing Search Engines in Heterogeneous Web Environments*

Rinat Khoussainov and Nicholas Kushmerick

Department of Computer Science, University College Dublin
Belfield, Dublin 4, Ireland
{rinat,nick}@ucd.ie

Abstract. Distributed heterogeneous search environments are an emerging phenomenon in Web search, in which topic-specific search engines provide search services, and metasearchers distribute user's queries to only the most suitable search engines. Previous research has explored the performance of such environments from the user's perspective (e.g., improved quality of search results). We focus instead on performance from the search service provider's point of view (e.g, income from queries processed vs. resources used to answer them). We analyse a scenario in which individual search engines compete for queries by choosing which documents to index. We propose the COUGAR algorithm that specialised search engines can use to decide which documents to index on each particular topic. COUGAR is based on a game-theoretic analysis of heterogeneous search environments, and uses reinforcement learning techniques to exploit the sub-optimal behaviour of its competitors.

1 Introduction

Heterogeneous search environments are a recent phenomenon in Web search. They can be viewed as a federation of *independently controlled* metasearchers and many specialised search engines. Specialised search engines provide focused search services in a specific domain (e.g. a particular topic). Metasearchers help to process user queries effectively and efficiently by distributing them only to the most suitable search engines for each query. Compared to the traditional search engines like Google or AltaVista, specialised search engines (together) provide access to arguably much larger volumes of high-quality information resources, frequently called the "deep" or "invisible" Web.

Previous work has mainly explored the performance of such heterogeneous search environments from the user's perspective (e.g., improved quality of search results). Examples include algorithms for search engine selection and result merging [1]. On the other hand, a provider of search services is more interested in the income from queries processed vs. resources used to answer them. To the best of our knowledge, little attention has been paid to performance optimisation of search engines from the service provider's point of view.

An important factor that affects performance of a specialised search engine in a heterogeneous search environment is *competition* with other independently controlled

---

* This research was supported by grant SFI/01/F.1/C015 from Science Foundation Ireland, and grant N00014-03-1-0274 from the US Office of Naval Research.

search engines. When there are many search engines available, users want to send their queries to the engine(s) that would provide the best possible results. Multiple search providers in a heterogeneous search environment can be viewed as participants in a search services market competing for user queries.

We examine the problem of performance-maximising behaviour for non-cooperative specialised search engines in heterogeneous search environments. We analyse a scenario in which individual search engines compete for queries by choosing to index documents for which they think users are likely to query. Our goal is to propose a method that specialised search engines can use to select on which topic(s) to specialise and how many documents to index on that topic to maximise their performance.

While the search engines in a heterogeneous search environment are independent in terms of selecting their content, they are not independent in terms of the performance achieved. Changes to parameters of one search engine affect the queries received by its competitors and, vice versa, actions of the competing engines influence the queries received by the given search engine. Thus, the utility of any local content change depends on the state and actions of other search engines in the system. The uncertainty about actions of competitors as well as the potentially large number of competing engines make our optimisation problem difficult. We show that naive strategies (e.g, blindly indexing lots of popular documents) are ineffective, because a rational search engine's indexing decisions should depend on the (unknown) decisions of its opponents.

Our main contributions are as follows:

- We formalise the issues related to optimal behaviour in competitive heterogeneous search environments and propose a model for performance of a specialised search engine in such environments.
- We provide game-theoretic analysis of a simplified version of the problem and motivate the use of the concept of *"bounded rationality"* [2]. Bounded rationality assumes that decision makers act sub-optimally in the game-theoretic sense due to incomplete information about the environment and/or limited resources.
- We propose a reinforcement learning procedure for topic selection, called COUGAR, which allows a specialised search engine to exploit sub-optimal behaviour of its competitors to improve own performance.

An evaluation of COUGAR in a simulation, driven by real user queries submitted to over 47 existing search engines, demonstrates the feasibility of our approach.

2 Problem Formulation

2.1 Search Engine Performance

We adopt an economic view on search engine performance from the service provider's point of view. Performance is a difference between the value of the search service provided (income) and the cost of the resources used to provide the service. The value of a search service is a function of the user queries processed. The cost structure in an actual search engine may be quite complicated involving many categories, such as storage, crawling, indexing, and searching. In our simplified version of the problem, we only take into account the cost of resources involved in processing search queries. (Note that we also obtained similar results for a more elaborated cost model that takes into account the cost of document crawling, storage, and maintenance [3].) Under these assumptions, we can use the following formula for search engine performance: $P = \alpha Q - \beta Q D$, where Q is the number of queries processed in a given time interval, D is the number of documents in the search engine index, α and β are constants.

αQ represents the service value: if the price of processing one search request for a user is α, then αQ would be the total income from service provisioning. $\beta Q D$ represents the cost of processing search requests. If x amount of resources is sufficient to process Q queries, then we would need $2x$ to process twice as many queries in the same time. Similarly, if x resources is enough to search in D documents for each query, then we would need $2x$ to search twice as many documents in the same time. Thus, the amount of resources (and, hence, the cost) is proportional to both Q and D, and so can be expressed as $\beta Q D$, where β is a constant reflecting the resource costs. An examination of the architecture of the FAST search engine (www.alltheweb.com) shows that our cost function is not that far from reality [4].

We assume that all search engines in our system use the same α and β constants when calculating their performance. Having the same β reasonably assumes that the cost of resources (per "unit") is the same for all search engines. Having the same α assumes, perhaps unrealistically, that the search engines choose to charge users the same amount per query. We leave to future work, however, optimisation of search engine performance in environments where engines may have different service pricing. With no service price differentiation, selection of search engines by the metasearcher depends on what documents the engines index. Therefore, the goal of each search engine would be to select the index content in a way that maximises its performance.

2.2 Metasearch Model

We assume a very generic model of how any reasonable metasearch system should behave. This will allow us to abstract from implementation details of particular metasearch algorithms (presuming that they approximate our generic model). It is reasonable to assume that users would like to send queries to the search engine(s) that contain the most relevant documents to the query, and the more of them, the better.

The ultimate goal of the metasearcher is to select for each user query to which search engines it should be forwarded to maximise the results relevance, while minimising the number of engines involved. The existing research in metasearch (e.g. [1]), however, does not go much further than simply ranking search engines. Since it is unclear how many top ranked search engines should be queried (and how many results requested), we assume that the query is always forwarded to the *highest ranked* search engine. In case several search engines have the same top rank, one is selected at random.

The ranking of search engines is performed based on the expected number of relevant documents that are indexed by each engine. Engine i that indexes the largest expected number of documents NR_i^q relevant to query q will have the highest rank.

We apply a probabilistic information retrieval approach to assessing relevance of documents [5]. For each document d, there is a probability $\Pr(rel|q,d)$ that this document will be considered by the user as relevant to query q. In this case, $NR_i^q =$

$\sum_{d \in i} \Pr(rel|q, d)$, where by $d \in i$ we mean the set of documents indexed by engine i. Obviously, the metasearcher does not know the exact content of search engines, so it tries to estimate NR_i^q from the corresponding content summaries.

If $\Pr(rel|q_1, d) = \Pr(rel|q_2, d), \forall d$ then queries q_1 and q_2 will look the same from both metasearcher's and search engine's points of view, even though the queries may differ lexically. All engines will have the same rankings for q_1 and q_2, and the queries will get forwarded to the same search engine. Therefore, all queries can be partitioned into equivalence classes with identical $\Pr(rel|q, d)$ functions. We call such classes *topics*. We assume in this paper that there is a fixed finite set of topics and queries can be assigned to topics. Of course, this it not feasible in reality. One way to approximate topics in practice would be to cluster user queries received in the past and then assign new queries to the nearest clusters.

2.3 Engine Selection for "Ideal" Crawlers

Let us assume that users only issue queries on a single topic. We will see later how this can be extended to multiple topics. It follows from Section 2.2, that to receive queries, a search engine needs to be the highest ranked one for this topic. It means that given an index size D, a search engine would like to have a document index with the largest possible NR_i. This can be achieved, if the engine indexes the D most relevant documents on the topic.

Population of search engines is performed by topic-specific (focused) Web crawlers [6]. Since it is very difficult to model a Web crawler, we assume that all search engines have "ideal" Web crawlers which for a given D can find the D most relevant documents on a given topic. Under this assumption, two search engines indexing the same number of documents $D_1 = D_2$ will have $NR_1 = NR_2$. Similarly, if $D_1 < D_2$, then $NR_1 < NR_2$ (assuming that all documents have $\Pr(rel|d) > 0$). Therefore, the metasearcher will forward user queries to the engine(s) containing the largest number of documents.

This model can be extended to multiple topics, if we assume that each document can only be relevant to a single topic. In this case, the state of a search engine can be represented by the number of documents D_i^t that engine i indexes for each topic t. A query on topic t will be forwarded to the engine i with the largest D_i^t.

2.4 Decision Making Process

The decision making process proceeds in series of fixed-length time intervals. For each time interval, search engines simultaneously and independently decide on how many documents to index on each topic. They also allocate the appropriate resources according to their expectations for the number of queries that users will submit during the interval. Since search engines cannot have unlimited crawling resources, we presume that they can only do incremental adjustments to their index contents that require the same time for all engines. The user queries submitted during the time interval are allocated to the search engines based on their index parameters (D_i^t) as described above. The whole process repeats in the next time interval.

Let $\hat{Q}_i^t$ be the number of queries on topic t that, according to expectations of search engine i, the users will submit. Then the total number of queries expected by engine

i can be calculated as $\hat{Q}_i = \sum_{t:D_i^t>0} \hat{Q}_i^t$. We assume that engines always allocate resources for the full amount of queries expected. Then the cost of resources allocated by engine i can be expressed as $\beta \hat{Q}_i D_i$, where $D_i = \sum_t D_i^t$ is the total number of documents indexed by engine i. The number of queries on topic t *actually forwarded* to engine i can be represented as

$$Q_i^t = \begin{cases} 0 & : \exists j, D_i^t < D_j^t \\ \frac{Q^t}{|B|} & : i \in B, B = \{b : D_b^t = \max_j D_j^t\} \end{cases}$$

where B is the set of the highest-ranked search engines for topic t, and Q^t is the number of queries on topic t *actually submitted* by the users. That is, the search engine does not receive any queries, if it is ranked lower than competitors, and receives its appropriate share when it is the top ranked engine (see Sections 2.2 and 2.3). The total number of queries forwarded to search engine i can be calculated as $Q_i = \sum_{t:D_i^t>0} Q_i^t$.

We assume that if the search engine receives more queries than it expected (i.e. more queries than it can process), the excess queries are simply rejected. Therefore, the total number of queries processed by search engine i equals to $\min(Q_i, \hat{Q}_i)$. Finally, the performance of engine i over a given time interval can be represented as follows: $P_i = \alpha \min(Q_i, \hat{Q}_i) - \beta \hat{Q}_i D_i$.

3 The COUGAR Approach

The decision-making process for individual search engines can be modelled as a multi-stage game [7]. At each stage, a matrix game is played, where players are search engines, actions are values of (D_i^t), and player i receives payoff P_i.

If player i knew the actions of its opponents and user queries at a future stage k, it could calculate the optimal response as the one maximising $P_i(k)$. For example, in case of a single topic it should play $D_i(k) = \max_{j \neq i} D_j(k) + 1$, if $\max_{j \neq i} D_j(k) + 1 < \alpha/\beta$, and $D_i(k) = 0$ otherwise (simply put, outperform opponents by 1 document if profitable, and do not incur any costs otherwise).

In reality, players do not know the future. Uncertainty about future queries can be largely resolved by reasonably assuming that user interests usually do not change quickly. That is, queries in the next interval are likely to be approximately the same as queries in the previous one. A more difficult problem is not knowing future actions of the opponents (competing search engines). One possible way around this would be to agree on (supposedly, mutually beneficial) future actions in advance. To avoid deception, players would have to agree on playing a Nash equilibrium [7] of the game, since then there will be no incentive for them to not follow the agreement. Agreeing to play a Nash equilibrium, however, becomes problematic when the game has multiple such equilibria. Players would be willing to agree on a Nash equilibrium yielding to them the highest (expected) payoffs, but the task of characterising all Nash equilibria of a game is NP-hard even given complete information about the game (as follows from [8]).

NP-hardness results and the possibility that players may not have complete information about the game and/or their opponents lead us to the idea of "bounded rationality" [2]. Bounded rationality assumes that players may not use the optimal strategies in the game-theoretic sense. Our proposal is to cast the problem of optimal behaviour in the game as a learning task, where the player would have to learn a strategy that performs well against its sub-optimal opponents.

Learning in games have been studied extensively in both game theory and machine learning. Some examples include fictious play and opponent modelling. Fictious play assumes that the other players are following some Markovian (possibly mixed) strategies, which are estimated from their historical play [9]. Opponent modelling assumes that opponent strategies are representable by finite state automata. The player learns parameters of the opponent's model from experience and then calculates the the best-response automaton [10]. We apply a more recent technique from reinforcement learning called GAPS (which stands for Gradient Ascent for Policy Search) [11]. In GAPS, the learner plays a parameterised strategy represented, e.g., by a finite state automaton, where parameters are probabilities of actions and state transitions. GAPS implements stochastic gradient ascent in the space of policy parameters. After each learning trial, parameters of the policy are updated by following the payoff gradient.

GAPS has a number of advantages important for our domain. It works in partially observable games (e.g. it does not require complete knowledge of the opponents' actions). It also scales well to multiple topics by modelling decision-making as a game with factored actions (where action components correspond to topics). The action space in such games is the product of factor spaces for each action component. GAPS, however, allows us to reduce the learning complexity: rather than learning in the product action space, separate GAPS learners can be used for each action component. It has been shown that such distributed learning is equivalent to learning in the product action space. As with all gradient-based methods, the disadvantage of GAPS is that it is only guaranteed to find a local optimum. We call a search engine that uses the proposed approach COUGAR, which stands for **CO**mpetitor **U**sing **G**APS **A**gainst **R**ivals.

3.1 Engine Controller Design

The task of the search engine controller is to change the state of the document index to maximise the engine performance. When making decisions, the engine controller can receive information about current characteristics of its own search engine as well the external environment in the form of observations.

The COUGAR controllers are modelled by non-deterministic Moore automata. A controller consists of a set of Moore automata (M^t), one for each topic, functioning synchronously. Each automaton is responsible for controlling the state of the search index for the corresponding topic. The following actions are available to each automaton M^t in the controller: *Grow* – increase the number of documents indexed on topic t by one; *Same* – do not change the number of documents on topic t; *Shrink* – decrease the number of documents on topic t by one. The resulting action of the controller is the product of actions (one for each topic) produced by each of the individual automata.

A controller's observations consist of two parts: observations of the state of its own search engine and observations of the opponents' state. The observations of its own state reflect the number of documents in the search engine's index for each topic. The observations of the opponents' state reflect the relative position of the opponents in the metasearcher rankings, which indirectly gives the controller partial information about the state of the opponents' index. The following three observations of the opponents' state are available for each topic t: *Winning* – there are opponents ranked higher for topic t than our search engine; *Tying* – opponents have either the same or a smaller rank for topic t than our search engine; *Losing* – the rank of our search engine for topic t is higher than opponents.

For T topics, the controller's inputs consist of T observations of the state of its own search engine (one for each topic) and T observations of the relative positions of the opponents (one per topic). Note, that the state of *all* opponents is summarised as a vector of T observations. Each of the Moore automata M^t in the COUGAR controller receives observations only for the corresponding topic t.

One may ask how the controller can obtain information about rankings of its opponents for a given topic. This can be done by sending a query on the topic of interest to the metasearcher and requesting a ranked list of search engines for the query. We also assume that the controller can obtain from the metasearcher information (statistics) on the queries previously submitted by user. This data are used in calculation of the expected number of queries for each topic $\hat{Q}_i^t$. In particular, for our experiments the number of queries on topic t expected by engine i in a given time interval k equals to the number of queries on topic t submitted by users in the previous interval (i.e. $\hat{Q}_i^t(k) = Q^t(k-1)$).

3.2 Learning Procedure

Training of the COUGAR controller to compete against various opponents is performed in series of simulation trials. Each simulation *trial* consists of 100 days, where each day corresponds to one state of the multi-stage game played. The search engines start with empty indices and then, driven by their controllers, adjust their index contents. In the beginning of each day, search engine controllers receive observations and simultaneously produce control actions (change their document indices). A query generator issues a stream of search queries for one day. The metasearcher distributes these queries between the search engines according to their index parameters on the day. The resulting reward in a simulation trial is calculated in the traditional for reinforcement learning way as a sum of discounted rewards from each day. After each trial, a learning step is performed. The COUGAR controller updates its strategy using the GAPS algorithm. That is, the action and state transition probabilities of the controller's Moore automata are modified using the payoff gradient (due to the lack of space see [11] for details of the update mechanism).

In our experiments, we simulated two competing search engines for a single and multiple topics. One search engine was using a fixed strategy, the other one was using the COUGAR controller. To simulate user search queries, we used HTTP logs obtained from a Web proxy of a large ISP. Since each search engine uses a different URL syntax for submission of requests, we developed URL extraction rules individually for 47 well-known search engines The total number of queries extracted was 657,861 collected over a period of 190 days. We associated topics with search terms in the logs. To simulate queries for n topics, we extracted the n most popular terms from the logs. The number of queries generated on topic t during a given time interval was equal to the number of queries with term t in the logs belonging to this time interval.

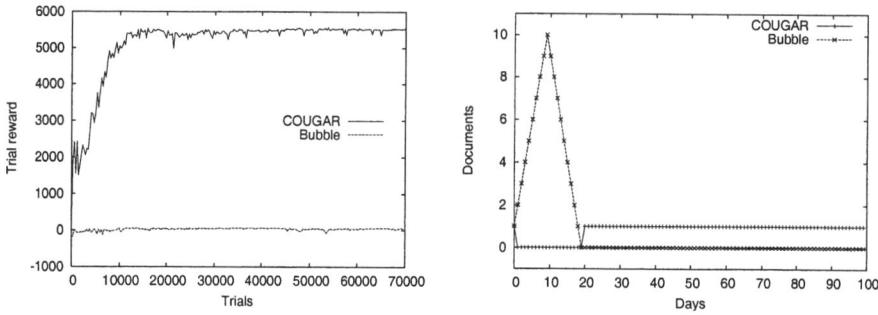

Fig. 1. "Bubble" vs COUGAR, single topic. Left: learning curve. Right: sample trial.

4 Results

4.1 "Bubble" Strategy

The "Bubble" strategy tries to index as many documents as possible without any regard to what competitors are doing. As follows from our performance formula (see Section 2.4), such unconstrained growing leads eventually to negative performance. Once the total reward falls below a certain threshold, the "Bubble" search engine goes bankrupt (i.e. it shrinks its index to 0 documents and retires until the end of the trial). This process imitates the situation in which a search service provider expands its business without paying attention to costs, eventually runs out of money, and quits. An intuitively sensible response to the "Bubble" strategy would be to wait until the bubble "bursts" and then come into the game alone. That is, a competitor should not index anything while the "Bubble" grows and should start indexing a minimal number of documents once the "Bubble" search engine goes bankrupt.

Figure 1 (left) shows how the performance of the COUGAR engine improved during learning for a single topic case. Once COUGAR reached a steady performance level, its resulting strategy was evaluated in a series of testing trials. Figure 1 (right) visualises a sample trial between the "Bubble" and the COUGAR engines by showing the number of documents indexed by the engines on each day of the trial.

In case of multiple topics, the "Bubble" was increasing (and decreasing) the number of documents indexed for each topic simultaneously. The COUGAR controller was using separate GAPS learners to manage the index size for each topic (as discussed in Section 3). Figure 2 shows the engines' behaviour (left) and performance (right) in a test trial with two different topics. Note that COUGAR has learned to wait until "Bubble" goes bankrupt, and then to win all queries for both topics.

4.2 "Wimp" Strategy

The "Wimp" controller used a more intelligent strategy. Consider it first for the case of a single topic. The set of all possible document index sizes is divided by "Wimp" into three non-overlapping sequential regions: "Confident", "Unsure", and "Panic". The

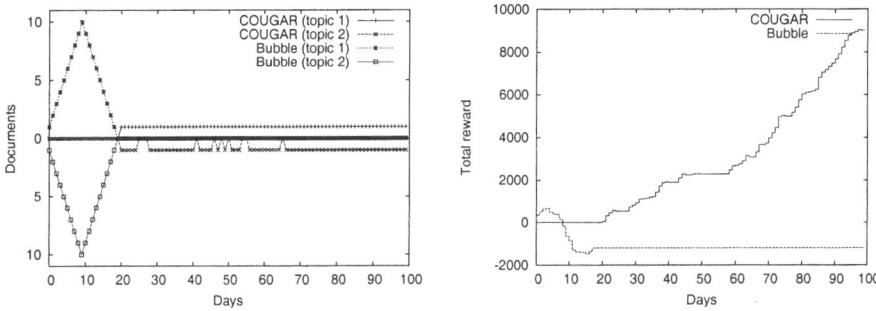

Fig. 2. "Bubble" vs COUGAR, multiple topics. Left: sample trial; the top half of Y axis shows the number of documents for topic 1, while the bottom half shows the number of documents for topic 2. Right: performance in a sample trial.

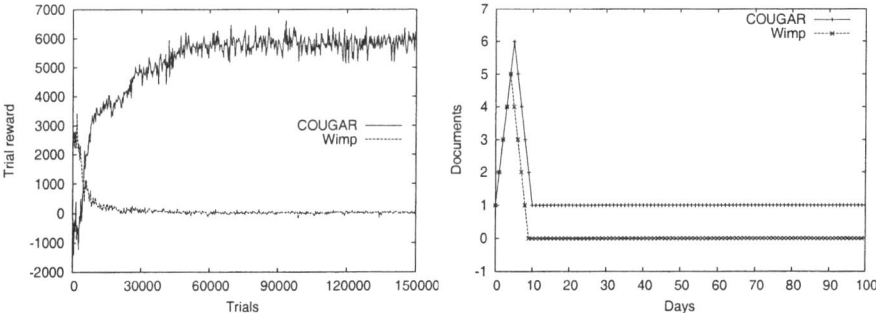

Fig. 3. "Wimp" vs COUGAR, single topic. Left: learning curve. Right: sample trial.

"Wimp's" behaviour in each region is as follows: *Confident* – the strategy in this region is to increase the document index size until it ranks higher than the opponent. Once this goal is achieved, the "Wimp" stops growing and keeps the index unchanged; *Unsure* – in this region, the "Wimp" keeps the index unchanged, if it is ranked higher or the same as the opponent. Otherwise, it retires (i.e. reduces the index size to 0); *Panic* – the "Wimp" retires straight away.

The overall idea is that the "Wimp" tries to outperform its opponent while in the "Confident" region by growing the index. When the index grows into the "Unsure" region, the "Wimp" prefers retirement to competition, unless it is already winning over or tying with the opponent. This reflects the fact that the potential losses in the "Unsure" region (if the opponent wins) become substantial, so the "Wimp" does not dare to risk.

Common sense tells us that one should behave aggressively against the "Wimp" in the beginning, to knock him out of competition, and then enjoy the benefits of monopoly. This is exactly what the COUGAR controller has learned to do as can be seen from Figure 3.

To generalise the "Wimp" strategy to multiple topics, it was modified in the following way. The "Wimp" opponent did not differentiate between topics of both queries

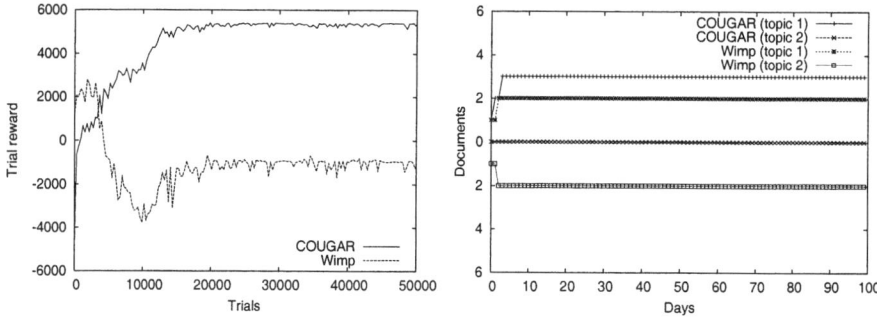

Fig. 4. "Wimp" vs COUGAR, multiple topics. Left: learning curve. Right: sample trial; the top half of Y axis shows the number of documents for topic 1, while the bottom half shows the number of documents for topic 2.

and documents. When assessing its own index size, the "Wimp" was simply adding the documents for different topics together. Similarly, when observing relative positions of the opponent, it was adding together ranking scores for different topics. Finally, like the multi-topic "Bubble", the "Wimp" was changing its index size synchronously for each topic. Figure 4 presents the learning curve (left) and a sample trial (right) respectively. COUGAR decided to specialise on the more popular topic, where it outperformed the opponent. The "Wimp" mistakenly assumed that it was winning in the competition, since its rank for both topics together was higher. In reality, it was receiving only queries for one topic, which did not cover its expenses for indexing documents on both topics.

4.3 Self-play

In the final set of experiments, we analysed behaviour of the COUGAR controller competing against itself. It is not guaranteed from the theoretical point of view that the gradient-based learning will always converge in self play. In practice, however, we observed that both learners converged to relatively stable strategies. We used the same setup with two different topics in the system. Figure 5 (left) shows that the players decided to split the query market: each of the search engines specialised on a different topic. Figure 5 (right) also shows the learning curves.

5 Related Work

The issues of performance (or profit) maximising behaviour in environments with multiple, possibly competing, decision makers have been addressed in a number of contexts, including multi-agent e-commerce systems and distributed databases.

In Mariposa [12], the distributed system consists of a federation of databases and query brokers. A user submits a query to a broker for execution together with the amount of money she is willing to pay for it. The broker partitions the query into sub-queries and finds a set of databases that can execute the sub-queries with the total cost not exceeding

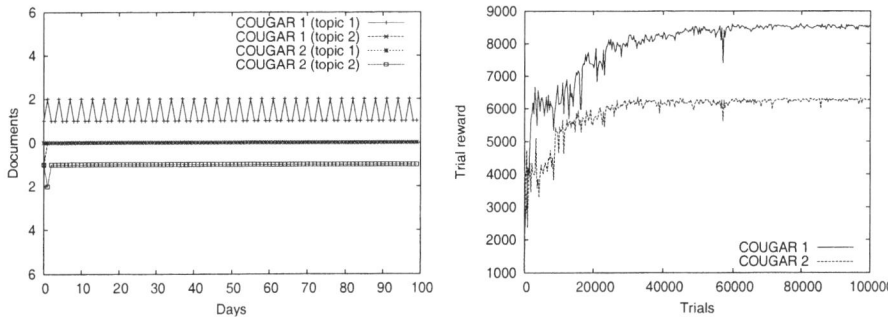

Fig. 5. COUGAR in self play, multiple topics. Left: sample trial; the top half of Y axis shows the number of documents for topic 1, while the bottom half shows the number of documents for topic 2. Right: learning curve.

what the user paid and the minimal processing delay. A database can execute a subquery only if it has all necessary data (data fragments) that are involved. The databases can trade data fragments (i.e. purchase or sell them) to maximise their revenues.

Trading data fragments may seem similar to the topic selection problem for specialised search engines. There are, however, significant differences between them. Acquiring a data fragment is an act of mutual agreement between the seller and the buyer, while search engines may change their index contents independently from others. Also, a proprietorship considerations are not taken into account.

Greenwald *et al* have studied behaviour dynamics of *pricebots*, automated agents that act on behalf of service suppliers and employ price-setting algorithms to maximise profits [13]. In the proposed model, the sellers offer a homogeneous good in an economy with multiple sellers and buyers. The buyers may have different strategies for selecting the seller, ranging from random to the selection of the cheapest seller on the market (bargain hunters), while the sellers use the same pricing strategy. A similar model but with populations of sellers using different strategies has been studied in [14]. The pricing problem can be viewed as a very simple instance of our topic selection task (namely, as a single topic case with some modifications to the performance model).

6 Conclusions and Future Work

The successful deployment of heterogeneous Web search environments will require that participating search service providers have effective means for managing the performance of their search engines. We analysed how specialised search engines can select on which topic(s) to specialise and how many documents to index on that topic to maximise their performance. We provided both an in-depth theoretical analysis of the problem and a practical method for automatically managing the search engine content in a simplified version of the problem. Our adaptive search engine, COUGAR, has managed to compete with some non-trivial opponents as shown by the experimental results. Most importantly, the same learning mechanism worked successfully against opponents using different strategies. Even when competing against other adaptive search engines (in our case itself), COUGAR has demonstrated a fairly sensible behaviour from the economic point of view. Namely, the engines have learned to segment the search services market with each engine occupying its niche, instead of a head-on competition.

We do not claim to provide a complete solution for the problem here, but we believe it is the promising first step. Clearly, we have made many strong assumptions in our models. One future direction will be to relax these assumptions to make our simulations more realistic. In particular, we intend to perform experiments with real documents and using some existing metasearch algorithms. This should allow us to avoid the assumption of the "single-topic" documents and also to assess how closely our metasearch model reflects real-life engine selection algorithms. We also plan to use clustering of user queries to derive topics in our simulations.

While we are motivated by the optimal behaviour for search services over document collections, our approach is applicable in more general scenarios involving services that must weigh the cost of their inventory of objects against the expected inventories of their competitors and the anticipated needs of their customers. For example, it would be interesting to apply our ideas to an environment in which large retail e-commerce sites must decide which products to stock. Another important direction would be to further investigate performance and convergence properties of the learning algorithm when opponents also evolve over time (e.g. against other learners). One possible approach here would be to use a variable learning rate as suggested in [15].

References

1. Gravano, L., Garcia-Molina, H.: GlOSS: Text-source discovery over the Internet. ACM Trans. on Database Systems **24** (1999) 229–264
2. Rubinstein, A.: Modelling Bounded Rationality. The MIT Press (1997)
3. Khoussainov, R., Kushmerick, N.: Performance management in competitive distributed Web search. In: Proc. of the IEEE/WIC Intl. Conf. on Web Intelligence. (2003) To appear.
4. Risvik, K., Michelsen, R.: Search engines and web dynamics. Computer Networks **39** (2002)
5. van Rijsbergen, C.J.: Information Retrieval. 2nd edn. Butterworths (1979)
6. Chakrabarti, S., van den Berg, M., Dom, B.: Focused crawling: A new approach to topic-specific Web resource discovery. In: Proc. of the 8th WWW Conf. (1999)
7. Osborne, M., Rubinstein, A.: A Course in Game Theory. The MIT Press (1999)
8. Conitzer, V., Sandholm, T.: Complexity results about Nash equilibria. Technical Report CMU-CS-02-135, Carnegie Mellon University (2002)
9. Robinson, J.: An iterative method of solving a game. Annals of Mathematics **54** (1951)
10. Carmel, D., Markovitch, S.: Learning models of intelligent agents. In: Proc. of the 13th National Conf. on AI. (1996)
11. Peshkin, L.: Reinforcement Learning by Policy Search. PhD thesis, MIT (2002)
12. Stonebraker, M., Devine, R., Kornacker, M., Litwin, W., Pfeffer, A., Sah, A., Staelin, C.: An economic paradigm for query processing and data migration in Mariposa. In: Proc. of the 3rd Intl. Conf. on Parallel and Distributed Information Systems. (1994) 58–67
13. Greenwald, A., Kephart, J., Tesauro, G.: Strategic pricebot dynamics. In: Proc. of the 1st ACM Conf. on Electronic Commerce. (1999) 58–67
14. Greenwald, A., Kephart, J.: Shopbots and pricebots. In: Proc. of the 16th Intl. Joint Conf. on AI. (1999) 506–511
15. Bowling, M., Veloso, M.: Rational and convergent learning in stochastic games. In: Proc. of the 17th Intl. Joint Conf. on AI. (2001)

Robust k-DNF Learning via Inductive Belief Merging

Frédéric Koriche and Joël Quinqueton

LIRMM, UMR 5506, Université Montpellier II CNRS
161, rue Ada 34392 Montpellier Cedex 5, France
{koriche,jq}@lirmm.fr

Abstract. A central issue in logical concept induction is the prospect of inconsistency. This problem may arise due to noise in the training data, or because the target concept does not fit the underlying concept class. In this paper, we introduce the paradigm of *inductive belief merging* which handles this issue within a uniform framework. The key idea is to base learning on a belief merging operator that selects the concepts which are as close as possible to the set of training examples. From a computational perspective, we apply this paradigm to robust k-DNF learning. To this end, we develop a greedy algorithm which approximates the optimal concepts to within a logarithmic factor. The time complexity of the algorithm is polynomial in the size of k. Moreover, the method bidirectional and returns one maximally specific concept and one maximally general concept. We present experimental results showing the effectiveness of our algorithm on both nominal and numerical datasets.

1 Introduction

The problem of logical concept induction has occupied a central position in machine learning [1,2]. Informally, a concept is a formula defined over some knowledge representation language called the *concept class*, and an example is a description of an instance together with a label, positive if the instance belongs to the unknown target concept and negative otherwise. The problem is to extrapolate or *induce* from a collection of examples called the *training set*, a concept in the concept class that accurately classifies future, unlabelled instances.

A useful paradigm for studying this issue is the notion of *version space* introduced by Mitchell in [1]. Given some concept class, the version space for a training set is simply the set of concepts in the concept class that are consistent with the data. Probably, the most salient feature of this paradigm lies in the property of *bidirectional learning* [3]. Namely, for admissible concept classes like k-DNF, k-CNF or Horn theories, every concept in a version space can be factorized from below by a maximally specific concept and from above by a maximally general concept. Thus, a version space incorporates two dual strategies for learning a target concept, one from a specific viewpoint (allowing errors of omission) and the other from a general viewpoint (allowing errors of commission). This bidirectional approach is particularly useful when the available data is not sufficient to converge to the unique identity of the target concept. From this perspective, Mitchell proposed to generate the set S of all maximally specific concepts and the set G of all maximally general concepts, using the so-called Candidate Elimination algorithm [1]. Since these sets are often expensive in space [4], Sablon and his colleagues [5] proposed to maintain only one maximally specific and one maximally general concept. Although their learning algorithm does not pretend to capture the whole solution set, it guarantees a linear space-complexity.

Unfortunately, the version-space paradigm have proven fundamentally limited in practice due to its inability to handle inconsistency. A set of examples is said to be *inconsistent* with respect to a given concept class if no concept in the class is able to distinguish the positive from the negative examples. In presence of inconsistency, any version space becomes empty (it is said to *collapse*) and hence, the learning algorithm can fail into trivialization. In fact, as noticed by Clark and Niblett [6], very few real world problems operate under consistent conditions. Inconsistency may arise due to the imperfectness of the "training set". For example, some observations may contain noise due to imperfect measuring equipments, or the available data can be collected from several, not necessarily agreeing sources. Inconsistency may also occur due the incompleteness of the "concept class". In practice, the target concept class is not known in advance, so the learner can use a hypothesis language which is inappropriate for the target concept. Nonetheless, even inconsistent environments may contain a great deal of valid information. Therefore, it seems important to develop alternative paradigms for *robust learners* that should allow to learn as much as possible given the training data and the concept class available.

Several authors have attempted to handle this issue by generalizing the standard paradigm of version spaces. Notably, Hirsh and Cohen [7, 8] consider inconsistency has a problem of reasoning about uncertainty. Informally, each example which is assumed to be corrupted gives rise to a set of supposed instances. The learner computes all version spaces consistent with at least one supposed instance originated from any observed example and then returns their intersection. As mentioned by the authors, this approach asks the question of how sets of supposed instances are acquired in practice. Moreover, consistency is *not* guaranteed to be recovered: if the sets of supposed instances are chosen inappropriately then the resulting version space may collapse, as in the standard case. Last, this scheme is basically limited because the number of version spaces maintained in parallel during the learning phase can grow exponentially.

In another line of research, Sebag [9, 10] develops a model of disjunctive version spaces which deals with inconsistency by using a voting mechanism. A separate classifier is learned for each positive training example taken with the set of all negative examples, then new instances are classified by combining the votes of these different hypothesis. The complexity of induction is shown to be polynomial in the number of instances. However, an important inconvenient of the approach is the poor comprehensibility of the resulting concept (typically a disjunction of conjunctions of disjunctions). Moreover, we loose the bidirectional property of version spaces since only maximally general concepts are learned.

In this study, we adopt a radically different approach inspired from *belief merging*, a research field that has received increasing attention in the database and the knowledge representation communities [11–13]. The aim of belief merging is to infer from a set of theories, expressed in some logical formalism, a new theory considered as the overall knowledge of the different sources. When the initial theories are consistent together, the result is simply the intersection of their models. However, in presence of inconsistency, a nontrivial operator must be elaborated. The key idea of the so-called "distance-based" merging operators is to select those models that are close as possible to the initial theories, using an appropriate metric in the space of all possible interpretations.

The main insight underlying our study is to base learning on a merging operator that selects the concepts which are as close as possible to the set of training examples. In the present paper, we apply this idea to robust k-DNF learning. As argued by Valiant [14, 15], the DNF family is a natural class for expressing and understanding real concepts in propositional learning.

In section 2, we present the paradigm of inductive belief merging. In this setting, we define a distance-based merging operator that introduces a preference bias in the k-DNF class, induced by the sum of the distances $d(\varphi, e)$ between a concept φ and each example e in the training set. The resulting "robust version space" is the set of all concepts whose distance to the training set is minimal. In section 3, we show that every concept in this version space can be characterized by a corresponding "minimal weighted cover" defined from the training set and the concept class. This establishes a close relationship between the learning problem and the so-called *weighted set cover* problem [16, 17]. Based on this correspondence, we develop in section 4 a greedy algorithm which builds a cover that approximates the optimum to within a logarithmic factor. The algorithm is bidirectional and returns the maximally specific k-DNF and the maximally general k-DNF generated from the approximate cover. The method is guaranteed to be polynomial in time and only uses a linear space.

From a conceptual point of view, a benefit of our paradigm is that it allows to characterize robust learning in terms of three distinguished biases, namely, the restriction bias imposed by the concept class, the preference bias defined by the merging operator, and the search bias given by the approximation algorithm. From an empirical point of view, we report in section 5 experiments on twenty datasets that show diversity in size, number of attributes and type of attributes. For almost all domains, we show that robust k-DNF learning is equal or superior to the popular C4.5 decision-tree learning algorithm [18, 19].

2 Inductive Belief Merging

In this section, we present the logical aspects of our framework. We begin to introduce some usual definitions in concept learning and then, we detail the notion of inductive belief merging.

2.1 Preliminaries

We consider a finite set V of boolean variables. A *literal* is either a variable v or its negation $\neg v$. A *term* is a conjunction of literals and a DNF formula is a disjunction of terms. In the following, we shall represent DNF as sets of terms and terms as sets of literals. Given a positive integer k, a k-term is a term that contains at most k literals and a k-DNF *concept* is a DNF composed of k-terms. Given two k-DNF concepts φ and ψ, we say that φ *is more specific than* ψ (or equivalently ψ *is more general than* φ) if φ is a subset of ψ.

An *instance* is a map x from V to $\{0,1\}$. Given an instance x and a formula φ, we say that x is *consistent* with φ if x is a logical model of φ. Otherwise, we say that x is *inconsistent* with φ. An *example* e is a pair (x_e, v_e) where x_e is an instance and v_e is a boolean variable. An example e is called positive if $v_e = 1$ and negative if $v_e = 0$. Given an example e and a formula φ, we say that e is *consistent* (resp. *inconsistent*) with φ if x_e is consistent (resp. inconsistent) with φ. Given a positive integer k and a positive (resp. negative) example e, the *atomic version space* of e with respect to k, denoted $C_k(e)$, is set of all k-DNF concepts that are consistent (resp. inconsistent) with e. Now, given a set of examples E, the *version space* of E with respect to k, denoted $C_k(E)$, is the set of all k-DNF concepts that are consistent with every positive example in E and that are inconsistent with every negative example in E. As observed by Hirsh in [8], the overall version space of E is simply the intersection of the atomic version spaces defined for each example in E:

$$C_k(E) = \bigcap_{e \in E} C_k(e).$$

A training set E is called *consistent* with respect to the k-DNF class if $C_k(E)$ is not empty, and *inconsistent* otherwise. When E is consistent, the aim of concept learning is then to find a concept φ in $C_k(E)$. However, in case of inconsistency, $C_k(E)$ collapses and the problem fails into triviality. So, it is necessary to generalize the notion of version space in order to handle this issue.

2.2 Learning via Merging

The key idea underlying our framework is to replace the "intersection" operator by a "merging" operator. To this end, we need some additional definitions. Given two DNF formulas φ and ψ, the *term distance* between φ and ψ, denoted $d(\varphi, \psi)$, is defined as the number of terms the two concepts differ:

$$d(\varphi, \psi) = |(\varphi \cup \psi) - (\varphi \cap \psi)|.$$

This notion of distance can be seen as the number elementary operations needed to transform the first concept into the second one. Now, given a k-DNF concept φ and an example e, the distance between φ and e with respect to k, denoted $d_k(\varphi, e)$, is defined by the minimum distance between this concept and the atomic version space of e:

$$d_k(\varphi, e) = \min\{d(\varphi, \psi) : \psi \in C_k(e)\}.$$

Intuitively, the distance between φ and e is the minimal number of k-terms that need to be added or deleted in order to correctly cover e. Specifically, if e is positive, then the distance between φ and e is the minimal number of k-terms that need to be *added* in φ in order to be consistent with x_e. From a dual point of view, if e is negative, then the distance is the minimal number of k-terms that need to be *deleted* in φ in order to be inconsistent with x_e.

Finally, given a k-DNF concept φ and a set of examples E, the distance between φ and E with respect to k, denoted $d_k(\varphi, E)$ is the sum of the distances between this concept and the examples that occur in E:

$$d_k(\varphi, E) = \sum_{e \in E} d_k(\varphi, e).$$

Interestingly, we observe that this distance induces a preference ordering over the k-DNF class defined by the following condition: φ is *more preferred than* ψ for E with respect to k if $d_k(\varphi, E) \leq d_k(\psi, E)$. It is easy to see that the preference relation is a total pre-order. Thus, we say that φ is a *most preferred* concept for E with respect to k if $d_k(\varphi, E)$ is minimal, that is, for every k-DNF formula ψ we have $d_k(\varphi, E) \leq d_k(\psi, E)$. Now, we have all elements in hand to capture the solution set of "learning via merging". Given a positive integer k and a training set E, the *inductive merging* of E with respect to k, denoted $\triangle_k(E)$, is the set of all most preferred concepts for E in the k-DNF class:

$$\triangle_k(E) = \{\varphi : \varphi \text{ is a } k\text{-DNF concept and } d_k(\varphi, E) \text{ is minimal}\}.$$

This model of robust induction embodies two important properties. First, it is guaranteed to *never* collapse. This is a direct consequence of the above definition. Second, inductive merging is a *generalization* of the standard notion of version space. Namely, if E is *consistent* with respect to the k-DNF concept class, then $\triangle_k(E) = C_k(E)$. This lies in the fact that $d(\varphi, E) = 0$ iff $\varphi \in C_k(E)$.

Example 1. Suppose that the training set E is defined by the following examples: $e_1 = (\{v_1, v_2\}, 1)$, $e_2 = (\{v_1, \neg v_2\}, 1)$, $e_3 = (\{\neg v_1, \neg v_2\}, 1)$, $e_4 = (\{v_1, \neg v_2\}, 0)$ and $e_5 = (\{\neg v_1, v_2\}, 0)$. Suppose further that the concept class is the set of all 1-DNF (simple disjuncts). Clearly, the version space $C_1(E)$ would collapse here. Now, consider the distances reported on the table below (we only examine non trivial disjuncts). We observe that $\triangle_k(E)$ includes two maximally specific concepts $\{v_1\}$ and $\{\neg v_2\}$, and one maximally general concept $\{v_1, \neg v_2\}$.

c	e_1	e_2	e_3	e_4	e_5	Σ
$\{\}$	1	1	1	0	0	3
$\{v_1\}$	0	0	1	1	0	2
$\{v_2\}$	0	1	1	0	1	3
$\{\neg v_2\}$	1	0	0	1	0	2
$\{\neg v_1\}$	1	1	0	0	1	3
$\{v_1, v_2\}$	0	0	1	1	1	3
$\{v_1, \neg v_2\}$	0	0	0	2	0	2
$\{\neg v_1, v_2\}$	0	1	0	0	2	3
$\{\neg v_1, \neg v_2\}$	1	0	0	1	1	3

3 A Representation Theorem

After an excursion into the logical aspects of the framework, we now provide a representation theorem that enables to characterize solutions in $\triangle_k(E)$ in terms of minimal weighted covers. As we shall see in the next section, this representation is particularly useful for constructing efficient approximation algorithms.

To this end, we need some additional definitions. Given a set of examples E and a k-term t, the *extension* of t in E, denoted $E(t)$ is the set of examples in E that are consistent with t. The *weight* of t in E, denoted $w(t, E)$ is the size of the extension of t in E. Given a set of examples E, a *cover* of E is a list of k-terms $\pi = (t_1, \cdots, t_n)$ such that every *positive* example e in E is consistent with at least one term t_i in π. Intuitively, the index i denotes the priority of the term t_i in the cover π, with the underlying assumption that 1 is the highest priority and n is the lowest priority. Given a cover π of E and a k-term t, the *extension* of t in E with respect to π is inductively defined by the following conditions:

$$E(t, \pi) = \begin{cases} E(t) & \text{if } t = t_1 \\ E(t) - \cup\{E(t_j, \pi) : 1 \leq j < i\} & \text{if } t = t_i \text{ for } 1 < i \leq n \\ \emptyset & \text{otherwise} \end{cases}$$

The *weight* of a k-term t in E with respect to π, denoted $w(t, \pi, E)$ is given by the size of $E(t, \pi)$. We notice that if t is not a member of the cover π then its weight is simply set to 0. Now, given a training set E, let E_n be the set of negative examples in E and let E_p be the set of positive examples in E. The following lemma states that the distance between a concept and a training set can be characterized in terms of weights.

Lemma 1. *For every k-DNF concept φ and every set of examples E:*

$$d(\varphi, E_n) = \sum_{t \in \varphi} w(t, E_n), \text{ and}$$

$$d(\varphi, E_p) = \min\{d(\varphi, \pi) : \pi \text{ is a cover of } E\} \text{ where } d(\varphi, \pi) = \sum_{t \notin \varphi} w(t, \pi, E_p).$$

Proof. The first property can be easily derived from the fact that, for every negative example e, $d(\varphi, e)$ is the number of terms t in φ which are consistent with e. Let us examine the second property. Let $E_p = E'_p \cup \{e\}$ and suppose by induction hypothesis that π' is a cover of E'_p such that $d(\varphi, \pi')$ is minimal. We know that $d(\varphi, E_p) = d(\varphi, E'_p) + d(\varphi, e)$. To this point, we remark that $d(\varphi, e) = 0$ if e is consistent with at least one term t in φ and 1 otherwise. First, assume that $d(\varphi, e) = 0$ and let t be a term in φ which is consistent with e. The cover π is defined as follows: $\pi = \pi'$, if π' covers E_p, and $\pi = \pi' \cup \{t\}$ otherwise. In both cases we have $\sum_{t \notin \varphi} w(t, \pi, E_p) = \sum_{t \notin \varphi} w(t, \pi', E'_p)$. Since $d(\varphi, e) = 0$, it follows that $d(\varphi, E_p) = d(\varphi, \pi)$, as desired. Second, assume that $d(\varphi, e) = 1$. Let t be an arbitrary k-term that is consistent with e. As previously, the cover π is defined by π' if π' covers e and $\pi' \cup \{t\}$, otherwise. In both cases, we have $\sum_{t \notin \varphi} w(t, \pi, E_p) = \sum_{t \notin \varphi} w(t, \pi', E'_p) + 1$. Since the right-hand side is the sum of $d(\varphi, E'_p)$ and $d(\varphi, e)$, we obtain $d(\varphi, E_p) = d(\varphi, \pi)$, as desired.

Now, we turn to the notion of "minimal weighted cover". Let T_k be the set of all k-terms generated from the boolean variables and let κ be the cardinality of T_k. Given a set of examples E and a cover π of E, the *weight* of π in E, denoted $w(\pi, E)$ is defined as follows:

$$w(\pi, E) = \sum_{i=1}^{\kappa} \min(w(t_i, E_n), w(t_i, \pi, E_p))$$

A cover π is called *minimal* if its weight is minimal, that is, for every other cover π' of E, we have $w(\pi, E) \leq w(\pi', E)$. Informally, the weight of a minimal cover corresponds to the optimal distance of the concepts in $\triangle_k(E)$. Furthermore, a minimal cover embodies a whole "lattice" of most preferred concepts. In particular, the *maximally specific concept* of π, denoted S_π is the set of all k-terms t in T_k such that $w(t, \pi, E_p) < w(t, E_n)$ and dually, the *maximally general concept* of π, denoted G_π, is the set of all k-terms t in T_k such that $w(t_i, E_n) \not> w(t_i, \pi, E_p)$. With these notions in hand, we are in position to give the representation theorem.

Theorem 1. *For every k-DNF concept φ and every set of examples E:*

$$\varphi \in \triangle_k(E) \text{ iff there exists a minimal cover } \pi \text{ of } E \text{ such that } S_\pi \subseteq \varphi \subseteq G_\pi.$$

Proof. Let π be a cover of E such that $d(\varphi, \pi)$ is minimal and let $\mu(t, \pi)$ be an abbreviation of $\min(w(t, E_n), w(t, \pi, E_p))$. Based on lemma 1, we can derive that $d(\varphi, E)$ is the sum of three parts:

$$d(\varphi, E) = \sum_{t \in \varphi}(w(t, E_n) - \mu(t, \pi)) + \sum_{t \notin \varphi}(w(t, \pi, E_p) - \mu(t, \pi)) + w(\pi, E).$$

Let φ' be a concept such that $\varphi' \in \triangle_k(E)$. Based on the above result, we have $d(\varphi', E) \geq w(\pi', E)$ where π' is a cover of E such that $d(\varphi', \pi')$ is minimal. Dually, let φ be a concept such that $S_\pi \subseteq \varphi \subseteq G_\pi$ for some minimal cover π of E. We may observe that $d(S_\pi, E) = d(G_\pi, E) = w(\pi, E)$ since, in both cases, the first part and the second part of the above equation are set to 0. Thus, $d(\varphi, E) \leq w(\pi, E)$. Therefore, we have $w(\pi, E) \leq w(\pi', E)$.

Now, suppose that $\varphi \notin \triangle_k(E)$. It follows that $d(\varphi, E) > d(\varphi' E)$. Therefore, we derive $w(\pi, E) > w(\pi', E)$, but this contradicts the above result. On the other hand, assume that φ' is not factorized by $S_{\pi'}$ and $G_{\pi'}$. As $w(\pi, E) \leq w(\pi', E)$, there are two cases. First, if $d(\pi', E) > w(\pi, E)$, we then obtain $d(\varphi', E) > d(\varphi, E)$. Therefore $\varphi' \notin \triangle_k(E)$, but this contradicts the initial assumption. Second, if $d(\pi', E) = d(\pi, E)$, then π' is a minimal cover of E. It follows that $S_{\pi'} \not\subseteq \varphi'$ or $\varphi' \not\subseteq G_{\pi'}$. In both situations, it is easy to derive $d(\varphi', E) > w(\pi' E)$. Thus, we obtain $d(\varphi', E) > d(\varphi, E)$. Therefore $\varphi' \notin \triangle_k(E)$, hence contradiction.

Example 2. Let us examine the training set E given in example 1. Based on the 1-DNF concept class, we may generate eight covers of E. Notably, we observe that $\pi = (v_1, \neg v_2)$ and $\pi' = (\neg v_2, v_1)$ are minimal covers of E. The weight of these covers is 2. In the first case, $S_\pi = \{v_1\}$ and in the second case $S_{\pi'} = \{\neg v_2\}$. Furthermore, we have $G_\pi = G_{\pi'} = \{v_1, \neg v_2\}$.

4 An Approximation Algorithm

As demonstrated in the previous section, the concept learning problem has close similarities with the so-called "weighted set cover" problem. This last problem is known to be NP-hard in the general case, yet efficient approximation algorithms have been proposed in the literature [16]. Based on these considerations, we develop in this section an approximation method that returns a cover which is as close as possible to the optimal distance.

The algorithm is detailed in figure 1. The intuitive idea underlying the algorithm is to select terms in a "greedy" manner, by choosing at each iteration the term that covers the most positive examples and the least negative ones.

Input: A training set E and an integer $k \geq 1$.
Output: The most specific concept S_π and the most general concept G_π of a k-DNF cover π of E.

1. Set $T = \{t : t \text{ is a } k\text{-term}\}$. Set $P = E_p$. Set $\pi = \varnothing$;
2. If $P = \varnothing$ then stop and output S_π and G_π.
3. Find a term $t \in T$ that minimizes the quotient $\frac{\min(w(t,E_n),w(t,P))}{w(t,P)}$, for $w(t,P) \neq 0$. In case of a tie, take t which maximizes $w(t,P)$;
4. Append t at the end of π. Set $P = P - P(t)$. Return to step 2.

Fig. 1. MERGEDNF(E, k).

An important feature of this algorithm is that it bidirectional: it returns a maximally specific concept *and* a maximally general concept, with respect to the cover that has been found. Furthermore the algorithm has the additional property that, while it does not always find a "minimal" cover, it tends to approximate such a cover to within a logarithmic factor.

Theorem 2. *For every k-DNF concept class and every training set E, if m is the number of positive examples and w^* is the weight of a minimal cover, then* MERGEDNF(E, k) *is guaranteed to find a cover of weight at most $(w^*+1)\ln(m)$.*

Proof. The demonstration is a variant of the proof given in [16]. In any iteration i, let e_i be a positive example that has not yet been covered by the algorithm. Let t be the first term to cover e_i. The cost of e_i, denoted cost(e_i), is given by the quotient $\frac{\min(w(t,E_n),w(t,P))}{w(t,P)}$. Let $P - P(t)$ the set of remaining elements. The size of this set is bounded by $m - i + 1$. In this case, the optimal solution can cover the remaining elements of at a weight at most $w^* + 1$. Therefore, we obtain cost$(e) \leq \frac{w^*+1}{m-i+1}$. It follows that the weight of the cover generated by the algorithm is at most $\sum_{i=1}^{m} \text{cost}(e) \leq \sum_{i=1}^{m} \frac{w^*+1}{i} = (w^* + 1)H_m$. Since $H_m \sim \ln(m)$, we obtain $(w^* + 1)\ln(m)$, as desired.

As a corollary of this proposition, we may determine that the worst-case time complexity of the algorithm is linear in the number of k-terms and polynomial in the number of examples. Let n be the number of boolean variables. For sake of simplicity, let us assume that E contains m positive examples and m negative examples. Step 1 of the algorithm requires only $O(mn^k)$ time. Moreover, the number of iterations of the algorithm is bounded by $O((m+1)\ln(m))$. This corresponds to the worst case where the optimal weight is given by the number of positive examples. Therefore, since step 3 requires $O(mn^k)$ time, the overall time bound of the algorithm is $O(m^2 n^k \ln(m))$.

5 Experiments

This section reports experimental validations of our learning scheme on a representative collection of datasets from the UCI Machine Learning Repository.

Based on the bidirectional property of the algorithm, the learner can choose between two classifiers for classifying test data, namely, the maximally specific concept and the maximally general concept generated from the cover. From this viewpoint, each training set was split into a learning set used to induce concepts from data and a test set used to select the best classifier. In all the experiments, the fraction of the training set used as internal test data was set to 5%. Each experiment was then decomposed into three stages: 1) learn the two concepts from the learning set, 2) select the best concept on the internal test set, and 3) validate the resulting concept on the remaining, external test set.

The twenty datasets are summarized in Table 1. For each benchmark problem, the first section gives the number of examples, the number of continuous and discrete attributes, the number of classes, and the percentage of examples in the majority class. The datasets are taken without modification from the UCI repository with one exception: in the "waveform" problem, a 300-example dataset was generated, as suggested in [19]. The last two sections provide an empirical comparison of our learning scheme with the C4.5 decision-tree learner. To measure generalization error, we ran ten different 10-fold cross validations for each dataset and averaged the results. The second section details the accuracy results obtained by MERGEDNF on 2-DNF formulas. Since the algorithm has been designed for two-class problems, the goal was to separate the most frequent class from the remaining classes. In case of tie, the target class was selected in a random way. Continuous data was discretized using the "equal-width binning method" [20]. The number of bins b was set to $b = \max(1, 2 \cdot \log(l))$ where l is the number of distinct observed values for each attribute.

Finally, the last column reports accuracy results obtained the C4.5 algorithm. We used C4.5 Release 8 that deals with noise by incorporating (by default) an error-based pruning technique and that handles continuous data using a method inspired by the Minimum Description Length principle. For all domains, the algorithm was run with the same default settings for all the parameters; no attempt was made to tune the system for these problems. Notice that the results are very similar to those reported by Quinlan in [19].

Table 1. Comparison of MERGEDNF with C4.5

Dataset	size	attributes cont	disc	classes nb	majority	MERGEDNF ($k=2$)	C4.5 Release 8
breast-w	699	9	–	2	65.52	97.55 ± 1.05	94.76 ± 1.94
colic	368	10	12	2	60.00	85.07 ± 2.29	85.08 ± 2.85
credit-a	690	6	9	2	55.51	88.39 ± 2.46	85.16 ± 2.24
credit-g	1000	7	13	2	70.00	82.52 ± 2.48	71.40 ± 2.94
diabetes	768	8	–	2	65.10	76.03 ± 2.72	74.46 ± 2.87
glass	214	9	–	6	35.51	82.33 ± 5.49	67.12 ± 7.18
heart-c	303	8	5	2	54.12	84.00 ± 3.87	76.72 ± 4.91
heart-h	294	8	5	2	63.95	93.07 ± 4.19	80.17 ± 3.12
heart-s	123	8	5	2	93.50	95.50 ± 3.51	93.12 ± 4.52
heart-v	200	8	5	2	74.50	88.30 ± 4.50	72.74 ± 6.02
hepatisis	155	6	13	2	54.84	88.67 ± 5.13	80.81 ± 5.91
hypo	3772	7	22	5	95.23	97.22 ± 0.53	99.49 ± 0.08
iris	150	4	–	3	33.33	97.37 ± 2.63	95.02 ± 1.92
labor	57	8	8	2	64.91	88.60 ± 7.11	82.55 ± 9.73
sick	3772	7	22	2	90.74	95.85 ± 0.72	98.64 ± 0.33
sonar	208	60	–	2	53.37	86.55 ± 5.82	73.09 ± 6.57
splice	3190	–	62	3	51.88	97.39 ± 1.05	94.18 ± 0.83
vehicule	846	18	–	4	25.77	91.45 ± 1.40	72.13 ± 0.40
voting	435	–	16	2	61.38	97.40 ± 1.32	94.83 ± 2.72
waveform	300	21	–	3	33.92	89.03 ± 3.05	74.16 ± 2.10

Of course, the comparison of MERGEDNF with C4.5 is biased since, notably, the two learners actually use different techniques for handling continuous data. Nevertheless, it is clear that, over these datasets, the inductive merging scheme is competitive with pruned-based decision-tree learning. Specifically, the accuracy results reveal that MERGEDNF, for 2-DNF formulas, is approximatively equal or superior to C4.5 Release 8 on 18 of the 20 datasets. The performance of the algorithm is particularly significant on noisy datasets like the "heart disease" family. In all these domains, MERGEDNF outperforms C4.5 even when pruning was employed. Furthermore, we observe that the algorithm is very effective on continuous datasets. The "glass", "sonar" and "waveform" domains are particularly notable examples. These benchmark problems are known to be difficult for machine-learning algorithms, due to overlapping classes and numerical noise. In these datasets, MERGEDNF also outperforms C4.5.

From a computational point of view, we observed that in our learning scheme the 2-DNF family offers an interesting compromise between the effectiveness of the learner and the time spent to generate covers. For almost all domains, the learning time was inferior to 10 seconds, using a Pentium IV-1.5GHz. For datasets containing a small number of attributes (e.g. "glass" or "iris"), the learning time was even smaller than 1 second. The only notable exception is the "splice" domain which needed approximatively 110 seconds.

In table 2, we briefly illustrated how the performance of the learner depends upon the choice of the parameter k. CPU times are given in seconds. Interest-

Table 2. Dependence among k for the MERGEDNF algorithm

Dataset	1-DNF		2-DNF		3-DNF	
	accuracy	cpu	accuracy	cpu	accuracy	cpu
glass	75.33 ± 6.02	0.007	82.33 ± 5.49	0.462	85.33 ± 4.60	2.740
heart-c	83.23 ± 3.62	0.013	84.00 ± 3.57	0.462	89.70 ± 3.13	5.950
heart-h	91.27 ± 5.21	0.021	93.07 ± 4.19	0.471	92.72 ± 4.57	5.615
heart-s	95.83 ± 3.15	0.006	95.50 ± 3.51	0.121	95.50 ± 3.25	1.235
heart-v	73.75 ± 5.19	0.012	88.30 ± 4.50	0.284	90.30 ± 3.82	3.175
iris	97.40 ± 3.30	0.002	97.37 ± 2.63	0.013	97.31 ± 2.44	0.041

ingly, we remark that the accuracy of the learner does not necessarily increase with k. On-going research investigates the use of model selection methods [21] in order to choose the appropriate value of k during the learning phase.

6 Conclusion

This study lies at the intersection of two research fields: concept learning and belief merging. On the one hand, the aim of concept learning is to induce from a set of examples a concept in an hypothesis language that is consistent with the examples. On the other hand, the aim of belief merging is to infer from a set of belief bases a new theory which is as consistent as possible with the initial beliefs. The main insight underlying this study has been to base induction on a belief merging operator that selects the concepts which are as close as possible from the training examples, using an appropriate distance measure.

Several directions of future research are possible. In this paper, we have restricted the paradigm of inductive merging to k-DNF concepts. An important issue is to extend this paradigm to other concept classes in both the propositional setting and the first-order setting. A first question here is whether an appropriate distance measure can be defined on these concept classes. A second question is whether an algorithm can be designed for generating concepts of minimal distance or, at least, approximating this optimum to within a small factor. Some classes, like k-CNF, are quite immediate. However, solving these questions for other concept classes, like Horn theories or first-order clausal theories, is more demanding. Another line of research is to generalize further the idea of inductive merging. To this end, a wide variety of aggregation operators have been proposed in the belief merging literature. Some authors use a "weighted-sum" for capturing the level of confidence of belief theories [11]. Other authors advocate "max" functions in order to satisfy some principles of arbitration [12]. To this point, it would be interesting to examine these operators in the setting of robust concept learning. For example, a "weighted-sum" would be particularly relevant for training examples that do not have the same level of confidence.

References

1. Mitchell, T.M.: Generalization as search. Artificial Intelligence **18** (1982) 203–226
2. Raedt, L.D.: Logical settings for concept-learning. Artificial Intelligence **95** (1997) 187–201
3. Bundy, A., Silver, B., Plummer, D.: An analytical comparison of some rule-learning programs. Artificial Intelligence **27** (1985) 137–181
4. Haussler, D.: Quantifying inductive bias: AI learning algorithms and Valiant's learning framework. Artificial Intelligence **36** (1988) 177–221
5. Sablon, G., Readt, L.D., Bruynooghe, M.: Iterative version spaces. Artificial Intelligence **69** (1994) 393–409
6. Clark, P., Niblett, T.: Induction in noisy domains. In: Proceedings of the 2nd European Working Session on Learning, Sigma Press (1987) 11–30
7. Hirsh, H., Cohen, W.W.: 12. In: Learning from data with bounded inconsistency: theoretical and experimental results. Volume I: Constraints and Prospects. MIT Press (1994) 355–380
8. Hirsh, H.: Generalizing version spaces. Machine Learning **17** (1994) 5–46
9. Sebag, M.: Delaying the choice of bias: a disjunctive version space approach. In: Proceedings of the 13th International Conference on Machine Learning, Morgan Kaufmann (1996) 444–452
10. Sebag, M.: Constructive induction: A version space-based approach. In: Proceedings of the 16th International Joint Conference on Artificial Intelligence, Morgan Kaufmann (1999) 708–713
11. Lin, J.: Integration of weighted knowledge bases. Artificial Intelligence **83** (1996) 363–378
12. Revesz, P.Z.: On the semantics of arbitration. Journal of Algebra and Computation **7(2)** (1997) 133–160
13. Konieczny, S., Lang, J., Marquis, P.: Distance based merging: A general framework and some complexity results. In: Proceedings of the 8th International Conference on Principles of Knowledge Representation and Reasoning, Morgan Kaufmann (2002) 97–108
14. Valiant, L.G.: Learning disjuctions of conjunctions. In: Proceedings of the 9th International Joint Conference on Artificial Intelligence. (1985) 207–232
15. Valiant, L.G.: Circuits of the Mind. Oxford University Press (1994)
16. Chvatal, V.: A greedy heuristic for the set covering problem. Mathematics of Operation Research **4** (1979) 233–235
17. Lund, C., Yannakakis, M.: On the hardness of approximating minimization problems. In: Proceedings of the 25th ACM Symposium on the Theory of Computing, ACM Press (1993) 286–295
18. Quinlan, J.R.: C4.5: Programs for Machine Learning. Morgan Kaufmann (1993)
19. Quinlan, J.R.: Improved use of continuous attributes in C4.5. Journal of Artificial Intelligence Research **4** (1996) 77–90
20. Dougherty, J., Kohavi, R., Sahami, M.: Supervised and unsupervised discretization of continuous features. In: Proceedings of the 12th International Conference on Machine Learning, Morgan Kaufmann (1995) 194–202
21. Kearns, M., Mansour, Y., Ng, A.Y., Ron, D.: An experimental and theoretical comparison of model selection methods. Machine Learning **27** (1997) 7–50

Logistic Model Trees

Niels Landwehr[1,2], Mark Hall[2], and Eibe Frank[2]

[1] Department of Computer Science
University of Freiburg
Freiburg, Germany
landwehr@informatik.uni-freiburg.de
[2] Department of Computer Science
University of Waikato
Hamilton, New Zealand
{eibe,mhall}@cs.waikato.ac.nz

Abstract. Tree induction methods and linear models are popular techniques for supervised learning tasks, both for the prediction of nominal classes and continuous numeric values. For predicting numeric quantities, there has been work on combining these two schemes into 'model trees', i.e. trees that contain linear regression functions at the leaves. In this paper, we present an algorithm that adapts this idea for classification problems, using logistic regression instead of linear regression. We use a stagewise fitting process to construct the logistic regression models that can select relevant attributes in the data in a natural way, and show how this approach can be used to build the logistic regression models at the leaves by incrementally refining those constructed at higher levels in the tree. We compare the performance of our algorithm against that of decision trees and logistic regression on 32 benchmark UCI datasets, and show that it achieves a higher classification accuracy on average than the other two methods.

1 Introduction

Two popular methods for classification are linear logistic regression and tree induction, which have somewhat complementary advantages and disadvantages. The former fits a simple (linear) model to the data, and the process of model fitting is quite stable, resulting in low variance but potentially high bias. The latter, on the other hand, exhibits low bias but often high variance: it searches a less restricted space of models, allowing it to capture nonlinear patterns in the data, but making it less stable and prone to overfitting. So it is not surprising that neither of the two methods is superior in general — earlier studies [10] have shown that their relative performance depends on the size and the characteristics of the dataset (e.g., the signal-to-noise ratio).

It is a natural idea to try and combine these two methods into learners that rely on simple regression models if only little and/or noisy data is available and add a more complex tree structure if there is enough data to warrant such structure. For the case of predicting a numeric variable, this has lead to 'model trees', which are decision trees with linear regression models at the leaves. These have been shown to produce good results [11]. Although it is possible to use model trees for classification tasks by transforming the classification problem into a regression task by binarizing the class [4], this approach produces several trees (one per class) and thus makes the final model harder to interpret.

A more natural way to deal with classification tasks is to use a combination of a tree structure and logistic regression models resulting in a single tree. Another advantage of using logistic regression is that explicit class probability estimates are produced rather than just a classification. In this paper, we present a method that follows this idea. We discuss a new scheme for selecting the attributes to be included in the logistic regression models, and introduce a way of building the logistic models at the leaves by refining logistic models that have been trained at higher levels in the tree, i.e. on larger subsets of the training data.

We compare the performance of our method against the decision tree learner C4.5 [12] and logistic regression on 32 UCI datasets [1], looking at classification accuracy and size of the constructed trees. We also include results for two learning schemes that build multiple trees, namely boosted decision trees and model trees fit to the class indicator variables [4], and a different algorithm for building logistic model trees called PLUS [8]. From the results of the experiments we conclude that our method achieves a higher average accuracy than C4.5, model trees, logistic regression and PLUS, and is competitive with boosted trees. We will also show that it smoothly adapts the tree size to the complexity of the data set.

The rest of the paper is organized as follows. In Section 2 we briefly review logistic regression and the model tree algorithm and introduce logistic model trees in more detail. Section 3 describes our experimental study, followed by a discussion of results. We discuss related work in Section 4 and draw some conclusions in Section 5.

2 Algorithms

This section begins with a brief introduction to the application of regression for classification tasks and a description of our implementation of logistic regression. A summary of model tree induction is also provided as this is a good starting point for understanding our method.

2.1 Logistic Regression

Linear regression performs a least-squares fit of a parameter vector β to a numeric target variable to form a model

$$f(x) = \beta^T \cdot x,$$

where x is the input vector (we assume a constant term in the input vector to accommodate the intercept). It is possible to use this technique for classification by directly fitting linear regression models to class indicator variables. If there

1. Start with weights $w_{ij} = 1/n$, $i = 1, \ldots, n$, $j = 1, \ldots, J$, $F_j(x) = 0$ and $p_j(x) = 1/J$ $\forall j$

2. Repeat for $m = 1, \ldots, M$:
   (a) Repeat for $j = 1, \ldots, J$:
       i. Compute working responses and weights in the jth class
       $$z_{ij} = \frac{y_{ij}^* - p_j(x_i)}{p_j(x_i)(1 - p_j(x_i))}$$
       $$w_{ij} = p_j(x_i)(1 - p_j(x_i))$$
       ii. Fit the function $f_{mj}(x)$ by a weighted least-squares regression of z_{ij} to x_i with weights w_{ij}
   (b) Set $f_{mj}(x) \leftarrow \frac{J-1}{J}(f_{mj}(x) - \frac{1}{J}\sum_{k=1}^{J} f_{mk}(x))$, $F_j(x) \leftarrow F_j(x) + f_{mj}(x)$
   (c) Update $p_j(x) = \frac{e^{F_j(x)}}{\sum_{k=1}^{J} e^{F_k(x)}}$

3. Output the classifier $\mathrm{argmax}_j F_j(x)$

Fig. 1. LogitBoost algorithm for J classes.

are J classes then J indicator variables are created and the indicator for class j takes on value 1 whenever class j is present and value 0 otherwise. However, this approach is known to suffer from masking problems in the multiclass setting [7].

A better method for classification is *linear logistic regression*, which models the posterior class probabilities $Pr(G = j|X = x)$ for the J classes via linear functions in x while at the same time ensuring they sum to one and remain in [0,1]. The model has the form[1]

$$Pr(G = j|X = x) = \frac{e^{F_j(x)}}{\sum_{k=1}^{J} e^{F_k(x)}}, \quad \sum_{k=1}^{J} F_k(x) = 0,$$

where $F_j(x) = \beta_j^T \cdot x$ are linear regression functions, and it is usually fit by finding maximum likelihood estimates for the parameters β_j.

One way to find these estimates is based on the LogitBoost algorithm [6]. LogitBoost performs forward stage-wise fitting of *additive logistic regression models*, which generalize the above model to $F_j(x) = \sum_m f_{mj}(x)$, where the f_{mj} can be arbitrary functions of the input variables that are fit by least squares regression. In our application we are interested in linear models, and LogitBoost finds the maximum likelihood linear logistic model if the f_{mj} are fit using (simple or multiple) linear least squares regression and the algorithm is run until convergence. This is because the likelihood function is convex and LogitBoost performs quasi-Newton steps to find its maximum.

The algorithm (shown in Figure 1) iteratively fits regression functions f_{mj} to a 'response variable' (reweighted residuals). The $x_1, \ldots, x_n$ are the training examples and the y_{ij}^* encode the observed class membership probabilities for

---
[1] This is the *symmetric* formulation [6].

instance x_i, i.e. y^*_{ij} is one if x_i is labeled with class j and zero otherwise. One can build the f_{mj} by performing multiple regression based on all attributes present in the data, but it is also possible to use a simple linear regression, selecting the attribute that gives the smallest squared error. If the algorithm is run until convergence this will give the same final model because every multiple linear regression function can be expressed as a sum of simple linear regression functions, but using simple regression will slow down the learning process and thus give a better control over model complexity. This allows us to obtain simple models and prevent overfitting of the training data: the model learned after a few iterations (for a small M) will only include the most relevant attributes present in the data, resulting in automatic attribute selection, and, if we use cross-validation to determine the best number of iterations, a new variable will only be added if this improves the performance of the model on unseen cases.

In our empirical evaluation simple regression together with (five fold) cross-validation indeed outperformed multiple regression. Consequently, we chose this approach for our implementation of logistic regression. We will refer to it as the *SimpleLogistic* algorithm.

2.2 Model Trees

Model trees, like ordinary regression trees, predict a numeric value given an instance that is defined over a fixed set of numeric or nominal attributes. Unlike ordinary regression trees, model trees construct a piecewise linear (instead of a piecewise constant) approximation to the target function. The final model tree consists of a decision tree with linear regression models at the leaves, and the prediction for an instance is obtained by sorting it down to a leaf and using the prediction of the linear model associated with that leaf.

The M5' model tree algorithm [13] — a 'rational reconstruction' of Quinlan's M5 algorithm [11] — first constructs a regression tree by recursively splitting the instance space using tests on single attributes that maximally reduce variance in the target variable. After the tree has been grown, a linear multiple regression model is built for every inner node, using the data associated with that node and all the attributes that participate in tests in the subtree rooted at that node. Then the linear regression models are simplified by dropping attributes if this results in a lower expected error on future data (more specifically, if the decrease in the number of parameters outweighs the increase in the observed training error). After this has been done, every subtree is considered for pruning. Pruning occurs if the estimated error for the linear model at the root of a subtree is smaller or equal to the expected error for the subtree. After pruning has terminated, M5' applies a 'smoothing' process that combines the model at a leaf with the models on the path to the root to form the final model that is placed at the leaf.

2.3 Logistic Model Trees

Given this model tree algorithm, it appears quite straightforward to build a 'logistic model tree' by growing a standard classification tree, building logistic regression models for all nodes, pruning some of the subtrees using a pruning criterion, and combining the logistic models along a path into a single model in some fashion. However, the devil is in the details and M5' uses a set of heuristics at crucial points in the algorithm — heuristics that cannot easily be transferred to the classification setting.

Fortunately LogitBoost enables us to view the combination of tree induction and logistic regression from a different perspective: iterative fitting of simple linear regression interleaved with splits on the data. Recall that LogitBoost builds a logistic model by iterative refinement, successively including more and more variables as new linear models f_{mj} are added to the committee F_j. The idea is to recursively split the iterative fitting process into branches corresponding to subsets of the data, a process that automatically generates a tree structure.

As an example, consider a tree with a single split at the root and two leaves. The root node N has training data T and one of its sons N' has a subset of the training data $T' \subset T$. Following the classical approach, there would be a logistic regression model M at node N trained on T and a logistic regression model M' at N' trained on T'. For classification, the class probability estimates of M and M' would be averaged to form the final model for N'.

In our approach, the tree would instead be constructed by building a logistic model M at N by fitting linear regression models trained on T as long as this improves the fit to the data, and then building the logistic model M' at N' by taking M and adding more linear regression models that are trained on T', rather than starting from scratch. As a result, the final model at a leaf consists of a committee of linear regression models that have been trained on increasingly smaller subsets of the data (while going down the tree). Building the logistic regression models in this fashion by refining models built at higher levels in the tree is computationally more efficient than building them from scratch.

However, a practical tree inducer also requires a pruning method. In our experiments 'local' pruning criteria employed by algorithms like C4.5 and M5' did not lead to reliable pruning. Instead, we followed the pruning scheme employed by the CART algorithm [2], which uses cross-validation to obtain more stable pruning results. Although this increased the computational complexity, it resulted in smaller and generally more accurate trees.

These ideas lead to the following algorithm for constructing logistic model trees:

– Tree growing starts by building a logistic model at the root using the LogitBoost algorithm. The number of iterations (and simple regression functions f_{mj} to add to F_j) is determined using five fold cross-validation. In this process the data is split into training and test set five times, for every training set LogitBoost is run to a maximum number of iterations (we used 200) and the error rates on the test set are logged for every iteration and summed up over the different folds. The number of iterations that has the lowest sum of errors is used to train the LogitBoost algorithm on all the data. This gives the logistic regression model at the root of the tree.

```
LMT(examples){
    root = new Node()
    alpha = getCARTAlpha(examples)
    root.buildTree(examples, null)
    root.CARTprune(alpha)
}

buildTree(examples, initialLinearModels) {
    numIterations = crossValidateIterations(examples, initialLinearModels)
    initLogitBoost(initialLinearModels)
    linearModels = copyOf(initialLinearModels)
    for i = 1...numIterations
        logitBoostIteration(linearModels,examples)
    split = findSplit(examples)
    localExamples = split.splitExamples(examples)
    sons = new Nodes[split.numSubsets()]
    for s = 1...sons.length
        sons.buildTree(localExamples[s], nodeModels)
}

crossValidateIterations(examples,initialLinearModels) {
    for fold = 1...5
        initLogitBoost(initialLinearModels)
        //split into training/test set
        train = trainCV(fold)
        test = testCV(fold)
        linearModels = copyOf(initialLinearModels)
        for i = 1...200
            logitBoostIteration(linearModels,train)
            logErrors[i] += error(test)
    numIterations = findBestIteration(logErrors)
    return numIterations
}
```

Fig. 2. Pseudocode for the LMT algorithm.

– A split for the data at the root is constructed using the C4.5 splitting criterion [12]. Both binary splits on numerical attributes and multiway splits on nominal attributes are considered. Tree growing continues by sorting the appropriate subsets of data to those nodes and building the logistic models of the child nodes in the following way: the LogitBoost algorithm is run on the subset associated with the child node, but starting with the committee $F_j(x)$, weights w_{ij} and probability estimates p_{ij} of the last iteration performed at the parent node (it is 'resumed' at step 2.a in Figure 1). Again, the optimum number of iterations to perform (the number of f_{jm} to add to F_j) is determined by five fold cross validation.
– Splitting continues in this fashion as long as more than 15 instances are at a node and a useful split can be found by the C4.5 splitting routine.
– The tree is pruned using the CART pruning algorithm as outlined in [2].

Figure 2 gives the pseudocode for this algorithm, which we call *LMT*. The method LMT constructs the tree given the training data examples. It first calls getCARTAlpha to cross-validate the 'cost-complexity-parameter' for the CART pruning scheme implemented in CARTPrune. The method buildTree grows the logistic model tree by recursively splitting the instance space. The argument initialLinearModels contains the simple linear regression functions already fit by LogitBoost at higher levels of the tree. The method initLogitBoost initializes the probabilities/weights for the LogitBoost algorithm as if it had already fitted the regression functions initialLinearModels (resuming Logit-Boost at step 2.a). The method crossValidateIterations determines the number of LogitBoost iterations to perform, and logitBoostIteration performs a single iteration of the LogitBoost algorithm (step 2), updating the probabilities/weights and adding a regression function to linearModels.

Handling of Missing Values and Nominal Attributes. To deal with missing values we calculate the mean (for numeric attributes) or mode (for categorical ones) based on all the training data and use these to replace them. The same means and modes are used to fill in missing values when classifying new instances.

When considering splits in the tree, multi-valued nominal attributes are handled in the usual way. However, regression functions can only be fit to numeric attributes. Therefore, they are fit to local copies of the training data where nominal attributes with k values have been converted into k binary indicator attributes.

Computational Complexity. The asymptotic complexity for building a logistic regression model is $O(n \cdot v^2 \cdot c)$ if we assume that the number of LogitBoost iterations is linear in the number of attributes present in the data[2] (n denotes the number of training examples, v the number of attributes, and c the number of classes). The complexity of building a logistic model tree is $O(n \cdot v^2 \cdot d \cdot c + k^2)$, where d is the depth and k the number of nodes of the initial unpruned tree. The first part of the sum derives from building the logistic regression models, the second one from the CART pruning scheme. In our experiments, the time for building the logistic regression models accounted for most of the overall runtime. Compared to simple tree induction, the asymptotic complexity of LMT is only worse by a factor of v. However, the nested cross-validations (one to prune the tree, one to determine the optimum number of LogitBoost operations) constitute a large (albeit constant) multiplying factor.

In the algorithm outlined above, the optimum number of iterations is determined by a five fold cross-validation for every node. This is the most computationally expensive part of the algorithm. We use two heuristics to reduce the runtime:

– In order to avoid an internal cross-validation at every node, we determine the optimum number of iterations by performing *one* cross-validation in the beginning of the algorithm and then using that number *everywhere* in the tree. This approach works surprisingly well: it never produced results that were significantly worse than those of the original algorithm. This indicates that the best number of iterations for LogitBoost does depend on the dataset — just choosing a fixed number of iterations for all of the datasets lead to significantly worse results — but not so much on different subsets of a particular dataset (as encountered in lower levels in the tree).

---

[2] Note that in our implementation it is actually bounded by a constant (500 for standalone logistic regression and 200 at the nodes of the logistic model tree)

- When performing the initial cross-validation, we have to select the number of iterations that gives the lowest error on the test set. Typically, the error will first decrease and later increase again because the model overfits the data. This allows the number of iterations to be chosen greedily by monitoring the error while performing iterations and stopping if the error starts to increase again. Because the error curve exhibits some spikes and irregularities, we keep track of the current minimum and stop if it has not changed for 25 iterations. Using this heuristic does not change the behavior of the algorithm significantly.

We included both heuristics in the final version of our algorithm, and all results shown for LMT refer to this final version.

3 Experiments

In order to evaluate the performance of our method and compare it against other state-of-the-art learning schemes, we applied it to several real-world problems. More specifically, we seek to answer the following questions in our experimental study:

1. How does LMT compare to the two algorithms that form its basis, i.e., logistic regression and C4.5? Ideally, we would never expect worse performance than either of these algorithms.
2. How does LMT compare to methods that build multiple trees? We include results for boosted C4.5 trees (using the AdaBoostM1 algorithm [5] and 100 boosting iterations), where the final model is a 'voting committee' of trees and for the M5' algorithm, which builds one tree per class when applied to classification problems.
3. How big are the trees constructed by LMT? We expect them to be much smaller than simple classification trees because the leaves contain more information. We also expect the trees to be pruned back to the root if a linear logistic model is the best solution for the dataset.

We will also give results for another recently developed algorithm for inducing logistic model trees called 'PLUS' (see Section 4 for a short discussion of the PLUS algorithm).

3.1 Datasets and Methodology

For our experiments we used 32 benchmark datasets from the UCI repository [1], given in the first column of Table 1. Their size ranges from under hundred to a few thousand instances. They contain varying numbers of numeric and nominal attributes and some contain missing values. For more information about the datasets, see for example [4].

For every dataset and algorithm we performed ten runs of ten fold stratified cross-validation (using the same splits into training/test set for every method). This gives a hundred data points for each algorithm and dataset, from which we

Table 1. Average classification accuracy and standard deviation.

Data Set	LMT	C4.5	SimpleLogistic	M5'	PLUS	AdaBoost.M1
anneal	99.5±0.8	98.6±1.0 •	99.5±0.8	98.6±1.1	99.4±0.8 (c)	99.6±0.7
audiology	84.0±7.8	77.3±7.5	83.7±7.8	76.8±8.6 •	80.6±8.3 (c)	84.7±7.6
australian	85.0±4.1	85.6±4.0	85.2±4.1	85.4±3.9	85.2±3.9 (m)	86.4±4.0
autos	75.8±9.7	81.8±8.8	75.1±8.9	76.0±10.0	76.6±8.7 (c)	86.8±6.8 ○
balance-scale	90.0±2.5	77.8±3.4 •	88.6±3.0	87.8±2.2 •	89.7±2.8 (m)	76.1±4.1 •
breast-cancer	75.6±5.4	74.3±6.1	75.6±5.5	70.4±6.8 •	71.5±5.7 (c) •	66.2±8.1 •
breast-w	96.3±2.1	95.0±2.7	96.2±2.3	95.9±2.2	96.4±2.2 (c)	96.7±2.2
german	75.3±3.7	71.3±3.2 •	75.2±3.7	75.0±3.3	73.3±3.5 (m)	74.5±3.3
glass	69.7±9.5	67.6±9.3	65.4±8.7	71.3±9.1	69.3±9.7 (c)	78.8±7.8 ○
glass (G2)	76.5±8.9	78.2±8.5	76.9±8.8	81.1±8.7	83.2±11.1(c)	88.7±6.4 ○
heart-c	82.7±7.4	76.9±6.6 •	83.1±7.4	82.1±6.7	78.2±7.4 (s)	80.0±6.5
heart-h	84.2±6.3	80.2±8.0	84.2±6.3	82.4±6.4	79.8±7.8 (c)	78.3±7.1 •
heart-statlog	83.6±6.6	78.1±7.4 •	83.7±6.5	82.1±6.8	83.7±6.4 (m)	80.4±7.1
hepatitis	83.7±8.1	79.2±9.6	84.1±8.1	82.4±8.8	83.3±7.8 (m)	84.9±7.8
horse-colic	83.7±6.3	85.2±5.9	82.2±6.0	83.2±5.4	84.0±5.8 (c)	81.7±5.8
hypothyroid	99.6±0.4	99.5±0.4	96.8±0.7 •	99.4±0.4	99.1±0.4 (c) •	99.7±0.3
ionosphere	92.7±4.3	89.7±4.4 •	88.1±5.3 •	89.9±4.2	89.5±5.2 (c)	94.0±3.8
iris	96.2±5.0	94.7±5.3	96.3±4.9	94.9±5.6	94.3±5.4 (c)	94.5±5.0
kr-vs-kp	99.7±0.3	99.4±0.4	97.4±0.8 •	99.2±0.5 •	99.5±0.4 (c)	99.6±0.3
labor	91.5±10.9	78.6±16.6•	91.9±10.4	85.1±16.3	89.9±11.5(c)	88.9±14.1
lymphography	84.7±9.6	75.8±11.0•	84.5±9.3	80.4±9.3	78.4±10.2(c)	84.7±8.4
pima-indians	77.1±4.4	74.5±5.3	77.1±4.5	76.6±4.7	77.2±4.3 (m)	73.9±4.8 •
primary-tumor	46.7±6.2	41.4±6.9 •	46.7±6.2	45.3±6.2	40.7±6.1 (c) •	41.7±6.5 •
segment	97.1±1.2	96.8±1.3	95.4±1.5 •	97.4±1.0	96.8±1.1 (c)	98.6±0.7 ○
sick	98.9±0.6	98.7±0.6	96.7±0.7 •	98.4±0.6 •	98.6±0.6 (c)	99.0±0.5
sonar	76.4±9.4	73.6±9.3	75.1±8.9	78.4±8.8	71.6±8.0 (c)	85.1±7.8 ○
soybean	93.6±2.5	91.8±3.2	93.5±2.7	92.9±2.6	93.6±2.7 (c)	93.3±2.8
vehicle	82.4±3.3	72.3±4.3 •	80.4±3.4	78.7±4.4 •	79.8±4.0 (m)	77.9±3.6 •
vote	95.7±2.8	96.6±2.6	95.7±2.7	95.6±2.8	95.3±2.8 (c)	95.2±3.3
vowel	94.1±2.5	80.2±4.4 •	84.2±3.7 •	80.9±4.7 •	83.0±3.7 (c) •	96.8±1.9 ○
waveform-noise	87.0±1.6	75.3±1.9 •	86.9±1.6	82.5±1.6 •	86.7±1.5 (m)	85.0±1.6 •
zoo	95.0±6.6	92.6±7.3	94.8±6.7	94.5±6.4	94.5±6.8 (c)	96.3±6.1

○, • statistically significant win or loss

calculated the average accuracy (percentage of correctly classified instances) and standard deviation. To correct for the dependencies in the estimates we used the corrected resampled t-test [9] instead of the standard t-test on these data points to identify significant wins/losses of our method against the other methods at a 5% significance level.

Table1 gives the average classification accuracy for every method and dataset, and indicates significant wins/losses compared to LMT. Table 2 gives the number of datasets on which a method (column) significantly outperforms another method (row). Apart from PLUS all algorithms are implemented in Weka 3.3.6 (including LMT and SimpleLogistic)[3]. Note that PLUS has three different modes of operation: one to build a simple classification tree, and two modes that build logistic model trees using simple/multiple logistic regression models. For all datasets, we ran PLUS in all three modes and selected the best result, indicated by (c),(s) or (m) in Table 1.

3.2 Discussion of Results

To answer our first question, we observe from Table 1 that the LMT algorithm indeed reaches at least accuracy levels comparable to both SimpleLogistic and

---
[3] Weka is available from www.cs.waikato.ac.nz/~ml

Table 2. Number of datasets where algorithm in column significantly outperforms algorithm in row.

	LMT	C4.5	SimpleLogistic	M5'	PLUS	AdaBoost.M1
LMT	-	0	0	0	0	6
C4.5	13	-	6	5	5	13
SimpleLogistic	6	3	-	4	4	10
M5'	8	0	1	-	1	12
PLUS	4	1	1	2	-	0
AdaBoost.M1	7	1	3	1	0	-

Table 3. Tree size.

Data Set	LMT	C4.5	PLUS	Data Set	LMT	C4.5	PLUS
anneal	1.8	38.0 o	15.8 o	ionosphere	4.6	13.9 o	13.5 o
audiology	1.0	29.9 o	47.6 o	iris	1.1	4.6 o	6.1 o
australian	2.5	22.5 o	2.0	kr-vs-kp	8.0	29.3 o	42.6 o
autos	3.0	44.8 o	42.2 o	labor	1.0	4.2 o	5.1 o
balance-scale	5.3	41.6 o	1.9 •	lymphography	1.2	17.3 o	14.9 o
breast-cancer	1.1	9.8 o	9.1 o	pima-indians	1.0	22.2 o	1.2
breast-w	1.4	12.2 o	1.2	primary-tumor	1.0	43.8 o	26.7 o
german	1.0	90.2 o	4.3 o	segment	12.0	41.2 o	65.9 o
glass	7.0	23.6 o	25.2 o	sick	14.1	27.4 o	30.0 o
glass (G2)	4.6	12.5 o	15.5 o	sonar	2.7	14.5 o	13.2 o
heart-c	1.0	25.7 o	6.2 o	soybean	3.7	61.1 o	42.4 o
heart-h	1.0	6.3 o	5.1	vehicle	3.5	69.5 o	1.0 •
heart-statlog	1.0	17.8 o	1.0	vote	1.1	5.8 o	5.8 o
hepatitis	1.1	9.3 o	1.5	vowel	5.2	123.3 o	156.9 o
horse-colic	3.7	5.9	6.6	waveform-noise	1.0	296.5 o	1.0
hypothyroid	5.6	14.4 o	12.9 o	zoo	1.0	8.4 o	9.5 o

o, • statistically significant increase or decrease

C4.5, it is never significantly less accurate. It outperforms SimpleLogistic on six and C4.5 on 13 datasets, and both methods simultaneously on two datasets. SimpleLogistic performs surprisingly well on most datasets, especially the smaller ones. However, on some larger datasets ('kr-vs-kp', 'sick', 'hypothyroid') its performance is a lot worse than that of any other method. Linear models are probably too restricted to achieve good performance on these datasets.

With regard to the second question, we can say that LMT achieves similar results as boosted C4.5 (although with strengths/weaknesses on different datasets). Comparing LMT with M5', we find better results for LMT on almost all datasets. Note that LMT also outperforms PLUS, even though the selection of the best result from the three modes for PLUS introduces an optimistic bias.

To answer our third question, Table 3 gives the observed average tree sizes (measured in number of leaves) for LMT, C4.5 and PLUS. It shows that the trees built by the LMT algorithm are always smaller than those built by C4.5 and mostly smaller than those generated by PLUS. For many datasets the average tree size for LMT is very close to one, which essentially means that the algorithm constructs a simple logistic model. To account for small random fluctuations, we will say the tree is pruned back to the root if the average tree size is less than 1.5. This is the case for exactly half of the 32 datasets, and consequently the results for LMT on these datasets are almost identical to those of SimpleLogistic. It can be seen from Table 1 that on all datasets (with the exception of 'vote') where the tree is pruned back to the root, the result for LMT is better than that for C4.5, so it is reasonable to assume that for these datasets using a simple logistic regression model is indeed better than building a tree structure. Looking at the sixteen datasets where the logistic model tree is not pruned back to the root, we observe that on 13 of them LMT is more accurate than SimpleLogistic. This indicates a tree is only built if this leads to better performance than a single logistic model. From these two observations we can conclude that our method reliably makes the right choice between a simple logistic model and a more elaborate tree structure.

We conclude that the LMT algorithm achieves better results than C4.5, SimpleLogistic, M5' and PLUS, and results that are competitive with boosted C4.5. Considering that a single logistic model tree is easier to interpret than a boosted committee of C4.5 trees we think that LMT is an interesting alternative to boosting trees. Of course, one could also boost logistic model trees — but because building them takes longer than building simple trees this would be computationally expensive.

4 Related Work

As mentioned above, model trees form the basis for the ideas presented here, but there has also been some interest in combining regression and tree induction into 'tree structured regression' in the statistics community. For example, Chaudhuri et al. [3] investigate a general framework for combining tree induction with node-based regression models that are fit by maximum likelihood. Special cases include poisson regression trees (for integer-valued class variables) and logistic regression trees (for binary class variables only). Chaudhuri et al. apply their logistic regression tree implementation to one real-world dataset, but it is not their focus to compare it to other state-of-the-art learning schemes.

More recently, Lim presents an implementation of logistic regression trees called 'PLUS' [8]. There are some differences between the PLUS system and our method: first, PLUS does not consider nominal attributes when building the logistic regression models, i.e. it reverts to building a standard decision tree if the data does not contain numeric attributes. Second, PLUS uses a different method to construct the logistic regression models at the nodes. In PLUS, every logistic model is trained from scratch on the data at a node, whereas in our method the final logistic model consists of a committee of linear models trained on nested subsets of the data, thus naturally incorporating a form of 'smoothing'. Furthermore, our approach automatically selects the best attributes to include in a logistic model, while PLUS always uses all or just one attribute (a choice that has to be made at the command line by the user).

5 Conclusions

This paper introduces a new method for learning logistic model trees that builds on earlier work on model trees. This method, called LMT, employs an efficient and flexible approach for building logistic models and uses the well-known CART algorithm for pruning. Our experiments show that it is often more accurate than C4.5 decision trees and standalone logistic regression on real-world datasets, and, more surprisingly, competitive with boosted C4.5 trees. Like other tree induction methods, it does not require any tuning of parameters.

LMT produces a single tree containing binary splits on numeric attributes, multiway splits on nominal ones, and logistic regression models at the leaves, and the algorithm ensures that only relevant attributes are included in the latter. The result is not quite as easy to interpret as a standard decision tree, but much more intelligible than a committee of multiple trees or more opaque classifiers like kernel-based estimators.

Acknowledgments

Many thanks to Luc de Raedt and Geoff Holmes for enabling Niels to work on his MSc at Waikato. Eibe Frank was supported by Marsden Grant 01-UOW-019.

References

1. C.L. Blake and C.J. Merz. UCI repository of machine learning databases, 1998. [www.ics.uci.edu/~mlearn/MLRepository.html].
2. L. Breiman, H. Friedman, J. A. Olshen, and C. J. Stone. *Classification and Regression Trees*. Wadsworth, 1984.
3. P. Chaudhuri, W.-D. Lo, W.-Y. Loh, and C.-C. Yang. Generalized regression trees. *Statistica Sinica*, 5:641–666, 1995.
4. Eibe Frank, Yong Wang, Stuart Inglis, Geoffrey Holmes, and Ian H. Witten. Using model trees for classification. *Machine Learning*, 32(1):63–76, 1998.
5. Yoav Freund and Robert E. Schapire. Experiments with a new boosting algorithm. In *Proc. Int. Conf. on Machine Learning*, pages 148–156. Morgan Kaufmann, 1996.
6. Jerome Friedman, Trevor Hastie, and Robert Tibshirani. Additive logistic regression: a statistical view of boosting. *The Annals of Statistic*, 38(2):337–374, 2000.
7. Trevor Hastie, Robert Tibshirani, and Jerome Friedman. *The Elements of Statistical Learning: Data Mining, Inference, and Prediction*. Springer-Verlag, 2001.
8. T.-S. Lim. *Polytomous Logistic Regression Trees*. PhD thesis, Department of Statistics, University of Wisconsin, 2000.
9. C. Nadeau and Yoshua Bengio. Inference for the generalization error. In *Advances in Neural Information Processing Systems 12*, pages 307–313. MIT Press, 1999.
10. C. Perlich and F. Provost. Tree induction vs logistic regression. In *Beyond Classification and Regression (NIPS 2002 Workshop)*, 2002.
11. J. R. Quinlan. Learning with Continuous Classes. In *5th Australian Joint Conference on Artificial Intelligence*, pages 343–348, 1992.
12. R. Quinlan. *C4.5: Programs for Machine Learning*. Morgan Kaufmann, 1993.
13. Y. Wang and I. Witten. Inducing model trees for continuous classes. In *Proc of Poster Papers, European Conf. on Machine Learning*, 1997.

Color Image Segmentation: Kernel Do the Feature Space

Jianguo Lee, Jingdong Wang, and Changshui Zhang

State Key Laboratory of Intelligent Technology and Systems
Department of Automation, Tsinghua University
Beijing, 100084, P. R. China
{lijg01,wangjd01}@mails.tsinghua.edu.cn
zcs@mail.tsinghua.edu.cn

Abstract. In this paper, we try to apply kernel methods to solve the problem of color image segmentation, which is attracting more and more attention recently as color images provide more information than gray level images do. One natural way for color image segmentation is to do pixels clustering in color space. GMM has been applied for this task. However, practice has shown that GMM doesn't perform this task well in original color space. Our basic idea is to solve the segmentation in a nonlinear feature space obtained by kernel methods. The scheme is that we propose an extension of EM algorithm for GMM by involving one kernel feature extraction step, which is called K-EM. With the technique based on Monte Carlo sampling and mapping, K-EM not only speeds up kernel step, but also automatically extracts good features for clustering in a nonlinear way. Experiments show that the proposed algorithm has satisfactory performance. The contribution of this paper could be summarized into two points: one is that we introduced kernel methods to solve real computer vision problem, the other is that we proposed an efficient scheme for kernel methods applied in large scale problems.

1 Introduction

Image segmentation [1] is an essential and critical topic in image processing and computer vision. Recently, color image segmentation attracts more and more attention mainly due to the following reasons: (1) Color images provide more information than gray level images do. (2) The power of computers is increasing rapidly, and PCs can deal with color images more easily.

Color image segmentation [2] can be viewed as an extension of gray level image segmentation, and there are various methods, which can be roughly categorized as three typical ways: (1) color space clustering based segmentation, (2) edge or contour detection based segmentation and (3) region or area extraction based segmentation. The basic idea of clustering based approach [3] is to directly cluster the pixels in color space by employing clustering algorithm such as k-means, Gaussian Mixture Models (GMM), etc. Edge based approach is a more global method. The basic idea is to firstly extract the edges using edges detectors such as Canny edge detector [4], secondly link the edges through edge linking and tracing methods, and consequently obtain the segmentation by using the linked closed edges. Region based approach [5], including region growing, region split and merge, attempts to group pixels into homogeneous regions.

In this paper, we address the problem of clustering based color image segmentation. In fact, image segmentation can be viewed as a hidden variable problem, i.e., segmenting an image into clusters involves determining which source cluster generates the image pixels. Based on this fact, a global mixture probabilistic model can be built up. For instance, GMM based on the basic Expectation-Maximization (EM) [6] algorithm is applied for image segmentation.

One serious problem of GMM based segmentation is how to choose a proper color representation for segmentation. The frequently used color spaces, including linear space such as RGB and YIQ color space, nonlinear space such as HSV and LUV color space [2], have been verified in practice to be not suitable for clustering [3, 7]. Thus two typical methods have been proposed towards the improvement. One is that Data-Driven Markov Chain Monte Carlo (DD-MCMC) [8] is employed to improve the performance of mixture probabilistic model for segmentation. The other is that Principal Components Analysis (PCA) is applied to find a characteristic color features space from mono- or hybrid- color spaces for detecting clusters [2]. However, two critical problems arose. One is that PCA is a linear method, but color image segmentation is more likely to be nonlinear. The other is that most clustering based approaches only utilize the color information, but do not utilize the geometrical or spatial information. All these motivate us to use kernel feature extraction method [9] instead of linear PCA to extract nonlinear features from both color and spatial information for clustering.

The basic idea of the proposed method is to extend EM algorithm to embed one kernel feature extraction step (K-Step), which does feature extraction and mapping to transform data from input space to nonlinear feature space (It should be emphasized that any kernel feature analysis methods can be utilized in K-Step, where in this paper Kernel PCA is adopted). The benefit of K-EM for GMM is that we could not only avoid the extremely large computational cost of kernel feature analysis, but also extend GMM to be capable of dealing with data sets with complex structures. The experiments show that the proposed method has satisfactory performance.

The rest of this paper is organized as follows. Section 2 presents the computational cost problem of kernel methods applied to large scale data sets, and proposes the K-EM algorithm for GMM to solve this problem. Section 3 demonstrates experimental results of the proposed algorithm on a synthetic data set and real world color image segmentation problems. Section 4 concludes.

2 K-EM Algorithm for GMM

As is known, EM algorithm often fails in data sets with complex structures (nonlinear and non-Gaussian). One possible way is to find a nonlinear map so that the data is projected and well clustered in the mapped feature space. That leads to the intuitive idea of our K-EM algorithm. In this section, we first introduce kernel feature analysis method and present great computational cost problem in kernel methods for large scale data sets. Secondly, we propose the speedup technique for Kernel PCA based on Monte Carlo sampling and mapping. Thirdly, we provide the whole K-EM algorithm for GMM. Finally, we give some discussions of the proposed algorithm and related work.

2.1 Kernel Feature Analysis

Kernel trick [10] is an efficient method for nonlinear data analysis early used in Support Vector Machine (SVM). The idea is that we could implicitly map input data into a high dimension feature space via a nonlinear function:

$$\begin{aligned} \Phi : X &\to H \\ x &\mapsto \phi(x) \end{aligned} \qquad (1)$$

And a similarity measure is defined from the dot product in H as follows:

$$k(x, x') \triangleq \langle \phi(x), \phi(x') \rangle \qquad (2)$$

where the kernel function $k(\cdot, \cdot)$ should satisfy *Mercer's condition* [9, 10].

Besides being successfully used in SVM, kernel trick has been transported to many other kinds of algorithms. Among which, Kernel Feature Analysis (KFA), including Kernel Principal Component Analysis (Kernel PCA) [11] and Kernel Fisher Discriminant (KFD) [9] etc, is a class of methods with the most influence.

KFA aims to extract features in a nonlinear way. In this paper, we apply Kernel PCA as our feature extractor. We must stress that any other kernel feature extraction method could be employed in our final framework. Given a set of $\{x_i\}_{i=1}^m \in R^d$, with zero means, using the nonlinear mapping and kernel trick defined as in (1) and (2), Kernel PCA mainly depends on the eigen-decomposition problem on a Gram matrix.

$$m\lambda\alpha = \mathbf{K}\alpha \qquad (3)$$

where $\alpha = (\alpha^1, \cdots, \alpha^m)^T$ is the expansion coefficient, λ is the eigen-value and $\mathbf{K}$ is the $m \times m$ Gram matrix with element $K_{ij} = \langle \phi(x_i), \phi(x_j) \rangle$.

To extract nonlinear features from a test point x, Kernel PCA computes dot product between $\phi(x)$ and the nth eigenvector v^n in feature space to obtain the projection $y = (y^1, \cdots, y^p)$.

$$y^n = \langle v^n, \phi(x) \rangle = \sum_{i=1}^{m} \alpha_i^n k(x_i, x) \quad n = 1, \cdots, p \qquad (4)$$

where p ($p < m$) is the dimension of extracted features space F, and p is automatically chosen according to the leading eigenvalues λ.

Kernel PCA is an efficient nonlinear method for feature extraction. The advantage of Kernel PCA is that data with complex structure could be well clustered in feature space. However, the computational cost problem arises when Kernel PCA is applied to large scale data sets.

As is known, through kernel trick, the computational cost of Kernel PCA is mainly determined by the eigen-decomposition problem, such as (3) for Kernel

PCA. Thus the computational cost directly depends on the size of Gram matrix **K**, i.e. the size of data sets. With the increase of size m, it is liable to meet with the curse of dimension. As is known, if m is large, e.g. larger than 5,000, currently it is impossible to finish the eigen-decomposition within hours even on the fastest PCs. Unfortunately, the size m is often very large in many cases, especially for data mining problems and pixels clustering based image segmentation (For example, m will be 16,384 for a not very large image with size 128×128). That is to say, the application of Kernel PCA method is seriously restricted by the size of data sets. Any attempt in this point is significative for the application of kernel methods. In the following subsection, we will focus on this point.

2.2 Speed up Kernel PCA by Monte Carlo Sampling and Mapping

Some techniques are proposed to handle the great computational cost problem in Kernel PCA. Most assume that the symmetry Gram matrix has a low rank. There are three typical techniques based on that assumption. The first technique is based on traditional Orthogonal Iteration or Lanzcos Iteration. The second is to make the Gram matrix sparse by sampling techniques [12]. The third is to apply Nyström method to speedup kernel machine [13]. However, all these methods still can't efficiently solve the vast-data problem such as pixel clustering based image segmentation. Moreover, none of these techniques has been successful in a practical problem.

Here, we also adopt this basic assumption, but reconsider the problem in a different way. Consider that samples forming the Gram matrix are drawn from a probabilistic distribution $p(x)$, thus the eigen-problem could be written down as a continuous form.

$$\int k(x,y)p(x)V_i(x)dx = \lambda_i V_i(y) \tag{5}$$

where λ_i, $V_i(y)$ are eigenvalue and eigenvector corresponding with the Gram matrix, and $k(\cdot,\cdot)$ is a given kernel function. Note that the eigenvalues are ordered so that $\lambda_1 > \lambda_2 \cdots$.

The integral on the left of Equation (5) could be approximated by using Monte Carlo method to draw a subset of samples $\{x_i\}_{i=1}^{N}$ according to $p(x)$.

$$\int k(x,y)p(x)V_i(x)dx \approx \frac{1}{N}\sum_{j=1}^{N} k(x_j,y)V_i(x_j) \tag{6}$$

Then plugging in $y = x_k$ for $j = 1,\cdots,N$, we obtain a matrix eigen-problem.

$$\frac{1}{N}\sum_{j=1}^{N} k(x_j,x_k)V_i(x_j) = \hat{\lambda}_i V_i(x_k) \tag{7}$$

where $\hat{\lambda}_i$ is the approximation of eigenvalue λ_i.

Fortunately, this approximation has been proved feasible and has bounded error performance [14]. This result is extremely beautiful. It indicates that we can approximate the eigenvalues of large size Gram matrix by using only a subset of samples.

Our proposed technique is based on this result. Considering data $x_i \in X$ with dimension d, Kernel PCA projects data x_i into feature space F to be y_i with dimension p, where $p \ll m$ holds true under the basic low rank assumption. Since eigenvalues are associated with eigenvectors, the corresponding eigenvectors of the approximated eigenvalues form a representative space D, which could be viewed as an approximation of feature space F. Our work will utilize this property to construct a representative space D to approximate feature space F in an iterative procedure.

Suppose sample x_i is drawn from known distribution $p(x)$, in other words, each sample $x_i \in X$ is associated with a known sampling weight $w(x_i)$. In most cases, especially in our color segmentation problem, $p(x)$ is not known. However it is possible using all samples to estimate a distribution $\hat{p}(x)$ to approximate $p(x)$. We just sample data set X according to $\hat{p}(x)$ independently T times to obtain T subset S_i $(1 \leqslant i \leqslant T)$, where S_i is a subset with N elements (with the low rank assumption, $N \ll m, N \geqslant p$) which are drawn from X according to $\hat{p}(x)$. Thus the sampling procedure could be viewed as Sampling Important Resampling (SIR) [15], which is one kind of Monte Carlo sampling method. Afterward, perform Kernel PCA on each S_i, and obtain representative space D_i. We apply Support Vector Regression (SVR) [10] to construct the mapping from S_i to D_i.

$$y = f_i(x), \ 1 \leqslant i \leqslant T \quad (8)$$

And T maps are combined together to be a nonlinear map from X to D as follows.

$$y = f(x) = \frac{1}{T} \sum_{i=1}^{T} f_i(x) \quad (9)$$

When a new sample x comes, it could be projected to the representative space D by (9). We should emphasize here that using SVR to learn the mapping is due to its capability of generalization, and the reason of using T subsets is that the ensemble of T subsets can make result with less variance and more robust.

The whole sampling, resampling and combining procedure could be viewed as development of bagging ensemble [16] technique.

However, there is still a sticking point in the speedup scheme. That is how to obtain the distribution $p(x)$ or how to provide sampling weight information. We can't provide the information in one step, but we adopt the idea from Sequential Monte Carlo method that we provide the information in an iterative procedure. That we first project all the samples into the representative space, then we estimate a distribution in the space and update the sampling weight according to the estimated distribution, and then we can draw samples according to the new sampling weight information. Iteratively running the procedure till convergence, we can obtain the expected result. This is achieved by efficiently combining Kernel PCA with GMM in the next subsection.

2.3 K-EM Algorithm for GMM

GMM is a kind of mixture density models, which assumes that each component of the probabilistic model is a Gaussian density. That is to say:

$$p(y|\Theta) = \sum_{i=1}^{M} \alpha_i G_i(y|\theta_i) \qquad (10)$$

where parameters $\Theta = (\alpha_1, \cdots, \alpha_M; \theta_1, \cdots, \theta_M)$ satisfy $\sum_{i=1}^{M} \alpha_i = 1$, $\alpha_i \geqslant 0$ and $G_i(y|\theta_i)$ is a Gaussian probability density function with parameter $\theta_i = (\mu_i, \Sigma_i)$.

EM [17] algorithm has been successfully used in generative models such as GMM. However, traditional EM for GMM often fails when structure of the data does not conform to mixture Gaussian assumption, especially for image pixels. Thus EM has been extended in many ways to overcome this problem.

D-EM [18] is one of the extensions of EM. It focuses mainly on two categorized semi-supervised learning problem, which has two categories with the minority samples labeled and the majority unlabeled. D-EM solves the problem by embedding a linear transformation step, which finds good fit of the data distributions as well as automatically selects good features. However, the linear transformation and two categorized learning framework limit its applications. Kernel trick is also introduced into D-EM [19], but the existed kernel version of D-EM did not start from the idea of speedup kernel feature extraction method in a probabilistic framework.

The proposed K-EM for GMM aims to extend D-EM in at least three aspects. The linear transformation will be replaced by Kernel PCA (In fact, any kernel feature analysis can be ultilized), the two categorized semi-supervised learning problem will be extended to multi-component clustering problem, and GMM provide sampling weight information so that Kernel PCA will be sped up greatly by Monte Carlo sampling and mapping technique.

The basic idea of K-EM for GMM is that it will efficiently combine two operations of Kernel PCA and parameters estimation of GMM. Kernel PCA extracts good features for GMM, whereas GMM provides sampling weight information needed by the proposed speedup technique of Kernel PCA. That is to say, in iteration step $(t-1)$, we estimate a distribution $p(y|\Theta^{(t-1)})$ in representative space D using GMM. Then we update the sampling weight of sample x_i by the following equation since each x_i corresponds to one y_i.

$$w^{(t-1)}(x_i) = \frac{p(y_i|\Theta^{(t-1)})}{\sum_{j=1}^{m} p(y_j|\Theta^{(t-1)})} \qquad (11)$$

Consequently, we do the sampling important resampling and mapping step according to the updated weight information and the scheme described in previous subsection.

To summarize, for a given data set X, the proposed K-EM algorithm for GMM iterates over three steps. That is "Expectation-Kernel feature extraction-Maximization". The detail algorithm of K-EM for GMM is shown in Table 1. The algorithm initializes all the samples with the same sampling weight $1/m$. In

Table 1. The detailed K-EM algorithm for GMM.

Input: Data set X
Output: Clustering parameters Θ of GMM
S1: Initialize all samples with the sampling same weight $1/m$, number of clusters C, largest iteration steps L, iterating counter $t = 0$, number of subsets T and size of subsets N.
S2: Iteration counter $t = t + 1$

- **E-Step** does sampling in set X according to sampling weight information by M-Step to obtain T subsets S_i.
- **K-Step** performs Kernel PCA on each subset S_i, projects data in S_i into the representative space D_i, then learns the mapping function (8) between the input space and the representative space of set S_i. The T learned maps are combined to obtain the final map by (9), thus all the samples in X are projected into the representative space D by (9).
- **M-Step** performs parameters Θ estimation of GMM and updates sampling weight of each sample by (11).

S3: Test whether convergence is reached or $t > L$. If not, loop back to $S2$, otherwise return parameters Θ and exit.

---

other words, the first E-Step performs a uniform sampling. The algorithm could not be terminated until the parameters converge or the presetting iteration steps are reached.

2.4 Discussion of the Algorithm

As we have mentioned in previous section, the problem we addressed is to apply eigen-decomposition based kernel methods to large scale data sets. If the data set size m is large enough, e.g. larger than 5,000, the eigen-decomposition is intractable. However, the time complexity of the proposed method depends upon the subset size N instead of whole data set size m, and N could be much less than m ($N \ll m$), thus the proposed method can solve the problem indirect but much more efficiently. That could be viewed as our motivation.

There are still some other related work besides D-EM and its kernel version. One of the most influential methods is the particle filter or bootstrap filter [20]. Particle filter also iteratively uses weight updating and important sampling, which is called Sequential Important Sampling (SIS). And in our algorithm, the samples in subset could be viewed as particles in particle filter, and size of them is also fixed. But there are still two obvious differences. First, particle filter only uses particles to approximate the data distribution, but our method projects all data into feature space and approximates the data distribution by GMM. Second, particle filter only performs in the input data space, whereas our method performs in a feature space by Kernel PCA.

The other one is spectral clustering [21]. Spectral clustering could be regarded as first using RBF (only using RBF) based kernel methods to extract features, and then performing clustering by k-means. It is not an iterative procedure. Moreover, it still can not deal with problems with large scale data set.

Our proposed method combines the idea of particle filter and that of spectral clustering, and could be regarded as a kernel extension of particle filter and a sequential version of spectral clustering in some sense.

3 The Experimental Results

To provide an intuitive illustration of the proposed algorithm, we firstly demonstrate the K-EM for GMM on a synthetic 2-D data set, and then on real world color image segmentation problem.

3.1 Synthetic 2-D Data Clustering

The synthetic data set with 2,000 samples is depicted in Fig 2. Traditional GMM based on basic EM, using coordinates of sample points as features, partitions the data set into two clusters as shown in Fig 2(b). The result is obviously not satisfying. As a comparison, the proposed K-EM for GMM is also employed this task using a polynomial kernel

$$k(x, x') = (x \cdot x')^d \tag{12}$$

with degree $d = 2$, and setting the representative dimension $p = 4$, subset S_i with size $N = 15$. In order to observe the sampling procedure easily, we just set number of subset $T = 1$. With these paramters, we achieve the promising results shown in Fig 2(a). Fig 2(c) shows the 15 samples drawn at the beginning of the algorithm, and Fig 2(d) shows the 15 samples drawn at the end of the algorithm. It is obvious that samples in Fig 2(d) provide more information about the structure of the data set than that of Fig 2(c).

What we still want to emphasize here is the running time compared with spectral clustering. On a Pentium4 2.0GHZ PC, the proposed algorithm could finish the whole clustering problem within 10 seconds, but spectral clustering need half an hour to achieve the same result using RBF kernel function

$$k(x, x') = \exp(-\gamma \|x - x'\|^2) \tag{13}$$

where sets $\gamma = 10$. We could see that the proposed algorithm achieves satisfied result as well as reduces the computational cost noticeably. All these demonstrate the power of the proposed algorithm.

3.2 Color Image Segmentation

In this part, we present some experiments on color image segmentation.

As Kernel PCA will project original color space to nonlinear space, the original color space we adopt is linear color space, that the RGB color space. As mentioned in the first section, the spatial information is also utilized for the

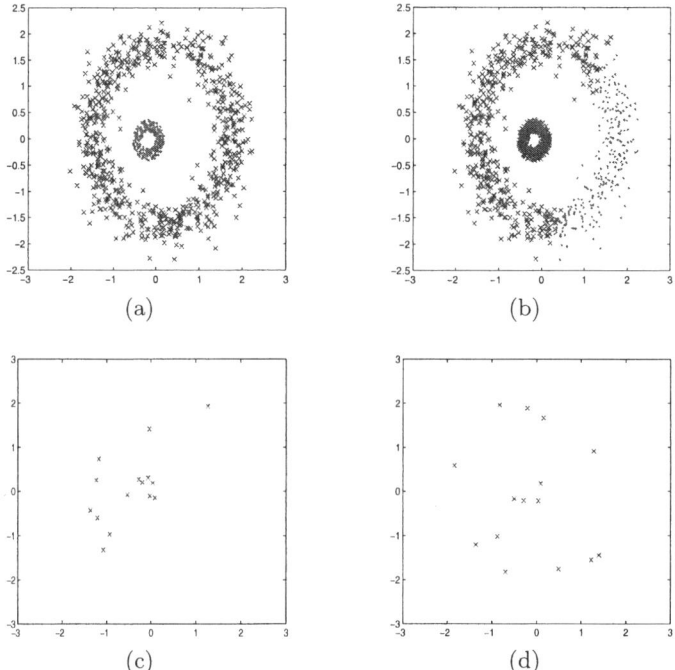

Fig. 1. Intuitive illustration of K-EM for GMM. (a) Clustering result by the proposed method. (b) Clustering result by GMM based on basic EM. (c) 15 Samples drawn at the beginning of the K-EM algorithm (marked by '×'). (d) 15 Samples drawn at the end of the K-EM algorithm.

clustering. The input features for our algorithm are $(r, g, b, x, y)^T$, where (x, y) is coordinate and (r, g, b) is RGB value of the corresponding pixel. We choose Kernel PCA as the kernel feature extraction method, and RBF kernel as in Equation (13) is used in all segmentation experiments. Some parameters could almost be fixed as dimension of subsets number $T = 10$, representative space $p = 7$, and samples in each subset $N = 400$ for most segmentation problem. Number of clusters C and parameter of RBF kernel γ need to be determined according to practice.

As a comparison, GMM based on basic EM also performs the same task. And it adopts the same clusters number as the proposed method, but only uses the RGB color space as the feature space for clustering.

Results are shown in Fig 2. First column depicts the original images, second column depicts the corresponding results by our K-EM for GMM, and the third column depicts the result by GMM based on basic EM. Both examples set the clusters number C to be three ($C = 3$). Parameter of RBF kernel is set to be $\gamma = 0.15$ and $\gamma = 1$ for Fig 2(b) and Fig 2(e) respectively. It is obvious that the results achieved by our method are satisfactory and much better than GMM based on basic EM.

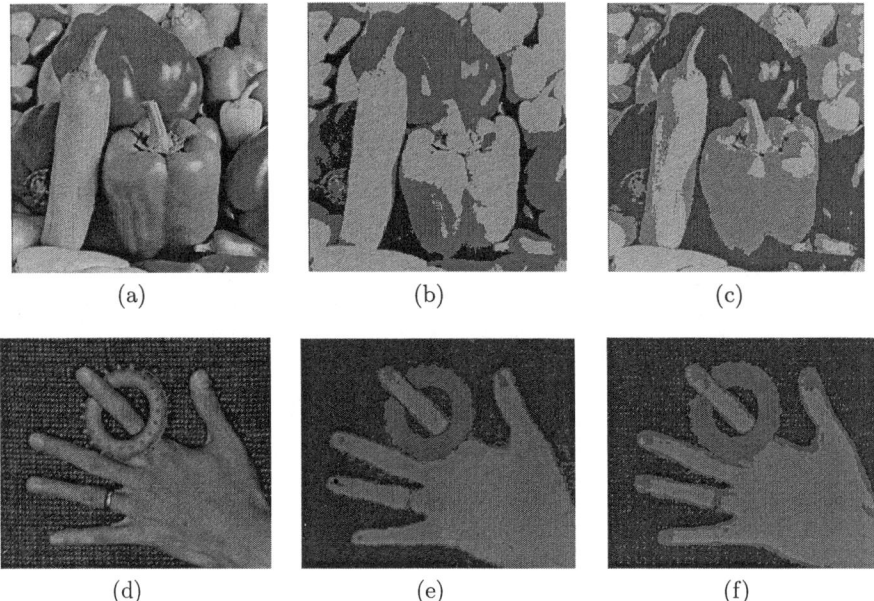

Fig. 2. Color Image segmentation results achieved by the proposed algorithm and basic GMM. Original images are depicted in the first column, the corresponding results by our K-EM for GMM are depicted in second column, and results by GMM based on basic EM are depicted in the third column. Both examples set the clusters number C to be three (C=3).

4 Conclusion

In this paper, we extend EM algorithm to K-EM by involving one kernel feature extraction (in this paper, kernel PCA) step. The proposed K-EM for GMM efficiently combines Kernel PCA and GMM, where GMM provides sampling weight information needed by the speedup technique of Kernel PCA, whereas Kernel PCA extracts good features for GMM. The advantage of the combination is that we could avoid the great computational cost, which could be encountered when directly performing eigen-decomposition of the Gram matrix in problems with large scale data sets. That is just the original intention of our proposed algorithm.

Experiments have been done on synthetic data set and real world color image segmentation problem by our algorithm. Results show that the algorithm has a satisfactory performance and does much better than GMM based on basic EM. The attempts in color image segmentation is significative since we present a way to solve real computer vision problem efficiently by kernel methods.

Since the proposed K-EM algorithm needs to preset the number of clusters C, our future work will focus on automatically selecting C with methods such as Reversible Jump Markov Chain Monte Carlo as in [22]. We also intend to integrate multi-scale information to improve the color image segmentation results.

Acknowledgement

The author would like to thank anonymous reviewers for their helpful comments, also thank Xing Yi and Chi Zhang for their helpful work on revising this paper.

References

1. Forsyth, D. and Ponce, J.: Computer Vision: A Modern Approach, Prentice Hall Press (2002)
2. Cheng, H., Jiang, X., et al: Color image segmentation: advances and prospects, Pattern Recognition, Vol. 34, (2001) 2259-2281
3. Roberts, S J.: Parametric and Non-Parametric Unsupervised Cluster Analysis, Pattern Recognition, Vol.30, No.2, (1997) 261-272
4. Canny, J. F.: A Computational Approach to Edge Detection, IEEE Trans. on PAMI, Vol.8, No.6, (1986) 679-698
5. Adams, R. and Bischof, L.: Seeded Region Growing, IEEE Trans. on PAMI, Vol. 16, No. 6, (1994)
6. Belongie, S., Carson, C., Greeenspan, H. and Malik, J.: Color and Texture Based Image Segmentation Using EM and Its Application to Content-Based Image Re-trieval, Proceeding of the International Conferences on Computer Vision (ICCV'98) (1998)
7. Comaniciu, D. and Meer, P.: Mean Shift: A Robust Approach toward Feature Space Analysis, IEEE Trans. on PAMI, Vol.24, No.5, (2002) 603-619
8. Tu, Z. and Zhu, S.C.: Image Segmentation by Data-Driven Markov Chain Monte Carlo, IEEE Trans. on PAMI, Vol.24, No.5, (2002) 657-673
9. Schölkopf, B. and Smola, A. J.: Learning with Kernels: Support Vector Machines, Regularization and Beyond, MIT Press, Cambridge, Massachusetts(2002)
10. Vapnik, V.: The Nature of Statistical Learning Theory, Springer-Verlag, 2nd Edition, New York (1997)
11. Schölkopf, B., Smola, A.J. and Müller, K R.: Nonlinear Component Analysis as a Kernel Eigenvalue Problem, Neural Computation, Vol.10, No.5, (1998) 1299-1319
12. Achlioptas, D., McSherry, F. and Schölkopf, B.: Sampling techniques for kernel methods. Advance in Neural Information Processing Systems (NIPS) 14, (2002)
13. Williams, C. and Seeger, M.: Using the Nyström Method to Speed Up Kernel Machines. Advance in Neural Information Processing Systems (NIPS) 13, (2001)
14. Taylor, J. S., Williams, C., Cristianini, N. and Kandola J.: On the Eigenspectrum of the Gram Matrix and Its Relationship to the Operator Eigenspectrum, N. CesaBianchi et al. (Eds.): ALT 2002, LNAI 2533, Springer-Verlag, Berlin Heidelberg (2002) 23-40
15. Andrieu, C., N. de Freitas, Doucet, A. and Jordan, M. I.: An introduction to MCMC for machine learning. Machine Learning, 50 (2003) 5-43
16. Breiman, L.: Bagging Predictors, Machine Learning, Vol. 20, No.2, (1996) 123-140
17. Bilmes, J. A.: A Gentle Tutorial on the EM Algorithm and its Application to Parameter Estimation for Gaussian Mixture and Hidden Markov Models, Technical Report, ICSI-TR-97-021, UC Berkeley (1997)
18. Wu, Y., Tian, Q. and Huang, T. S.: Discriminant-EM Algorithm with Application to Image Retrieval, Proceeding of the IEEE Conferences on Computer Vision and Pattern Recognition (CVPR' 00), (2000) 222-227

19. Wu, Y., Huang, T. S. and Toyama, K.: Self-Supervised Learning for Object Recognition based on Kernel Discriminant-EM Algorithm. Proceeding of the International Conferences on Computer Vision (ICCV'01), (2001) 275-280
20. Doucet, A., Nando de Freitas and Gordon, N. (ed): Sequential Monte Carlo in Practice, Springer-Verlag (2001)
21. Ng, A. Y., Jordan, M. I. and Weiss, Y., On Spectral Clustering: Analysis and an algorithm, Advance in Neural Information Processing Systems (NIPS) 14, (2002)
22. Kato, Z.: Bayesian Color Image segmentation using reversible jump Markov Chain Monte Carlo, CWI Research Report PNA-R9902, ISSN 1386-3711, (1999)

Evaluation of Topographic Clustering and Its Kernelization

Marie-Jeanne Lesot, Florence d'Alché-Buc, and Georges Siolas

Laboratoire d'Informatique de Paris VI
8, rue du capitaine Scott
F-75 015 Paris, France
Marie-Jeanne.Lesot@lip6.fr

Abstract. We consider the topographic clustering task and focus on the problem of its evaluation, which enables to perform model selection: topographic clustering algorithms, from the original Self Organizing Map to its extension based on kernel (STMK), can be viewed in the unified framework of constrained clustering. Exploiting this point of view, we discuss existing quality measures and we propose a new criterion based on an F-measure, which combines a compacity with an organization criteria and extend it to their kernel-based version.

1 Introduction

Since their definition by Kohonen [1], Self Organizing Maps have been applied in various domains (see [2]), such as speech recognition, image analysis, robotics or organization of large databases. They solve a topographic clustering task, i.e. pursue a double objective: as any clustering method, they aim at determining significant subgroups within the whole dataset; simultaneously they aim at providing information about the data topology through an organized representation of the extracted clusters, such that their relative distance reflects the dissimilarity of the data they contain.

We consider the problem of the results evaluation, which is an important step in a learning process. Defining a quality measure of the obtained model enables to perform model comparison and thus model selection. Many criteria have been proposed but most of them fail to take into account the double objective of clustering and organization.

To address the evaluation question, we show that the various topographic clustering approaches can be viewed as solving a constrained clustering problem, the difference lying in the expression of the constraint which conveys the organization demand. We propose a new criterion which estimates the map's quality by combining, through an F-measure [3], an evaluation of its clustering quality with a measure of its organization quality; we apply it to classic and kernel-based maps to perform hyperparameter selection and data encoding comparison.

2 Constrained Clustering

We divide the various formalizations proposed for topographic clustering and summarized in table 1, p. 269. in four categories and highlight the way they express the constraint.

2.1 Neural Networks

A first category of topographic algorithms is based on a neural network representation. Each neuron is associated with a position z_r and a weight vector w_r which represents a cluster center and has the same dimension as the input data. A topology is defined on this neurons set, through a $K \times K$ neighborhood matrix, where K is the number of nodes. It is defined as a decreasing function of the distance between positions, e.g.

$$h_{rs} = \exp\left(-\frac{\|z_r - z_s\|^2}{2\sigma_h^2}\right) \quad . \tag{1}$$

The *Self Organizing Maps* (SOM) algorithm introduced by Kohonen [1] is defined by the following iterative learning rule:

$$w_r(t+1) = w_r(t) + \alpha_t h_{rg(x_t)}(t)(x_t - w_r(t)) \tag{2}$$

$$\text{with } g(x_t) = \arg\min_s \|x_t - w_s\|^2 \quad ,$$

where x_t is a data point; the neighborhood term h_{rs} and the learning rate α_t decrease during the learning procedure; $g(x_t)$ denotes the winning node, i.e. x_t nearest neuron in terms of weight. At each step, the similarity between a data point and its winning node is increased; as a result, similar data are assigned to the same node, whose weight vector corresponds to an average representant of its associated data. Moreover, through the coefficient $h_{rg(x_t)}$, a data point modifies the weights of its node's neighbors: the organization constraint is expressed as an influence sphere around the winning node, which affects its neighbors. The parameter $\sigma_h(t)$ monitors the width of the influence areas and thus the distance at which the organization constraint is still to be felt.

Heskes [4] showed that the learning rule (2) cannot be derived from an energy function when the data follow a continuous distribution, and therefore lacks theoretical properties (see also [5]). Thus, he proposes to train the network by optimizing an energy function that leads to a slightly different map, which still fulfills the topographic clustering aims. In the case of a finite dataset $X = \{x_i, i = 1..N\}$, it is defined as

$$E = \frac{1}{N}\sum_{i=1}^{N}\sum_{r=1}^{K} h_{rg(x_i)}\|x_i - w_r\|^2 \text{ with } g(x_i) = \arg\min_s \sum_{t=1}^{K} h_{st}\|x_i - w_t\|^2 \quad . \tag{3}$$

Thus, the winning node is not only x_i nearest neighbor as in SOM, but takes into account the resemblance to neighbor nodes. If h is defined as in (1), $\forall r, h_{rr} = 1$, we propose to write $E = E_1 + E_2$ with

$$E_1 = \frac{1}{N}\sum_{i=1}^{N} \|x_i - w_{g(x_i)}\|^2 \quad \text{and} \quad E_2 = \frac{1}{N}\sum_{i=1}^{N}\sum_{r \neq g(x_i)} h_{rg(x_i)}\|x_i - w_r\|^2, \tag{4}$$

and thus to interpret E in a constrained clustering context: E_1 equals the cost function optimized by the k-means algorithm. E_2 imposes the organization: when it is minimum, neighbor cells, corresponding to high $h_{rg(x_i)}$ values, have similar weight vectors. Indeed, $\|w_{g(x_i)} - w_r\|^2 \leq \|w_{g(x_i)} - x_i\|^2 + \|x_i - w_r\|^2$ where the first term is low because of E_1 minimization and the second because of the term $h_{rg(x_i)}\|x_i - w_r\|^2$ in E_2.

The parameter σ_h can be interpreted in a regularization framework: it monitors the relative importance of the main goal, clustering, and the imposed constraint, and thus the number of free parameters. When it is low, most h_{rs} terms are zero and the dominant term in E is E_1; when E_2 becomes prevalent (for high σ_h values), the map falls in a degenerate state where only the furthest nodes on the grid are non empty. Indeed, for such neurons, the weight is exclusively determined by the constraint and not by a tradeoff taking into account its assigned data, which enables to maximize organization.

Graepel, Burger and Obermayer [6] propose a deterministic annealing scheme to optimize this cost function, which leads to global and stable minima; beside the weights w_r, it provides assignment probabilities $p(x_i \in C_r) \in [0,1]$, where $C_r = \{x_i/g(x_i) = r\}$. The associated algorithm is called *Soft Topographic Vector Quantization* (STVQ).

2.2 Markov Chains

Luttrell [7] considers topographic clustering as a noisy coding-transmission-decoding process, which he models by a specific Markov chain, called Folded Markov Chain (FMC): it consists in a chain of probabilistic transformations followed by the chain of the inverse (in a Bayes' sense) transformations.

He shows that SOM are a specific case of a two-level FMC. The first level corresponds to the coding step, which is equivalent to a clustering phase: it assigns data according to rule defined in equation (3) and codes them by the corresponding vector. The second level represents the transition probability to other clusters, it is fixed *a priori* and enables to express the constraint in the same way as a normalized neighborhood matrix (see [6]). The optimized cost function is defined as the reconstruction cost; it is equivalent to the function (3) if the neighborhood matrix is normalized.

2.3 Probability Distribution Modelling

Other formalizations aim at explicitely modelling the data probability distribution.

Utsugi [8] considers a bayesian framework to learn a gaussian mixture, constrained through a smoothing prior on the set $\mathcal{W} = \{w_r, 1 \le r \le K\}$. The prior is based on a discretized differential operator D:

$$p(\mathcal{W}/\alpha) = \prod_{j=1}^{d} C \exp\left(-\frac{\alpha}{2}\|Dw_{(j)}\|^2\right) \quad \text{with} \quad C = \left(\frac{\alpha}{2\pi}\right)^{l/2} (\det{}^+ D^T D)^{\frac{1}{2}} \,, \tag{5}$$

where $w_{(j)}$ is the vector of the jth components of the centers, $l = \text{rank}(D^T D)$, and $\det{}^+ D^T D$ denotes the product of the positive eigenvalues of $D^T D$. Thus, a weights set is *a priori* all the more probable as its components have a low amplitude evolution, as expressed by the differential operator D. The centers w_r are learnt by maximizing the penalized data likelihood, computed as a gaussian mixture with this prior on centers; α monitors the importance of the constraint.

Bishop, Svensén and Williams [5] also consider a gaussian mixture, based on a latent variable representation: a data $x \in \mathcal{R}^d$ is generated by a latent variable $z \in \mathcal{L}$ of lower dimension $l < d$, through a function ψ of parameters $\mathcal{A}$: $x = \psi(z; \mathcal{A})$. Denoting by β the variance of a gaussian noise process, and defining $p(z)$ as the sum of functions centered at nodes of a grid in $\mathcal{L}$, $p(z) = 1/K \sum_{r=1}^{K} \delta(z - z_r)$, $p(x)$ is defined as

$$p(x/\mathcal{A}, \beta) = \frac{1}{K} \sum_{r=1}^{K} \left(\frac{\beta}{2\pi}\right)^{\frac{d}{2}} \exp\left(-\frac{\beta}{2} \|\psi(z_r; \mathcal{A}) - x\|^2\right), \qquad (6)$$

which corresponds to a constrained gaussian mixture: the centers $\psi(z_r; \mathcal{A})$ cannot evolve independently, as they are linked through the function ψ, whose parameters $\mathcal{A}$ are to be learnt. The continuity of $\psi(\cdot; \mathcal{A})$ imposes the organization constraint: two neighbor points z_A and z_B are associated with two neighbor images $\psi(z_A; \mathcal{A})$ and $\psi(z_B; \mathcal{A})$.

Heskes [9] shows that the energy function (3) can be interpreted as a regularized gaussian mixture: in a probabilistic context, it can be written as the data likelihood plus a penalization term, defined as a deviation of the learnt center w_r from the value imposed by organization $\tilde{w}_r = \sum_s h_{rs} w_s$. The solution must find a tradeoff between adapting to the data and abiding by a low deviation, thus it solves a constrained clustering task.

2.4 Kernel Topographic Clustering

Graepel and Obermayer [10] propose an extension of topographic clustering, called Soft Topographic Mapping with Kernels (STMK), using the kernel trick: it is based on a non-linear transformation $\phi : \mathcal{R}^d \to \mathcal{F}$ to a high, or infinite, dimensional space, called the feature space; it must enable to highlight relevant correlations which may remain unnoticed in the input space. STMK transposes the cost function (3) in $\mathcal{F}$, by appplying STVQ to $\phi(x_i)$; the centers, denoted w_r^ϕ, then belong to $\mathcal{F}$. The cost function becomes

$$E^\phi = \frac{1}{N} \sum_{i=1}^{N} \sum_{r=1}^{K} h_{rg(x_i)} \|\phi(x_i) - w_r^\phi\|^2 \text{ with } g(x_i) = \arg\min_s \sum_{t=1}^{K} h_{st} \|\phi(x_i) - w_t^\phi\|^2.$$

Provided w_r^ϕ is searched as a linear combination of $\phi(x_i)$, as $w_r^\phi = \sum_i a_{ir} \phi(x_i)$, the computations are expressed solely in terms of dot products $< \phi(x_i), \phi(x_j) >$ [10]. Thus, defining a kernel function k such that $< \phi(x_i), \phi(x_j) >= k(x_i, x_j)$, it is possible to optimize E^ϕ without doing costly calculations in the high dimensional space $\mathcal{F}$. This algorithm being a direct transposition of STVQ to $\phi(x_i)$, it has the same interpretation in terms of constrained clustering, in the feature space.

3 Topographic Clustering Evaluation

Table 1 summarizes the previous algorithms. Whichever choice is made, the result map must be evaluated, to determine its validity and possibly to perform *a posteriori* model selection: in topographic clustering, it implies choosing the appropriate neighborhood parameter and the adequate size of the grid[1], plus the kernel parameter in the kernelized approach. According to the previous constrained clustering framework, maps must be

---
[1] assuming the dimension of the visualization space is 2.

Table 1. Summary of some caracteristics of topographic clustering algorithms (see section 2).

Designation	Principle	Learning algorithm	Probabilistic modelling	Constraint expression	Associated references
SOM	neural net	iterative rule	no	influence areas	[2]
STVQ	neural net	deterministic	possible	influence	[6,4,9]
STMK		annealing		area	[10]
FMC	probabilistic transformation	EM	yes	probabilistic influence	[7]
Utsugi	gaussian + prior	EM	yes	smooth weight differential	[8]
Bishop et al.	latent variable	EM	yes	continous gene--ration process	[5]

assessed along two lines: their clustering capacity and their respect of the constraint, i.e. their organization. Yet most existing measures only take into account one aspect; using the notations of section 2.1, we discuss some of the existing criteria.

3.1 Clustering Quality

Kohonen [2] proposes to use the classic criterion called quantization error, which is the cost function of the k-means algorithm and is defined as the cost of representing a data x by the center of the cluster it is assigned to:

$$qC_1 = \frac{1}{N} \sum_{i=1}^{N} \|x_i - w_{g(x_i)}\|^2 = \frac{1}{N} \sum_{r=1}^{K} \sum_{i/x_i \in C_r} \|x_i - w_r\|^2 \quad . \tag{7}$$

For topographic clustering, contrary to clustering, the center of a cluster and its mean are distinct, as centers are influenced by their neighbors due to the organization constraint. Thus, computing the distance to centers introduces a bias in the homogeneity measure, and under-estimates the clustering quality. We propose to measure the cost obtained when representing a data by the mean of the cluster $\bar{x}_r$:

$$qM_1 = \frac{1}{N} \sum_{i=1}^{N} \|x_i - \bar{x}_{g(x_i)}\|^2 = \frac{1}{N} \sum_{r=1}^{K} \sum_{i/x_i \in C_r} \|x_i - \bar{x}_r\|^2 \quad . \tag{8}$$

Only the identified subgroups intervene in the measure, which makes it a justified clustering quality criterion.

Compacity can also be measured by the average variance of clusters [11]:

$$qM_2 = \frac{1}{K^*} \sum_{r=1}^{K} \frac{1}{|C_r|} \sum_{i/x_i \in C_r} \|x_i - \bar{x}_r\|^2 \quad K^* = \text{number of non empty clusters.} \tag{9}$$

One can notice that qM_1 is also a weighted average variance, whose weighting coefficients are $|C_r|K^*/N$ i.e. the quotient between the cluster cardinal and an average cluster cardinal, under an equi-distribution assumption.

Some learning algorithms, like STVQ, provide assignment probabilities $p(x_i \in C_r)$ which are normalized so that $\forall i, \sum_r p(x_i \in C_r) = 1$ and equal the conditional probabilities $p(C_r/x_i)$. They lead to a probabilistic quantization error, qM_1^p computed by averaging the individual probabilistic errors, and a probabilistic variance mean qM_2^p:

$$qM_1^p = \frac{1}{N}\sum_{i=1}^{N}\gamma(x_i) \quad \text{with} \quad \gamma(x_i) = \sum_{r=1}^{K} p(C_r/x_i)\|x_i - \bar{x}_r\|^2 \quad , \tag{10}$$

$$qM_2^p = \frac{1}{K^*}\sum_{r=1}^{K}\sigma^2(C_r) \quad \text{with} \quad \sigma^2(C_r) = \sum_{i=1}^{N} p(x_i/C_r)\|x_i - \bar{x}_r\|^2 \quad , \tag{11}$$

$$\text{where} \quad \bar{x}_r = \frac{1}{\sum_j p(x_j \in C_r)}\sum_{i=1}^{N} p(x_i \in C_r)x_i \quad . \tag{12}$$

Likewise, one can define a probabilistic equivalent to qC_1. As previously, the differences between qM_1^p and qM_2^p come from normalization coefficients: considering equiprobable data, $p(x_i/C_r) = p(C_r/x_i)/\sum_{j=1}^{N} p(C_r/x_j)$.

3.2 Organization Quality

The organization criteria can be divided in three groups. The first measure was proposed by Cottrell and Fort [12] for one dimensional maps, as the number of inversions, i.e. the number of direction changes, which evaluates the line organization. It was generalized to higher dimensions by Zrehen and Blayo [13].

A second category is based on the data themselves and uses the winning nodes: if the map is well organized, then for each data the two best matching units must be adjacent on the grid. This principle has inspired measures such as the topographic error [14], Kaski and Lagus criterion [15], or the Hebbian measure [16].

Some organization measures are computed using only the neurons, without the data, which leads to an important computational saving and is more independent from the learning dataset. They evaluate the correlation between the distance in terms of weights and the distance imposed by the grid, that is $dW_{rs} = \|w_r - w_s\|^2$ and $dG_{rs} = \|z_r - z_s\|^2$. Indeed, the aim of organization is that the nearer the nodes the higher their similarity in terms of weight vectors. Bauer and Pawelzik [17] evaluate the conservation of ordering between nodes sorted by dW or dG. Flexer [18] evaluates the organization by a measure of correlation on the distance matrices. It only considers the map itself, without taking into account the data whose role is reduced to the training phase. Denoting for any $K \times K$ matrix A, $\Sigma A = \sum_{i,j} A_{ij}$, and $N_A = (\Sigma A^2 - (\Sigma A/K)^2)$, he uses the Pearson correlation:

$$\rho = \frac{\sum dG dW - \frac{\sum dG \sum dW}{K^2}}{\sqrt{N_G N_W}} \in [-1, 1] \quad . \tag{13}$$

3.3 Combination

The previous measures do not consider the double objective of topographic clustering, but only one of its aspects; only two measures evaluate the compromise quality.

In the case of probabilistic formalizations, the result can be evaluated by the penalized likelihood of validation data. This measure evaluates the two objectives as it integrates the probability distribution on the weights, which expresses the constraint.

Independently of the learning algorithm, one can use as criterion a weighted quantization error $q_w = E$, where E is the function (3) whose decomposition (4) shows it considers both clustering and organization. Yet, it does not enable to select an optimal σ_h value if the h matrix is not normalized: when σ_h is small, most $h_{rg(x_i)}$ terms are low; it appears that when σ_h increases, the augmentation of the number of summing terms entails a more important increase than the decrease of cost due to a better organization. Thus, q_w augments, without its reflecting a real deterioration of the map's quality.

4 Proposed Criterion

To evaluate globally a topographic map, we propose a criterion combining a clustering quality measure with an organization measure, which we extend to kernel-based maps.

4.1 Classic Topographic Clustering

To measure the clustering quality, we choose a normalized expression $\tilde{q}_p = q/\eta$ of the criteria presented in section 3.1, $q = qC_1^p$, qM_1^p, or qM_2^p. The normalization aims at making the measure independent of the data norm scale. We propose to define:

$$\eta = \frac{1}{N}\sum_{i=1}^{N} \|x_i - \bar{x}\|^2 \quad \text{with } \bar{x} = \frac{1}{N}\sum_{i=1}^{N} x_i \quad . \tag{14}$$

If $q = qM_1^p$ or qC_1^p, η is interpreted as an *a priori* quantization error, obtained when all data are coded by the mean of the dataset. If $q = qM_2^p$, η is seen as the variance of the dataset before any subdivision. The criterion $\tilde{q}_p = q/\eta$ constitutes a clustering quality measure which varies in the interval $[0, 1]$ and must be minimized.

As organization measure, we choose a criterion derived from the Pearson correlation

$$c = \frac{1+\rho}{2} \in [0,1] \quad . \tag{15}$$

$\tilde{q}_p$ only depends on the data, c on the weight vectors, which makes them independent. We combine them through the F-measure defined by Van Rijsbergen [3] and classically used in the Information Retrieval field to combine recall and precision. We apply it to c and $1 - \tilde{q}_p$ which are both to be maximized and define the global criterion $\mathcal{Q}_b$

$$\mathcal{Q}_b = \frac{(1+b^2)(1-\tilde{q}_p)c}{b^2(1-\tilde{q}_p)+c} \quad , \tag{16}$$

which must be maximized too. b is a weighting parameter controlling the relative importance of the two aims in the evaluation: if $b = 2$ for instance, $\mathcal{Q}_b$ rewards a high organization four times more than a good clustering. Thus this classic measure offers a mean to agregate in a single quantity the two criteria, and provides a numerical value, which always belong to the interval $[0,1]$, to compare different maps; its advantage comes from the flexibility provided by the b agregation weight which allows the user to define numerically a tradeoff level between the two objectives.

4.2 Kernel-Based Topographic Clustering

The evaluation of the kernel-based topographic map requires us to compute the previous measure without computations in the feature space. $\tilde{q}_p^\phi$ imposes to evaluate $\|\phi(x_i)-\bar{x}_r^\phi\|$ and η^ϕ; both can be expressed solely with the kernel matrix $k_{ij} = k(x_i, x_j)$: denoting $p_{ir} = p(C_r/x_i)$ et $\alpha_{ir} = p_{ir}/\sum_j p_{jr}$, we have

$$\|\phi(x_i) - \bar{x}_r^\phi\|^2 = k_{ii} - 2\sum_{j=1}^N \alpha_{jr} k_{ij} + \sum_{j,l=1}^N \alpha_{jr}\alpha_{lr} k_{jl}$$

$$\eta^\phi = \tfrac{1}{N}\sum_{i=1}^N \|\phi(x_i) - \bar{x}^\phi\|^2 = \tfrac{1}{N}\left(\sum_{i=1}^N k_{ii} - \tfrac{1}{N}\sum_{i,j=1}^N k_{ij}\right) \quad .$$

Thanks to the normalisation η^ϕ, a small $\tilde{q}_p^\phi$ value is not due to the kernel itself, but indicates that the corresponding feature space defines a data encoding which highlights the presence of homogenous subgroups in the dataset.

The adaptation of c^ϕ requires to compute $dW_{rs} = \|w_r^\phi - w_s^\phi\|^2$. Using the decomposition $w_r = \sum_i a_{ir}\phi(x_i)$, we have $dW_{rs}^\phi = \sum_{i,l=1}^N k_{il}(a_{ir}a_{lr} - 2a_{ir}a_{ls} + a_{is}a_{ls})$.

The global quality of the map is then computed without too important additional costs as the F-measure between $1-\tilde{q}_p^\phi$ and c^ϕ:

$$\mathcal{Q}_b^\phi = \frac{(1+b^2)(1-\tilde{q}^\phi)c^\phi}{b^2(1-\tilde{q}^\phi)+c^\phi} \quad . \tag{17}$$

5 Numerical Experiments

The numerical experiments highlight the relevance of the proposed criterion for map evaluation, and model selection including the algorithm hyperparameters (grid size K and neighborhood parameter σ_h), the kernel hyperparameters (type and parameter) and the data encoding. They are based on the STMK algorithm applied to a 2D square map. Indeed, STMK contains the classic maps as a special case, using the linear kernel $k(x,y) = (x \cdot y)/d$ which is equivalent to the scalar product in the input space.

5.1 Criterion Validation and Hyperparameter Selection

We study the behavior of the proposed criterion on an artificial 2D database, varying the hyperparameters. The base is generated by two distributions: a gaussian centered along a parabolic curve, and an isotropic gaussian (see fig. 1). As the data belong to $\mathcal{R}^2$, the resulting clusters can be visually displayed, by representing data belonging to a same node with a same symbol; the organization is represented by joining the means

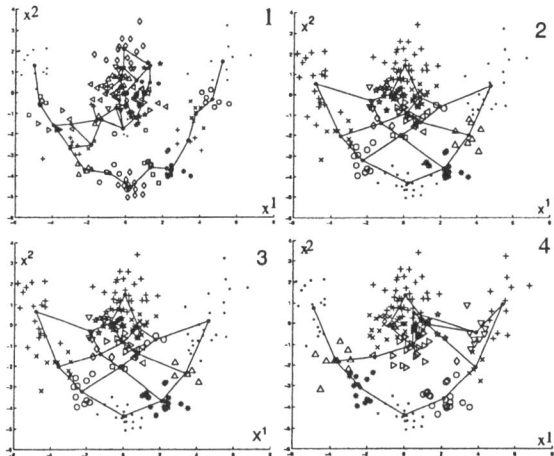

Fig. 1. Maps obtained with the optimal hyperparameter values. 1. Best linear map for $\mathcal{Q}_{0.5}$, $(K, \sigma_h) = (49, 0.30)$. 2. Best linear map for $\mathcal{Q}_2$, $(K, \sigma_h) = (16, 0.28)$. 3. Best 4x4 gaussian map for $\mathcal{Q}_2^\phi$, $(\sigma_h, \sigma_k) = (0.28, 1)$. 4. Best 4x4 polynomial map for $\mathcal{Q}_2^\phi$, $(\sigma_h, m_k) = (0.28, 2)$.

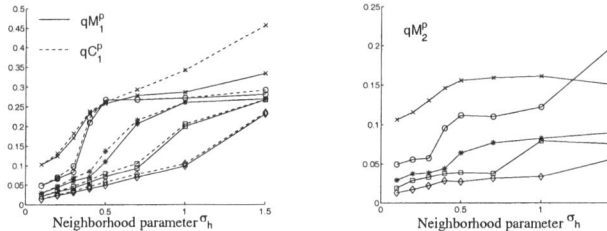

Fig. 2. Variation of the clustering criteria qC_1^p, et qM_1^p on the left, qM_2^p on the right, as functions of the neighborhood parameter σ_h for various grid sizes $K = \kappa^2$. Caption: x $\Leftrightarrow \kappa = 3$, o $\Leftrightarrow \kappa = 4$, * $\Leftrightarrow \kappa = 5$, □ $\Leftrightarrow \kappa = 6$, ◇ $\Leftrightarrow \kappa = 7$.

(computed in $\mathcal{R}^2$) of non empty clusters corresponding to adjacent nodes (in the kernel-based case, the centers w_r^ϕ belong to the feature space $\mathcal{F}$, and cannot be represented).

Figure 2 represents, for the linear kernel, the evolution of the clustering criteria qC_1^p, and qM_1^p (left), and qM_2^p (right), as functions of σ_h for various K values. All are monotonous functions of K and σ_h: the clustering quality is higher if the number of clusters is high and the organization constraint is low; thus they are not sufficient to select optimal parameter values. One can notice that the difference between qC_1^p and qM_1^p remains low; yet, as qM_1^p evaluates the clustering quality using only the identified data subgroups, it appears as more satisfying on an interpretation level. Lastly the range of qM_2^p (right graph) is smaller than that of qC_1^p and qM_1^p: it is less discriminant and thus less useful to compare maps. In the following, we shall keep the qM_1^p measure.

Figure 3 represents the evolution of $\mathcal{Q}_{0.5}$ (left) and $\mathcal{Q}_2$ (middle), for a linear kernel. They are not monotonous and indicate optimal values, which depend on b. We chose to test $b = 0.5$ and $b = 2$ to favor respectively each objective: for $b = 0.5$, clustering is considered as the main task, thus the optimal K value is the highest tested value,

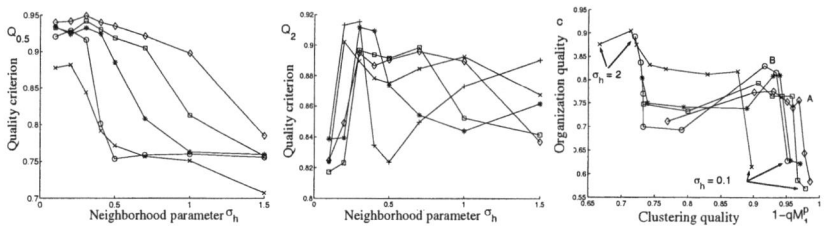

Fig. 3. Variations of $\mathcal{Q}_{0.5}$ on the left, $\mathcal{Q}_2$ in the middle, as functions of σ_h; on the right, "trajectory" of the map in the $(1-\tilde{q}, c)$ plane when σ_h varies; for different grid sizes $K = \kappa^2$. Caption: $\times \Leftrightarrow \kappa = 3, \circ \Leftrightarrow \kappa = 4, * \Leftrightarrow \kappa = 5, \square \Leftrightarrow \kappa = 6, \Diamond \Leftrightarrow \kappa = 7$.

$K = 49$; if $b = 2$, the organization demand is stronger, large grids which are difficult to organize obtain a lower score, and the optimum is $K = 16$.

The right graph of fig. 3 shows the "trajectory" of the map in the $(1-\tilde{q}, c)$ plane, when σ_h varies, for different grid sizes, and highlights σ_h influence: small σ_h lead to a high quality clustering, but a poor organization. The parameter b, which expresses the relative importance of the two objectives in the evaluation phase enables the user to define the tradeoff level he desires: the points denoted A and B correspond to the optima associated with $\mathcal{Q}_{0.5}$ and $\mathcal{Q}_2$ and represent two different compromises. From our experiments, it seems that $b = 2$ is a good compromise in a visualisation framework.

Graphs 1 and 2 of fig. 1 show the maps obtained with the optimal (K, σ_h) values for $\mathcal{Q}_{0.5}$ and $\mathcal{Q}_2$ respectively. For $b = 0.5$, the clusters have low variances, but their organization is not satisfying: the chain of clusters associated with the parabolic data is too sensitive to data. For $b = 2$, it is more regular, and the map distinguishes between the two generative sources; it reflects the intern structure of data, in particular their symmetry. In the following, we conserve the value $b = 2$, which better reflects the visualisation goal, and consider 4x4 maps.

We tested STMK with the polynomial kernel k_p and the gaussian kernel k_g

$$k_p(x, y) = \left(\frac{x \cdot y}{d} + 1\right)^{m_k} \qquad k_g(x, y) = \exp\left(-\frac{\|x-y\|^2}{2\sigma_k^2 d}\right) \quad . \tag{18}$$

Figure 4 represents $\mathcal{Q}_2^\phi$ as a function of σ_h for various values of σ_k (resp. m_k), for k_p and k_g. It shows that a large σ_h range leads to similar results. It also indicates that the gaussian kernel outperforms the linear one: $\mathcal{Q}_2^\phi$ optimal value is 0.941 in the gaussian case, and 0.917 in the linear case. The associated graphs (2 et 3, fig. 1) are very similar, the evaluation difference has a double reason: the slight assignment differences are in favor of the gaussian kernel; moreover, even identical clusters appear as more compact in the feature space than in the input space and lead to a better score. This is justified as the higher compacity leads to a faster convergence (5.3 times faster with these parameter values). According to $\mathcal{Q}_2^\phi$, the polynomial kernel gives poor results which is confirmed by the graphical representation (graph 4, fig. 1): the optimal polynomial map enables to distinguish the two sources but lacks organization.

This artificial base highlights the fact that the quality criterion based on the F-measure enables to select the hyperparameters values that indeed correspond to opti-

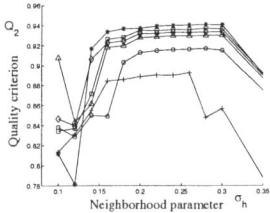 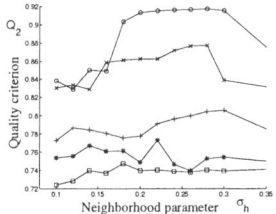

Fig. 4. Variations of Q_2^ϕ, for gaussian (left) and polynomial (right) kernels, as function of σ_h. ○ corresponds to the linear map ; right, x to $\sigma_k = 0.1$, + to $\sigma_k = 0.5$, ∗ to $\sigma_k = 1$, □ to $\sigma_k = 1.5$, ◇ to $\sigma_k = 1.7$, △ to $\sigma_k = 2$; left x to $m_k = 2$, + to $m_k = 3$, ∗ to $m_k = 4$, □ to $m_k = 5$.

Table 2. Best gaussian parameter combinations for various databases. The correspondance with the newsgroups is: 1 = alt.atheism, 2 = comp.graphics, 3 = rec.autos, 4 = rec.sport.hockey, 5 = sci.crypt, 6 = sci.electronics, 7 = soc.religion.christian, 8 = talk.politics.guns.

Dataset content	tfidf encoding (500 attributes)					mppca encoding (20 attributes)				
	σ_h	σ_k	$1-\tilde{q}^\phi$	c^ϕ	Q_2^ϕ	σ_h	σ_k	$1-\tilde{q}^\phi$	c^ϕ	Q_2^ϕ
$\mathcal{D}_1$: 2, 3, 5, 8	0.14	2	0.43	0.73	0.645	0.18	0.5	0.66	0.79	0.761
$\mathcal{D}_2$: 1, 2, 6, 8	0.14	1.5	0.36	0.72	0.601	0.22	1	0.69	0.78	0.762
$\mathcal{D}_3$: 3, 4, 6, 7	0.14	1.7	0.32	0.74	0.582	0.24	1.5	0.69	0.79	0.769

mal maps, by both rewarding good maps and penalizing bad ones. It also enables to highlight the relevance of kernels in solving a topographic clustering problem.

5.2 Data Encoding Comparison

We applied the proposed criterion to compare two document encodings: the *tfidf* method and a semantic based representation, called *mppca*, proposed by Siolas and d'Alché-Buc [19]. The latter exploits, through Fisher score extraction, a generative document model combined with a generative word model which captures semantic relationships between words thanks to a mixture of probabilistic PCAs. The dataset is built from the 20 newsgroup database[2] by selecting 100 texts of four different newsgroups. These 400 documents are encoded either by a 20 PCA mixture learnt on a 4x200-text set, or by the *tfidf* also learnt on this set, with a 500-word vocabulary. Table 2 presents the caracteristics of the best 7x7 gaussian maps. It shows the relevance of the semantic based model for the topographic clustering task: it leads to far better results, both globally and individually on clustering and organization. These tests on an unsupervised learning task confirm the results obtained in a supervised framework [19].

6 Conclusion

We have presented topographic clustering algorithms, from the original formulation by Kohonen of Self Organizing Maps to the Soft Topographic Mapping with Kernel extension which enables to use the kernel functions, in the same context of constrained

---
[2] http://www.ai.mit.edu/people/jrennie/20Newsgroups/

clustering, and considered the map evaluation problematic. We defined a new criterion which flexibly combines by an F-measure a clustering quality criterion with an organization criterion. The numerical experiments show it constitutes an efficient map comparison tool and enables to perform hyperparameter selection. Its main advantage lies in its flexibity which makes it possible for the user to explicitely define the tradeoff level between the two contradictory objectives of self organizing maps; thus it adapts itsef to the user's demands.

The next step of our work consists in applying bootstrap or other robust statistical method of estimnation to the proposed evaluation measure. The perspectives also include the application of the criterion to micro-array data where visualization is at the heart of the problematic and where such a criterion would enable to objectively select the best maps.

References

1. Kohonen, T.: Analysis of a simple self-organizing process. Biol. Cybern. **44** (1982) 135–140
2. Kohonen, T.: Self Organizing Maps. Springer (2001)
3. Van Rijsbergen, C.J.: Information Retrieval. Butterworth, London (1979)
4. Heskes, T.: Energy functions for self organizing maps. In Oya, S., Kaski, E., eds.: Kohonen Maps. Elsevier, Amsterdam (1999) 303–316
5. Bishop, C., Svensén, M., Williams, C.: GTM: The generative topographic mapping. Neural Computation **10** (1998) 215–234
6. Graepel, T., Burger, M., Obermayer, K.: Phase transitions in stochastic self-organizing maps. Physical Review E **56** (1997) 3876–3890
7. Luttrell, S.: A Bayesian analysis of self-organizing maps. Neural Computation **6** (1994) 767–794
8. Utsugi, A.: Hyperparameter selection for self organizing maps. Neural Computation **9** (1997) 623–635
9. Heskes, T.: Self-organizing maps, vector quantization, and mixture modeling. IEEE TNN **12** (2001) 1299–1305
10. Graepel, T., Obermayer, K.: Fuzzy topographic kernel clustering. In: Proc. of the 5th GI Workshop Fuzzy Neuro Systems, W. Brauer (1998) 90–97
11. Rezaee, M., Lelieveldt, B., Reiber, J.: A new cluster validity index for the fuzzy c-means. Pattern Recognition Letters **19** (1998) 237–246
12. Cottrell, M., Fort, J.: Etude d'un processus d'auto-organisation. Annales de l'Institut Poincaré **23** (1987) 1–20
13. Zrehen, S., Blayo, F.: A geometric organization measure for Kohonen's map. In: Proc. of Neuro-Nîmes. (1992) 603–610
14. Kiviluoto, K.: Topology preservation in Self Organizing Maps. In: Proc. of Int. Conf. on Neural Networks. Volume 1., IEEE Neural Networks Council (1996) 294–299
15. Kaski, S., Lagus, K.: Comparing self-organizing maps. In: Proc. of ICANN. (1996) 809–814
16. Polani, D., Gutenberg, J.: Organization measures for self-organizing maps. In: Proc. of the Workshop on Self-Organizing Maps, HUT (1997) 280–285
17. Bauer, H., Pawelzik, K.: Quantifying the neighborhood preservation of self-organizing feature maps. IEEE TNN **3** (1992) 570–579
18. Flexer, A.: On the use of self organizing maps for clustering and visualization. Intelligent Data Analysis **5** (2001) 373–384
19. Siolas, G., d'Alché Buc, F.: Mixtures of probabilistic PCAs and Fisher kernels for word and document modeling. In: Proc. of ICANN. (2002) 769–776

A New Pairwise Ensemble Approach for Text Classification

Yan Liu, Jaime Carbonell, and Rong Jin

School of Computer Science
Carnegie Mellon University
5000 Forbes Ave, Pittsburgh, USA
{yanliu,jgc,rong+}@cs.cmu.edu

Abstract. Text classification, whether by topic or genre, is an important task that contributes to text extraction, retrieval, summarization and question answering. In this paper we present a new pairwise ensemble approach, which uses pairwise Support Vector Machine (SVM) classifiers as base classifiers and "input-dependent latent variable" method for model combination. This new approach better captures the characteristics of genre classification, including its heterogeneous nature. Our experiments on two multi-genre collections and one topic-based classification datasets show that the pairwise ensemble method outperforms both boosting, which has been demonstrated as a powerful ensemble approach, and Error-Correcting Output Codes (ECOC), which applies pairwise-like classifiers for multiclass classification problems.

1 Introduction

Text classification, the problem of assigning documents to predefined categories, is an active research area in both information retrieval and machine learning. It plays an important role in information extraction and summarization, text retrieval, and question-answering. In general, text classification includes topic-based text classification and text genre-based classification. Topic-based text categorization, which is classifying documents according to their topics, has been intensively studied before [24, 26]. However, texts can also be written in many genres, for instance: scientific articles, news reports, movie reviews, and advertisements. Genre is defined on the way a text was created, the way it was edited and published, the register of language it uses, and the kind of audience to whom it is addressed [16].

Previous work on genre classification recognized that this task differs from topic-based categorization [16, 7]. A single genre, such as "written newswire" may encompass a range of topics, e.g., *sports, politics, crime, technology, economy and international events*. On the other hand, many articles on the same topics can be written in different genres. Therefore, the genre-topic mapping is many to many. Genre collections, such as ours discussed later, contain different genre covering with the same topic, *newswire, radio news and TV news*, in order to evaluate automated genre classification independent of topic classification. One way in which these two classification problems differ is that in general genre classification seldom exhibits individual features that highly predict a category, unlike topic classification, where words such as "umpire" and "RBI" directly predict the "baseball" category and indirectly the "sports" category.

Given the task of genre classification, the next questions are: How can we build accurate methods according to the characteristics of the genre data? Can we partially reuse the extensive body of work on topic classification? This paper explores aspects of these questions.

There have been many attempts to extract meaningful linguistic features to improve the prediction accuracy, such as POS tagging, parsing, number of punctuation, and layout features. However, many of those features (such as POS tagging or parsing) require high computational costs with little performance improvement; furthermore, for some text sources such as video, capitalization, punctuation and other such information are lost in the automatically speech-recognized transcript from the audio stream. Therefore it is useful to address genre classification using "bag of words" features only, which is the same for topic-based classification. Thus, instead of extracting other potential features, we focus on identifying the characteristics of the data in genre classification and propose suitable learning models accordingly.

Typically, most data for genre classification are collected from the web, through newsgroups, bulletin boards, and broadcast or printed news. They are multi-source, and consequently have different formats, different preferred vocabularies and often significantly different writing styles even for documents within one genre. Namely, the data are *heterogenous*. To illustrate this point, we provide an excerpt of two documents from the same genre, "bulletin-board", in our collected corpus:

- Example-1: *GSA announces weekly Happy Hours! Where: Skibo Coffeehouse When: Friday's 5-7pm What: Beer, Soda and Pizza Why: A chance to meet graduate students from all across campus. See you this Friday!*
- Example-2: *Hi guys, I don't know whether there is an informal party or not although different people kept saying there might be one... So if there is nothing, we can go to Cozumel tonight cuz there will be a live Latin band tonight starting at 9:30pm. But if there is anything else, then let me know.*

Heterogeneity is an important property shared by many other problems, such as scene classification and handwritten digit recognition. However, typical studies in topic-based classification assume homogenous data and tight distributions[1]. Extending classification for high-variance heterogeneous data is an interesting topic that has not been investigated, and is the primary focus of this paper.

Since the data are acquired from different sources and thus rather heterogeneous, a single classification model might not be able to explain all the training data accurately. One apparent solution to this problem is to divide the heterogeneous data into a set of relatively homogeneous partitions, train a classification model over each partition and combine the predictions of individual models. In

---

[1] The primary exception is Topic-Detection and Tracking (TDT) where multiple news sources are tracked in an on-line categorization task [1, 25].

this way, each sub-model captures only one aspect of the decision boundary. The idea of creating multiple models on the training data and combining the predictions of each model is essentially the ensemble approach, and there have been many studies on this subject. Several ensemble approaches have been successfully applied to text classification tasks, including boosting [8], Error-Correcting Output codes (ECOC) [6], hierarchical mixture model [22] and automated survey coding [12]. Alternative approaches such as stacking [23] and earlier meta-classifier approaches [2] do not partition the data, but rather combine classifiers each of which attempts to classify all data over the entire category space.

In this paper, we examine different ensemble methods for text classification. In particular, we propose an "input dependent latent variable" approach for model combination, which automatically directs each test example to the most appropriate classification model within the ensemble. We use this method as the framework to solve genre classification problems. Although our discussion is focused on multi-class classification framework, it is not difficult to extend to multi-label classification problems. The rest of the paper is organized as follows: in Section 2 we give an in-depth discussion of the popular ensemble approaches for topic-based text classification. Then we present our pairwise ensemble approach in Section 3. We compare our method with other ensemble methods on four datasets, including one artificial dataset, two genre datasets and one topic-based classification data. Finally, we give conclusion and hint at future work.

2 Popular Ensemble Approaches for Text Classification

Generally speaking, an ensemble approach involves two stages, namely model generation and model combination. In this section, we examine the model generation and model combination strategies in the popular ensemble approaches for the topic-based classification. Since genre classification also uses "bag of words" features, hopefully we can reuse some of the successful learning methods from topic classification to help genre classification.

Bagging involves a "bootstrap" procedure for model generation: each model is generated over a subset of the training examples using random sample with replacement (the sample size is equal to the size of the original training set). From a statistical point of view, this procedure asymptotically approximates the models sampled from the Bayesian posterior distribution. The model combination strategy for bagging is majority vote. Simple as it is, this strategy can reduce variance when combined with model generation strategies. Previous studies on bagging have shown that it is effective in reducing classification errors [4].

Boosting As a general approach to improving the effectiveness of learning, boosting [8] has been the subject of both theoretical analysis and practical applications. Unlike bagging, in which each model is generated independently, boosting forces the base classifier to focus on the misclassified examples in previous iterations. In this way, each new model can compensate for the weakness of previous models and thus correct the inductive bias gradually [17]. Applying boosting to text categorization tasks, Schapire and Singer evaluated AdaBoost on the benchmark corpus of Reuters news stories and obtained results comparable to Support Vector Machines and k-Nearest Neighbor methods [21], which are among the top classifiers for text classification evaluation [24, 14]. Empirical studies on boosting and bagging show that while both approaches can substantially improve accuracy, boosting exhibits greater benefits [19, 9]. Therefore, we provide only the results of boosting in our comparative experiments.

ECOC is an ensemble approach for solving multiclass categorization problems originally introduced by Dieterich and Bakiri[6]. It reduces a k-class classification problem into L ($L \leq k$) binary classification problems and combines the predictions of those L classifiers using the nearest codeword (for example, by Hamming distance). The *code matrix* R (an $k \times L$ matrix) defines how each sub-model is generated. There have been many code matrixes proposed, such as Dense matrix and BCH codes [20]. Recent work has demonstrated that ECOC offers improvement over the standard *one-against-all* method in text classification and provided theoretical evidence for the use of random codes [3, 11].

3 Pairwise Ensemble Approaches

From the discussion in section 2, we can see that most of those methods have complex model generation procedures and demonstrate considerable empirical improvement. However, they may not be the best choices for classification problems with heterogeneous data for two reasons: 1) In order to capture the heterogeneous characteristics of the data, it would be desirable to divide the training data into several relatively homogenous subsets. However, most algorithms do not intentionally do so. 2) The combination strategies are rather simple. To better solve the heterogenous classification problems, we propose the pairwise ensemble approach. The key idea of our algorithm is:
– build pairwise classifiers to intentionally divide the training data into relatively less heterogeneous sets so that each base classifier focuses on only one aspect of the decision boundary;
– combine the results using the "input-dependent latent variable" approach, which can consider the particular properties of each testing example and dynamically determine the appropriateness of each base classifiers.

3.1 Model Generation by Pairwise Classification

Since our data are quite heterogenous, it presents difficulties to the classical *one-against-all* method, which is implied in our experiment results in section 4. A natural idea would be applying pairwise classification method to discover the exact difference between each pair of genres and then combine the predictions of the individual classifiers. One big advantage of this approach is that each sub-classifier only need capture one local aspect of the training data while in the single model approach it has to fit all the aspects of the entire training data, which can average out important local distinctions.

Building pairwise classifier for multi-class classification problems is not a new idea and many attempts have been made to build ensemble approaches, such as ECOC [6], pairwise coupling [13], and round robin ensemble [10]. However, there has been little prior work on automatically combining individual pairwise classifier results in a meaningful way.

3.2 A General "Latent Variable" Approach for Combining Models

After the pairwise classifiers have been built, the remaining problem is how to combine the results. Linear combination methods, such as weighted voting, are inappropriate for the pairwise classification because each individual classifier only captures local information. One sub-classifier may be good for some examples, but not necessarily for all the testing data. Thus, a better strategy is to build a set of "gates" on top of the individual models and ask the "gate" to tell whether the corresponding model is good at capturing the particular patterns of the input test data. We would call this "input-dependent latent variable" because those gates can be thought as latent variables that determine the right models for each input data. Next, we give a formal description of this strategy.

Given the input data $\mathbf{x}$ and a set of ensemble models $M = \{m_1, m_2, \ldots, m_n\}$, our goal is to compute the posterior probability $P(y|\mathbf{x}, M)$. As shown in Figure-1, each gate, i.e. hidden variable, is responsible for choosing whether its corresponding classifier should be used to classify the input pattern. More precisely, let h_i stand for the hidden variable corresponding to the i_{th} classification model; the value of h_i can be 1 or 0, with 1 representing that the i_{th} model is selected for classifying the input example and 0 otherwise. By using the hidden variables, we can expand the posterior probability as a sum as follows:

$$P(y|\mathbf{x}, M) = \sum_{k_i \in \{0,1\}} P(y, h_1 = k_1, h_2 = k_2, \ldots, h_n = k_n | \mathbf{x}, M).$$

By assuming that the selection of a classification model is independent from the selection of another, we can simplify the joint probability as follows:

$$P(y, h_1 = k_1, h_2 = k_2, \ldots, h_n = k_n | \mathbf{x}, M)$$
$$= \prod_{i=1}^{n} P(h_i = k_i | \mathbf{x}, M) \times P(y | h_1 = k_1, \ldots, h_n = k_n, \mathbf{x}, M).$$

Consider building an exponential model with a set of features $\{\ln P(y|\mathbf{x}, m_1), \ldots, \ln P(y|\mathbf{x}, m_n)\}$, then $P(y|h_1 = k_1, \ldots, h_n = k_n, \mathbf{x}, M) = \frac{1}{Z} \exp \sum_i \alpha_i \ln P(y|\mathbf{x}, m_i)$. To incorporate h_i into the equation above, we set α_i to k_i, with the intuition that the prediction of a model is given high weight if the model is suitable for the input pattern and low weight otherwise. In this way, we get

$$P(y|h_1 = k_1, \ldots, h_n = k_n, \mathbf{x}, M) \approx \frac{1}{Z} \prod_{i=1}^{n} P^{k_i}(y|\mathbf{x}, m_i). \quad (1)$$

We drop the normalization factor Z, rewriting the previous equation as a proportionality, and then the joint probability can be derived as follows:

$$P(y, h_1 = k_1, h_2 = k_2, \ldots, h_n = k_n | \mathbf{x}, M) \propto \prod_{i=1}^{n} P(h_i = k_i | \mathbf{x}, M) P^{k_i}(y|\mathbf{x}, m_i).$$

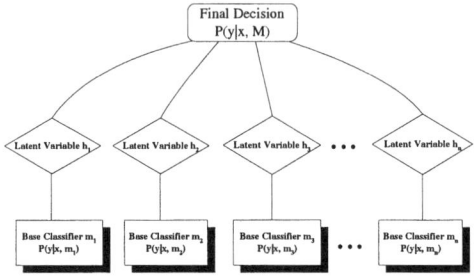

Fig. 1. The Structure of the Latent Variable Approach.

Therefore

$$P(y|\mathbf{x}, M) \propto \sum_{k_i \in \{0,1\}} \prod_{i=1}^{n} P(h_i = k_i|\mathbf{x}, M) P^{k_i}(y|\mathbf{x}, m_i)$$

$$= \prod_{i=1}^{n} \sum_{k_i \in \{0,1\}} P(h_i = k_i|\mathbf{x}, M) P^{k_i}(y|\mathbf{x}, m_i)$$

$$\propto \prod_{i=1}^{n} \{P(h_i = 1|\mathbf{x}, M) P(y|\mathbf{x}, m_i) + P(h_i = 0|\mathbf{x}, M)\}.$$

By assuming $P(h_i = 0|\mathbf{x}, M) \to 1$ [2], we have

$$P(y|\mathbf{x}, M) \propto \prod_{i=1}^{n} \{P(h_i = 1|\mathbf{x}, M) P(y|\mathbf{x}, m_i) + 1\}.$$

In this way we can further simplify by expanding only to the first order and ignoring the high order terms that usually express the interaction between different models, which are usually very small in value. At last, we get the approximation:

$$P(y|\mathbf{x}, M) \propto \sum_{i=1}^{n} P(h_i = 1|\mathbf{x}, M) P(y|\mathbf{x}, m_i) \qquad (2)$$

As indicated in (2), there are two major components: $P(h_i = 1|\mathbf{x}, M)$, i.e. the component describing how likely it is the i_{th} classifier should be used for classifying the input example, and $P(y|\mathbf{x}, m_i)$, i.e. the component determining the likelihood that class y is the true class label given the input $\mathbf{x}$ and the classification model m_i. At first glance, (2) looks very similar to the linear combination strategies except that the combination factor is $P(h_i = 1|\mathbf{x}, M)$. However, unlike the linear combination strategies whose combination weights is the same for all inputs, the weights in the latent variable approach are strongly connected with the input example by the conditional probability $P(h_i = 1|\mathbf{x}, M)$.

---

[2] During the developing process, we have made two assumptions ((1) and this one). In section 4 we will show that our approach demonstrates significant improvement over other methods even with those simplifying assumptions.

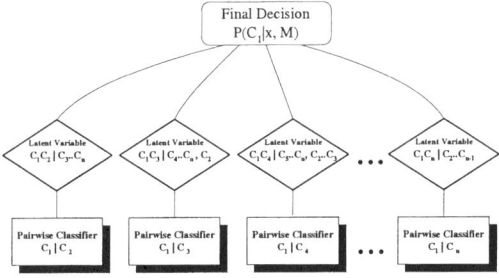

Fig. 2. The Structure of the Pairwise Ensemble Approach for Class C_1.

3.3 "Latent Variable" Approach for Pairwise Classifier

Given the latent variable approach as the framework, the remaining problem is to estimate the conditional probability $P(h_i = 1|\mathbf{x}, M)$, i.e. the likelihood that the i_{th} model should be used for class prediction given the input $\mathbf{x}$. Since each individual classifier is a pairwise classifier to differentiate two classes, say C_i and C_j, a simple method to estimate $P(h_i = 1|\mathbf{x}, M)$ is to build a binary classifier on top of each base classifier to differentiate examples that belong to these two classes (C_i and C_j) and those that do not. The underlying idea is that the likelihood for a model to be used for classifying an input datum $\mathbf{x}$ is equal to the likelihood that $\mathbf{x}$ is similar with the examples to train the model.

To make it more clear, let n be the number of classes and $M_{C_i|C_j}$ represent the pairwise classifier to differentiate class C_i and C_j. On the top level, we will have another classifier $M_{C_i, C_j | \overline{C_{i,j}}}$ to differentiate whether the examples belong to one of classes C_i, C_j or not. Figure 2 shows the structure of the model for class C_1. Compared with (2), for the pairwise ensemble approach

$$P(y = C_1|\mathbf{x}, m_{1i}) = P(y = C_1|\mathbf{x}, y \in \{C_1, C_i\}, m_{1i}),$$
$$P(h_i = 1|\mathbf{x}, M_1) = P(y \in \{C_1, C_i\}|\mathbf{x}, M_1).$$

For each class C_i, we build a structure like this and compute the corresponding score of the test examples. For multiclass problem, typical in genre classification, we can assign the test example to either the class label with the highest score (R-cut) or the classes whose scores are above some preset thresholds (S-cut) [26]. In this way, our approach can be extended to multi-label classification problems by assigning all the class labels above a given threshold to each test instance.

3.4 Related Work and Discussion

Our work is related to several approaches, including hierarchical mixture of experts (HME) [15] and pairwise coupling [13]. HME uses similar ideas to dynamically determine the most appropriate model for testing examples. However, it requires much higher computational costs because it applies an EM algorithm to estimate the latent variables. Pairwise coupling also incurs high costs in the

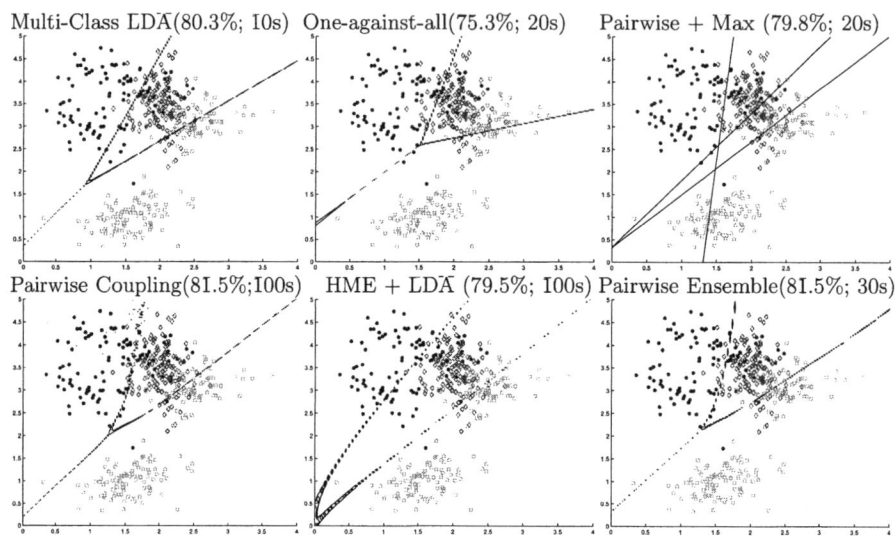

Fig. 3. Comparison of time and accuracy of Different Ensemble Approaches. Subtitle lists method, accuracy and estimated running time $C1 \rightarrow *(black), C2 \rightarrow \sqcap(blue), C3 \rightarrow \diamond(red)$.

test phase due to its iterative search procedures. Therefore it would be difficult to directly apply those two methods to text classification problems. In order to provide a rough idea on the efficiency and effectiveness of those ensemble methods, we followed the experiments in [13] and generated a synthetic dataset of 3 classes with the data in each class generated from a mixture of Guassians. We use Linear Discriminative Analysis (LDA) as base classifiers. The results and the decision boundary are shown in Figure 3. From the results, we can see that pairwise ensemble and pairwise coupling are the best in terms of accuracy, and our method is much faster.

4 Empirical Validation

In our experiments we chose two datasets for genre-based classification evaluation. Collection I consists of 12,259 documents from 10 genres (for details see Table 1). We split the corpus into a training set of 9,236 documents and a test set of 3,023 documents. The Radio-news, TV-news and Newswire are part of the TDT2 [1] and we extracted documents from the same time period in order to ensure similar contents and thus minimize the information provided due to different topics instead of different genres. The rest of the documents were collected from the web. Collection II, provided by Nigel Dewdney, consists of about 3,950 documents from 17 genres (see Table 2 for details). We split the corpus into a training set of 3,000 documents and a test set of 950 documents. Compared with collection I, collection II contains more genres, but they are easier to distinguish.

Table 1. Document Distribution in Collection I.

Genre	Newswire	Radio	TV	Message	Ad.	FAQ	Politics	Bulletin	Review	Search Result
Number	2082	1810	1145	1106	1091	1063	999	998	996	969

Table 2. Document Distribution in Collection II.

Genre	Jokes	Recipe	Quotes	Tips	Newspages	Advice	Poetry	Horoscopes	Conference
Number	315	302	293	270	252	243	231	223	211
Genre	Resume	Company	Personal	Interview	Article	Search	Homepages	Classified	
Number	203	202	200	201	201	201	202	200	

Table 3. Comparison of Results for Collection I.

Method	Micro-Avg F_1		Macro-Avg F_1		Error Rate
One-against-all + SVM	0.8757	n/a	0.8780	n/a	11.6%
Pairwise Ensemble + SVM	**0.8965**	+2.3%	**0.9003**	+2.5%	10.4%
Boosting + SVM	0.8695	-0.7%	0.8726	-0.6%	12.4%
ECOC + SVM	0.8720	-0.4%	0.8758	-0.3%	12.8%

Table 4. Comparison of Results for Collection II.

Method	Micro-Avg F_1		Macro-Avg F_1		Error Rate
One-against-all + SVM	0.9013	n/a	0.8755	n/a	9.1%
Pairwise Ensemble + SVM	**0.9495**	+5.3%	**0.9432**	+7.7%	5.1%
Boosting + SVM	0.8903	-1.2%	0.8620	-1.5%	9.9%
ECOC + SVM	0.9126	+1.3%	0.9026	+3.1%	8.7%

We pre-processed the documents, including down-casing, tokenization, removal of punctuation and stop words, stemming and supervised statistical features selection using the χ^2-max criterion. The optimal feature set size was chosen separately by 10-fold cross validation. Finally we chose 14,000 features and 10,000 features for Collection I and Collection II, respectively. Document vectors based on these feature sets were computed using the SMART *ltc* version of TF-IDF term weighting [5]. For the evaluation metric, we used error rate and a common effectiveness measure, F_1, defined to be [26]: $F_1 = \frac{2rp}{r+p}$ where F_1 is the *harmonic average* of precision p and recall r. To measure overall effectiveness we use both the *micro-average* (effectiveness computed from the sum of per-category contingency tables) and the *macro-average* (unweighted average of effectiveness across all categories).

4.1 Experimental Results

In our experiments we used Support Vector Machines, one of the most powerful classifiers in previous text classification evaluation [26], relying on the SVM_{Light} package [14]. Table 3 & 4 shows the results by different ensemble approaches and their improvement over the baseline on Collection I & II respectively.

We use the result of SVM with linear kernel, without any ensemble methods as baseline. For boosting, we use the AdaBoost algorithm with SVM, tuned

Table 5. Comparison Results of Three Genres within the Same Topic (F_1 measure).

	Newswire	Radio-news	TV-news	Macro-Avg F_1
One-against-all + SVM	0.9297	0.7635	0.7572	0.8168
Pairwise Ensemble + SVM	0.9337	0.7838	0.8240	0.8472
Boosting+SVM	0.9327	0.7529	0.7603	0.8153
ECOC+SVM	0.8894	0.7669	0.8073	0.8212

for the optimal number of training iterations and report the best results (the corresponding training iteration is 10 and 5 respectively for collection I and II). For ECOC, we use SVM as the base classifier and apply a 63-bit random coding for both collections, which is also used in [11] for their experiments. SVM is used for both base classifiers and the top level gate classifier in pairwise ensemble.

From the results, we can see the pairwise ensemble approach performs consistently the best among the four methods in terms of error minimization and both Micro-F_1 and Macro-F_1 measurement. Boosting SVM decreased performance over the baseline for both collections, which is a sign of overfitting. In fact, we tried boosting other classifiers, such as Decision Tree and Naive Bayes. Although boosting SVM deteriorates the performance, it gives the best result compared to other boosted classifiers. ECOC method achieved some improvement on Collection II but decreased the performance for the other collection. This implies that ECOC is not a generally effective method to improve classification accuracy.

In order to more clearly evaluate automated genre classification, independent of topic classification, we listed in Table 5 the detailed results of three genres in Collection I, i.e., *Newswire, Radio-news and TV-news*, which have been intentionally collected on the same topics to minimize the information provided due to different topics instead of different genres. From the results, we can see that the performance on those three categories is much lower than the average result over the whole collection with ten categories. This implies that it is more difficult and challenging to distinguish genre within the same topic. On the other hand, our approach achieves the best performance on all the three categories, especially for TV-news, which improves abut 9% over the baseline in F_1 measure.

4.2 Extension for Topic-Based Text Classification

We have shown that the pairwise ensemble approach is effective to improve the performance of genre classification. Since we use only word features for genre classification, which is the same with the topic-based classification, it is a natural question to ask whether our method is also good for topic-based text classification. To answer the question, we tested our methods on the Newsgroups dataset [18], one of commonly used datasets for text classification. The dataset contains 19,997 documents evenly distributed across 20 classes. We used the cleaned-up version of the dataset[3], removed stop words as well as the words that occur only

---

[3] This cleaned-up version is downloaded from
http://www.ai.mit.edu/people/jrennie/ecoc_svm

Table 6. Comparison of Results for 20Newsgroup.

Method	Micro-Avg F_1		Macro-Avg F_1		Error Rate
One-against-all + SVM	0.9009	n/a	0.8941	n/a	9.3%
Pairwise Ensemble + SVM	**0.9333**	+3.6%	**0.9257**	+3.5%	6.8%
Boosting + SVM	0.9020	+0.1%	0.8967	+0.3%	9.1%
ECOC + SVM	0.9159	+1.7%	0.9025	+1.0%	8.4%

once, with the final vocabulary size being about 60,000. We randomly select 80% of the documents per class for training and the remaining 20% for testing (15199 training documents and 3628 test documents). This is the same pre-processing and splitting as in the McCallum and Nigam experiments [18].

Table 6 lists the results of comparing different ensemble approaches on the newsgroup dataset. For boosting, the training iteration was 10 by cross-validation and all other parameter settings are the same with previous experiments. The results imply that the pairwise ensemble approach works well for this text classification dataset, in fact significantly better that baseline SVM or boosting SVM.

5 Conclusion and Future Work

In this paper, we identified the heterogeneity of genre data and presented our new pairwise ensemble approach to capture this characteristic. Empirical studies on two genre datasets and one topic-based datasets show that our method achieved the best performance among all the popular ensemble approaches we have tried, including boosting and ECOC. However, is pairwise ensemble truly dominant in general? Answering that question would require much larger scale empirical studies, but is definitely an important issue. Another line of research involves discovering the limitations of pairwise ensemble, such as the computational tractability as the category space grows and potential paucity of data to train all pairwise classifiers. One solution would be selecting only category pairs with sufficient training data and smoothing the decisions via the baseline classifier. Empirical validation for these extensions would be a natural next step.

Acknowledgments

This work presented in this paper was funded in part by the National Science Foundation Award # EIA-0225656. Any opinions or findings in this material are those of the authors and do not necessarily reflect those of the sponsor.

References

1. J. Allan, J. Carbonell, G. Doddington, J. Yamron, and Y. Yang. Topic detection and tracking pilot study: Final report. 1998.
2. P. N. Bennett, S. T. Dumais, and E. Horvitz. Probabilistic combination of text classifiers using reliability indicators: Models and results. In *SIGIR'02*, 2002.

3. A. Berger. Error-correcting output coding for text classification. In *IJCAI'99: Workshop on machine learning for information filtering*, 1999.
4. L. Breiman. Bagging predictors. *Machine Learning*, 24(2):123–140, 1996.
5. C. Buckley, G. Salton, and J. Allan. The effect of adding relevance information in a relevance feedback environment. In *SIGIR-94*, pages 292–300, 1994.
6. T. G. Dietterich and G. Bakiri. Solving multiclass learning problems via error-correcting output codes. *Journal of Artificial Intelligence Research*, 2:263–286, 1995.
7. A. Finn, N. Kushmerick, and B. Smyth. Genre classification and domain transfer for information filtering. In *Proceedings of ECIR-02*, 2002.
8. Y. Freund and R. E. Schapire. A decision-theoretic generalization of on-line learning and an application to boosting. In *European Conference on Computational Learning Theory*, pages 23–37, 1995.
9. Y. Freund and R. E. Schapire. Experiments with a new boosting algorithm. In *International Conference on Machine Learning*, pages 148–156, 1996.
10. J. Fürnkranz. Round robin rule learning. In *Proceedings of the 18th International Conference on Machine Learning (ICML-01)*, pages 146–153, 2001.
11. R. Ghani. Using error-correcting codes for text classification. In *Proceedings of 17th International Conference on Machine Learning*, pages 303–310, 2000.
12. D. Giorgetti and F. Sebastiani. Multiclass text categorization for automated survey coding. In *ACM Symposium on Applied Computing*, pages 798–802, 2003.
13. T. Hastie and R. Tibshirani. Classification by pairwise coupling. In *Advances in Neural Information Processing Systems*, volume 10. The MIT Press, 1998.
14. T. Joachims. Text Categorization with Support Vector Machines: Learning with Many Relevant Features. In *European Conference on Machine Learning (ECML)*, pages 137–142, Berlin, 1998. Springer.
15. M. I. Jordan and R. A. Jacobs. Hierarchical mixtures of experts and the EM algorithm. *Neural Computation*, 6:181–214, 1994.
16. B. Kessler, G. Nunberg, and H. Schütze. Automatic detection of text genre. In *Proceedings of the Thirty-Fifth ACL and EACL*, pages 32–38, 1997.
17. Y. Liu, Y. Yang, and J. Carbonell. Boosting to correct the inductive bias for text classification. In *Proc. of CIKM'02*, 2002.
18. A. McCallum and K. Nigam. A comparison of event models for naive bayes text classification. In *AAAI-98 Workshop on Learning for Text Categorization*, 1998.
19. J. R. Quinlan. Bagging, boosting, and c4.5. *Proceedings of the 13th National Conference on Artifitial Intelligence on Machine Learning*, pages 322–330, 1996.
20. J. Rennie. Improving multi-class text classification with support vector machine. *Master's thesis, Massachusetts Institute of Technology*, 2001.
21. R. Schapire and Y. Singer. Boosttexter: Aboosting-based system for text categorization. In *Machine Learning*, volume 39(1/3), pages 135–168, 2000.
22. K. Toutanova, F. Chen, K. Popat, and T. Hofmann. Text classification in a hierarchical mixture model for small training sets. In *Proc. of CIKM'01*, 2001.
23. D. Wolpert. Stacked generalization. *Neural Networks*, pages 241–259, 1992.
24. Y. Yang. An evaluation of statistical approaches to text categorization. *Journal of Information Retrieval*, 1(1/2):67–88, 1999.
25. Y. Yang, J. Carbonell, R. Brown, J. Lafferty, T. Pierce, and T. Ault. Multi-strategy learning for topic detection and tracking. In *TDT99 book*. Kluwer Academic Press.
26. Y. Yang and X. Liu. A re-examination of text categorization methods. In *SIGIR'99*, pages 42–49, 1999.

Self-evaluated Learning Agent in Multiple State Games

Koichi Moriyama[1] and Masayuki Numao[2]

[1] Department of Computer Science, Tokyo Institute of Technology.
2–12–1, Ookayama, Meguro, Tokyo, 152–8552, Japan
moriyama@mori.cs.titech.ac.jp
[2] The Institute of Scientific and Industrial Research, Osaka University.
8–1 Mihogaoka, Ibaraki, Osaka, 567–0047, Japan
numao@ai.sanken.osaka-u.ac.jp

Abstract. Most of multi-agent reinforcement learning algorithms aim to converge to a Nash equilibrium, but a Nash equilibrium does not necessarily mean a desirable result. On the other hand, there are several methods aiming to depart from unfavorable Nash equilibria, but they are effective only in limited games. Based on them, the authors proposed an agent learning appropriate actions in PD-like and non-PD-like games through self-evaluations in a previous paper [11]. However, the experiments we had conducted were static ones in which there was only one state. The versatility for PD-like and non-PD-like games is indispensable in dynamic environments in which there exist several states transferring one after another in a trial. Therefore, we have conducted new experiments in each of which the agents played a game having multiple states. The experiments include two kinds of game; the one notifies the agents of the current state and the other does not. We report the results in this paper.

1 Introduction

We investigate the use of reinforcement learning in a multi-agent environment. Many multi-agent reinforcement learning algorithms have been proposed to date [6, 4, 2, 13, 1]. Almost all of them aim to converge to a combination of actions called Nash equilibrium. In game theory, a Nash equilibrium is a combination of actions of rational players. However, this combination is not optimal in some games such as the prisoner's dilemma (PD) [14]. There are, on the other hand, several methods aiming to depart from undesirable Nash equilibria and proceed to a better combination by handling rewards in PD-like games [7, 8, 23]. However, since they use fixed handling methods, they are inferior to normal reinforcement learning in non-PD-like games.

In our previous paper [11], we have constructed an agent learning appropriate actions in both PD-like and non-PD-like games through self-evaluations. The agent has two conditions for judging whether the game is like PD or not and two self-evaluation generators — one generates self-evaluations effective in PD-like games and the other generates them effective in non-PD-like games. The agent selects one of the two generators according to the judgement and generates a self-evaluation for learning. We showed results of experiments in several iterated games and concluded that the proposed method was effective in both PD-like and non-PD-like games.

However, the experiments were *static* ones in which there was only one state. The versatility for PD-like and non-PD-like games is indispensable in *dynamic* environments in which there exist several states transferring one after another in a trial. Therefore, we have conducted new experiments in each of which the agents played a game having multiple states. The experiments include two kinds of game; the one notifies the agents of the current state and the other does not. We report the results in this paper.

This paper consists of six sections. In Section 2, we introduce the generators and the conditions proposed in the previous paper. We show in Section 3 the new experiments that we have conducted in two kinds of game played by the agents. In Section 4, we discuss the result of the experiments and of this study itself. Related works are shown in Section 5. Finally, we conclude the paper and point out future works in Section 6.

2 Generating Self-evaluation

This section introduces our method proposed in the previous paper [11].

2.1 Background and Objectives

In game theory, an actor is called a *player*. A player maximizes his own payoff and assumes that all other players do similarly. A player i has a set of actions Σ_i and his strategy σ_i is defined by a probability distribution over Σ_i. When σ_i assigns probability 1 to an action, σ_i is called a *pure* strategy and we refer to it as the action. $\sigma \equiv (\sigma_i)$ is a vector of strategies of players in a game, and σ_{-i} is a vector of strategies of players excluding i. A payoff of player i is defined as $f_i(\sigma) \equiv f_i(\sigma_i, \sigma_{-i})$. Then the *best response* of player i for σ_{-i} is a strategy σ_i satisfying

$$f_i(\sigma_i, \sigma_{-i}) = \max_{\tau_i} f_i(\tau_i, \sigma_{-i}).$$

The vector σ is a *Nash equilibrium* if, for all i, σ_i is the best response for σ_{-i}. On the other hand, the vector σ is *Pareto optimal* if there is no vector ρ satisfying

$$\forall i \quad f_i(\rho) \geq f_i(\sigma) \quad \text{and} \quad \exists j \quad f_j(\rho) > f_j(\sigma).$$

It means that there is no combination of strategies in which someone gets more payoff than σ without those who get less.

Generally, a Nash equilibrium is not Pareto optimal. Table 1 shows a game having only a single Nash equilibrium, which is not Pareto optimal. This game is an example of the *prisoner's dilemma* (PD) [14]. In this game, since the best response of a player is D regardless of the other player's action, there is only one Nash equilibrium $\sigma = (D, D)$; but it is not Pareto optimal because (C, C) is the role of ρ in the definition.

In reinforcement learning, an actor is called an *agent* and it learns from cycles of action selection and reward acquisition [18]. Although reinforcement learning is for a single agent environment, there are many proposals to extend it for a multi-agent environment [6, 4, 2, 13, 1]. However, almost all of them aim to converge to a Nash equilibrium without considering Pareto optimality. Hence, in a PD game of Table 1, they will converge to an unfavorable result $\sigma = (D, D)$ purposely.

Table 1. Prisoner's Dilemma [14]. Player A selects a row and B selects a column. Each takes cooperation C or defection D. (x,y) refers to the payoff of A and B, respectively

A \ B	C	D
C	(2,2)	(0,3)
D	(3,0)	(1,1)

On the other hand, there are several proposals to have the combination of actions depart from undesirable Nash equilibria and proceed to a better combination in PD-like games through reinforcement learning with reward handling methods [7,8,23]. However, since the methods of these proposals are fixed and applied unconditionally, the methods are inferior to normal reinforcement learning in non-PD-like games. Hence, when we equip agents with these methods, we have to check the game in advance. These cannot also be used in an environment changing from game to game.

Hence, in the previous paper [11], we have constructed an agent learning appropriate actions in both PD-like and non-PD-like games. The agent has two reward handling methods and two conditions for judging the game. We call the handled rewards *self-evaluations* and the reward handling methods *self-evaluation generators*. Each generator generates self-evaluations appropriate in either PD-like or non-PD-like games, and the conditions judge whether the game is like PD or not. In each learning cycle, the agent judges the game through the conditions, selects one of the two generators according to the judgement, generates a self-evaluation, and learns through the evaluation.

Before introducing the generators and the conditions in detail, we classify games in the next subsection.

2.2 Classification of Symmetric Games

We classify *symmetric* games into four classes in terms of game theory. A symmetric game is that in which all players have a common set of actions Σ and a common payoff function f. A Nash equilibrium which consists only of pure strategies is called a *pure strategy Nash equilibrium* (PSNE), and a PSNE in which all players' actions are identical is called a *symmetric PSNE* (SPSNE). Here, we classify a symmetric game into one of the following class by a set of SPSNEs N and a set of Pareto optimal combinations of actions P of the game.

Independent: $N \neq \emptyset$, $N \subset P$
All SPSNEs are Pareto optimal.
Boggy: $N \neq \emptyset$, $N \cap P = \emptyset$
None of SPSNEs are Pareto optimal.
Selective: $N \neq \emptyset$, $N \cap P \neq \emptyset$, $N \not\subset P$
There are Pareto optimal SPSNEs and non-Pareto optimal SPSNEs.
Rival: $N = \emptyset$
There is no SPSNE.

For a game in the *independent* class, the combination of actions is desirable when all players select rational actions independently. Conversely, the combination is unfavorable for a game in the *boggy* class. In the game, the players actually get less if all of them select the more profitable action. This is the origin of the name "boggy". PD is in this class. In a game in the *selective* class, it is a problem which SPSNE is desirable. The *rival* class consists of games having some gainers and some losers (e.g. a game in which a player has to yield a way to another). In the two-person two-action case, the independent and the boggy classes are both in Categories I and IV[1] of Weibull [21], and the selective and the rival classes are in Categories II and III, respectively.

2.3 Generating Self-evaluation

In this paper, we use *Q-learning* [20] that is a representative reinforcement learning method. Q-learning updates the *Q-function* representing estimates of future rewards from each cycle of action selection and reward acquisition. At time t, an agent recognizes the current state s_t, takes an action a_t, obtains a reward r_{t+1}, and recognizes the next state s_{t+1}. Afterwards, Q-learning updates the Q-function Q_t as follows.

$$Q_t(s, a) = Q_{t-1}(s, a) \quad \text{if } s \neq s_t \text{ or } a \neq a_t, \\ Q_t(s_t, a_t) = Q_{t-1}(s_t, a_t) + \alpha\, \delta_t. \tag{1}$$

In the update rule, δ_t is a temporal difference (TD) error:

$$\delta_t \triangleq r_{t+1} + \gamma \max_a Q_{t-1}(s_{t+1}, a) - Q_{t-1}(s_t, a_t). \tag{2}$$

The agent selects an action using the Q-function with a randomizing method, e.g. the softmax method [18], that adds some randomness to the selection.

We now introduce two self-evaluation generators. In an agent A_i at time t, a self-evaluation $r'_{i,t+1}$ is generated by adding a term $\lambda_{i,t+1}$ to a reward $r_{i,t+1}$, which is then used to update the Q-function. We omit the subscript i showing "the agent itself (A_i)" in the following.

$$r'_{t+1} \triangleq r_{t+1} + \lambda_{t+1}. \tag{3}$$

We propose two λ's, which we call the *neighbor's rewards* (NR) and the *difference of rewards* (DR). NR is effective for a game in the boggy class and DR is effective for a game in the independent class.

$$\lambda^{NR}_{t+1} \triangleq \sum_{A_k \in N_i \setminus A_i} r_{k,t+1} \tag{4}$$

$$\lambda^{DR}_{t+1} \triangleq r_{t+1} - r_t \tag{5}$$

In Formula 4, $N_i \setminus A_i$ is a set of agents that excludes A_i from a set of A_i's neighbors, N_i. NR is effective in a game in which the neighbors' rewards decrease as the agent selects profitable actions. Since DR emphasizes the difference between the present reward and the last reward, it makes the agent sensitive to change of rewards and the agent has a tendency to take self-interested actions.

---
[1] Categories I and IV are the same except for action names.

Table 2. Auto-Select (AS-) AA, AR, and RR: Q-functions for the judgement

AS-	Formula 6	Formula 7
AA	Q^{act}	Q^{act}
AR	Q^{act}	Q^{recog}
RR	Q^{recog}	Q^{recog}

Although NR and DR are effective in games in the boggy class and in the independent class, respectively, they are harmful when their use is reversed because the two classes are the opposite. Therefore, we have to devise how the agent appropriately selects the two λ's according to the game. In the previous paper, we have proposed two conditions by the following formulae for judging the class of game and selecting λ.

$$Q_{t-1}(s_t, a) < 0 \quad \text{for all } a, \tag{6}$$

$$r_{t+1} < Q_{t-1}(s_t, a_t) - \gamma \max_a Q_{t-1}(s_{t+1}, a). \tag{7}$$

Formula 6 means that there is no hope whatever action the agent currently selects. Formula 7 is derived from the TD error (Formula 2). This formula shows that the current situation is worse than what the agent learned, because it shows that the present reward is less than the estimate calculated from the learned Q-function on the assumption that the TD error is 0, i.e. the learning is completed. We can think that the agents should refrain from taking self-interested actions that bring such worse situation. Thus, we make a rule that NR is used as a self-evaluation generator if at least one of these formulae is satisfied; DR is used otherwise. We call this rule *auto-select* (AS).

In Formula 7, the left-hand side is the present reward (r). It becomes a subject of discussion because, in this paper, the Q-function is learned by *self-evaluations* (r'), not by rewards. Accordingly, we also introduce a normal Q-function for the judgement. We call this normal Q-function Q^{recog} because it is used for recognizing games, and refer to the Q-function learned by self-evaluations as Q^{act} because it is used for action selection. Since the discussion is not concerned with Formula 6, we are able to introduce two types of agent; one uses Q^{act} and the other uses Q^{recog} in Formula 6. We call them AS-AR and AS-RR, respectively. We also introduce AS-AA that uses Q^{act} in both formulae [10]; it can be thought to substitute rewards for self-evaluations in Formula 7. Table 2 shows the relation of ASs.

In summary, the proposed agents AS-AA, AS-AR, and AS-RR learn actions in the following cycle:

1. Sense the current state s_t.
2. Select and take an action a_t by Q^{act} with a randomizing method.
3. Obtain a reward r_{t+1} and sense the next state s_{t+1}.
4. Recognize the game by Formulae 6 and 7, then select λ_{t+1}.
5. Generate a self-evaluation r'_{t+1} from r_{t+1} and λ_{t+1} by Formula 3.
6. Update Q^{act} by Q-learning with $s_t, a_t, r'_{t+1}, s_{t+1}$ and Q^{recog} by Q-learning with $s_t, a_t, r_{t+1}, s_{t+1}$.
7. Back to 1.

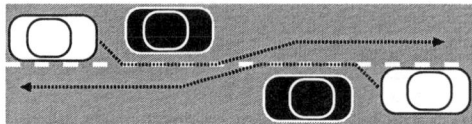

Fig. 1. Narrow Road Game: Black cars are parking on the road. Two white cars simultaneously appear at both side of the road

3 Experiments

We have conducted three experiments using two kinds of game having multiple states played by multiple homogeneous agents. One kind is called *Markov games* or *stochastic games* [6, 4] in which each agent is notified of the current state, and the other kind is *state-unknown games* in which each agent is not informed of the state. We used seven types of agents for comparison: *random* (RD), *normal* (NM), the *neighbors' rewards* (NR), the *difference of rewards* (DR), and the three types of *auto-select* (AS-AA, AS-AR, and AS-RR). RD selects actions randomly, and NM learns by normal Q-learning.

Each experiment was conducted twenty-five times. Q-functions were initialized to 0 in each trial. We used the softmax method [18] as a randomizing method for action selection and a parameter of the method called temperature was set to 1. Learning rate α and discount factor γ in Formula 1 were both set to 0.5.

3.1 Markov Game

A Markov game [6, 4] has several matrix games each of which has a label called *state*. In the game, the combination of all player's actions makes a state transfer to another and every player knows which state he is in now.

Here we use a game named Narrow Road Game. Suppose a road with two parking cars and two cars which simultaneously appear at both sides of the road (Figure 1). Each car selects one of actions: GO or WAIT. Both cars want to pass the narrow point as soon as possible. However, if both take GO, they cannot pass because of the point. If both take WAIT, on the other hand, nothing changes.

Each car (agent) receives a reward 1 when it takes GO and succeeds in passing and −0.5 when it fails to pass or it takes WAIT. A cycle is finished after both agents have passed or they have taken four actions. Every agent learns after every reward acquisition and knows whether the opposite remains and how many actions they have taken. After one agent succeeds in passing, it gets out of the cycle, and the remaining agent takes an action again. Then if the remaining agent takes GO, it passes unconditionally, and otherwise, it has to take an action again. These are summarized in Figure 2. Since payoff matrices (i.e. states) change with the number of agents and every agent knows which state it is in now, this is a Markov game. The set of neighbors, N_i, in Formula 4 includes all agents in a game.

Figure 3 shows the average of summed reward of two agents at the 100th cycle in 25 trials. In each cycle, the rewards each agent obtains are accumulated and two agents' accumulated rewards are summed. The maximum summed reward is 1.5 when

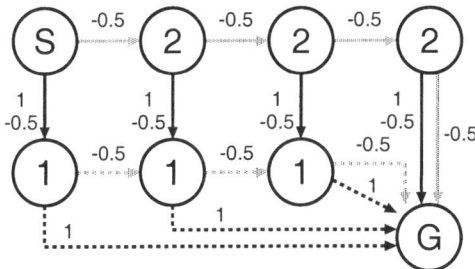

Fig. 2. State Transition in Narrow Road Game: A circle and an arrow show a state and a state transition, respectively. A number in a circle shows how many agents are remaining. Black arrows show transitions in the case in which one of the agents succeeds in passing, and gray ones show transitions in other cases. Dashed arrows show transitions by one remaining agent. Numbers with an arrow show payoff with each transition. With a solid black arrow, the upper number is payoff for the going agent and the lower is payoff for the waiting agent

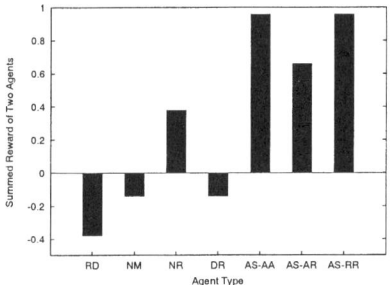

Fig. 3. Result of Narrow Road Game: It shows the average of summed reward of two agents at the 100th cycle in 25 trials

one agent passes at the first action phase (i.e. the other waits) and the other passes at the second, and the minimum is −4 when both fail to pass in four action phases.

From the figure, we can see the following:

- The three AS versions outperform the other methods. However, as a result of paired t-tests, there is no significant difference between the result of AS-AR and those of other methods. AS-AA and AS-RR are also not significantly different from NR.
- The summed reward about 1 in AS-AA and AS-RR means that the probability of taking more than two action phases is less than a half.

3.2 State-Unknown Games

The previous subsection shows the experimental result of a Markov game. In a Markov game, every agent is able to know which state it is in now. However, in a real situation, we cannot precisely know the current state in many cases and we have to guess it.

Therefore, in this subsection, we show the results of two experiments in state-unknown games.

We used the *tragedy of the commons* (TC) type games. TC is introduced by Hardin [3], in which there is an open pasture with several rational herdsmen each of whom grazes cattle in the pasture. Since each herdsman tries to maximize his profit, each one brings as many cattle as possible to the pasture. If all herdsmen bring their cattle unlimitedly, however, it is overgrazing and the pasture goes wild. This is the tragedy.

Mikami et al. [7] conducted an experiment consisting of ten agents. In a cycle, each agent takes one of three actions (*selfish*, *cooperative*, and *altruistic*) simultaneously and receives a reward. An action a_i of an agent A_i ($i = 0, 1, ..., 9$) follows a base reward $R(a_i)$ and a social cost $C(a_i)$. R is 3, 1, and −3 and C is +1, ±0, and −1 when the agent takes a selfish, a cooperative, and an altruistic action, respectively. After all agents take actions, A_i receives a reward r_i defined as

$$r_i \triangleq R(a_i) - \sum_j C(a_j).$$

The set of A_i's neighbors, N_i, in Formula 4 is defined as

$$N_i \triangleq \{A_k \mid k = (i+j) \bmod 10, \, j = 0, 1, 2, 3\},$$

and A_i uses the combination of actions of N_i as a state in Q-learning. A_i is able to know only the combination, not all agents' actions.

In our previous paper [11], we modified the cost C as $+c$, ± 0, and $-c$ when the agent took a selfish, a cooperative, and an altruistic action, respectively. c was a constant common for all agents and the game was identical with Mikami's when $c = 1$. We showed the results of two experiments, $c = 1$ and $c = 0$, which were in the boggy class and in the independent class, respectively, and concluded that the proposed methods (ASs) were effective in both games.

In this paper, the cost parameter c is changed *without informing agents* in each trial. Since the results in the previous paper were at the 3000th cycle, we changed the parameter c in a trial after 3000 cycles and continued the trial further 3000 cycles. We have conducted two experiments; the parameter c is changed from 1 (boggy) to 0 (independent) and vice versa. We show the results at the 6000th cycle (i.e. the 3000th cycle after the change) with the previous results for comparison. We look at the results of the experiments with those of Mikami's *average filter* (AF)[2] [7] and of our past method called the *general filter* (GF) [9].

Figure 4 shows the average of summed reward of ten agents at the 6000th cycle in 25 trials. From the figure we can see that, in the experiment from $c = 1$ (boggy) to 0 (independent), the results are considerably different from the previous static ones, especially those of ASs. On the other hand, the results are similar in the experiment from $c = 0$ to 1.

---

[2] They proposed two types of AF; but due to space constraint, only the result of type 1 is shown here.

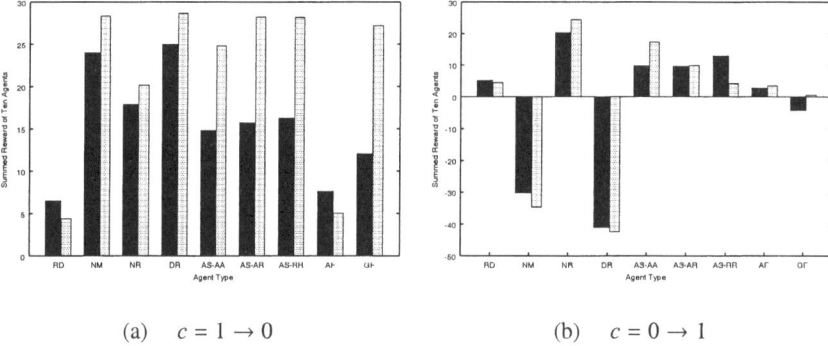

(a) $c = 1 \rightarrow 0$ (b) $c = 0 \rightarrow 1$

Fig. 4. Result of the Tragedy of the Commons: Each thick, black bar shows the average of summed reward of ten agents at the 6000th cycle (i.e. the 3000th cycle after change) in 25 trials. Each thin, gray bar shows the result at the 3000th cycle in 25 trials of a previous static experiment with changed c, i.e. 0 in (a) and 1 in (b) [11]

4 Discussion

In Narrow Road Game, ASs are the best of all. It seems slightly strange because ASs only chose NR or DR that were worse than ASs, but we can be convinced if we interpret as the game requiring agents to use NR and DR properly. In fact, when two agents are remaining, which is in the rival class, one agent has to give a way to the other and NR may be effective in this class. On the other hand, when only one is remaining, which is in the independent class, it has to go decisively and DR is effective in this class.

In state-unknown games, although the result of '0 to 1' is not affected by the change, the result of '1 to 0' is worse than that of $c = 0$. It is because an agent's policy learned before the change had deleterious effect on its actions after the change. Since $c = 1$ is in the boggy class, the agent mainly learned through NR before the change. Hence, the agent's Q^{act} function for altruistic actions must have been more than that for selfish actions. The function for cooperative actions may also have been. On the other hand, not only selfish actions, but also cooperative ones bring positive rewards after the change in this game. Therefore, even if altruistic actions were withdrawn appropriately by learning after the change, the action the agent would choose may have been not the selfish one, which is desirable in $c = 0$, but the cooperative one. Consequently, if the agent learns through same Q-functions before and after the change, we cannot avoid this problem even if we humans choose NR and DR properly. Thus, in order to learn appropriate actions in these games, what we have to improve is, probably, not the conditions for selecting self-evaluation generators, but the selected generators, i.e. NR and DR.

We have constructed an agent which is able to learn suitable actions in *several* games by means of Q-learning with self-evaluations instead of rewards. As far as we know, no such work yet exists in a reinforcement learning context. There are indeed some works which handles reward functions for learning suitable actions [7, 8, 23], but they differ from this work because each of them performs for only *one* game. If we use their works for constructing agents, we have to decide in advance whether we are to use them according to the game. If we use this work, on the other hand, it will surely reduce problem of judging the game.

This work aims to discover suitable conditions or *meta-rules* for learning. In this paper, we introduce two conditions for judging the boggy game. Although we can introduce other meta-rules, it will be difficult. Thus, we should devise methods for constructing meta-rules themselves. It becomes a meta-learning problem [19] in a learning context. We can also search function space of self-evaluations by genetic algorithm.

5 Related Works

Although there are only a few works which handle rewards for learning suitable actions in a reinforcement learning context, there are several methods in a genetic algorithm (GA) context. Mundhe et al. [12] proposed several fitness functions for the tragedy of the commons. Their proposed fitness functions are used if a received reward is less than the best of the past; otherwise, normal functions are used. Thus, unlike Mikami's [7] and Wolpert's [23], they are conditionally used but only applied to games in the boggy class.

There are a few works aiming to obtain meta-rules. Schmidhuber et al. [17] proposed a reinforcement learning algorithm called the *success story algorithm* (SSA). It learns when it evaluates actions in addition to normal actions. Zhao et al. [24] used the algorithm in a game in which agents have to cooperate to gain food, as they escape from a pacman. In a GA context, Ishida et al. [5] proposed agents each of which had its own fitness function called *norm*. If the agent's accumulated reward becomes under a threshold, the agent dies and a new one having a new norm takes the agent's place. They conducted only an experiment in the tragedy of the commons.

Uninformed changes in state-unknown games are similar to *concept drifts* in a symbolic learning context, which are changes of concepts driven by some hidden contexts. A learner in the environment having concept drifts usually uses a kind of windowing method to cast off expired inputs. Widmer et al. [22] presented a flexible windowing method which modified the window size according to the accuracy of learned concepts to the input sequence in order to follow the concept drifts more flexibly. They also proposed a learner that reuses some old concepts learned before. Sakaguchi et al. [16] proposed a reinforcement learning method having the forgetting and reusing property. In their method, if the TD error is over a threshold, a learner shifts the current Q-function to an adequate one it has or creates a new Q-function if it does not have. They conducted experiments only in single agent environments.

In game theory, each player takes defection in the prisoner's dilemma (PD). However, when humans play the game, the result is different from that of theories. Rilling et al. [15] requested thirty-six women to play PD and watched their brains by functional Magnetic Resonance Imaging (fMRI). They reported that several parts of reward processing in their brains were activated when both players cooperated, and explained that rewards for cooperation were then *generated in their brains*. This shows that there are common features in a human's brain processes and in the proposed method of this work.

6 Conclusion

Most of multi-agent reinforcement learning methods aim to converge to a Nash equilibrium, but a Nash equilibrium does not necessarily mean a desirable result. On the other hand, there are several methods aiming to depart from unfavorable Nash equilibria, but they are effective only in limited games. Hence, we have constructed an agent learning appropriate actions in many games through reinforcement learning with self-evaluations.

First we defined a symmetric pure strategy Nash equilibrium (SPSNE) and categorized symmetric games into four classes — independent, boggy, selective, and rival — by SPSNE and Pareto optimality. Then we introduced two self-evaluation generators and two conditions for judging games in the boggy class. We proposed three types of methods, which were auto-select (AS-) AA, AR, and RR.

We have conducted experiments in Narrow Road Game and state-unknown games. The result of Narrow Road Game shows that the versatility for PD-like and non-PD-like games is indispensable in games having multiple states. In '0 to 1' state-unknown game, there is no effect from the change, thus the proposed methods (ASs) seem robust to multiple states. On the other hand, the result of '1 to 0' state-unknown game shows that there exist games in which ASs are fragile. However, discussion about this ineffectiveness in Section 4 points out that the fragility is derived from not the conditions for selecting self-evaluation generators, but the selected generators.

We are able to point out several future works. First, since we have conducted only empirical evaluation in this paper, we have to evaluate the proposed methods theoretically. Next, since we have classified only symmetric games, we need to extend the class definition so that it can deal with asymmetric games. Furthermore, we conducted experiments only in simple games with homogeneous agents, and thus, we have to conduct experiments in more complex problems which consist of heterogeneous agents and evaluate the proposed methods by the results.

References

1. M. Bowling and M. Veloso. Multiagent learning using a variable learning rate. *Artificial Intelligence*, 136:215–250, 2002.
2. C. Claus and C. Boutilier. The Dynamics of Reinforcement Learning in Cooperative Multi-agent Systems. In *Proc. 15th National Conference on Artificial Intelligence, AAAI-98*, pages 746–752, Madison, Wisconsin, U.S.A., 1998.
3. G. Hardin. The Tragedy of the Commons. *Science*, 162:1243–1248, 1968.
4. J. Hu and M. P. Wellman. Multiagent Reinforcement Learning: Theoretical Framework and an Algorithm. In *Proc. 15th International Conference on Machine Learning, ICML'98*, pages 242–250, Madison, Wisconsin, U.S.A., 1998.
5. T. Ishida, H. Yokoi, and Y. Kakazu. Self-Organized Norms of Behavior under Interactions of Selfish Agents. In *Proc. 1999 IEEE International Conference on Systems, Man, and Cybernetics*, Tokyo, Japan, 1999.
6. M. L. Littman. Markov games as a framework for multi-agent reinforcement learning. In *Proc. 11th International Conference on Machine Learning, ML'94*, pages 157–163, New Brunswick, New Jersey, U.S.A., 1994.

7. S. Mikami and Y. Kakazu. Co-operation of Multiple Agents Through Filtering Payoff. In *Proc. 1st European Workshop on Reinforcement Learning, EWRL-1*, pages 97–107, Brussels, Belgium, 1994.
8. S. Mikami, Y. Kakazu, and T. C. Fogarty. Co-operative Reinforcement Learning By Payoff Filters. In *Proc. 8th European Conference on Machine Learning, ECML-95*, (Lecture Notes in Artificial Intelligence 912), pages 319–322, Heraclion, Crete, Greece, 1995.
9. K. Moriyama and M. Numao. Constructing an Autonomous Agent with an Interdependent Heuristics. In *Proc. 6th Pacific Rim International Conference on Artificial Intelligence, PRICAI-2000*, (Lecture Notes in Artificial Intelligence 1886), pages 329–339, Melbourne, Australia, 2000.
10. K. Moriyama and M. Numao. Construction of a Learning Agent Handling Its Rewards According to Environmental Situations. In *Proc. 1st International Joint Conference on Autonomous Agents and Multi-Agent Systems, AAMAS-2002*, pages 1262–1263, Bologna, Italy, 2002.
11. K. Moriyama and M. Numao. Generating Self-Evaluations to Learn Appropriate Actions in Various Games. Technical Report TR03-0002, Department of Computer Science, Tokyo Institute of Technology, 2003.
12. M. Mundhe and S. Sen. Evolving agent societies that avoid social dilemmas. In *Proc. Genetic and Evolutionary Computation Conference, GECCO-2000*, pages 809–816, Las Vegas, Nevada, U.S.A., 2000.
13. Y. Nagayuki, S. Ishii, and K. Doya. Multi-Agent Reinforcement Learning: An Approach Based on the Other Agent's Internal Model. In *Proc. 4th International Conference on MultiAgent Systems, ICMAS-2000*, pages 215–221, Boston, Massachusetts, U.S.A., 2000.
14. W. Poundstone. *Prisoner's Dilemma*. Doubleday, New York, 1992.
15. J. K. Rilling, D. A. Gutman, T. R. Zeh, G. Pagnoni, G. S. Berns, and C. D. Kilts. A Neural Basis for Social Cooperation. *Neuron*, 35:395–405, 2002.
16. Y. Sakaguchi and M. Takano. Learning to Switch Behaviors for Different Environments: A Computational Model for Incremental Modular Learning. In *Proc. 2001 International Symposium on Nonlinear Theory and its Applications, NOLTA-2001*, pages 383–386, Zao, Miyagi, Japan, 2001.
17. J. Schmidhuber, J. Zhao, and N. N. Schraudolph. Reinforcement Learning with Self-Modifying Policies. In [19], pages 293–309, 1997.
18. R. S. Sutton and A. G. Barto. *Reinforcement Learning: An Introduction*. MIT Press, Cambridge, MA, 1998.
19. S. Thrun and L. Pratt, editors. *Learning to Learn*. Kluwer Academic Publishers, Norwell, MA, 1997.
20. C. J. C. H. Watkins and P. Dayan. Technical Note: Q-learning. *Machine Learning*, 8:279–292, 1992.
21. J. W. Weibull. *Evolutionary Game Theory*. MIT Press, Cambridge, MA, 1995.
22. G. Widmer and M. Kubat. Learning in the Presence of Concept Drift and Hidden Contexts. *Machine Learning*, 23:69–101, 1996.
23. D. H. Wolpert and K. Tumer. Collective Intelligence, Data Routing and Braess' Paradox. *Journal of Artificial Intelligence Research*, 16:359–387, 2002.
24. J. Zhao and J. Schmidhuber. Solving a Complex Prisoner's Dilemma with Self-Modifying Policies. In *From Animals to Animats 5: Proc. 5th International Conference on Simulation of Adaptive Behavior*, pages 177–182, Zurich, Switzerland, 1998.

Classification Approach towards Ranking and Sorting Problems

Shyamsundar Rajaram[1], Ashutosh Garg[2], Xiang Sean Zhou[3], and Thomas S. Huang[1]

[1] University of Illinois, Urbana, IL
{rajaram1,t-huang}@uiuc.edu
[2] IBM Almaden Research Center, San Jose, CA
ashutosh@us.ibm.com
[3] Siemens Corporate Research, Princeton, NJ
xzhou@scr.siemens.com

Abstract. Recently, ranking and sorting problems have attracted the attention of researchers in the machine learning community. By ranking, we refer to categorizing examples into one of K categories. On the other hand, sorting refers to coming up with the ordering of the data that agrees with some ground truth preference function. As against standard approaches of treating ranking as a multiclass classification problem, in this paper we argue that ranking/sorting problems can be solved by exploiting the inherent structure present in data. We present efficient formulations that enable the use of standard binary classification algorithms to solve these problems, however the structure is still captured in our formulations. We further show that our approach subsumes the various approaches that were developed in the past. We evaluate our algorithm on both synthetic datasets and for a real world image processing problem. The results obtained demonstrate the superiority of our algorithm over multiclass classification and other similar approaches for ranking/sorting data.

1 Introduction

Consider the problem of ranking movies. The goal is to predict if a movie fan will like a certain movie or not. One can probably extract a number of features like - actors playing the lead role, setting of the movie (urban or rural), type of movie (romantic or a horror movie etc). Based on this, a set of possible ratings for a movie could be - *run-to-see, very-good, good, only-if-you-must, do-not-bother,* and *avoid-at-all-cost*. At another time, given a list of movies one might like to obtain a ordered list where the order in the list represents his preferences or choices. Here we observe that, in both these problems, the labels themselves do not carry much meaning. The information is captured by the relative ranks or order given to the movies. Henceforth, we refer to the first problem as ranking problem and the second problem as sorting problem.

Most of the research in the machine learning community has gone into developing algorithms which are good for either classification or regression. Given that, some of the researchers have attempted to solve the ranking and sorting problems by posing them as either multiclass classification or regression problems. In this paper, we argue that this is not the right approach. If the ranking problem is posed as a classification problem then the inherent structure present in ranked data is not made use of and hence generalization ability of such classifiers is severely limited. On the other hand, posing the task of sorting as a regression problem leads to a highly constrained problem.

This paper starts with the theoretical analysis relating the problem of sorting with classification. We show that the VC-dimension of a linear classifier is directly related to the rank-dimension (defined later) of a linear classifier. We use the intuition developed by studying the complexity of sorting/ranking problems to show how these can be reduced to a standard classification problem. This reduction enables use of both powerful batch learning algorithms like SVM and online classification algorithms like Winnow and Perceptron. The online version of our algorithm subsumes the previously proposed algorithm Pranking [2] and at the same time is much easier to implement. Further, in many ranking problems, because of the users preference, only few features may be active at any given time and as such Winnow [9] is a better choice than Perceptron. We further extend the results presented in the paper to handle the case when it may not be possible to learn a linear ranker in the original data space. In particular, we make use of kernel methods and show how one can learn a non linear ranker for both the ranking and sorting problems. This formulation is similar in spirit to the work by [4], however in our approach there is a significant reduction in the computational complexity.

At this point, we would like to note that the basic problem formulation presented in this paper is different from the formulation that has been assumed in algorithms like Cranking [7]. The model adopted in the latter is specifically meant to learn the sorting of the data based on the ordering of the data given by other experts. The problem considered in this paper however deals with the case when we actually do not have the orderings from individual experts but instead have some feature based representation of the data. For example, given some documents/images that need to be sorted or ranked, we will extract the features from these documents/images and learn a ranker on top of these. This is the view which has also been adopted in [2,4].

Recently, there has also been work to solve the problem of multiclass classification by considering ordering information in class attributes, thereby posing it as a ranking problem. In [3], Frank et al. transform the data in such a way that the k-class ordinal classification problem reduces to $k - 1$ binary class problems. Krammer et al. [13] use a modification of S-CART (Structural Classification And Regression Trees) to perform ordinal classification. The algorithm that we propose in this paper, can be easily adapted to solve the problem of multiclass classification if the ordering of the classes are known.

The organization of the paper is as follows. We start off by explaining some notations and give the formal definition of the problem. We will also explain the model adopted to solve the problem. In Sec. 3, we give the relationship between the rank-dimension and VC-dimension of a linear classifier. Sec. 4 gives the main result of the paper. In this section, we show how one can reduce the ranking and sorting problems to a classification problem. Based on the results from this section, we show how one can use SVM and other kernel algorithms in Sec. 5. Finally, in Sec. 6 we give results on both synthetic data and test our ranking algorithm on a novel image processing problem.

2 Notations and Problem Definition

Consider a training sample of size m say $S = \{(x_1, y_1), (x_2, y_2), ..., (x_m, y_m)\}$, $x_i \in \mathcal{X}, y_i \in \mathcal{Y}$ where $\mathcal{X}$ is the domain from which each training example comes and $\mathcal{Y}$ is the space from which labels are assigned to each example. The labels y_i are referred to as the ranks given to the examples. As mentioned earlier, in this paper we have adopted a feature based representation of the data and we assume that $\mathcal{X}$ is n dimensional space of reals $\Re^n$. Under this, for any $x_i, x_j \in \mathcal{X}$ we have $x_i - x_j \in \mathcal{X}$.

For ranking problem, $\mathcal{Y} = \{1, ..., K\}$ where K is the maximum rank that can be taken by any example. This is similar to the multiclass classification problem. However the spirit of the ranking problem is very different. The ranks relate to the degree of interest/confidence a person has in that instance. Given an example with rank k, all the examples with rank less than k are less interesting and all the examples with rank more than k are more interesting. Such a relationship/viewpoint does not exist in case of multi-class classification problem. In general we will assume that K (the maximum rank) is fixed for a given problem and will treat the case when K is same as the size of the dataset separately. We refer to this latter case as the *sorting problem*. In the sorting problem, each training example has a distinct rank (this rank will be referred to as the order in the dataset) which refers to the relative position of that instance in the dataset. In this case, one cannot treat it as a multiclass problem as the number of classes depend on the size of the data and the interest is in learning a function that can give relative ordering instead of absolute class labels.

2.1 The Ranking Model

In this paper, we adopt a functional approach to solve the ranking problem. Given a data point x or a set of data points S, we learn a ranker $f : \mathcal{X} \to \mathcal{Y}$. Depending upon whether K is fixed or it is m, our choice of function f will be different. In general, when $K < m$ is fixed, we will refer to it as the ranking problem where as when $K = m$, we will refer to it as the sorting problem.

In this paper, we assume that *there exists an axis in some space such that when data is projected on to this axis, the relative position of the data points captures the model of user preferences*. In the case of the sorting problem, we will treat f to be a linear function whose value is the signed distance from some hyperplane h. That is $f(x_i) = h^T x_i$. The information about the relative order of the datapoints will be captured by the distance from the hyperplane. During the testing phase, given a set of datapoints, the sorted set of datapoints with respect to their order will be obtained by sorting them with respect to the raw value $f(x)$.

We will adopt a similar framework to solve the ranking problem. However, in this case, in addition to learning h (as in the previous case), we also learn a number of thresholds $(K-1)$ corresponding to the different ranks that will be assigned to data. The learned classifier in this case will be expressed as $(h, \theta_1, ..., \theta_{K-1})$ with the thresholds satisfying $\theta_1 < \theta_2 ... < \theta_{K-1}$. The ranking rule in this case is

$$f(x) = \begin{cases} 1 & \text{if } h^T x < \theta_1, \\ i & \text{if } \theta_{i-1} < h^T x < \theta_i, \ i \neq 1, K \\ K & \text{if } \theta_{K-1} < h^T x \end{cases} \quad (1)$$

Although, this model of ranking may seem too simplistic, as we show in Sec. 3 it is quiet powerful and we give some analysis relating VC-dimension of the learned classifier to what we call rank-dimension of the data. Later in Sec. 5, we will show how one can extend the above framework to the case where learning needs to be done in a space different from the original space. In such a case, learning is done in some high dimensional space by making use of kernels for the mapping.

3 Complexity of Ranking vs Classification

It has been argued [1] that the ranking problem is much harder than the classification problem. Although this is true in the particular view adopted by [1], in this paper we present an alternate viewpoint. We analyze the complexity of the ranking problem from the view of the VC-dimension. We define the variant of the VC-dimension, called rank-dimension, for the ranking problem as follows: if the data points are ranked with respect to the value of the functional evaluated on a particular data point, then we say that the rank dimension of the functional is the maximum number of points that can be ranked in any arbitrary way using this functional.

Theorem 1. *The rank dimension of a linear functional is same as its VC-dimension. Following the notation given in Sec. 2, it holds for all $x_i, x_j \in \mathcal{X}$ we also have $x_i - x_j \in \mathcal{X}$ and $x_j - x_i \in \mathcal{X}$*

Proof. Let us consider the case of linear classifier $h \in \Re^n$. Say one observes a set of m points $S = \{x_1, x_2, ..., x_m\}$, with the corresponding ranks $y_1, y_2, ..., y_m$.

Clearly if we can rank a set of m points in any arbitrary way using a functional, then we can always shatter them (at the cost of one additional dimension corresponding to the threshold). Consider a subset $S_0 \subset S$ such that we want to label all the points that belong to S_0 as negative and all the points that belong to S but not to S_0 as positive (i.e. $S \backslash S_0$). Now, if we rank all the points in such a way so that the rank of all the points in S_0 is less than the rank of all the points in $S \backslash S_0$ then we can do the classification by just thresholding based on the rank. This shows that the rank-dimension of any functional cannot be more than the "VC-dimension" of the same functional.

We know that the VC-dimension of a linear classifier in n dimensional space is $n + 1$. That is any set of $n + 1$ points (assuming general positions) in n dimensional space can be shattered by a n dimensional linear classifier. Now we show that any set of $n + 1$ points can be ranked in any arbitrary way using a linear classifier in n dimensional space. Given any arbitrary ranking of the points, lets re-label the points such that $rank(x_1) < rank(x_2) < ... < rank(x_{n+1})$. Define a new set of points $S' = \{0, x_2 - x_1, x_3 - x_2, ..., x_{n+1} - x_n\}$. Now, if we label the points as $\{-1, 1, 1, ..., 1\}$. The cardinality of set S' is $n + 1$ (n-difference vectors and one 0 vector.) Also it is easy to see that all points in S' lie in $\Re^n$. Now, from the VC-dimension theory, we know that there exists a linear classifier in n dimensional space that can shatter S' according to the labelling given above. Let this linear classifier be h, with classification as $sign(h^T x)$. Then for correct classification $h^T(x_i - x_{i-1}) > 0 \Rightarrow h^T x_i > h^T x_{i-1}$. That is the distance of the original points from the hyperplane does corresponds to the specified ranking. Hence, we have shown that any pair of $n + 1$ points can be ranked in any arbitrary fashion by a n dimensional classifier and at the same time we have also shown that the rank dimension cannot be more than the VC-dimension. This shows that the rank-dimension of any classifier is same as its VC-dimension.

This is a very interesting result as it shows that the complexity of the hypothesis space for the two problems is same. However, as of now, we are not clear about the relation between the growth function for the two problems. Further, the relation between the computational complexity of the two problems has to be studied.

4 Ranking, Sorting and Classification

In the previous section, we saw the close relationship between the classification and the sorting problem. It is clear that if we can solve a sorting problem then we can also solve a ranking problem (by giving any arbitrary order to all the data points within the same rank class). However, it turns out that computationally both problems demand individual treatment. In this section, we present two approaches to solve this problem. The first is referred to as the difference space approach while the second is referred to as the embedded space approach.

4.1 Difference Space Approach

Given a training set S, define a new set S_d of difference vectors $x_{ij}^d = x_i - x_j$; $\forall i, j : y_i \neq y_j$ and their corresponding labels $y_{ij}^d = sign(y_i - y_j)$. This leads to a dataset[1] of size $O(m^2)$. Learning a linear classifier for this problem would be same as learning a ranker h. Once such a ranker is learned, the thresholds for the ranking problem can easily be computed. This formulation is same as the one proposed by [4]. Computational complexity of most of the learning algorithms depend on the size of the training data and a quadratic increase in the size of the data will certainly make most of the existing algorithms impractical. Hence, we propose to generate difference vectors only among the adjacent rank classes. Formally, given a training set S, obtain a new set S_d made up of difference vectors $x_{ij}^d = x_i - x_j$; $\forall i, j : y_i = y_j + 1$ and their corresponding labels $y_{ij}^d = +1$. This would result in a dataset with only positive examples. Again, most standard classification algorithms behave well if the number of positive examples is close to the number of negative examples. To get around this problem, once such a dataset is obtained, multiply each example x_{ij}^d and the corresponding label y_{ij}^d by q_{ij} where q_{ij} is a random variable taking values $\{-1, 1\}$ with equal probabilities. Clearly, learning a linear classifier over this dataset will give a ranker h which will be same as the one obtained in the previous case. The size of the dataset in this case is $O(\frac{m^2}{K})$. For a small K (which is the case in most K-ranking problems) this is still too large to handle. However, interestingly, for the sorting problem, the size of the new dataset is of the same order as the size of the old dataset and therefore this problem can be solved easily. Next, we present an approach that specifically handles the ranking problem without exploding the size of the training dataset.

4.2 Embedded Space Approach

In this section, we present a new framework to handle the ranking problem which can be seen as the main contribution of this paper. It is a novel formulation that allows one

---

[1] The different elements of this dataset are not independent of one another.

to map a ranking problem to a standard classification problem without increasing the size of the dataset. The embedded space approach presented in this section is similar in spirit to the model presented in [12], however as we will see shortly in our model, the dimension of the new space does not grow linearly as the one presented in their paper. Fig. 1 graphically depicts the ranking framework. The distance from the hyperplane h of a datapoint x is mapped to a one dimensional space. In this space, $\theta_1,..,\theta_{K-1}$ are the different thresholds against which the distance is compared. Note that $h^T x_j$; $\forall x_j$ having rank i results in a range represented by its left end point θ_{i-1} and its right end point θ_i. Define $\alpha_i = \theta_{i+1} - \theta_i$; $1 \leq i \leq K-1$. For the data items belonging to rank 1, there is no lower bound and for all the data items belonging to rank K there is no upper bound. By construction, it is easy to see that $\alpha_i > 0$; $\forall i$. Note that data point x_j having rank $i > 1$ will satisfy, (assuming $\alpha_0 = 0$.)

$$h^T x_j > \theta_{i-1}; \quad h^T x_j + \alpha_{i-1} > \theta_i; \quad h^T x_j + \sum_{k=i-1}^{K-2} \alpha_k > \theta_{K-1} \quad (2)$$

Similarly, for an example with rank $i < K$, (assuming $\theta_K = \infty$, $\alpha_{K-1} = 0$)

$$h^T x_j < \theta_i; \quad h^T x_j + \alpha_i < \theta_{i+1}; \quad h^T x_j + \sum_{k=i}^{K-2} \alpha_k < \theta_{K-1} \quad (3)$$

Based on this observation, define $\bar{h} = [h \; \alpha_1 \; \alpha_2 \ldots \alpha_{K-2}]$ and for an example x_j with rank $1 < i < K$, define $\bar{x}_j^+, \bar{x}_j^-$ as $n + K - 2$ dimensional vectors with

$$\bar{x}_j^+[l] = \begin{cases} x_j[l] & 1 \leq l \leq n, \\ 0 & n < l < n+i-1, \\ 1 & n+i-1 \leq l \leq n+K-2. \end{cases} \quad \bar{x}_j^-[l] = \begin{cases} x_j[l] & 1 \leq l \leq n, \\ 0 & n < l < n+i, \\ 1 & n+i \leq l \leq n+K-2. \end{cases} \quad (4)$$

For an example x_j with rank $i = 1$, we define only $\bar{x}_j^-$ as above and for an example with rank $i = K$, we define only $\bar{x}_j^+$ again as above. This formulation assumes that $\theta_{K-1} = 0$. It is easy to see that one can assume this without loss of generality (by increasing the dimension of x by 1 one can get around this.) Once we have defined $\bar{x}_j^+, \bar{x}_j^-$, the ranking problem simply reduces to learning a classifier $\bar{h}$ in $n + K - 2$ dimensional space such that $\bar{h}^T \bar{x}_j^+ > 0$; and $\bar{h}^T \bar{x}_j^- < 0$. This is a standard classification problem with at most $2m$ training examples, half of which have label $+1$ (examples $\bar{x}_j^+$) and rest have label -1 (examples $\bar{x}_j^-$). Even though, the overall dimension of the data points and the weight vector h is increased by $K - 2$, this representation limits the number of training data points to be $O(m)$. Note that although, we have slightly increased the

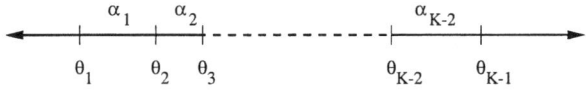

Fig. 1. Graphical representation of the ranking framework.

dimension (by $K - 2$), the number of parameters that needs to be learned is still the same (the classifier and the thresholds). Interestingly, any linear classification method can now be used to solve this problem. It is easy to prove that if there exists a classifier that learns the above rule with no error on the training data then all the α_i's are always positive which is a requirement for the classification problem to be same as ranking problem. Next we show how one can use kernel classifiers (SVM) to solve the ranking problem for datasets where there may not exist a linear ranker.

5 Kernel Classifiers - SVM

In many real world problems it may not be possible to come up with a linear function that would be powerful enough to learn the ranking of the data. In such a scenario, standard practice is to make use of kernels which allow nonlinear mapping of data. We will denote a kernel as $\mathcal{K}(\cdot, \cdot) = \phi^T(\cdot)\phi(\cdot)$ which corresponds to using the non-linear mapping $\phi(\cdot)$ over the original feature vector.

Solving Sorting Problems. For the sorting problem, we propose to learn a linear classifier over the difference feature vectors and then use this learned classifier to sort the data. While using non linear mapping ϕ with corresponding kernel $\mathcal{K}$, this would imply

$$\text{Learn } h: \ y_{ij}^d(\phi(h)^T \phi(x_{ij}^d)) > 0 \Rightarrow h: \ y_{ij}^d(\phi(h)^T \phi(x_i - x_j)) > 0 \quad (5)$$

However, we note that $\phi(x_i - x_j) \neq \phi(x_i) - \phi(x_j)$ because $\phi()$ is a non linear mapping. To get around this, we adopt a different strategy (also proposed in [4]). Instead of solving the classification problem over the difference vector in the original space, we solve the classification problem over the difference vectors in the projected space.

$$\text{Learn } h: \ y_{ij}^d(\phi(h)^T(\phi(x_i) - \phi(x_j))) > 0 \quad (6)$$

Interestingly, it can be solved easily by defining a new kernel function(It can be easily verified that this is a Kernel function) as

$$\mathcal{K}(x_i - x_j, x_l - x_m) = \mathcal{K}(x_i, x_l) + \mathcal{K}(x_j, x_m) - \mathcal{K}(x_i, x_m) - \mathcal{K}(x_j, x_l) \quad (7)$$

Solving Ranking Problems. For solving the ranking problem, we have proposed the mapping given in Eqn. 4. One has to be careful in using kernel classifiers with this mapping. To see this, note that if x_j has rank i, then $\bar{h}^T \bar{x}_j^+ > 0 \Rightarrow h^T x_j > \theta_{i-1}$; $\bar{h}^T \bar{x}_j^- < 0 \Rightarrow h^T x_j > \theta_i$ but $\mathcal{K}(\bar{h}, \bar{x}_j^+) = \phi(\bar{h})^T \phi(\bar{x}_j^+) > 0 \not\Rightarrow \phi(h)^T \phi(x_j) > \theta_{i-1}$ This is again because of the nonlinearity of the mapping $\phi()$. However, one can again get around this problem by defining a new kernel function. For a kernel function $\mathcal{K}$ and the corresponding mapping ϕ, lets define a new kernel function $\overline{\mathcal{K}}$ and with the corresponding mapping $\bar{\phi}()$ as

$$\bar{\phi}(\bar{x}) = [\phi(x), \bar{x}[n+1:n+K-2]]; \quad \bar{\phi}(\bar{h}) = [\phi(h), \bar{h}[n+1:n+K-2]] \quad (8)$$

Note that, only the first n dimensions of $\bar{x}$ corresponding to x are projected to a higher dimensional space. The new kernel function can hence be decomposed into sum of two kernel functions where the first term is obtained by evaluation of kernel over the first n

dimensions of the vector and second term is obtained by evaluating a linear kernel over the remaining dimensions.

$$\overline{\mathcal{K}}(\bar{x}_i, \bar{x}_j) = \mathcal{K}(x_i, x_j) + \bar{x}_i[n+1:n+K-2]^T \bar{x}_j[n+1:n+K-2] \quad (9)$$

However, when using the SVM algorithm with kernels one has to be careful as when working in the embedded space, learning algorithms minimize the norm of $\bar{h}$ and not h as should have been the case. In the next section, we introduce the problem of ordinal regression and show how one can get around this problem.

5.1 Reduction to Ordinal Regression

In this section, we show how one can actually get around the problem of minimizing $||h||$ as against minimizing $||\bar{h}||$. We want to solve the following problem

$$\text{minimize } \frac{1}{2} \| h \|^2; \quad \text{subject to } \bar{y}_j^{+/-}(\bar{h}^T \bar{x}_j^{+/-} + b) > 0 \quad (10)$$

Based on the analysis in Sec. 4, the inequality in the above formulation for x_j with rank y_j can be written as,

$$-b - \sum_{l=n+1}^{n+k-2} \bar{h}(l) \bar{x}_j^-(l) = \theta_{y_j} > h^T x_j > -b - \sum_{l=n+1}^{n+k-2} \bar{h}(l) \bar{x}_j^+(l) = \theta_{y_j-1}; \quad 1 < i \le K$$

In this analysis, we will assume that with respect to threshold θ_i's, there is a margin of at least ϵ such that for any datapoint x_j with corresponding rank y_j, we have

$$\theta_{y_j-1} + \epsilon < h^T x_j; \quad 1 < y_j \le K$$

Now, the problem given in Eqn. 10 can be reframed as

$$\text{minimize } \frac{1}{2} \| h \|^2; \quad \text{subject to } h^T x_j < \theta_{y_j}; \ \forall 1 \le y_j < K \ \ h^T x_j > \theta_{y_j-1} + \epsilon; \ 1 < y_j \le K$$

This leads to the following lagrange formulation,

$$L_P = \frac{1}{2} \| h \|^2 + \sum_{j=1}^{m-m_K} \gamma_j^+ (h^T x_j - \theta_{y_j}) + \sum_{j=m_1+1}^{m} \gamma_j^- (\theta_{y_j-1} + \epsilon - h^T x_j) - \sum_j \gamma_j^+ - \sum_j \gamma_j^-$$

where m_i refers to number of elements having rank 'i'. The ranker h is obtained by minimizing the above cost function under the positivity constraints for γ_j^+ and γ_j^-. Dual formulation L_d of the above problem can be obtained by following steps as in [11],

$$L_d = -\frac{1}{2} \sum_{i=1}^{n} \sum_{j=1}^{n} (\gamma_i^- - \gamma_i^+)(\gamma_j^- - \gamma_j^+) \mathcal{K}(x_i, x_j) - \sum_j \gamma_j^+ - \sum_j \gamma_j^- \quad (11)$$

with constraints,

$$\sum_{p=m_{i-1}+1}^{m_i} \gamma_p^+ = \sum_{p=m_i+1}^{m_{i+1}} \gamma_p^-; \quad \forall i \in [2, K-1] \quad (12)$$

Table 1. (left)Comparison of sorting algorithms for linear data. (right) Comparison of sorting algorithms for nonlinear data.

Algorithm	Ave. No. of Transpositions
Perceptron	36.31
Winnow	35.68
linear-SVM	**30.92**

Algorithm	Ave. No. of Transpositions
Perceptron	62771
Winnow	62840
kernel-SVM	**1456.4**

We have introduced $\gamma_l^+, \gamma_m^- \forall l \in [n_{K-1}+1, n_K]$ and $m \in [1, n_1]$ for simplicity of notation. These are deterministic quantities with value 0. It is interesting to note that, Eqn. 11 has the same form as a regression problem. The value of θ_i's is obtained using Kuhn Tucker conditions.

6 Experiments

In this section, we present experimental results of the various algorithms that have been outlined in this paper. We start off by giving results obtained on synthetic data and then we show results of the performance of ranking for a novel image processing application.

6.1 Synthetic Data

Sorting. First, we compare the performance of Perceptron, Winnow and SVM for sorting problem on linear data. Linear data is obtained by generating N dimensional data x_i; $1 \leq i \leq m$. Data points are sorted based on the value of inner product $w^T x_i$ where w is a randomly generated N dimensional vector. In the following experiments we choose $N = 5, M = 700$ with 200 examples as training data and rest as test data. The performance of the three algorithms was analyzed by computing the minimum number of adjacent transpositions [7] needed to bring the sorting produced by the learned ranker $\hat{Y}$ to the ground truth Y.

In Table. 1, we show the averaged number of transpositions normalized by the length of the sequence for the three methods. It can be observed that linear-SVMs are slightly better than the online learning rules.

Next we compare the performance of the three algorithms on nonlinear data. The data was generated as above with the addition of quadratic non-linearity in the data when obtaining the ground truth sorting. Table. 1 shows the performance of the three algorithms. A radial basis function is used as kernel and it is clear from the results that kernel-SVMs handle non linear data very well. Fig. 2 shows an instance of sorting performed by kernel SVMs for nonlinear data. In this figure, the data is plotted with respect to the ground truth sorting. It is clearly evident that the non-linear SVM is able to capture the inherent nonlinearity.

Ranking. In addition to various ranking algorithms proposed in the paper, one can treat ranking as a multiclass classification problem. We present a comparison of various ranking algorithms on synthetic data and study how their behavior varies with the increase in number of classes/ranks. In particular, we analyze ranking algorithms namely

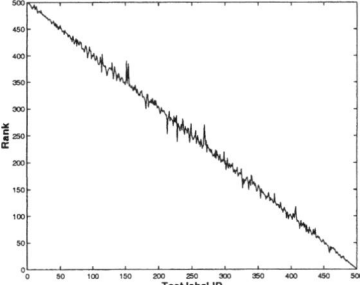

Fig. 2. An example of sorting done using kernel-SVM for nonlinear data. The ideal ranking is a straight line.

Table 2. (left)Comparison of Ranking algorithms for linear data. The rows represent the values of K and the columns correspond to the algorithms A1:SVM using ordinal regression, A2:multi-class SVM, A3:SVMs using appending, A4:Perceptron, A5:Winnow. (right) Comparison of K-ranking algorithms for nonlinear data. The rows represent different K values ranging from 3 to 10 and the columns correspond to the algorithms A1:SVM using ordinal regression, A2:multi-class SVM, A3:SVMs using appending, A4:Perceptron, A5:Winnow.

	A1	A2	A3	A4	A5
K=3	7.8	15.6	7.2	10.1	9.1
K=4	8.3	34.7	8.3	7.0	6.2
K=5	4.5	52.2	4.5	9.0	5.6
K=6	5.1	68.2	5.9	10.6	6.0
K=7	9.8	72.5	9.8	8.3	8.5
K=8	7.7	82.0	7.7	8.9	8.1
K=9	8.5	83.6	8.2	11.1	9.1
K=10	8.0	93.3	7.8	9.6	6.2

	A1	A2	A3	A4	A5
K=3	22.9	51.9	24.3	78.6	83.2
K=4	29.3	65.5	29.0	95.1	97.0
K=5	35.1	87.4	34.8	105.5	105.5
K=6	37.6	93.6	37.7	113.6	108.2
K=7	36.1	104.3	35.6	114.4	116.1
K=8	30.9	107.5	31.1	116.0	111.8
K=9	40.7	108.6	41.1	116.8	117.1
K=10	38.3	118.0	38.2	123.2	130.3

Perceptron, Winnow, SVM using ordinal regression, multi-class SVM and SVMs using appending (by mapping the data to new embedded space as explained in Sec. 4. Multi-class SVM learns K classifiers where each classifier distinguishes one class corresponding to particular rank from the rest of the classes. SVM using ordinal regression and SVM using appending are implementation of the theory discussed in Sec. 5.1 and Section. 4 respectively. Linear data is generated and sorted as before. Now the sorted set is divided into K equally sized groups and labels are assigned to them ranging from $[1, K]$ such that, any item in group i must be placed lower than any other element in group $i - 1$ with respect to some linear hyperplane (unknown to the algorithm). The results are tabulated in Table. 2.

Next, we give the results for the case when there is no linear ranker. Nonlinear data is again generated as discussed earlier Table. 2 shows the results obtained in tabular format. It is clear from both Table. 2 that SVMs using ordinal regression and appending do significantly better than the multi-class SVMs because the former methods capture the inherent structure in the data.

6.2 Automatic Image Focusing

A very nice application of ranking datasets is to rank images I capturing a particular scene based on the level of focus and hence perform defocusing by picking the image which has the highest rank among all the images. We choose this particular application [6] [10][5] to demonstrate the applicability of ranking formulation presented in the paper towards solving the task of automatically extracting the best focused image.

To study the image focusing problem, we started by experimenting with synthetic data. 50 images were take from the corel database. As has been argued in literature, Gaussian blurring is closely related to the noise in a badly focused image and hence we used this method to obtain images which are not focused properly. In particular, each image is blurred two times giving us three images with varying level of focus. The more the blurring is, the worse is the appearance of the image. This whole process resulted in 150 images with varying level of focus. Each of these images were resized to obtain a 120x80 image resulting in a 9600 dimensional vector. Instead of representing the image in such crude form, we use Gabor 2D wavelets [8] to represent each of the image by a 64 dimensional vector. The ranking algorithm discussed earlier is used with rbf(radial basis function) kernel to learn the ranking function. The learned function is then evaluated on the remaining 120 images corresponding to 40 different scenes (three images correspond to each scene). For each scene, the testing task is to figure out the clearest (best focused) image out of the three images. In 95% of the cases (that is in all but two cases), the original image (without Gaussian noise) is picked as the best focused image.

The real test of the algorithm is when it is subject to real data. To do this, we used a digital camera (IBM Web camera) and captured 42 scenes from it. For each scene, three images were taken by manually distorting the focus. Some of these images are shown in Fig. 3. Note that the difference between the focused and unfocused image is very minor (this makes the problem very hard). To test it, we used a novel approach in which we took small amount of real data (since we want to test it on as much real data as possible) – 5 scenes and used all the synthetic data as the training set. Again all the images were of size – 120x80 resulting in a 9600 dimensional feature vector. As with synthetic data, the Gabor signatures are used to represent these image as a 64 dimensional vector. Again, we made use of our ranking algorithm with rbf kernel function to learn the ranker. When tested on remaining 37 scenes, we found that except for 2 cases, in 35 cases the algorithm picked the correct image. Some of the images ranked by our system are presented in Fig. 3. The strength and generalization capabilities of the algorithm are clearly evident from the fact that the classifier which was learned with only a small number of real training images (and synthetic images) did so well on the test data.

7 Summary

In this paper, we have presented an algorithm to reduce both sorting and ranking problems to a binary classification problem. We have also shown how one can make use of kernels to solve these problems in higher dimensional spaces. Moreover, our reduction of the ranking problem to a binary classification problem results in a straightforward

Fig. 3. Some synthetic(top row) and real(bottom row) images used to test our system.

application of online/batch classification algorithms. The main contribution of the paper is that training can be done with linear amount of data using a novel formulation of the ranking problem. Our results on synthetic and real data shows that these algorithms are viable and can be used in practice.

References

1. W. Cohen, R. Schapire, and Y. Singer. Learning to order things. *Artificial Intelligence Research*, 10:243–279, 1999.
2. K. Crammer and Y. Singer. Pranking with ranking. In T. G. Dietterich, S. Becker, and Z. Ghahramani, editors, *Advances in Neural Information Processing Systems 14*, Cambridge, MA, 2002. MIT Press.
3. E. Frank and M. Hall. A simple approach to ordinal classification. *Lecture Notes in Computer Science*, 2167:145–??, 2001.
4. R. Herbrich, T. Graepel, and K. Obermayer. Large margin rank boundaries for ordinal regression. *Advances in Large Margin Classifiers, MIT press*, pages 115–132, 2000.
5. B. K. P. Horn. Focusing. *Technical Report AIM-160, Massachusetts Institute of Technology*, May 1968.
6. R. A. Jarvis. Focus optimisation criteria for computer image processing. *Microscope*, 24(2):163–180, 1976.
7. G. Lebanon and J. Lafferty. Cranking: Combining rankings using conditional probability models on permutations. In *Proceedings of the 19th International Conference on Machine Learning (ICML)*, San Francisco, CA, 2002. Morgan Kaufmann Publishers.
8. T. S. Lee. Image representation using 2d gabor wavelets. *IEEE Transactions on Pattern Analysis and Machine Intelligence*, 18(10):959–971, 1996.
9. N. Littlestone. Learning quickly when irrelevant attributes abound: A new linear threshold algorithm. *Machine Learning*, 2(4):115–132, 1988.
10. J. F. Schlag, A. C. Sanderson C. P. Neumann, and F. C. Wimberly. Implementation of automatic focusing algorithms for a computer vision system with camera control. *Technical Report CMU-RI-TR-83-14, Carnegie Mellon University*, August 1983.
11. A. Smola and B. Schlkopf. A tutorial on support vector regression. In *NeuroCOLT2 Technical Report NC2-TR-1998-030*, 1998.
12. D. Roth S. Har-Paled and D. Zimak. Constraint classification: A new approach to multiclass classification. In *13th Interntional Conference on Algorithmic Learning Theory*, pages 365–379, 2002.
13. B. Pfahringer S. Kramer, G. Widmer and M. de Groeve. Prediction of ordinal classes using regression trees. In *International Syposium on Methodologies for Intelligent Systems*, pages 426–434, 2000.

Using MDP Characteristics to Guide Exploration in Reinforcement Learning

Bohdana Ratitch and Doina Precup

McGill University, Montreal, Canada
{bohdana,dprecup}@cs.mcgill.ca,
http://www.cs.mcgill.ca/{~sonce,~dprecup}

Abstract. We present a new approach for exploration in Reinforcement Learning (RL) based on certain properties of the Markov Decision Processes (MDP). Our strategy facilitates a more uniform visitation of the state space, a more extensive sampling of actions with potentially high variance of the action-value function estimates, and encourages the RL agent to focus on states where it has most control over the outcomes of its actions. Our exploration strategy can be used in combination with other existing exploration techniques, and we experimentally demonstrate that it can improve the performance of both undirected and directed exploration methods. In contrast to other directed methods, the exploration-relevant information can be precomputed beforehand and then used during learning without additional computation cost.

1 Introduction

One of the key features of reinforcement learning (RL) is that a learning agent is not instructed what actions it should perform; instead, the agent has to evaluate all available actions [13], and then decide for itself on the best way of behaving. This creates the need for an RL agent to actively explore its environment, in order to discover good behavior strategies. Ensuring an efficient exploration process and balancing the risk of taking exploratory actions with the benefit of information gathering are of great practical importance for RL agents, and have been the topic of much recent research, e.g., [14,7,2,4,12].

Existing exploration strategies can be divided into two broad classes: undirected and directed methods. *Undirected methods* are concerned only with ensuring *sufficient* exploration, by selecting all actions infinitely often. The ε-greedy and Boltzman exploration strategies are notable examples of such methods. Undirected methods are very popular because of their simplicity, and because they do not have additional requirements of storage or computation. However, they can be very inefficient for certain domains. For example, in deterministic goal directed tasks with a positive reward received only upon entering the goal state, undirected exploration is exponential in the number of steps needed for an optimal agent to reach the goal state [14]. On the other hand, by using some information about the course of learning, the same tasks can be solved in time polynomial in the number of states and maximum number of actions available in each state [14]. The impact of exploration is believed to be even more important for stochastic environments. *Directed exploration* strategies attempt not only to ensure a sufficient amount of exploration, but also to make the exploration *efficient*, by using additional information about the learning process. These techniques often aim to achieve a more uniform exploration of the state space, or to balance the relative profit of discovering new information versus exploiting current knowledge. Typically, directed methods keep track of information regarding the learning process and/or learn a model of the system. This requires extra computation and storage in addition to the resources needed by general on-line RL algorithms, in order to make better exploration decisions. More details on existing exploration methods are given in Section 2.2.

In this paper, we present a new directed exploration approach, which takes into account the properties of the Markov Decision Process (MDP) being solved. In prior work [9], we introduced several attributes that can be used to provide a quantitative characterization of MDPs. Our approach to exploration is based on the use of the two attributes: state transition entropy and forward controllability. The state transition entropy provides a characterization of the amount of stochasticity in the environment. Forward controllability measures how much the agent's actions actually impact the trajectories that the agent follows. Our prior experimental results [9] suggest that these attributes significantly affect the quality of learning for on-line RL algorithms with function approximation, and that this effect is due in part to the amount of exploration in MDPs with different characteristics. In this paper, we show how to use these MDP attributes in combination with both undirected and directed existing exploration methods.

Using MDP attributes can improve the exploration process in three ways. First, it encourages a more homogeneous visitation of the state space, similar to other existing directed methods. Second, it encourages more frequent sampling for actions with potentially high variance in their action-value estimates. Finally, it encourages the learning agent to focus more on the states in which its actions have more impact. One important difference between our exploration strategy and other directed techniques is that the extra information we use reflects only properties of the task at hand, and does not depend on the history of learning. Hence, this information does not carry the bias of previous, possibly unfortunate exploration decisions. Additionally, in some cases the MDP attributes can be pre-computed beforehand and then used during learning without any additional computational cost. The attributes' values can also be transferred between tasks if the agent is faced with solving multiple related tasks in an environment in which the dynamics does not change much. The attributes can also be estimated during learning, which would require only a small constant amount of additional resources in contrast to most other directed methods.

The rest of the paper is organized as follows. In Section 2, we provide background on RL and existing exploration approaches. The details of the proposed exploration method are presented in Section 3. Empirical results are discussed in Section 4. The directions for future work are presented in Section 5.

2 Background

2.1 RL Framework

We assume the standard RL framework, in which a learning agent is situated in a dynamic stochastic environment and interacts with it at discrete time steps. The environment assumes states from some *state space S* and the agent chooses actions from some *action space A*. On each time step, in response to the agent's actions, the environment undergoes state transitions governed by a stationary probability distribution $P^a_{ss'}$, where $s, s' \in S, a \in A$. At the same time, the agent receives a numerical *reward* from the environment, $R^a_{ss'} \in \Re$, which reflects the one-step desirability of the agent's actions. State transitions and rewards are, in general, stochastic and satisfy the *Markov property*: their distributions depend only on the current state of the environment and the agent's current action and are independent of the past history of interaction. The goal of the agent is to adopt a *policy* (a way of choosing actions) $\pi : S \times A \rightarrow [0, 1]$ that optimizes a *long-term performance* criterion, called *return*, which is usually expressed as a cumulative function of the rewards received on successive time steps. Such a learning problem is called a Markov Decision Process (MDP). Many RL algorithms estimate *value functions* which can be viewed as utilities of states and actions. Value functions are estimates of the expected returns and take into account any uncertainty pertaining to the environment or the agent's action choices. For instance, the *action-value function* associated with a policy π, $Q^\pi : S \times A \rightarrow \Re$, is defined as:

$$Q^\pi(s,a) = E_\pi \{r_{t+1} + \gamma r_{t+2} + \ldots | s_t = s, a_t = a\}$$

where $\gamma \in (0, 1]$ is the discount factor. The optimal action value function, Q^*, is defined as the action-value function of the best policy: $Q^*(s,a) = \max_\pi Q^\pi(s,a)$. In this paper, we focus on RL algorithms that estimate the optimal action-value function from samples obtained by interacting with the environment.

2.2 Exploration in RL

The goal of an exploration policy is to allow the RL agent to gather experience with the environment in such a way as to find the optimal policy as quickly as possible, while also gathering as much reward as possible during learning. This goal can be itself cast a learning problem, often called *optimal learning* [6]. Solving this problem would require the agent to have a probabilistic model of the uncertainty about its own knowledge of the environment, and to update this model as learning progresses. Solving the optimal learning problem then becomes equivalent to solving the partially observable MDP (POMDP) defined by this model, which is generally intractable. However, various heuristics can be used to decide which exploration policy to follow, based only on certain aspects of the uncertainty about the agent's knowledge of the environment.

As discussed in Section 1, existing exploration techniques can be grouped in two main categories: undirected and directed methods. Undirected methods ensure that each action will be selected with non-zero probability in each visited state. For instance, the ε-*greedy exploration strategy* selects the currently greedy action (the best according to the current estimate of the optimal action-value function $Q(s,a)$), in any given state, with probability $(1 - \varepsilon)$, and selects a uniformly random action with probability ε. Another popular choice for undirected exploration, the *Boltzman distribution* assigns probability $\pi(s,a)$ of taking action a in state s as $\pi(s,a) = e^{\frac{Q(s,a)}{\tau}} / \sum_{b \in A} e^{\frac{Q(s,b)}{\tau}}$, where τ is a positive temperature parameter that decreases the amount of randomness as it approaches zero. When using on-policy RL algorithms, such as SARSA [13], the exploration rate (ε in the ε-greedy exploration and τ in Boltzman exploration) has to decrease to zero with time in an appropriate manner [11] in order to ensure convergence to the optimal (deterministic) policy. In practice, however, constant exploration rates are often used.

Directed exploration methods typically keep some information about the state of knowledge of the agent, estimating certain aspects of its uncertainty. The action to be taken is usually selected by maximizing an evaluation function that combines action-values with some kind of *exploration bonuses*, δ_i:

$$N(s,a) = K_0 Q(s,a) + K_1 \delta_1(s,a) + ... + K_k \delta_k(s,a) \quad (1)$$

Exploration is driven mainly by the exploration bonuses that change over time. The positive constants K_i control the exploration-exploitation balance.

Directed exploration methods differ in the kind of exploration bonuses they define, which reflect different heuristics regarding what states are important to revisit. For example, counter-based methods [14] direct exploration toward the states that were visited least frequently in the past. Recency-based exploration [14, 12] prefers instead the states that were visited least recently. In both of these cases, the result is a more homogeneous exploration of the state space. Error-based exploration [10] prefers actions leading to states whose value changed most in past updates. Interval Estimation (IE) [3, 16], as well as its global equivalent, IEQL+ [7], bias exploration toward actions that have the highest variance in the action value samples. In the value of information strategy [1, 2], the exploration-exploitation tradeoff is solved with a myopic approximation of the value of perfect information. The E^3 algorithm [4] learns a model of the MDP. Based on the estimated accuracy of this model and a priori knowledge of the worst-case mixing time of the MDP and the maximum attainable returns, E^3 explicitly balances the profit of exploitation and the possibility of efficient exploration. Due to this balancing, E^3 provably achieves near-optimal performance in polynomial time. However, there is little practical experience available with this algorithm.

3 Using MDP Attributes for Exploration

Similarly to many directed exploration methods, the goal of our approach is to ensure a more uniform visitation of the state space, while also gathering quickly the samples most needed to estimate well the action value function. In order to achieve this goal, we focus on using two attributes that can be used to characterize MDPs: state transition entropy (STE) and forward controllability (FC). In prior work [9], we found that these attributes had a significant effect on the speed of learning and quality of the solution found by on-line RL algorithms. This effect seemed to be due mostly to their influence on the RL agent's exploration of the state space. Both attributes can be computed for each state-action pair (s,a) based on the MDP model (if it is known) or they can be estimated based on sample transitions. The basic idea of our strategy is to favor exploratory actions which exhibit high values of STE, FC, or both of these features. We will now explain the details of our approach.

State transition entropy (STE) measures the amount of stochasticity due to the environment's state dynamics. Let $O_{s,a} \in S$ denote a random variable representing the outcome (next state) of the transition from state s when the agent performs action a.

Using the standard information-theoretic definition of entropy, STE for a state-action pair (s,a) can be computed as follows [5]:

$$STE(s,a) = H(O_{s,a}) = -\sum_{s' \in S} P^a_{s,s'} \log P^a_{s,s'} \quad (2)$$

A high value of $STE(s,a)$ means that there are many possible next states s' (with $P^a_{s,s'} \neq 0$) which occur with similar probabilities. If in some state s, actions a_1 and a_2 are such that $STE(s,a_1) > STE(s,a_2)$, the agent is more likely to encounter more different states by taking action a_1 than by taking action a_2. This means that giving preference to actions with higher STE could achieve a more homogeneous exploration of the state space. Empirical evidence that a homogeneous visitation of the state space can be helpful is present in [13], where the performance of Q-learning with an ε-greedy behavior policy is compared with the performance of Q-learning performed by picking states uniformly randomly. The experiments were performed on discrete random MDPs with different branching factors. Note that a large branching factor means a high STE value for all states. In these tasks, the ε-greedy on-policy updates resulted in better solutions and faster learning mainly for the deterministic tasks (with branching factor 1). As the branching factor (and thus STE) increased, performing action-value updates uniformly across the state space led to better solutions in the long run, and to better learning speed.

Another potential consequence of a high value of $STE(s,a)$ is a large variance of the action-value estimates for (s,a). In on-policy learning methods, such as SARSA [13], the action value of a state-action pair (s,a) is updated toward a *target estimate* obtained after taking action a:

$$Q(s,a) \leftarrow (1-\alpha)Q(s,a) + \alpha\underbrace{[R^a_{ss'} + \gamma Q(s',a')]}_{\text{Target for }(s,a)}, \alpha \in (0,1)$$

These target estimates are drawn according to the probability distribution of the next state s'. If $STE(s,a)$ is high, there will be many possible next states, and consequently the variance in the target estimates could be higher. In prior experiments using the SARSA(0) learning algorithm with linear function approximation [9], we observed that in environments with high STE values, there was a trade-off in the quality of the approximation achieved between the positive effect of "natural" exploration and the negative effect of high variance in the target action-value estimates used by the algorithm. In order to get a good estimate of $Q(s,a)$ when the target values have high variance, more samples are needed. By encouraging the exploration of actions with high STE values, our strategy ensures that we will collect enough samples. This idea is reminiscent of the IE directed exploration method [3], but we do not rely on explicitly estimating the variance of the action value samples, which would be much more expensive in terms of both storage and computation.

The *controllability* of a state s is a normalized measure of the information gain when predicting the next state based on knowledge of the action taken, as opposed to making the prediction before an action is chosen (a similar, but not identical, attribute is used by Kirman [5]). Let $O_s \in S$ denote a random variable representing the outcome of a uniformly random action in state s. Let $O_s \in S$ denote a random variable representing the outcome of a uniformly random action in state s. Let A_s denote a random variable representing the action taken in state s. We consider A_s to be chosen from a uniform distribution. Given the value of A_s, information gain is the reduction in the entropy of O_s: $H(O_s) - H(O_s|A_s)$, where

$$H(O_s) = -\sum_{s' \in S} \left(\frac{\sum_{a \in A} P^a_{s,s'}}{|A|}\right) \log\left(\frac{\sum_{a \in A} P^a_{s,s'}}{|A|}\right); \quad H(O_s|A_s) = -\sum_{a \in A} \frac{1}{|A|} \sum_{s' \in S} P^a_{s,s'} \log(P^a_{s,s'})$$

The controllability in state s is defined as:

$$C(s) = \frac{H(O_s) - H(O_s|A_s)}{H(O_s)} \quad (3)$$

If all actions are deterministic, then $H(O_s|A_s) = 0$ and $C(s) = 1$. If $H(O_s) = 0$ (all actions deterministically lead to the same state), then $C(s)$ is defined to be 0. The *forward controllability* (FC) of a state-action pair is the expected controllability of the next state:

$$FC(s,a) = \sum_{s' \in S} P^a_{s,s'} C(s') \quad (4)$$

Favoring actions with high FC will direct an RL agent toward states in which it has a lot of control on the next state transitions, by making appropriate action choices. Having such control enables the agent to reap higher returns in environments where some trajectories are more profitable than others, as shown in our prior experiments [9]. At the same time, actions with high FC lead to states in which different actions have very different outcomes. Hence, from such states, the agent is likely to explore the state space more uniformly. A third reason to favor actions with high values of $FC(s,a)$ is that, similarly to the case of high STE, such actions can potentially have high variance in the targets used to update their action values, $Q(s,a)$. If a resulting state, s', is highly controllable, the actions a' available there could lead to very different next states, and hence $Q(s',a')$ is likely to have high variance. As a result, gathering more samples from (s,a) should increase the speed of learning.

The idea of guiding exploration based on the values of the STE and FC attributes can easily be incorporated in both undirected and directed exploration techniques. For instance, consider the case of the ε-greedy exploration strategy. The greedy action is still chosen with probability $(1-\varepsilon)$. When a choice to explore is made (with probability ε), the exploratory action is selected according to a Boltzman distribution:

$$\pi(s,a) = \frac{e^{\frac{K_1 * STE(s,a) + K_2 * FC(s,a)}{\tau}}}{\sum_{b \in A} e^{\frac{K_1 * STE(s,b) + K_2 * FC(s,b)}{\tau}}} \quad (5)$$

where τ is the temperature parameter. The nonnegative constants K_1 and K_2 can be used to adjust the relative contribution of each term. Of course, STE and FC can be used with probability distributions other than Boltzman as well.

In directed exploration, the STE and FC attributes can be used as additional exploration bonuses, and hence can be easily incorporated in most existing methods. In this case, the behavior policy deterministically picks the action maximizing the function:

$$N(s,a) = K_0 Q(s,a) + K_1 STE(s,a) + K_2 FC(s,a) + \sum_j K_j \delta_j(s,a) \quad (6)$$

where $\delta_j(s,a)$ can be any exploration bonuses based on data about the learning process, such as counter-based, recency-based, error-based or IE-based bonuses. In this case, the trade-off between exploitation and exploration can be controlled by tuning the parameters K_i associated with each term.

Note that our exploration approach uses only characteristics of the environment, which are *independent of the learning process*. Thus, the information needed can be gathered prior to learning. This can be done if the transition model is known, or if the agent has an access to a simulator, with which it can interact to estimate the attributes from sampled state transitions[1]. Also, the attributes' values can be carried over if the task changes slightly (e.g., in the case of goal-directed tasks in which the goal location moves over time). Alternatively, the attributes can be computed during learning based on observed state transitions. This can be done efficiently by incremental methods for entropy estimation [15] and mean estimation with a forgetting factor for FC. In this case, only a small constant amount of extra computation per time step is needed. This is in contrast to most other directed exploration methods, which not only rely on estimation of transition probabilities, but also require more computation to re-evaluate their exploration-relevant information on every time step, e.g., [14,4,12,3,16,2]. At the same time, the exploration-relevant information based on the learning history used in other directed techniques can carry the bias of previous (possibly unsuccessful) exploration decisions and value estimates.

4 Experimental Results

In order to assess empirically the merit of using STE and FC as heuristics for guiding exploration, we experimented with using these attributes together with ε-greedy exploration (as a representative of undirected methods) and recency-based exploration (as a representative of directed methods). We chose recency-based exploration among the directed exploration techniques because in previous experiments [14] it compared favorably to other directed methods, while being less sensitive to the tuning of its parameters. At the same time, this method is conceptually close to attribute-based exploration, in that it encourages a homogeneous exploration of the state space. Hence, it is interesting to see whether the use of MDP attributes can give any additional benefit in this case.

The attributes were incorporated into the ε-greedy strategy as shown in (5). We used parameter settings $K_1, K_2 \in \{0,1\}$, $\tau = 1$ and $\varepsilon \in \{0.1, 0.4, 0.9\}$. The recency-based technique was combined with the attributes based on the idea of additive exploration bonuses, as shown in (6), where we used one recency-based exploration bonus, $\delta(s,a)$. As before, we used $K_1, K_2 \in \{0,1\}$. The constant corresponding to the value function was set to $K_0 \in \{1, 10, 50\}$ and the constant corresponding to the recency bonus was $K_3 = 1$. The learning algorithm used was tabular SARSA(0) with a decreasing learning rate $\alpha(s_t, a_t) = \frac{1.25}{0.5 + n(s_t, a_t)}$, where $n(s_t, a_t)$ is the number of visits to a state-action pair (s_t, a_t) at time t. The action values $Q(s,a)$ were initialized to zero at the beginning of learning.

---

[1] Note that even if the MDP model is known, it is often not feasible to apply dynamic programming methods and the issue of efficient exploration is still important. As suggested in [17], model-based exploration methods are in fact superior to model-free methods in many cases.

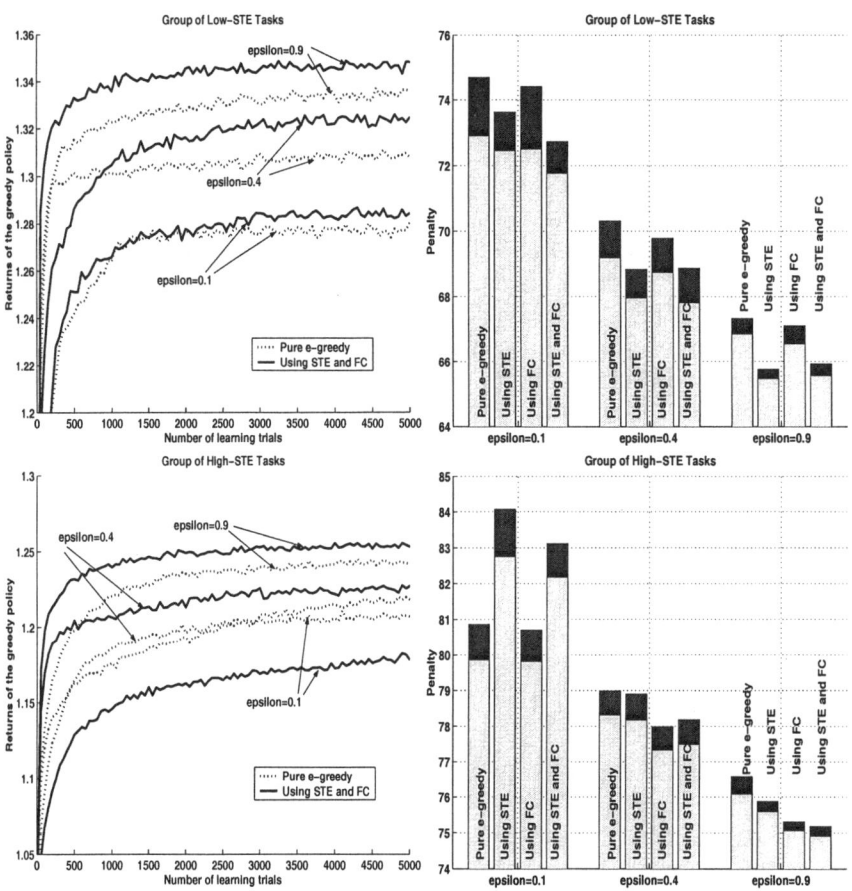

Fig. 1. Performance of ε-greedy exploration (pure and attribute-based) for low-STE (top) and high-STE tasks (bottom)

The experiments were conducted on randomly generated MDPs with 225 states and 3 actions available in every state. The branching factor for these MDPs varied randomly between 1 and 20 across the states and actions. Transition probabilities and rewards were also randomly generated, with rewards drawn uniformly from [0, 1]. At each state, there was a 0.01 probability of terminating the episode. These random MDPs were divided in four groups of five tasks each. Two of the groups contained MDPs with "low" average STE values ($avg(STE(s,a)) < 1.7$), and the other two groups contained MDPs with "high" STE values ($avg(STE(s,a)) \in [1.7, 2.7]$). This grouping allowed us to investigate whether the overall amount of stochasticity in the environment influences the effect of the attributes on exploration. The two groups on each STE level differed in that one of them (which we will call the *test group*) had a large variation in the attribute values for different actions, while the other one (the *control group*) had similar values of the attributes across all states and actions. In the control groups, we would expect to see no effect of using the attributes, because the exploration decisions at all states and actions should be mostly unaffected by the attribute values. Hence, we use the control groups to test the possibility of observing any effect "by chance". The experimental results presented below are for the case, where the attributes where precomputed from simulation of the MDPs prior to learning. Preliminary experiments, where the attributes were computed during learning, indicate qualitatively similar results.

We use two measures of performance for the exploration algorithms under consideration. The first measure is an estimate of the return of the greedy policy produced by the algorithms at different points in time. After every 50 trials, we take the greedy policy with respect to the current action values and we run this policy from 50 fixed test states, uniformly sampled from the state space. We run 30 trials from each such state, then we average these returns over the trials and over the 50 states. Because we are using different tasks, with different optimal value functions (and hence different upper bounds on the performance that can be achieved), it is difficult to compare greedy returns directly, without any normalization. Hence, we normalize the average greedy return by the average return of the uniformly random policy from the same 50 states (computed over 30 trials). In our prior experiments [9] we found that this normalization yields very similar results to normalizing by the return of the optimal policy. Of course, using the optimal policy would generally give the best normalization, but the optimal policy cannot always be computed by independent means.

The second performance measure that we use is aimed at providing a quantitative measure of both the speed of learning and the quality of the solution obtained. It is often difficult to compare different algorithms in terms of both of these measures, because one algorithm may have a steeper learning curve, but a more erratic (or worse) performance in the long run. In order to assess these kinds of differences, we use the following penalty measure for each run:

$$P = \sum_{t=1}^{T} \frac{t}{T}(R_{max} - R^t), \quad (7)$$

where R_{max} is an upper limit of the (normalized) return of the optimal policy[2], R^t is the (normalized) greedy return after trial t and T is the number of trials. In this way, failure to achieve the best known performance is penalized more after more learning trials have occurred. This measure gives a lower penalty to methods that achieve good solutions earlier and do not deviate from them. In our experiments, we compute one penalty for every independent run of every algorithm (which can be viewed as a "summary" for the run).

The results of the experiments are presented in Figure 1, for the ε-greedy strategy, and in Figure 2, for recency-based exploration. The performance measures are computed in terms of the normalized greedy returns, averaged over the 5 MDPs in each group and over 30 runs for each MDP. The left panels represent learning curves for the normalized greedy returns, while the right panels represent the average penalty measure over the runs, computed using (7). Light lower portions of the bars represent mean penalty, and they are topped with standard deviation (dark portions).

We also performed statistical tests to verify whether the observed performance differences are statistically significant. Because we are interested in both the asymptotic

---
[2] This limit can be either known or estimated as a maximum return ever observed for a task.

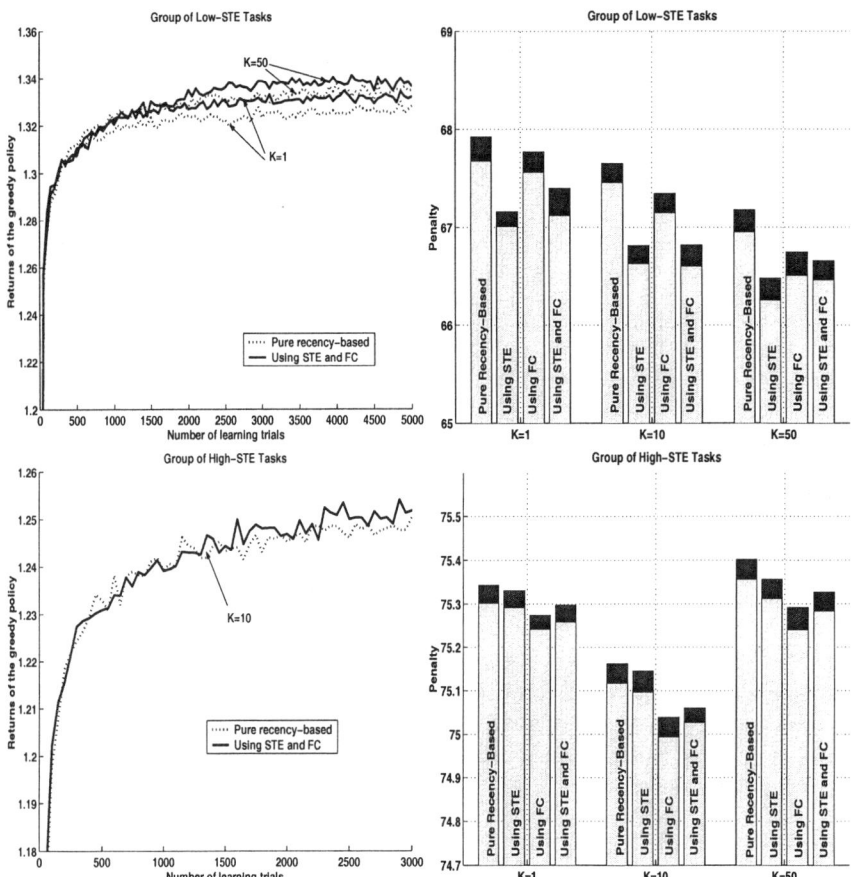

Fig. 2. Performance of pure and attribute-based recency exploration for the low-STE (top) and high-STE tasks (bottom)

performance and the speed of learning, we used a randomized ANOVA procedure [8] to compare the learning curves of the different algorithms. This procedure is more appropriate than the conventional one for comparing learning curves, because it does not rely on the assumption of homogeneity of co-variance, which is violated when there are carry-over effects. We performed the analysis separately on the learning curves for each task. We also performed two-way ANOVA of the penalty measure averaged over the 5 MDPs in each group. In this case, one factor was the tunable parameter for the "pure" exploration strategy (ε for the ε-greedy and K for the recency-based) and the other factor was the variant of the corresponding strategy (pure vs. using the attribute(s)).

As shown in Figure 1, incorporating the attributes into the ε-greedy strategy has a positive effect both for the low-STE and for the high-STE test, in all cases except $\varepsilon = 0.1$ in high-STE environments. The randomized ANOVA test for learning curves showed a difference in the performance between the pure strategy and each of the three attribute-based variants at the level of significance no smaller than $p = 0.008$ for each task and for each setting of ε. The penalty measure graphs show that the positive effect of using STE becomes more significant as ε increases, and this trend is especially pronounced in the case of the high-STE tasks. In this case, most estimates $Q(s,a)$ have high variance, but with a small exploration rate, many actions are not sufficiently sampled. Using STE allows more samples to be gathered for such actions, and hence improve the solution quality. FC has a greater positive effect for the high-STE tasks, as can be seen from the penalty graphs in the right panels of Fig.1, mainly because it improves the speed of learning (the learning curves are not shown here, due to lack of space). This shows that encouraging the agent to learn about states where it can better control the course of state transitions is helpful especially given a background of high overall stochasticity. The two-way ANOVA test on the penalty measure showed that the positive effect of using the attributes is significant.

Figure 2 presents the same performance measures when incorporating the attributes in the recency-based exploration strategy. The recency-based method is significantly more robust to the tuning of its main parameter, K_0 than the ε-greedy strategy is to the tuning of ε. With all the settings of K_0, the performance of this strategy is close to the best performance of the ε-greedy strategy (obtained at $\varepsilon = 0.9$). However, using the MDP attributes further improves performance of the recency-based method as well, although the effects appear to be smaller than in the case of the ε-greedy method (we believe this is due to a ceiling effect). Although the differences appear to be small, the statistical tests show that most differences are significant. In particular, the randomized ANOVA test shows a significant difference between learning curves in the low-STE group at the level no smaller than $p = 0.04$ for all tasks and all attribute versions. For the high-STE tasks, significance levels range from $p = 0.04$ for the version using only FC to $p = 0.226$ for the version using only STE. The two-way ANOVA on the penalty measure is also less significant for the recency-based strategy in the high-STE group ($p = 0.03$ for comparison of the pure vs. FC-based variant and $p = 0.11$ for pure vs. STE-based variant). Similar to the case of the ε-greedy strategy, FC appears to have a greater positive effect for the high-STE tasks.

For both the ε-greedy and recency-based strategies, in most cases, using STE and FC together produces an improvement which is very similar to the best improvement obtained by using either one of the attributes in isolation. For the low-STE test group, the STE attribute brings a bigger performance improvement, whereas for the high-STE test group, FC has a bigger effect. Thus, it would be reasonable to always use the combination of two attributes to achieve the best improvement. Note that the improvements were obtained without tuning any additional parameters, both for the ε-greedy and the recency-based methods.

The results of the experiments conducted on the control groups did not reveal any effect of using the attributes with either the ε-greedy or recency-based exploration. This reinforces our conclusion that the effects observed on the test groups are not spurious.

5 Conclusions and Future Work

In this paper, we introduced a novel exploration approach based on the use of specific MDP characteristics. Exploration decisions are made independently of the course of learning so far, based only on properties of the environment. Our technique facilitates a more homogeneous exploration of the state space, a more extensive sampling of actions with a potentially high variance of the action-value function estimates and encourages the agent to focus on states where it has most control over the outcomes of its actions. In our experiments, using these attributes improved performance for both undirected (ε-greedy) and directed (recency-based) exploration in a statistically significant way. The improvements were obtained without tuning any additional parameters. The attribute values can be pre-computed before the learning starts, or they can be estimated during learning. In the latter case, the amount of additional storage and computation is much less compared to other directed techniques.

We are currently conducting a more detailed empirical study using toy hand-crafted MDPs in order to better understand the circumstances under which the use of MDP attributes to guide exploration is most beneficial. We also plan to investigate the use of other attributes, e.g. the risk of taking exploratory actions and variance of immediate rewards.

References

1. Dearden, R., Friedman, N., Russell, S.: Bayesian Q-learning. In Proc. AAAI (1998) 761-768
2. Dearden, R., Friedman, N., Andre, D.: Model-Based Bayesian Exploration. In Proc. of the 15th UAI Conference (1999) 150-159
3. Kaelbling, L.P.: Learning in embedded systems (1993) Cambridge, MIT Press
4. Kearns, M., Singh, S.: Near-Optimal Reinforcement Learning in Polynomial Time. In Proc. of the 15th ICML (1998) 260-268
5. Kirman, J.: Predicting Real-Time Planner Performance by Domain Characterization. Ph.D. Thesis, Brown University (1995)
6. Kumar, P.R.: A survey of some results in stochastic adaptive control. SIAM Journal of Control and Optimization **23** (1985) 329-338
7. Meuleau, N., Bourgine, P.: Exploration of Multi-State Environments: Local Measures and Back-Propagation of Uncertainty. Machine Learning **35**(2) (1999) 117-154
8. Piater, J.H., Cohen, P.R., Zhang,X., Atighetchi, M.: A Randomized ANOVA Procedure for Comparing Performance Curves. In Proc. of the 15th ICML (1998) 430-438
9. Ratitch, B., Precup,D.: Characterizing Markov Decision Processes. In Proc. of the 13th ECML (2002) 391-404
10. Schmidhuber, J.H.: Adaptive Confidence and Adaptive Curiosity. Technical Report FKI-149-91, Technische Universitat Munchen (1991)
11. Singh, S., Jaakkola, T., Littman, M.L.,Szepesvari, C.: Convergence Results for Single-Step On-Policy Reinforcement Learning Algorithms. Machine Learning, **39** (2000) 287-308
12. Sutton, R.: Integrated architecture for learning, planning and reacting based on approximating dynamic programming. In Proc. of the 7th ICML (1990) 216-224
13. Sutton, R.S., Barto, A.G.: Reinforcement Learning. An Introduction. The MIT Press (1998)
14. Thrun,S.B.: Efficient Exploration in Reinforcement Learning. Technical Report CMU-CS-92-102. School of Computer Science, Carnegie Mellon University (1992)
15. Vignat C., Bercher, J.-F.: Un estimateur récursif de l'entropie. 17ème Colloque GRETSI, Vannes (1999) 701-704
16. Wiering, M.A., Schmidhuber, J.: Efficient Model-Based Exploration. In Proc. of the 5th International Conference on Simulation of Adaptive Behavior (1998) 223-228
17. Wiatt, J.: Exploration and Inference in Learning from Reinforcement. Ph.D. Thesis. University of Edingburg (1997)

Experiments with Cost-Sensitive Feature Evaluation

Marko Robnik-Šikonja

University of Ljubljana
Faculty of Computer and Information Science
Tržaška 25, 1001 Ljubljana, Slovenia
Marko.Robnik@fri.uni-lj.si

Abstract. Many machine learning tasks contain feature evaluation as one of its important components. This work is concerned with attribute estimation in the problems where class distribution is unbalanced or the misclassification costs are unequal. We test some common attribute evaluation heuristics and propose their cost-sensitive adaptations. The new measures are tested on problems which can reveal their strengths and weaknesses.

1 Introduction

Feature (attribute) evaluation is an important component of many machine learning tasks, e.g., feature subset selection, constructive induction, decision and regression tree learning. In feature subset selection we need a reliable and practically efficient method for estimating the relevance of the features to the target concept, so that we can tackle learning problems where hundreds or thousands of potentially useful features describe each input object. In the constructive induction we try to enhance the power of the representation language and therefore introduce new features. Typically many candidate features are generated and again we have to evaluate them in order to decide which to retain and which to discard. While constructing a decision or regression tree the learning algorithm at each interior node selects the splitting rule (feature) which divides the problem space into subspaces. To select an appropriate splitting rule the learning algorithm has to evaluate several possibilities and decide which would partition the given problem most appropriately. Feature rankings and numerical estimates provided by evaluation algorithms are also an important source of information for a human understanding of certain tasks.

While historically the majority of machine learning research have been focused on reducing the classification error, there also exists a corpus of work on cost-sensitive classification where all errors are not equally important (see on-line bibliography [13]). In general, differences in importance of errors are handled through the cost of misclassification.

This work is concerned with the cost-sensitive attribute estimation and we assume that costs can be presented with the cost matrix C, where $C(i,j)$ is the cost (could also be benefit) associated with prediction that an example belongs to the class τ_j where in fact it belongs to the class τ_i. The optimal prediction for an example $\mathbf{x}$ is the class τ_i that minimizes the expected loss:

$$L(\mathbf{x}, \tau_i) = \sum_{j=1}^{c} P(\tau_j|\mathbf{x})C(j,i),$$

where $P(\tau_j|\mathbf{x})$ is the probability of the class τ_j given example $\mathbf{x}$. The task of a learner is therefore to estimate these conditional probabilities. Feature evaluation measure need not be cost-sensitive for decision tree building, as shown by [1,3,4]. However, cost-sensitivity is a desired property of an algorithm which tries to rank or weight features according to their importance. Such ranking can be used for feature selection and feature weighting or shown to human experts to confirm/expand their domain knowledge. This is especially important in the fields like medicine where experts posses great deal of intuitive knowledge.

We will investigate some properties of attribute evaluation measures, like how do they behave on imbalanced data sets, scale with increasing number of classes, whether they detect (conditional) dependencies between attributes and to what extent they are cost-sensitive. We propose several cost-sensitive variants of common attribute evaluation measures and test them on artificial data sets which can reveal their properties.

Throughout the paper we use the notation where each learning instance $I_1, I_2, ..., I_n$ is represented by an ordered pair $(\mathbf{x}_k, \tau)$, where each vector of attributes $\mathbf{x}_k$ consists of individual attributes A_i, $i = 1, ..., a$, (a is the number of attributes) and is labeled with the target value τ_j, $j = 1, ..., c$ (c is the number of class values). Each discrete attribute A_i has values a_1 through a_{m_i}. Notation $I_{i,j}$ presents the value of j-th attribute for the instance I_i, and $I_{i,\tau}$ presents its class value. We write $p(a_{i,k})$ for the probability that the attribute A_i has value a_k, $p(\tau_k)$ is the probability of the class τ_k, and $p(\tau_j|a_{i,k})$ is the probability of the class τ_j conditioned by the attribute A_i having the value a_k.

The paper is organized into 5 sections. In Section 2 we review some selected attribute evaluation measures and in Section 3 we test how imbalanced class distribution affects their performance. In Section 4 we describe how to extend these measures to use the information from the cost matrix and in Section 5 we evaluate the proposed extensions. Section 6 concludes the work.

2 Attribute Evaluation Measures

The problem of attribute estimation has received much attention in the literature. There are several measures for estimating attributes' quality. In classification problems these are e.g., Gini index [1], Gain ratio [11], Relief [5], ReliefF [6], MDL [7], and DKM [2].

Except Relief and ReliefF all these attribute evaluation measures are impurity based, meaning that they measure impurity of the class value distribution. They assume the conditional (upon the class) independence of the attributes, evaluate each attribute separately and not take the context of other attributes into account. In problems which possibly involve much feature interactions these measures are not appropriate. Relief and ReliefF do not make this assumption and can correctly evaluate attributes in problems with strong dependencies between the attributes. We will first present measures based on impurity followed by ReliefF.

2.1 Impurity Based Measures

These measures evaluate each attribute separately by measuring impurity of the splits resulting from partition of the learning instances according to the values of the evaluated attribute. The general form of all impurity based measures is:

$$M(A_i) = i(\tau) - \sum_{j=1}^{a_{m_i}} p(a_{i,j}) i(\tau | a_{i,j}) ,$$

where $i(\tau)$ is the impurity of class values before the split, and $i(\tau | a_{i,k})$ is the impurity of class values after the split on $A_i = a_{k,j}$. By subtracting weighted impurity of the splits from the impurity of unpartitioned instances we measure gain in the purity of class values resulting from the split. Larger values of $M(A_i)$ imply pure splits and therefore good attributes. We cannot directly apply these measures to numerical attributes, but we can use any of the number of discretization techniques first and then evaluate discretized attributes. We consider three measures as examples of impurity based attribute evaluation.

Gain Ratio [11] is implemented in C4.5 program and is the most often used impurity based measure. It is defined as

$$GR(A_i) = \frac{\sum_{i=1}^{c} p(\tau_i) \log p(\tau_i) - \sum_{j=1}^{a_{m_i}} \sum_{i=1}^{c} p(\tau_i | a_{i,j}) \log p(\tau_i | a_{i,j})}{\sum_{j=1}^{a_{m_i}} p(a_{i,j}) \log p(a_{i,j})} . \quad (1)$$

Its gain part tries to maximize the difference of entropy (which serves as impurity function) before and after the split. To prevent excessive bias towards multiple small splits the gain is normalized with the attribute's entropy.

DKM [2] has the following form of impurity function:

$$i(\tau) = 2\sqrt{p(\tau_{max})(1 - p(\tau_{max}))} , \quad \text{where} \quad p(\tau_{max}) = \max_{i=1}^{c} p(\tau_i) \quad (2)$$

is the most probable class value (the one which labels the split). Drummond and Holte [3] have shown that for binary attributes this function is invariant to changes in the proportion of different classes, i.e. it is cost-insensitive.

MDL is based on Minimum Description Length principle and measures the quality of attributes as their ability to compress the data. The difference in coding length before and after the value of the attribute is revealed corresponds to the difference in impurity. Kononenko [7] has shown empirically that this criterion has the most appropriate bias concerning multi-valued attributes among a number of other impurity-based measures. It is defined as:

$$MDL(A_i) = \frac{1}{n}\left(\log_2\binom{n}{n_{1.},...,n_{c.}} - \sum_{j=1}^{a_{m_i}}\log_2\binom{n_{.j}}{n_{1j},...,n_{cj}}\right.$$
$$\left. + \log_2\binom{n+c+1}{c-1} - \sum_{j=1}^{a_{m_i}}\log_2\binom{n_{.j}+c-1}{c-1}\right) \quad (3)$$

Here n is the number of training instances, $n_{i.}$ the number of training instances from class i, $n_{.j}$ the number of instances with j-th value of given attribute, and n_{ij} the number of instances from class i with j-th value of the attribute.

2.2 ReliefF

ReliefF algorithm [6,12] is an extension of Relief [5]. Unlike Relief it is not limited to two class problems, is more robust, and can deal with incomplete and noisy data. The idea of Relief and ReliefF is to evaluate partitioning power of attributes according to how well their values distinguish between similar instances. An attribute is given a high score if its values separate similar observations with different class and do not separate similar instances with the same class values. ReliefF samples the instance space, computes the differences between predictions and values of the attributes and forms a statistical measure for the proximity of the probability densities of the attribute and the class. Assigned quality evaluations are in the range $[-1, 1]$.

Pseudo code of the algorithm is given on Figure 1. ReliefF randomly selects an instance R_i (line 3), and then searches for k of its nearest neighbors from the same class, called nearest hits H (line 4), and also k nearest neighbors from each of the different classes, called nearest misses $M(t)$ (lines 5 and 6). It updates the quality estimation W_v for all attributes depending on their values for R_i, hits H and misses $M(t)$ (lines 7 and 8). The process is repeated for m times.

The update formula balances the contribution of hits and all the misses, and averages the result of m iterations:

$$W_v = W_v - \frac{1}{m}\mathrm{con}(A_v, R_i, H) + \frac{1}{m}\sum_{\substack{t=1\\t \neq R_{i,\tau}}}^{c}\frac{p(\tau_t)\mathrm{con}(A_v, R_i, M(C))}{1 - p(R_{i,\tau})} \quad (4)$$

where $\mathrm{con}(A_v, R_i, S)$ is the contribution of k nearest instances from the set S (hits or misses). In the simplest case it can be an average difference of attribute's

Algorithm ReliefF
Input: for each training instance a vector of attribute values and the class value
Output: the vector W with the evaluation for each attribute

1. **for** v = 1 **to** a **do** $W_v = 0$
2. **for** i = 1 **to** m **do begin**
3.   randomly select an instance R_i
4.   find k nearest hits H
5.   **for** each class $t \neq R_{i,\tau}$ **do**
6.   from class t find k nearest misses $M(t)$
7.   **for** v = 1 **to** a **do**
8.   update W_v according to Eq. (4)
9. **end;**

Fig. 1. Pseudo code of ReliefF algorithm.

values for k instances:

$$\text{con}(A_v, R_i, S) = \frac{1}{k} \sum_{j=1}^{k} \text{diff}(A_v, R_i, S_j) \ .$$

Here diff(A_v, I_t, I_u) denotes the difference between the values of the attribute A_v for two instances I_t and I_u. For nominal and numerical attributes, respectively, it can be defined as:

$$\text{diff}(A_v, I_t, I_u) = \begin{cases} 0; & I_{t,v} = I_{u,v} \\ 1; & \text{otherwise} \end{cases}, \quad \text{diff}(A_v, I_t, I_u) = \frac{|I_{t,v} - I_{u,v}|}{\max_{l=1}^{n} I_{l,v} - \min_{l=1}^{n} I_{l,v}} \ . \quad (5)$$

In this work we use exponentially decreasing weighted contribution of instances ranked by distance ($k = 70$, $\sigma = 20$ as recommended by [12]):

$$\text{con}(A_v, R_i, S) = \frac{\sum_{j=1}^{k} \text{diff}(A_v, R_i, S_j) e^{-\left(\frac{\text{rank}(R_i, S_j)}{\sigma}\right)^2}}{\sum_{l=1}^{k} e^{-\left(\frac{\text{rank}(R_i, S_l)}{\sigma}\right)^2}} \ .$$

In (4) the contribution of each misses' class is weighted with the prior probability of that class $p(\tau_t)$. Since the contributions of hits and misses in each step should be in $[0, 1]$ and also symmetric, the misses' probabilities have to sum to 1. As the class of hits is missing in the sum we have to divide each probability weight with factor $1 - p(R_{i,\tau})$.

Selection of k hits and k misses from each class instead of just one hit and miss and weighted update of misses is the basic difference to Relief. It ensures greater robustness of the algorithm concerning noise and favorable bias concerning multi-valued attributes and multi-class problems.

Table 1. Characteristics of the problems.

name	c	class distribution	a	#inf	#rnd	n	ε distribution by (7)
C2u	2	0.5, 0.5	9	4	5	1000	0.05 0.95
C2i	2	0.9, 0.1	9	4	5	1000	0.31 0.69
C3u	3	0.33, 0.33, 0.33	11	6	5	1000	0.06 0.18 0.76
C3i	3	0.8, 0.15, 0.05	11	6	5	1000	0.33 0.30 0.37
C5u	5	0.2, 0.2, 0.2, 0.2, 0.2	15	10	5	1000 0.01 0.01 0.03 0.06 0.89
C5i	5	0.5, 0.3, 0.15, 0.04, 0.01	15	10	5	1000 0.16 0.17 0.22 0.12 0.33
C2xu	2	0.5, 0.5	13	8	5	1000	0.05 0.95
C2xi	2	0.9, 0.1	13	8	5	1000	0.31 0.69
C3xu	3	0.33, 0.33, 0.33	17	12	5	1000	0.06 0.18 0.76
C3xi	3	0.8, 0.15, 0.05	17	12	5	1000	0.33 0.30 0.37
C5xu	5	0.2, 0.2, 0.2, 0.2, 0.2	25	20	5	1000 0.01 0.01 0.03 0.06 0.89
C5xi	5	0.5, 0.3, 0.15, 0.04, 0.01	25	20	5	1000 0.16 0.17 0.22 0.12 0.33

3 Imbalanced Data Sets

Misclassification costs are often closely related with imbalanced distribution of class values in the data set (rare classes usually being of higher interest). We first test an ability of described measures to detect attributes which identify minority class values and, for now, we do not assume any knowledge of costs. For that matter we constructed three problems, C2, C3 and C5 with 2, 3, and 5 class values (available labels are c1, c2, c3, c4, or c5). For each class value (2, 3, or 5) we construct two binary attributes A-c?-90 and A-c?-70 (with values 0 and 1). Each binary attribute identifies one class value in 90% or 70% of the cases (e.g., the value of attribute A-c2-90 is 1 in 90% of the cases where the instance is labeled with c2; if label is different from c2, the attribute's value is randomly assigned). In each problem we also have 5 binary random attributes (R-50, R-60, R-70, R-80, and R-90), with 50%, 60%, 70%, 80%, and 90% of 0 values.

To test detection of conditional dependencies we transformed C2, C3 and C5 in such a way, that we replaced each of the informative binary attributes with two attributes, which are XOR of the original attribute (e.g., A-c2-90 is replaced with X1-c2-90 and X2-c2-90, where their values are assigned in such a way that the parity bit of the two attributes equals the value of A-c2-90). We call the transformed problems C2x, C3x, and C5x, respectively.

To observe how the distribution of class values influences the evaluation measures we formed two versions of each problem, one with uniform distribution of class values (data sets with suffix 'u') and one with imbalanced distribution of class values (data sets with suffix 'i'), so altogether 12 data sets. Distribution of class values and characteristics of the problems are given in Table 1.

We begin our analysis with two class problems. Note that for all measures higher score means better attribute, but the scores are not comparable between measures or across problems.

Left-hand side of Table 2 gives evaluations for the problem where class values are uniformly distributed (C2u problem). All the measures give expected rankings, i.e, attributes identifying values in 90% of the cases have higher scores than 70% attributes. All informative attributes were assigned higher scores than R_{max}, which is the highest score assigned to one of the five random attributes. If its value is larger than the value of some informative attribute that attribute is indistinguishable from random attributes for the respective measure.

Right-hand side of Table 2 contains evaluations for the two class, imbalanced problem (C2i). As before impurity-based measures rank 90% attributes higher than 70% attributes, and they also rank higher the attributes identifying more probable class. ReliefF, on the contrary ranks the minority class higher. The reason for this as well as for the high score of random attribute (R-50) becomes evident if we consider the space of attributes and its role in (4). The negative update of nearest hits in this two cases is likely to be zero (nearest instances have the same values of attributes), and so the positive update of nearest misses is not canceled for random attributes and the attributes identifying minority class.

Table 2. Feature evaluations for C2u and C2i.

	C2u, uniform					C2i, imbalanced				
measure	A-c1-90	A-c1-70	A-c2-90	A-c2-70	R_{max}	A-c1-90	A-c1-70	A-c2-90	A-c2-70	R_{max}
Gain ratio	0.171	0.022	0.193	0.027	0.001	0.078	0.007	0.031	0.017	0.002
DKM	0.110	0.015	0.122	0.018	0.001	0.045	0.007	0.039	0.020	0.003
MDL	0.149	0.018	0.164	0.022	-0.003	0.041	0.002	0.026	0.012	-0.002
ReliefF	0.156	0.033	0.130	0.029	0.008	0.185	0.137	0.301	0.183	0.141

Similar results for three class problems are collected in Table 3. Due to space constraints we omit results for A-c1-70 and A-c2-70, as they show similar trend than A-c3-70, but are always assigned higher scores. With uniform class distribution (left-hand side of the table) all measures except DKM separate informative from random attributes and rank 90% attributes higher than 70% attributes. The values of DKM are completely uninformative (after the split the probability of the majority class is around 0.5, giving high impurity impression). With imbalanced class distribution (p(0)=0.8, p(1)=0.15, p(2)=0.05; right-hand side of the table), all measures rank attributes identifying more frequent classes higher than attributes identifying less frequent classes, 90% attributes higher than 70% attributes, and do not distinguish between A-c3-70 and random attribute with maximal score. ReliefF improves its behavior compared to two class problems, because of more attributes (distances are larger and hits start to normalize the excessive contributions of the misses) and because of its normalizing factor for misses in (4). We get similar results and trends for 5 class problems so we skip the details.

In all problems where informative attributes are replaced with two XOR-ed attributes (C2xi, C2xu, C3xi, C3xu, C5xi, C5xu) the impurity functions do not differentiate between informative and random attributes, while ReliefF does, except for 70% attributes and the best random attribute (R-50). As it is well established fact that ReliefF can detect attributes with strong interactions and

Table 3. Feature evaluations for C3u and C3i.

measure	C3u, uniform					C3i, imbalanced				
	A-c1-90	A-c2-90	A-c3-90	A-c2-70	R_{max}	A-c1-90	A-c2-90	A-c3-90	A-c3-70	R_{max}
Gain ratio	0.138	0.118	0.121	0.029	0.002	0.223	0.066	0.028	0.002	0.002
DKM	-0.055	-0.053	-0.054	-0.038	-0.014	0.121	0.040	0.002	0.001	0.004
MDL	0.123	0.103	0.109	0.021	-0.001	0.149	0.057	0.019	-0.006	-0.000
ReliefF	0.108	0.093	0.086	0.027	0.006	0.262	0.191	0.127	0.094	0.096

impurity based measures cannot this is an expected result but shows that this ability exists in the imbalanced data sets as well. We skip the details.

The attribute evaluation measures we described so far did not take cost information into account. Surely, if such information is available we want that measures take it into account and give higher scores to attributes identifying classes whose misclassification cost is higher. We present such measures in the next section.

4 Implanting Cost-Sensitivity

There are different techniques how to incorporate cost information into learning. The key idea is to use expected cost of misclassification [1,13]. Following [8], we define expected cost of misclassifying an example that belongs to the i-th class as

$$\varepsilon_i = \frac{1}{1-p(\tau_i)} \sum_{\substack{j=1 \\ j \neq i}}^{c} p(\tau_j) C(i,j) \qquad (6)$$

and than change the probability estimates for class values:

$$p'(\tau_i) = \frac{p(\tau_i)\varepsilon_i}{\sum_{j=1}^{c} p(\tau_j)\varepsilon_j} . \qquad (7)$$

We use (7) in (1) and (2) to make Gain ratio and DKM cost sensitive. In (1) conditional probabilities $p(\tau_i | a_{i,j})$ are also computed in the spirit of (7). We call the respective measures GRatioC and DKMc. This adaptation has the same effect as sampling the data proportionally to (7). MDL uses length of the code instead of probabilities, so we cannot use this approach, but we can sample the data according to (7) and run MDL (3) on the resulting data set. The resulting measure is referred to as MDLs.

For two class problems [8] have adapted Relief[1] to use cost by changing its update formula[2]:

$$W_v = W_v - \text{diff}(A_v, R_i, H)/m + \frac{\varepsilon_{R_i,\tau}}{\sum_{j=1}^{c} p(\tau_j)\varepsilon_j} \text{diff}(A_v, R_i, M))/m . \qquad (8)$$

---
[1] Relief uses one nearest hit H and one nearest miss M, so we use diff instead of con.
[2] This formula was typeset incorrectly in [8] (confirmed by M. Kukar, personal communication). Eq. (8) is the correct version which was actually implemented.

This adaptation (called ReliefK in results below) is tailored for two class problems. As we were not satisfied with its performance on multi-class problems we tried different multi-class extensions and used $p'(\tau_i)$ instead of $p(\tau_i)$ in (4). We denote this extension with ReliefFp'. If we use just the information from cost matrix and do not take prior probabilities into account, similarly to (6) and (7), we compute average cost of misclassifying an example that belongs to the i-th class as

$$\alpha_i = \frac{1}{1-c} \sum_{\substack{j=1 \\ j \neq i}}^{c} C(i,j) . \tag{9}$$

The prior probability of class value becomes

$$\bar{p}(\tau_i) = \frac{\alpha_i}{\sum_{j=1}^{c} \alpha_i} . \tag{10}$$

We use $\bar{p}(\tau_i)$ instead of $p(\tau_i)$ in (4) and call this version ReliefF$\bar{p}$. For two class problems ReliefF, ReliefFp', and ReliefF$\bar{p}$ are identical.

Another idea how to use the cost information stems from the generalized form of ReliefF [12]:

$$W_v^G = \sum_{I_t, I_u \in \mathcal{I}} \text{similarity}(\tau, I_t, I_u) \cdot \text{similarity}(A_v, I_t, I_u) ,$$

where I_t and I_u are appropriate samples drawn from the instance population $\mathcal{I}$. For attribute similarity ReliefF uses negative diff function (5) and for class similarity it uses

$$\text{similarity}(\tau, I_t, I_u) = \begin{cases} 1 \; ; \; I_{t,\tau} = I_{u,\tau} \\ -1 \; ; \; I_{t,\tau} \neq I_{u,\tau} \end{cases} , \tag{11}$$

which together gives exactly updates for hits and misses in original Relief. The obvious place to use cost information is therefore (11), which affects the update formula (4). We used cost information in the form of expected and average cost. Using the expected cost, the contribution of class differences in hits costs $\varepsilon_{R_i,\tau}$, and different class of miss prevents the actual cost, so (4) changes to

$$W_v = W_v - \varepsilon_{R_i,\tau} \text{con}(A_v, R_i, H)/m$$
$$+ \sum_{\substack{t=1 \\ t \neq R_{i,\tau}}}^{c} \frac{p(\tau_t) C(R_{i,\tau}, \tau_t) \text{con}(A_v, R_i, M(t))/m}{1 - p(R_{i,\tau})} . \tag{12}$$

We call this measure ReliefFeC. While its updates are symmetric for hits and misses, note that they are not normalized to [0,1], so the scores of the attributes are not necessary normalized to [-1,1] . If we use just cost information (no priors) then we can use average cost of misclassification (ReliefFaC variant)

$$W_v = W_v - \alpha_{R_i,\tau} \text{con}(A_v, R_i, H)/m$$
$$+ \sum_{\substack{t=1 \\ t \neq R_{i,\tau}}}^{c} \frac{C(R_{i,\tau}, \tau_t) \text{con}(A_v, R_i, M(t))/m}{c-1} . \tag{13}$$

For two class problems ReliefFec and ReliefFac are identical.

We assumed that $C(i,i) = 0$, i.e., that predicting correct class implies no cost. If we are using benefit matrix instead of cost matrix, this is usually not the case, and we suggest using actual $C(i,i)$ instead of expected and average cost as normalizing factor for hits in (12) and (13).

Alternatively, instead of using costs directly, we can change the sampling to reflect the cost matrix as in [1,10]. While this approach may not reflect all the details of cost matrix, it may still work well in practice. We made sampling of random instances of class j in ReliefF (line 3 on Figure 1) proportional to (7). The resulting measure is called ReliefFs. In the next section we test how these measures exploit cost information.

5 Using Cost Information

Following the arguments of [4] and [9] not all cost matrixes are sensible and realistic. We try to test our measures with realistic cost matrixes, e.g., detecting exception for C2, progressive health risk for C3 and financial loss for C5 problems:

$$C2: \begin{bmatrix} 0 & 1 \\ 20 & 0 \end{bmatrix} \quad C3: \begin{bmatrix} 0 & 1 & 1 \\ 5 & 0 & 1 \\ 20 & 5 & 0 \end{bmatrix} \quad C5: \begin{bmatrix} 0 & 1 & 1 & 1 & 1 \\ 2 & 0 & 1 & 1 & 1 \\ 5 & 4 & 0 & 1 & 1 \\ 10 & 9 & 6 & 0 & 1 \\ 100 & 99 & 96 & 91 & 0 \end{bmatrix}$$

The right-most column of Table 1 presents the probability distributions by (7) computed from the given class distributions and cost matrixes.

In Table 4 we give results for two and three class problems with imbalanced distribution (C2i and C3i). Uniform distribution is nonrealistic with cost matrix information, so we skip these results. A-70$_{min}$ denotes 70% attribute with minimal score and R_{max} random attribute with maximal score.

For two class problem C2i (left-hand side of Table 4) MDLc and all variants of ReliefF reflect cost-sensitivity, i.e., they evaluate A-c2-90 as better than A-c1-90 (c2 has higher cost assigned, so attribute identifying it is more useful). These measures also separate 90% attributes from the random attributes. Only MDLs separates 70% attribute with minimal score from random attributes for 2 class problems, while none of the measures cannot do that for 3 and 5 class problems, which means, that random attributes are more difficult to detect in the cost-sensitive context. GRatioC and DKMc are also cost-sensitive but fail to separate A-c1-90 from the random attributes.

For three class problem C3i (right-hand side of Table 4) MDLs, ReliefF$\bar{p}$, ReliefFp' and GRatioC are the most cost-sensitive (which can be seen by comparing results with Table 3), followed by ReliefFeC and ReliefFac. ReliefFs and ReliefK are cost-sensitive to a lesser extent. DKMc once again fails completely for multi-class problems as the changed probability distribution moved towards the uniform distribution.

Table 4. Cost-sensitive feature evaluations for C2i and C3i.

measure	C2i				C3i				
	A-c1-90	A-c2-90	A-70$_{min}$	R$_{max}$	A-c1-90	A-c2-90	A-c3-90	A-70$_{min}$	R$_{max}$
GRatioC	-0.029	0.114	0.000	0.000	0.177	0.132	0.169	0.009	0.020
DKMc	-0.007	0.083	0.000	0.000	-0.035	-0.032	-0.032	-0.029	0.000
MDLs	0.095	0.189	0.021	-0.000	0.185	0.106	0.144	0.003	0.007
ReliefK	0.078	0.107	0.000	0.034	0.125	0.034	0.044	0.008	0.018
ReliefFp'	0.185	0.306	0.137	0.141	0.286	0.200	0.195	0.136	0.133
ReliefF$\bar{p}$	0.185	0.306	0.137	0.141	0.306	0.208	0.252	0.171	0.166
ReliefFeC	0.236	0.335	-0.125	-0.072	0.405	0.029	0.092	-0.132	-0.020
ReliefFaC	0.236	0.335	-0.125	-0.072	0.352	0.105	0.182	-0.001	0.000
ReliefFs	0.083	0.123	-0.045	-0.025	0.167	0.025	0.050	-0.049	-0.006

These findings are even more radical for the five class problem C5i, where only ReliefF$\bar{p}$, ReliefFp', MDLs and GRatioC can separate 90% attributes from random ones. ReliefFeC and ReliefFaC use (6) and (9) to normalize its hits so they are less stable when large differences between entries in cost matrix are not reflected by sufficiently large number of instances. ReliefFs also suffers from insufficient number of instances, while ReliefK is not properly normalized for multi-class problems.

In problems with XOR-ed attributes ReliefF based measures are cost-sensitive and can differentiate between informative and random attributes, while impurity based measures cannot.

6 Conclusions

We have investigated the performance of common attribute evaluation measures in problems where the class distribution is imbalanced and in problems with unequal misclassification costs. For that matter we constructed several data sets and adapted existing measures. Impurity based measures were adapted by including expected misclassification costs into class probabilities or through sampling. Adaptations of ReliefF stemmed from the expected misclassification cost, average misclassification cost, general form of ReliefF, and cost stratified sampling.

Imbalanced data sets cause no problems to Gain ratio, MDL and ReliefF, while DKM works only for two class problems. Only ReliefF detects highly dependent attributes.

In problems with unequal misclassification costs only MDLs and two variants of ReliefF, which use probability estimates (7) and (10) in the update formula (4), reliably exploit information from cost matrix. Cost-sensitive adaptation of Gain ratio fails to detect all important attributes in two class problem, while DKM is useless for multi-class problems. ReliefF variants retain its ability to detect highly dependent attributes.

While feature evaluation measures need not be cost-sensitive for decision tree building, in further work we want to test this hypothesis the presented measures. We will also investigate feature selection and weighting in the cost-sensitive context.

References

[1] Leo Breiman, Jerome H. Friedman, Richard A. Olshen, and Charles J. Stone. *Classification and regression trees*. Wadsworth Inc., Belmont, California, 1984.

[2] Thomas G. Dietterich, Michael Kerns, and Yishay Mansour. Applying the weak learning framework to understand and improve C4.5. In Lorenza Saitta, editor, *Machine Learning: Proceedings of the Thirteenth International Conference (ICML'96)*, pages 96–103. Morgan Kaufmann, San Francisco, 1996.

[3] Chris Drummond and Robert C. Holte. Exploiting the cost (in)sensitivity of decision tree splitting criteria. In *Proceedings of the Seventeenth International Conference on Machine Learnintg (ICML-2000)*, pages 239–246, 2000.

[4] Charles Elkan. The foundations of cost-sensitive learning. In *Proceedings of the Seventeenth International Joint Conference on Artificaial Intelligence (IJCAI'01)*, 2001.

[5] Kenji Kira and Larry A. Rendell. A practical approach to feature selection. In D. Sleeman and P. Edwards, editors, *Machine Learning: Proceedings of International Conference (ICML'92)*, pages 249–256. Morgan Kaufmann, San Francisco, 1992.

[6] Igor Kononenko. Estimating attributes: analysis and extensions of Relief. In Luc De Raedt and Francesco Bergadano, editors, *Machine Learning: ECML-94*, pages 171–182. Springer Verlag, Berlin, 1994.

[7] Igor Kononenko. On biases in estimating multi-valued attributes. In *Proceedings of the International Joint Conference on Artificial Intelligence (IJCAI'95)*, pages 1034–1040. Morgan Kaufmann, 1995.

[8] Matjaž Kukar, Igor Kononenko, Ciril Grošelj, Katarina Kralj, and Jure Fettich. Analysing and improving the diagnosis of ischaemic heart disease with machine learning. *Artificial Intelligence in Medicine*, 16:25–50, 1999.

[9] Dragos D. Margineantu. On class-probability estimates and cost-sensitive evaluation of classifiers. In *Workshop on Cost-Sensitive Learning at the Seventeenth International Conference on Machine Learning (WCSL at ICML-2000)*, 2000.

[10] Dragos D. Margineantu and Thomas G. Dietterich. Bootstrap methods for the cost-sensitive evaluation of classifiers. In *Machine Learning: Proceedings of Seventeenth International Conference on Machine Learning (ICML'2000)*, pages 583–590. Morgan Kaufmann, San Francisco, 2000.

[11] J. Ross Quinlan. *C4.5: Programs for Machine Learning*. Morgan Kaufmann, San Francisco, 1993.

[12] Marko Robnik-Šikonja and Igor Kononenko. Theoretical and empirical analysis of ReliefF and RReliefF. *Machine Learning Journal*, 2003. URL http://www.kluweronline.com/issn/0885-6125/. (forthcoming, available also as technical report at http://lkm.fri.uni-lj.si/rmarko/).

[13] Peter D. Turney and Olcay Boz. On-line cost-sensitive learning bibliography, 1996-2001. URL http://home.ptd.net/ olcay/cost-sensitive.html.

A Markov Network Based Factorized Distribution Algorithm for Optimization

Roberto Santana

Institute of Cybernetics, Mathematics, and Physics (ICIMAF),
Calle 15, entre C y D, Vedado, C-Habana, Cuba
Rsantana@icmf.inf.cu

Abstract. In this paper we propose a population based optimization method that uses the estimation of probability distributions. To represent an approximate factorization of the probability, the algorithm employs a junction graph constructed from an independence graph. We show that the algorithm extends the representation capabilities of previous algorithms that use factorizations. A number of functions are used to evaluate the performance of our proposal. The results of the experiments show that the algorithm is able to optimize the functions, outperforming other evolutionary algorithms that use factorizations.

Keywords: Genetic algorithms, EDA, FDA, evolutionary optimization, estimation of distributions.

1 Introduction

In the application of Genetic Algorithms (GAs) [4] to a wide class of optimization problems is essential the identification and mixing of building blocks. It has been early noticed that the Simple GA (SGA) is in general unable to accomplish these two tasks for difficult problems (e.g. deceptive problems). Perturbation techniques, linkage learners and model building algorithms are among the alternatives proposed to improve GAs. They try to identify the relevant interactions among the variables of the problem, and to use them in an efficient way to search for solutions.

Estimation Distribution Algorithms (EDAs) [10] are evolutionary algorithms that do not use the crossover and mutation operators. They construct in each generation a probabilistic model of the selected solutions. The probabilistic model must be able to capture a number of relevant relationships in the form of statistical dependencies among the variables. Dependencies are then used to generate solutions during a sampling step. It is expected that the generated solutions share a number of characteristics with the selected ones. In this way the search is led to promising areas of the search space. The interested reader is referred to [5] for a good survey that covers the theory, and a wide spectrum of EDAs applications.

One efficient way of estimating a probability distribution is by means of factorizations. A probability distribution is factorized when it can be computed as the product of functions defined on subsets of the variables. A subclass of EDAs includes the algorithms that use factorizations of the probability distribution. In this paper we call to this subclass Factorized Distribution Algorithms (FDAs)[1] [9].

FDAs have outperformed other evolutionary algorithms in the optimization of complex additive functions, and deceptive problems with overlapping variables [9]. However, a shortcoming of FDAs is that the probabilistic model they are based on is constrained to represent a limited number of interactions. In this paper we investigate the issue of extending the representation capabilities of FDAs. To this end we introduce the Markov Network FDA (MN-FDA), a new type of FDA based on an undirected graphical model, and able to represent the so called "invalid" factorizations [9].

The paper is organized as follows. In section 2 we discuss the problem of obtaining a factorization of the probability. Section 3 presents the main steps for learning an approximate factorization from data. Section 4 explains the way the sampling step has been implemented. We introduce the MN-FDA in section 5. Section 6 presents the functions used in our experiments. We discuss the numerical results of the simulation. Section 7 analyzes the MN-FDA in the context of recent related research on evolutionary computation, we also present in this section the conclusions of our paper.

2 Factorization of a Probability

The central problem of FDAs is how to efficiently estimate a factorization of the joint probability of the selected individuals. To compute a factorization the theory of graphical models is usually employed. The following definitions will help in the explanation of our proposal.

Let $X = (X_1, X_2, \cdots, X_n)$ represent a vector of integer random variables, where n is the number of variables of the problem. $x = (x_1, x_2, \cdots, x_n)$ is an assignment to the variables, and $p(x)$ is a joint probability distribution to be modeled. Each variable of the problem has associated one vertex in an undirected graph $G = (V, E)$. The graph G is a conditional independence graph respect to $p(x)$ if there is no edge between two vertices whenever the pair of variables is independent given all the remaining variables.

Definition 1. *Given a graph G, a clique in G is a fully connected subset of V. We reserve the letter C to refer to a clique. The collection of all cliques in G is denoted as $\mathcal{C}$. C is maximal when it is not contained in any other clique. C is the maximum clique of the graph if it is the clique in $\mathcal{C}$ with the highest number of vertices.*

Definition 2. *A junction graph (JG) of the independence graph G is a graph where each node corresponds to a maximal clique of G, and there exists an edge*

---
[1] In the literature the term FDA is frequently used to name a particular type of Factorized Distribution Algorithms. Our definition covers it, and other algorithms that use factorizations.

between two nodes if their corresponding cliques overlap. A labeled junction graph is a JG that has an associated ordering of the nodes with a distinguished node called the root, and satisfies that a node belongs to the graph if at least one the variables in the cliques is not contained in the previous nodes in the ordering.

Definition 3. *A junction tree (JT) is a single connected junction graph. It satisfies that if the variable X_k is a member of the junction tree nodes i and j, then X_k is a member of every node on the path between i and j. This property is called the* running intersection property.

If the independence graph G is chordal, an exact factorization of the probability, based on the cliques of the graph, exists. The factorization can be represented using a JT. If G is not chordal, a chordal super-graph of G can be found by adding edges to G in a process called triangulization. The problem is that we can not guarantee that the maximum clique of the super-graph will have a size that would make feasible the calculation of the marginal probabilities. The problem of finding a triangulization with maximum clique of minimum size is NP-complete.

Our goal is to find an approximate factorization that contains as many dependencies as possible, but without adding new edges to the graph. An exact factorization would comprise all the dependencies represented in the independence graph. We will assume that approximate factorizations of the probability are more precise as they include more of the dependencies represented in the independence graph. The approximate factorization will be represented using a labeled JG. The algorithm for learning the probabilistic model has five main steps.

Algorithm 1: Model learning
---
1. Learn an independence graph G from the data (the selected set of solutions).
2. If necessary, refine the graph.
3. Find the set L of all the maximal cliques of G.
4. Construct a labeled JG from L.
5. Find the marginal probabilities for the cliques in the JG.

3 Learning an Approximate Factorization

In this section we consider in detail the different steps for learning an approximate factorization from data.

3.1 Learning of an Independence Graph

The construction of an independence graph from the data can be accomplished by means of independence tests. To determine if an edge belongs to the graph, it is enough to make an independence test on each pair of variables given the rest. Nevertheless, from an algorithmic point of view it is important to reduce the order of the independence tests. Thus, we have adopted the methodology followed previously by Spirtes [12]. The idea is to start from a complete undirected graph, and then try to remove edges by testing for conditional independence between the linked nodes, but using conditioning sets as small as possible.

To evaluate the independence tests we use the Chi-square independence test. If two variables X_i and X_j are dependent with a specified level of significance α, they are joined by an edge. α is a parameter of the algorithm. In the general case we can assume that each edge $i \sim j$ in the initial independence graph is weighted with a value $w(i,j)$ stressing the pairwise interaction between the variables. This information might be available from prior information, or from the statistical tests conducted on the data (the value of the chi-square test). When such information is not available we assume that all the values of the dependencies are equal to a parameter w' (i.e. $w(i,j) = w', \forall i \sim j \in E$).

3.2 Refinement of the Graph

When the independence graph is very dense, we can expect that the dimension of the cliques will increase. An alternative to solve this problem is, in a step previous to the calculation of the cliques, to make the graph sparser. One way of doing this is allowing a maximum number of incident edges to each vertex. If the vertex has more than r incident edges, those with the lower weights are removed. In this way the size of the maximum clique will be always smaller or equal than r. Our refinement algorithms avoids introducing a bias in the way the edges are removed. However, it has a main drawback: it could be the case that there exist more than $MaxEdges$ variables depending from a single one, but the maximum clique where this variable is included be smaller than r. In this case, the procedure that eliminates the edges would remove dependencies from the graph without a real need to do so. We have not found a better practical solution to this problem.

3.3 Maximal Cliques of the Graph

To find all the cliques of the graphs the Ken and Kerbash algorithm [1] is used. This algorithm uses a branch and bound technique to cut off branches that can lead to cliques. Once all the cliques have been found they are stored in a list L, and their weights are calculated from the information about dependencies. The weight of any subgraph G' of G is calculated as $W(G') = \sum_{i \sim j \in G'} w(i,j)$. In this way the weights of the maximal cliques $w(C_i)$ are calculated.

3.4 Construction of the Labeled JG

Algorithm 2 receives the list of cliques L with their weight, and outputs a list L' of the cliques in the labeled JG. The first clique in L' is the root, and the labels of cliques in the labeled JG correspond to their position in the list. Each clique in the labeled JG is a subset of a clique in L.

Algorithm 2: Algorithm for learning a JG

1. Order the cliques in L in a decreasing order according to their weights
2. Add element $L(1)$ to list L'
3. Remove element $L(1)$ from L
4. While L is not empty
5.   Find the first element C in L such that $C \cap (L'(1) \cup L'(2) \cdots \cup L'(NCliques)) \neq C$, and the number of variables in $C \cap L'(1) \cap L'(2) \cdots \cap L'(NCliques)$ is maximized
6.   If $C = \emptyset$ Remove all the elements in L
7.   else Insert C in L'

We focus now on step 5 of algorithm 2. The condition of maximizing the number of variables in $C \cap (L'(1) \cup L'(2) \cdots \cup L'(NCliques))$ states that the clique C in L that has the highest number of overlapping variables with all the variables already in L', will be added to L'. The number of overlapping variables has to be less than the size of the clique, constraint meaning that at least one of the variables in C has not appeared before. If there exist many cliques with maximum number of overlapped variables, the one that appears first in L is added to L'. On the other hand, if the maximum number of overlapped variables is zero, then there exists in the JG more than one connected component. In this case we have a set of junction graphs, however we have preferred to abuse the notation and call it JG, whether it has one or more connected components. Finally, the addition of cliques stops when all the variables are already in the JG.

Marginal probabilities are found by calculating the number of counts associated to each configuration, and normalizing. In the implementation, the learned model's parameters can be changed by adding a perturbation in the form of probabilistic priors.

3.5 Description of an Example of the Learning Algorithm

We introduce an example of the application of algorithm 1. The information about the dependencies among the 12 variables of a given problem is represented by the independence graph shown in figure 1 (left). Let us suppose that the maximum number of incident edges allowed is 6. In the refinement step only edges incident to the vertex x_5 has to be removed. If information were available about the dependencies of each link, the two edges with the weakest dependencies would be removed. In the present example we assume that all the dependencies are equally strong, and two arbitrary edges ($x_1 \sim x_5$ and $x_5 \sim s_{10}$) are removed. The refined graph is shown in figure 1 (right).

In the next step all the maximal cliques of the graph are found. There are 9 maximal cliques, all of order 3. Also in this case the cliques have the same weight, therefore we arbitrarily select the clique (x_1, x_2, x_3) as the root.

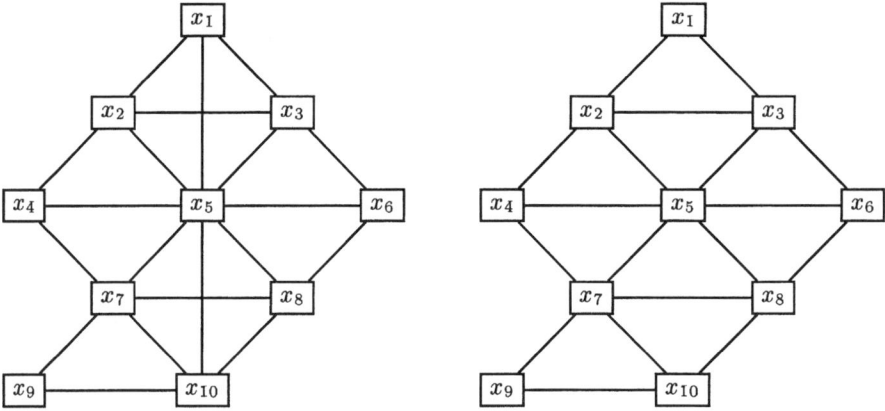

Fig. 1. Original and refined independence graphs.

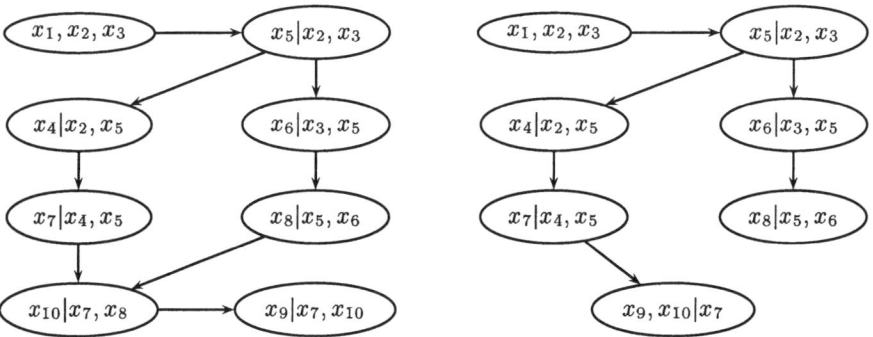

Fig. 2. Ordered junction graph and junction tree.

Construction of the ordered JG: In the first step the clique with maximum overlapping with all the variables already in the ordered JG is (x_2, x_3, x_5). In the next step either of the cliques (x_2, x_4, x_5) or (x_3, x_5, x_6) can be incorporated. Figure 2 (left) shows the final JG. In the cliques shown in the figure, each new variable incorporated to the graph is represented to the left of the bar. Only eight of the cliques are included in the ordered JG, the clique (x_5, x_7, x_8) is missing. Its absence is explained because the algorithm for finding the ordered JG can not guarantee that all the dependencies will be captured. On the other hand, the factorization represented by the labeled JG is invalid because there exists a cycle comprising different cliques.

Construction of the JT: Figure 2 (left) shows the JT obtained using the algorithm. Notice that the JT can represent less dependencies than the JG. As the JT prohibits the existence of cycles, the clique (x_{10}, x_7, x_8) can not be fully represented.

4 Sampling of the Approximate Factorization

Points are sampled from the labeled JG following the order determined by the labels. The variables corresponding to the first clique in the JG are instantiated sampling from the marginal probabilities. For the rest of cliques, each subset of variables that has not been instantiated is sampled conditionally on the variables already instantiated that belong to the clique. The process is very similar to Probabilistic Logic Sampling (PLS) [3], when it is used in junction trees. There exists however an important difference. The definition of JT discards the existence of cycles. A labeled JG can contain cycles, and this fact allows the representation of more interactions, but it does not essentially change the performance of the sampling algorithm. The reason is that in every step of the JG sampling algorithm, the conditioning and conditioned subsets of variables belong to the clique whose variables are being sampled.

5 MN-FDA

Our algorithm is called Markov Network FDA (MN-FDA), its pseudo-code is presented in algorithm 3. The main difference between it and previous FDAs based on undirected models is that it uses as its probabilistic model a labeled JG while previous FDAs based on undirected graphical models [9, 11] represent the factorizations using a JT.

Algorithm 3: MN-FDA

1. Set $t \Leftarrow 0$. Generate $N \gg 0$ points randomly.
2. **do** {
3.   Select a set S of $k \leq N$ points according to a selection method.
4.   Learn a labeled JG from the data.
5.   Calculate the marginal probabilities for all the cliques in the JG.
6.   Generate a the new population sampling from the JG.
7. $t \Leftarrow t + 1$
8. } **until** Termination criteria are met

In all the experiments presented in this paper the algorithm used to learn the independence graph only considered independence tests up to third order. The level of significance α was set to 0.75. This choice was motivated by the need of capturing as many dependencies as possible. Even if some of the found dependencies might be false, this is preferable that missing some of the real dependencies. The number of allowed neighbors for the refinement algorithms was sct to 8.

5.1 Computational Cost of the MN-FDA

The number of operations needed to make the independence tests is upper bounded by $O(Nn^3)$. The worst complexity of the refinement algorithm is bounded by $O(n^2 log(n))$. It has been calculated considering the case when after the independence tests, the graph remains complete. The time complexity of the Bron and Kerbosch algorithm is not calculated in their original work [1]. However from comparisons with other algorithms for which bounds have been calculated the worst comp lexity of the algorithm can be estimated as $O(\mu^2)$, where μ is the number of maximal cliques. When there are at most k edges for each variable and $k << n$, a bound for the number of cliques can be given by kn, and the complexity of the Bron and Kerbosh algorithm roughly estimated as $O(\mu^2) \approx O(n^2)$. The complexity of learning the parameters depends on the size of the population N, the number of cliques μ, and their size. The order of this step is $O(N\mu) \approx O(Nn^2)$. Th e total complexity of the MN-FDA is $O(Nn^3)$.

6 Experiments

In our experiments we compare the behavior of the MN-FDA with the following FDAs: The FDA^* [9], it uses a fixed model of interactions, only the parameters of the cliques are learned in each generation. The Univariate Marginal Distribution Algorithm (UMDA) [6], which uses a model that assumes all the variables are independent. In every step, the algorithm makes a parametric learning of the univariate probabilities. The Tree-FDA [11] uses a probability model where each variable is conditioned on at most one parent. The Learning FDA (LFDA) [8] is a FDA that uses a Bayesian probabilistic model.

First, a number of functions commonly used to evaluate evolutionary algorithms are presented. A practical problem used in the experiments is also described. All the problems used in the experiments are defined on binary variables. The numerical results and the analysis of the experiments are presented afterward.

6.1 Functions Used in the Experiments

Deceptive functions were introduced by Goldberg to show the deceptive nature of the GAs behavior, and to address the problems given by the convergence to local optima of the function. The following 4 elementary deceptive functions of k variables are used to define some of the additive functions used in our experiments. They are defined in terms of the unitation value $u(x) = \sum_{i=1}^{n} x_i$. Each entry of the table shows the evaluation of the corresponding deceptive function when the unitation value of the subset of variables it is evaluated on is u.

u	0	1	2	3	4	5
f^3_{dec}	0.9	0.8	0	1		
f^4_{dec}	3	2	1	0	4	
$IsoT_1$	m	0	0	0	0	0
$IsoT_2$	m	0	0	0	0	$m-1$

$$Onemax(x) = \sum_{i=1}^{n} x_i \qquad (1)$$

$$f_{3deceptive}(x) = \sum_{i=1}^{i=\frac{n}{3}} f^3_{dec}(x_{3i-2}, x_{3i-1}, x_{3i}) \qquad (2)$$

$$Deceptive_4(x) = \sum_{i=1}^{i=\frac{n}{4}} f^4_{dec}(x_{4i-3}, x_{4i-2}, x_{4i-1}, x_{4i}) \qquad (3)$$

$$F_{IsoP}(n, m, k, x) = \left(\sum_{i=1}^{n} x_i\right) \qquad (4)$$
$$+ k \cdot (m+1)((1-x_1) \cdots (1-x_m) x_{m+1} \cdots x_n)$$

When analyzing interactions between variables it is important to consider interactions that do not depend on the linear codification of solutions. To this end we considered function $F_{IsoTorus}$ (5) where x_{up}, x_{left}, etc., are defined as the appropriate neighbors, wrapping around.

$$F_{IsoTorus}(x) = IsoT_1(x_{1-m+n}, x_{1-m+n}, x_1, x_2, x_{1+m}) +$$
$$\sum_{i=2}^{n} IsoT_2(x_{up}, x_{left}, x_i, x_{right}, x_{down}) \qquad (5)$$

Function *BigJump* (6) was introduced in [7]. A valley has to be crossed in order to reach the global optimum of this function. The bigger the parameter m is for this function, the wider the valley. k can be increased to give bigger weight to the maximum.

$$BigJump(u, n, m, k) = \begin{cases} u & for\ 0 \leq u \leq n-m \\ 0 & for\ n-m \leq u \leq m \\ k \cdot n & for\ \quad u = m \end{cases} \qquad (6)$$

The generalized Ising model (7) is described by the energy functional (Hamiltonian) where L is the set of sites called a lattice. Each spin variable σ_i at site $i \in L$ either takes the value 1 or value -1. A specific choice of values for the spin variables is called a configuration. The constants J_{ij} are the interaction coefficients. In our experiments we take $h_i = 0$, $\forall i \in L$. The ground state is the configuration with minimum energy.

$$H = -\sum_{i<j \in L} J_{ij} \sigma_i \sigma_j - \sum_{i \in L} h_i \sigma_i \qquad (7)$$

6.2 Numerical Results

In all the experiments we use the truncation selection. In the following tables n is the number of variables, N is the population size, $succ$ is the number of times the optimum was reached in 100 experiments, gen the average number of generations to convergence, $\hat{f}$ the average fitness of the best found solutions, and $eval$ is the average number of evaluations needed to find the optimum.

Table 1. Comparison between the MN-FDA with other FDAs for unitation functions.

	OneMax				BigJump(30,3,1)				Deceptive4		
n	Alg.	N	$succ.$	n	Alg.	N	$succ.$	n	Alg.	N	$succ.$
30	UMDA	30	75	30	UMDA	200	100	32	UMDA	800	0
30	LFDA$_{0.25}$	100	2	30	LFDA$_{0.25}$	200	58	32	FDA*	100	81
30	LFDA$_{0.5}$	100	38	30	LFDA$_{0.5}$	200	96	32	LFDA$_{0.25}$	800	92
30	LFDA$_{0.75}$	100	80	30	LFDA$_{0.75}$	200	100	32	LFDA$_{0.5}$	800	72
30	LFDA$_{0.25}$	200	71	30	LFDA$_{0.25}$	400	100	32	LFDA$_{0.75}$	800	12
30	MN-FDA	30	72	30	MN-FDA	100	92	32	MN-FDA	600	90
30	MN-FDA	100	98	30	MN-FDA	200	100	32	MN-FDA	800	100

In table 1 results of the MN-FDA for different functions are compared with results published in [7] for the UMDA and the LFDA. For the functions considered in our experiments, results of the LFDA were available in [7] only for the values of the LFDA parameter α presented in the table[2]. In these functions the MN-FDA achieved equal or better results than the LFDA. We have observed that the learning algorithm used by the MN-FDA easily detects variables that are independent. The BN learning algorithms used by Bayesian FDAs may have problems recognizing independence, particularly if α is small.

In table 2 we have included the results for the UMDA, the Tree-FDA, and the LFDA for other functions. In all the cases $N = 1000$, the truncation parameter is 0.15 and the maximum number of generations is 25. For the LFDA, $\alpha = 0.5$.

For function $f_{3deceptive}$ the results of the MN-FDA are the best. For function $F_{IsoTorus}$ LFDA finds the optimum more times than the MN-FDA, however its average fitness is lower. For function F_{IsoP} the LFDA achieved the best results, although the difference is not as significant as in the case of the $f_{3deceptive}$. The UMDA was not able to solve the problems with interactions.

We have generated 4 random instances of the Ising model for different number of variables ($n \in \{25, 36, 49, 64\}$). For each of the instances we investigate two different issues. First, the influence of using the prior information about the interactions of the variables. MN-FDA^s is a Markov Network FDA that does not learn the independence graph from the data. In this case, the lattice where the Ising model is defined serves as the independence graph. The maximum size of the

---

[2] Parameter α has different meanings in the LFDA and the MN-FDA, although in the LFDA it also serves to specify the density of the Bayesian network.

Table 2. Comparison between the MN-FDA with other FDAs for different functions.

	$f_{3deceptive}$			$F_{IsoTorus}$			F_{IsoP}		
	succ.	$\hat{f}$	gen	succ.	$\hat{f}$	gen	succ.	$\hat{f}$	gen
MN-FDA	77	11.97	8.0	78	210.78	5.8	69	1190.69	5.0
UMDA	0	0	0	17	175.01	8.7	0	0	0
Tree-FDA	36	11.92	10.47	75	209.30	6.2	65	1190.65	4.9
LFDA	45	11.91	6.4	85	210.55	6.0	76	1190.75	4.6

Table 3. Results of the MN-FDA for different Ising instances.

Inst.	N	MN-FDA^s		MN-FDA	
		succ.	eval.	succ.	eval.
I^{25}	200	100	849	43	1163
I^{36}	400	86	2316	41	2453
I^{49}	700	82	3841	36	4201
I^{64}	700	67	6031	28	6641

cliques is equal 2. The second issue we study is the scaling of the algorithm when the population size is fixed to 1000, and the coefficient of truncation selection is $T = 0.15$.

The results of these experiments are shown in table 3. An analysis of the results reveals the convenience of using prior information about the optimization problem for increasing the efficiency of the MN-FDA. The small population size that is enough for the convergence of the MN-FDA^s is not sufficient for the MN-FDA. As expected, when the number of variables increases, a higher population size is needed to solve the problem.

7 Conclusions

In this paper we have presented a FDA that approximates the probability distribution determined by selection using a labeled JG. The JG is found by calculating the maximal cliques of a Markov Network that can be given as an input or learned from the data. Our work is related with previous work by Muehlenbein et al. [9], where approximate factorizations were recognized as an alternative for modeling probabilistic distributions. Our research, that has led to a different way of finding these approximations, is also related with the work presented by Brown et al. [2] in the application of MRFs to GAs. They have used probabilistic models of GA fitness functions to generate new solutions. Our work shows a number of relevant differences with this approach: The use of statistical tests to learn the structure of interactions. In [2] the structure of the interactions is known a priori. The construction of the JG from the MN, and the use of PLS on the JG. In [2] the Metropolis algorithm is used to generate new solutions.

The results of our experiments show that the MN-FDA is able to optimize theoretical functions as well as functions derived from practical problems, outperforming other evolutionary algorithms. The MN-FDA generalizes other FDAs by learning factorizations that have not to be valid. More theoretical investigation is needed to determine bounds for the convergence of the MN-FDA. Other practical optimization problems must be tried to assess the performance of the algorithm.

References

1. C. Bron and J. Kerbosch. Algorithm 457—finding all cliques of an undirected graph. *Communications of the ACM*, 16(6):575–577, 1973.
2. D. F. Brown, A. Garmendia-Doal, and J. A. W. McCall. Markov random field modelling of royal road genetic algorithms. In P. Collet, editor, *Proceedings of EA 2001*, volume 2310 of *Lecture Notes in Computer Science*, pages 65–76. Springer Verlag, 2002.
3. M. Henrion. Propagating uncertainty in Bayesian networks by probabilistic logic sampling. *Uncertainty in Artificial Intelligence*, 2:317–324, 1988.
4. J. H. Holland. *Adaptation in natural and artificial systems*. University of Michigan Press, Ann Arbor, MI, 1975.
5. P. Larrañaga and J. A. Lozano. *Estimation Distribution Algorithms. A new tool for Evolutionary Optimization*. Kluwer Academic Publishers, Boston/Dordrecht/London, 2001.
6. H. Mühlenbein. The equation for response to selection and its use for prediction. *Evolutionary Computation*, 5(3):303–346, 1997.
7. H. Mühlenbein and T. Mahnig. *Theoretical Aspects of Evolutionary Computing*, chapter Evolutionary Algorithms: From Recombination to Search Distributions, pages 137–176. Springer Verlag, Berlin, 2000.
8. H. Mühlenbein and T. Mahnig. Evolutionary synthesis of Bayesian networks for optimization. *Advances in Evolutionary Synthesis of Neural Systems, MIT Press*, pages 429–455, 2001.
9. H. Mühlenbein, T. Mahnig, and A. Ochoa. Schemata, distributions and graphical models in evolutionary optimization. *Journal of Heuristics*, 5(2):213–247, 1999.
10. H. Mühlenbein and G. Paaß. From recombination of genes to the estimation of distributions I. Binary parameters. In A. Eiben, T. Bäck, M. Shoenauer, and H. Schwefel, editors, *Parallel Problem Solving from Nature - PPSN IV*, pages 178–187, Berlin, 1996. Springer Verlag.
11. R. Santana, A. Ochoa, and M. R. Soto. The Mixture of Trees Factorized Distribution Algorithm. In *Proceedings of the Genetic and Evolutionary Computation Conference GECCO-2001*, pages 543–550, San Francisco, CA, 2001. Morgan Kaufmann Publishers.
12. P. Spirtes, C. Glymour, and R. Scheines. *Causation, Prediction and search*. Lecture Notes in Statistics. Springer-Verlag, New York, 1993.

On Boosting Improvement:
Error Reduction and Convergence Speed-Up

Marc Sebban and Henri-Maxime Suchier

EURISE – Université Jean Monnet de Saint-Etienne
23, rue du Dr Paul Michelon, 42023 Saint-Etienne cedex 2, France
{Marc.Sebban,Henri.Maxime.Suchier}@univ-st-etienne.fr

Abstract. Boosting is not only the most efficient ensemble learning method in practice, but also the one based on the most robust theoretical properties. The adaptive update of the sample distribution, which tends to increase the weight of the misclassified examples, allows to improve the performance of any learning algorithm. However, its ability to avoid overfitting has been challenged when boosting is applied to noisy data. This situation is frequent with the modern databases, built thanks to new data acquisition technologies, such as the Web. The convergence speed of boosting is also penalized on such databases, where there is a large overlap of probability density functions of the classes to learn (large Bayesian error). In this article, we propose a slight modification of the weight update rule of the algorithm ADABOOST. We show that by exploiting an adaptive measure of a local entropy, computed from a neighborhood graph built on the examples, it is possible to identify not only the *outliers* but also the examples located in the Bayesian error region. Taking into account this information, we correct the weight of the examples to improve the boosting performances. A broad experimental study shows the interest of our new algorithm, called *i*ADABOOST.

1 Introduction

A large number of studies in machine learning have focused during the last decade on classifier aggregation methods, which aim at improving by voting techniques the performances of a single classifier. Among these methods, the most usually used are probably *bagging* [1], *arcing* [2], and *boosting* [3, 4]. In this article, we only focus on this third approach, which received over the last few years a spectacular interest. The two main reasons for this growing popularity are probably due, on the one hand to its simplicity of implementation, and on the other hand to the large number of recently enacted theorems on bounds, margins, or boosting convergence [5, 6]. Boosting is known to improve the performances of any learning algorithm, assumed *a priori* unstable, called *weak learner*. The strategy consists in successively training the algorithm (T times) on various probability distributions $D_t(x)$ over the learning sample LS, and in combining the resulting classifiers (called *weak hypotheses*) in an efficient single classifier H. The central point of boosting, and its algorithm ADABOOST [7, 8] (see Algorithm

1), is the weight update rule. At each round, the current distribution favors the weights of examples mislabeled $(y(x) \neq h_t(x))$ by the previous hypothesis, that characterizes well the *ada*ptivity of *Ada*BOOST.

The first experimental results have shown that boosting seems to be immune against overfitting. Actually, not only the empirical error on the learning sample decreases exponentially with the number of iterations, but also the generalization error drops, even when the empirical error reaches its minimum (even 0). These results incited over the last few years researchers to find theoretical justifications for this behavior. These works made it possible to establish the link between boosting and margin maximization[1] [5], and in particular (i) to show that it is possible to bound the theoretical error by a term decreasing with the margin increase, and (ii) to prove that margins on the training examples increase with the boosting iterations. Parallel to these fundamental results, some studies on boosting are concerned with the improvement of the algorithm ADABOOST, which is today confronted with two main problems.

Data : A learning sample LS, a number of iterations T, a weak learner WL
Result : An aggregated classifier H

```
Initialize distribution:
```
$\forall x \in LS, \; D_1(x) = \frac{1}{|LS|}$;
```
for t = 2 to T do
```
  $h_t = $ `WL` (LS, D_t);
  $\epsilon_t = \sum_{e: y(x) \neq h_t(x)} D_t(x)$; $\alpha_t = \frac{1}{2} \log(\frac{1-\epsilon_t}{\epsilon_t})$;
```
  Distribution Update
```
  /* $\forall x \in LS, D_{t+1}(x) = \frac{D_t(x) e^{-\alpha_t y(x) h_t(x)}}{Z_t}$ */;
  /*Z_t is a Normalization Factor*/ ;

Return H s.t. $H(x) = \frac{1}{T}(\sum_{t=1}^{T} \alpha_t h_t(x))$;

Algorithm 1: Pseudo-code of ADABOOST.

Firstly, the emergence of very large but often strongly noisy modern databases forces the researchers to study and improve the noise tolerance capacities of boosting. Indeed, while the success of ADABOOST is indisputable, there is increasing evidence that the algorithm is quite susceptible to noise [9], resulting in overfitting. Recent works then tried to limit these risks of overfitting. ADABOOST tending (wrongly) to exponentially increase the weight of the *outliers*, some algorithms aim at controlling the update rule [10–12].

Secondly, the other drawback of the *real world* databases is not directly relating to boosting performances in terms of error, but rather on the convergence speed of ADABOOST. We will see in this article that in the presence of a high *overlap* between the probability densities of the classes, the optimal error of the learning algorithm is reached after many iterations (T very large). In other words, ADABOOST "loses" time, and thus iterations, by reweighting examples which

---
[1] The margin expresses the degree of confidence in the class prediction for an example.

theoretically do not deserve any attention, since they belong to the Bayesian error region. Such instances are frequent in the modern databases, which often present a non-null Bayesian error. The rare studies aiming at increasing the convergence speed [13] are more theoretical than usable in practice.

In this article, we deal with the two problems previously mentioned. We propose a modification of the weight update rule which (i) keeps the exponential function to not challenge the error bounds, (ii) but avoids applying it to noisy data and (iii) sets to zero the weights of examples in Bayesian region. In order to detect, at a given step t, not only the noisy data but also those at the border of the classes, we use information contained in a neighborhood graph built on the learning set. The graph is constructed only once, and only the node weights vary during the boosting procedure. We compute from the neighborhood of each example an entropy allowing to evaluate the level of local information. This non-monotone function thus makes it possible to assess, with the current weights, if each example deserves or not to be reweighted. Our procedure consists in assigning to each example a coefficient which estimates, in a way, the confidence that one can have in the new weight $D_{t+1}(x)$ calculated in ADABOOST.

This article is organized as follows. In Section 2, we present a synthetic state of the art of the main approaches, past or in progress, dealing with boosting improvement. Section 3 is devoted to the presentation of our new weight update rule, and to our algorithm iADABOOST. In Section 4, we carry out a broad experimental study aiming at comparing, on many databases, the performances of ADABOOST and iADABOOST, in terms of error and convergence speed.

2 State of the Art

In this section, we carry out a survey on the main methods aiming at improving boosting. We divide them in two categories according to their goal: managing noisy data and dealing with the speed of convergence.

2.1 Noise Tolerance

An experimental study was presented in [9], aiming in particular at comparing the performances of boosting and bagging, on a large number of benchmarks. The main information highlighted in this study is the weak tolerance of both methods to noisy data. More surprisingly, ADABOOST reaches a higher error rate than bagging. Dietterich gives a convincing explanation of the reason of this behavior. He shows that boosting tends to assign the examples to which noise was added much higher weight than other instances. As a result, hypotheses generated in later iterations cause the combined hypothesis to overfit the noise. In order to illustrate this phenomenon, ADABOOST was run on an *a priori* linearly separable sample, artificially corrupted by a given percentage of noise (see Fig. 1). We used *stumps* (decision trees with only a root node) to learn the data. *Stumps* have all the characteristics of good weak hypotheses [10] because they have, according to the *bias-variance* terminology, a low variance and a high bias. Fig. 1 also shows

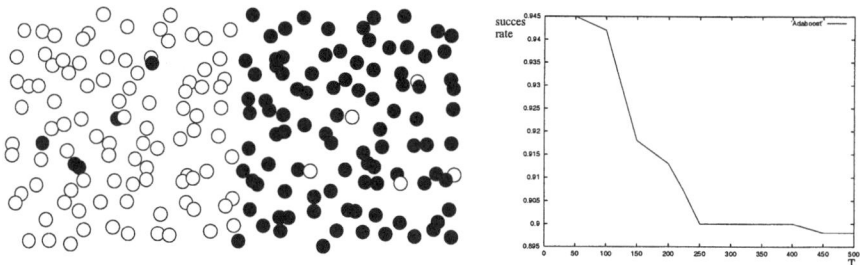

Fig. 1. An example of overfitting on noisy data. ADABOOST finds the right separator as of the first iteration. It then constraints itself to learn outliers, leading to an overfitting.

the results in terms of success rate estimated by cross-validation, over the first 500 iterations. It is clearly seen that ADABOOST quickly diverges, confirming the overfitting phenomenon on noisy data.

To improve the noise tolerance, two different strategies can be considered. Since ADABOOST is noise sensitive, a first approach would consist in removing noisy data before the boosting procedure. This kind of preprocessing is a matter for *prototype selection* (PS) which tries to *a priori* delete irrelevant or noisy data [14,15]. PS aims not only at reducing storage complexity of costly algorithms but also at improving their performances. To reach these goals, three main types of examples have to be suppressed with efficient heuristics (see Fig. 2). The first category corresponds to outliers (example 1 on the figure). The second concerns examples located in the Bayesian error region (example 2), which do not bring discriminant information to the classifier. The last category represents the instances at the center of a cluster (example 3). Since those examples are correctly labeled by instances located on the convex hull of the cluster, they can be considered as useless, and thus suppressed to reduce storage constraints.

The second approach for treating noisy data aims at taking them into account during the induction process, *i.e.* during the construction of the weak hypotheses. Generally, suggested strategies to avoid overfitting propose a modification of the weight update rule. In MADABOOST [12], the modification is very simple. Because the uncontrolled growth of the weights seems to be the root of the problems of ADABOOST, MADABOOST bounds the weight assigned to each example by its initial probability. In this way, the weights of the examples can not become arbitrarily large as it happens in ADABOOST. While the drawback of this approach is that the boosting speed is much slower than the one for ADABOOST, the authors prove that their moderate weight scheme has the boosting properties. In [11], Freund presents an adaptive version of his "boost by majority" algorithm, suggested in [3], in a new algorithm, called BROWNBOOST. In this approach, the algorithm is optimized to minimize the training error within a pre-assigned number k of boosting iterations. As the algorithm approaches its predetermined end, it becomes less and less likely that examples which have large negative margins will become correctly labeled. According to this remark, Freund uses the following weighting function, which corresponds in fact to the

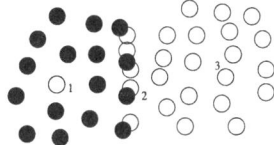

Fig. 2. Categories of irrelevant examples.

probability density of a binomial variable, which depends on k, on the index i of the current iteration, on the number of correct classifications made so far, and on the success probability $1 - \gamma$ imposed to each weak hypothesis.

$$\alpha_r^i = \binom{k-i-1}{\lfloor \frac{k}{2} \rfloor - r}(\frac{1}{2}+\gamma)^{\lfloor \frac{k}{2} \rfloor - r}(\frac{1}{2}-\gamma)^{\lfloor \frac{k}{2} \rfloor - i - 1 + r}$$

This is a non-monotone function, which looks quite like the exponential function for small negative margins. But beyond a certain value, the weight drops, particularly at the end of the k iterations. The advantage of this approach is that outliers will probably be detected, and their weight will thus stop to increase. However, they can be too lately identified, leading to a negative influence on the resulting hypothesis. In GENTLE ADABOOST [10], the authors also use a weighting scheme that uses a function with a lower growth than the exponential one. Boosting is viewed as an approximation to additive modeling on the logistic scale. By fitting an additive model of different and potentially simple functions, it expands the class of functions that can be approximated. Eventually, in [16], the authors present boosting as an optimization problem, in which slack variables are introduced, that permits to relax the constraint over high weighted examples, which are the ones having the worst negative margins.

2.2 Convergence Speed

If the negative impacts of noisy data on boosting performances have been frequently mentioned in the literature, the causes of a slowing down of convergence have rarely been studied. However, we can easily assess the consequences of a high level of density overlap. Indeed, the weight of examples located in Bayesian error region are alternatively increased, because mislabeled, and decreased to allow the correct classification of examples of the other class. This, of course, has an impact on the final classifier H, which will generally need more iterations, and thus more weak hypotheses, to reach its optimum. To illustrate our remarks, ADABOOST was run on an artificial sample containing a Bayesian error of 20%. Fig. 3 shows the success rate over 500 iterations. It can be seen that the optimal success rate of 80%, known *a priori*, is nearly reached after 400 iterations.

In order to reduce the number of weak hypotheses, we proposed in [13] to modify Schapire and Singer's theorem [6], pointed out below, which proves that the minimization of the error is ensured by minimizing each Z_t.

Theorem 1. *The following bound holds on the training error of H:*

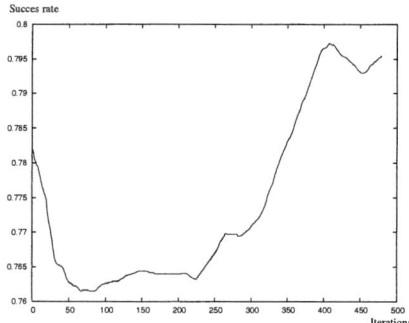

Fig. 3. An example of delayed convergence due to the presence of an overlap.

$$\frac{|\{i : H(x) \neq y_i\}|}{m} \leq \prod_t Z_t$$

We modified this theorem in [13] by integrating Bayes risk, allowing to encompass situations where many examples are sharing the same description. Consider the learning sample $LS = (x_1, y(x_1)), ..., (x_m, y(x_m))$ containing m examples with representation x and class $y(x)$. We define $n^+(x)$ and $n^-(x)$ respectively as the number of positive and negative examples sharing this representation. Let

$$\delta(x) = \frac{|n^+(x) - n^-(x)|}{(n^+(x) + n^-(x))}$$

Theorem 2. *The following bound holds on the training error of H:*

$$\frac{|\{i : H(x) \neq y_i\}|}{m} \leq (\prod_t Z_t) E_{D_{T+1}}[\delta(x)] + \epsilon^*$$

where ϵ^* is the minimal error on LS and $E_{D_{T+1}}[\delta(x)]$ is the expectation of $\delta(x)$ on distribution D_{T+1}, such that

$$D_{T+1}(x') = \frac{e^{-y(x') \sum_t \alpha_t h_t(x')}}{m \prod_t Z_t}$$

The interest of this theorem is to integrate Bayes risk in this upper bound. It suggests to annihilate the effect of the examples located in the Bayesian error region, the reweighting process favoring those for which $\delta(x)$ is highly in favor of one class. We modified the distribution $D_t(x)$ with the following update rule:

$$\forall x', D'_t(x') = \frac{\sum_{x \in LS*} D_t(x')[\pi(x, x')]\delta(x)}{\sum_{x'' \in LS} \sum_{x \in LS*} D_t(x'')[\pi(x, x'')]\delta(x)}$$

Where $LS*$ represents the set of examples containing only one instance of a given representation, where $[\pi(x, x')] = 1$ if the predicate "x and x' are identical descriptions" is true and $[\pi(x, x')] = 0$ if not. Note that if $LS* = LS$, we then have Schapire and Singer's results. The first expected effect of this theorem is related to a faster convergence to the optimal risk. From artificial experiments in feature selection [13], we have observed that the construction of up to 30% weak hypotheses can be saved. Nevertheless, from a practical point of view, the situations where the representation of two examples from different classes is strictly the same are very rare, especially with high representation dimensions. In the next section, we will try, through the use of the information contained in a neighborhood graph, to estimate if an example is potentially located in the Bayesian region, even if it does not share its representation with other examples.

Note that other approaches, which do not belong to the two categories stated before, also tried to improve boosting performances. For example, algorithm iBOOST [17] aims at specializing weak hypotheses on examples they are supposed to correctly label. Thanks to boolean variables, each example is weighted in $H(x)$ by a coefficient representing its adequacy with each h_t. The experimental results show a quite good improvement of ADABOOST. In [18], a new boosting algorithm is proposed, in which a test example gets the class of the weighted majority of examples having received the same proportion of vote among the T weak hypotheses. Noise tolerance as well as margin growth are also theoretically studied there. Finally, through REGIONBOOST [19], a new hypothesis weighting scheme is proposed. Weighting is evaluated at the moment of the vote thanks to the k nearest neighbors of the example to label. This approach permits to specialize each classifier on specific areas of the representation space. In spite of a performance improvement, the results show a certain noise sensitivity.

3 The Algorithm iADABOOST

The different strategies listed above for dealing with noisy data are not totally satisfying. Firstly, definitively removing noisy data during a preprocessing stage does not provide a moderate decision rule. Beyond the gain in terms of storage requirements, wrongly removed examples could lead to dramatic effects on the classifier performances. Secondly, as we said before, the step-by-step discovery of noisy data as done in BROWNBOOST is not also completely relevant. Actually, an outlier could have time to damage the final classifier. Moreover, the use of functions different from the exponential one (as in MADABOOST), is likely to call into question some theoretical results on bounds. Finally, the use of the efficient soft margins [16] does not solve the problems linked to bi-modal distributions (with two peaks of density), where relevant instances could be seen as outliers, using weak learners such as stumps. To avoid forcing ADABOOST to learn either noisy data or examples that would become too hard to learn during the boosting process, we are going to build a local information criterion around each example. This one will allow us not only to estimate overfitting risks, but also to evaluate if an example is located in the Bayesian error region. We build a geometrical graph, which will permit us to measure the information around each example. We consider here a very simple graph, the k-nearest-neighbor graph (kNN) [20], built on LS.

Definition 1. Let $N(x)$ be the neighborhood of x such that, $N(x) = \{x' \in LS/x'$ is one of the kNN of x using the Euclidean distance$\}$.

Note that it is possible to use other graphs, such as Gabriel graph, Relative Neighborhood graph, minimal spanning tree, Delaunay triangulation [21]. The properties of the kNN graph, and in particular the fact of having an error rate bounded by twice the Bayesian error [22], led us to choose this graph.

Definition 2. Let $n_t^+(x)$ (resp. $n_t^-(x)$), be the sum of the weights $D_t(x')$ of the examples x' having the same label as x (resp. opposite label of x) in $N(x)$.

$$n_t^+(x) = \sum_{x' \in N(x): y(x') = y(x)} D_t(x') \qquad n_t^-(x) = \sum_{x' \in N(x): y(x') \neq y(x)} D_t(x')$$

Definition 3. Let $I_t(x)$, the level of confidence in the new weight $D_{t+1}(x)$, at iteration t. $I_t(x)$ is an application from $[-1, +1]$ in $[0, 0.25]$, defined as follows:

$$I_t(x) = |\gamma_t(x)|(1 - |\gamma_t(x)|) \quad \text{where} \quad \gamma_t(x) = \frac{n_t^+(x) - n_t^-(x)}{n_t^+(x) + n_t^-(x)}$$

In order to have a coefficient ranging between 0 and 1, we will rather use $4I_t(x)$ for measuring the confidence in $D_{t+1}(x)$. In order to adjust the weights, we use the following reweighting scheme, where Z'_t is the new normalization coefficient.

$$D'_{t+1}(x) = \frac{4I_t(x)D_{t+1}(x)}{Z'_t}$$

The function $I_t(x)$ is graphically described in Fig. 4. Note that this function was built by merging two ideas coming from boosting and prototype selection. The first makes it possible to solve problems due to the systematic exponential growth of the weight of mislabeled examples. We aim here at using a non-monotone function, while if necessary keeping the exponential update for examples which deserve it. Note that for negative values of $\gamma_t(x)$, $I_t(x)$ looks like the binomial distribution used in [3], except that it does not depend on the iteration index, and can detect an outlier right at the beginning of the process.

The second idea takes into account the different categories of irrelevant examples listed in prototype selection. $I_t(x)$ deals with outliers, overlaps and clusters as well. Indeed, irrelevant examples will be detected by a null $|\gamma_t(x)|$ (Bayesian error region), or equal to 1 (outlier or center of cluster). In all cases, $I_t(x)$ will then be equal to 0, and the example will be annihilated. Between these two minima, the confidence in $D_{t+1}(x)$ is a non-monotone function of $\gamma_t(x)$, which expresses the information level around each example. We introduced all these ideas in a new algorithm, called iADABOOST. Its pseudocode (see Algorithm 2) strongly looks like to ADABOOST's one, since the main modification concerns the information collected within the neighborhood graph, and its use in the computation of the confidence coefficient of $D_{t+1}(x)$.

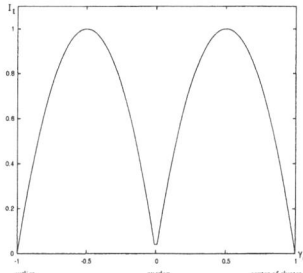

Fig. 4. The function $I_t(x)$.

Data : A learning sample LS, a number of iterations T, a weak learner WL
Result : An aggregated classifier H

Build the k nearest neighbor graph on LS ;
Initialize distribution: $\forall x \in LS, \; D_1(x) = \frac{1}{|LS|}$;
for $t = 2$ to T do
$\quad h_t =$ WL (LS, D_t);
$\quad \epsilon_t = \sum_{e: y(x) \neq h_t(x)} D_t(x)$ and $\alpha_t = \frac{1}{2} \log(\frac{1-\epsilon_t}{\epsilon_t})$;
$\quad$ Distribution Update: $\forall x \in LS \; D_{t+1}(x) = D_t(x) e^{-\alpha_t y(x) h_t(x)}$;
$\quad$ and $D'_{t+1}(x) = \frac{4 I_t(x) D_{t+1}(x)}{Z'_t}$;
$\quad$ where $I_t(x) = |\gamma_t(x)|(1 - \gamma_t(x)|)$ and $\gamma_t(x) = \frac{|n^+(x) - n^-(x)|}{(n^+(x) + n^-(x))}$;
Return H s.t. $H(x) = \frac{1}{T}(\sum_{t=1}^{T} \alpha_t h_t(x))$;

Algorithm 2: Pseudo-code of iADABOOST..

4 Experimental Results

The goal of this section is to compare, in terms of error and convergence speed, the algorithms ADABOOST and iADABOOST. Again, we use here stumps as weak hypotheses, and a 10-fold-cross-validation procedure. The kNN graph is built using different values of k. The results listed in this section are those obtained with the optimal value. In order to highlight the ability of iADABOOST to deal with both problems of noisy data and class overlap, we achieved two types of experiments. In the first part, we worked on 11 databases of the UCI repository [23][2], in which we introduced 10% of noise. This way to proceed ensures then the presence of a minimum number of outliers in order to test the efficiency of our approach. The second series of experiments aims at controlling the ability of iADABOOST to improve the speed of convergence. We built a learning sample with two linearly separable classes, and we artificially generated a density overlap of $\alpha\%$ of each distribution (α varying from 10 to 50%).

---

[2] They have been selected in the limited set of bi-class databases provided by the UCI.

Table 1. Performances in terms of success on 11 bases of the UCI repository.

BASE	STUMP % succ	ADABOOST % succ	iADABOOST k	iADABOOST % succ
WHITE HOUSE	85.89	85.21	5	85.89
PIMA	66.05	67.61	14	69.17
IONOSPHERE	65.61	70.90	5	74.61
GLASS	64.00	68.8	6	69.3
VEHICLE	60.89	67.7	7	68.5
TIC-TAC-TOE	59.45	68.25	8	69.57
XD6	55.80	69.71	6	69.53
HEART	73.38	72.28	4	73.39
ECHOCARDIOGRAM	55.05	65.43	7	66.92
BREAST	81.79	84.64	5	87.35
CAR	71.60	74.19	10	74.20
AVERAGE	67.23	72.25	7	73.49

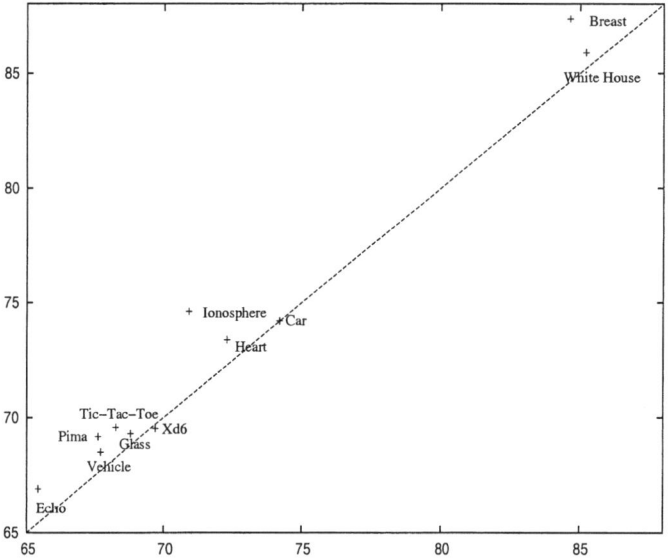

Fig. 5. Scatter plot on 11 databases.

Tab. 1 shows results obtained during the first study. We indicated the success rate (% *succ*) for ADABOOST and *i*ADABOOST. In order to show the effect of boosting, we also mentioned the success rate (*stump*) obtained with only one weak hypothesis built from the initial distribution. Finally the optimal value of k is indicated for each base. Note that in order to ensure a better comparison, the same folds were used during the cross-validation. The observation of the results shows that the positive effects of *i*ADABOOST are indisputable. Indeed, on 10 bases, our algorithm improves the performances of ADABOOST. On all the 11 databases, the gain with our method is about 1.2 (72.25 vs 73.49), that is highly statistically significant, using a Student test. Another concise way to display the results is proposed in Fig. 5. Each dot represents a database. A dot over the bisecting line expresses that *i*ADABOOST is better than ADABOOST.

Table 2 presents the results about the convergence speed of both algorithms. Several remarks can be made. The first one is relative to the iteration from which the algorithm has reached its optimum. Except for a small overlap level (10%), iADABOOST always reaches its optimum before ADABOOST. The second characterizes the difference between the two algorithms in terms of convergence. Indeed the higher the overlapping rate is, the higher the difference between the two convergence iterations $(T_2 - T_1)$ becomes. ADABOOST is less and less efficient for quickly learn the two classes. Finally we tested, thanks to a measure of dispersion, if iADABOOST is more stable than ADABOOST. We calculated the standard deviation (σ_1 and σ_2) over the success rates, from the stabilization iteration of iADABOOST to the end (T=1000). One can note that globally, our algorithm offers a higher stability (ranging from 0.1 to 0.3) than ADABOOST, which is more disturbed by the successive weight updates (from 0.26 to 1.51).

Table 2. Performances in terms of convergence speed.

OVERLAP.	iADABOOST		ADABOOST		$T_2 - T_1$
	T_1	σ_1	T_2	σ_2	
10 %	200	0.29	200	0.30	0
20 %	150	0.11	250	0.26	100
30 %	170	0.24	350	0.56	180
40 %	300	0.24	800	0.82	500
50 %	375	0.28	1000	1.51	625

5 Conclusion

We proposed in this article a modification of the weight update of ADABOOST in order to better take into account, not only noisy data, penalizing the success rate of the final classifier, but also the examples located in the Bayesian error region, slowing boosting convergence. Beyond the excellent performances obtained by our algorithm iADABOOST, we are currently working on theoretical justifications of such an update, and its effects on error bounds. It will be also important to theoretically verify that the use of this update rule does not call into question the main principles of boosting, and that margins keep on increasing with the number of iterations.

References

1. Breiman, L.: Bagging predictors. Machine Learning **24** (1996) 123–140
2. Breiman, L.: Bias, variance, and arcing classifiers. Technical Report 460, Department of Statistics, University of California, Berkeley (1996)
3. Freund, Y.: Boosting a weak learning algorithms by majority. Information and Computation **121** (1995) 256–285
4. Schapire, R.E.: The strength of weak learnability. Machine Learning (1990)
5. Schapire, R.E., Freund, Y., Bartlett, P.L., Lee, W.S.: Boosting the margin: a new explanation for the effectiveness of voting methods. Annals of Statistics **26** (1998) 1651–1686

6. Schapire, R.E., Singer, Y.: Improved boosting algorithms using confidence-rated predictions. In Press, A., ed.: Eleventh Annual Conference on Computational Learning Theory. (1998) 80–91
7. Freund, Y., Schapire, R.: A decision-theoretic generalization of online learning and an application to boosting. International Journal of Computer and System Sciences **55(1)** (1997) 119–139
8. Freund, Y., Schapire, R.E.: Experiments with a new boosting algorithm. In Kaufmann, M., ed.: Thirteenth International Conference on Machine Learning. (1996) 148–156
9. Dietterich, T.G.: An experimental comparison of three methods for constructing ensembles of decision trees: bagging, boosting, and randomization. Machine Learning (1999) 1–22
10. Friedman, J., Hastie, T., Tibshirani, R.: Additive logistic regression: a statistical view of boosting. Technical report (1998)
11. Freund, Y.: An adaptive version of the boost by majority algorithm. Machine Learning **43** (2001) 293–318
12. Domingo, C., Watanabe, O.: Madaboost: a modification of adaboost. In Press, A., ed.: Third Annual Confernce on Computational Learning Theory. (2000) 180–189
13. Nock, R., Sebban, M.: A bayesian boosting theorem. Pattern Recognition Letters **22 (3-4)** (2001) 413–419
14. Sebban, M., Nock, R., Lallich, S.: Stopping criterion for boosting-based data reduction techniques: from binary to multiclass problems. In: Journal of Machine Learning Research. (2003)
15. Wilson, D., Martinez, T.: Reduction techniques for exemplar-based learning algorithms. Machine Learning (1998)
16. Ratsch, G., Onoda, T., Muller, K.R.: Regularizing adaboost. In: M.S. Kearns, S.A. Solla, and D.A. Cohn, editors, conference NIPS. (1998)
17. Kwek, S., Nguyen, C.: iboost: Boosting using an i nstance-based exponential weighting scheme. In Springer Verlag, L.., ed.: Thirteenth European Conference on Machine Learning. (2002) 245–257
18. Nock, R., Lefaucheur, P.: A robust boosting algorithm. In: Thirteenth European Conference on Machine Learning. (2002)
19. Maclin, R.: Boosting classifiers regionally. In: AAAI/IAAI. (1998) 700–705
20. Cover, T., Hart, P.: Nearest neighbor pattern classification. IEEE Trans. Inform. Theory **IT13** (1967) 21–27
21. Preparata, F., Shamos, M.: Pattern recognition and scene analysis. Springer Verlag (1985)
22. Breiman, L., Friedman, J., Olshen, R., Stone, C.: Classification and regression trees with misclassification costs. Chapman and Hall (1984)
23. Merz, C.J., Murphy, P.M.: Uci repository of machine learning databases. www.ics.uci.edu/mlearn/mlrepository.html (1996)

Improving SVM Text Classification Performance through Threshold Adjustment

James G. Shanahan and Norbert Roma

Clairvoyance Corporation, 5001 Baum Boulevard, Suite 700,
Pittsburgh, PA 15213-1854, USA
{jimi,n.roma}@clairvoyancecorp.com

Abstract. In general, support vector machines (SVM), when applied to text classification provide excellent precision, but poor recall. One means of customizing SVMs to improve recall, is to adjust the threshold associated with an SVM. We describe an automatic process for adjusting the thresholds of generic SVM which incorporates a user utility model, an integral part of an information management system. By using thresholds based on utility models and the ranking properties of classifiers, it is possible to overcome the precision bias of SVMs and insure robust performance in recall across a wide variety of topics, even when training data are sparse. Evaluations on TREC data show that our proposed threshold adjusting algorithm boosts the performance of baseline SVMs by at least 20% for standard information retrieval measures.

1 Introduction

Generic support vector machines (SVMs) [19] provide excellent performance on a variety of learning problems including: handwritten character recognition [8], face detection [15] and most recently text categorization [6]. However, when generic SVMs are applied to text classification[1], their performance, while being competitive with other approaches (e.g., Rocchio, naïve Bayes) from a precision perspective, is not competitive from a recall perspective [6], [17].

Several attempts have been made to improve the recall of SVMs while not adversely affecting precision in a text classification context. The first category of such attempts falls under the label of uneven margin-based learning [12]. Here, a simple margin-based version of the perceptron learning algorithm is used to learn a model that has a pre-specified required positive and negative margin. The required positive and negative margins are heuristically determined using cross-validation on the training corpus. The second category of proposed SVM improvements for text classification is cost-based and is also incorporated into the SVM learning algorithm. To counter the imbalance of positive training documents to negative training documents,

---

[1] Text classification is a very active area of research and application in information management and is concerned with assigning a document to one or more pre-specified categories or classes.

a higher cost is associated with the misclassification of positive documents than with negative documents [20]. Tuning the asymmetric misclassification cost can provide significant improvement, though this process can be prohibitively expensive. The final category of proposed SVM improvements for text classification is based on post-processing or thresholding the output value (or margin/score) of the learnt SVM. This is generally an inexpensive one-dimensional optimization problem which can lead to significant improvement in performance measures.

This post-processing thresholding step is independent of the learning step. The critical step in thresholding is to determine the value, known as the threshold, at which a decision changes from labeling a document as positive to labeling a document as negative. Many of the approaches to thresholding that have been developed in other fields (such as information retrieval) can be applied directly in thresholding the score output of SVMs. Though thresholding has received a lot attention in the information retrieval sub-field of adaptive filtering, optimizing thresholds remains a challenging problem. The main challenge arises from a lack of labeled training data. Due to limited amounts of training data, standard approaches to information retrieval use the same data for both model fitting (learning) and threshold optimization. Consequently, this often biases the threshold to high precision, i.e., overfits the training data.

The following provides a brief overview of information retrieval-based thresholding approaches: Yang presents an empirical study of a variety of thresholding strategies for text categorization using k nearest neighbors [22]; Zhai. et al. present a beta-gamma thresholding algorithm for adaptive filtering, which has been adapted in the thresholding strategy proposed in this paper [23]; Zhang and Callan propose a maximum likelihood estimation of filtering thresholds [24]; Ault and Yang introduce a margin-based local regression approach for predicting optimal thresholds for adaptive filtering [2]; Arampatzis describe a score-distributional threshold optimization approach [1].

Some of these IR approaches have been adapted already for thresholding SVMs. Cancedda et al. report one such approach to adjusting the threshold of SVMs based upon a Gaussian modeling process of the SVM scores (output value) for positive and negative documents for each category [3]. This Gaussian model is then used to generate sample document scores and an optimal threshold is set to the score corresponding to maximum utility on the cumulative utility curve for the generated labeled scores. This approach, combined with asymmetric learning, has led to huge improvements in recall and precision, though it is hard to discern how much improvement can be attributed to the asymmetric cost learning strategy or to the thresholding strategy. This impact of adjusting the threshold will become clearer later in this paper when we show that it can boost significantly the performance of baseline SVMs for text classification.

In this paper, we adapt a procedure of setting the threshold of the learnt SVM using the beta-gamma thresholding technique, developed previously for adaptive text filtering using information retrieval-based filters [22], a more challenging task than text classification. In addition, we present a novel and very cheap technique for selecting the parameters of the threshold adjustment strategy automatically, based upon cross fold validation. This paper is organized as follows: Section 2 describes the proposed threshold adjustment algorithm after a brief overview of generic linear SVM modeling; Section 3 describes the experimental setup, detailing the explored variables and datasets used to evaluate the proposed approach; Section 4 presents the results of evaluations of the proposed approach and compares these to other approaches; Section 5 presents some concluding remarks.

2 Proposed Thresholding Approach

The proposed threshold adjustment algorithm is performed immediately after learning an SVM. In this section, we first present some background material on SVMs and then present the proposed threshold adjusting algorithm.

2.1 Support Vector Machines

Though support vector machines (SVM) were originally introduced by Vapnik in 1979 [19], and have provided state-of-the-art performance for a variety of learning problems (and in some cases better than state-of-the-art), it is only recently that they have gained popularity in the text retrieval and classification community. Geometrically (for linear support vector machines), a learnt SVM model can be seen as a hyperplane that separates a set of positive examples (belonging to the positive class) from a set of negative examples (negative class). This is illustrated in Figure 1, where H is a hyperplane that separates positive class examples (denoted by "+") and negative class examples (denoted by "-"). Mathematically a hyperplane can be represented as follows:

$$\left(\sum_{i=1}^{n} w_i x_i\right) + b = 0 \qquad (1)$$

This can be written more succinctly in vector format as $<W,X>+b=0$. Here W is known as a weight vector and corresponds to the normal vector to the separating hyperplane, H, and X is an input vector or document. b denotes the perpendicular distance from the hyperplane to the origin. n represents the number of input variables, in the case of text, this can be viewed as the number of words (or phrases, etc.) that are used to describe a document. The classification rule for an unlabeled document, X, using a support vector machine with separating hyperplane (W, b), is as follows:

$$Class(X) = Sign(\langle W, X \rangle + b) \qquad (2)$$

The distance from the hyperplane to the nearest positive or negative examples is known as the margin of the SVM. Learning a linear SVM can be simply thought of as searching for a hyperplane (i.e., the weights and bias values) that separates the data with the largest margin. As a result, learning for linearly separable data can be viewed as the following optimization problem:

$$\text{minimize}\left(\frac{\|w\|^2}{2}\right) \quad \text{subject to: } y_i(\langle W, X_i \rangle + b) \geq 1 \quad \forall \ i = 1,...,n \qquad (3)$$

where X_i is training example with label y_i and $||W||$ is the L^2 norm of the weight vector (i.e, $\sqrt{\Sigma^n_{i=1}(w_i * w_i)}$). In the case of non-linear separablity, two alternative formulations have been proposed: one is based upon slack variables; and the other is based upon using non-linear kernels (see [20] for more details). The slack variable or soft formulation of SVM learning [4] allows, but penalizes, examples that fall on the wrong side of the supporting hyperplanes (H_+ and H_- in Figure 1), i.e., false positives or false negatives. Different or asymmetric costs can be associated with false negatives and false positives. In practice, learning SVMs is more efficiently conducted in a dual space [19]. For our current study, two variations of the dual space Sequential Minimal Optimization (SMO) learning algorithm [16] were implemented and evaluated: SMOK1 and SMOK2, corresponding to modification 1 and modification 2, respectively, as proposed by Keerthi et al. [7]. Our current implementation caters only for symmetric false positive and false negative costs.

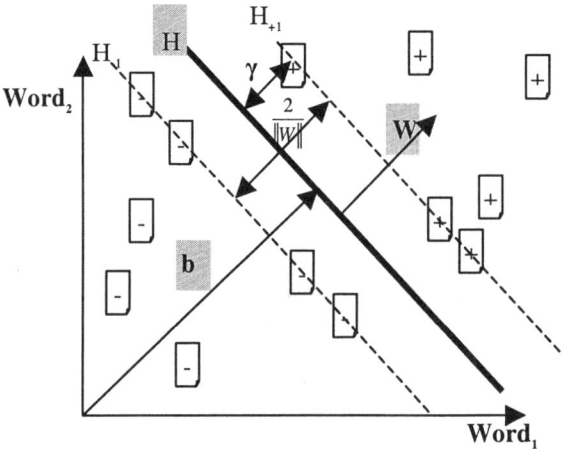

Fig. 1. A support vector machine in a two-dimensional input space, $Word_1 \times Word_2$, denoted by the hyperplane, H. Each document is associated with a category, ("+" or "-"). The support vectors correspond to the examples on the hyperplanes H_{+1} and H_{-1}.

2.2 Thresholding Adjusting Algorithm for SVMs

Optimizing thresholds is a challenging problem because the limited amount of training available is generally required for training the base model, thereby, resulting in a situation where it is rare to have an independent sample solely for threshold optimization. Standard approaches in text classification and retrieval use the same data for both model fitting (learning) and threshold optimization [22]. Consequently, this often biases the threshold to high precision, i.e., the threshold overfits the training data. SVM learning algorithms focus on finding the hyperplane that maximizes the margin since this criterion provides a good upper bound of the generalization error. Learning based on this criterion leads to models with very good ranking ability (demonstrated empirically by the results in Section 4). However, the resulting separating hyperplane tends to be too conservative (high precision oriented). The natural threshold value for SVM learning and classification is zero (see Equation 2). Here, we propose to combine the powerful ranking ability of SVMs with the beta-gamma thresholding algorithm [22] to reset the threshold of the learnt SVM in order to overcome this precision-oriented limitation. The powerful ranking ability of SVMs is only exploited for threshold adjustment, and is not used in classification (as each document is classified independently of each other). The beta-gamma thresholding algorithm relaxes the SVM threshold from zero, i.e., translates the SVM hyperplane towards the denser class (i.e., the class with more training data). In addition to adapting the beta-gamma algorithm for adjusting the SVM threshold, we propose a novel means for setting the parameters of this algorithm – beta and gamma – using a cheap cross validation mechanism.

We first present the core beta-gamma thresholding strategy, and subsequently describe how this can be used with cross validation to empirically determine the beta and gamma parameters. The beta-gamma thresholding strategy consists of the following steps and uses as input a category label, C, a labeled dataset, T, of documents consisting of both positive and negative examples of C, a learnt SVM, M, that models the category C, β, the threshold adjustment parameter, and *UtilityMeasure*, a utility measure that models the user's expectations:

SetSVMThresholdUsingBetaGamma(C, T, M, β, UtilityMeasure)
1. Rank the thresholding dataset, T, using the SVM, M, as scoring function, thereby yielding a ranked document list R consisting of tuples *<Document$_i$, SVMScore$_i$>*.
2. Generate the cumulative utility curve for R, i.e., for each document in the ranked list R compute the cumulative utility using the utility measure *UtilityMeasure*.
3. Determine the rank or indices of the maximum utility point on the cumulative curve and the first zero utility point following the maximum utility point. Denote these respectively as i_{Max}, and i_{Zero}. Assign the variables θ_{Max} and θ_{Zero} the output scores of the SVM, M, for the documents associated with the maximum and zero utility points respectively, i.e., the SVM scores of the documents at rank i_{Max}, and i_{Zero}. (See Figure 2 for a graphic illustration of this step.)
4. Return the threshold, θ, which is calculated as follows:

$$\theta = \beta \theta_{zero} + (1-\beta) \theta_{Max} \qquad (4)$$

In the procedure outlined above, β is either provided heuristically or determined using the beta-gamma cross-validation procedure outlined below. The following is a more sophisticated version of this threshold adjustment algorithm (Equation 4) that takes into account the number of positive training examples used in T:

$$\theta = \alpha \theta_{zero} + (1-\alpha) \theta_{Max}$$
$$\alpha = \beta + (1-\beta) e^{-p\gamma}. \qquad (5)$$

In this equation, p denotes the number of positive documents in the thresholding dataset, T. The γ component of this threshold relaxation formulation provides a mechanism to *further* relax the threshold based entirely upon β (Equation 4). This will have biggest impact on the threshold when there are very few documents. Once, again, as is the case for β, γ is either provided heuristically or determined using the beta-gamma cross-validation procedure outlined below.

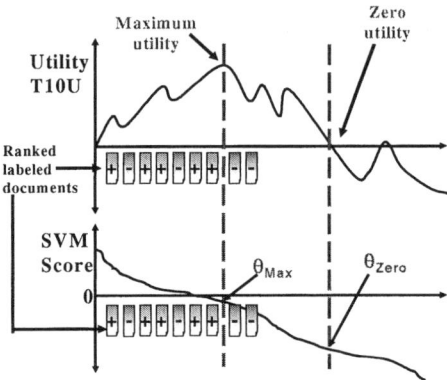

Fig. 2. Determining θ_{Max} and θ_{Zero} using a ranked list of training documents.

Now, we outline a procedure based upon n-fold cross validation to automatically determine the values of β and γ in the threshold relaxation procedure. It consists of the following steps and uses as input a category label, C, a labeled dataset, T, of documents consisting of both positive and negative examples of C (for example, T could be a subset or the complete training dataset), a learnt SVM, M, that models the category C, β, the threshold adjustment parameter, *UtililtyMeasure*, a utility measure that models the user's expectations, βs (valid values for β are positive or negative real numbers), the set of possible beta values, γs, the set of possible gamma values, and n, the number of folds that will be used in parameter selection.

SelectOptimalSVMThreshold(C, T, M, UtililtyMeasure, βs, γs, n)
1. Partition the data into n non-overlapping subsets of the data ensuring that both positive and negative documents are present in each fold or subset.
2. Foreach each combination of β and γ values in βs and γs do steps 3 and 4
3. Foreach fold n
   - Set T_n to the n-1 folds
   - Set θ = *SetSVMThresholdUsingBetaGamma(C, T_n, M, β, γ, UtililtyMeasure)*
   - Set Utility$_{\beta\gamma}$ = Calculate the utility for M and the threshold, θ, over the fold n. See Equation 6 for an explanation of how to use an adjusted threshold in conjunction with an SVM.
4. Compute the average utility as follows: Utility$_{\beta\gamma}$= Utility$_{\beta\gamma}$/n
5. End Foreach
6. Calculate the optimal threshold, θ_{Opt}, using the β and γ combination that has the highest average utility Utility$_{\beta\gamma}$ as follows: *SetSVMThresholdUsingBetaGamma(C, T, M, β, γ, UtililtyMeasure)*
7. Return θ_{Opt}.

The SVM classification rule is altered slightly as follows to accommodate the adjusted threshold:

$$Class(X) = Sign(\langle W, X \rangle + b - \theta_{Opt}) \qquad (6)$$

For our experiments, we adapted the *T10U* linear utility measure (see Table 2) for threshold optimization, as this provides an intuitive user utility model that generally leads to improved recall and precision when used as a cost function in learning [17].

3 Experimental Setup

This section describes the experimental variables, the experimental performance measures and the datasets used for this study. The parameters settings explored in the experiments reported in this paper are summarized in Table 1. All are pretty much self-explanatory, apart from how a document is represented. We represent a document as a vector of terms that is derived as follows: we replace all numerical and punctuation characters by spaces and eliminate stop-words such as articles and prepositions, etc.; each term is associated with a TFxIDF weight, where TF denotes the frequency of a term in a document, and IDF is calculated based on the distribution of the term in the training corpus [18]. In all experiments the document vectors were normalized to unit length.

In our analysis, we examined several information retrieval performance measures which are presented in Table 2 along with their definitions.

Table 1. Learning decision variables and explored values.

Decision Variable	Explored Values
Learning Algorithm	SMOK2
C (Upper bound for Lagrange multipliers)	0.4, 0.8, 0.9, 1, 2, 5
Tolerance	0.001
Type of kernel	Linear
Sampling Ratio	Used all training data
Number of terms k	Use all terms
Term types	White space delimited tokens with numbers, punctuation, and stopwords removed
Term weighting	TF_IDF

For our current study, we have performed an evaluation of learning threshold adjusted SVM classifiers (TSVMs) on the following classification corpora: Reuters-21578 ModApte split collection [10] and TREC2001 corpus [17]. The main reasons for choosing these corpora include the following: these corpora are commonly used in benchmarking text classification problems; the Reuters-21578 corpus is a manageable size thereby enabling extensive experimentation (without being computationally prohibitive). The details of each corpus are presented below.

3.1 Reuters-21578 (ModApte Split)

The Reuters-21578 collection contains 12,902 newswire stories that had been classified into 118 categories (e.g., corporate acquisitions, earnings, money market, grain, and interest) [10]. We followed the ModApte split in which 75% of the stories (9603 stories) are used to build classifiers, while the remaining 25% (3299 stories) are used to test the accuracy of the resulting models in reproducing the manual category assignments. Only 90 categories are modeled in our experiments. These 90 categories were selected based upon having at least one training and one testing example.

Though only 90 categories were modeled, the examples belonging to the non-modeled categories were used for training and testing.

3.2 TREC 2001 Corpus

The TREC 2001 Corpus, officially known as "Reuters Corpus, Volume, English Language, 1996-08-20 to 1997-08-19", contains one year of Reuters newswire stories in English, corresponding to 1.5 GB of data, or 810,000 news stories taken from the period August 1996 – August 1997. Each story has been assigned one or more category labels from 84 possibilities. The training dataset is limited to the last 12 days of August 1996 (corresponding to approximately 23,000 examples); the remaining 11 months are designated as test data. More information about this corpus can be found at http://about.reuters.com/researchandstandards/corpus [17].

Table 2. Evaluation measures and their definitions, where R^+, N^+, R^-, and N^- are true positives, false positives, false negatives and true negatives respectively.

Evaluation Measure	Definition
Precision	$p = \dfrac{R^+}{R^+ + N^+}$
Recall	$r = \dfrac{R^+}{R^+ + R^-}$
F_β	$F_\beta = \dfrac{(\beta^2 + 1) * p * r}{(\beta^2 * p) + r}$
T10U/ *T11U*	$T10U = T11U = 2R^+ - 1N^+$
T10SU	$T10SU = \dfrac{\max(T10U, MinU) - MinU}{MaxU - MinU}$ where $MaxU = 2*(R^+ + R^-)$ and $MinU = -100$
T11SU	$T11SU = \dfrac{\max(T11NU, MinNU) - MinNU}{1 - MinNU}$ where $T11NU = \dfrac{T11U}{MaxU}$ and $MinNU = -0.5$

4 Results and Empirical Observations

In the case of all examined corpora, a topic-specific binary classifier was learned from the training data that models the topic (positive examples) and the not-topic (negative examples). The values explored for β were restricted to the following list: {-0.05, 0.0, 0.05, 0.1, 0.15, 0.2, 0.25, 0.3, 0.35, 0.4, 0.45, 0.5, 0.55, 0.6, 0.65, 0.7, 0.75, 0.8}, while γ was set to 100 (effectively disabled). The γ parameter was disabled after noticing no discernable improvement from using it in the context of classification, though this parameter proved to be crucial in an adaptive text filtering context [22], where a topic is defined differently and its definition is adapted over time; usually a topic is defined in terms of a focused query and a small number of explicitly labeled documents; and its definition is refined over time upon receiving user feedback.

The proposed thresholding approach is compared against the following approaches: baseline (unthresholded) SVMs; other threshold adjusting SVM approaches; asymmetric (misclassification costs) SVMs; and traditional IR approaches.

Figure 3 compares the results for the Reuters-21578 corpus between the threshold adjusted SVMs and baseline SVMs for each topic with respect to the T11SU evaluation measure. For this graph of results, and for subsequent graphs of results, the horizontal axis represents the topics (considered in a corpus), ranked in decreasing order of the number of positive training data available for that topic. This graph has two primary vertical or y axes; the left vertical axis corresponds to the log (base 10) of number of training documents; the right vertical axis corresponds to the difference in performance for the indicated measure (T11SU in the case of Figure 3) between the threshold adjusted SVM (denoted as *SVMThresh*) and the baseline SVM. Positive bars for this measure correspond to an improvement in performance when threshold adjustment is used. Table 3 presents the macro-average results for precision, recall, Fbeta, and T11SU for the Reuters-21578 corpus.

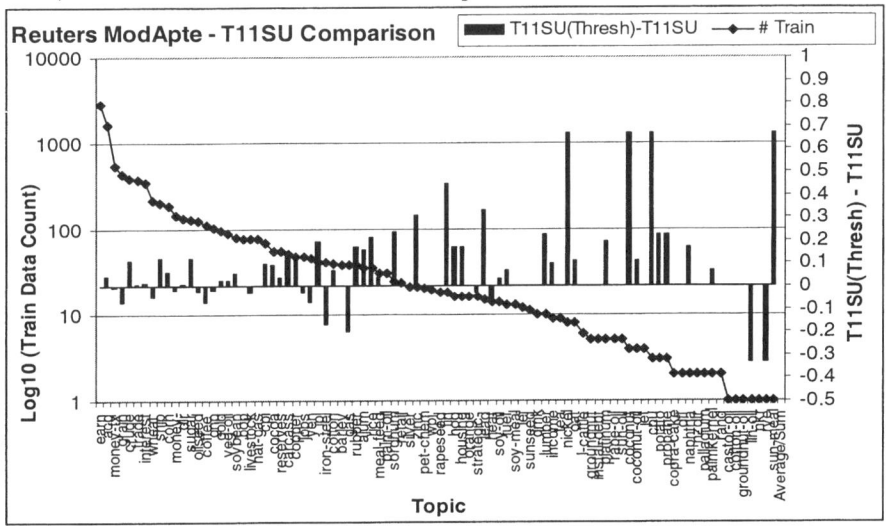

Fig. 3. The difference in T11SU performance for the Reuters-21578 corpus.

Table 3. A results comparison for the Reuters 87 ModApte corpus.

Approach	T11SU	$F_{\beta=0.5}$	Precision	Recall
CC Thresholded SVMs	0.61	0.57	0.64	0.48
Linear SVM	0.54	0.48	0.58	0.33

Overall, we can see that adjusting the threshold using the beta-gamma procedure boosts the performance of the baseline SVM on all examined evaluation measures at a macro level for the Reuter-21578 corpus (Table 3). Examining each topic from a T11SU perspective (Figure 3), we notice that the biggest improvement in T11SU performance comes from topics that have fewer than *fifty* positive training documents, topics that have traditionally being very difficult to model. Overall, 80% of the topics have improved or have not been adversely affected by this procedure.

Figure 4 compares the results for the TREC 2001 corpus between the threshold adjusted SVMs and baseline SVMs for each topic with respect to the T10SU evaluation measure. Table 4 presents the macro-average results for precision, recall, Fbeta, and T11SU for the TREC 2001 corpus. The K-NN result in Table 4 corresponds to a k nearest neighbor approach [2]. The IR result is achieved using traditional information retrieval filters [1]. The RBF SVM result in Table 4 was achieved using SVMs and radial basis kernels [13].

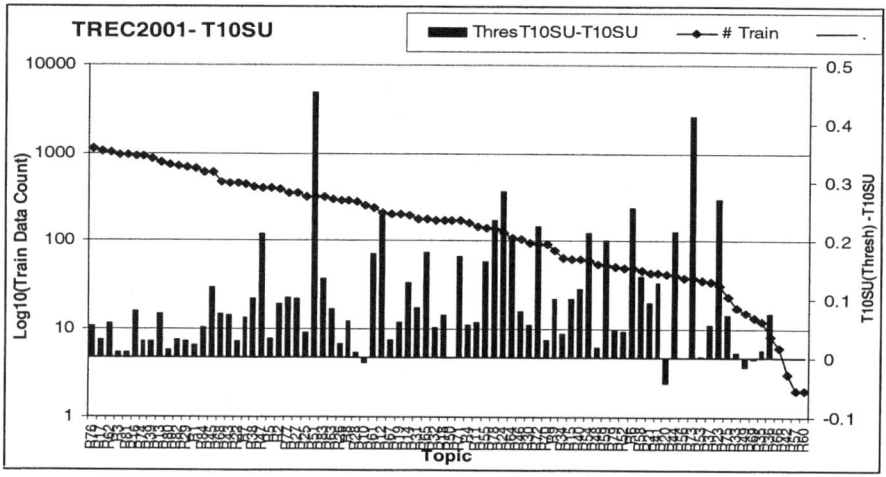

Fig. 4. The difference in T10SU performance for the TREC2001 corpus.

Table 4. A results comparison for the TREC2001 corpus.

Approach	T10SU	$F_{\beta=0.5}$	Precision	Recall
Asymmetric SVM [11]	0.41	0.60	0.75	0.45
CC Thresholded SVMs	0.40	0.56	0.64	0.50
K-NN [2]	0.32	0.49	0.63	0.36
Linear SVM	0.31	0.50	0.75	0.31
IR [1]	0.31	0.51	0.57	0.41
RBF SVM [13]	0.28	0.46	0.55	0.44

Adjusting the threshold of the SVM for the TREC2001 topics has boosted recall and therefore led to over 20% improvement in terms of T11SU performance over baseline SVMs (linear SVM), while not effecting precision. This performance is comparable with the best performer for this text classification task that was prepared by Lewis [11]. Lewis's submission was generated using asymmetric SVMs. The following observations can be made when we compare evaluation measures for our threshold adjusted experiment and Lewis's asymmetric run: first of all, due to the expensive cross fold validation required for determining the asymmetric costs of the SVM learning, training Lewis's asymmetric SVMs took two orders of magnitude more time to learn than our threshold adjusted SVMs (i.e., 500 hours for Lewis's experiment versus 5 hours for our experiment); Lewis's experiment with asymmetric SVMs provides 14% better precision than our threshold adjusted run; our threshold adjusted run provides 11% better recall than Lewis's run; this would seem to suggest that asymmetric SVMs and adjusting the threshold are addressing two independent aspects of the problem, which if combined could boost performance even further.

5 Conclusions

We have presented a novel SVM threshold adjusting algorithm. It uses cross validation to automatically determine the optimal parameters for the beta-gamma algorithm, which are subsequently used to relax the threshold of the class model. The proposed approach boosts the recall performance of baseline SVMs for text classification, while not adversely affecting precision. The gain in performance for examined TREC corpora is over 20% for standard information retrieval measures when compared to baseline SVMs. The extra cost of performing this threshold adjustment is small, in that it is a one-dimensional optimization problem. Adjusting the threshold of SVMs is just one technique for boosting the performance of SVMs. Combining our threshold adjustment algorithm with other techniques, such as asymmetric cost-based learning of SVMs, should lead to even better performance. This is part of ongoing work. A more detailed comparison between the proposed approach and other thresholding approaches that have or can be applied to the task of threshold adjustment for SVMs is currently being carried out. In addition, since the proposed thresholding approach is independent of the learnt model, using it in conjunction with other types of models will also form an interesting aspect of future work.

Acknowledgements

We thank David Evans, David Hull and Diane Kelly for their useful comments.

References

1. Arampatzis A., Unbiased S-D Threshold Optimization, Initial Query Degradation, Decay, and Incrementality, for Adaptive Document Filtering, *Tenth Text Retrieval Conference (TREC-2001)*, (2002), 596-605
2. Ault T., Yang Y., kNN, Rocchio and Metrics for Information Filtering at TREC-10, *Tenth Text Retrieval Conference (TREC-2001)*, (2002), 84-93
3. Cancedda N. et al., Kernel Methods for Document Filtering, Eleventh Text Retrieval Conference (TREC-2002), 2003
4. Cortes, C., Vapnik, V., Support vector networks. *Machine Learning*, (1995) 20:273-297
5. Evans, D.A., Shanahan, J., Tong, X., Roma, N., Stoica, E., Sheftel, V., Montgomery, J., Bennett, J., Fujita, S., Grefenstette, G. Topic Specific Optimization and Structuring. *Tenth Text Retrieval Conference (TREC-2001)*, (2002), 132-141

6. Joachims, T. Text categorization with support vector machines: Learning with many relevant features. In *Proceedings 10th European Conference on Machine Learning (ECML)*, Springer Verlag, (1998)
7. Keerthi, S.S., Shevade, S.K., Bhattacharyya, C., Murthy, K.R.K. *Improvements to Platt's SMO algorithm for SVM classifier design*. Technical report, Dept of CSA, IISc, Bangalore, India, (1999)
8. LeCun, Y., Jackel, L. D., Bottou, L., Cortes, C., Denker, J. S., Drucker, H., Guyon, I., Muller, U. A., Sackinger, E., Simard, P. and Vapnik, V. Learning algorithms for classification: A comparison on handwritten digit recognition. *Neural Networks: The Statistical Mechanics Perspective*, (1995), 261-276
9. Lewis, D.D., Schapire, R.E., Callan, J.P., and Papka, R. Training algorithms for linear text classifiers, In *Int'l ACM Conf. on Research and Development in Information Retrieval* (SIGIR-96), (1996), 298-306.
10. Lewis D. D., The Reuters-21578 text categorization test collection. http://www.research.att.com/~lewis/reuters21578.html. Checked on 11 May 1998; Timestamp Tue Jan 20 21:07:21 EST (1998).
11. Lewis D. D., Applying Support Vector Machines to the TREC-2001 Batch Filtering and Routing Tasks, *Tenth Text Retrieval Conference (TREC-2001)*, (2002), 286-294
12. Li, Y., Zaragoza, H., Herbrich, R., Shawe-Taylor, J., Kandola, J.S. The Perceptron Algorithm with Uneven Margins. *ICML 2002*: 379–386
13. Mayfield J., McNamee P., Costello C., Piatko C., Banerjee A., JHU/APL at TREC 2001: Experiments in Filtering and in Arabic, Video, and Web Retrieval, at TREC-10, *Tenth Text Retrieval Conference (TREC-2001)*, (2002), 322-332
14. Morik, K., Brockhausen, P., Joachims, T. Combining statistical learning with a knowledge-based approach - A case study in intensive care monitoring. *Proc. 16th Int'l Conf. on Machine Learning (ICML-99)*, (1999)
15. Osuna, E., Freund, R., and Girosi, F. Training support vector machines: An application to face detection. In *Proceedings of Computer Vision and Pattern Recognition '97*, (1997), 130-136
16. Platt, J. Fast training of SVMs using sequential minimal optimization. In: B. Scholkopf, C. Burges, and A. Smola (Eds.) *Advances in Kernel Methods – Support Vector Learning*, MIT Press, (1998).
17. Robertson S., Soboroff I., The TREC 2001 Filtering Track Report, *Tenth Text Retrieval Conference (TREC-2001)*, (2002), 26–37.
18. Salton G., Introduction to Modern Information Retrieval, Verlag: Mc Graw Hill, New York, (1983).
19. Vapnik, V., The Nature of Statistical Learning Theory, Springer-Verlag, (1995)
20. Vapnik, V., Statistical Learning Theory, Wiley, (1998)
21. Voorhees E.M., Overview of TREC 2002, Eleventh Text Retrieval Conference (TREC-2002), (2002), 1–16
22. Yang Y., A study on thresholding strategies for text categorization, Proceedings of ACM SIGIR Conference on Research and Development in Information Retrieval (SIGIR'01), (2001), 137-145
23. Zhai, C., Jansen, P., Stoica, E., Grot, N., Evans, D.A. Threshold Calibration in CLARIT Adaptive Filtering. *Seventh Text Retrieval Conference (TREC-7)*, (1999), 149–156
24. Zhang, Y. and Callan, J. "YFilter at TREC-9". In *Proceedings of the Ninth Text REtrieval Conference (TREC-9)*, (pp. 135-140). National Institute of Standards and Technology, (2001), 500-249

Backoff Parameter Estimation for the DOP Model

Khalil Sima'an and Luciano Buratto*

Institute for Logic, Language and Computation (ILLC)
University of Amsterdam, The Netherlands
simaan@science.uva.nl; lburatto@citri.iq.usp.br

Abstract. The Data Oriented Parsing (DOP) model currently achieves state-of-the-art parsing on benchmark corpora. However, existing DOP parameter estimation methods are known to be biased, and ad hoc adjustments are needed in order to reduce the effects of these biases on performance. In contrast with earlier work, in this paper we show that the DOP parameters constitute a hierarchically structured space of correlated events (rather than a set of disjoint events). The correlations between the different parameters can be expressed by an asymmetric relation called "backoff". Subsequently, we present a novel recursive estimation algorithm that exploits this hierarchical structure for parameter estimation through discounting and backoff. Finally, we report on experiments showing error reductions of up to 15% in comparison to earlier estimation methods.

1 Introduction

The Data Oriented Parsing (DOP) model currently exhibits state-of-the-art performance on benchmark corpora [1]. A DOP model is trained on a treebank[1] by extracting all subtrees of the treebank trees and employing them as the basic rewrite events (or productions) of a formal grammar. The problem of how to estimate the probabilities of the subtrees from the treebank turns out *not* as straightforward as originally thought. So far, there exist three suggestions for parameter estimation [2, 3, 1]. As shown in [3, 4] and in the present paper, all three estimation procedures turn out to be biased in an unintuitive manner. Therefore, the problem of how to estimate the DOP parameters in a productive, yet computationally reasonable manner, remains unsolved.

Parameter estimation for DOP is complex due to two unique aspects of the model: (1) a parse-tree in DOP is often generated through multiple, different rewrite derivations, and (2) the model consists of treebank subtrees of arbitrary size. These two aspects distinguish DOP from other existing models that are predominantly based on the paradigm of History-Based Stochastic Models (HBSG)

---

* We thank Rens Bod, Detlef Prescher and the reviewers for their comments.
[1] A treebank is a sample of parse-sentence pairs drawn from a domain of language use; the parses are the correct syntactic structures as perceived by humans.

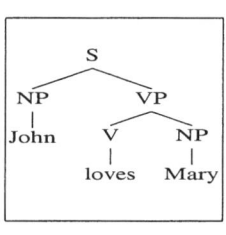

Fig. 1. A toy treebank

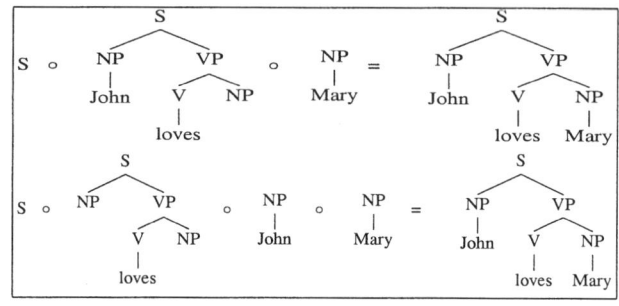

Fig. 2. Two different derivations of the same parse

[5]. An HBSG generates every parse-tree through a unique derivation involving rewrite production that can be considered, to a large extent, disjoint events. This allows for simpler estimation procedures and more efficient parsing algorithms than is possible for current DOP models.

This paper addresses the DOP parameter estimation from a different angle than preceding work. Crucially, we observe that the space of subtrees of a DOP model does not merely constitute a set of disjoint events, but that it constitutes a hierarchical space. This space is structured by a partial order between the different derivations of the same subtree; the more independence assumptions a derivation involves, the lower it is in this hierarchy, just like different n-gram orders of the same word string. This partial order between a subtree and its derivations is characterized by the relation of "backoff", defined in the sequel. Subsequently, a DOP model can be viewed as an interpolation of different orders of derivations: a subtree, the derivations of that subtree obtained by one, two, ... independence assumptions between smaller subtrees. Based on this observation we suggest to combine the different derivations through *backoff*, rather than interpolation. This view leads to a simple, yet powerful recursive estimation procedure. The new DOP model, Backoff DOP, leads to improved parsing results. We report on experiments that show a 10-15% error reduction on a treebank on which the original DOP model already achieves excellent results.

2 The DOP Model

Like other treebank models, DOP extracts a finite set of rewrite productions, called *subtrees*, from the training treebank together with probability estimates. A connected subgraph of a treebank tree t is called a *subtree* iff it consists of one or more context-free productions[2] from t. Following [2], the set of rewrite productions of DOP consists of *all* the subtrees of the treebank trees. Figure 3 exemplifies the set of subtrees extracted from the treebank of Figure 1.

---

[2] Note that a non-leaf node labeled p in tree t dominating a sequence of nodes labeled $c_1, \cdots, c_n$ consists of a graph that represents the context-free production: $p \to c_1 \cdots c_n$.

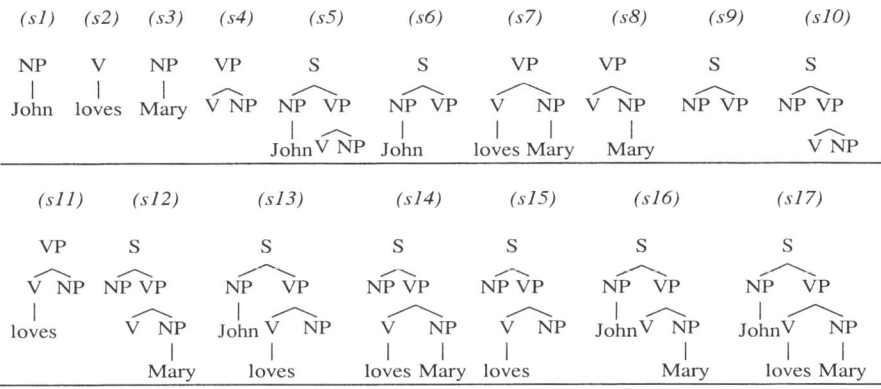

Fig. 3. The subtrees of the treebank in Figure 1

DOP employs the set of subtrees in a Stochastic Tree-Substitution Grammar (STSG): an TSG is a rewrite system similar to Context-Free Grammars (CFGs), with the difference that TSG productions are subtrees of arbitrary depth[3].

A TSG derivation proceeds by combining subtrees using the substitution operation ∘ starting from the start symbol S of the TSG. In contrast with CFG derivations, multiple TSG derivations may generate the same parse[4]. For example, the parse in Figure 1 can be derived at least in two different ways as shown in Figure 2. In this sense, the DOP model deviates from other contemporary models, e.g. [8,9], that belong to the so-called History-Based Stochastic Grammar (HBSG) family [5].

An Stochastic TSG (STSG) is a TSG extended with a probability mass function P over the set of subtrees: the probability of subtree t, that has root label R_t, is given by $P(t|R_t)$, i.e. for every nonterminal A: $\sum_{\{t|R_t=A\}} P(t \mid A) = 1$. Given a probability function P, the probability of a derivation $D = S \circ t_1 \circ \cdots \circ t_n$ is defined by $P(D \mid S) = \prod_{i=1}^{n} P(t_i|R_{t_i})$. The probability of a parse is defined by the sum of the probabilities of all derivations in the STSG that generate that parse.

When parsing an input sentence U under a DOP model, the preferred parse T is the Most Probable Parse (MPP) for that sentence: $\arg\max_T P(T|U)$. However, the problem of computing the MPP is known to be intractable [10]. In contrast, the calculation of the Most Probable Derivation (MPD) D for the input sentence U i.e., $\arg\max_D P(D|U)$, can be done in time cubic in sentence length.

In this paper we address another difficulty that arises from the property of the multiple derivations per parse with regard to the DOP model: how to estimate the model parameters (i.e. subtree probabilities) from a treebank.

---

[3] The depth of a tree is the number of edges along the longest path from the root to a leaf node.
[4] Note the difference between parses and subtrees: the first are generated, complex events while the latter are atomic, rewrite events.

3 Existing DOP Estimators

All three existing DOP estimators are biased, either by giving too much probability mass to large/small subtrees or by overfitting the training data.

(1) Subtree relative Frequency: The first instantiation of a DOP model is due to [11] and is referred to as DOP_{rf}. In this model, the probability estimates of subtrees extracted from a treebank are given by a relative frequency estimator. Let $f(t)$ represent the number of times t occurred in the bag of subtrees extracted from the treebank. Then the probability of t in DOP_{rf} is estimated as: $P_{rf}(t|R_t) = \frac{f(t)}{\sum_{t':R_{t'}=R_t} f(t')}$.

Using heuristics to limit the unwanted biases, the model achieved 89.7% in labelled recall and precision on the Wall Street Journal treebank [1]. Despite good performance, DOP_{rf} estimator has been shown to be biased and inconsistent [4]. As argued in [3], DOP_{rf} overestimates the probability of large subtrees. Furthermore, DOP_{rf}'s good performance can be attributed to limitations on the set of subtrees extracted from the treebank (e.g. subtree depth upper bounds). These constraints reduce the model's bias, leading to improved performance.

(2) Bonnema's Estimator: In [3], an alternative estimator for DOP is proposed. It assumes that every treebank parse represents a *uniform distribution* over all possible derivations that generated that parse in the model. Thus, the probability of a subtree t is estimated by taking the relative frequency of t along with the fraction of derivations of the treebank parses in which t participates. This leads to the following estimate: $P(t|R_t) = 2^{-N(t)} P_{rf}(t|R_t)$, where $N(t)$ is the number of non-root nonterminal nodes of subtree t and P_{rf} is the original DOP_{rf}'s relative frequency estimator. The estimator defines a new DOP model which we refer to as DOP_{Bon} model. Next we show that the DOP_{Bon} estimator is biased towards smaller subtrees.

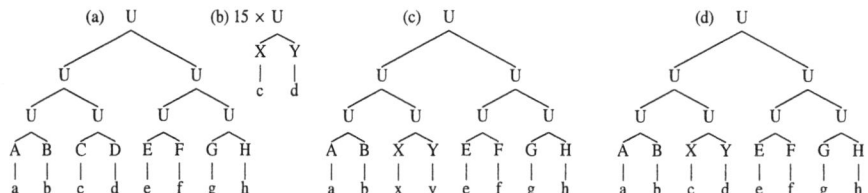

Fig. 4. /Example illustrating DOP_{Bon}'s bias towards small subtree fragments. Given the training treebank (a–c), the correct parse to $abcdefgh$ should be (a). DOP_{Bon} model chooses (d) instead

Consider the treebank in Figure 4(a–c) with 17 subtrees. According to the treebank, the correct analysis for string $abcdefgh$ should be the one in Figure 4(a). DOP_{Bon}, however, prefers the parse in Figure 4(d). In other words, a derivation that was actually seen in the treebank (i.e. the parse tree yielding $abcdefgh$ in Figure 4(a)) becomes less likely than a newly constructed parse involving the subtree in Figure 4(b)!

(3) Maximum-Likelihood: One might say that DOP_{rf} estimator is biased because it is not a Maximum-Likelihood (ML) estimator. This is in fact the approach taken in [12], where the Inside-Outside algorithm is used for estimation of DOP model parameters from a treebank under the assumption that the model has a hidden element (the derivations that generated the parses of the treebank). However, as [3] pointed out, ML for DOP results in a model that overfits the treebank. We exemplify this next.

Let be given a treebank with trees τ_1, τ_2, both having the same root label X. The ML probability assignment to the subtrees extracted from this treebank is given as follows: for τ_1 and τ_2, $P(\tau_1|X) = P(\tau_2|X) = 1/2$; for all other X-rooted subtrees t, $P(t|X) = 0$. In other words, probability zero is given to all parses not present in the treebank, resulting in a model that overfits the data and has no generalization power.

4 A New Estimator for DOP

In this section we develop a completely different approach to parameter estimation for DOP than earlier work. Consider the common situation where a subtree[5] t is equal to a tree generated by a derivation $t_1 \circ \cdots \circ t_n$ involving multiple subtrees $t_1 \cdots t_n$. For example, subtree *s17* (Figure 3) can be constructed by different derivations such as *(s16 ∘ s2)*, *(s14 ∘ s1)* and *(s15 ∘ s1 ∘ s3)*. We will refer to subtrees that can be constructed from derivations involving other subtrees with the term *complex subtrees*.

For every complex subtree t, we restrict[6] our attention only to the derivations involving pairs of subtrees; in other words, we focus on subtree t such that there exist subtrees t_1 and t_2 such that $t = (t_1 \circ t_2)$. In DOP, the probability of t is given by $P(t|R_t)$. In contrast, the derivation probability is defined by $P(t_1 \circ t_2 | R_{t_1}) = P(t_1|R_{t_1})P(t_2|R_{t_2})$. However, according to the chain rule (note that $R_t = R_{t_1}$)

$$P(t_1 \circ t_2 | R_{t_1}) = P(t_1|R_{t_1})P(t_2|t_1, R_{t_1})$$

Therefore, the derivation $t_1 \circ t_2$ embodies an independence assumption realized by the approximation[7]: $P(t_2|t_1) \approx P(t_2|R_{t_2})$. This approximation involves a so-called *backoff*, i.e. a weakening of the conditioning context from $P(t_2|t_1)$ to $P(t_2|R_{t_2})$. Hence, we will say that the derivation $t_1 \circ t_2$ constitutes *a backoff* of subtree t and we will write $(t \geq_{bfk} t_1 \circ t_2)$ to express this fact.

---

[5] According to the definitions in section 2, the term "subtree" is reserved for the tree-structures that DOP extracts from the treebank.

[6] Because DOP takes all subtrees of the treebank, if complex subtree t has a derivation $t_1 \circ t_2 \circ \cdots \circ t_n$, then the tree resulting from $t_1 \circ t_2$ is a complex subtree also. For example, in Figure 3, *s17* can be derived through *(s15 ∘ s1 ∘ s3)*; *s15 ∘ s1* generates subtree *s13*. Hence, derivations of t that involve more than two subtrees can be separarted into (sub)derivations that involve pairs of subtrees, each leading to a complex subtree. Therefore, for any complex subtree t, we may restrict our attention to derivations involving only pairs of subtrees i.e., $t = t_1 \circ t_2$.

[7] Note that R_{t_2} is part of t_1 (the label of the substitution site).

The backoff relation $\geq_{bfk}$ between a subtree and a pair of other subtrees allows for a partial order between the derivations of the subtrees extracted from a treebank. A graphical representation of this partial order is a directed acyclic graph which consists of a node for each pair of subtrees t_i, t_j that constitute a derivation of another complex subtree. A directed edge points from a subtree t_i in a node[8] to another node containing a pair of subtrees $\langle t_j, t_k \rangle$ iff $t_i \geq_{bfk} t_j \circ t_k$. We refer to this graph as the *backoff graph*. A portion of the backoff graph for the subtrees of Figure 3 is shown in figure 5 (where $s0$ stands for a subtree consisting of a single node labeled S – the start symbol).

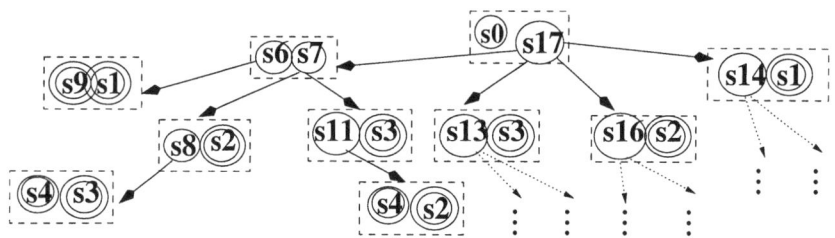

Fig. 5. A portion of the backoff graph for the subtrees in Figure 3

We distinguish two sets of subtrees: initial and atomic. Initial subtrees do not participate in a backoff derivation of any other subtree. In Figure 3, subtree $s17$ is the only initial subtree. Atomic subtrees are subtrees for which there are no backoffs. In Figure 3, these are subtrees of depth one (double circled in the backoff graph).

In the DOP model (under any estimation procedure discussed in section 3), the probablity of a parse-tree is defined as the sum of the probabilities of all derivations that generate this parse-tree. This means that DOP interpolates, linearly and with uniform weights, derivations involving subtrees from different levels of the backoff graph; this is similar to the way Hidden Markov Models interpolate different Markov orders over, e.g. words, for calculating sentence probability. Hence, we will refer to the different levels of subtrees in the backoff graph as the *Markov orders*.

Backoff DOP: Crucially, the partial order over the subtrees, embodied in the backoff graph, can be exploited for turning DOP into a "backedoff model" as follows. A subtree is generated by a sequence of derivations *ordered by the backoff relation*. This is in sharp contrast with existing DOP models that consider the different derivations leading to the same subtree as a set of *disjoint* events. Next, after we review smoothing and Katz Backoff, we present the estimation procedure that accompanies this new realization of DOP as a recursive backoff over the different Markov orders.

---

[8] In a pair $\langle t_h, t_i \rangle$ or $\langle t_i, t_h \rangle$ that constitutes a node.

Estimation vs. Smoothing: It is common to *smooth* a probability distribution $P(t|X,Y)$ by a backoff distribution e.g. $P(t|X)$. The smoothing of $P(t|X,Y)$ aims at dealing with the problem of sparse-data (whenever the probability $P(t|X,Y)$ is zero). $P(t|X)$ can be used as an approximation of $P(t|X,Y)$ under the assumption that t and Y are independent. Smoothing, then, aims at enlarging the space of non-zero events in the distribution $P(t|X,Y)$. Hence, the goal of smoothing differs from our goal. While smoothing aims at filling the zero gaps in a distribution, our goal is to estimate the distribution (a priori to smoothing it). Despite these differences, we employ a backoff method for parameter estimation by *redistributing probability mass among DOP model subtrees*.

Katz Backoff: [6,7] is a smoothing technique based on the discounting method of Good-Turing (GT) [13,7]. Given a higher order distribution $P(t|X,Y)$, Katz backoff employs the GT formula for discounting from this distribution leading to $P_{GT}(t|X,Y)$. The probability mass that was discounted $(1 - \sum_t P_{GT}(t|X,Y))$ is distributed over the lower order distribution $P(t|X)$.

Estimation by Backoff: We assume initial probability estimates P_f based on frequency counts, e.g. as in DOP_{rf} or DOP_{Bon}. The present backoff estimation procedure operates iteratively, top-down over the backoff graph, starting with the initial and moving down towards the atomic subtrees. In essense this procedure *transfers, stepwisely, probability mass* from complex subtrees to their backoffs.

Let P^c represent the current probability estimate resulting from i previous steps of re-estimation (initially, for $i = 0$, $P^0 := P_f$). After i steps, the edges of the backoff graph lead to the *current layer* of nodes. For every t, a subtree in a node from the current layer in the backoff graph, an edge e outgoing from t stands for the relation $(t \geq_{bfk} t_1 \circ t_2)$, where $\langle t_1, t_2 \rangle$ is the node at the other end of edge e. We know that $P^c(t_2|t_1)$ is backedoff to $P^c(t_2|R_{t_2})$ since $P^c(t|R_t) = P^c(t_1|R_{t_1})P^c(t_2|t_1)$ and $P^c(t_1 \circ t_2) = P^c(t_1|R_{t_1})P^c(t_2|R_{t_2})$. We adapt the Katz method to estimate the Backoff DOP probability P_{bo} as follows:

$$P_{bo}(t_2|t_1) = \begin{cases} P^c_{GT}(t_2|t_1) + \alpha(t_1)\, P_f(t_2|R_{t_2}) & [\mathrm{P}^c(\mathrm{t}_2|\mathrm{t}_1) > 0] \\ \alpha(t_1)\, P_f(t_2|R_{t_2}) & \texttt{otherwise} \end{cases}$$

where $\alpha(t_1)$ is a normalization factor that guarantees that the sum of the probabilities of subtrees with the same root label is one. Simple arithmetic leads to the following formula: $\alpha(t_1) = 1 - \sum_{t_2: f(t_1,t_2)>0} P^c_{GT}(t_2|t_1)$. Using the above estimate of $P_{bo}(t_2|t_1)$, the other backoff estimates are calculated as follows:

$$P_{bo}(t|R_t) := P_f(t_1|R_{t_1})\, P^c_{GT}(t_2|t_1) \qquad P_{bo}(t_1|R_{t_1}) := (\, 1 + \alpha(t_1)\,)\, P_f(t_1|R_{t_1})$$

Before the next step $i+1$ takes place over the next layer in the backoff graph, the current probabilities are updated as follows: $P^{i+1}(t_1|R_{t_1}) := P_{bo}(t_1|R_{t_1})$.

Note that P_{bo} is a proper distribution in the sense that for all nonterminals A: $\sum_t P(t|A) = 1$. This is guaranteed by the redistribution of the reserved probability mass at every step of the procedure over the layers of the backoff graph. Furthermore, we note that the present method is *not* a smoothing method since it applies Katz Backoff for redistributing probability mass *only* among subtrees that *did occur* in the treebank. The present method does not address probability estimation for unknown/unseen events.

Current Implementation: The number of subtrees extracted from a tree-bank is extremely large. In this paper, we choose to apply the Katz backoff only to $t \geq_{bfk} t_1 \circ t_2$ iff t_2 is a lexical subtree i.e., $t_2 = X \to w$ where X is a Part of Speech (PoS) tag and w a word. Our choice has to do with the importance of lexicalized subtrees and the overestimation that accompanies their relative frequency. All experiments reported here pertain to applying the backoff estimation procedure to this limited set of subtrees (while the probabilities of all other subtrees are left untouched).

5 Empirical Results

OVIS Corpus and Evaluation Metrics: The experiments were carried out on the OVIS corpus, a Dutch language, speech-based, dialogue system that provides railway information to human users over ordinary telephone lines [14]. The corpus contains 10,049 syntactically and semantically annotated utterances which are answers given by users to the system's questions (e.g. "From where to where do you want to travel?"). Utterances are annotated by a phrase-structure scheme with syntactic+semantic labels.

The corpus was randomly split into two sets: i) a training set with 9,049 trees; ii) a test set with 1,000 trees. The experiments were carried out using the same train/test split, unless stated otherwise. We report results for sentences that are at least two-word long (as 1 word sentences are easy). Without 1-word sentences, the average sentence length is 4.6 words/sentence.

Three accuracy measures were employed: exact match and recall/precision (F-score) of labeled bracketing [15]. Furthermore, we compate models using the *error reduction ratio*, the ratio between the percent point improvement of model 1 over model 2 normalized by the global error of model 2.

Subtree space was reduced by means of four upper bounds on their shape: 1) depth (d), 2) number of lexical items (l), 3) number of substitution sites (n) and 4) number of consecutive lexical items (L). Most Probable Derivation (**MPD**) and Most Probable Parse (**MPP**) were used as the maximization entities to select the preferred parse[9].

Naming convention: We tested the new estimator under two different counting strategies: DOP_{rf} and DOP_{Bon}. The following naming convention was used: **DOP_{rf}** (as in [2]), **DOP_{Bon}** (as in [3]), **$BF\text{-}DOP_{rf}$** (backoff estimator applied to DOP_{rf} frequencies), and **$BF\text{-}DOP_{Bon}$** (backoff estimator applied to DOP_{Bon} frequencies).

Accuracy vs. Depth Upper Bound: Figure 6 shows exact match results as a function of subtree depth upper bound. The subtrees were restricted to at most 2

---

[9] A complete specification of the algorithms for extracting the MPD and MPP can be found in [16, 17].

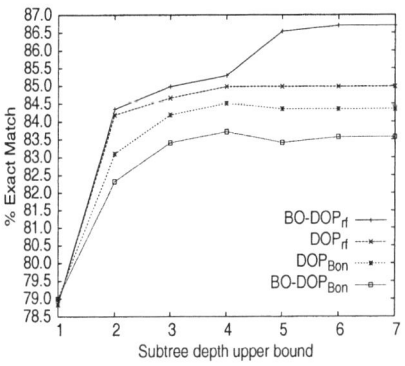 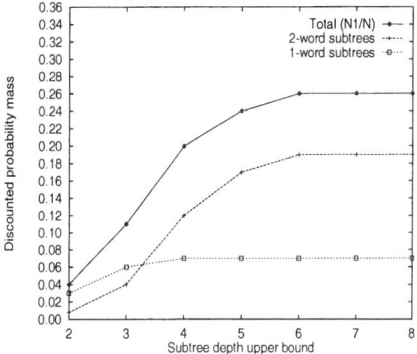

Fig. 6. Exact match as a function of subtree depth upper bound ($l2n4$, MPD)

Fig. 7. Probability mass discounted from subtrees as a function of depth upper bound ($l2n4$)

words and 4 substitution nodes ($l2n4$). This yields small subtree spaces: for depth 7, this corresponds to 172,050 subtrees. For all depth upper bounds, $BF\text{-}DOP_{rf}$ achieved the best results followed by DOP_{rf}, DOP_{Bon} and $BF\text{-}DOP_{Bon}$. $BF\text{-}DOP_{rf}$ improved on DOP_{rf} by 1.72 percent points at depth 6, an increase of 2.02%. This corresponds to an error reduction of 11.4%. When compared to DOP_{Bon}, error reduction rose to about 15%. F-score results followed the same pattern. At depth 6, $BF\text{-}DOP_{rf}$ reached 95.33%; DOP_{rf}, 94.73%; DOP_{Bon}, 94.5% and $BF\text{-}DOP_{Bon}$, 94.33%. Error reduction of $BF\text{-}DOP_{rf}$ with respect to DOP_{rf} reached 11.3% and with respect to DOP_{Bon}, 15.7%.

The good perfomance of $BF\text{-}DOP_{rf}$ over DOP_{rf} may be explained by its reduced bias towards large subtrees. $BF\text{-}DOP_{Bon}$'s poor perfomance, on the other hand, is a result of increasing even further DOP_{Bon}'s bias towards smaller subtrees. The lesson here is: if one has to choose between biased estimators, choose the one favoring larger subtrees; they are able to capture more linguistically relevant dependencies.

Probability Mass Transfer: Figure 7 shows discounted probability mass as a function of subtree depth upper bound. The probability mass discounted from 2-word subtrees is bigger than the mass discounted from 1-word subtrees[10]. This happens because the number of hapax legomena (subtrees that occur just once) tends to increase for higher d and l upper bounds, since more large subtrees with rare word combinations are allowed into the distribution. More hapax legomena results in higher discounting rates according to the Good-Turing method. Thus, the probability mass discounted from n-word subtrees is, in general, bigger than the mass discounted from (n-1)-subtrees. Consequently, the magnitude of the probability transfer across Markov orders gradually decreases as the recursive estimation procedure approaches atomic subtrees. The property of decreasing

---

[10] n-word subtrees are subtrees having exactly n words in their leaf nodes.

discounts avoids the pitfall of overestimating small subtrees (c.f. DOP_{Bon}) and, at the same time, reduces the overestimation of large subtrees (c.f. DOP_{rf}).

Most Probable Parse and Derivation: The next set of experiments used distributions obtained with parameters l7n2L3. These settings allow for testing the models quickly, since they generate relatively small subtree spaces (133,308 subtrees for depth 7). Longer cascade effects can also be observed, since the models can backoff from 7-word subtrees to 0-word ones. Figures 8 and 9 show exact

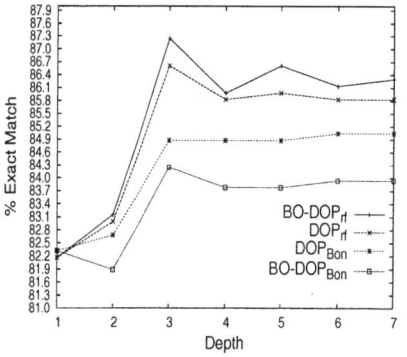

Fig. 8. Exact match as a function of depth upper bound (l7n2L3,MPD)

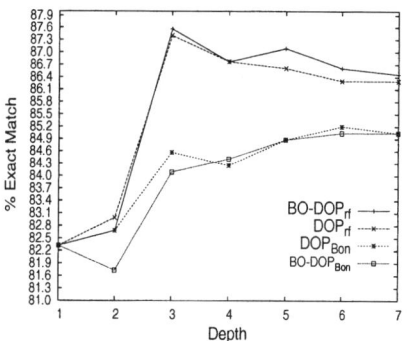

Fig. 9. Match as a function of depth upper bound (l7n2L3, MPP, Monte Carlo sample size: 5,000)

match results as a function of depth upper bound and maximization entity. Note that they follow the same pattern observed in the results with l2n4. Unlike those, however, maximum accuracy is achieved here at depth 3, not 6.

MPP has better performance than MPD. This shift is stronger for DOP_{rf} and $BF\text{-}DOP_{Bon}$. One possible explanation is that MPP allows for recovering part of the joint dependencies lost by the independence assumption underlying MPD. Moreover, contrary to MPP, MPD assumes that the probability of a parse is concentrated in a single derivation, which might lead to wrong results.

Consistency Across Splits: To test whether the results above are due to some random property of the train/test split, experiments were carried out with fixed parameters l7n2L3d3 and varying train/test splits. The number of trees was kept constant: 9,049 for training; 1,000 for testing. Depth 3 was chosen because most models achieved their best results with this setting, which might indicate fluctuation. Four experiments were carried out. Experiment 1 (Exp1) refers to the split used so far, Experiments 2, 3 and 4 (Exp2, Exp3, Exp4) refer to different splits obtained through random drawings from the OVIS corpus. Note that different splits yield distinct models with different generative powers. Therefore, performance can greatly vary.

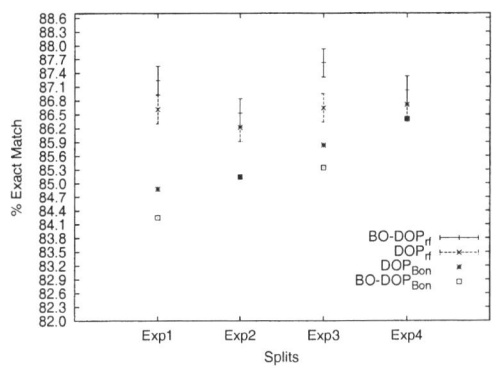

Fig. 10. Exact match for fixed depth 3 as a function of training/test set splits (l7n2d3L3,MPD)

Figure 10 shows that the pattern previously observed, with $BF\text{-}DOP_{rf}$ achieving the best results and $BF\text{-}DOP_{Bon}$ the worst, is conserved across the splits. The improvement, although persistent, is not statistically significant. $BF\text{-}DOP_{rf}$'s performance mean of 87.10% is not significantly different from DOP_{rf}'s mean of 86.54%, with 95% confidence according to the t-test (interval: ±0.3097%).

Exp3 was the only one that reached statistical significance. It is important to emphasize that the wide range of the confidence interval is due to the small sample size. Definitive conclusions can only be drawn once a larger number of experiments is carried out. Moreover, these results refer to a single 'cut' in the parameter space and it is possible that different parameter combinations will result in significant differences. In any case, these results do not contradict the relative ranking between $BF\text{-}DOP_{rf}$ and DOP_{rf}.

6 Conclusions

The main point of this paper is that the DOP parameters constitute a hierarchically structured space of highly correlated events. We presented a novel estimator for the DOP model based on this observation by expressing the correlations in terms of backoff. We provided empirical evidence for the improved performance of this estimator over existing estimators.

We think that the hierarchical structuring of the space of DOP parameters can be exploited within a Maximum-Likelihood estimation procedure. The space structure can be seen to express some parameters as functions of other parameters.

Future work will address (1) formal aspects of the new estimator (bias and inconsistency questions), (2) a Maximum-Likelihood variant for DOP that incorporates the observations discussed in this paper, and (3) further experiments on larger treebanks, and less constrained DOP models.

References

1. Bod, R.: What is the minimal set of fragments that achieves maximal parse accuracy? In: Proceedings of the 39th Annual Meeting of the Association for Computational Linguistics (ACL'2001). (2001)

2. Bod, R.: Enriching Linguistics with Statistics: Performance models of Natural Language. PhD dissertation. ILLC dissertation series 1995-14, University of Amsterdam (1995)
3. Bonnema, R., Buying, P., Scha, R.: A new probability model for data oriented parsing. In Dekker, P., ed.: Proceedings of the Twelfth Amsterdam Colloquium. ILLC/Department of Philosophy, University of Amsterdam, Amsterdam (1999) 85–90
4. Johnson, M.: The DOP estimation method is biased and inconsistent. Computational Linguistics **28(1)** (2002) 71–76
5. Black, E., Jelinek, F., Lafferty, J., Magerman, D., Mercer, R., Roukos, S.: Towards History-based Grammars: Using Richer Models for Probabilistic Parsing. In: Proceedings of the 31st Annual Meeting of the ACL (*ACL'93*), Columbus, Ohio (1993)
6. Katz, S.: Estimation of probabilities from sparse data for the language model component of a speech recognizer. IEEE Transactions on Acoustics, Speech and Signal Processing (ASSP) **35(3)** (1987) 400–401
7. Chen, S., Goodman, J.: An empirical study of smoothing techniques for language modeling. Technical Report TR-10-98, Harvard University (1998)
8. Chelba, C., Jelinek, F.: Exploiting syntactic structure for language modeling. In Boitet, C., Whitelock, P., eds.: Proceedings of the Thirty-Sixth Annual Meeting of the Association for Computational Linguistics and Seventeenth International Conference on Computational Linguistics, San Francisco, California, Morgan Kaufmann Publishers (1998) 225–231
9. Charniak, E.: A maximum entropy inspired parser. In: Proceedings of the 1st Meeting of the North American Chapter of the Association for Computational Linguistics (NAACL-00), Seattle, Washington, USA (2000) 132–139
10. Sima'an, K.: Computational complexity of probabilistic disambiguation. Grammars **5(2)** (2002) 125–151
11. Bod, R.: A computational model of language performance: Data Oriented Parsing. In: Proceedings of the 14th International Conference on Computational Linguistics (COLING'92), Nantes (1992)
12. Bod, R.: Combining semantic and syntactic structure for language modeling. In: Proceedings ICSLP-2000. (2000)
13. Good, I.: The population frequencies of species and the estimation of population parameters. Biometrika **40** (1953) 237–264
14. Scha, R., Bonnema, R., Bod, R., Sima'an, K.: Disambiguation and Interpretation of Wordgraphs using Data Oriented Parsing. Technical Report #31, Netherlands Organization for Scientific Research (NWO), Priority Programme Language and Speech Technology, *http : //grid.let.rug.nl : 4321/* (1996)
15. Black et al., E.: A procedure for Quantitatively Comparing the Syntactic Coverage of English Grammars. In: Proceedings of the February 1991 DARPA Speech and Natural Language Workshop, San Mateo, CA., Morgan Kaufman (1991) 306–311
16. Sima'an, K.: Learning Efficient Disambiguation. PhD dissertation (University of Utrecht). ILLC dissertation series 1999-02, University of Amsterdam, Amsterdam (1999)
17. Bod, R.: Beyond Grammar: An Experience-Based Theory of Language. CSLI Publications, California (1998)

Improving Numerical Prediction
with Qualitative Constraints

Dorian Šuc and Ivan Bratko

Faculty of Computer and Information Science, University of Ljubljana,
Tržaška 25, 1000 Ljubljana, Slovenia
{dorian.suc,ivan.bratko}@fri.uni-lj.si

Abstract. The usual numerical learning methods, that are primarily concerned with finding a good numerical fit to the data, often make predictions that do not correspond to the qualitative mechanisms in the domain of modelling or a domain expert's intuition. Consistency of numerical predictions with a given qualitative model is helpful when a numerical model is used for explanation of phenomena in the modelled domain, but can also considerably improve numerical accuracy. In this paper we present a novel approach to numerical machine learning called Qfilter. Qfilter is a numerical regression method that can take into account qualitative background knowledge to give *qualitatively faithful numerical prediction*. The results on a set of domains including population dynamics show considerable prediction accuracy improvements compared to the usual numerical learners. As qualitative domain knowledge is often available in practice, Qfilter's ability to exploit such knowledge should be beneficial in many applications.

1 Introduction

1.1 Qualitative Problems of Numerical Learning

Methods of numerical machine learning, such as regression tree learning and locally weighted regression (LWR), often make predictions that a knowledgeable user finds obviously incorrect. A domain expert finds such errors incorrect not so much in numerical, but in qualitative terms. Often there are a priori known qualitative constraints in the domain of application, and for numerical predictions to make sense, the predictions should be consistent with such constraints.

For example, consider a container filled with water. Let there be an open drain at the bottom of the container, and water is draining out. Suppose we want to make predictions about the amount of water at various times. Although exact numerical predictions of the amount may be hard, obviously these predictions will have to satisfy some qualitative constraints, such as: (1) the amount can never be negative, and (2) the amount of water in the container can never be increasing. Suppose that we have examples of measurements of the amount of water in time, obtained from past behavior of the draining process that started at different initial amounts. We then use standard methods of numerical machine learning to make predictions of the amount at future times, starting with some new initial amount. Unfortunately, state-of-the-art numerical learning techniques will typically produce predictions that do not completely respect the above mentioned qualitative constraints even when the learning data is noise-free. Šuc et al. [1] give pertinent experimental results with the draining process, using M5 regression and model trees [2] and LWR [3] (implementation in Weka; [4]).

Such qualitative errors of numerical predictors are undesirable particularly because they make numerical results difficult to interpret. The underlying mechanism in the domain is usually best explained in qualitative terms. However, this is obscured by qualitative errors in numerical predictions.

1.2 Qfilter

In this paper we introduce a numerical learning method, called Qfilter. Qfilter accepts as input a set of numerical data points and a set of qualitative constraints, and performs numerical regression so that the predicted numerical values respect the given qualitative constraints. In a typical application of Qfilter, the qualitative constraints are provided by the domain expert as (qualitative) background knowledge. Such constraints are typically part of domain knowledge. For example, in biological modelling the growth rate of a population is qualitatively proportional to the current size of the population and to the amount of food available to the population. Another possibility of applying Qfilter is within the Q^2 learning, described below. In this context, qualitative constraints do not have to come from a domain expert.

In Section 2 we define the type of qualitative constraints and qualitative trees accepted by Qfilter. In Section 3 we describe the Qfilter algorithm. Section 4 presents experiments with Qfilter and a comparison with standard numerical prediction methods. Section 5 gives conclusions.

1.3 Relation of Qfilter to Q^2 Learning

To rectify the qualitative problems of numerical learning, Šuc et al. [1] proposed "qualitatively faithful quantitative learning", called Q^2 learning for short. In experiments with a complex industrial modelling problem, Q^2 learning not only improved the predictions qualitatively, but also numerically. Numerical predictions with Q^2 were considerably more accurate than those obtained with the mentioned numerical learning methods.

Q^2 learning consists of two stages:

1. Induce a qualitative model from numerical examples. Program QUIN ([5, 6]) that induces qualitative trees from numerical data can be used for this.
2. Transform a qualitative model induced in stage 1 into a quantitative model (i.e. a numerical function) that fits well the given numerical data and is consistent with the qualitative constraints in the qualitative tree. This transformation is called Q2Q transformation (qualitative-to-quantitative).

The Q2Q transformation in [1] was based on piece-wise linear regression where these linear functions were determined heuristically using LWR on a grid

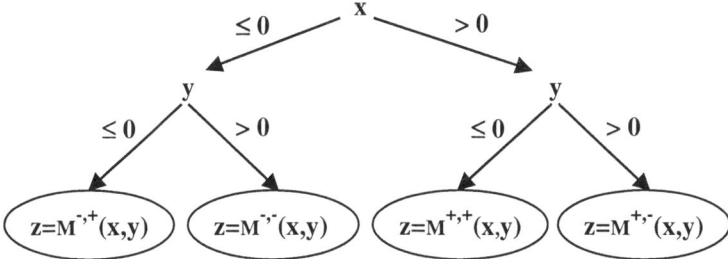

Fig. 1. A qualitative tree that describes the qualitative relations between class Z and attributes X and Y for the function $Z = X^2 - Y^2$. The rightmost leaf, applying when attributes X and Y are positive, says that Z is strictly increasing in its dependence on X and strictly decreasing in its dependence on Y.

of selected points. Although this method worked well in the experiments, it was ad hoc in that there was no guarantee that the so obtained heuristic functions would completely respect the qualitative constraints. The Qfilter approach introduced in this paper is a better founded and better performing method for Q2Q transformation.

2 Qualitative Trees for Knowledge Representation

In this section we describe a formalism for the representation of qualitative background knowledge. We represent qualitative knowledge in the form of so-called qualitative trees that are described below and proved to be useful and understandable in several different applications [5, 7, 1]. In these applications qualitative trees were induced from numerical examples by program QUIN [5, 6]. In this paper we assume that they are given, e.g. defined by a domain expert, and study the advantages in terms of prediction accuracy.

Qualitative trees are similar to decision trees but model qualitative relations between the class and the attributes. As in decision trees, the internal nodes in a qualitative tree specify conditions that split the attribute space into subspaces. In a qualitative tree, however, each leaf specifies a region in the attribute space where some monotonicity constraints hold. These monotonicity constraints are represented by what we call *qualitatively constrained functions* (QCFs for short). A simple example of QCF is: $Y = M^+(X)$. This says that Y is a monotonically increasing function of X. In general, QCFs can have more than one argument. For example, $Z = M^{+,-}(X, Y)$ says that Z monotonically increases in X and monotonically decreases in Y. We say that Z is positively related to X and negatively related to Y. If both X and Y increase, then according to this constraint, Z may increase, decrease or stay unchanged. In such a case, a QCF cannot make an unambiguous prediction of the qualitative change in Z as explained below.

Figure 1 gives an example of a qualitative tree. This qualitative tree is a qualitative model of the function $Z = X^2 - Y^2$ and describes how Z qualitatively depends on attributes X and Y. The tree partitions the attribute space into four regions that correspond to the four leaves of the tree. A different QCF applies in each of the leaves. The QCF $Z = M^{+,-}(X, Y)$ applies in the rightmost leaf, where both X and Y are positive.

Qualitatively constrained functions are inspired by the qualitative proportionality predicates Q_+ and Q_- as defined by Forbus [4] and are also a generalization of the qualitative constraint M^+, as used in QSIM [9]. A QCF constrains the qualitative change of the class variable in response to the qualitative changes of the attributes. Namely, a QCF $M^{s_1,\ldots,s_m}$, $s_i \in \{+, -\}$ represents an arbitrary function $\Re^m \mapsto \Re$ with m continuous attributes that respects the qualitative constraints given by signs s_i. The qualitative constraint given by sign $s_i = +$ ($s_i = -$) requires that the function is strictly increasing (decreasing) in its dependence on the i-th attribute. We say that the function is *positively related* (negatively related) to the i-th attribute. $M^{s_1,\ldots,s_m}$ represents any function which is, for all $i = 1, \ldots, m$ positively (negatively) related to the i-th argument, if $s_i = +$ ($s_i = -$).

Note that the qualitative constraint given by sign $s_i = +$ only states that when the i-th attribute increases, the QCF will also increase, *barring other changes*. It can happen that a QCF with the constraint $s_i = +$ decreases even if the i-th attribute increases, because of a change in another attribute. For example, consider the behaviour of gas pressure in a container given by equation $Pres \times Vol/Temp = const$. We can express the qualitative behaviour of gas pressure by QCF $Pres = M^{+,-}(Temp, Vol)$. This constraint allows that the pressure decreases even if the temperature increases, because of a change in the volume. Notice however, that the qualitative behaviour of gas is not consistent with the constraint $Pres = M^+(Temp)$.

QCFs are concerned with qualitative changes. Qualitative change q_i in the i-th attribute is the sign of change in that variable. This can be either *positive*, *negative* or *zero* change. For simplicity, we ignore zero changes in the next paragraphs. QCF-prediction $P(s_i, q_i)$ is the qualitative change of the class variable predicted according to a single (i-th) attribute. QCF-prediction is positive if s_i and q_i are both positive or both negative, and is negative otherwise. *Qualitative ambiguity*, i.e. ambiguity in the class's qualitative change appears whenever there exist both positive and negative QCF-predictions according to different attributes. A qualitatively constrained function is *consistent* with a pair of examples if there exists an attribute whose QCF-prediction is equal to the class's qualitative change. We say that this example pair is QCF-consistent. A qualitatively constrained function is *consistent* with a set of examples if it is consistent with all possible example pairs, i.e. when all possible examples pairs are QCF-consistent.

3 Qfilter

3.1 Idea and Example

Here we describe algorithm Qfilter that, given a set of examples and a qualitative tree, adjusts the class values in such a way that they are consistent with

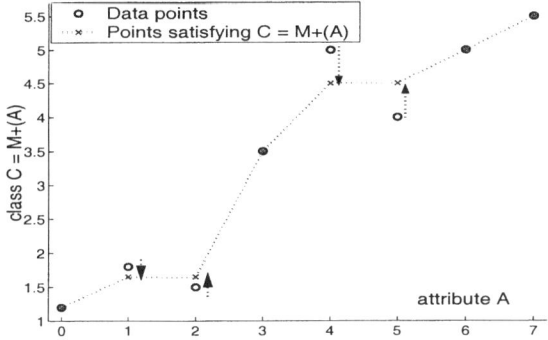

Fig. 2. Achieving consistency with QCF $C = M^+(A)$: since the QCF requires that class C is strictly increasing in attribute A, class values c_i (denoted by circles) are changed into $c_i + d_i$ (denoted by crosses) by minimizing the sum of squared changes d_i. The arrows denote the class changes d_i.

the qualitative tree. Namely, Qfilter is an optimization procedure that finds the minimal required quadratic changes in class values to achieve qualitative consistency with the qualitative tree. In one respect Qfilter can be viewed as a filter that smooths the data and removes the qualitative errors introduced by the measurement errors, but here we use it to remove the qualitative errors made by numerical predictors, as it will be explained later.

Let us first observe a simple example illustrated in Figure 2. We have eight examples (a_i, c_i), $i = 0, 1, .., 7$ described with the values of class C and attribute A. The examples are not consistent with the given QCF $C = M^+(A)$, because the QCF requires that $c_{i+1} > c_i$ which is violated at $i = 1$ and $i = 4$.

To achieve consistency with $C = M^+(A)$, class values should be changed into $c_i + d_i$, where the unknown parameter d_i denotes the change in i-th class value. Class changes d_i are constrained by QCF imposed inequalities: $c_{i+1} + d_{i+1} > c_i + d_i$ where $i = 0, 1, .., 6$. This gives the optimization problem that can be formulated in matrix notation by writing the inequalities as $\mathbf{A}\mathbf{d} > \mathbf{b}$, where $\mathbf{d}$ is a vector of unknown parameters d_i, vector $\mathbf{b}$ has elements $b_i = c_i - c_{i+i}$, and matrix $\mathbf{A}$ has elements $a_{i,i} = -1$, $a_{i,i+1} = 1$ and zeros elsewhere. Therefore finding minimal quadratic changes in class values that achieve consistency with a given QCF can be posed as the optimization problem:

$$\text{find vector } \mathbf{d} \text{ that minimizes } \mathbf{d}^T\mathbf{H}\mathbf{d}$$
$$\text{such that } \mathbf{A}\mathbf{d} > \mathbf{b} \tag{1}$$

In the above formulation matrix $\mathbf{H}$ is the identity matrix. In general $\mathbf{H}$ can be changed to differently penalize the changes in class values. For example, we could change $\mathbf{H}$ to require that the classes of examples that have higher confidence are changed less. The above stated optimization problem is a kind of *quadratic programme* and can be efficiently solved by a number of methods. We used a quadratic programming solver in Matlab [10–12]. Since the criterion function

$d^T H d$ with diagonal matrix H is a convex function, and because the linear constraints $A d > b$ define a convex hull, any local minimum of the criterion function is a globally optimal solution.

Note that in the above formulation the values of attribute A are not mentioned at all. However the ordering of attributes values, i.e. $a_{i+1} > a_i$, was used together with QCF $C = M^+(A)$ to set the ordering of class values, i.e. $c_{i+1} > c_i$. A different ordering of attribute values would require a different ordering of class values, depending also on the QCF. When more than one attributes are used in a QCF, finding an appropriate ordering of class values is not as trivial as in the example above and is explained in the next section.

3.2 Details of the Qfilter Algorithm

Qfilter handles each leaf of a qualitative tree separately. It first splits the examples according to the qualitative tree and then change class values to achieve consistency with a QCFs in the corresponding leaf. As mentioned above, Qfilter uses the attributes' values and the QCF to find an appropriate ordering of class values, poses the optimization problem in the form given by Equation 1, and solves it by using quadratic programming methods. To explain how to find an appropriate ordering of class values we first define two useful terms, and then explain some properties of QCFs. Since in general not all of the attributes appear in a QCF, we call an attribute that appears in a QCF a *QCF-attribute*. We call a QCF that doesn't have a negative dependance on an attribute, i.e. is positively related with all QCF-attributes, a *pure-positive QCF*.

The first interesting QCF property is that an arbitrary QCF can be, by appropriate changes in attributes, replaced by a pure-positive QCF. It is easy to check that a QCF that is negatively related with attribute A_i and positively related with all other attributes, is equivalent to a pure-positive QCF, where the attribute A_i is replaced by $\hat{A}_i = -A_i$. For example QCF $M^{+,-}(A_1, A_2)$ is equivalent to QCF $M^{+,+}(A_1, \hat{A}_2)$, where $\hat{A}_2 = -A_2$. Therefore we can simply multiply by minus one (or any other negative number) all the negatively related QCF-attributes to get a pure-positive QCF. Actually multiplying by minus one all negatively related QCF-attributes is the first step in Qfilter. In the rest of this section we assume that a given QCF is a pure-positive QCF.

The second interesting QCF property is that a QCF defines a partial ordering of class values and that a pure-positive QCF is consistent with a set of examples if the class value of every example e is greater than the class values of every example from a set called $F_{sg}(e)$. More formally, we show that a pure-positive QCF is consistent with a set of examples if, and only if:

$$\forall e, f \in \text{Examples} : f \in F_{sg}(e) \Rightarrow c_e > c_f \qquad (2)$$

where $F_{sg}(e)$ is the set of examples f_{sg} that are smaller than e in every QCF-attribute and there is no example f_s that is in every attribute smaller than e and in every QCF-attribute greater than f_{sg}. This is explained in the next paragraphs. We show this by using the QCF consistency criterion that requires that all possible example pairs are QCF-consistent. A first simplification is that we do not need to check all possible example pairs. A pure-positive QCF is consistent with a set of examples if every example e is QCF-consistent with all the examples f_s that are *smaller than e in every QCF-attribute*. The set of such examples is denoted by $F_s(e)$. Namely, example pairs of e and examples f_{amb} that are in one QCF-attribute grater than e, and in another QCF-attribute smaller than e are QCF-consistent with any pure-positive QCF. QCF-consistencies of example pairs of e and examples f_g, that are in all QCF-attributes grater than e, are checked when examples f_g are checked. Since the relation "is smaller than e in every QCF-attribute" is transitive, we need to check the consistency only for the "largest" examples from $F_{sg}(e) \subseteq F_s(e)$, i.e. examples $f_{sg} \in F_s(e)$ with the property that in F_s there is no example that is in every QCF-attribute greater than example f_{sg}. Since all the examples from $F_{sg}(e)$ are smaller than e in every QCF-attribute, a pure-positive QCF requires that the class value of example e is greater than the class value of every example from the set $F_{sg}(e)$, i.e. $\forall f \in F_{sg}(e) : c_e > c_f$.

The ordering of class values given by Equation 2 is used to set the inequality constraints, i.e. matrix $\mathbf{A}$ and vector $\mathbf{b}$ from Equation 1. For each $f \in F_{sg}(e)$ we add one (say i-th) constraint $c_e + d_e > c_f + d_f$, therefore vector $\mathbf{b}$ has elements $b_i = c_f - c_e$, and matrix $\mathbf{A}$ has elements $a_{i,f} = -1$, $a_{i,e} = 1$ and zeros elsewhere.

3.3 Qfilter for Numerical Prediction

The basic idea of using Qfilter for numerical prediction is to apply it, with a given qualitative tree, on predictions of an arbitrary numerical learner. A numerical predictor is usually trained on a set of learning examples, where "correct" class values are given. For this reason it is quite natural to provide the learning examples also to Qfilter. In this case Qfilter is supplied with the learning examples with "correct" class values together with test examples with predictions of class values. Qfilter then adjusts the class values of both learning and test examples to fit a qualitative tree. It is quite obvious that using also learning examples usually helps Qfilter. This is especially evident when adjusting a prediction of a test example that is close to some learning examples.

One possible improvement of Qfilter is to also use the confidence estimate in numerical prediction if it is provided by the numerical predictor. In this case, Qfilter would change the class values with higher confidence less, for the price of bigger changes of class values that have lower confidence. This is achieved by simply changing matrix $\mathbf{H}$ in Equation 1 from identity to a diagonal matrix with $h_{i,i} = w_i$, where weight w_i is computed from predictor's confidence estimate in i-th class value. Of course, the computation of weight w_i depends on the type and scale of confidence estimate, but would generally be smaller if a numerical predictor is more confident in i-th class prediction.

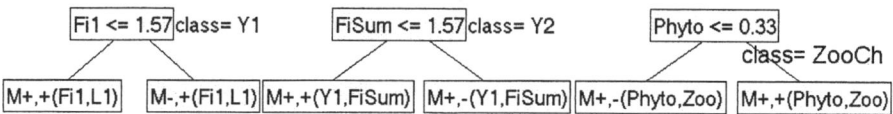

Fig. 3. Qualitative trees used with Qfilter in domains *RoboY1*, *RoboY2atrY1* and in the population dynamics domain *ZooChange*. Note that 1.57 in the first two trees is an approximation of $\frac{\pi}{2}$ where $\sin(\Phi)$ changes from an increasing to a decreasing function.

4 Experimental Results

Here we compare the numerical accuracy of locally weighted regression [3] (LWR) and Qfilter. Qfilter was used to adjust the LWR predictions according to given qualitative trees. We used a standard procedure to optimize LWR. Namely, LWR optimized the Gaussian kernel width that is used to weigh the neighbor examples according to the mean squared local cross validation error at the point of prediction.

We experimented with different learning set sizes and different noise in class variable. We used normally distributed zero-mean noise. Noise percentage p % means that the standard deviation of noise is d_c $p/100$ where d_c denotes the difference between maximal and minimal class value. First we describe experiments in four artificial domains and then experiments in a more complex population dynamics domain.

4.1 Artificial Domains

Here we describe experiments in four artificial domains. The first is the domain called *Quad* with attributes X and Y and class $Z = X^2 - Y^2$. Attributes X and Y are uniformly distributed between -10 and 10. Qfilter used LWR predictions and the qualitative tree given in Figure 1 and explained in Section 2.

The second set of domains consists of three domains, called *RoboY1*, *RoboY2* and *RoboY2atrY1*. Here we model a planar two-link, two joint robot arm. The angle in the shoulder joint is denoted by Φ_1 and the angle in the elbow joint is denoted by Φ_2. Angle Φ_1 is between zero and π, while Φ_2 is between $-\pi/2$ and $\pi/2$. When the arm is in horizontal position Φ_1 and Φ_2 are both zero. The first link, i.e. the link from shoulder to elbow, is extendible with length L_1 ranging from 2 to 10. The second link has fixed length $L_2 = 5$. The first learning problem is to predict y-coordinate of the first link end, i.e. $Y1 = L_1 \sin(\Phi_1)$. This problem is called *RoboY1*. For Qfilter we used the qualitative tree given in Figure 3.

The second learning problem is to predict y-coordinate of the second link end, i.e. $Y2 = L_1 \sin(\Phi_1) + 5 \sin(\Phi_1 + \Phi_2)$. Here we helped the learners with a derived attribute $\Phi_{sum} = \Phi_1 + \Phi_2$, i.e. the deflection of the second link from the horizontal. We experimented with two versions of this learning problem. In domain *RoboY2* we used the attributes L_1, Φ_1, Φ_2 and Φ_{Sum}. In domain *RoboY2atrY1* we also used the correct $Y1$ as an attribute. We generated examples where angles Φ_1 and Φ_2 and link length L_1 are uniformly distributed in their possible

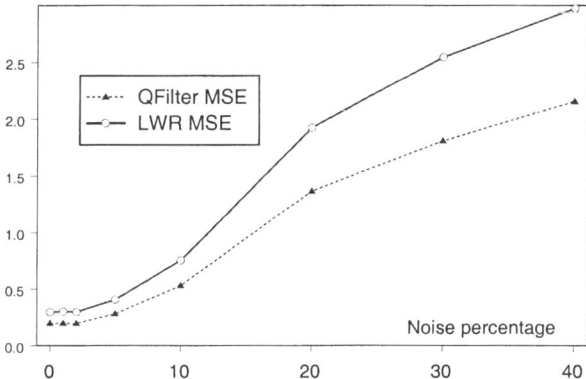

Fig. 4. Noise curve in domain *RoboY1* with 100 learning examples: on x-axis is noise percentage and on y-axis is LWR (line with circles) and Qfilter (dotted line with triangles) mean squared error.

ranges. Qualitative tree used with domain *RoboY2atrY1* is given in Figure 3. Qualitative tree used with domain *RoboY2* has four leaves, with the same root node as qualitative tree for domain *RoboY2atrY1*, but with $Y1$ replaced by the qualitative tree for $Y1$.

We experimented with different learning set sizes and different noise in class variable. We used a test set of 200 examples without noise. Table 1 gives the comparison of LWR and Qfilter mean squared errors (MSE) with 100 learning examples and various noise levels. All the results are averages on 10 sets of randomly selected learning and test examples. With all four learning problems the improvement of Qfilter with respect to LWR is obvious. Qfilter usually reduces LWR MSE by more than 20 %. The MSE reduction usually increases with increased noise. Figure 4 shows a typical noise curve in domain *RoboY1*.

We also experimented with different learning set sizes. For an illustration, we give the results with learning from examples with no noise in domain *RoboY1* in Table 1. When we used only 10 or 20 learning examples the Qfilter reduction of error is relatively small, since none of the learners is able to generalize well from such a small learning set. But as the learning set increases, Qfilter can take advantage of given qualitative knowledge. After a certain learning set size, the reduction of error decreases with increasing learning set. However, the reduction in error is usually still visible even when we use relatively large learning set. Of course this depends on the difficulty of the domain. When a numerical learner gives predictions that are consistent with a given qualitative tree, Qfilter does not change them.

4.2 Population Dynamics Domain

The last domain models a dynamic behavior of an aquatic ecosystem that involves populations of zooplankton and phytoplankton, and inorganic nutrient nitrogen that are denoted by variables *Zoo*, *Phyto* and *Nut*, respectively. The

Table 1. Comparison of LWR and Qfilter accuracy. The first table gives MSE with 100 learning examples and various noise levels in all the described domains. Since the changes in zooplankton are small, the values of MSE given for the domain ZooChange are multiplied by 10^3. The second table gives MSE in domain RoboY1 when different number of learning examples with no noise were used. All the results are averages on 10 sets of learning examples.

Domain name	class variable	no noise MSE LWR; Qfilter	5 % n. MSE LWR; Qfilter	20 % n. MSE LWR; Qfilter
Quad	$Z = X^2 - Y^2$	98.4 ; 84.7	149.3 ; 114.6	765.6 ; 554.7
RoboY1	$Y1 = L_1 \sin(\Phi_1)$	0.298 ; 0.196	0.407 ; 0.280	1.924 ; 1.367
RoboY2	$Y2 = L_1 \sin(\Phi_1) + 5 \sin(\Phi_{sum})$	2.618 ; 2.305	3.078 ; 2.612	6.823 ; 5.167
RoboY2atrY1	$Y2$ as above, using attr. $Y1$	0.940 ; 0.691	1.324 ; 0.968	3.665 ; 2.707
ZooChange	$ZooCh(t) = Zoo(t+1) - Zoo(t)$	0.015 ; 0.008	0.112 ; 0.102	2.269 ; 1.889

Domain name	20 learn. ex. MSE LWR; Qfilter	50 l.ex. MSE LWR; Qfilter	100 l.ex. MSE LWR; Qfilter	300 l.ex. MSE LWR; Qfilter
RoboY1	3.690 ; 3.421	1.201 ; 0.933	0.298 ; 0.196	0.019 ; 0.018

model assumes closed ecosystem with no inflow and consists of two consumption interactions. Namely, phytoplankton consumes nitrogen, and zooplankton consumes phytoplankton. This results in complex time behavior of the variables.

Our learning task is to predict the change in zooplankton $ZooChange(t)$, i.e. the difference between the zooplankton population at the next and the current time point $(ZooCh(t) = Zoo(t+1) - Zoo(t))$, given the values of zooplankton, phytoplankton, and nutrient at the current time point. We used experimental data that was kindly provided by Ljupčo Todorovski and Sašo Džeroski who previously experimented in this domain and give a more elaborate description of the domain [13]. The experimental data was generated by the following differential equations model:

$$\dot{Nut} = 2 - Phyto\, Nut$$
$$\dot{Phyto} = 0.1 - \frac{Phyto}{7} - \frac{Phyto}{5} + 0.7\, PhytoNut - 0.5\, \frac{Zoo\, Phyto}{Phyto + 0.5} \quad (3)$$
$$\dot{Zoo} = -0.1\, Zoo + 0.25\, \frac{Zoo\, Phyto}{Phyto + 0.5}$$

In contrast to other experimental domains we do not use a qualitative model that would completely correspond to the actual numerical behavior of the population dynamics model. Instead we use a heuristic qualitative tree given in Figure 3. This qualitative tree was obtained by qualitative abstraction of $\dot{Zoo}$ in Equation 3 and assumes constant values of the variables between the current and the next time point. It is just an approximate qualitative model an expert might give and has the following interpretation. Since zooplankton feeds on phytoplankton, a larger phytoplankton population enables a bigger positive change in zooplankton. The change of zooplankton is also positively related to the zooplankton population, since the growth rate of a population is positively related to the size of the population. But if the phytoplankton population is too small (below 0.33 in qualitative tree in Figure 3) to provide enough food for zooplankton, then the change in zooplankton will be negatively related to the zooplankton population.

The data consists of ten traces generated by simulating a numerical model from ten randomly chosen triples of starting values for variables *Zoo*, *Phyto* and *Nut*. Each simulation lasts for 100 time steps and gives 100 examples, each example being described with attributes $Nut(t)$, $Phyto(t)$ and $Zoo(t)$. The class variable *ZooCh* was computed as the difference in zooplankton population between two consecutive points in time, i.e. $ZooCh(t) = Zoo(t+1) - Zoo(t)$. The learning examples were randomly selected from the first five traces, and the test examples were randomly selected from second five traces. We used 100 learning and 100 test examples. The results in Table 1 are averages of learning from ten random selections of examples. These results show that even an approximate qualitative model can help Qfilter to improve numerical accuracy.

In the experiments with Weka [4] implementation of M5 regression and model trees [2], qualitative errors were even more obvious, as illustrated also in [1]. For this reason the accuracy improvements of Qfilter with respect to model and regression trees were usually bigger.

5 Conclusions

We presented a novel approach to numerical machine learning called Qfilter. Qfilter is a numerical regression method that can take into account qualitative background knowledge expressed as a qualitative tree with qualitatively constrained functions in the leaves of the tree. As qualitative domain knowledge is often available in practice, Qfilter's ability to exploit such knowledge should be beneficial in many applications. One desirable consequence of using such qualitative knowledge is improved accuracy of numerical predictions. Another desirable property is that the resulting numerical regression model is qualitatively consistent with known qualitative relations in the domain of application.

There are several directions in which Qfilter can be extended. As noted in Section 3.3, a possible improvement is to use the confidence estimate in numerical prediction provided by the numerical predictor to change less the class values that have higher confidence estimate. Experiments with using the size of confidence intervals provided by LWR show that this can additionally improve Qfilter accuracy. Qfilter as presented in this paper, requires a numerical learner and it does not provide an explicit model. However, the quadratic programming approach can easily be extended to induce a piecewise linear model that is consistent with a given qualitative model. Another interesting point is that Qfilter finds minimal sum of squared changes of class values to achieve consistency with a given qualitative model. In this respect it gives the error of numerical data w.r.t. qualitative model or vice versa and provides a bridge between qualitative and numerical models.

In the experiments in several domains, Qfilter always improved the accuracy of numerical predictions compared to standard regression methods. Improvements in accuracy were observed even in cases when the qualitative constraints applied were only approximate. In the experiments, the improvements were observed consistently when varying the amount of learning examples and the degree of noise in the data. In this paper we assumed that qualitative trees are given. An appealing alternative would be to use induced qualitative trees. QUIN, depending on the noise, often induced similar qualitative trees as used here.

Acknowledgements

The work reported in this paper was partially supported by the European Fifth Framework project Clockwork and the Slovenian Ministry of Education, Science and Sport.

References

1. Šuc, D., Vladušič, D., Bratko, I.: Qualitatively faithful quantitative prediction. In: Proceedings of the 18th International Joint Conference on Artificial Intelligence. (2003) August, 2003, Acapulco, Mexico.
2. Quinlan, J.: Learning with continuous classes. In: Proc. of the 5th Australian Joint Conference on Artificial Intelligence, Singapore, World Scientific (1992) 343–348
3. Atkeson, C., Moore, A., Schaal, S.: Locally weighted learning. Artificial Intelligence Review **11** (1997) 11–73
4. Witten, I., Frank, E.: Data Mining: Practical Machine Learning Tools and Techniques with Java Implementations, Chapter 8. Morgan Kaufmann, San Francisco (2000) 265–320
5. Šuc, D.: Machine Reconstruction of Human Control Strategies. PhD thesis, Faculty of Computer and Information Sc., University of Ljubljana, Slovenia (2001)
6. Šuc, D., Bratko, I.: Induction of qualitative trees. In De Raedt, L., Flach, P., eds.: Proc. of the 12th European Conf. on Machine Learning, Springer (2001) 442–453
7. Šuc, D., Bratko, I.: Qualitative reverse engineering. In Sammut, C., Hoffmann, A., eds.: Proc. of the 19th International Conf. on Machine Learning, Morgan Kaufmann (2002) 610–617
8. Forbus, K.: Qualitative process theory. Artificial Intelligence **24** (1984) 85–168
9. Kuipers, B.: Qualitative simulation. Artificial Intelligence **29** (1986) 289–338
10. The MathWorks, I.: Matlab software. (2003) http://www.mathworks.com.
11. Coleman, T.F., Li, Y.: A reflective Newton method for minimizing a quadratic function subject to bounds on some of the variables. SIAM Journal on Optimization **6** (1996) 1040–1058
12. Gill, P.E., Murray, W., Wright, M.H.: Quadratic programming. In: Practical Optimization. Academic Press, London, England (1981) 177–184
13. Todorovski, L., Džeroski, S.: Using domain knowledge on population dynamics modeling for equation discovery. In: Proceedings of the 12th European Conference on Machine Learning, Springer (2001) 478–490

A Generative Model for Semantic Role Labeling

Cynthia A. Thompson[1], Roger Levy[2], and Christopher D. Manning[2]

[1] School of Computing, University of Utah
Salt Lake City, UT 84112
cindi@cs.utah.edu
http://www.cs.utah.edu/~cindi
[2] Departments of Linguistics and Computer Science, Stanford University
Stanford, CA 94305
{rog,manning}@stanford.edu

Abstract. Determining the semantic role of sentence constituents is a key task in determining sentence meanings lying behind a veneer of variant syntactic expression. We present a model of natural language generation from semantics using the FrameNet semantic role and frame ontology. We train the model using the FrameNet corpus and apply it to the task of automatic semantic role and frame identification, producing results competitive with previous work (about 70% role labeling accuracy). Unlike previous models used for this task, our model does not assume that the frame of a sentence is known, and is able to identify *null-instantiated roles*, which commonly occur in our corpus and whose identification is crucial to natural language interpretation.

1 Introduction

A central goal of natural language processing is domain-independent understanding. A useful step towards that goal is the assignment of semantic roles to the (syntactic) constituents of a sentence. Having semantic roles allows one to recognize semantic arguments of a situation, even when expressed in different syntactic configurations. For example the role of an *instrument*, such as a *hammer*, can be recognized, regardless of whether its expression is as the subject of the sentence (*the hammer broke the vase*) or via a prepositional phrase headed by *with*. This paper attempts the task of learning to automatically assign such roles. Identifying such roles and the relationships between them can in turn serve as support for inference about a sentence's meaning, for antecedent resolution, or for other understanding or parsing tasks such as prepositional phrase attachment or word sense disambiguation.

This paper develops a generative model from which one can infer role labels, given sentence constituents and a word from that sentence that is a *predicator*, which takes semantic role arguments. We learn the parameters for this model from a body of examples provided by the FrameNet corpus [1]. The problem and some elements of our approach are similar to that of [2], but the work differs by use of a generative, not a discriminative, model, and by assuming less known information for making the role assignment. A difficulty of this task is that there is limited data available annotated with semantic roles, in comparison to syntactic parsing. As an illustration of this, in the model developed by [2] the most accurate rules only covered 50% of the unseen examples. To overcome the limited amount of training data, we would ultimately like to apply *bootstrapping*, in which limited labeled data are combined with unlabeled data to produce a more accurate model than that trained on unlabeled data alone [3, 4]. Generative models are a natural choice in the case of combining fully and partially annotated data. First, we need to test their capabilities on fully annotated data, such as it exists. This is the focus of the current paper.

Our work can be compared and contrasted with much past work in information extraction [5–7], in which the goal is to extract from text words or phrases that fill a role, such as "acquiring company" or "vehicle," and in which there are often multiple roles of interest. In particular, recent work such as [5] uses Hidden Markov Models, including induction over the structure of the model, for the labeling task. The model we use is similar, but while our goal is also to identify which roles are filled, and identify the words that fill them, we additionally aim to identify the overarching relationship that holds between the roles. We call this relationship the *frame*. Secondly, information extraction normally uses a small number of very domain specific roles, while our corpus has a large number of roles, with many types of roles that apply across domains. The techniques of information extraction may not scale well to large numbers of roles. Also, in information extraction, the labeling task is somewhat tied, semantically, to the domain at hand. These methods also tend to rely on regular structure, such as capitalization or indicator terms drawn from a closed class. Finally, the currently annotated semantic data is primarily at the sentence level, versus entire texts for information extraction.

The acquisition of selectional preferences, or the tendency of verbs to prefer arguments of a particular type, is a second closely related area [8, 9]. In this line of research statistical models are typically trained on parsed sentences to determine verb-subject or verb-direct object relationships. Such information can be useful for prepositional phrase attachment or to help determine the semantic class of a previously unseen word.

In this paper, we show that our generative model for role labeling produces results competitive with previous work in this area. In addition, our model is flexible enough to be used for annotating additional data, thus improving the model and the pool of data available for other researchers. Second, it has the advantage of capturing the case when roles are *null instantiated* in a particular sentence: they are not overtly expressed but their presence is understood implicitly in discourse. While our model handles these roles, we leave to future work a full evaluation of this ability. Finally, it can identify which constituents correspond to role labels of a particular given predicator.

2 Background

In this section we discuss the FrameNet Corpus, the previous work on labeling roles by Gildea and Jurafsky, and the role labeling task in more detail.

2.1 The FrameNet Corpus

FrameNet [1] is a large-scale, domain-independent computational lexicography project organized around the motivating principles of lexical semantics: that systematic correlations can be found between the meaning components of words, principally the semantic roles associated with events, and their combinatorial properties in syntax. This principle has been instantiated at various levels of granularity in different traditions of linguistic research; FrameNet researchers work at an intermediate level of granularity, termed the *frame*. Examples of frames include MOTION_DIRECTIONAL, CONVERSATION, JUDGMENT, and TRANSPORTATION. Frames consist of multiple *lexical units*—a items corresponding to a sense of a word. Examples for the MOTION_DIRECTIONAL frame are *drop* and *plummet*. Also associated with each frame is a set of semantic *roles*. Examples for the MOTION_DIRECTIONAL frame include the moving object, called the THEME; the ultimate destination, the GOAL; the SOURCE; and the PATH.

In addition to frame and role definitions, FrameNet has produced a large number of role-annotated sentences; the sentences are drawn primarily from the British National Corpus. There are two releases of the corpus, FrameNet I and FrameNet II[1]; we present results from both, but have so far focused primarily on the former. For each annotated example sentence, a lexical unit of interest, one which takes arguments, is identified. We will call this word the *predicator*[2]. The words and phrases which participate in the predicator's meaning are labeled with their roles, and the entire sentence is labeled with the relevant frame. Finally, the corpus also includes syntactic category information for each role. We give some examples below, with the frame listed in braces at the beginning, the predicator in bold, and each relevant constituent labeled with its role and phrase type. Note that the last example has a DRIVER role that is null instantiated.

{MOTION_DIRECTIONAL} Mortars lob heavy shells high into the sky so that $[^{NP}_{THEME}$ they] **drop** $[^{PP}_{PATH}$ down] $[^{PP}_{GOAL}$ on the target] $[^{PP}_{SOURCE}$ from the sky].

{ARRIVING} He heard the sound of liquid slurping in a metal container as $[^{NP}_{THEME}$ Farrell] **approached** $[^{NP}_{GOAL}$ him] $[^{PP}_{SOURCE}$ from behind].

{TRANSPORTATION} $[^{NULL}_{DRIVER}]$ $[^{NP}_{CARGO}$ The ore] was **boated** $[^{PP}_{GOAL}$ down the river].

Our focus here is on the FrameNet corpus, but another semantically annotated corpus is under development, called the Proposition Bank [10]. This corpus, based on adding semantics to the Penn English Treebank, is projected to soon be larger than FrameNet, and involves comprehensive rather than selective annotation of a corpus. However, it does not incorporate the rich frame typology of FrameNet, and only a somewhat limited role typology; while roles are specified for each verb, there is no generalization across verbs. Finally, Proposition Bank labels only verbs, leaving nouns and adjectives for a later stage; FrameNet includes all three. Since we desire rich semantic information in preference to a large corpus, we use FrameNet annotations as our source of training data. Our methods, however, would generalize to Proposition Bank.

2.2 Gildea & Jurafsky's Discriminative Model

Gildea and Jurafsky (2002) (henceforth, G&J) were the first to apply a statistical learning technique to the FrameNet data. They describe a discriminative model for deter-

---

[1] Also, confusingly known as version 0.75 and version 1.0, respectively.

[2] What we call the *predicator* is called the *target* in the FrameNet theory, and what we are calling a *(semantic) role* is called in FrameNet a *frame element*, while what we call a *constituent* or *argument head*, [2] call simply the *head*. We have found that most people find the FrameNet terminology rather confusing, and so have adopted alternative terms here.

mining the most probable role for a constituent given the frame, the predicator and some other features whose description we defer until later in the paper. They evaluate their model on a pre-release version of the FrameNet I corpus, which at that time contained about 50,000 sentences and 67 frame types. Their model was trained by first using the parser of Collins [11], and deriving features from that parse, the original sentence, and the correct FrameNet annotation of that sentence. Their work differs from ours in a number of important respects. Firstly, in all their experiments, they assume that the *frame* is already known, as well as the predicator of interest. While one could certainly imagine first determining the frame from the sentence (for example, one could use the model presented here to do that), their use of a discriminative approach makes it less straightforward to do joint inference over the choice of frame and semantic roles for constituents, as one would wish to do, whereas that is a natural thing to do within a generative model. Secondly, since their discriminative model assigns roles to constituents in the sentence, there is no natural way to handle unexpressed arguments, and they do not attempt to. But unexpressed arguments are common in natural languages, and again are naturally handled in a generative model. Moreover, most of their work assigns roles to constituents individually and independently. Later in their paper, they do develop and consider joint inference over all the semantic roles of a predicator, but this is more naturally done using the kind of model we present here. Finally, although this remains a promissory note, we believe that a generative model will be a better basis for extension via bootstrapping to unlabeled data.

2.3 The Role Labeling Task

With respect to the FrameNet corpus, several factors conspire to make the task of role-labeling challenging, with respect to the features available for making the classification. These results are likely to hold across other theories and methodologies for semantic role determination. The challenges also imply that constructing a hand-built semantic role identifier would prove a daunting task. First, it is not always predictable from the syntactic relationship between two phrases whether they stand in a semantic relationship. Second, many words that may participate in a role have a wide variety of possible roles in which they may participate. There are also many generic roles such as TIME and PLACE that can be indicated by almost any word. Third, the internal structure of a syntactic constituent is not always a good predictor of the role it receives. The prepositional phrase *in the hole*, for example, can be a LOCATION, as in *she sat in the hole*, or a GOAL of movement, as in *she jumped in the hole*. Finally, as mentioned earlier, in many cases roles are null instantiated, which is widespread in many languages; an English example is passive sentences with no specified agent, such as *the cake was eaten*. Thus, the only evidence for the presence of such roles is contextual.

With respect to the relationships between predicators, frames, and roles, further difficulties arise. A leading idea of FrameNet is that there is considerable variety to the semantic role types available in a particular event (for example, PERCEPTION events and COMMERCE events have very different participants). Thus, identifying the frame that is relevant for a particular sentence and predicator narrows the search for roles. However, many predicators are ambiguous with respect to their frame. Further, not all lexical units of a particular frame necessarily have the same distribution of roles. For example, *drop* and *plummet* have lexical entries in the MOTION_DIRECTIONAL frame, but SOURCE is rare for *plummet*, yet quite common for *drop*. As a result, for the task of automatic role assignment a mixture of predicator-specific and frame-specific statistics are potentially useful to deal with sparseness of a particular predicator or role.

3 A Generative Model for Sentence-Role Labeling

Our goal is to identify frames and roles, given a natural language sentence and predicator. As discussed above, G&J's approach to this problem was to determine the most probable role for each constituent of the sentence, given the frame, the predicator and some other features. However, this does not capture null instantiation, or roles that are not reified in the sentence. In addition, a model should ideally capture the relationships between frames and roles, determining which constituents are likely roles for which predicator. To address these concerns we turn to a generative model to determine the sequence of role labels for a sentence. In other words, our model defines a joint probability distribution over predicators, frames, roles, and constituents. While the model is fully general in its ability to determine these variables, in this paper it is only tested on its ability to determine roles and frames when given *both* a list of constituents and a single predicator. The generative model, illustrated in Figure 1, functions as follows. First, a predicator, S, is chosen, which then generates a frame, F. The frame generates

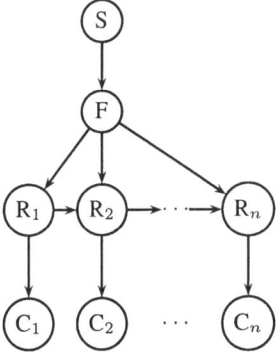

Fig. 1. Role Tagger

a (linearized) role sequence, R_1 through R_n which in turn generates each constituent of the sentence, C_1 through C_n. Note that, conditioned on a particular frame, the model is just a Hidden Markov Model. The sentence-to-constituent mapping is discussed in more detail in Section 3.1.

The model is complicated slightly by the fact that some sentence constituents do not correspond to a labeled semantic role. We handle these constituents with an idea from machine translation: that of the null source. A second complication is the null instantiations, which are also captured by a null, but in this case it is the emission which is a null. Henceforth, null sources will be described by an UNK (unknown) role to avoid confusion with null emissions. We will discuss an example with an unknown role in Section 3.1, and gave an example of a null emission in Section 2.1.

The joint probability for a FrameNet example in this model is

$$P(\mathbf{C}, \mathbf{R}, F, S) = P(S) \times P(F|S) \times P(\mathbf{R}|F, S) \times P(\mathbf{C}|\mathbf{R}, F, S),$$

where $\mathbf{C}$ is the vector of constituent heads, $\mathbf{R}$ is the role vector that generates them, F is the frame, and S is the predicator word. The third and fourth terms of this equation involve sequences. For the role sequence, we usually make a Markov assumption that each word's role is dependent only on the previous role in the sequence. Thus:

$$P(\mathbf{R}|F, S) = \prod_i P(R_i|R_1 \cdots R_{i-1}, F) \approx \prod_i P(R_i|R_{i-1}, F)$$

where the R_i are the roles in the sequence. The Markov assumption has been effective in language modeling and tagging and so seems a good assumption to begin with.

Finally, our basic model assumes that constituent emissions are independent of the frame and predicator given the sequence of roles, that each emission depends only on the role that generated it, and that constituents are independent of each other. Thus:

$$P(\mathbf{C}|F, S, \mathbf{R}) \approx P(\mathbf{C}|\mathbf{R}) = \prod_i P(C_i|R_i),$$

where C_i are the elements of $\mathbf{C}$ and R_i are the corresponding elements of $\mathbf{R}$. This can be compared to a part of speech tagging model where words are independent of each other given the tags, and depend only on the tag in the same position in the sequence. The independence of the constituents and the frame and predicator given the roles seems quite reasonable, given that most roles are frame-specific, and the whole rationale of FrameNet is that frames are sufficiently fine-grained that roles for predicators inside a single frame behave similarly. Adding further dependencies might be expected to only exacerbate the problem of sparseness in the data.

3.1 Training the Model

The FrameNet corpus contains annotations for all of the model components described above. To simplify the model, we chose to represent each constituent by its phrasal category together with the head word of that constituent. Since the FrameNet annotations do not include head word information, we determined the heads using simple heuristics. This representation and the method of head-finding are familiar from the statistical parsing literature ([12]). This data then provides a set of constituents with correctly annotated roles for a given sentence, where it is known which constituents correspond to roles and what the appropriate predicator is for those roles. For example, for the example below, the training example would be: S=rode; F=TRANSPORTATION; R_1=DRIVER; C_1=Anne/NP; R_2=VEHICLE; C_2=donkey/NP; R_3=AREA; C_3=on/PP.

{TRANSPORTATION} "On 26th May [$^{NP}_{DRIVER}$ Anne] **rode** [$^{NP}_{VEHICLE}$ a donkey] [$^{PP}_{AREA}$ on the beach]," the letter said.

Most of the parameters for the model are estimated using a straightforward maximum likelihood estimate based on fully labeled training data. Emission probabilities need to be smoothed, due to the sparseness of head words. During training, all words seen only once are replaced by the phrase type label of the constituent of which they are a head. This gives a phrasal-class based model, which is itself smoothed with a uniform phrasal class prior, and the probability of generating unseen words belong to a certain class is estimated as simply a constant (representing $P(word|class)$) times the probability of the phrasal class. Therefore, statistics are gathered both for the probabilities of roles generating each phrase type plus head combination, and there is a backoff model of roles generating a phrase type, and some unknown word within that type.

In an actual semantic parsing application, it would not be known which constituents bear a role of which predicators. We could make use of a syntactic parse in determining constituents that are candidates for roles. In a first approximation of this, we used a parser to determine constituents and their phrase types, and combined these with the FrameNet annotations. For this purpose, we restricted ourselves to training and testing on examples whose annotated predicator is a verb, since these are dealt with in a straightforward manner. The "sentence" level of the model in this case includes only the verb phrase whose head is the predicator, and its subject and arguments. If a constituent is identified in the parse but not in the FrameNet annotation, we label it as an UNK role. Again, this treatment is similar to the case of null emissions in a statistical machine translation model. For this format, the example above would have an additional role inserted at the beginning, with role=UNK and constituent=On/PP.

3.2 Producing the Semantic Role Labels

At inference time, the goal is to produce a sequence of role labels, given a sequence of constituents and a predicator. As just discussed, these constituents may be the head/phrase-type pairs from the FrameNet data, or the head/phrase-type pairs that are the result of parsing a sentence in the corpus and extracting the verb phrase with its subject and arguments. The role-labeling procedure is dependent on the frame, itself a hidden variable at labeling time. If the frame were known, we could simply use the HMM Viterbi algorithm, with the roles as the hidden states and the constituent heads and their phrase type as the emissions. In that case, we would use transition probabilities from only the frame of interest. Because we currently add empty constituents for the null instantiated roles whether using parsing information or not, our Viterbi sequence is of the same length as the input constituent sequence.

For the emission probabilities, there are two options, since a particular role can appear in multiple frames. One option is to condition the emission probabilities also on the frame. That is, the emission probabilities are calculated from only those role/constituent pairs that originally appeared in the given frame. A second option is to calculate emission probabilities for a role over all frames in the training data, since this arguably would provide more evidence and mitigate sparse data problems to some extent. However, the second option also leads to a potential problem, that of words unseen in the given frame but seen as emissions of the role in other frames. We compare both options in the results.

If the frame is not known, the more realistic case, then we have several options. We could just change the model and make the roles a combination of a role and a frame, but then the Viterbi sequence might change frames part way through, which seems unsatisfactory, given the intended semantics of the model. We could marginalize out the frame variable. In practice, given that most roles are particular to individual frames, doing such a marginalization would probably give results little different to our current results, but this also seems conceptually wrong, since we're wanting to do inference for the most likely frame and roles underlying a sentence. So instead we calculate the most probable configuration of all the hidden variables. This generalized Viterbi algorithm is a straightforward instance of max-propagation algorithms for Bayesian networks [13].

For this case, this is equivalent to the less efficient operation of simply finding all frames with $P(F|S) > 0$, compute the role sequence probabilities given the transition probabilities for that frame and the emission probabilities across all frames, and then choosing the maximum product of the prior probability of the frame for the predicator and the probability returned by the HMM Viterbi algorithm.

4 Experimental Results

To test the above model, we trained it on annotated FrameNet data, randomly dividing the data into a training set and an unseen test set. Each frame was randomly split so that 70% of its examples were in the training set and 10% were in the test set. We report on three types of accuracy. First, role labeling accuracy is the number of constituents correctly labeled. Since we label all constituents, this makes the familiar metrics of *recall* and *precision* equivalent. We micro-average by adding up the number of correct labels for *all* examples and dividing by the number of total labels for all examples, so this is not an average accuracy per-sentence, though we have done the calculations both ways, and for these experiments the two figures are quite close to each other. Second, we report the percent of sentences for which all roles are correctly labeled, or full sentence accuracy. Finally, frame accuracy is calculated as the proportion of sentences for which the correct frame was chosen based on the predicator.

For a baseline comparison, we computed the accuracy of a zeroth-order Markov model, treating all transition probabilities between roles as uniform. We also computed the accuracy of choosing, for all constituents, the most common role given the predicator, and the accuracy of choosing the most common role given the frame, where the most common frame ($\arg\max_F P(F|S)$) for the known predicator is chosen.

4.1 Results: Annotated Roles

Our first set of experiments trained and tested our model from the correctly annotated sentences of the FrameNet corpus, together with constituent heads as determined by a parser. We performed most of our experiments on FrameNet I, but ran some experiments with FrameNet II as well[3]. The constituents' heads were chosen by some simple

---

[3] We regard the FrameNet I results as broadly comparable with those of G&J, though the data sets are not exactly the same, and there are various other differences (we guess the frame whereas they assume it; except in parsing experiments, we use the phrasal category given in FrameNet, whereas they always use phrasal categories returned by a parser, even when using the constituent extent information given by FrameNet). We have recently obtained G&J's data, and hope to provide a more precise comparison in future work.

Table 1. FrameNet I Experimental Results. Key: Role=Role labeling accuracy, Full=full sentence accuracy, Frame=Frame choice accuracy. Trn=Training Set, Tst=Test Set

System	Trn Role	Tst Role	Trn Full	Tst Full	Tst Frame
FirstOrder	86.1%	79.3%	75.4%	65.3%	97.5%
ZeroOrder	–	60.0%	–	34.6%	96.5%
BasePredicator	39.9%	39.2%	10.5%	10.2%	N/A
BaseFrame	37.8%	37.6%	9.2%	9.5%	N/A

Table 2. FrameNet I Arg Max versus all Sequences

System	Role	Full	Frame
First All	79.3%	65.3%	97.5%
First ArgMax	77.2%	63.2%	94.8%
Zero All	60.0%	34.6%	96.5%
Zero ArgMax	58.8%	33.4%	94.8%

heuristics, but their labels correspond to the Phrase Type labels from FrameNet. These tests are similar but not identical to the analysis in Section 4.2 of G&J.

The first results are on 36,805 training sentences, containing a total of 82,169 constituents, and 5299 test sentences containing 11,833 constituents. There are 78 frames, 139 possible role labels, and 1,385 predicators. We obtain 86.1% role labeling accuracy on the training data, 79.3% on the test data. For full sentence accuracy, we obtained 75.4% accuracy on the training data and 65.3% on the test data. Finally, the correct frame was chosen for 98.1% of training sentences and 97.5% of the test sentences. Table 1 summarizes these and the remainder of our results for this data set. We did not measure the training accuracy in the zeroth-order case. These results are roughly comparable to results of 78.5% on test data for G&J's model on data with constituents marked, and they cite a similar result for BasePredicator of 40.6%. We can at least conclude that performance is similar.

We also measured the benefit of exploring all sequences versus only the sequence for the frame with the highest probability given the predicator. The difference is shown in Table 2, for training accuracy only in the First Order and Zero Order case. The differences are about two percentage points in most cases.

Our next set of results are on FrameNet II, where we evaluated only the ArgMax case. Training on 70% and testing on 10% resulted in a corpus of 89,900 training sentences and 12,990 test sentences. Here there are 282 frames, 423 possible role labels, and 4,712 predicators. The performance results on the test set, shown in Table 3, are somewhat weaker than for FrameNet I, but not overly so, considering the increased number of roles and frames.

In analysis of the role labeling results, we noticed two major sources of error. The first is words unseen in a particular frame but not "rare" over the whole corpus. We could partially address this with a held-out mass for unseen words that is weighted by the prevalence of rare words of each phrase type. Second, some cases are just very difficult, for example, prepositions commonly heading more than one type of role can induce ambiguity, one example being Instrument/Manner ambiguity on *with*-marked

Table 3. FrameNet II Experimental Results

System	Role	Full	Frame
FirstOrder	73.9%	63.7%	88.7%
ZeroOrder	61.3%	43.0%	89.3%

Table 4. Parse Model Experimental Results

System	Trn Role	Tst Role	Trn Full	Tst Full
FirstOrder	81.0%	70.1%	58.1%	39.5%
ZeroOrder	78.8%	67.8%	50.7%	34%
BasePredicatorParse	35.4%	33.2%	1.0%	0.7%

roles. We also have difficulties with roles in frames such as Differentiation, which contains roles for Phenomena, Phenomenon1, and Phenomenon2, or Conversation, with its Interlocutors, Interlocutor1, and Interlocutor2 roles. These roles are semantically similar, and we would need a richer syntactic representation to differentiate them.

4.2 Results: All Constituents

In the next set of experiments, we evaluated the system, together with a parser, on the ability to both determine which constituents correspond to roles, and to label those constituents. To do so, we used our statistical parser [14] to parse only the sentences used in the previous section which have a verbal predicator. The parser was trained on Brown and about half of the Wall Street Journal. Our generative model was trained as described above, with the inclusion of UNK roles for constituents not corresponding to a labeled role. At role labeling time, the verb phrases as determined by the parser are presented to the model with (the labeled heads of) their subject and arguments, with the main verb as the predicator. The model now has the option of choosing UNK role labels.

Because of the difficulty in matching parse constituents with their appropriate role labels in the annotated data, the size of the data set for these tests is considerably smaller than that above. We used only the verb phrases corresponding to known frames, but with the UNK roles included. There are are 13,782 training examples, 1,558 test examples, 55 frames, and 980 different predicators. Also, there are 117 unique roles and 43,937 constituents. On this task, the system obtained 81% role labeling accuracy on the training set and 70.1% on the test set. Full sentences were considerably more difficult to get right, with 58.1% training accuracy and 39.5% test accuracy. Frame choice accuracy was 94.5% on the training data and 93.3% on the test data. These results are summarized in Table 4. The only figure G&J give for full sentence accuracy is 38% for a system that had to determine both which constituents correspond to roles, and what those role labels should be, which is again roughly comparable to our 39.5% performance on the test set.

4.3 Discussion

Our model and these results can be compared and contrasted with those of G&J. Some of the features used by G&J are similar to those used by our model. Both models use the phrase type and head word of each constituent. Both models incorporate the predicator, but in different ways. Our model assumes the predicator is either explicitly given or assumes that each main verb in the sentence is a predicator. A future version could determine the probability that each head word is a predicator.

In addition to these features, G&J introduce several other features. First, the *Governing Category* determines for noun phrases, whether an S or VP most closely dominates the phrase. This feature may provide similar information to that given by our Markov chain. Second, their *Path* feature follows the parse tree from the predicator to the constituent, represented as the string of nonterminals encountered. The final two features missing from our model but present in theirs are whether the main verb phrase of the sentence is in active or passive *Voice*, and the *Position* of the constituent, before or after the predicator. However, these are partially captured by linear order and phrasal constituent type. On the other hand, they always assume knowledge of the frame, and because they only labeled the roles of actual sentence constituents, their model does not include null instantiated roles, nor is it obvious how to extend it to do so.

Finally, our ultimate use for this model is not just role labeling, but to estimate parameters when the training data is only partially observed. In that case, using the maximum likelihood estimate is statistically sound, whereas maximizing the conditional likelihood would not be and a generative model is to be preferred.

5 Conclusion and Future Work

We have described and evaluated a successful generative model for semantic role labeling. Our results to date are encouraging but more remains to be done. While small improvements, such as better unknown word handling, can be made to the model, we also see several larger issues that need to be addressed. To do role boundary detection a more sophisticated model is necessary, since under some circumstances non-verbal predicators assign roles to syntactically non-local constituents. Also, while it is fairly straightforward to generalize the current model to the case of multiple predicators per sentence, an articulated theory of when constituents can take roles from multiple predicators is still under development in FrameNet, and would require further articulation in our theory. Finally, it would also be useful to incorporate some extra syntactic information, such as predicator position, and the presence of coordination, and to model role-shuffling operations such as passivization, imperative forms, and extraposition, since these operations, if not modeled, can obscure linguistically motivated generalizations about the linear order of roles.

Acknowledgments

This work was supported in part by the Advanced Research and Development Activity (ARDA)'s Advanced Question Answering for Intelligence (AQUAINT) Program, and in part by an IBM Faculty Partnership Award to the final author.

References

1. Baker, C.F., Fillmore, C.J., Lowe, J.B.: The Berkeley FrameNet project. In: COLING-ACL. (1998)
2. Gildea, D., Jurafsky, D.: Automatic labeling of semantic roles. Computational Linguistics **28** (2002) 245–288
3. Riloff, E., Jones, R.: Learning dictionaries for information extraction by multi-level bootstrapping. In: Sixteenth National Conference on Artificial Intelligence. (1999) 474–479
4. Nigam, K., McCallum, A.K., Thrun, S., Mitchell, T.M.: Learning to classify text from labeled and unlabeled documents. In: Proceedings of AAAI-98, 15th Conference of the American Association for Artificial Intelligence, Madison, AAAI Press (1998) 792–799
5. Freitag, D., McCallum, A.: Information extraction with HMM structures learned by stochastic optimization. In: Proceedings of AAAI. (2000) 584–589
6. Leek, T.: Information extraction using hidden Markov models. Master's thesis, U C San Diego (1997)
7. Huffman, S.: Learning information extraction patterns from examples. In Wermter, S., Scheler, G., Riloff, E., eds.: Connectionist, Statistical and Symbolic Approaches to Learning for Natural Language Processing. Springer-Verlag (1996) 246–260
8. Resnik, P.S.: Selection and Information: a class-based approach to lexical relationships. PhD thesis, University of Pennsylvania (1993)
9. Rooth, M., Riezler, S., Prescher, D., Carroll, G., Beil, F.: Inducing a semantically annotated lexicon via em-based clustering. In: 37th Annual Meeting of the ACL. (1999)
10. Kingsbury, P., Palmer, M., Marcus, M.: Adding semantic annotation to the penn treebank. In: Proceedings of the Human Language Technology Conference, San Diego, California (2002)
11. Collins, M.J.: Three generative, lexicalised models for statistical parsing. In: ACL 35/EACL 8. (1997) 16–23
12. Collins, M.: Head-Driven Statistical Models for Natural Language Parsing. PhD thesis, University of Pennsylvania (1999)
13. Cowell, R.G., Dawid, A.P., Lauritzen, S.L., Spiegelhalter, D.J.: Probabilistic Networks and Expert Systems. Springer-Verlag, New York (1999)
14. Klein, D., Manning, C.D.: Fast exact inference with a factored model for natural language parsing. In: Advances in Neural Information Processing Systems. Volume 15., MIT Press (2003)

Optimizing Local Probability Models
for Statistical Parsing

Kristina Toutanova[1], Mark Mitchell[2], and Christopher D. Manning[1]

[1] Computer Science Department, Stanford University,
Stanford, CA 94305-9040, USA
{kristina,manning}@cs.stanford.edu
[2] CSLI, Stanford University,
Stanford, CA 94305, USA
markmitchell@fastmail.fm

Abstract. This paper studies the properties and performance of models for estimating local probability distributions which are used as components of larger probabilistic systems — history-based generative parsing models. We report experimental results showing that memory-based learning outperforms many commonly used methods for this task (Witten-Bell, Jelinek-Mercer with fixed weights, decision trees, and log-linear models). However, we can connect these results with the commonly used general class of deleted interpolation models by showing that certain types of memory-based learning, including the kind that performed so well in our experiments, are instances of this class. In addition, we illustrate the divergences between joint and conditional data likelihood and accuracy performance achieved by such models, suggesting that smoothing based on optimizing accuracy directly might greatly improve performance.

1 Introduction

Many disambiguation tasks in Natural Language Processing are not easily tackled by off-the-shelf Machine Learning models. The main challenges posed are the complexity of classification tasks and the sparsity of data. For example, syntactic parsing of natural language sentences can be posed as a classification task — given a sentence s, find a most likely parse tree t from the set of all possible parses of s according to a grammar G. But the set of classes in this formulation varies across sentences and can be very large or even infinite.

A common way to approach the parsing task is to learn a generative history-based model $P(s,t)$, which estimates the joint probability of a sentence s and a parse tree t [2]. This model breaks the complex (s,t) pair into pieces which are sequentially generated, assuming independence on most of the already generated structure. More formally, the general form of the history-based parsing model is $P(t) = \prod_{i=1}^{n} P(y_i|x_i)$. Here the parse tree is generated in some order, where every generated piece y_i (future) is conditioned on some context x_i (history).

The most important factors in the performance of such models are (*i*) the chosen generative model, including the representation of parse tree nodes, and (*ii*) the method for estimating the local probability distributions needed by the model. Due to the sparseness of NLP data, the method of estimating the local distributions $P(y_i|x_i)$ plays a very important role in building a good model. We will sometimes refer to this problem as smoothing.

The goals of the paper are three-fold: (*i*) to empirically evaluate the accuracy achieved by previously proposed and new local probability estimation models; (*ii*) to characterize the form of a kind of memory-based models that performed best in our study, showing their relation to deleted interpolation models; and (*iii*) to study the relationship among joint and conditional likelihood, and accuracy for models of this type.

While various authors have described several smoothing methods, such as using a deleted interpolation model [5], or a decision tree learner [13], or a maximum entropy inspired model [3], there has been a lack of comparisons of different learning methods for local decisions within a composite system. Because our ultimate goal here is to have good classifiers for choosing trees for sentences according to the rule $t = \arg\max_{t'} P(s,t')$, where the model $P(s,t')$ is a product of factors given by the local models $P(y_i|x_i)$, one can not isolate the estimation of local probabilities $P(y_i|x_i)$ as a stand-alone problem, choosing a model family and setting parameters to optimize the likelihood of test data. The bias-variance tradeoff may be different [9]. We find interesting patterns in the relationship between joint and conditional data likelihood and accuracy performance achieved by such compound models, suggesting that heavier smoothing is needed to optimize accuracy and that fitting a small number of parameters to optimize it directly might greatly improve performance.

The experimental study shows that memory-based learning outperforms commonly used methods for this task (Witten-Bell, Jelinek Mercer with fixed weights, decision trees, and log-linear models). For example, an error reduction of 5.8% in whole sentence accuracy is achieved by using memory-based learning instead of Witten-Bell, which is used in the state-of-the art model [5].

2 Memory-Based and Deleted Interpolation Models

In this section we demonstrate the relationship between deleted interpolation models and a class of memory-based models that performed best in our study.

2.1 Deleted Interpolation Models

Deleted interpolation models estimate the probability of a class y given a feature vector (context) of n features, $P(y|x_1, \ldots, x_n)$, by linearly combining relative frequency estimates based on subsets of the full context $(x_1, \ldots, x_n)$, using statistics from lower-order distributions to reduce sparseness and improve the estimate. To write out an expression for this estimate, let us introduce some notation. We will denote by S_j subsets of the set $\{1, \ldots, n\}$ of feature indices. S_j can take on 2^n values ranging from the empty set to the full set $\{1, \ldots, n\}$. We will denote by X_S the tuple of feature values of X for the features whose indices are in S. For example $X_{\{1,2,3\}} = (x_1, x_2, x_3)$. For convenience, we will add another set, denoted by $*$, which we will use to include in the interpolation the uniform distribution $P(y) = \frac{1}{V}$, where V is the number of possible classes y. The general form of estimate is then:

$$\tilde{P}(y|X) = \sum_{S_i \subseteq \{1,\ldots,n\} \vee S_i = *} \lambda_{S_i}(X) \hat{P}(y|X_{S_i}) \qquad (1)$$

Here $\hat{P}$ are relative frequency estimates and $\hat{P}(y|X_*) = \frac{1}{V}$ by definition. The interpolation weights λ are shown to depend on the full context $X = (x_1, \ldots, x_n)$ as well as the specific subset S_i of features. In practice parameters as general as that are never estimated. For strictly linear feature subsets sequences, methods have been proposed to fit the parameters by maximizing the likelihood of held-out data through EM while tying parameters for contexts having equal or similar counts[1].

2.2 (A Kind of) Memory-Based Learning Models

We will show that a broad class of memory-based learning methods have the same form as Equation 1 and are thus a subclass of deleted interpolation models. While [18] have noted that memory-based and back-off models are similar in the way they use counts and in the way they specify abstraction hierarchies among context subsets, the exact nature of the relationship is not made precise. They emphasize the case of 1-nearest neighbor and show that it is equivalent to a special kind of strict back-off (non-interpolated) model. Our experimental results suggest that a number of neighbors K much larger than 1 works best for local probability estimation in parsing models. The exact form of the interpolation weights λ as dependent on contexts and their counts is therefore crucial for combining more specific and more general evidence. We will look at memory-based learning models determined by the following parameters:

- K, the number of nearest neighbors.
- A distance function $\Delta(X, X')$ between feature vectors. This function should depend only on the *positions* of matching/mis-matching features.
- A weighting function $w(X, X')$, which is the weight of neighbor X' of X. We will assume that the weight is a function of the distance, i.e. $w(X, X') = w(\Delta(X, X'))$.

Let us denote by $N_K(X)$ the set of K nearest neighbors of X. The probability of a class y given X is estimated as:

$$\tilde{P}(y|X) = \frac{\sum_{X' \in N_K(X)} w(\Delta(X, X'))\delta(y, y')}{\sum_{X' \in N_K(X)} w(\Delta(X, X'))} \quad (2)$$

Here y' is the label of the neighbor X', and $\delta(y, y') = 1$ iff $y = y'$, and 0 otherwise. For nominal attributes, as always used in conditioning contexts for natural language parsers, the distance function commonly distinguishes only between matches and mismatches on feature values, rather than specifying a richer distance between values. We will limit our analysis to this case as specified in the conditions above. In the majority of applications of k-NN to natural language tasks, simple distance functions have been used [6][2].

---

[1] When not limited to linear subsets sequences, it is possible to optimize tied parameters, but EM is difficult to apply and we are not aware of work trying to optimize interpolation parameters for models of this more general form.

[2] Richer distance functions have been proposed and shown to be advantageous [18, 12, 8]. However, such distance functions are harder to acquire and using them raises significantly the computational complexity of applying the k-NN algorithm. When simple distance functions are used, clever indexing techniques make testing a constant time operation.

The distance function $\Delta(X, X')$ will take on one of 2^n values depending on the indices of the matching features between the two vectors. In practice we will add V artificial instances to the training set, one of each class (to avoid zero probabilities). These instances will be at an additional distance value δ_{smooth} which will normally be larger that the other distances. We require that the distance $\Delta(X, X')$ be no smaller than $\Delta(X, X'')$ if X'' matches X on a superset of the attributes on which X' matches.

The commonly used overlap distance function, $\Delta(X, X') = \sum_{i=1}^{n} w_i \delta(x_i, x'_i)$, satisfies these constraints. Every feature has an importance weight $w_i \geq 0$. This is the distance function we have used in our experiments, but it is more restrictive than the general case for which our analysis holds, because it has only $n + 1$ parameters — the w_i and δ_{smooth}. The general case would require $2^n + 1$ parameters.

We go on to introduce one last bit of notation. We will say that the schema S of an instance X' with respect to an instance X is the set of feature indices on which the two instances match. (We are herer using similar terminology to [18]). It is clear that the distance $\Delta(X, X')$ depends only on the schema S of X' with respect to X. The same holds true for the weight of X' with respect to X. We can therefore think of the K nearest neighbors as groups of neighbors that have the same schema. Let us denote by $S_K(X)$ the set of schemata of the K nearest neighbors of X. We assume that instances in the same schema are either all included or excluded from the nearest neighbors set. The same assumption has commonly been made before [18]. We have the following relationships between schemata $S' \leq S$ if the schema S' is more specific than S, i.e. the set of feature indices S' is a superset of the set S. We will use $S' \prec S$ for immediate precedence, i.e. $S' \prec S$ iff $S' \leq S$ and there are no schemata between the two in the ordering. We can rearrange Equation 2 in terms of the participating schemata and then after an additional re-bracketing, we obtain the same form as Equation 1.

$$\tilde{P}(y|X) = \sum_{S_j \in S_K(X)} \lambda_{S_j}(X) \hat{P}(y|X_{S_j}) \qquad (3)$$

The interpolation coefficients have the form:

$$\lambda_{S_j}(X) = \frac{(w(\Delta(S_j)) - \sum_{S_j \prec S'_j, S'_j \in S_K(X)} w(\Delta(S'_j)))}{Z(X)} c(X_{S_j}) \qquad (4)$$

$$Z(X) = \sum_{S_j \in S_K(X)} \left(w(\Delta(S_j)) - \sum_{S_j \prec S'_j, S'_j \in S_K(X)} w(\Delta(S'_j)) \right) c(X_{S_j}) \qquad (5)$$

This concludes our proof that memory-based models of this type are a subclass of deleted interpolation models. It is interesting to observe the form of the interpolation coefficients. We can notice that they depend on the total number of instances matching the feature subset as is usually true of other linear subsets deleted interpolation methods such as Jelinek-Mercer smoothing and Witten-Bell smoothing. However they also depend on the counts of more general subsets as seen in the denominator. The different counts are weighted according to the function w.

In practice the most widely used deleted interpolation models exclude some of the feature subsets and estimates are interpolated from a linear feature subsets order. These models can be represented in the form:

$$\dot{P}(y|x_1,\ldots,x_n) = \lambda_{x_1,\ldots,x_n}\hat{P}(y|x_1,\ldots,x_n) + (1 - \lambda_{x_1,\ldots,x_n})\tilde{P}(y|x_1,\ldots,x_{n-1}) \quad (6)$$

The recursion is ended with the uniform distribution as above. Memory-based models will be subclasses of deleted interpolation models of this form if we define $\Delta(S) = \Delta(\{1,\ldots,i\})$, where i is the largest numbers such that $\{1,\ldots,i\} \geq S$. If such i does not exist $\Delta(S) = \Delta(\{\})$ or $\Delta(*)$ for the artificial instances.

3 Experiments

We investigate these ideas via experiments in probabilistic parse selection from among a set of alternatives licensed by a hand-built grammar in the context of the newly developed Redwoods HPSG treebank [14]. HPSG (Head-driven Phrase Structure Grammar) is a modern constraint-based lexicalist (unification) grammar, described in [15].

The Redwoods treebank makes available syntactic and semantic analyses of much greater depth than, for example, the Penn Treebank. Therefore there are a large number of features available that could be used by stochastic models for disambiguation. In the present experiments, we train generative history-based models for derivation trees. The derivation trees are labeled via the derivation rules that build them up; an example is shown in Figure 1. All models use the 8 features shown in Figure 2. They estimate the probability $P(expansion(n)|history(n))$, where *expansion* is the tuple of node labels of the children of the current node and *history* is the 8-tuple of feature values. The results we obtain should be applicable to Penn Treebank parsing as well, since we use many similar features such as grand-parent information and build similar generative models.

The accuracy results we report are averaged over a ten-fold cross-validation on the data set summarized in Table 1. Accuracy results denote the percentage of test sentences for which the highest ranked analysis was the correct one. This measure scores whole sentence accuracy and is therefore stricter than the labelled precision/recall measures, and more appropriate for the task of parse selection[3].

Table 1. Annotated corpus used in experiments: The columns are, from left to right, the total number of sentences, average length, average lexical ambiguity (number of lexical entries per token), average structural ambiguity (number of parses per sentence), and the accuracy of choosing at random

sentences	length	lex ambiguity	struct ambiguity	random baseline
5312	7.0	4.1	8.3	25.81%

3.1 Linear Feature Subsets Order

In this first set of experiments, we compare memory-based learning models restricted to linear order among feature subsets to deleted interpolation models using the same

---
[3] Therefore we should expect to obtain lower figures for this measure compared to labelled precision/recall. As an example, the state of the art unlexicalized parser [11] achieves 86.9% F measure on labelled constituents and 30.9% exact match accuracy.

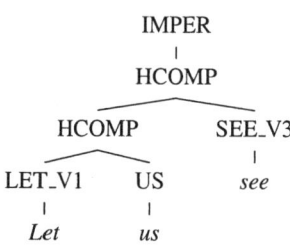

No.	Name	Example
1	Node Label	HCOMP
2	Parent Node Label	HCOMP
3	Node Direction	left
4	Parent Node Direction	none
5	Grandparent Node Label	IMPER
6	Great Grandparent Label	yes
7	Left Sister Node Label	HCOMP
8	Category of Node	verb

Fig. 1. Example of a Derivation Tree

Fig. 2. Features over derivation trees

linear subsets order. The linear interpolation sequence was the same for all models and was determined by ordering the features of the history by gain-ratio. The resulting order was: 1, 8, 2, 3, 5, 4, 7, 6 (see Table 2). Numerous methods have been proposed for estimation of parameters for linearly interpolated models[4]. In this section we survey the following models:

Jelinek Mercer with a fixed interpolation weight λ for the lower-order model (and $1 - \lambda$ for the higher-order model). This is a model of the form of Equation 6, where the interpolation weights do not depend on the feature history. We report test set accuracy for varying values of λ. We refer to this model as **JM**.

Witten-Bell smoothing [17] uses as an expression for the weights : $\lambda(x_1, \ldots, x_i) = \frac{c(x_1,\ldots,x_i)}{c(x_1,\ldots,x_i)+d\times|y:c(y,x_1,\ldots,x_i)>0|}$. We refer to this model as **WBd**. The original Witten-Bell smoothing[5] is the special case with $d = 1$, but use of an additional parameter d which multiplies the number of observed outcomes in the denominator is commonly used in some of the best-performing parsers and named-entity recognizers [1,5].

Memory-based models restricted to linear sequence, with varying weight function and varying values of K. The restriction to linear sequence is obtained by defining the distance function to be of the special form described at the end of section 2. We define the distance function as follows for subsets of the linear generalization sequence: $\Delta(\{1,\ldots,n\}) = 0, \cdots, \Delta(\{\}) = n, \Delta(*) = n+1$. We implemented several weighting methods, including inverse, exponential, information gain, and gain-ratio. The weight functions inverse cubed(**INV3**) and inverse to the fourth (**INV4**) worked best. They are defined as follows: $INV3(d)=(1/(d+1))^3$ $INV4(d)=(1/(d+1))^4$. We refer to these models as **LKNN3** and **LKNN4**, standing for linear k-NN using weighting **INV3** and linear k-NN using weighting function **INV4** respectively.

Figure 3 shows parse selection accuracy for the three models discussed above — JM in (a), WBd in (b) and LKNN3 and LKNN4 in (c). We can note that the maximal performance of JM (79.14% at $\lambda = .79$) is similar to the maximal performance of WBd (79.60% at $d = 20$). The best accuracies are achieved when the smoothing

---

[4] In addition to models of the form of Equation 6 there are models that use modified distributions (not the relative frequency). Comparison to these other good models (e.g., forms of Kneser-Ney and Katz smoothing [4] is not the subject of this study and would be an interesting topic for future research.

[5] *Method C*, also used in [4].

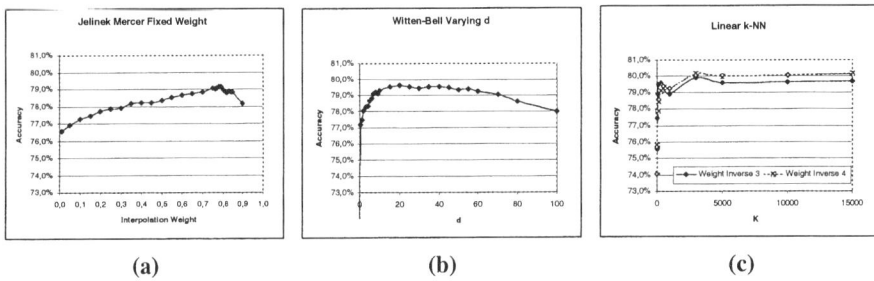

Fig. 3. Linear Subsets Deleted Interpolation Models: Jelinek Mercer (JM) (*a*) Witten-Bell (*b*) and k-NN (*c*)

is much heavier than we would expect. For example, one would think that the higher order distributions should normally receive more weight, i.e. $\lambda < .5$ for JM. Similarly, for Witten-Bell smoothing, the value of d achieving maximal performance is larger than expected. WB is an instance of WBd and we see that it does not achieve good accuracy. [5] reports that values of d between 2 and 5 were best. The over-smoothing issue is related to our observations on the connection between joint likelihood, conditional likelihood, and parse selection accuracy, which we will discuss at length in Section 4.

The best performance of LKNN3 is 79.94% at $K = 3,000$ and the best performance of LKNN4 is 80.18% at $K = 15,000$. Here we also note that much higher values of K are worth considering. In particular, the commonly used $K = 1$ (74.07% for LKNN4) performs much worse than optimal. The difference between LKNN4 at $K = 15,000$ and JM at $\lambda = 0.79$ is statistically significant according to a two-sided paired t-test at level $\alpha = .05$ (p-value=.024). The difference between LKNN4 and the best accuracy achieved by WBd is not significant according to this test but the accuracy of LKNN4 is more stable across a broad range of K values and thus the maximum can be more easily found when fitting on held-out data.

We saw that using k-NN to estimate interpolation weights in a strict linear interpolation sequence works better than JM and WBd. The real advantage of k-NN, however, can be seen when we want to combine estimates from more general feature contexts but do not limit ourselves to strict linear deleted interpolation sequences. The next section compares k-NN in this setting to other proposed alternatives.

3.2 General k-NN, Decision Trees, and Log-Linear Models

In this second group of experiments we study the behavior of memory-based learning not restricted to linear subset sequences, using different weighting schemes and number of neighbors, comparing this result to the performance of decision trees and log-linear models. The next paragraphs describe our implementation of these models in more detail.

For k-NN we define the distance metric as follows: $\Delta(\{i_1, \ldots, i_k\}) = n - k$; $\Delta(\{\}) = n, \Delta(*) = n + 1$. We report the performance of inverse weighting cubed (INV3) and inverse weighting to the fourth(INV4) as for linear k-NN. We refer to these two models as KNN3 and KNN4 respectively.

Table 2. Best Parse Selection Accuracies Achieved by Models

Model	KNN4	DecTreeWBd	LogLinSingle	LogLinPairs	LogLinBackoff
Accuracy	80.79%	79.66%	78.65%	78.91%	77.52%

Decision trees have been used previously to estimate probabilities for statistical parsers [13][6]. We found that smoothing the probability estimates at the leaves by linear interpolation with estimates along the path to the root improved the results significantly, as reported in [13]. We used WBd and obtained final estimates by linearly interpolating the distribution at the leaf up to the root and the uniform distribution. We can think of this as having a different linear subset sequence for every leaf. The obtained model is thus an instance of a deleted interpolation model ([13]). We denote this model as DecTreeWBd.

Log-linear models have been successfully applied to many natural language problems, including conditional history-based parsing models [16], part-of-speech tagging, PP attachment, etc. In [3], the use of a "maximum entropy inspired" estimation technique leads to the currently best performing parser[7]. The space of possible maximum entropy models that one could build is very large. In our implementation here, we are using only binary features over the history and expansion of the following form: $f_{v_{i1},...,v_{ik},expansion}(x'_1,...,x'_n, expansion') = 1$ iff $expansion' = expansion$ and $x_{i1} = v_{i1} \cdots x_{ik} = v_{ik}$. Gaussian smoothing was used by all models. We trained three models differing in the type of allowable features (templates).

- Single attributes only. This model has the fewest number of features. Here we allow the features to be defined by specifying a value for a single attribute for a history. We denote this model LogLinSingle.
- This model includes features looking at the values of pairs of attributes. However, we did not allow all pairs of attributes, but only pairs including attribute number 1 (the node label). These are a total of 8 pairs (including the singleton set containing only attribute 1). We denote this model LogLinPairs.
- This final model mimics the linear feature subsets deleted interpolation models of section 3.1. It uses all subsets in the linear sequence, which makes for 9 subsets. We denote this model LogLinBackoff.

Figure 4 shows the performance of k-NN using the two inverse weighing functions for varying values of K and DecTreeWBd for varying values of d. Table 2 shows the best results achieved by KNN4, DecTreeWbd and the three log-linear models.

The results suggest that memory-based models perform better than decision trees and log-linear models in combining information for probability estimation. The difference between the accuracy of KNN4 and WBd is 5.8% error reduction and is statis-

---

[6] We induce decision trees using gain-ratio as a splitting criterion (information gain divided by the entropy of the attribute). We stopped growing the tree when all samples in a leaf had the same class, or when the gain ratio was 0.

[7] In [3], estimates based on different feature subsets are multiplied and the model has a form similar to that of a log-linear model. The obtained distributions are not normalized but are close to summing to one.

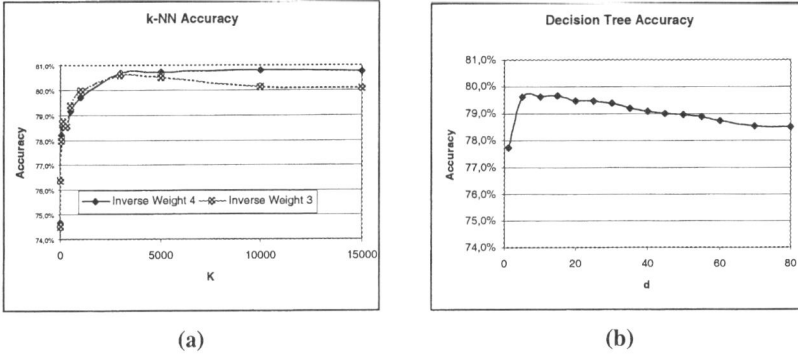

Fig. 4. k-NN using INV3 and INV4 (*a*) and DecTreeWBd (*b*)

tically significant at level $\alpha = 0.01$ according to a two-sided paired t-test (*p*-value= 0.0016).

This result agrees with the observation in [7] that memory-based models should be good for NLP data, which is abundant with exceptions and special cases. The study in [7] is restricted to the classification case and $K = 1$ or other very small values of K are used. Here we have shown that these models work particularly well for probability estimation. Relative frequency estimates from different schemata are effectively weighted based on counts of feature subsets and distance-weighting. It is especially surprising that these models performed better than log-linear models. Log-linear/logistic regression models are the standardly promoted statistical tool for these sorts of nominal problems, but actually we find that simple memory-based models performed better. The log-linear models we have surveyed perform more abstraction (by just including some features) and are less easily controllable for overfitting; abstracting away information is not expected to work well for natural language according to [7].

4 Log-Likelihoods and Accuracy

Our discussion up to now included only parse selection results. But what is the relation to the joint likelihood of test data (likelihood according to a model of the correct parses) or the conditional likelihood (the likelihood of the correct parse given the sentence)? Work in smoothing for language models optimizes parameters on held-out data to maximize the joint likelihood, and measures test set performance by looking at perplexity (which is a monotonic function of the joint likelihood) [4]. Results on word error rate for speech recognition are also often reported [10], but the training process does not specifically try to minimize word error rate (because it is hard). In our experiments we observe that much heavier smoothing is needed to maximize accuracy than to maximize joint log-likelihood.

We show graphs for the model JM for the joint log-likelihood averaged per expansion, and the conditional log-likelihood averaged per sentence in Figure 5 (*a*). The corresponding accuracy curve is shown in Figure 3 (*a*). The graph in 5 (*b*) shows joint and conditional log-likelihood curves for model KNN4; its accuracy curve is in Figure 4 (*a*).

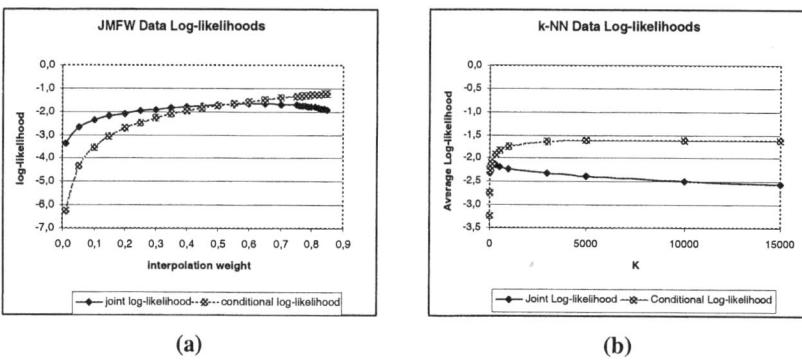

Fig. 5. JM (*a*) and k-NN using INV4(*b*)

The pattern of the points of maximum for the test data joint log-likelihood, conditional log-likelihood and parse selection accuracy is fairly consistent across smoothing methods. The joint likelihood increased in the beginning with smoothing up to point, and then started to decrease. The accuracy followed the pattern of the joint likelihood, but the peak performance was reached long after the best settings for joint likelihood (and before the best settings for conditional likelihood). This relationship between the maxima — first joint log-likelihood, followed by the accuracy maximum holds for all surveyed models. This phenomenon could be partly explained by reference to the increased significance of the variance in classification problems [9]. Smoothing reduces the variance of the estimated probabilities. In models of the kind we study here, where many local probabilities are multiplied to obtain a final probability estimate, assuming independence between model sub-parts, the bias-variance tradeoff may be different and over-smoothing even more beneficial. There exist smoothing methods that would give very bad joint likelihood but still good classification as long as the estimates are on the right side of the decision boundary. We can also note that, for the models we surveyed, achieving the highest joint likelihood did not translate to being the best in accuracy. For example, the best joint log-likelihood was achieved by DecTreeWBd followed very closely by WBd. The joint log-likelihood achieved by linear k-NN was worse and the worst was achieved by general k-NN (which performed best in accuracy). Therefore fitting a small number of parameters for a model class to optimize validation set accuracy is worth it for choosing the best model.

Another interesting phenomenon is that the conditional log-likelihood continued to increase with smoothing and the maximum was reached at the heaviest amount of smoothing for almost all surveyed models — JM, WBd, DecTreeWBd, and KNN3. For the other forms of k-NN the conditional log-likelihood curve was more wiggly and peaked at several points going up and down. We explain this increase in conditional log-likelihood with heavy smoothing by the tendency of such product models to be over-confident. Whether they are wrong or right, the conditional probability of the best parse is usually very close to 1. The conditional log-likelihood can thus be improved by making the model less confident. Additional gains are possible even long after the best smoothing amount for accuracy.

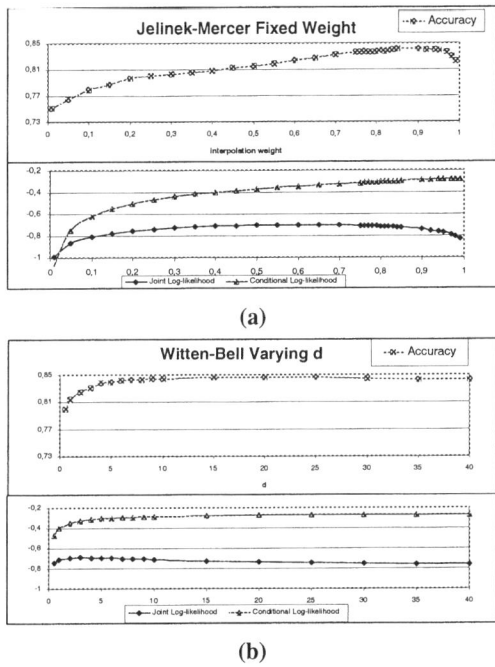

Fig. 6. PP Attachment Task: Jelinek-Mercer with Fixed Weight λ for the higher order model (a) and Witten-Bell WBd for varying d (b)

One could think that this phenomenon may be specific to our task — selection of the best parse from a set of possible analyses, and not from all parses to which the model would assign non-zero probability. To further test the relationship between likelihoods and accuracy, we performed additional experiments on a different domain. The task is PP (prepositional phrase) attachment given only the four words involved in the dependency — v, n_1, p, n_2, such as e.g. *eat salad with fork*. The attachment of the PP phrase p, n_2 is either to the preceding noun n_1 or to the verb v. We tested a generative model for the joint probability $P(Att, V, N_1, P, N_2)$, where Att is the attachment and can be either noun or verb. We graphed the likelihoods and accuracy achieved when using Jelinek-Mercer with fixed weight and Witten-Bell with varying parameter d, as for the parsing experiments. Figure 6 shows curves of accuracy, (scaled) joint log-likelihood and conditional log-likelihood. We see that the pattern described above repeats.

5 Summary and Future Work

The problem of effectively estimating local probability distributions for compound decision models used for classification is surprisingly unexplored. We empirically compared several commonly used models to memory-based learning and showed that memory-based learning achieved superior performance. The added flexibility of an interpolation sequence not limited to a linear feature sets generalization order paid off for the task of building generative parsing models. Further research is necessary studying the performance of memory-based models — such as comparing to Kneser-Ney and Katz smoothing, and fitting the k-NN weights on held-out data.

Our experimental study of the relationship among joint and conditional likelihood, and classification accuracy conveyed interesting regularities for such models. A more theoretical quantification of the effect of the bias and variance of the local distributions on the overall system performance is a subject of future research.

References

1. D. M. Bikel, S. Miller, R. Schwartz, and R. Weischedel. Nymble: a high-performance learning name-finder. In *Proceedings of the Fifth Conference on Applied Natural Language Processing*, pages 194–201, 1997.
2. E. Black, F. Jelinek, J. Lafferty, D. M. Magerman, R. Mercer, and S. Roukos. Towards history-based grammars: Using richer models for probabilistic parsing. In *Proceedings of the 31st Meeting of the Association for Computational Linguistics*, pages 31–37, 1993.
3. E. Charniak. A maximum entropy inspired parser. In *NAACL*, 2000.
4. S. F. Chen and J. Goodman. An empirical study of smoothing techniques for language modeling. In *Proceedings of the Thirty-Fourth Annual Meeting of the Association for Computational Linguistics*, pages 310–318, 1996.
5. M. Collins. Three generative, lexicalised models for statistical parsing. In *Proceedings of the 35th Meeting of the Association for Computational Linguistics and the 7th Conference of the European Chapter of the ACL*, pages 16–23, 1997.
6. W. Daelemans. Introduction to the special issue on memory-based language processing. *Journal of Experimental and Theoretical Artificial Intelligence*, 11:3:287—292, 1999.
7. W. Daelemans, A. van den Bosch, and J. Zavrel. Forgetting exceptions is harmful in language learning. *Machine Learning*, 34:1/3:11—43, 1999.
8. I. Dagan, L. Lee, and F. Pereira. Similarity-based models of cooccurrence probabilities. *Machine Learning*, 34(1-3):43–69, 1999.
9. J. Friedman. On bias variance 0/1-loss and the curse-of-dimensionality. *Journal of Data Mining and Knowledge Discovery*, 1(1), 1996.
10. J. T. Goodman. A bit of progress in language modeling: Extended version. In *MSR Technical Report MSR-TR-2001-72*, 2001.
11. D. Klein and C. D. Manning. Accurate unlexicalized parsing. In *Proceedings of the 41st Annual Meeting of the Association for Computational Linguistics*, 2003.
12. L. Lee. Measures of distributional similarity. In *37th Annual Meeting of the Association for Computational Linguistics*, pages 25–32, 1999.
13. D. M. Magerman. Statistical decision-tree models for parsing. In *Proceedings of the 33rd Meeting of the Association for Computational Linguistics*, 1995.
14. S. Oepen, K. Toutanova, S. Shieber, C. Manning, D. Flickinger, and T. Brants. The LinGo Redwoods treebank: Motivation and preliminary applications. In *COLING 19*, 2002.
15. C. Pollard and I. A. Sag. *Head-Driven Phrase Structure Grammar*. University of Chicago Press, 1994.
16. A. Ratnaparkhi. A linear observed time statistical parser based on maximum entropy models. In *EMNLP*, pages 1—10, 1997.
17. I. H. Witten and T. C. Bell. The zero-frequency problem: Estimating the probabilities of novel events in adaptive text compression. *IEEE Trans. Inform. Theory*, 37,4:1085—1094, 1991.
18. J. Zavrel and W. Daelemans. Memory-based learning: Using similarity for smoothing. In *Joint ACL/EACL*, 1997.

Extended Replicator Dynamics as a Key to Reinforcement Learning in Multi-agent Systems

Karl Tuyls*, Dries Heytens, Ann Nowe, and Bernard Manderick

Computational Modeling Lab
Department of Computer Science
Vrije Universiteit Brussel, Belgium
{ktuyls@,dheytens@,asnowe@info,bmanderi@}vub.ac.be

Abstract. Modeling learning agents in the context of Multi-agent Systems requires an adequate understanding of their dynamic behaviour. Evolutionary Game Theory provides a dynamics which describes how strategies evolve over time. Börgers et al. [1] and Tuyls et al. [11] have shown how classical Reinforcement Learning (RL) techniques such as Cross-learning and Q-learning relate to the Replicator Dynamics (RD). This provides a better understanding of the learning process. In this paper, we introduce an extension of the Replicator Dynamics from Evolutionary Game Theory. Based on this new dynamics, a Reinforcement Learning algorithm is developed that attains a stable Nash equilibrium for all types of games. Such an algorithm is lacking for the moment. This kind of dynamics opens an interesting perspective for introducing new Reinforcement Learning algorithms in multi-state games and Multi-Agent Systems.

1 Introduction

In this paper a new RL algorithm, based on the Replicator Dynamics (RD) from Evolutionary Game Theory (EGT), is introduced. Several authors have already noticed and proved that the RD can emerge from several RL schemes. Börgers et al. [1] have shown that the RD can emerge from Cross learning and the authors [10, 11] have shown that the RD emerge from Learning Automata and Boltzmann Q-learning. This emergence offers a lot of advantages. For instance, these evolutionary dynamics open a new perspective in understanding and fine tuning the learning process in games and more general in Multi-Agent Systems (MAS). Learning can be very time consuming, especially when you need to fine tune some parameters. As the experiments in Tuyls et al. illustrate [10, 11], plotting the direction field of the RD beforehand in one-state games gives information on how to initialize the learning agents so that they end up in the most interesting attractors. As these previous results show, convergence is not always guaranteed for some particular kind of games. For this reason we adapted the

---

* Author funded by a doctoral grant of the institute for advancement of scientific technological research in Flanders (IWT)

RD to an extended evolutionary dynamics which describes the desired behaviour from the Reinforcement Learning (RL) agents. After this, the accompanying RL algorithm of these Extended Replicator Dynamics (ERD) will be developed.

The outline of the paper is as follows, in section 2 we elaborate on the RD from EGT and on the important connection with RL, more specifically the Cross learning model. Section 3 describes how the RD are extended to satisfy the need of convergence to certain attractors in certain games. After this we describe the new RL algorithm matching this ERD. Section 4 describes the experiments, confirming the results from section 3. Finally, we end with a conclusion.

2 Selection Dynamics and Cross Learning

In this section we elaborate on an important result of Börgers and Sarin [1]. They showed that in an appropriately constructed time limit, the Cross learning model converges to the Replicator Equations. Also it is shown [10,11] how the RD emerge from Learning Automata and Boltzmann Q-learning. The perspective of evolutionary dynamics in reinforcement learning offers a lot of advantages. First, it becomes possible to understand RL in terms of evolutionary dynamics, i.e. selection and mutation mechanisms, second it allows to fine tune the learning process in advance. In this paper a new RL algorithm will be developed based on the replicator equations, which behaves as one desires. This means that the learning process is guaranteed to converge to a stable Nash equilibrium in all types of one-state games. In a first subsection we briefly explain the RD, as we will alter these dynamics in section 3. After this the Cross learning model will be explained, as this model will serve as a basis for a new RL algorithm in section 3.

2.1 The Replicator Equations

The basic concepts and techniques developed in EGT were initially formulated in the context of evolutionary biology [13, 9]. In this context, the strategies of all the players are genetically encoded (called genotype). Each genotype refers to a particular behavior which is used to calculate the payoff of the player. The payoff of each player's genotype is determined by the frequency of other player types in the environment.

One way in which EGT proceeds is by constructing a dynamic process in which the proportions of various strategies in a population evolve. Examining the expected value of this process gives an approximation which is called the RD. Simpy stated, an abstraction of an evolutionary process usually combines two basic elements: selection and mutation. Selection favors some varieties over others, while mutation provides variety in the population. RD highlights the role of selection, it describes how systems consisting of different strategies change over time. They are formalized as a system of differential equations. Each replicator (or genotype) represents one (pure) strategy. This strategy is inherited by all the offspring of that replicator. The general form of a replicator dynamic is the following:

$$\frac{dx_i}{dt} = [(A\mathbf{x})_i - \mathbf{x} \cdot A\mathbf{x}]x_i \tag{1}$$

In equation (1), x_i represents the density of strategy i in the population, A is the payoff matrix which describes the different payoff values each individual replicator receives when interacting with other replicators in the population. The state of the population ($\mathbf{x}$) can be described as a probability vector $\mathbf{x} = (x_1, x_2, ..., x_J)$ which expresses the different densities of all the different types of replicators in the population. Hence $(A\mathbf{x})_i$ is the payoff which replicator i receives in a population with state x and $\mathbf{x} \cdot A\mathbf{x}$ describes the average payoff in the population. The growth rate $\frac{dx_i}{dt}/x_i$ of the population share using strategy i equals the difference between the strategy's current payoff and the average payoff in the population. For further information we refer the reader to [13, 2].

In this paper the players are reinforcement learners. We consider a game to be played between the members of two different populations, each population representing one reinforcement learner. As a result, we need two systems of differential equations: one for the row player (P) and one for the column player (Q). This setup corresponds to a RD for asymmetric games. If $A = B^t$, equation (1) would again emerge.

This translates into the following replicator equations for the two populations:

$$\frac{dp_i}{dt} = [(A\mathbf{q})_i - \mathbf{p} \cdot A\mathbf{q}]p_i \tag{2}$$

$$\frac{dq_i}{dt} = [(B\mathbf{p})_i - \mathbf{q} \cdot B\mathbf{p}]q_i \tag{3}$$

As can be seen in equation (2) and (3), the growth rate of the types in each population is now determined by the composition of the other population. Note that, when calculating the rate of change using these systems of differential equations, two different payoff matrices (A and B) are used for the two different players.

2.2 The Cross Learning model

The cross learning model is a special case of the standard reinforcement learning model [1]. The model considers several agents playing the same normal form game repeatedly in discrete time. At each point in time, each player is characterized by a probability distribution over her strategy set which indicates how likely she is to play any of her strategies. At each time step (indexed by n), a player chooses one of her strategies based on the probabilities which are related to each isolated strategy. As a result a player can be represented by a probability vector:

$$p(n) = (p_1(n), ..., p_r(n))$$

In case of a 2-player game with payoff matrix U, player k ($k \in 1, 2$) gets payoff U_{ij}^k when player 1 chooses strategy i and player 2 chooses strategy j.

Players do not observe each others' strategies and payoffs, they are uninformed players. After each stage they update their probability vector, according to,

$$p_i(n+1) = U_{ij} + (1 - U_{ij})p_i(n) \tag{4}$$

$$p_{i'}(n+1) = (1 - U_{ij})p_{i'}(n) \tag{5}$$

where $0 \leq U_{ij} \leq 1$. Equation (4) expresses how the probability of the selected strategy (i) is updated and equation (5) expresses how all the other strategies $i' \neq i$ are adjusted. The probability vector of $Q(n)$ is updated in an analogous manner. This entire system of equations defines a stochastic update process for the players $\{p^k(n)\}$. This process is called the "Cross learning process" in [1]. Börgers and Sarin showed that in an appropriately constructed continuous time limit, this model converges to the asymmetric, continuous time version of the replicator dynamics, see section 2.

3 Extending the Replicator Equations and the Cross Learning Model

The reasons for changing the RD and looking for a new dynamics become clear from [10, 11]. In one-state games it is impossible for Cross learning and Learning Automata to guarantee convergence to a stable Nash equilibrium in all types of games. In Boltzmann Q-learning a Nash equilibrium can be attained, but there is no guarantee for stability. If a dynamical system can be found that offers these guarantees, we can construct a reinforcement learning algorithm in an analogous manner with the same behaviour of this adapted dynamical system. This makes the approach of replicator equations very interesting and promising toward multi-state games and Multi-Agent Systems.

In the first subsection we will alter the traditional replicator equations in such a manner that in all classes of games the players will converge to a particular Nash equilibrium (see section 4). These new equations are referred to as the Extended Replicator Dynamics (ERD). In the second subsection we will present the accompanying learning algorithm of the changed dynamics based on the Cross learning model.

3.1 Developing an Extended Replicator Dynamics

When constructing an altered selection dynamics, we take the replicator dynamics and its interpretation as a starting point. In replicator dynamics, the probabilities a players has over its strategies are changed greedily with respect to payoff in the present. In this section a method is shown to change this probabilities over strategies not only with respect to payoff growth in the present but also to payoff growth in the future. We call those players that act so as to optimize future payoff extended Cross learners and the class of dynamics associated extended dynamics.

There are of course different ways to build such extended players. The most obvious is to use a linear approximation of the evolution of fitness in time. This is the approach we use here.

For the ERD we compose the following equation f,

$$f(x) = RD(x) + (dRD(x)/dt) * \eta \tag{6}$$

were RD(x) is,

$$\frac{dx_i}{dt} = [(A\mathbf{x})_i - \mathbf{x} \cdot A\mathbf{x}]x_i \tag{7}$$

and η is the parameter that determines how far in the future we need to look.

The composition of equation 6 can best be understood as follows. When using the classical replicator equations (i.e. RD(x)), we act greedily toward payoff in the present. When adding our second term,

$$(dRD(x)/dt) * \eta \tag{8}$$

we act greedily toward payoff in the future. From an analytical point of view, the second term gives actions that are winning fitness (whether its fitness is negative or positive) a positive push toward a higher chance of getting selected. On the other hand, actions that are losing fitness (again whether its fitness is negative or positive) are given a negative push toward a lower chance of getting selected. This extends the traditional replicator equations. The algorithm we used to calculate this dynamics can be found in algorithm 1. It will be referred to as the ERD algorithm since it extends the tradional $RD(x)$ with the future. This extended evolutionary dynamics succeeds in converging to a stable Nash Equilibrium (NE) in all 3 categories of 2*2 games. Experiments confirming this can be found in section 4.

In the next section the reinforcement learning algorithm based on these extended dynamics is developed.

3.2 Developing an Extended RL-Algorithm

To develop a RL-algorithm based on the Extended Replicator Dynamics, we start from the result of Börgers and Sarin. They showed that in an appropriately constructed continuous time limit, this model converges to the asymmetric, continuous time version of the replicator dynamics [1]. Recall that we extended these dynamics with the following acceleration term,

$$(dRD(x)/dt) * \eta \tag{9}$$

expressing that we act greedily toward payoff in the future. So for the part of the RD we can rely on the Cross algorithm of Börgers and Sarin. For the part of equation 9 we calculate an approximation in algorithm 2.

Step a of the algorithm is nothing more than the calculation of Cross Learning. Step b calculates the approximation of the ERD, where the *accel* variable

Algorithm 1 The algorithm used to calculate extended replicator dynamics.

Parameters:

η How far in the future we look for calculating future fitness growth.
stepSize Determines how large steps we take in the updaterule
$a_{1..r}$ The actions a available to the players p.
$p(n) - (p_1(n), ..., p_r(n))$ The chances for p playing a_i.
$RD_{a_i(n)}$ The replicator dynamics function of action a from player p at timestep n according to the current position of all player's strategies. This implicitly defines the game being played.

For all actions a_i.

1. Calculate an approximation to the replicator dynamics acceleration in the current position of all player's strategies in Δ.
   $acceleration_{a_i(n)} := RD_{a_i(n-1)} - RD_{a_i(n-2)};$
2. Ensure payoff positivity. It turns our dynamics into one that is stable in a NE.
   if($\neg(((RD_{a_i(n)} > 0) \land (RD_{a_i(n)} + \eta * acceleration_{a_i(n)} > 0)) \lor$
   $((RD_{a_i(n)} < 0) \land (RD_{a_i(n)} + \eta * acceleration_{a_i(n)} < 0)))$
   $\{acceleration_{p_a} := 0;\}$
3. Adjust the strategy according to:
   $f_{a_i(n)} := stepSize * RD_{a_i(n)} + \eta * acceleration_{a_i(n)};$ f is the function we are approximating
   $p_i(n) := p_i(n) + f_{a_i(n)}$

contains the approximation of equation 9. Furthermore payoff positivity is ensured. Payoff positivity means that strategies that earn above (below) average have positive (negative) growth rates. Actually, with payoff positivity we ensure that there is stability in all Nash equilibria. Step c executes the update of the probabilities of the different actions and updates the acceleration term (or the payoff in the future). To finalize, the probabilities are normalized.

In the next section we will show experiments in all classes of games with this algorithm and it will become clear that it always converges to the Extended Replicator Dynamics.

4 Experiments

In this section we describe some experiments that illustrate the mathematical derivation of section 3. The experiments have been conducted with 2 × 2 games. The general payoff matrices, A for the first player and B for the second, are defined in table 1. The family of 2 × 2 games is usually classified in three subclasses, as follows[5],

Subclass 1: if $(a_{11} - a_{21})(a_{12} - a_{22}) > 0$ or $(b_{11} - b_{12})(b_{21} - b_{22}) > 0$, at least one of the 2 players has a dominant strategy, therefore there is just 1 strict equilibrium.

Algorithm 2 An algorithm for RL based on extended replicator dynamics.

Parameters:

η How far in the future we look for calculating future fitness growth.
$stepSize$ Determines how large steps we take in the updaterule
$a_{1..r}$ The actions a available to the players p.
$p(n) = (p_1(n), ..., p_r(n))$ The chances for p playing a_i.
$\overrightarrow{accel}$ A variable containing an approximative current acceleration for each $p_i(n)$.
θ Learningrate for learning $\overrightarrow{accel}$.
$\overrightarrow{formerSpeed}$ A variable containing an approximative speed for each a_i.
$Env(\overrightarrow{a_i})_p$ The function returning the immediate payoff from the environment to player p when all players have acted according to $\overrightarrow{a_i}$. This implicitly defines the game being played.
Act_p The function defining the action selection method.

For all players p
  1. $\overrightarrow{actions}_p := Act_p;$
For all players p
  1. $\overrightarrow{rewards}_p := Env(\overrightarrow{actions})_p$
For all players p
  1. For all actions a_i
     (a) Calculate CrossLearning.
         if $(a_i == \overrightarrow{actions}_p)$
         then {
         $CrossLearning := \overrightarrow{rewards}_p * (1 - p_i(n));$ }
         else {
         $CrossLearning := -\overrightarrow{rewards}_p * p_i(n);$}
     (b) Calculate extended RD approximation, making sure we retain payoff positive.
         if$(sign(CrossLearning) == sign(CrossLearning + \overrightarrow{accel}_{a_i}))$
         then $ExtendRDLearning := CrossLearning + \overrightarrow{accel}_{a_i};$
         else $ExtendRDLearning := 0;$
     (c) Perform the updaterule and calculation of $\overrightarrow{accel}_{a_i}$.
         $p_i(n) := p_i(n) + stepSize * extendRDLearning;$
         $\overrightarrow{accel}_{a_i} := \overrightarrow{accel}_{a_i} + \theta * ((stepSize * CrossLearning - \overrightarrow{formerSpeed}_{a_i}) - \overrightarrow{accel}_{a_i});$
         $\overrightarrow{formerSpeed}_{a_i} := stepSize * CrossLearning;$ }
  2. Normalize the $p_i(n)$ so that their sum is 1.

Subclass 2: if $(a_{11} - a_{21})(a_{12} - a_{22}) < 0, (b_{11} - b_{12})(b_{21} - b_{22}) < 0$, and $(a_{11} - a_{21})(b_{11} - b_{12}) > 0$, there are 2 pure equilibria and 1 mixed equilibrium.

Subclass 3: if $(a_{11} - a_{21})(a_{12} - a_{22}) < 0, (b_{11} - b_{12})(b_{21} - b_{22}) < 0$, and $(a_{11} - a_{21})(b_{11} - b_{12}) < 0$, there is just 1 mixed equilibrium.

The first subclass includes those type of games where each player has a dominant strategy, as for instance the prisoners dilemma. However it includes a larger collection of games since only 1 of the players needs to have a dominant strategy.

Table 1. The left matrix (A) defines the payoff for the row player, the right matrix (B) defines the payoff for the column player.

$$A = \begin{pmatrix} a_{11} & a_{12} \\ a_{21} & a_{22} \end{pmatrix} \quad B = \begin{pmatrix} b_{11} & b_{12} \\ b_{21} & b_{22} \end{pmatrix}$$

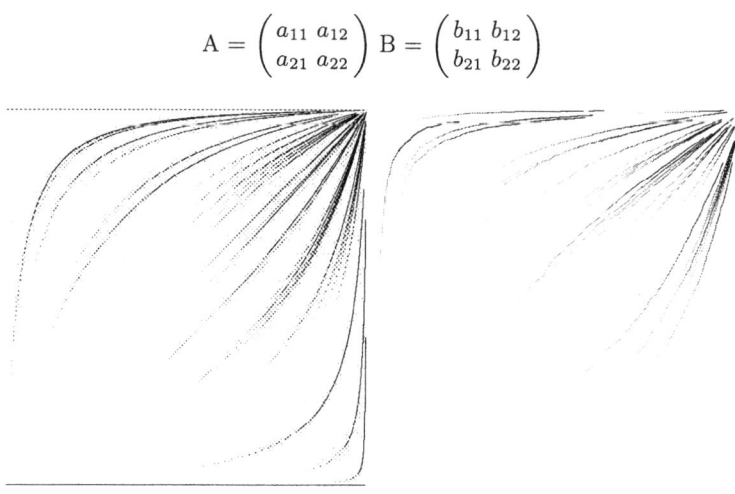

Fig. 1. *Left*: The direction field of the ERD of the prisoners game. *Right*: The paths induced by the learning process

In the second subclass none of the players has a dominated strategy. But both players receive the highest payoff by both playing their first or second strategy. This is expressed in the condition $(a_{11} - a_{21})(b_{11} - b_{12}) > 0$. The third subclass only differs from the second in the fact that the players do not receive their highest payoff by both playing the first or the second strategy. This is expressed by the condition $(a_{11} - a_{21})(b_{11} - b_{12}) < 0$. In the following three subsections we describe the results of the experiments conducted in each subclass. In all subclasses we used the following general settings,

- η is set at 300
- *stepsize* is set to 0.003
- *theta* is set to 0.0006

4.1 Category 1: Prisoners Dilemma

In category 1 we considered the prisoners dilemma game [13, 3]. In this game both players have a dominant strategy, more precisely *defect*. The payoff matrices for this game are as follows,

$$\begin{pmatrix} 1 & 5 \\ 0 & 3 \end{pmatrix} \text{ and } \begin{pmatrix} 1 & 0 \\ 5 & 3 \end{pmatrix}$$

In figure 1 the replicator dynamic of the game is plotted using the differential equations of 6.

More specifically, the figure on the left illustrates the direction field of the extended replicator dynamics and the figure on the right shows the learning

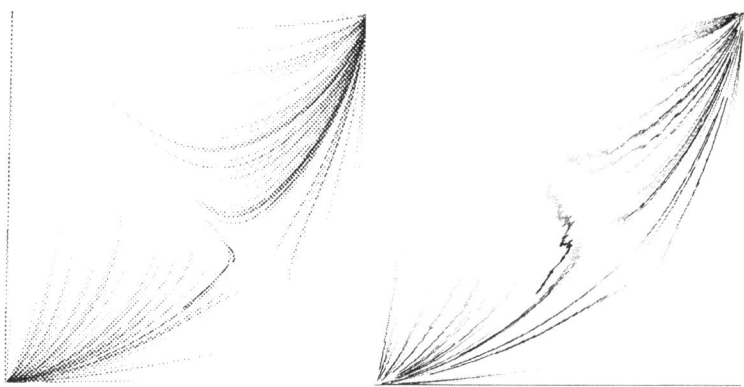

Fig. 2. *Left*: The direction field of the RD of the battle of the sexes game. *Right*: The paths induced by the learning proces

process of algorithm 1. We plotted for both players the probability of choosing their first strategy (in this case defect). So, the first players probabilities are on the X-axis and the second players probabilities on the Y-axis. As starting points for the learning process we generated 50 random points. In every point a learning path starts and converges to the equilibrium at the point $(1,1)$. As you can see all the sample paths of the reinforcement learning process approximate the paths of the RD.

4.2 Category 2: Battle of the Sexes

For the second game we considered the battle of the sexes game, defined by the following payoff matrices [13, 3]:

$$\begin{pmatrix} 2 & 0 \\ 0 & 1 \end{pmatrix} \text{ and } \begin{pmatrix} 1 & 0 \\ 0 & 2 \end{pmatrix}$$

Figure 2 demonstrates the results. On the left you see the direction field of this game, on the right the sample paths induced by the learning process. You can see 3 equilibria: two pure equilibra at $(0,0)$ and at $(1,1)$, and one mixed at $(2/3, 1/3)$. Now we have convergence to the 2 strict equilibria. The third equilibrium is very unstable as you can see in the direction field plot. This instability is the reason why it will not emerge from the learning process on the long run. Again we used a grid of random starting points.

4.3 Category 3:

The third class consists of the games with a unique mixed equilibrium. We considered the following game,

$$\begin{pmatrix} 2 & 3 \\ 4 & 1 \end{pmatrix} \text{ and } \begin{pmatrix} 3 & 1 \\ 2 & 4 \end{pmatrix}$$

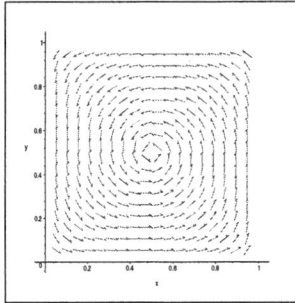

Fig. 3. The direction field plot of the RD for subclass 3

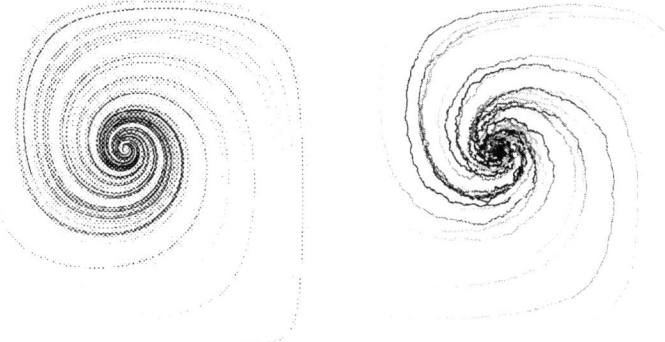

Fig. 4. *Left*: The direction field of the RD. *Right*: The paths induced by the learning process

Typical for the traditional RD in this class of games is that the interior trajectories define closed orbits around the equilibrium point. Figure 3 illustrates this.

This type of game shows an important difference with our ERD and the matching learning algorithm. ERD and the matching learning algorithm will not circle but converge to the mixed Nash equilibrium. This is illustrated in figure 4. Moreover the equilibrium is stable, meaning that the learning process will not abandon it. The long-run learning dynamics are illustrated in the figure on the right. Again we used a grid of random starting points for the learning process.

5 Conclusion

In this paper it is shown that the RD from EGT are an adequate basis for reinforcement learning in games. This opens a new perspective on developing reinforcement learning algorithms for multi-state games and Multi-Agent Systems.

More precisely we showed that with an extension of the traditional replicator equations (ERD), Nash equilibria can be attained in all kind of games. Based on this new dynamics we constructed a RL-algorithm that converges to this extended replicator dynamics. In [12] we showed that for the matter of one-state games Cross learning is the simplest learning model (over Learning Automata, Q-learning) and suffices to attain the same results as the other learning models. It turned out that the Cross model keeps things most simple in the sense of setting parameters and computational effort. The experiments confirmed that with the Cross model, the Nash equilibria can be reached in the most elegant way. Therefore this new algorithm, extending Cross Learning and guaranteeing a stable Nash equilibrium, is sufficient for any type of one-state game.

In a next phase, these results will be extended to multiple state games. Developing such algorithms will be based on Learning Automata and Q-learning, two possible techniques for multi-state games. In both techniques the connection with the Replicator Dynamics has been proved [10, 11].

References

1. Börgers, T., Sarin, R., Learning Through Reinforcement and Replicator Dynamics. Journal of Economic Theory, Volume 77, Number 1, November 1997.
2. Hofbauer, J., Sigmund, K., Evolutionary Games and Population Dynamics, Cambridge University Press, 1998.
3. Gintis, C.M., Game Theory Evolving. Princeton University Press, June 2000.
4. Narendra, K., Thathachar, M., Learning Automata: An Introduction. Prentice-Hall (1989).
5. Redondo, F.V., Game Theory and Economics, Cambridge University Press, (2001).
6. Schneider, T.D., Evolution of biological information. journal of NAR, volume 28, pages 2794 - 2799, 2000.
7. Stauffer, D., Life, Love and Death: Models of Biological Reproduction and Aging. Institute for Theoretical physics, Köln, Euroland, 1999.
8. Sutton, R.S., Barto, A.G. : Reinforcement Learning: An introduction. Cambridge, MA: MIT Press (1998).
9. L. Samuelson, Evolutionary Games and Equilibrium Selection, MIT Press, Cambridge, MA, 1997.
10. Tuyls, K., Lenaerts, T., Verbeeck, K., Maes, S. and Manderick, B, Towards a Relation Between Learning Agents and Evolutionary Dynamics. Proceedings of BNAIC 2002. KU Leuven, Belgium.
11. Tuyls, K., Verbeeck, K. and Lenaerts, T., A Selection-Mutation model for Q-learning in MAS. Accepted at AAMAS 2003. Melbourne, Australia.
12. Tuyls, K., Verbeeck, K., and Maes, S. On a Dynamical Analysis of Reinforcement Learning in Games: Emergence of Occam's Razor. Accepted at CEEMAS 2003.
13. Weibull, J.W., Evolutionary Game Theory, MIT Press, (1996).

Visualizations for Assessing Convergence and Mixing of MCMC

Jarkko Venna, Samuel Kaski, and Jaakko Peltonen

Neural Networks Research Centre
Helsinki University of Technology
P.O. Box 9800, FIN-02015 HUT, Finland
{jarkko.venna,samuel.kaski,jaakko.peltonen}@hut.fi

Abstract. Bayesian inference often requires approximating the posterior distribution with Markov Chain Monte Carlo (MCMC) sampling. A central problem with MCMC is how to detect whether the simulation has converged. The samples come from the true posterior distribution only after convergence. A common solution is to start several simulations from different starting points, and measure overlap of the different chains. We point out that Linear Discriminant Analysis (LDA) minimizes the overlap measured by the usual multivariate overlap measure. Hence, LDA is a justified method for visualizing convergence. However, LDA makes restrictive assumptions about the distributions of the chains and their relationships. These restrictions can be relaxed by a recently introduced extension.

1 Introduction

Probabilistic generative modeling is one of the theoretical foundations of current mainstream machine learning and data analysis. Bayesian inference makes very accurate but computationally intensive predictions possible, and gives rigorous methods for model selection and complexity control. In a nutshell, the uncertainty in the data is converted into uncertainty of the model parameters in the form of a distribution. Inference of parameter values and of predictions is then done based on this distribution.

Bayesian inference is potentially very powerful but closed-form solutions are seldom available. Inference has to be based on either sophisticated approximation methods or simulations with Markov Chain Monte Carlo (MCMC) [1] sampling. MCMC sampling is a very versatile yet computationally intensive procedure. The main practical problem of MCMC is how to assess whether the simulation has converged. The resulting samples come from the true distribution only after convergence.

There are several strategies for monitoring convergence [2]. Often in practice convergence is assessed by starting the simulation from several different initial conditions, and by monitoring when the different simulation chains become sufficiently mixed together. The mixing can be monitored visually on scatter plots of the MCMC samples against all pairs of variables, which is of course feasible only for models with few parameters. An alternative is to measure convergence quantitatively; measures of the overlap of the different sampling chains have been proposed by Brooks and Gelman [3]. The measures have the problem that rules of thumb are required for deciding whether the simulation has converged or not, and hence they are often complemented with visualizations. The other advantage of visualizations is that they are useful also for analyzing reasons of convergence problems.

It turns out that the main multivariate convergence measure equals the cost function of a one-dimensional LDA (for a definition of LDA see [4]), a method that discriminates between data classes. Here the classes are the different sampling chains. Our first main result or suggestion is to use LDA for visual evaluation of convergence. It has a rigorous criterion for visualizing convergence and complements the existing quantitative measures. Our second main result is an extension of the LDA visualization by applying a less restrictive measure of the overlap of the chains, resulting in a connection with a recent extension of discriminant analysis.

2 Bayesian Modeling in a Nutshell

In Bayesian modeling the relationship between the data y and the parameters $\boldsymbol{\theta}$ of the model is defined by the *likelihood* $p(y|\boldsymbol{\theta})$. Knowledge about the parameter values before observing the data is given by the *prior distribution* $p(\boldsymbol{\theta})$. By combining these we get the *posterior distribution* that represents our knowledge about the parameter values after observing the data. The posterior can be calculated from the prior and likelihood with the Bayes formula

$$p(\boldsymbol{\theta}|y) = \frac{p(y|\boldsymbol{\theta})p(\boldsymbol{\theta})}{\int p(y|\boldsymbol{\theta})p(\boldsymbol{\theta})d\boldsymbol{\theta}}, \qquad (1)$$

where $\int p(y|\boldsymbol{\theta})p(\boldsymbol{\theta})d\boldsymbol{\theta}$ is a normalizing term.

While in maximum likelihood estimation a single parameter value is sought, in Bayesian data analysis the result is the whole posterior distribution. This makes it possible to take our uncertainty about the parameter values into account in inference. A Bayesian model can be used to predict new values $\tilde{y}$ according to the posterior predictive distribution

$$p(\tilde{y}|y) = \int p(\tilde{y}|\boldsymbol{\theta})p(\boldsymbol{\theta}|y)d\boldsymbol{\theta} , \qquad (2)$$

where the uncertainty of the parameter values has been taken into account by integrating over the posterior distribution.

In practice the posterior distribution is usually not known in closed form and has to be approximated. A common method for approximation is MCMC sampling. MCMC generates samples x_t that are distributed proportionally to the posterior distribution. These samples can be used to estimate any statistic of the distribution and integrals over the posterior get approximated with sums over samples.

3 Monitoring Convergence Using Multiple Sequences

3.1 Measuring Convergence

One of the most common methods for monitoring MCMC convergence is the potential scale reduction factor (PSRF) proposed by Gelman and Rubin [5]. Multiple MCMC sequences are started from different (overdispersed) initial points and compared. At convergence the chains should come from the same distribution, which is assessed by comparing the variance and mean of each chain to the variance and mean of the combined chain.

The PSRF is defined for one-dimensional data as follows. A number (m) of parallel chains are started, with $2n$ samples each. Only the last n potentially better converged samples from each chain are used. The between-chain variance B/n and pooled within-chain variance W are defined by

$$\frac{B}{n} = \frac{1}{m-1} \sum_{j=1}^{m} (\bar{x}_{j\cdot} - \bar{x}_{\cdot\cdot})^2 \text{ and} \tag{3}$$

$$W = \frac{1}{m(n-1)} \sum_{j=1}^{m} \sum_{t=1}^{n} (x_{jt} - \bar{x}_{j\cdot})^2 , \tag{4}$$

where $\bar{x}_{j\cdot}$ is the mean of the samples in chain j and $\bar{x}_{\cdot\cdot}$ is the mean of the combined chains.

By taking the sampling variability of the combined mean into account we get a pooled estimate for the posterior variance

$$\hat{V} = \frac{n-1}{n} W + \left(1 + \frac{1}{m}\right) \frac{B}{n}. \tag{5}$$

Finally an estimate $\hat{R}$ of PSRF is obtained by dividing the pooled posterior variance estimate with the pooled within chain variance,

$$\hat{R} = \frac{\hat{V}}{W}. \tag{6}$$

If the chains have converged, the PSRF is close to one, which makes it a useful indicator of convergence. It is not a perfect indicator, however, since it does not guarantee convergence. The chains might not have traveled the whole state space yet and might discover possible new areas of high probability. Additionally, it does not take higher-order moments into account, only the mean and variance, and it is applicable to only one variable at a time.

Brooks and Gelman [3] have extended the PSRF to a multivariate version, MPSRF. It is defined, similarly to the univariate PSRF, in terms of the estimate of the posterior covariance matrix $\hat{\mathbf{V}}$, which we get from (5) by replacing the scalar variances B/n and W with the covariance matrices

$$\frac{\mathbf{B}}{n} = \frac{1}{m-1} \sum_{j=1}^{m} (\bar{\mathbf{x}}_{j\cdot} - \bar{\mathbf{x}}_{\cdot\cdot})(\bar{\mathbf{x}}_{j\cdot} - \bar{\mathbf{x}}_{\cdot\cdot})^T \text{ and} \qquad (7)$$

$$\mathbf{W} = \frac{1}{m(n-1)} \sum_{j=1}^{m} \sum_{t=1}^{n} (\mathbf{x}_{jt} - \bar{\mathbf{x}}_{j\cdot})(\mathbf{x}_{jt} - \bar{\mathbf{x}}_{j\cdot})^T . \qquad (8)$$

In the multivariate case the comparison of within-chain variance to the pooled variance requires comparing the matrices. Brooks and Gelman chose to summarize the comparison by a maximum root statistic which gives the maximum scale reduction factor of any linear projection of $\mathbf{x}$. The estimate $\hat{R}^p$ of MPSRF is defined by

$$\hat{R}^p = \max_{\mathbf{a}} \frac{\mathbf{a}^T \hat{\mathbf{V}} \mathbf{a}}{\mathbf{a}^T \mathbf{W} \mathbf{a}} \qquad (9)$$

$$= \frac{n-1}{n} + \left(\frac{m+1}{m}\right) \max_{\mathbf{a}} \frac{\mathbf{a}^T \mathbf{B} \mathbf{a}/n}{\mathbf{a}^T \mathbf{W} \mathbf{a}} \qquad (10)$$

$$= \frac{n-1}{n} + \left(\frac{m+1}{m}\right) \lambda_1, \qquad (11)$$

where the λ_1 is the largest eigenvalue of the matrix $\mathbf{W}^{-1}\mathbf{B}/n$.

This criterion is very closely related to linear discriminant analysis (LDA). The goal of (a one-dimensional) LDA is to find the linear transformation $y = \mathbf{a}^T \mathbf{x}$ that maximizes the variance between classes, relative to the variance within classes. More formally, LDA solves the problem

$$\max_{\mathbf{a}} \frac{\mathbf{a}^T \mathbf{B}_{ss} \mathbf{a}}{\mathbf{a}^T \mathbf{W}_{ss} \mathbf{a}} , \qquad (12)$$

where $\mathbf{B}_{ss}$ and $\mathbf{W}_{ss}$ are the between and within sum of squares and cross products (SSCP) matrices which differ only by a constant scale from the corresponding covariance matrices. This is a generalized eigenvalue problem, and its solution $\mathbf{a}$ is the eigenvector corresponding to the largest eigenvalue of $\mathbf{W}_{ss}^{-1} \mathbf{B}_{ss}$.

Hence, disregarding the constants, MPSRF equals the cost function of (a one-dimensional) LDA. In other words, optimizing the LDA is equivalent to choosing the component that best detects convergence, in the sense of MPSRF. Monitoring convergence by MPSRF or by the LDA cost function is equivalent; if the chains can be discriminated, then they have not converged.

3.2 Visualizing Convergence

Current practice. It is common practice to complement the convergence measures by visualizations of the MCMC chains. Visualizations are useful especially when analyzing reasons of convergence problems. Convergence measures can only tell that the simulations did not convergence, not why they did not.

MCMC chains have traditionally been visualized in three ways. Each variable in the chain can be plotted as a separate time series, or alternatively the marginal distributions can be visualized as histograms. The third option is a scatter or contour plot of two parameters at a time, possibly showing the trajectory of the chain on the projection. The obvious problem with these visualizations is that they do not scale up to large models with lots of parameters. The number of displays would be large, and it would be hard to grasp the underlying high-dimensional relationships of the chains based on the component-wise displays.

Some new methods have been suggested. For three dimensional distributions advanced computer graphics methods can be used to visualize the shape of the distribution [6]. Alternatively, if the outputs of the models can be visualized in an intuitive way, the chain can be visualized by animating the outputs of models corresponding to successive MCMC samples [7]. These visualizations are, however, applicable only to special models.

A principled way of visualizing convergence. The worst problem with the straightforward visualization methods is that they lack the means to focus on visualizing variables or dimensions that are relevant for convergence. This worsens the problems caused by the required large number of plots.

In the previous Section (3.1) it was noted that the MPSRF measure of MCMC convergence (10) is closely related to linear discriminant analysis (LDA). We will use this connection to justify the use of LDA to visualize the convergence of the MCMC sampler.

In summary, LDA finds a projection that best separates the classes in the sense of maximizing the between-class variation relative to within-class variation. For a one-dimensional projection this was shown to be equivalent to choosing MPSRF as the criterion for the projection.

There is no reason to confine the visualization to be one-dimensional. LDA chooses the second direction or projection axis to be the eigenvector corresponding to the second largest eigenvalue, etc. A K-dimensional LDA then maximizes $\sum_{k=1}^{K} \lambda_k$, the relative between-chain variance representable by the K directions together. This criterion could actually be used as an alternative convergence criterion to MPSRF; it takes directly into account deviation in several directions instead of only the dominant one.

When LDA is used to visualize MCMC convergence we in effect try to find a linear transformation that visualizes the convergence problems as clearly as possible, in the sense of the (extended) MPSRF measure.

3.3 Informative Components

Brooks and Gelman [3] noted that any statistic calculated from the separate chains should be equal to the one calculated from the combined chain when the chains have reached convergence, as the distributions should then be the same. The LDA connection above resulted from comparing means and variances. We propose that instead of comparing a statistic, a more general measure would result from comparing the distributions themselves. A natural measure is the mutual information between the distributions and the chain index. The difference between this and the LDA (MPSRF) criterion is discussed below.

Problems with LDA. LDA assumes that each class is normally distributed with the same covariance matrix in each class. If the assumptions are correct, LDA discriminates between two classes optimally. This does not hold in general, however, in particular not before MCMC convergence for small data.

Another problem surfaces when generalizing LDA to several classes. The objective considers only pairwise divergences between classes, and no longer corresponds to optimal discrimination. See the Appendix for details.

To address the above problems, we suggest to complement LDA-based analysis with a generalization of LDA. The projection is linear but the assumptions about the distribution of data are relaxed.

Relevant component analysis. A recent method for finding *informative* or *relevant* components directly maximizes their class-prediction power [8]. Formally, the conditional (log) likelihood

$$L = \sum_{(\mathbf{x},c)} \log p(c|\mathbf{W}^T\mathbf{x}) \qquad (13)$$

of classes is maximized within the subspace formed by the components. Here $\mathbf{x}$ is the sample, c is its class, and $\mathbf{W}$ is the (orthogonal) projection matrix whose columns are the component directions. The optimal projection is specific to the number of components sought. The well-defined objective for finite data, the likelihood, is asymptotically equivalent to the mutual information between components and classes. The task of finding such components was coined *relevant component analysis* (RCA). A sketch of the connection between LDA and RCA is presented in the Appendix.

In this paper the c are the different chains, and RCA maximizes the (log) likelihood of correctly guessing which MCMC chain each sample is from. For converged chains one cannot (asymptotically) do better than a random guess; hence, large likelihood indicates non-convergence which can be assessed visually from the RCA projection.

With finite data, we do not know the exact densities $p(c|\mathbf{W}^T\mathbf{x})$, but we can optimize the projection parameters by using a nonparametric estimate $\hat{p}(c|\mathbf{W}^T\mathbf{x})$ in the projection space. Since this estimate is non-parametric, RCA makes no distributional assumptions. For details on RCA and its optimization, see [8]. Technically, we replaced the stochastic gradient in [8] by conjugate (batch) gradient optimization.

The main justification for using RCA here is that it maximizes a flexible measure of separation of the classes. It remains an empirical question of how much the RCA improves the LDA-based visualizations. In Section 4.2 we apply both methods to assess convergence in a relatively simple task.

4 Analysis of a MCMC Run

To demonstrate visual analysis of a MCMC sampler we have chosen a data set that contains reaction times for schizophrenics and nonschizophrenics. The model and the problem are described in the book Bayesian Data Analysis [9] (Example 16.4, p.426) and were also used to illustrate the use of the PSRF measure in the original article [5].

The data consist of (log) reaction time measurements from 11 nonschizophrenics and 6 schizophrenics. Each person had their reaction time measured 30 times. It is believed that schizophrenics suffer from attentional deficit on some measurements as well as an overall motor reflex retardation.

For the nonschitzophrenics the reaction time is modeled as a random-effects model with a distinct mean α_j for each person and a common variance σ_y^2. The reaction times for the schizophrenics are modeled with a two-component Gaussian mixture. With probability $(1 - \lambda)$ there is no attention lapse and the response time has mean α_j and variance σ_y^2. With probability λ there is a delay and the response time has mean $\alpha_j + \tau$ and the same variance σ_y^2. To address the question about the amount of motor reflex retardation a hierarchical population model is devised. The means of the reaction times α_j are modeled to be normally distributed with a mean μ for the nonschizophrenics and a mean $\mu + \beta$ for the schizophrenics. The model can be expressed as

$$y_{ij}|\alpha_j, \zeta_{ij}, \phi \sim \mathrm{N}(\alpha_j + \tau\zeta_{ij}, \sigma_y^2), \tag{14}$$

$$\alpha_j|\zeta_{ij}, \phi \sim \mathrm{N}(\mu + \beta S_j, \sigma_\alpha^2), \tag{15}$$

$$\zeta_{ij}|\phi \sim \mathrm{Bernoulli}(\lambda S_j), \tag{16}$$

where $\phi = (\sigma_\alpha^2, \beta, \lambda, \tau, \mu, \sigma_y^2)$ contains the hyperparameters and y_{ij} is the response i from person j. The term S_j is an indicator that equals 1 for schizophrenics and 0 for nonschizophrenics, and ζ_{ij} is an unobserved indicator that equals 1 if the observation arose from a delayed response and 0 otherwise.

The hyperparameters in ϕ are assigned a noninformative uniform prior density. Additionally, τ, σ_α^2 and σ_y^2 are restricted to be positive. The mixture parameter λ is further restricted to the interval $[0.001, 0.999]$. As all necessary conditional distributions were readily available, Gibbs sampling, a form of MCMC, was used.

Ten chains of 1500 samples each were generated from random starting positions. The MPSRF measure showed that the sampling had not converged. Calculating the univariate PSRF measures for the 23 variables we were interested in (all except the indicator variables ζ_{ij}) showed that several variables had not converged. At this point we still had no idea what had gone wrong with the sampler, or was the convergence just slow.

4.1 Visualization with LDA

Gaining insight on the problem. In order to better understand the behavior of the chains we visualized a part of the simulation, samples $[200, 600]$ around the point 350 after which the MPSRF measure seemed to have stabilized at a high value.

It is clear from the LDA projection (Fig. 1) that there are five distinct clusters in the sample set. By color coding (not shown) the different chains with different

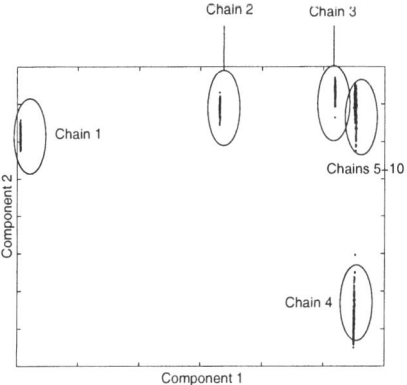

Fig. 1. Two-dimensional LDA projection of all samples from the interval [200, 600]. The ellipses have been drawn by hand to mark the chains.

colors it was easy to identify the chains. Six of the chains were clustered together and the other four formed a separate cluster each. Three of the chains were separated from the main cluster on discriminative component 1 and one on component 2. We additionally checked whether any of the separate chains could still be moving toward the common cluster, by color coding based on sampling time. There was no visible hint of that.

Verifying the findings. A further study showed that four of the chains had ended up in a degenerate part of the parameter space, that is, in a part where the mixture model has collapsed to a one-component model, already very soon after the initialization. For three of these chains (chains 1, 2, and 3) the probability of a sample being generated by a delayed mixture component was so low that no samples were assigned to it. This was apparent already by a quick look at the one-dimensional time series plots of these chains. The delay parameter τ had not changed at all from the starting position.

The reason for the fourth chain appearing separated is the reverse. Nearly all samples came from the mixture component representing delayed measurements, and hence the β and τ could not be identified separately. It was harder to diagnose the problem with this chain because the time series plots looked normal. The LDA visualization in Figure 1 helped to quickly identify the problem areas.

Checking the behavior of the sampler near convergence. At this point we could have modified our model or our sampler to remove the problems. If there are a sufficient number of chains, a rapid alternative is to discard the degenerate ones. We computed the MPSRF measure again for the remaining chains. It is clear from Figure 2a that this time convergence has been reached after about 350 samples. For a demonstration we created a new LDA projection showing only the nondegenerate chains. In Figure 2b we can see that there are two 'tails' from chains which are moving toward the common distribution. By color coding the

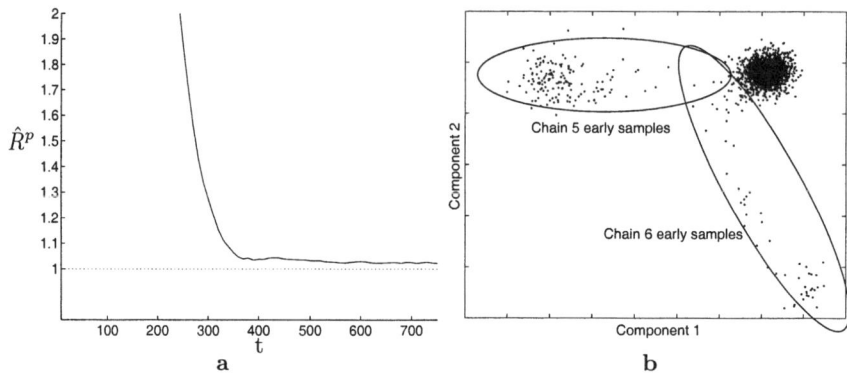

Fig. 2. a) MPSRF measure calculated from the nondegenerate chains (5-10). b) LDA projection of the nondegenerate samples from the interval [200, 600]. The ellipses have been drawn by hand to mark early samples from chains 5 and 6. The samples can be visualized by a time-based color code.

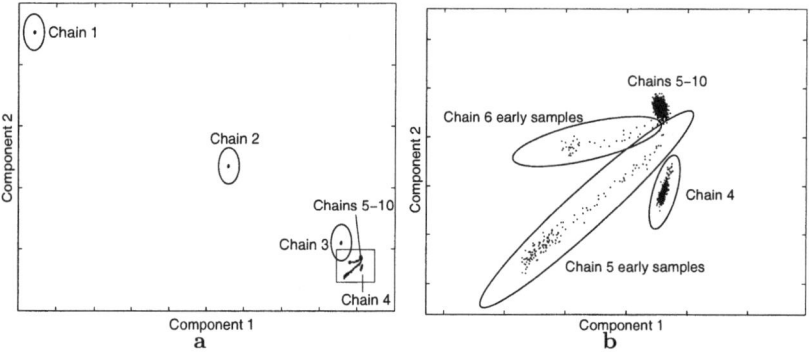

Fig. 3. a) 2D RCA projection of all samples from the interval [200, 600]. b) Enlarged view of the box in lower right corner of **a**.

samples based on time we verified that the samples were indeed early samples and that the two chains became combined with the other chains after the early samples. Thus we could conjecture that the simulation had converged this time.

4.2 Visualization with RCA

We finally compare qualitatively the less restrictive RCA projection with LDA to verify that it gives the same or better insights on convergence.

From the two-dimensional RCA projection of all samples from the interval [200, 600] (Fig. 3) we can see that RCA has discovered the same five clusters as LDA. Four of the clusters are composed of a single chain each, and the last consisted of six chains. In addition, RCA has found the two 'tails' of samples, generated by two chains converging toward the multi-chain cluster. These are the same 'tails' that were found using LDA on the nondegenerate chains (Fig. 2b).

Chains 1 and 2 are far from the others in both the LDA and the RCA visualizations. However, the LDA visualization kept the chain 4 far apart as well, whereas RCA placed it closer to chains 5-10 and instead separated the 'tails' of early samples of chains 5 and 6. Since the chain 4 can still be discriminated well, this yields a more informative projection.

In conclusion, RCA visualization displayed all the discovered convergence properties in a single two-dimensional visualization. No additional studies were required as with LDA. (A visualization corresponding to Figure 2b was computed just in case, and revealed only the same properties.)

5 Discussion

We have shown how to create visualizations for MCMC convergence analysis with linear discriminant analysis (LDA). Problems can be identified quickly using only a few visualizations. Justification for LDA comes from its connection to a common convergence measure: Its goal is to separate the different simulation chains, and if it is successful the simulation has not converged. This was demonstrated in a case study.

It is straightforward to extend the black-and-white visualizations of this Proceedings with color coding. If the different chains are colored differently it is easy to distinguish them in the figures. Coloring samples with shades that change as a function of time brings visible the evolution of the chains during sampling. Further possibilities for extensions are coloring according to the likelihood of the sampled models, or coloring according to the prior or posterior density of the samples. This would clearly show how much the posterior differs from the prior, for example.

If more details about the behavior of the sampler are of interest, some more technical measures like acceptance ratio or autocorrelation within a window around the sample could be visualized by the color code. This could possibly identify areas where the sampler is performing poorly. These ideas could be combined in an interactive visualization tool aimed at easy exploratory analysis of the behavior of a MCMC sampler.

Even though LDA can be used for principled visualizations of MCMC chains, it is based on assumptions that often do not hold. It assumes normally distributed chains, which usually does not hold, and that the covariance matrices of the chains are the same, which holds only after convergence. A new method, RCA, is based on a more flexible measure of the overlap of the simulation chains: The likelihood of predicting the chains, which asymptotically becomes the mutual information. These theoretical connections justify the use of the RCA, and it was demonstrated to work better than LDA in a small case study.

Finally, the objective function of RCA could additionally serve as a measure of convergence, when compared with a naive estimate that simply predicts the overall chain proportions. If the values are different, MCMC has not converged.

Acknowledgments

This work was supported by the Academy of Finland, grants 1164349 and 52123.

References

1. W.R.Gilks, S. Richardson, and D.J.Spiegelhalter. *Markov Chain Monte Carlo in Practice*. Interdisciplinary Statistics. Chapman & Hall/CRC, Boca Raton, Florida, 1995.
2. Stephen Brooks and Andrew Gelman. Some issues in monitoring convergence of iterative simulations. In *Proceedings of the Section on Statistical Computing*. ASA, 1998.
3. Stephen Brooks and Andrew Gelman. General methods for monitoring convergence of iterative simulations. *Journal of Computational and Graphical Statistics*, 7:434–456, 1998.
4. Neil H. Timm. *Applied Multivariate Analysis*. Springer Texts in Statistics. Springer-Verlag, New York, 2002.
5. Andrew Gelman and Donald B. Rubin. Inference from iterative simulation using multiple sequences. *Statistical Science*, 7:457–472, 1992.
6. Edward J. Wegman and Qiang Luo. On methods of computer graphics for visualizing densities. *Journal of Computational and Graphical Statistics*, 11:137–162, 2002.
7. Nicole A. Lazar and Joseph B. Kadane. Movies for the visualization of MCMC output. *Journal of Computational and Graphical Statistics*, 11:836–874, 2002.
8. Samuel Kaski and Jaakko Peltonen. Informative Discriminant Analysis. In *Proceedings of ICML-2003, The Twentieth International Conference on Machine Learning*, 2003. In press.
9. Andrew Gelman, John B. Carlin, Hal S. Stern, and Donald B. Rubin. *Bayesian Data Analysis*. Texts in Statistical Science. Chapman & Hall/CRC, Boca Raton, Florida, 1995.
10. S. Theodoridis and K. Koutroumbas. *Pattern Recognition*. Academic Press, San Diego, CA, 1999.

Appendix: Connection between LDA and RCA

Reformulating LDA. For simplicity, consider only the first LDA component $\mathbf{a}$. Denote $\sigma_\mathbf{a}^2 = \mathbf{a}^T \mathbf{W}_{ss} \mathbf{a}/N$, where N is the total number of samples. The LDA objective equals the variance of class centers along the projection direction, relative to the within-class variance:

$$\frac{\mathbf{a}^T \mathbf{B}_{ss} \mathbf{a}}{\mathbf{a}^T \mathbf{W}_{ss} \mathbf{a}} = \frac{1}{N \sigma_\mathbf{a}^2} \mathbf{a}^T \mathbf{B}_{ss} \mathbf{a} = \sum_c \frac{n_c}{N} \frac{(\mathbf{a}^T (\bar{\mathbf{x}}_{c.} - \bar{\mathbf{x}}_{..}))^2}{\sigma_\mathbf{a}^2} . \quad (17)$$

Since, for a scalar variable x, $E_{x_1,x_2}[(x_1 - x_2)^2] = 2E[x^2] - 2(E[x])^2 = 2E[(x - E[x])^2]$, the objective further equals (up to a constant multiplier) the weighted sum of squared distances between class pairs:

$$\frac{2}{N \sigma_\mathbf{a}^2} \mathbf{a}^T \mathbf{B}_{ss} \mathbf{a} = \sum_{c_1,c_2} \frac{n_{c_1} n_{c_2}}{N^2} \frac{(\mathbf{a}^T (\bar{\mathbf{x}}_{c_1.} - \bar{\mathbf{x}}_{c_2.}))^2}{\sigma_\mathbf{a}^2} . \quad (18)$$

Since $\mathbf{a}^T\mathbf{a} = 1$, each Gaussian class has a variance of $\sigma_{\mathbf{a}}^2$ along the projection dimension. Then, for each pair of classes c_1 and c_2, the rightmost term equals the squared *Mahalanobis distance* of the projected class centers along the projection. This in turn equals the following *symmetrized Kullback-Leibler divergence* between the distributions along the projection [10]:

$$\frac{1}{\sigma_{\mathbf{a}}^2}(\mathbf{a}^T(\bar{\mathbf{x}}_{c_1.} - \bar{\mathbf{x}}_{c_2.}))^2 = D_{KL}(p(\mathbf{a}^T\mathbf{x}|c_1), p(\mathbf{a}^T\mathbf{x}|c_2)) + D_{KL}(p(\mathbf{a}^T\mathbf{x}|c_2), p(\mathbf{a}^T\mathbf{x}|c_1)) \quad (19)$$

LDA thus maximizes a sum of symmetrized Kullback-Leibler divergences between the classes along the projection, weighted by the fractions $n_{c_1} n_{c_2}/N^2$.

Improving the cost function. Optimizing the above objective (18) does not result in optimal discrimination. We will improve it in two steps. First, for each class pair (c_1, c_2), replace the symmetrization in (19) with the *Jensen-Shannon divergence*. This helps to reinterpret the objective in a form that can be easily generalized. For brevity, denote $y = \mathbf{a}^T\mathbf{x}$, denote the proportions of the class prior probabilities by $p_{c_1} = p(c_1)/(p(c_1)+p(c_2))$ and $p_{c_2} = p(c_2)/(p(c_1)+p(c_2))$, and set $q(y) = p_{c_1}p(y|c_1) + p_{c_2}p(y|c_2) = p(y|c_1 \vee c_2)$, where $c_1 \vee c_2$ referes to the distribution containing only clases c_1 and c_2. The Jensen-Shannon divergence is

$$\begin{aligned}
D_{JS}(p(y,c_1), p(y,c_2)) &= p_{c_1} D_{KL}(p(y|c_1), q(y)) + p_{c_2} D_{KL}(p(y|c_2), q(y)) \\
&= p_{c_1} \int p(y|c_1) \log \frac{p(y|c_1)}{q(y)} dy + p_{c_2} \int p(y|c_2) \log \frac{p(y|c_2)}{q(y)} dy \\
&= \int \sum_{c=c_1,c_2} p(y|c) p_c \log \frac{p(y|c)}{q(y)} dy = I(y, c|c_1 \vee c_2) . \quad (20)
\end{aligned}$$

LDA then finds (roughly, due to the different symmetrization) the direction that maximizes the sum of pairwise mutual informations between classes, weighted by the class proportions. This suggests the natural extension to consider more than just pairwise class interactions, and maximize the complete mutual information $I(c, y)$ between classes and projected data. It can be shown that as the amount of data grows, the likelihood objective of RCA asymptotically equals $I(c, y)$, up to a constant. RCA is then a finite-data implementation of an LDA extension.

A Decomposition of Classes via Clustering to Explain and Improve Naive Bayes

Ricardo Vilalta[1] and Irina Rish[2]

[1] Department of Computer Science
University of Houston
4800 Calhoun Rd., Houston TX 77204-3010, USA
vilalta@cs.uh.edu
[2] IBM T.J. Watson Research Center
19 Skyline Dr., Hawthorne N.Y. 10532, USA
rish@us.ibm.com

Abstract. We propose a method to improve the probability estimates made by Naive Bayes to avoid the effects of poor class conditional probabilities based on product distributions when each class spreads into multiple regions. Our approach is based on applying a clustering algorithm to each subset of examples that belong to the same class, and to consider each cluster as a class of its own. Experiments on 26 real-world datasets show a significant improvement in performance when the class decomposition process is applied, particularly when the mean number of clusters per class is large.

1 Introduction

Probabilistic classifiers constitute a major venue of research in data mining, pattern recognition, and machine learning. Successful applications are found in speech recognition, document classification, and medical diagnosis, among many others. We focus on a popular probabilistic classifier based on the assumption of attribute independence, also known as Naive Bayes; the performance of this simple classifier is unexpectedly often similar to other classifiers unrestrained by the attribute independence assumption. Although the reasons explaining the competitiveness of Naive Bayes remain unclear, several studies have revealed useful information; examples include studies about the conditions for its optimality [2]; its geometric properties [15]; and how the product distribution implied by the independence assumption compares to most other joint distributions with the same set of marginals [5].

This paper reports on a method to improve the performance of Naive Bayes by attending to the distribution of examples in the input-output space. We work on the characterization and transformation of data rather than on the algorithm design. The idea is to transform the data by decomposing each class into clusters; this is useful to avoid the effects of poor class conditional probabilities based on product distributions when each class spreads into multiple regions. In contrast, most previous work looks at improving the algorithm design alone; examples include adjusting the estimated probabilities [12], improving probability estimates

[7,14], and combining Naive Bayes with other models [8]. Some previous work does transform the data by searching for attribute dependencies to construct new features [4]; our approach differs in that the transformation is made over the class distribution by looking at each cluster as a new class. Our main idea is to augment the number of original classes according to the example distribution to improve the probability estimations made by Naive Bayes.

Our experimental results, obtained using 26 datasets from the University of California at Irvine repository, enable us to provide an explanation for the competitiveness of Naive Bayes in real-world domains. In summary, most domains exhibit a distribution characterized by few clusters per class; a situation where Naive Bayes is known to perform well. In these cases the performance of our proposed approach is almost identical to Naive Bayes. But when a domain is characterized by many clusters per class (on average) the estimation of class-conditional probabilities is biased, and Naive Bayes performs poorly. In these cases our approach can improve the performance of Naive Bayes significantly. The fact that few domains exhibit many clusters per class explains why Naive Bayes often appears at the same level of performance as other (more sophisticated) algorithms.

This paper is organized as follows. Section 2 introduces background information on classification, probabilistic classifiers, and Naive Bayes. Section 3 explains why Naive Bayes is expected to yield poor probability estimates under certain kinds of input-output distributions. Section 4 describes our class decomposition approach to improve and explain the performance of Naive Bayes. Section 5 compares our class-decomposition approach to local learning. Section 6 reports our experimental analysis. Finally, Section 7 gives a summary and discusses future work.

2 Preliminaries

Let $(A_1, A_2, \cdots, A_n)$ be an n-component vector-valued random variable, where each A_i represents an attribute or feature; the space of all possible attribute vectors is called the input space $\mathcal{X}$. Let $\{y_1, y_2, \cdots, y_k\}$ be the possible classes, categories, or states of nature; the space of all possible classes is called the output space $\mathcal{Y}$. A classifier receives as input a set of training examples $T = \{(\mathbf{x}, y)\}$, where $\mathbf{x} = (a_1, a_2, \cdots, a_n)$ is a vector or point of the input space and y is a point of the output space. We assume T consists of independently and identically distributed (i.i.d.) examples obtained according to a fixed but unknown joint probability distribution ϕ in the input-output space $\mathcal{Z} = \mathcal{X} \times \mathcal{Y}$. The outcome of the classifier is a function h (or hypothesis) mapping the input space to the output space, $h : \mathcal{X} \to \mathcal{Y}$. Function h can then be used to predict the class of previously unseen attribute vectors.

We consider the case where a classifier defines a discriminant function for each class $g_j(\mathbf{x})$, $j = 1, 2, \cdots, k$ and chooses the class corresponding to the discriminant function with highest value (ties are broken arbitrarily):

$$h(\mathbf{x}) = y_m \texttt{ iff } g_m(\mathbf{x}) \geq g_j(\mathbf{x}) \tag{1}$$

In probabilistic classifiers the discriminant functions are the posterior probabilities of a class given the input vector $\mathbf{x}$, $P(y_j|\mathbf{x})$. Using Bayes rule[1]:

$$g_j(\mathbf{x}) = P(y_j|\mathbf{x}) = \frac{P(\mathbf{x}|y_j)P(y_j)}{P(\mathbf{x})} \qquad (2)$$

where $P(y_j)$ is the a priori probability of class y_j, $P(\mathbf{x}|y_j)$ is called the likelihood of y_j with respect to $\mathbf{x}$ or the class-conditional probability, and $P(\mathbf{x})$ is the evidence factor [3]. Since the evidence factor $P(\mathbf{x})$ is constant for all classes we can dispense with it. Assuming all attributes are independent given the class yields the following discriminant function used by Naive Bayes:

$$g_j(\mathbf{x}) = P(y_j) \prod_i^n P(a_i|y_j) \qquad (3)$$

where a_i is the value of attribute A_i in vector $\mathbf{x}$. The main idea is to approximate the joint input-output distribution through a product distribution by assuming attribute independence. While this is clearly unrealistic in many real-world applications, experimental results have repeatedly demonstrated that Naive Bayes often performs as well as other algorithms that make no attribute independence assumption. Our goal in this paper is to relate the performance of Naive Bayes to the characteristics of a domain; the derived analysis shows a clear mechanism to improve the performance of this probabilistic classifier.

3 A Perspective View of Naive Bayes

Although the behavior of Naive Bayes has been explained from different perspectives [2, 15, 5], an understanding of the degree of match between different target distributions and the set of assumptions or bias embedded by the algorithm remains unclear. In this section we identify a kind of distributions for which the product approximation of Naive Bayes may result in multiple misclassifications; we name this problem the *class-dispersion problem*.

3.1 Maximum Entropy and Approximating Distributions

We begin by studying the implication behind a product approximation. Our main assumption is that the set of training examples T is drawn from an unknown but fixed probability distribution ϕ that defines $P(x, y)$ for every point in the input-output space. Naive Bayes assumes distribution ϕ can be approximated through a product of low order components (i.e., product of marginals) assuming attribute independence given the class (equation 3). The following definitions will be instrumental in characterizing the approximation used by Naive Bayes.

---

[1] We assume features take on discrete values; we then have probability masses, rather than probability densities.

Definition 1. A distribution $\phi_{\max}$ over the input-output space $\mathcal{Z}$ is called a maximum entropy distribution if it assumes equal probabilities over all elements in $\mathcal{Z}$ (i.e., if it corresponds to a uniform distribution over all possible elements in $\mathcal{Z}$). The entropy of $\phi_{\max}$, denoted as $H_{\phi_{\max}}$, is as high as possible:

$$H_{\phi_{\max}} = -\sum_{i=1}^{|\mathcal{Z}|} \frac{1}{|\mathcal{Z}|} \log \frac{1}{|\mathcal{Z}|} = \log |\mathcal{Z}| \qquad (4)$$

where $|\mathcal{Z}|$ is the size of the input-output space.

Definition 2. The information contained in a probability distribution ϕ over the input-output space $\mathcal{Z}$, defined as I_ϕ, is the difference between the entropy of the maximum entropy distribution and the actual entropy of ϕ:

$$I_\phi = H_{\phi_{\max}} - H_\phi \qquad (5)$$

where H_ϕ is defined as follows

$$H_\phi = -\sum_{i=1}^{|\mathcal{Z}|} P_i \log P_i \qquad (6)$$

and each P_i is the probability of element i in Z according to ϕ.

An interpretation of Definition 2 is straightforward: a flat distribution where all elements are assigned equal probabilities carries no information, whereas the more peaked a distribution, the higher the information conveyed by such distribution [9].

We now consider the problem of approximating a true distribution ϕ using an approximation ϕ'. Let us suppose all we know about ϕ is a set of low order component distributions L. All we require from approximation ϕ' is that it must reduce to the same set of low order components in L (i.e., that it can be expressed as function of the low order components in L). Approximating distributions can be categorized by the amount of information they contain. If the approximation is based on the idea of providing the least amount of additional information beyond the set of low order components, then we have a maximum entropy approximating distribution.

Definition 3. Let ϕ be the true distribution over the input-space $\mathcal{Z}$ and let L be a set of low order components to which ϕ can be reduced. An approximating distribution of ϕ with respect to L is called a maximum entropy approximating distribution, denoted as $\phi'_{\max_L}$, if among all distributions ϕ'_L that reduce to the same set of low order components L, $\phi'_{\max_L}$ is the one with maximum entropy or less information:

$$I_{\phi'_{\max_L}} \leq I_{\phi'_L} \qquad (7)$$

for all distributions ϕ'_L that reduced to the same set of low order components L.

3.2 The Product Approximation of Naive Bayes

We now return to the product approximation followed by Naive Bayes. It can be shown that a product approximation contains the smallest amount of information (or maximum entropy) of all possible approximations to ϕ that reduce to the same set of low order components. In other words, Naive Bayes is a maximum entropy approximating distribution [9]. We formalize this as follows: Let L be the set of low order components used by Naive Bayes. That is, for every class y_j, let $L = \{P(y_j), P(a_1|y_j), P(a_2|y_j), \cdots, P(a_n|y_j)\}$. Let ϕ_L^{NB} be the product approximation corresponding to Naive Bayes, and let ϕ'_L be any other approximation different from Naive Bayes that reduces to the same set of low order components in L. Then irrespective of the nature of ϕ'_L, it is always true that ϕ'_L contains more (or equal) information than ϕ_L^{NB}.

What is the implication behind the product approximation of Naive Bayes? In brief, such approximation tries to reconstruct the true distribution from the set of low order components assuming as little additional information as possible; hence the distribution is maximally *flat*. Naive Bayes displays a *homogeneous* class distribution on all regions of examples for which the set of low order components is identical.

As an illustration, Figure 1-left shows an input-output distribution on two classes: positive ($y_1 = +$) and negative ($y_2 = -$). We assume a two-dimensional space where attribute A_1 takes on three values, and attribute A_2 takes on two values. Since we have equal class proportions ($P(+) = P(-) = \frac{1}{2}$), the classification depends on the likelihoods only. Figure 1-right shows the approximation made by Naive Bayes. The product approximation tends to smooth all probabilities. According to Naive Bayes the distribution is now the same along $A_2 = 1$, with a likelihood ratio in favor of the negative class, and along $A_2 = 2$, with a likelihood ratio in favor of the positive class.

Consider example $\mathbf{x} = (A_1 = 2, A_2 = 1)$ as shown in Figure 1. Bayes (optimal) classifier assigns $\mathbf{x}$ to class positive (Figure 1-left). The situation changes completely for Naive Bayes (Figure 1-right). Since $P(A_1 = 2|+) = P(A_1 = 2|-) = \frac{1}{3}$, the classification for $\mathbf{x}$ hinges on $P(A_2 = 1|y)$ exclusively; Naive Bayes assigns $\mathbf{x}$ to class negative because $P(A_2 = 1|-) = \frac{2}{3} > P(A_2 = 1|+) = \frac{1}{3}$. The mistake incurred by Naive Bayes stems from the assumption behind a maximal entropy distribution. The existence of regions that are class uniform is blurred by Naive Bayes's vision; these regions are simply averaged altogether when projected onto each attribute.

3.3 The Class-Dispersion Problem

The problem we are addressing is characteristic of distributions where clusters of examples that belong to the same class are dispersed throughout the input space. We call this the *class-dispersion problem*. In this case, clusters are hard to identify because a single-dimensional projection of the data loses their spatial information. This is related to the small disjunct problem in classification [6], where the existence of many small disjuncts (i.e., class-uniform clusters covering

2	$P(+)=1.0$ $P(-)=0.0$	$P(+)=0.0$ $P(-)=1.0$	$P(+)=1.0$ $P(-)=0.0$	2	$P(+)=\frac{2}{3}$ $P(-)=\frac{1}{3}$	$P(+)=\frac{2}{3}$ $P(-)=\frac{1}{3}$	$P(+)=\frac{2}{3}$ $P(-)=\frac{1}{3}$
1	$P(+)=0.0$ $P(-)=1.0$	$P(+)=1.0$ $P(-)=0.0$	$P(+)=0.0$ $P(-)=1.0$	1	$P(+)=\frac{1}{3}$ $P(-)=\frac{2}{3}$	$P(+)=\frac{1}{3}$ $P(-)=\frac{2}{3}$	$P(+)=\frac{1}{3}$ $P(-)=\frac{2}{3}$

Fig. 1. (left) The true distribution of examples in the input-output space. (right) The maximum-entropy approximation made by Naive Bayes. Example **x** is incorrectly classified by Naive Bayes.

few examples) may account for a significant amount of the total error rate. Our focus, however, is based on the distribution of clusters rather than their coverage.

Our intuition is that Naive Bayes may perform better on domains where the examples of one class are clustered together. This intuition has some theoretical justification. For example, a Boolean target function made of a disjunction (conjunction) of all attributes (or their negations) has only a single example of class 0 (1 for conjunction) and yields optimal (error-free) performance for Naive Bayes [2]. The optimality of Naive Bayes can be easily proven for a more general case of two-class problems where one of the classes is assigned to a single point [11], but the attributes are nominal rather than Boolean. We have extended this result showing that probability distributions having almost all the probability mass concentrated in one example are well approximated through a product distribution (see [11] for proof):

Theorem 1. *If for some* $0 \leq \delta \leq 1$, $\exists\, \mathbf{x}^* = (a_1^*, ..., a_n^*)$ *such that* $P(a_1^*, ..., a_n^* | y_j) \geq 1 - \delta$, *then* $\forall \mathbf{x} = (a_1, ..., a_n)$, $|P(\mathbf{x}|y_j) - \prod_i^n P(a_i|y_j)| \leq n\delta$.

In these cases, although a product approximation does not guarantee good performance of Naive Bayes, it makes it more likely in practice. Nevertheless, as the target distribution changes such that each class groups into multiple clusters, the chances of misclassifications incurred by Naive Bayes increase greatly. This is because Naive Bayes tends to smooth out the class-conditional probabilities. In cases when instances of the same class are scattered, computing marginals (i.e. single-dimensional projections) of the data may result in significant loss of information.

4 Decomposing Classes into Clusters

Our solution to the class-dispersion problem can be summarized through a two-step process: 1) identify class-uniform clusters of examples in the training set, and 2) relabel each cluster as a new class of examples. The new dataset differs from the original training set in the class labelling: there is now an additional

Algorithm 1: Mapping-Process
Input: clustering method C, dataset T
Output: new dataset T'
MAPPING-PROCESS(C,T)
(1)   Separate T into subsets $\{T_j\}$
(2)   where $T_j = \{(\mathbf{x}, y) \in T | y = y_j\}$
(3)   **foreach** T_j
(4)   Apply clustering C on T_j
(5)   Let $\{C_p^j\}$ be the set of clusters
(6)   **foreach** example $e = (\mathbf{x}, y_j)$
(7)   Let p be the cluster index for $\mathbf{x}$
(8)   Create example $e' = (\mathbf{x}, y'_j)$
(9)   where $y'_j = (y_j, p)$
(10)   Add e' to T'
(11)   **end**
(12)   **end**
(13)   **return** T'

Fig. 2. The process to transform dataset T into a new dataset T' using a clustering algorithm.

number of classes. Naive Bayes is then trained over the new dataset. During classification, performance can be assessed by simply assigning each example back to its original class. A general description of our approach follows.

4.1 The Data Transformation

Let $T = \{(\mathbf{x}, y)\}$ be the input dataset. Our first step is to map T into another dataset T' through a class-decomposition process. The mapping leaves the input space $\mathcal{X}$ intact but changes the output space $\mathcal{Y}$ into a (possibly) larger space $\mathcal{Y}'$ (i.e., $|\mathcal{Y}'| \geq |\mathcal{Y}|$, where $|\cdot|$ is the cardinality of the space).

The second step is to train Naive Bayes on T' to obtain hypothesis h'. The hypothesis acts over the transformed output space $h' : \mathcal{X} \to \mathcal{Y}'$. The classification of a new input vector $\mathbf{x}$ is obtained by applying a function g over $h'(x)$ that will essentially bring the class label back to the original output space, $g : \mathcal{Y}' \to \mathcal{Y}$.

4.2 The Mapping Process

The first step in the transformation process is shown in Algorithm 1 (Figure 2). We proceed by first separating dataset T into sets of examples of the same class. That is T is separated into different sets of examples $T = \{T_j\}$, where each T_j comprises all examples in T labelled with class y_j, $T_j = \{(\mathbf{x}, y) \in T | y = y_j\}$.

For each set T_j we apply a clustering algorithm C to find sets of examples (i.e., clusters) grouped together according to some distance metric over the input space. Let $\{C_p^j\}$ be the set of such clusters. We map the set of examples in T_j into a new set T'_j by renaming every class label to indicate not only the class but also the cluster to which each example belongs. One simple way to do this

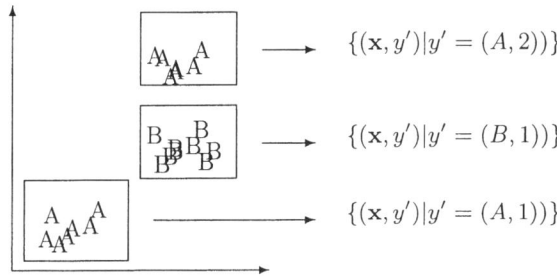

Fig. 3. The mapping process relabels examples to encode both class and cluster.

is by making each class label a pair (a, b), where the first element represents the original class and the second element represents the cluster that the example falls into. In that case, $T'_j = \{(\mathbf{x}, y'_j)\}$, where $y'_j = (y_j, p)$ whenever example $\mathbf{x}$ is assigned to cluster C^j_p.

An illustration of the transformation above is shown in Figure 3. We assume a two-dimensional input space where examples belong to either class A or B. Let's suppose the clustering algorithm separates class A into two clusters, while class B is grouped into one single cluster. The transformation relabels every example to encode class and cluster label. As a result, dataset T' has now three different classes.

Finally the new dataset T' is simply the union of all sets of examples of the same class relabelled according to the cluster to which each example belongs, $T' = \bigcup_{j=1}^{k} T'_j$.

4.3 The Classification Process

During the second step, Naive Bayes is trained over the new dataset T' producing a hypothesis h' mapping points from input space $\mathcal{X}$ to the new output space $\mathcal{Y}'$. Each discriminant function has the same form as Equation 3, but the number of discriminant functions is now (possibly) larger, according to how much the decomposition process divided up each class into multiple clusters.

When classifying a new input vector $\mathbf{x}$, hypothesis h' will output a prediction consisting of a class label and a cluster label, $h(\mathbf{x}) = (y_j, p)$, corresponding to original class y_j and cluster C^j_p. To know the actual prediction in the original output space $\mathcal{Y}$ we simply apply a function g that removes the second element of the pair, $g(y_j, p) = y_j$. Essentially, we predict class label y_j whenever example $\mathbf{x}$ is assigned to any of the clusters of class y_j.

The decomposition process aims at eliminating the cases where a class spreads out into multiple regions. As each cluster is transformed into a class of its own, the class-dispersion problem vanishes. The result is a new input-output space where each class sits in a tight region. By reducing the class-dispersion problem, the conditional probabilities estimated by Naive Bayes better conform with the assumption of a product distribution (i.e., of a maximum-entropy distribution).

5 Locality, Capacity, and the Class Decomposition Process

A better understanding of our approach can be gained by looking at the difference between locality, capacity, and the class-decomposition process. Naive Bayes is a global classifier: it makes use of all available data to estimate its parameters (i.e., a priori and class-conditional probabilities). As such it fails to detect local class variations given the same set of low order components. Failing to detect those variations is a byproduct of the attribute-independence assumption; Naive Bayes is a learning machine with low capacity (i.e., low flexibility in the decision boundaries). To solve this problem one may introduce a form of locality in the global classifier, in which parameters are estimated based only on the neighborhood of the example x being classified.

The class decomposition process discussed in Section 4 introduces an alternative view to local classification: instead of focusing on local regions of the input space, we can augment the number of discriminant functions according to the class distribution. That is, one can add more decision boundaries but retain their low flexibility. By augmenting the number of discriminant functions, the capacity of the algorithm is in fact increased, but the flexibility of the boundaries remains the same. The trick lies in the clustering phase that in fact pre-identifies local structures in the data. In addition, separating classes into clusters simply reduces the dependencies between attributes, but retains all examples for analysis. The class-cluster encoding computed during the transformation process (Figure 3) does not result in a loss of information with respect to the original sample distribution.

6 Experiments

We now report on a series of experiments that compare Naive Bayes (NB) with a modified version (NB′) that computes the transformation described in Section 4. Our datasets (26 domains) can be obtained from the University of California at Irvine repository [1]. In what follows, predictive accuracy on each dataset is obtained using stratified 10-fold cross-validation, averaged over 5 repetitions; tests of significance use a two-tailed t-student distribution. The clustering algorithm follows the Expectation Maximization (EM) technique [10]; it groups examples into clusters by modelling each cluster through a probability density function. Each example in the dataset has a probability of class membership and is assigned to the cluster with highest posterior probability. The number of clusters is estimated using cross-validation. Implementations of Naive Bayes and EM are part of the WEKA machine-learning class library [13], set with default values. Runs were performed on a RISC/6000 IBM model 7043-140.

Table 1 displays our results. The first column describes the domains used for our experiments. The second and third columns report on the accuracy of Naive Bayes; the second column corresponds to the standard version and the third column to the version using the transformation described in Section 4 (numbers

Table 1. Predictive accuracy on real-world domains for Naive Bayes with and without the transformation process. Numbers enclosed in parentheses represent standard deviations.

Domain	Naive Bayes NB	Naive Bayes with transformation NB'	Δ Accuracy	Number of Clusters		
				Mean	Min	Max
Anneal	86.64 (0.06)	96.48 (0.09)	9.84*	3.4	1.0	5.0
Audiology	72.17 (0.20)	72.17 (0.20)	0.00	1.0	1.0	1.0
Autos	57.89 (0.25)	71.83 (0.80)	13.94*	2.66	1.0	5.0
Balance-Scale	90.48 (0.05)	90.48 (0.05)	0.00	1.0	1.0	1.0
Breast-Cancer	73.30 (0.15)	73.72 (0.26)	0.42	2.5	2.0	3.0
Breast-W	95.98 (0.01)	95.98 (0.01)	0.00	1.0	1.0	1.0
Colic	78.50 (0.17)	78.50 (0.17)	0.00	1.0	1.0	1.0
Credit-G	75.05 (0.27)	73.26 (0.13)	−1.79	4.0	3.0	5.0
Diabetes	75.49 (0.07)	74.98 (0.10)	−0.51	3.0	1.0	5.0
Heart-C	83.18 (0.07)	84.16 (0.09)	0.98*	2.0	1.0	3.0
Heart-H	84.22 (0.24)	83.52 (0.12)	−0.70	4.0	2.0	6.0
Heart-Statlog	84.28 (0.15)	84.28 (0.15)	0.00	1.0	1.0	1.0
Hepatitis	84.24 (0.25)	85.71 (0.13)	1.47	2.5	1.0	4.0
Ionosphere	82.25 (0.13)	90.12 (0.15)	7.87*	4.5	1.0	8.0
Iris	95.36 (0.07)	95.96 (0.37)	0.60	3.3	2.0	5.0
Chess	87.18 (0.35)	90.62 (0.06)	3.44*	9.5	9.0	10.0
Labor	94.08 (0.42)	94.08 (0.42)	0.00	1.0	1.0	1.0
Lymph	83.79 (0.18)	83.79 (0.18)	0.00	1.0	1.0	1.0
Mushroom	94.01 (0.23)	99.83 (0.01)	5.82*	5.5	5.0	6.0
Tumor	51.20 (0.21)	51.20 (0.21)	0.00	1.0	1.0	1.0
Segment	79.73 (0.09)	87.89 (0.68)	8.16*	4.57	1.0	11.0
Sick	93.84 (0.39)	98.70 (0.04)	4.86*	8.5	6.0	11.0
Vehicle	44.96 (0.17)	73.73 (0.03)	28.77*	8.0	6.0	10.0
Vote	90.07 (0.03)	95.60 (0.13)	5.53*	2.5	2.0	3.0
Vowel	63.79 (0.15)	92.05 (0.11)	28.26*	6.3	4.0	9.0
Zoo	94.92 (0.16)	97.02 (0.00)	2.10*	1.28	1.0	2.0
Average	80.63	85.22	4.58	3.42	2.19	4.80

enclosed in parentheses represent standard deviations). The fourth column shows the improvement in accuracy that comes with our proposed approach (an asterisk at the top right of each number implies the difference is significant at the $p = 0.01$ level). The last columns shows average values for the mean, minimum, and maximum number of clusters per class for every dataset.

Our results show how the transformation process improves the accuracy of Naive Bayes in most of the datasets used for our experiments. Where no improvement is observed the difference is not statistically significant; in the extreme case where each class is grouped into one single cluster, the performance of our proposed approach is identical to Naive Bayes. In some other domains, the improvement goes up to approximately 28% points (e.g., Vehicle and Vowel). The average improvement in accuracy is of approximately 4.5% points. Figure 4 (left) shows the difference between our approach (NB') and Naive Bayes (NB) (y-axis) where domains are ordered according to the mean number of clusters per class (x-axis). Most significant differences correspond to domains with many clusters per class (we note the increase is not monotonic).

In addition, our results shed some light on the competitiveness of Naive Bayes in real-world domains. Figure 4 (right) shows a histogram of the mean number of clusters per class for each dataset. Most datasets exhibit a distribution characterized by few clusters per class, a situation that favors the assumption behind a product distribution. Few datasets exhibit many clusters per class, which explains why Naive Bayes often appears at the same level of performance as other (more sophisticated) algorithms.

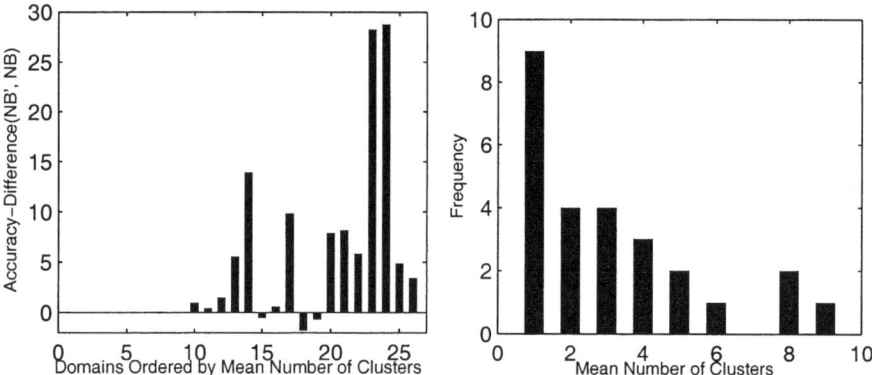

Fig. 4. (left) Accuracy difference between Naive Bayes with the transformation and Naive Bayes standard. (right) A histogram of domains based on the mean number of clusters per class.

7 Summary and Future Work

We propose a method to improve the probability estimates made by Naive Bayes by applying a clustering algorithm to each subset of class-uniform examples; the result is a new output space where each cluster is assigned a new class label. Our experimental analysis shows a significant improvement in performance when the class decomposition process is applied, especially when the mean number of clusters per class is large. The competitiveness of Naive Bayes reported in previous work is explained by the fact that many real-world datasets decompose into few clusters per class, a situation that favors the product distribution assumption followed by Naive Bayes.

Our study assumes an effective clustering algorithm in charge of the class decomposition process. The choice of the clustering algorithm bears relevance to the effectiveness of our approach; future work will explore if our results hold for different clustering algorithms. In addition, we note that the parameters of the clustering algorithm can be adjusted based on the performance of Naive Bayes (e.g., by varying the number of clusters).

Finally, since our proposed approach does not alter the algorithm design, it can be employed outside the boundaries of Naive Bayes, serving as a framework to improve the performance of classifiers that exhibit poor performance when the dataset is characterized by many clusters per class, as is the case with linear classifiers. We plan to address this in future work; our goal is to understand how the class-decomposition process can serve as a general framework to improve classification performance.

References

1. Blake C.L., Merz C.J.: UCI, Repository of machine learning databases. University of California, Irvine, Dept. of Information and Computer Sciences (1998). http://www.ics.uci.edu/~mlearn/MLRepository.html.
2. Domingos P., Pazzani M.: On the Optimality of the Simple Bayesian Classifier Under Zero-One Loss. Machine Learning 29, pp. 103–130 (1997).
3. Duda R. O., Hart P. E., Stork D. G.: Pattern Classification. John Wiley Ed. 2nd Edition (2001).
4. Friedman N., Geiger D., Goldzmidt M.: Bayesian Network Classifiers. Machine Learning 29, pp. 131-163 (1997).
5. Garg A., Roth D.: Understanding Probabilistic Classifiers. European Conference on Machine Learning, Lecture Notes in Artificial Intelligence, pp. 179-191 (2001).
6. Holte R.C., Acker L.E., Porter B.W.: Concept Learning and the Problem of Small Disjuncts. Eleventh International Joint Conference on Artificial Intelligence, Morgan Kaufmann, pp. 813-818 (1989).
7. Kohavi R., Becker B., Sommerfield D.: Improving Simple Bayes. European Conference on Machine Learning (1997).
8. Kohavi R.: Scaling Up the Accuracy of Naive-Bayes Classifiers: A Decision-Tee Hybrid. International Conference on Knowledge Discovery and Data Mining (1996).
9. Lewis P.M.: Approximating Probability Distributions to Reduce Storage Requirements. Information and Control, 2, pp. 214-225 (1959).
10. McLachlan G., Krishnan T.: The EM Algorithm and Extensions. John Wiley and Sons (1997).
11. Rish I., Hellerstein, J., Jayram, T.: An Analysis of Naive Bayes on Low-Entropy Distributions. IBM T.J. Watson Research Center, RC91994 (2001).
12. Webb G. I., Pazzani M. J.: Adjusted Probability Naive Bayes Induction. Tenth Australian Joint Conference on Artificial Intelligence. Springer-Verlag, pp. 285-295 (1998).
13. Witten I. H., Frank E.: Data Mining: Practical Machine Learning Tools and Techniques with Java Implementations. Academic Press, London U.K. (2000).
14. Zadrozny B., Elkan C.: Obtaining Calibrated Probability Estimates From Decision Trees and Naive Bayesian Classifiers. International Conference on Machine Learning (2001).
15. Zhang H., Ling C. X.: Geometric Properties of Naive Bayes in Nominal Domains. European Conference on Machine Learning, pp. 588–599 (2001).

Improving Rocchio with Weakly Supervised Clustering

Romain Vinot and François Yvon

GET/ENST, 46 rue Barrault,
75634 Paris Cedex, France
{romain.vinot, francois.yvon}@enst.fr

Abstract. This paper presents a novel approach for adapting the complexity of a text categorization system to the difficulty of the task. In this study, we adapt a simple text classifier (Rocchio), using weakly supervised clustering techniques. The idea is to identify sub-topics of the original classes which can help improve the categorization process. To this end, we propose several clustering algorithms, and report results of various evaluations on standard benchmark corpora such as the Newsgroups corpus.

1 Introduction

The automated categorization of documents [16] into predefined classes has progressively emerged as one of the most popular task in the area of Text Mining technologies. The categorization paradigm provides a very general framework for many practical applications such as filtering, routing, indexation, tracking... Historically, research in automated text categorization was developped promoted by the Information Retrieval community, in the context of text indexation. In the past five to ten years, this task has been rediscovered by the Machine Learning community and has since been the subject of many empirical studies [20], demonstrating the applicability and efficiency of Machine Learning algorithms such as Support Vector Machines [6] and Boosting techniques [14].

The Rocchio algorithm [12], originally proposed as a means to improve information retrieval (IR) systems, is conceptually one of the simplest text categorization algorithm. As such, it has been shown to be, in many experimental conditions, less successful than other approaches, such as SVMs or k-NN. Various improvements of this algorithm have been proposed, eg. in [17] [1] [15] or [9], which have been effective in increasing the performance of this methodology.

As discussed for instance in [19], Rocchio is especially well suited in contexts for applications where (i) the number of classes is high; (ii) the n-best answers (rather than just the first one) are taken into account and (iii) class labels are noisy. This seems to happen in practical applications, especially when categories cannot be directly linked with the thematic content of documents. Conversely, we have experimentally demonstrated that classes with heterogeneous content can badly impair its performance. This behaviour is in line with the simplicity of the underlying statistical model and of the learning procedure.

In this paper, we investigate several procedures allowing Rocchio to automatically adapt its complexity to the data using a weakly supervised clustering. The idea is to identify *useful* subclasses in the training data, and to use these to refine the decision surface; each new subclass increasing the overall model complexity. The main novelty of this work lies in our attempt to discover these subclasses in such a way that the resulting partition actually improves the final decision rule.

The idea of using unsupervised clustering to improve supervised classification is not entirely new, and has already been suggested in several contexts. In the context of the k-nearest neighbors algorithm, many authors have advocated unsupervised clustering as a means to organise very large instance sets, thus speeding up the k-nn computation.

In the context of the (TREC) batch filtering task, [4] and [11] incrementally cluster incoming data into subclasses of the original classes. These clusters are then used as (new) regular class labels : any document falling into cluster S of class C is eventually labelled as C. Both papers use rather different classification algorithms (Rocchio for the former paper, and SVM for the latter), but neither yield fully conclusive results. In any case, this optimisation does not seem to increase overall performance. One should note that in this approach, clustering and classification are viewed as two separate and unrelated processes.

The motivations of [3] for using unsupervised clustering are clearer: these authors explicitely aim at structuring an heterogeneous corpus of training texts, in the context of a filtering task. Relevant texts are first partitionned into N clusters, using *autoclass* [2]. Test documents are then classified as follows: for each subclass a relevance judgement is separately computed; these judgements are then linearly combined, using a perceptron. This procedure seems to provide the authors an effective means to isolate those clusters which provide the most relevant judgements.

The idea of [7] is to use clustering techniques in order to make the k-nn decision rule less sensible to noisy data, and more like a linear classifier. Proceeding bottom-up, their algorithm recursively aggregates training instances, subject to the condition that (i) they belong to the same class and (ii) they are sufficiently close in the representational space. Test documents are then classified according to the following two-steps procedure: first compute the similarity with each cluster using Rocchio or the Widrow-Hoff rule; then linearly combine these similarities to compute the final label. This procedure provides a significant improvement both over a "pure" k-nn approach and a "pure" linear decision.

This paper is organised as follows: in Section 2 we present the Rocchio algorithm and discuss its main advantages and drawbacks. Section 3 explains how this baseline is improved with a weakly supervised clustering procedure. We describe two algorithms which aim at creating such clusters which may prove beneficial for the decision procedure. Section 4 reports and discusses experimental results obtained on 3 different textual databases and Section 5 presents some conclusions and directions for future work.

2 Rocchio

Rocchio is a text classifier originally introduced in [12] to improve information retrieval systems with relevance feedback. It uses the vector space model [13]: every text d is represented by a vector $[d]$ in R^n (with n the number of distinct words in the corpus), each coordinate d_w can be computed from the frequency $\text{fr}(w, d)$ of word w in d in several manners. One of the most used formulation is :

$$d_w = TFIDF(w,d) = \log(1 + \text{fr}(w,d)) * \log(\frac{N}{N(w)}) \qquad (1)$$

where N is the number of documents in the corpus and $N(w)$ the number of documents in which w occurs at least once. This formula allocates a higher weight to words which simultaneously occur frequently in the document while occuring only in a few documents. Each vector $[d]$ is then normalized according to: $d_w = \frac{d_w}{\sqrt{\sum_w d_w^2}}$ in $[d]$ so as to reduce the distortion caused by the length of documents. A prototypical profile $[c]$ is computed for each class c according to :

$$c_w = \frac{t}{N_c} \sum_{d \in c} d_w - \frac{1-t}{N_{\bar{c}}} \sum_{d \notin c} d_w \qquad (2)$$

with N_c the number of documents in c, $N_{\bar{c}}$ the number of documents not in c and t a free parameter between 0 and 1 . These profiles are defined as the centroid of the examples (with a positive coefficient for examples in the class and a negative one for the others). These vectors are also normalized. In the context of a routing task, $t = 1$ is a usual choice, meaning that in this case, negative examples do not contribute to the centroids.

Classification of new documents is performed by computing the euclidian distance between the document vector and the prototype vector of each class; the document is then assigned to the nearest class. As all vectors (prototypes and documents) are normalized, euclidian distance is equivalent to cosine similarity or dot product, which is used for implementation reasons.

In the context of this paper, Rocchio exhibits two important characteristics :

- The decision rule computed by Rocchio is a linear separator (hyperplane) in the vector space. It gives Rocchio the same expressivity as a Perceptron classifier. As [8] shows on filtering tasks, the accuracy of Rocchio with dynamic feedback is comparable to that of a neural network trained with a gradient descent algorithm.
- The learning model of Rocchio is a generative one. Parameters are optimized to match the data, not to discriminate the different classes. Generative models usually have lower asymptotic performance value than discriminative ones, but they converge to their optimal performance faster, especially when there is lots of parameters to estimate (which is the case in the textual classification domain) [10].

We have shown in [19] that Rocchio is robust in the presence of noise and very effective for routing tasks with a high number of classes. On the other hand, its inability to take into account the substructure of classes (such as different subtopics) is a significant drawback compared to others approaches. Rocchio vastly underperforms other algorithms when classes contain intermixed subtopics: when some subtopics of different classes are nearer than subtopics of the same class (for example in the case of spam filtering, the subtopic on software advertisement can be closer to legitimate emails than to other subtopics of spams such as ones with pornographic content). In the remainder of this paper, we will call classes with such intermixed subtopics "heterogeneous classes". Figure 1 shows an example of homogeneous and heterogeneous classes in terms of relative positioning of subtopics in the vector space.

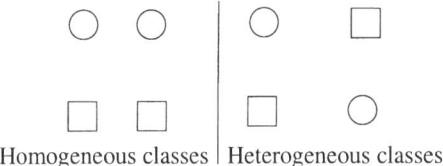

Homogeneous classes | Heterogeneous classes

Fig. 1. Homogeneous and heterogeneous corpus (round and square classes have two subtopics).

These difficulties in dealing with classes with intermixed subtopics come from the generative model used by Rocchio. It assumes that each class has a spherical shape and that the information of the centroid is sufficient to correctly describe a class. Training is accordingly straightforward, because one only has to compute the centroid of all examples for each class. But in cases where the data does not match this model, Rocchio will perform poorly.

To avoid these shortcomings, one need to allow Rocchio to use more complex models while at the same time preserving its simple learning process. This can be achieved with the use of a clustering algorithm which will split the classes into coherent sub-classes. A prototype is then computed for each cluster, as if it were a class in its own right. New examples are labelled according to the class of the nearest prototype. We call this class of algorithms Multi-Prototypes Rocchio (MPR). Even if this procedure can be used with any classifier, it is especially tailored to avoid Rocchio's shortcomings.

Rocchio can be seen as a neural network with no hidden layer. Weights are not learned by a back-propagation algorithm but simply computed as the mean of weights of all examples. Clusters are analog to a hidden layer having as many neurons as clusters. Weights of connection between initial layer and hidden layer are still computed by the mean of examples, weights between the hidden layer and the final layer are binary values according to the class of the cluster. Propagation of weights are different in MPR, because classification is based on the nearest prototype (the hidden neuron with the highest weight) instead of a weighted sum of all hidden layers. With this analogy, we see that the clustering allows to change the complexity of the underlying model.

Moreover, preliminary experiments [19] show that the use of subclasses can be very useful for heterogeneous classes but not for homogeneous ones. The model complexity (in other words number of clusters) must not be chosen according to the data but driven by the accuracy of Rocchio. There is no need to separate two subtopics of the same class if they are not mixed with any subtopic of another class. This suggests that clustering must be performed using a discriminative approach rather than a generative one.

Most of the clustering algorithms described in introduction don't meet these requirements, because the clustering process is independent of the categorization one. They don't try to directly optimize the accuracy of the induced classifier (with the exception of the GIS algorithm from Lam).

3 Clustering Algorithms

We want to devise a clustering algorithm which detects clusters in heterogeneous classes but not those in homogeneous classes. This condition can be turned into a mathematical criterion in various ways. We have explored two different criteria: the first one is based on the relative positioning of clusters, the second one is more directly error-driven and based on example categorization. Both are integrated into a top-down hierarchical clustering (at each step, we split one cluster into two new smaller clusters). As both criteria uses the class labels of examples, this procedure is not entirely unsupervised, thus the term "weakly supervised".

3.1 Notations

Let $\mathcal{C} = \{c_1, ..., c_k\}$ be a set of k classes, N the number of examples and $\Pi = \{\Pi_1, ..., \Pi_p\}$ the unknown partition of examples. $c(x)$ is the class of example x and $c(\Pi_i)$ the class labels of the examples in Π_i. Clusters are only allowed to split the existing classes. The partition must then verify:

$$\forall (x,y) \ \Pi(x) = \Pi(y) \Rightarrow c(x) = c(y) \tag{3}$$

3.2 Top-Down Clustering

Our algorithm starts with one cluster per class. At each step, we want to split the cluster with the largest dispersion of its documents. Following [5], we measure the dispersion with the square-root of the average pairwise similarity between documents:

$$\begin{aligned} ||c||^2 &= \sum_w c_w^2 = \frac{1}{N_c^2} \sum_w \left(\sum_{d \in c} d_w \right)^2 \\ &= \frac{1}{N_c^2} \sum_w \left(\sum_{d1,d2 \in c} d1_w d2_w \right) \\ &= \frac{1}{N_c^2} \sum_{d1,d2 \in c} [d1][d2] \end{aligned} \tag{4}$$

So we choose the cluster with the smallest norm and apply any clustering algorithm to create two subclusters. We choose K-Means for its simplicity. The resulting split is tested against the criterion. If the division is not accepted, we try with the cluster with the second smallest norm and so on until no more split is accepted.

Algorithm 1 Top-down clustering with criterion

Parameter: A criterion θ
Π initial partition with one cluster per class.
$S = \emptyset$
while $S \neq \Pi$ **do**
  $p = \operatorname{argmin}_{p \in \Pi - S}(\|p\|)$
  Apply *2-means* on p. Let p_1 and p_2 be the two clusters.
  if θ is verified **then** {Split is accepted}
    $\Pi = \Pi - p + p_1 + p_2$
    $S = \emptyset$
  else
    $S = S + p$
  end if
end while

3.3 Criterion *RP*: With Relative Positioning of Clusters

$$\forall i, j \; c(\Pi_i) = c(\Pi_j) \Rightarrow \exists k, \; c(\Pi_k) \neq c(\Pi_i) \text{ and } \begin{cases} d(\Pi_i, \Pi_k) \leq d(\Pi_i, \Pi_j) \\ d(\Pi_j, \Pi_k) \leq d(\Pi_i, \Pi_j) \end{cases} \quad (5)$$

This constraint means that for each pair of clusters of the same class, there must exist a third cluster of another class *between* the two (see figure 2 for a small illustration). This constraint is obviously satisfied with one cluster per class. The criterion we used aims at maximizing the number of clusters, while keeping the constraint satisfied.

Fig. 2. Illustration of the "zone between two clusters".

Given the highly combinatorial nature of the problem, we have used a approximation, which relies on a greedy algorithm. At each step of the clustering process, we only test if the two newly constructed clusters verify our criterion. The global constraint is not garanteed because we do not verify it for all the other pairs of clusters.

An additional threshold controls the clusters size, preventing to built too small solutions, which are often noisy and unreliable : clusters are never accepted if they contain less than N_0 examples. Without this filtering, the algorithm will create noisy clusters covering very few examples. These clusters will then allow more splits to be accepted. In our experiments, we have found that without filtering, the algorithm finishes with lots of very small clusters which is clearly not what we want. We have chosen $N_0 = 20$ for all our experiments.

3.4 Criterion DC: With Training Documents Categorization

$$\text{Min } \left| \left\{ x | \exists \Pi_1, \Pi_2 \text{ s.t. } \begin{array}{c} c(\Pi_1) = c(\Pi_2) = c(x) \\ \Pi_1, \Pi_2 \text{ nearest clusters of } x \end{array} \right\} \right| \qquad (6)$$

This formula expresses the fact that we want to minimize the number of examples for which the two nearest prototypes are in the same class. The idea is that if this is true for a lots of examples, then we don't need to distinguish those two prototypes. As before, this formula is obviously minimal with one cluster per class. Whenever a second cluster is created for any class, there is almost always at least one example which does not satisfy the criterion anymore. The constraint (6) has been relaxed as follows: new clusters are accepoted if less than $m * min(|p_1|, |p_2|)$ examples of the two clusters do not satisfy the constraint anymore, with m a free parameter. Experiments show that results are not very sensitive to the value of m (we have tried from $m = 0.5$ to $m = 5$ with no significant differences).

Finally, we also need to point out that this constraint only take into account correctly classified examples, which implicitly lowers the influence of noisy examples. This explains why there is no need to filter small clusters, filtering being already implicitly performed by the criterion.

4 Experiments and Results

4.1 Corpora

We have used three different corpora: Newsgroups, Spam and Mail Center.

The *Newsgroups* corpus, collected by Ken Lang, contains 20000 messages, evenly distributed in 20 classes, each class corresponding to a different Usenet newsgroup[1]. A list of Newsgroups is given in table 1. Two new corpora were then derived: the first one is obtained by merging newsgroups with the same Usenet prefix[2], leading to a partition of messages into 4 homogeneous classes; the second one results from the merging of unrelated newsgroups into four superclasses, so as to have intermixed subclusters. This corpus is later referred as the heterogeneous corpus.

The *Spam* corpus contains 2193 emails. The task is here to discriminate junk or unsollicited emails from the legitimate ones. The corpus contains 1460 spams for 733 legitimate emails. Messages in English and in French are mixed in the two classes.

The *Mail Center* corpus contains 2393 emails received by a customer service classified in 40 categories (see [18] for more information regarding this corpus). Messages are mostly written in French.

In all our experiments, two third of the corpus is used for training and the remaining part is used for testing.

---

[1] The corpus can be downloaded at
http://www-2.cs.cmu.edu/afs/cs/project/theo-20/www/data/news20.html
[2] We have placed *soc.religion.christian*, *alt.atheism* and *misc.forsale* in the most similar classes so as to have super-classes with homogeneous sizes.

Table 1. List of groups for the newsgroups corpus.

1. comp.graphics	11. alt.atheism	**Base 1**: non mixed subclusters
2. comp.windows.x	12. sci.electronics	C1 : 1,2,3,4,5
3. comp-os.ms-windows.misc	13. sci.crypt	C2 : 6,7,8,9,10,11
4. comp.sys.mac.hardware	14. sci.space	C3 : 12,13,14,15
5. comp.sys.ibm.pc.hardware	15. sci.med	C4 : 16,17,18,19,20
6. talk.politics.guns	16. misc.forsale	
7. talk.politics.mideast	17. rec.sport.baseball	**Base 2**: Intermixed subclusters
8. talk.politics.misc	18. rec.sport.hockey	C1 : 1,2,6,12,16
9. talk.religion.misc	19. rec.autos	C2 : 3,7,8,13,17
10. soc.religion.christian	20. rec.motorcycles	C3 : 4,9,10,14,18
		C4 : 5,11,15,19,20

Table 2. Performance measure: Acc-1/Acc-2. Bold values show the best algorithm for each corpus. There is no Acc-2 measure for the Spam corpus since it contains only two classes.

	Newsgroups			Spam	Mail
	normal	heterogeneous	homogeneous		Center
Rocchio	0.810/0.921	0.754/0.921	0.892/0.973	0.771/.	0.508/0.724
K-NN	0.844/**0.944**	0.864/**0.970**	0.932/0.983	0.930/.	0.535/0.649
SVM	**0.865**/0.932	**0.890**/0.968	**0.959/0.990**	**0.974**/.	**0.578**/0.713
clustered-SVM	..	0.878/0.960	0.940/0.984	0.978/.	0.532/0.698
K-Means	0.810/0.921	0.815/0.944	0.904/0.973	0.959/.	0.527/0.726
Greedy clustering	0.809/0.921	0.804/0.943	0.908/0.975	0.948/.	0.560/0.729
Criterion RP	0.813/0.924	0.818/0.942	0.905/0.972	0.964/.	0.522/0.723
Criterion DC	0.818/0.922	0.813/0.932	0.907/0.973	0.962/.	0.562/**0.731**

4.2 Accuracy Measures

Experiments have been performed for all corpora with the following algorithms: K nearest neighbors, Support Vector Machine, simple Rocchio, Clustered-SVM, MPR with K-Means, criterion-based clustering and a greedy division clustering. The greedy clustering always splits the cluster with the smallest norm. Clustered-SVM is similar to the work of [11]: after clustering, a SVM is learned for each cluster and new documents are assigned to the class of the best cluster. For algorithms where the number of clusters must be provided (such as K-Means), we have used the number found by criterion-based clustering. To compare algorithms, we have used a more general performance measure than usual accuracy. Acc-n is defined as the pourcentage of test examples for which the correct class is found in one of the n-best answers of the algorithm. This measure seems to provide a reasonable estimate of actual performance in applicative contexts involving a human validation [18]. We have shown in [19] that Rocchio performs comparatively much better with Acc-n ($n > 1$) than with Acc-1.

Results presented in table 2 suggest the following comments:
- SVM constantly outperforms all other algorithms for the Acc-1 measure.
- Clustered-SVM is always lower than simple SVM, as in [11]. This confirms that clustering is useful for Rocchio but not necessarily for other classifiers.
- For the three newsgroups corpora, MPR is only slightly better than Rocchio and always worse than k-NN or SVM.
- For Spam and Mail Center databases, the improvement over Rocchio is very sensible and MPR surpasses k-NN and even SVM for Mail Center with Acc-2.
- MPR improves Rocchio more for Acc-1 than for Acc-2.
- The different clustering algorithms have a very similar behaviour. The main advantage of our criterion-based clustering is its ability to automatically determine the "right" number of clusters. Overall, the DC criterion is more stable and accurate and is used for the rest of our experiments.

4.3 Discussions about Number of Clusters Found by MPR

Both implementations of MPR are also able to create useful clusters to improve overall accuracy. Unlike K-Means or any unsupervised clustering, they are able to choose the right number of clusters.

This fact is confirmed by an examination of the results on the Newsgroups homogeneous and heterogeneous corpora. For this experiments, the right number of clusters is known in advance: for the homogeneous corpus we expect clustering to be useless, whereas for the heterogeneous, we expect to get better results by recovering the 20 initial classes. Experimental results are reported in table 3. Obviously, MPR is able to see a difference between these two simulated corpora and to pick up an approximately correct number of clusters.

Table 3. Number of clusters found by each algorithm.

	homogeneous	heterogeneous
Optimal	4 or 20	20
Criterion RP	6.2 (0.905)	22 (0.818)
Criterion DC	5.4 (0.905)	14 (0.813)

A second way to check that the number of clusters is correct is to do an exhaustive search. To this end, we have used the greedy clustering with an increasing number of clusters. Each of these is then integrated in the classifier. Results are presented on Figure 3. Our criterion seems to always find just a little less clusters than the optimum value, the resulting accuracy being slightly lower than the maximum found by greedy clustering. Overall, we think that the criterion-based clustering is able to find an appropriate number of clusters.

4.4 Influence of Corpus Size

Rocchio is very efficient and often outperforms other algorithms when the training corpus contains very few examples per class. The clustering algorithms pre-

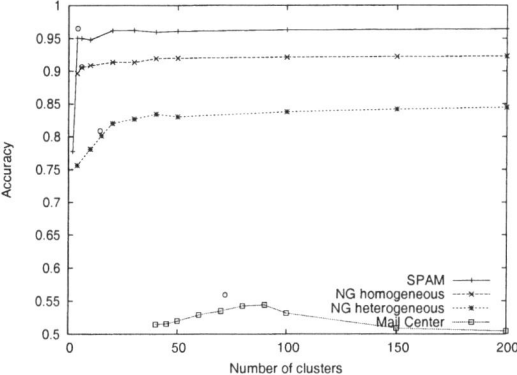

Fig. 3. Accuracy with increasing numbers of clusters. The dots represent number of clusters and accuracy for MPR with criterion DC.

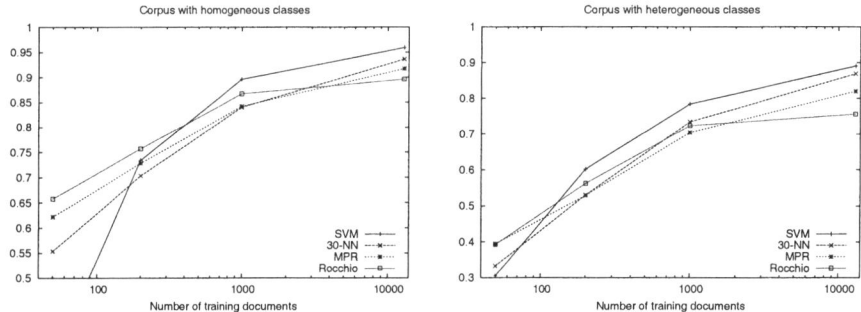

Fig. 4. Accuracy according to the number of learning examples.

sented here require an important number of examples to be able to create statistically coherent clusters. To see how the combination of clustering and Rocchio behaves on a small corpus, we have performed additional experiments with corpora of varying size.

Results are reported on Figure 4. As expected, Rocchio outperforms all others classifiers with fery few documents but its learning curve rapidly flattens. MPR is a compromise between Rocchio and k-NN / SVM with better accuracy than k-NN or SVM with few examples and better than Rocchio with lots of examples.

5 Conclusion and Future Work

We have presented here a weakly supervised clustering algorithm and demonstrate the usefulness of this learning procedure when used in conjonction with a Rocchio classifier for text categorization tasks. Unlike related work, this algorithm tries to use the supervision data (class labels) to guide clustering. We think this is the main reason for the difference of results between [11] and our work.

This strategy provides the clustering algorithm with a well-behaved stopping criterion, which allows to automatically discover the right number of clusters. The criterion based on performance measures seems to be the most accurate and most stable one. Using this weakly supervised clustering, we have successfully managed to improve Rocchio's performance, with errors rate dropping between 4 % and 84 % depending on the corpus. These differences in performance confirms that Rocchio can use some extra information regarding the internal organization of clusters, but this information is not useful for all corpora. In our experiments, we found that the number of useful subclusters is relatively small, thus preserving the efficiency of Rocchio during the classification phase. We have also identified an important characteristic of our clustering algorithm: it requires more documents than a simple Rocchio classifier; in fact using it with a too small corpus can even lower accuracy.

Our clustering algorithm allows to discover some hidden structure on any textual database in a way that is beneficial for the classifier Rocchio. We plan to investigate the use of similar unsupervised clustering techniques for other tasks including forgetting of past examples after a concept shift and management of a temporal stream of documents by monitoring these clusters.

References

1. Chris Buckley and Gerard Salton. Optimization of relevance weights. In *Proceedings of the Eighteenth Annual International ACM SIGIR Conference of Research and Development in Information Retrieval*, pages 351–357, 1995.
2. P. Cheeseman, J. Kelly, M. Self, J. Stutz, W. Taylor, and D. Freeman. Autoclass: A bayesian classification system. In *Proceedings of the Fifth International Conference on Machine Learning*, pages 54–64, Ann Arbor, June 1988. Morgan Kaufmann Publishers.
3. H. de Kroon, T. Mitchell, and E. Kerckhoffs. Improving learning accuracy in information filtering. In *International Conference on Machine Learning - Workshop on Machine Learning Meets HCI*, 1996.
4. D. Eichmann, M. Ruiz, P. Srinivasan, N. Street, C. Chris, and F. Menczer. A cluster based approach to tracking, detection and segmentation of broadcast news. In *Proceedings of the DARPA Broadcast News Workshop*, pages 69–76, 1999.
5. Eui-Hong Han and George Karypis. Centroid-based document classification: Analysis and experimental results. In *Principles of Data Mining and Knowledge Discovery*, pages 424–431, 2000.
6. Thorsten Joachims. Text categorization with support vector machines: Learning with many relevant features. In *ECML-98, Tenth European Conference on Machine Learning*, pages 137–142, 1998.
7. Wai Lam. Using a generalized instance set for automatic text categorization. In *Proceedings of SIGIR-98, 21th ACM International Conference on Research and Development in Information Retrieval*, pages 81–89, 1998.
8. David D. Lewis, Robert E. Schapire, James P. Callan, and Ron Papka. Training algorithms for linear text classifiers. In *Proceedings of SIGIR-96*, pages 298–306, Zürich, CH, 1996.
9. Alessandro Moschitti. A study on optimal parameter tuning for rocchio text classifier. In *proceedings of the 25th European Conference on Information Retrieval Research (ECIR)*, Pisa, Italy, 2003.

10. Andrew Y. Ng and Michael I. Jordan. On discriminative vs. generative classifiers: A comparison of logistic regression and naive bayes. *Neural Information Processing Systems*, 2001.
11. J-H Oh, K-S Lee, D-S Chang, C. Won Seo, and K-S Choi. Trec-10 experiments at kaist: Batch filtering and question answering. In *Proceedings of The Tenth Text REtrieval Conference (TREC-10)*, pages 347–354, 2001.
12. Joseph John Rocchio. *The SMART Retrieval System: Experiments in Automatic Document Processing*, chapter 14, Relevance Feedback in Information Retrieval, pages 313–323. Gerard Salton (editor), Prentice-Hall Inc., New Jersey, 1971.
13. Gerard Salton, A. Wong, and C.S. Yang. A vector space model for information retrieval. *Communications of the ACM*, 18(11):613–620, November 1975.
14. Robert E. Schapire and Yoram Singer. BoosTexter: A boosting system for text classification. *Machine Learning*, 39(2/3):135–168, 2000.
15. Robert E. Schapire, Yoram Singer, and Amit Singhal. Boosting and rocchio applied to text filtering. In W. Bruce Croft, Alistair Moffat, Cornelis J. van Rijsbergen, Ross Wilkinson, and Justin Zobel, editors, *Proceedings of SIGIR-98, 21st ACM International Conference on Research and Development in Information Retrieval*, pages 215–223, Melbourne, AU, 1998. ACM Press, New York, US.
16. Fabrizio Sebastiani. Machine learning in automated text categorization. *ACM Computing Surveys*, 34(1):1–47, 2002.
17. Amit Singhal, Mandar Mitra, and Christopher Buckley. Learning routing queries in a query zone. In *Proceedings of SIGIR-97, 20th ACM International Conference on Research and Development in Information Retrieval*, pages 25–32, Philadelphia, US, 1997.
18. Romain Vinot and François Yvon. Semi-automatic response in a Mail Center. In *ASMDA 2001, 10th International Symposium on Applied Stochastic Models and Data Analysis*, pages 992–997. Université de Technologie de Compiègne, 2001.
19. Romain Vinot and François Yvon. Quand simplicité rime avec efficacité : Analyse d'un catégoriseur de textes. In *Colloque International sur la Fouille de Texte (CIFT'02)*, pages 17–26, Tunisie, 2002.
20. Yiming Yang. An evaluation of statistical approach to text categorization. *Journal of Information Retrieval*, 1(1/2):67–88, 1999.

A Two-Level Learning Method for Generalized Multi-instance Problems

Nils Weidmann[1,2], Eibe Frank[2], and Bernhard Pfahringer[2]

[1] Department of Computer Science, University of Freiburg
Freiburg, Germany
weidmann@informatik.uni-freiburg.de
[2] Department of Computer Science, University of Waikato
Hamilton, New Zealand
{eibe,bernhard}@cs.waikato.ac.nz

Abstract. In traditional multi-instance (MI) learning, a single positive instance in a bag produces a positive class label. Hence, the learner knows how the bag's class label depends on the labels of the instances in the bag and can explicitly use this information to solve the learning task. In this paper we investigate a generalized view of the MI problem where this simple assumption no longer holds. We assume that an "interaction" between instances in a bag determines the class label. Our two-level learning method for this type of problem transforms an MI bag into a single meta-instance that can be learned by a standard propositional method. The meta-instance indicates which regions in the instance space are covered by instances of the bag. Results on both artificial and real-world data show that this two-level classification approach is well suited for generalized MI problems.

1 Introduction

Multi-instance (MI) learning has received a significant amount of attention over the last few years. In MI learning, each training example is a bag of instances with a single class label, and one assumes that the instances in a bag have individual, but unknown, class labels. The bag's class label depends in some way on the unknown classifications of its instances. The assumption of how the instances' classifications determine their bag's class label is called the *multi-instance assumption*. In existing approaches to MI learning, a bag is assumed to be positive if and only if it contains at least one positive instance. This assumption was introduced because it seemed to be adequate in the MI datasets used so far [1]. We refer to it as the *standard* MI assumption.

In this paper we explore a generalization of the standard assumption by extending the process that combines labels of instances to form a bag label. In the standard MI case, one instance that is positive w.r.t. an underlying propositional concept makes a bag positive. Instead of a single underlying concept, we use a set of underlying concepts and require a positive bag to have a certain number of instances in each of them.

We introduce three different generalized MI concepts. In *presence-based* MI datasets, a bag is labeled positive if it contains at least one instance in each of the underlying concepts; a *threshold-based* MI dataset requires a concept-dependent minimum number of instances of each concept; and in a *count-based* MI dataset, the number of instances per concept is bounded by an upper as well as a lower limit. These three types of MI concepts form a hierarchy, i.e. *presence-based* ⊂ *threshold-based* ⊂ *count-based*. Note that the standard MI problem is a special case of a presence-based MI concept with just one underlying concept. Consequently any learner able to solve our generalized MI problem should perform well on standard MI data.

In generalized MI problems, the learner has much less prior knowledge about the way the class label is determined by the instances in a bag, making this type of problem more difficult. We introduce the idea of *two-level-classification* (TLC) to tackle generalized MI problems. In the first step, this method constructs a single instance from a bag. This so-called *meta-instance* represents regions in the instance space and has an attribute for each of theses regions. Each attribute indicates the number of instances in the bag that can be found in the corresponding region. Together with the bag's class label, the meta-instance can be passed to a standard propositional learner in order to learn the influence of the regions on a bag's classification.

This paper is structured as follows. Section 2 gives an overview over the standard multi-instance problem and introduces notational conventions. In Section 3, we give definitions for our three generalizations of the MI problem. The two-level classification method is outlined in Section 4, and experiments with the algorithm on artificial data and the Musk problems are described in Section 5. We summarize our findings in Section 6.

2 The Standard Multi-instance Setting

In traditional supervised learning, each learning example consists of a fixed number of attributes and a class label. However, sometimes only a collection of instances can be labeled. For these cases, Dietterich et al. [1] introduced the notion of a multi-instance problem, where a "bag" of instances is given a class label. The motivating task was to predict whether a certain molecule is active or not. This is determined by its chemical binding properties, which again depend on the shape of the molecule. A molecule occurs in different shapes (conformations), because some of its internal bonds can be rotated. If at least one of the conformations of the molecule binds well to certain receptors, the molecule expresses a "musky" smell and is therefore considered active. In the Musk problems, a bag corresponds to a molecule, and the instances are its conformations.

In this paper, we follow the notation of Gärtner et al. [2]. $\mathcal{X}$ denotes the instance space, Ω is the set of class labels. In MI learning, the class is assumed to be binary, so $\Omega = \{\top, \bot\}$. A MI concept is a function $\nu_{MI} : 2^{\mathcal{X}} \to \Omega$. In the standard MI case, this function is defined as

$$\nu_{MI}(X) \Leftrightarrow \exists x \in X : c_I(x)$$

where $c_I \in \mathcal{C}$ is a concept from a concept space $\mathcal{C}$ (usually called the "underlying concept"), and $X \subseteq \mathcal{X}$ is a set[1] of instances. In this type of problem, a learner can be sure that every instance that is encountered in a negative bag is also a negative instance w.r.t. the underlying concept. Thus, it can focus on identifying positive instances using axis-parallel rectangles [1], neural networks [3], or the Diverse Density algorithm [4]. However, in this paper we are interested in a more generalized problem that leads to a harder learning task.

3 Generalized Multi-instance Problems

We extend the assumption of how a bag's label is determined by the classifications of its instances. In the standard MI case, a single instance that is positive in the underlying concept causes the bag label to be positive. In our case, we do no longer assume a single concept. Instead, a set of underlying concepts is used, each of which contributes to the classification. We assume that criteria based on the number of instances in each concept determine the bag's class label. Below we introduce generalizations of the standard MI concept that are based on three different types of criteria.

These more general problems cannot be solved simply by identifying positive instances that never occur in negative bags, because an instance in a negative bag can still be positive w.r.t. one of the underlying concepts. In other words, a positive instance does not necessarily cause a bag to be positive. Only if a sufficient number of instances of other concepts is present in the bag, the bag's label is positive. Thus a learning method for this task must take all instances in the bag into account.

To formalize our generalized view on MI learning, we redefine the MI concept function ν_{MI} introduced in the last paragraph. The data representation is unchanged, which means that we are given bags $X \subseteq \mathcal{X}$ with class labels in $\{\top, \bot\}$. The generalized MI concept function operates on a *set* of underlying concepts $C \subset \mathcal{C}$. We also need a counting function $\Delta : 2^{\mathcal{X}} \times \mathcal{C} \rightarrow \mathbb{N}$, which counts the members of a given concept in a bag.

3.1 Presence-Based MI Concepts

Our first generalization is defined in terms of the presence of instances of each concept in a bag. For example, an MI concept of this category is "only if instances of concept c_1 and instances of concept c_2 are present in the bag, the class is positive". Formally, a presence-based MI concept is a function $\nu_{PB} \colon 2^{\mathcal{X}} \rightarrow \Omega$, where for a given set of concepts $C \subset \mathcal{C}$,

$$\nu_{PB}(X) \Leftrightarrow \forall c \in C : \Delta(X, c) \geq 1$$

The following example (introduced in [5]) illustrates a presence-based MI concept. Assume we are given a set of bunches of keys. A bunch corresponds to a

---
[1] For notational convenience, we assume that all the instances in a bag are distinct.

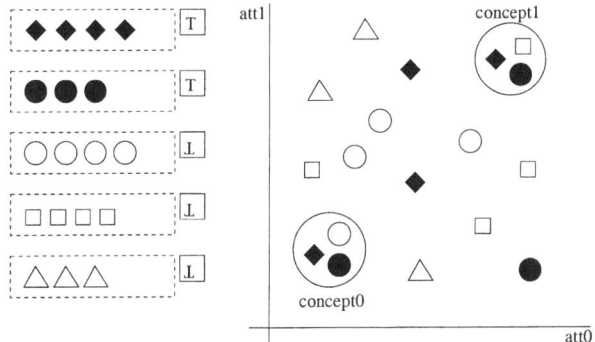

Fig. 1. A multi-instance dataset with a presence-based MI concept. Instances in a two-dimensional instance space (attribute att0 and attribute att1) are assigned to five bags (◆, ●, ○, □ and △). Two concepts (concept0 and concept1) are given as circles. The instance in a circle are part of the corresponding concept. ◆ and ● are positive bags, because they have instances in both concept0 and concept1

bag, the keys are its instances. The task is to predict if an unseen bunch can be used to open a locked door. If this door has only one lock, every bunch with at least one key for that lock would be positive. This corresponds to a standard MI learning problem. However, assume there are n different locks that need to be unlocked before the door can be opened. This is an example for a presence-based MI concept, because we need at least one instance (one key) of each of the n concepts (the locks) to classify a bag as positive. Thus the standard MI problem is a special case of this presence-based concept with $|C| = 1$.

Figure 1 visualizes a presence-based MI concept in a two-dimensional instance space. Note that presence-based MI problems have been introduced before as "multi-tuple problems" in an ILP-based setting [6]. The instances are all part of the same instance space, thus the number of underlying database relations is 1. In the ILP definition of standard MI learning, a hypothesis consists of a single rule using only one tuple variable. This rule corresponds to what we call the underlying concept. Multi-tuple problems are the relaxation of this definition, where an arbitrary number of rules can be used. These correspond to our set of concepts. Thus, because presence-based MI problems can be embedded into the ILP framework, they can, at least in principle, be solved by ILP learners. Another generalization of the MI problem called "multi-part problem" has been introduced in an ILP-based setting [5]. In this type of problem no explicit assumption is made about how the instances in a bag contribute to the bag's classification.

3.2 Threshold-Based MI Concepts

Instead of the mere presence of certain concepts in bag, one can require a certain number of instances of each concept to be present simultaneously. If for each concept, the corresponding number of instances of that concept exceeds a given threshold (which can be different for each concept), the bag is labeled positive and negative otherwise. Formally, we define a threshold-based MI concept function ν_{TB} as

$$\nu_{TB}(X) \Leftrightarrow \forall c_i \in C : \Delta(X, c) \geq t_i$$

where $t_i \in \mathbb{N}$ is called the "lower threshold for concept i". An extension of the "key-and-lock" example mentioned above illustrates a count-based MI concept. Assume the door has more than just one lock of each type, and that the keys have to be used simultaneously in order to open the door, i.e. we need one key for each lock. Here, we need at least as many keys for each type of lock as there are locks of this type in the door. In a such a dataset, each positive bag (a bunch of keys) has to have a minimum number of keys (the instances) of each type of lock (the concepts).

3.3 Count-Based MI Concepts

The most general concepts in our hierarchy are count-based MI concepts. These require a maximum as well as a minimum number of instances of a certain concept in a bag. This can be formalized as

$$\nu_{CB}(X) \Leftrightarrow \forall c_i \in C : t_i \leq \Delta(X, c) \leq z_i$$

where $t_i \in \mathbb{N}$ is again the lower threshold and $z_i \in \mathbb{N}$ is called the "upper threshold for concept i". Imagine the following learning example for this type of problem. We are given daily statistics of the orders processed by an company. An order is usually assigned to one the company's departments. We want to predict if the company's workload is within an optimal range, where none of the departments processes too few orders (because its efficiency would be low), or gets too many orders (because it would be overloaded). In a MI representation of this problem, bags are collections of orders (the instances) of a certain day, and the class label indicates whether the company was within an effective workload on that day. Each of the underlying concepts C assigns an order to a department. In order for the company to perform efficiently on a certain day, each of the departments has to work within its optimal range, i.e. the number of instances of this concept must be bounded from below and above. These bounds can be different for each concept.

4 Two-Level Classification

Although ILP-based learners can be used for presence-based MI problems, there appears to be no method capable of dealing with threshold- and count-based MI concepts. In particular, learners relying on the standard MI assumption are doomed to fail, because they aim at identifying positive instances that are not present in a negative bag. In our generalized view, this is usually not the case.

Taking a closer look at the way MI data are created, there are two functions that determine a bag's class label. First, there is a function that assigns an instance in a bag to a concept, a mono-instance concept function. Second, there is the MI concept function that computes a class label from the instances in a bag, given their concept membership by the first function. Thus, a two-level approach to learning seems appropriate. At the first level, we try to learn the structure of the instance space $\mathcal{X}$, and at the second level we try to discover the interaction that leads to a bag's class label. Let us discuss the second level first.

4.1 Second Level: Exploring Interactions

Assume we are given the concept membership functions c_i for all concepts $c_i \in C$. Then we can transform a bag X into a meta-instance with $|C|$ numerical attributes whose values indicate the number of instances in the bag that are members of the respective concept. Assigning the bag's class label to this newly created instance, we end up with a single instance appropriate for propositional learning. Processing all the MI bags in this way results in a propositional dataset that can be used as input for a propositional learner. However, we are not given the concept membership functions, and inducing each c_i directly is not possible, because we neither know the number of concepts that are used, nor the instances' individual class labels. Instead, we are only given a class label for the bag as a whole. However, it turns out that a decomposition of the instance space into "candidate" regions for each concept is possible, enabling the learner to recover the true MI concept at the second level. This is described in the next section.

4.2 First Level: Structuring the Instance Space

In the first level of our classification procedure, we construct a single instance from an MI bag. The attributes in this instance represent regions of the instance space, and an attribute's value is simply the number of instances in the bag that pertain to the corresponding region. One possible approach for identifying the regions would be clustering. However, this discards information given by the bag label. If we label each instance with its bag's label, regions with a high observed proportion of positive instances will be candidate components for concepts (see Figure 1). Hence, the "clustering" method should be sensitive to changes in the class distribution.

Consequently, we use a standard decision tree for imposing a structure on the instance space because it is able to detect these changes. The decision tree is built on the set of all instances contained in all bags, labeled with their bag's class label. The weight of each instance in a bag X is set to $\frac{1}{|X|} \cdot \frac{N}{b}$, where N denotes the sum of all the bag sizes and b the number of bags in the dataset. This gives bags of different size the same weight and makes the total weight equal to the number of instances. Information gain is used as the test selection measure. A node in the tree is not split further when the weight of its instances sums up to less than 2, and no other form of pruning is used. A unique identifier is assigned to each node of the tree. Using this tree, we convert a bag into a single instance with one numerical attribute for each node in the tree. Each attribute

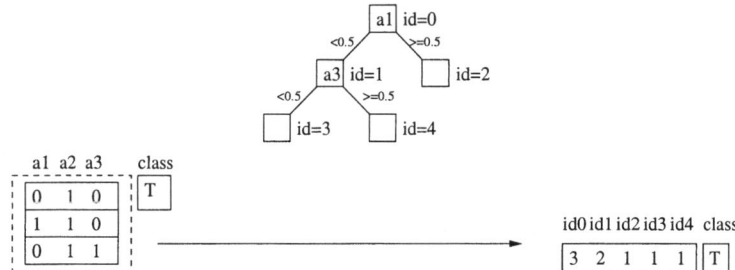

Fig. 2. Constructing a single instance from a bag with three instances and three attributes a1, a2 and a3. A decision tree with five nodes is used to identify regions in the instance space. The constructed single instance (right) has an attribute for each node in the tree, that counts the number of instances in the bag pertaining to that node

counts how many instances in the bag are assigned to the corresponding node in the tree. See Figure 2 for an illustration.

4.3 Attribute Selection

Attribute selection (AS) can be applied to refine the classifier. If the decision tree is not able to find the region representing a concept, classification at the meta-level will fail. Attributes that do not contribute to the classification of individual instances could be picked as splitting attributes in the tree and thus cause an incorrect representation of the concept regions. Attribute selection tries to eliminate these attributes. In our experiments, we used the method proposed in [7], which evaluates a given subset of attributes by cross-validations on this subset. Note that the cross-validation is performed at the bag level using both levels of TLC. We used backward selection, which starts with all attributes and subsequently eliminates attributes that worsen the performance. Of course, this method is computationally expensive and increases the runtime of the two-level classifier considerably.

5 Experiments

We have evaluated the performance of TLC using both artificial and real-world data. The only publicly available real-world data stems from the Musk problem [1], and for this problem it is very likely that methods able to deal with the standard MI assumption are sufficient. We therefore focus on artificially created datasets, where the performance on different types of MI concepts can be shown, and where we know that the various properties of our three types of problem hold.

Assuming that the first-level classifier can identify concepts over the instance space properly, the second-level learner must be able to learn intervals in the meta-attributes that are responsible for a positive classification. In our experiments, we used Logit-boosted decision stumps [8] with 10 boosting iterations, because they are able to do so, are well-known to be accurate general-purpose classifiers and performed well in initial experiments.

We compare the results of TLC both with and without attribute selection to the Diverse Density (DD) algorithm [4] and the MI Support Vector Machine [2]. Both have been designed for standard MI problems, although the latter does not exploit the MI assumption in any way. In the DD algorithm, we used an initial scaling parameter of 1.0. The MI Support Vector Machine was based on an RBF kernel, a γ-parameter of 0.6 and a C-parameter of 1.0.

5.1 Artificial Datasets

For the artificial datasets in our experiments we used bitstrings of different length l as instances, i.e. $\mathcal{X} = \{0,1\}^l$. The length l of the bitstring is the sum of the number of relevant attributes l_r and the number of irrelevant attributes l_i. Concepts c are bitstrings in $\{0,1\}^{l_r}$, i.e. an instance is member of a concept c_i if and only if its first l_r attributes match the bit pattern c_i.

The construction of an artificial dataset of a certain type (either presence-, threshold-, or count-based) works as follows. We randomly select different bitstrings of length l_r as concepts. A positive bag is first filled with instances of the different concepts according to the type of data we want to create: for presence-based MI concepts, at least one instance of each concept is added to the positive bag; for a threshold-based MI concept at least t_i instances of each concept c_i are added; and for a count-based MI concept, we add at least t_i and at most z_i instances of concept c_i. Since we choose different bitstrings representing the concepts, instances cannot be member of two concepts at the same time. In a second step, a number of random instances that are not member of any concept are added to the bag. These are created by uniformly drawing instances from the instance space $\{0,1\}^l$ and ensuring that they are not member of any of the concepts. These "irrelevant" instances are designed to make learning problem harder and more realistic.

Negative bags are constructed by first creating a positive bag in the way described above and then converting it into a negative bag. Since a negative bag must not satisfy the used MI concept, we need to negate at least one condition imposed on one of the concepts C. For a presence-based concept, we need to remove all the instances of at least one concept c_i, for a threshold-based concept the number of instances of at least one concept c_i must be less than t_i, and for a count-based concept, the number of instances of at least one concept must be increased or decreased so that it is either less than t_i or greater that z_i. Every possible subset of C except the empty set can be negated to create a negative bag. We choose uniformly from these $2^{|C|}-1$ possibilities. Increasing/decreasing the number of instances of a concept in bag can be done by replacing random instances by instances of the respective concept or replacing some of the concept's instances by random instances. After negation, the bag has the same size as before, thus the average bag size of positive and negative bags is the same.

Table 1. Results for presence-based MI data using only one underlying concept

	DD	MI SVM	TLC without AS	TLC with AS
1-5-0	100 ± 0	94.35 ± 0.74	100 ± 0	100 ± 0
1-5-5	100 ± 0	92.26 ± 0.95	100 ± 0	100 ± 0
1-5-10	100 ± 0	90.74 ± 0.76	100 ± 0	100 ± 0
1-10-0	99.57 ± 0.59	96.20 ± 0.85	97.46 ± 0.92	97.07 ± 0.3
1-10-5	99.41 ± 0.54	94.67 ± 1.35	97.57 ± 0.87	96.11 ± 1.57
1-10-10	99.8 ± 0.44	91.66 ± 2.3	97.85 ± 0.89	94.34 ± 2.66

Table 2. Results for presence-based MI data using two or three underlying concepts

	MI SVM	TLC without AS	TLC with AS
2-5-0	80.96 ± 1.9	100 ± 0	100 ± 0
2-5-5	81.17 ± 1.79	88.38 ± 11.91	100 ± 0
2-5-10	79.21 ± 1.66	78.64 ± 13.15	100 ± 0
2-10-0	84.18 ± 0.52	99.01 ± 1.32	97.56 ± 1.38
2-10-5	82.0 ± 1.53	85.18 ± 10.07	96.67 ± 1.58
2-10-10	80.74 ± 0.79	86.63 ± 8.69	94.45 ± 4.54
3-5-0	82.0 ± 2.13	100 ± 0	100 ± 0
3-5-5	82.12 ± 0.98	81.93 ± 2.9	99.98 ± 0.04
3-5-10	81.43 ± 0.96	86.32 ± 6.48	98.49 ± 1.74
3-10-0	84.39 ± 1.25	95.68 ± 3.78	94.73 ± 2.91
3-10-5	84.27 ± 1.44	78.07 ± 0.91	87.41 ± 6.24

Presence-based MI Datasets. We created presence-based datasets with concepts of length 5 and 10, hence $l_r = 5$ or $l_r = 10$, respectively. Some of our datasets required two concepts to be present in the positive bags ($|C| = 2$), in some we used three concepts ($|C| = 3$). To generate a positive bag, the number of instances in a concept was chosen randomly from $\{1, ..., 10\}$ for each concept. The number of random instances was selected with equal probability from $\{10|C|, ..., 10|C|+10\}$. Hence the minimal bag size in this dataset was $|C| + 10|C|$ and the maximal bag size $20|C| + 10$. We trained the classifiers on five different training sets with 50 positive and 50 negative bags each. Tables 1 and 2 show the average accuracy on a test set with 5,000 positive and 5,000 negative bags and the standard deviation of the five runs. The parameters of the dataset are given as $\langle |C| \rangle - \langle l_r \rangle - \langle l_i \rangle$, e.g. 3-10-5 has three concepts, 10 relevant and 5 irrelevant attributes.

The results in Table 1 show that each of the MI learners can deal well with presence-based MI concepts using only one underlying concept (corresponding to the standard MI assumption). DD cannot deal with more than one underlying concept and its performance is not competitive, therefore it is not included in Table 2. The MI SVM does not make explicit use of the standard MI assumption and surprisingly, its similarity measure enables it to perform well on these presence-based datasets (Table 2). The TLC method discovers the underlying MI concept perfectly in most cases, if no irrelevant attributes are used. Irrelevant attributes make it hard for the decision tree to represent the true underlying concepts, which in turn worsens the performance of the classifier (e.g. for dataset

Table 3. Results for threshold-based MI data

	MI SVM	TLC without AS	TLC with AS
42-5-0	84.35 ± 3.07	100 ± 0	100 ± 0
42-5-5	81.54 ± 2.24	95.93 ± 9.1	100 ± 0
42-5-10	81.59 ± 0.4	84.67 ± 14.31	100 ± 0
42-10-0	86.28 ± 1.33	99.35 ± 0.45	97.02 ± 1.65
42-10-5	85.36 ± 0.92	88.65 ± 10.12	96.58 ± 1.91
42-10-10	83.93 ± 0.36	84.59 ± 8.08	95.89 ± 2.05
275-5-0	84.75 ± 1.03	97.2 ± 2.78	97.2 ± 2.78
275-5-5	83.9 ± 1.29	90.62 ± 6.57	97.94 ± 2.83
275-5-10	82.73 ± 0.85	86.42 ± 5.39	93.75 ± 6.63
275-10-0	88.66 ± 1.12	95.44 ± 1.21	97.68 ± 1.57
275-10-5	87.05 ± 0.75	86.92 ± 6.56	90.44 ± 4.63

2-5-10). However, the attribute selection method eliminates the irrelevant attributes, enabling the classifier to give good results even on datasets with a high ratio of irrelevant attributes (dataset 2-5-10 and 3-5-5).

Threshold-based MI Datasets. We created threshold-based datasets using $l_r = 5$ or $l_r = 10$ and two or three concepts. We chose thresholds $t_1 = 4$ and $t_2 = 2$ for six datasets and $t_1 = 2$, $t_2 = 7$ and $t_3 = 5$ for another five datasets. For positive bags, the number of instances of concept c_i was chosen randomly from $\{t_i, ..., 10\}$. To form a negative bag, we replaced at least $(\Delta(X, c_i) - t_i - 1)$ instances of a concept c_i in a positive bag X by random instances. The minimal bag size in this dataset is $\sum_i t_i + 10|C|$, the maximal size is $20|C| + 10$. Table 3 shows the results. The parameters of the dataset are given as $\langle t_1..t_n \rangle - \langle l_r \rangle - \langle l_i \rangle$. For example, 42-10-0 has at least 4 instances of the first concept and 2 instances of the second concept in a positive bag, with 10 relevant and 0 irrelevant attributes.

Even though threshold-based MI concepts are harder to learn than presence-based ones, the results for the MI SVM show that it can deal quite well with these datasets. However, TLC achieves better results, although the variance of the results can be high (datasets 42-5-10 and 275-5-5) if no attribute selection is performed. We did not apply attribute selection in conjunction with the MI SVM, because Table 3 shows that its performance is not greatly affected by irrelevant attributes.

Count-based MI Datasets. Our count-based MI datasets are based on 5 or 10 relevant attributes. We used the same value for both thresholds t_i and z_i, because we considered this an interesting special case. In the following, we refer to this value as z_i. Hence, the number of instances of concept c_i is exactly z_i in a positive bag. For six datasets, we set $z_1 = 4$ and $z_2 = 4$, and for five other datasets, $z_1 = 2$, $z_2 = 7$ and $z_3 = 5$. A negative bag can be created by either increasing or decreasing the required number z_i of instances for a particular c_i. We chose a new number from $\{0, ..., z_i - 1\} \cup \{z_i + 1, ..., 10\}$ with equal probability. If this number was less than z_i, we replaced instances of concept c_i by random instances, if it was greater, we replaced random instances by instances of concept

Table 4. Results for count-based MI data

	MI SVM	TLC without AS	TLC with AS
42-5-0	52.78 ± 2	99.55 ± 0.64	99.35 ± 0.92
42-5-5	52.7 ± 1.04	57.89 ± 11.09	85.22 ± 21.65
42-5-10	53.83 ± 1.46	57.63 ± 7.64	70.9 ± 25.94
42-10-0	55.21 ± 1.76	90.89 ± 6.25	92.76 ± 1.64
42-10-5	54.62 ± 0.5	57.8 ± 8.55	92.78 ± 2.45
42-10-10	55.59 ± 2.81	51.05 ± 1.6	65.1 ± 20.35
275-5-0	54.31 ± 2.07	95.15 ± 2.4	95.15 ± 2.4
275-5-5	51.6 ± 0.45	55.2 ± 6.13	83.87 ± 17.67
275-5-10	52.34 ± 0.5	50.33 ± 0.72	56.94 ± 11.64
275-10-0	54.52 ± 1.54	87.85 ± 4.26	89.86 ± 3.4
275-10-5	54.5 ± 1.81	54.11 ± 4.79	83.5 ± 17.88

Table 5. Results for musk-datasets

	DD	MI SVM	TLC without AS
musk1	88.9	86.4 ± 1.1	88.69 ± 1.64
musk2	82.5	88.0 ± 1.0	83.13 ± 3.23

c_i. The minimal bag size in this dataset is $\sum_i z_i + 10|C|$, the maximal possible bag size is $20|C| + 10$. Accuracy results are given in Table 4. The parameters of the dataset are given as $\langle z_1..z_n \rangle - \langle l_r \rangle - \langle l_i \rangle$. For example dataset 42-5-5 requires exactly 4 instances of the first concept and 2 instances of the second concept in a positive bag, using 5 relevant and 5 irrelevant attributes.

The results for the count-based MI data (Table 4) show that the TLC method is able to learn this type of concept, even if a reasonable number of irrelevant attributes is involved. In datasets with a very high ratio of irrelevant attributes (dataset 275-5-10), even TLC fails, because the underlying concepts cannot be identified accurately enough. Attribute selection improves the performance of TLC, but only in some of the five runs, which leads to high variance. The results show that the MI SVM cannot learn count-based MI concepts; its performance is only slightly better than the default accuracy.

5.2 Musk Datasets

We have also evaluated the performance of TLC on the Musk datasets used by Dietterich et al. [1]. As described above, we used a boosted decision stump with 10 boosting iterations at the second level. At the first level, we used a standard pruned C4.5 tree [9]. However, performance improved after equal-width discretization based on ten intervals, representing the split points as binary attributes [10], and our results are based on the discretized data. We performed 10 runs of 10-fold cross-validation and give their average accuracy and standard deviation in Table 5. The results for the MI SVM are an average value of 1000 runs of randomly leaving out 10 bags and training the classifier on the remaining ones [2], using a γ-parameter of $10^{-5.5}$. The results for the DD algorithm were achieved by twenty runs of a 10-fold cross-validation [4]. Table 5 shows that TLC can successfully be applied to the Musk data.

6 Conclusions and Further Work

We have presented three different generalizations of the multi-instance assumption. Two-level classification is an elegant way to tackle these learning problems, and as our results show, it performs well on artificial data representing all three types of problems. A simple form of attribute selection increases the performance considerably in cases where a high ratio of irrelevant attributes makes it hard to discover the underlying instance-level concepts. On the Musk data, our algorithm performs comparably with state-of-the-art methods for this problem. Further work includes the application of a different clustering technique at the first level to structure the instance space and the application of our method to an image classification task.

Acknowledgments

Many thanks to Luc de Raedt and Geoff Holmes for enabling Nils to work on his MSc at Waikato University. Eibe Frank was supported by Marsden Grant 01-UOW-019. Xin Xu provided the implementation of the DD algorithm, and Thomas Gärtner the code of the MI-Kernel SVM.

References

1. Dietterich, T.G., Lathrop, R.H., Lozano-Perez, T.: Solving the Multiple Instance Problem with Axis-Parallel Rectangles. Artificial Intelligence **89** (1997) 31–71
2. Gärtner, T., Flach, P.A., Kowalczyk, A., Smola, A.J.: Multi-Instance Kernels. In: Proc. 19th Int. Conf. on Machine Learning, Morgan Kaufmann, San Francisco, CA (2002) 179–186
3. Ramon, J., De Raedt, L.: Multi Instance Neural Networks. In: Proc. ICML Workshop on Attribute-Value and Relational Learning. (2000)
4. Maron, O., Lozano-Pérez, T.: A Framework for Multiple-Instance Learning. In: Advances in Neural Information Processing Systems. Volume 10., MIT Press (1998)
5. Zucker, J.D., Chevaleyre, Y.: Solving multiple-instance and multiple-part learning problems with decision trees and decision rules. Application to the mutagenesis problem. In: Internal Report, University of Paris 6. (2000)
6. De Raedt, L.: Attribute-Value Learning Versus Inductive Logic Programming: The Missing Links. In: Proc. 8th Int. Conf. on ILP, Springer (1998) 1–8
7. Kohavi, R., John, G.H.: Wrappers for Feature Subset Selection. Artificial Intelligence **97** (1997) 273–324
8. Friedman, J., Hastie, T., Tibshirani, R.: Additive logistic regression: A statistical view of boosting. Annals of Statistics **28** (2000) 307–337
9. Quinlan, R.: C4.5: Programs for Machine Learning. Morgan Kaufmann (1993)
10. Frank, E., Witten, I.: Making Better Use of Global Discretization. In: Proc. 16th Int. Conf. on Machine Learning, Morgan Kaufmann (1999) 115–123

Clustering in Knowledge Embedded Space

Yungang Zhang[1], Changshui Zhang[1], and Shijun Wang[1]

State Key Laboratory of Intelligent Technology and Systems
Department of Automation, Tsinghua University, Beijing 100084, China
{zyg00,zcs,wsj02}@mails.tsinghua.edu.cn

Abstract. Cluster analysis is a fundamental technique in pattern recognition. It is difficult to cluster data on complex data sets. This paper presents a new algorithm for clustering. There are three key ideas in the algorithm: using mutual neighborhood graphs to discover knowledge and cluster data; using eigenvalues of local covariance matrixes to express knowledge and form a knowledge embedded space; and using a denoising trick in knowledge embedded space to implement clustering. Essentially, it learns a new distance metric by knowledge embedding and makes clustering become easier under this distance metric. The experiment results show that the algorithm can construct a quality neighborhood graph from a complex and noisy data set and well solve clustering problems.

1 Introduction

Cluster analysis is the automatic identification of groups of similar objects. The discovered clusters serve as the foundation for other data mining and analysis techniques. There have been many works on cluster analysis. Existing clustering algorithms, such as K-means [1], PAM [2], CLARANS [3], DBSCAN [4], CURE [5], and ROCK [6] are designed to find clusters that fit some static models. These algorithms will breakdown if the model is not adequate to capture the characteristics of clusters. Most of these algorithms breakdown when the data set consists of clusters that are of different shapes, densities and sizes [7].

This paper presents a new clustering algorithm. There are three key ideas in the algorithm. The first is using mutual neighborhood graphs to discover knowledge and cluster data. The second is using eigenvalues of local covariance matrixes to express knowledge and embedding knowledge into the input space to form a knowledge embedded space. MNN (Mutual Nearest Neighbor) distance in the knowledge embedded space is used as the new distance metric instead of Euclidean distance in the input space. The third is using a denoising trick in knowledge embedded space to implement clustering. Essentially, it learns a new distance metric by knowledge embedding and makes clustering become easier under this distance metric. The experiment results show that the algorithm can cluster data of different shapes, densities and sizes correctly.

The rest of this paper is organized as follows: Section two gives basic notions and an overview of related work. Section three describes the new method in detail. Section four explains several experiments using the new method. Section five gives some discussions. Section six presents conclusions.

2 Basic Notions and Related Work

The basic ideas of our algorithm are elicited by LLE [8,9]. LLE showed us an efficient way to use local information to solve nonlinear problems. First, it constructs a neighborhood graph. Next, it discovers the information of reconstruction weights from the neighborhood graph. Finally, it carries out nonlinear dimensionality reduction by using the reconstruction weights. Our algorithm is similar to LLE except it solves clustering problems. First, a mutual neighborhood graph is constructed. For ideal data sets, all points belonging to the same cluster are connected in the neighborhood graph. Any points belonging to different clusters are not connected. However, in practice, due to noise and the complexity of the data set, different clusters are often connected. We must split them from each other. Then, local information useful for clustering is discovered and embedded into input space and a knowledge embedded space is formed. Finally, clustering can be done by the use of this information and different clusters can be split from each other.

The local information used in our algorithm is eigenvalues of local covariance matrixes. This is an extension of local principal component analysis methods [10–12]. Our method directly uses all the eigenvalues of local covariance matrixes to represent local knowledge rather than only analyzing local principal components. The advantage is that it contains all the information about local shape and local size rather than local dimension. In section 3.4 and 3.5, we will see that eigenvalues are useful for denoising of input data and λ knowledge that are pivotal steps for clustering.

The Kernel-based method [13–15] is a typical solution for nonlinear problems. The key idea of which is to transform nonlinear data sets in the input space into linear data sets in a high dimensional feature space. Essentially, it is still finding a new distance metric by space transformation. The primary difficulty of kernel-based methods is that it is difficult to choose a proper kernel function to perform this task. In our method, we also construct a high dimension space, an easily formed knowledge embedded space. The purpose is to analyze useful information for clustering, not translate nonlinear data sets into linear data sets.

3 NK Algorithm

Our algorithm is called NK algorithm. It means mutual neighborhood graph construction by knowledge embedding. "N" indicates neighborhood and "K" indicates Knowledge. This section describes the NK algorithm in detail. First, some basic concepts are defined, and then the details of the algorithm are given.

3.1 Definitions

Here are the basic concepts used in NK algorithm which will be explained in the next six subsections. The input of the algorithm is a data set X, with N points:

$$X = \{\boldsymbol{x}_1, \ldots, \boldsymbol{x}_N\}, \boldsymbol{x}_i \in R^d \qquad (1)$$

N is the number of points and d is the dimension number of input data.

Definition 1: Set $\omega_i = \{x_i, x_{i_1}, \ldots, x_{i_K}\}$ $(i = 1, \ldots, N)$ is called the local neighborhood of x_i, where K is the number of neighbors and x_{i_l} $(l = 1, \ldots, K)$ denotes the lth nearest neighbor of x_i. For convenience, x_{i_0} is used to denote x_i and ω_i is rewritten as $\omega_i = \{x_{i_0}, \ldots, x_{i_K}\}$.

Definition 2: Local covariance matrix of ω_i is:

$$S_i = \frac{1}{K+1} \sum_{l=0}^{K} (x_{i_l} - m_i)(x_{i_l} - m_i)^T, \quad (2)$$

where $m_i = \frac{1}{K+1} \sum_{l=0}^{K} x_{i_l}$ is the average of ω_i.

Definition 3: $\lambda_i = [\lambda_{i1}, \ldots, \lambda_{id}]^T$ $(i = 1, \ldots, N, \lambda_{i1} \geq \cdots \geq \lambda_{id})$ is the vector of eigenvalues of S_i and is called the local feature of x_i. The knowledge represented by local feature is called λ knowledge.

Definition 4: A neighborhood graph is an undirected weighted graph $G = (X, E)$, where X is the set of data points and E is the set of edges between neighbors with weights e_{ij} to represent the distance. When MNV (Mutual Neighborhood Values) [16] are used as the weights, the neighborhood graph is called a mutual neighborhood graph and the distance represented by MNV is called MNN distance. If x_i and x_j are not neighbors, let $e_{ij} = 0$, indicating there is no edge between them; otherwise, e_{ij} is the MNV of x_i and x_j:

$$e_{ij} = \begin{cases} L_{ij}, x_j \in \omega_i \\ 0, x_j \notin \omega_i \end{cases}, \quad (3)$$

where L_{ij} is the mutual neighborhood value of the pair of points x_i and x_j. If x_j is the pth nearest neighbor of x_i and x_i is the qth nearest neighbor of x_j, then $L_{ij} = p + q - 2, p, q = 1, \ldots, K$ [16].

Definition 5: Inadaptability of ω_i is defined as follows:

$$a_i = \frac{1}{d} \sum_{j=1}^{d} \frac{\lambda_{ij}}{\bar{\lambda}_{ij}}, \quad (4)$$

where λ_{ij} is the jth element of λ_i, $\bar{\lambda}_{ij} = \frac{1}{K} \sum_{t \in \{i_1, \ldots, i_K\}} \lambda_{tj}$, λ_t $(t = i_1, \ldots, i_K)$ is the vector of eigenvalues of S_t. i_l $(l = 1, \ldots, K)$ is the subscript of x_{i_l} which is the lth nearest neighbor of x_i.

3.2 Mutual Neighborhood Graph Construction

The first step is mutual neighborhood graph construction: Calculate the Euclidean distance of each pair of x_i and x_j; Calculate the mutual neighborhood value $L = \{L_{ij}\}$; Find the K nearest neighbors for each point x_i according to mutual distance L_{ij}.

This is a K-NN method which is suitable for our algorithm, when K is fixed, the eigenvalues of a local covariance matrix represent the distribution of the local data, which helps us to learn knowledge from the data. Furthermore, mutual nearest neighbor distance is used instead of Euclidean distance. As we know, MNN distance contains important knowledge for nonlinear problems and makes it easier for the points with similar densities to cluster together. We regard local density as important knowledge for clustering, so MNN distance is more suitable here than traditional Euclidean distance.

3.3 Distance Metric Learning by Knowledge Embedding

The second step is to discover knowledge from the mutual neighborhood graph. After mutual neighborhood graph construction, the neighborhood of each data point is identified. As a result, local covariance matrix S_i and its eigenvalues λ_i can be computed. Then we get local knowledge for each point and the knowledge embedded space is formed by combine x_i with λ_i: $y_i = \begin{bmatrix} x_i \\ \lambda_i \end{bmatrix}$, where y_i is the corresponding point of x_i in knowledge embedded space. In the next subsections two steps of denoising are performed which are the pivotal steps in NK algorithm.

The distance metric used in our algorithm is MNN distance in the knowledge embedded space rather than Euclidean distance in input space. If two points are close in this distance metric, it means that in the input space, their coordinates are close and local features are similar. How this metric is used for clustering will be discussed in section 5.

3.4 Denoising of Input Data

When data set has some background noise, clustering becomes difficult. We should remove background noise from data set. By the use of λ knowledge, this task can be done easily. As we know, background noise is usually very sparse. So its eigenvalues of local covariance matrix are much larger than other points. Then, background noise can be removed by using a threshold $E(\lambda_i) + P_{noise} * D(\lambda_i)$, where $E(\lambda_i)$ and $D(\lambda_i)$ are the mean and variance of λ_i respectively, and P_{noise} is a parameter. How to choose P_{noise} will be discussed in section 5.

3.5 Denoising of λ Knowledge

In neighborhood graphs, there are often some edges connecting two points that are not actually neighbors. These are called false edges. In Fig. 1, the edges between layers are false edges. Where there is a false edge, the corresponding eigenvalues of the local covariance matrix cannot represent the correct local feature of the neighborhood. We consider this as some kind of noise of λ knowledge. An efficient algorithm must be used to remove the false edges and this is called the denoising of λ knowledge.

Inadaptability a_i is defined for false edge finding. In Fig. 2, x_i is a point with false edges. ω_i is the corresponding neighborhood. x_j is a neighbor of x_i who has no false edges and ω_j is x_j's neighborhood. λ_i and λ_j are corresponding eigenvalues. Obviously, the elements of λ_i tend to be larger than λ_j's. So neighborhoods with false edges can be found by comparing their eigenvalues. There may be clusters with different densities and eigenvalues in a sparse cluster will be larger than those in a dense cluster. So we compare eigenvalues only between neighbors and define inadaptability as definition 5, where λ_{ij} is the jth element of λ_i, $\bar{\lambda}_{ij}$ is the mean of the jth eigenvalue of $\lambda_{i_l}(l=1,\ldots,K)$. So the similarity between ω_i and ω_{i_l} can be measured by a_i. If ω_i and ω_{i_l} are similar, a_i is small; otherwise a_i is large. Then ω_i with false edges whose corresponding a_i is larger than a threshold is selected. $E(a_i)+P_{false}*D(a_i)$ is used as the threshold, where $E(a_i)$ and $D(a_i)$ are the mean and variance of a_i $(i=1,\ldots,N)$ and P_{false} is a parameter. How to choose P_{false} will be discussed in section 5.

Each ω_i with false edges is denoised by a steepest descent method. First, calculate the mean of the neighborhood $m_i = \frac{1}{K+1}\sum_{l=0}^{K} x_{i_l}$. Then, calculate the distance between x_{i_l} and m_i. Next, remove the point with the maximal distance from ω_i and repeat this procedure until the inadaptability on the rest points is smaller than the threshold $E(a_i) + P_{false} * D(a_i)$.

After denoising, a well constructed mutual neighborhood graph is obtained. It is called a denoised mutual neighborhood graph.

3.6 Clustering in Knowledge Embedded Space

In the last step, we cluster data in knowledge embedded space. Start from arbitrary node x_i, find its K nearest neighbors, $x_{i_1},\ldots,x_{i_K}$. Then find the K nearest neighbors of each x_{i_l}, etc. Combining all these points together results in a cluster. All the clusters can be obtained in the same way. It is obvious that the number of clusters is determined automatically.

3.7 Summarization of the Algorithm

The algorithm is presented in detail in Table 1.

4 Experiments

4.1 Clustering

Fig. 1–4 are experiment results of a two-layer Swiss roll which is a typical nonlinear problem. In the first step, there were many false edges between layers. All the points will be clustered into one cluster, see Fig. 1. Our algorithm can cluster all the points correctly, because it uses a denoising trick to remove the false edges, see Fig. 4.

Fig. 5–8 are experiments on data sets of many clusters with different shapes, densities, sizes and also with some background noise. The data sets comes from

Table 1. NK algorithm

Step 1: Mutual neighborhood graph construction

- Calculate the Euclidean distance matrix $D = \{d_{ij}\}, i, j = 1, \ldots, N$.
- Calculate the mutual neighborhood value matrix, $L = \{L_{ij}\}$.
- Find the K nearest neighbors for each point x_i under MNN distance.

Step 2: Knowledge embedding

- Calculate local covariance matrix S_i of each point x_i.
- Calculate eigenvalues λ_i of S_i.

Step 3: Denoising of input data.

- Calculate the threshold $E(\lambda_i) + P_{noise} * D(\lambda_i)$ and remove noise points.
- Construct a new mutual neighborhood graph on the denoised input data.

Step 4: Denoising of λ knowledge.

- Recalculate eigenvalues λ_i of each point x_i.
- Calculate inadaptability a_i of each point x_i.
- Calculate the threshold $E(a_i) + P_{false} * D(a_i)$ and select out ω_i with false edges whose corresponding a_i is larger than the threshold $E(a_i) + P_{false} * D(a_i)$.
- Denoising ω_i with false edges by a steepest descent method:
  a) calculate the mean of the neighborhood $m_i = \frac{1}{K+1} \sum_{l=0}^{K} x_{i_l}$
  b) calculate the distance d_i^l between x_{i_l} and m_i, x_{i_l} is the lth neighbor of x_i.
  c) Find x_{i_s} whose corresponding d_i^s is the maximum in all $d_i^l, l = 1, \ldots, K$. Remove the point x_{i_s} from ω_i and remove the point x_i from ω_{i_s}. It means to break the edges between x_i and x_{i_s}
  d) Repeat c) until the inadaptability on the rest points is smaller than the threshold.

Step 5: Clustering in knowledge embedded space.

---

[17]. All the points can be correctly clustered and background noise is removed. To keep the figure legible, only parts of the points are shown and background noise is not shown.

4.2 Enhanced Isomap

The algorithm was also used to construct the neighborhood graph for ISOMAP [18]. For complex data sets, there are often some false edges in the neighborhood graph which prevent ISOMAP from reducing dimensionality correctly. After removing these false edges, ISOMAP was able to find the structure of complex data sets much more accurately (see Fig. 9).

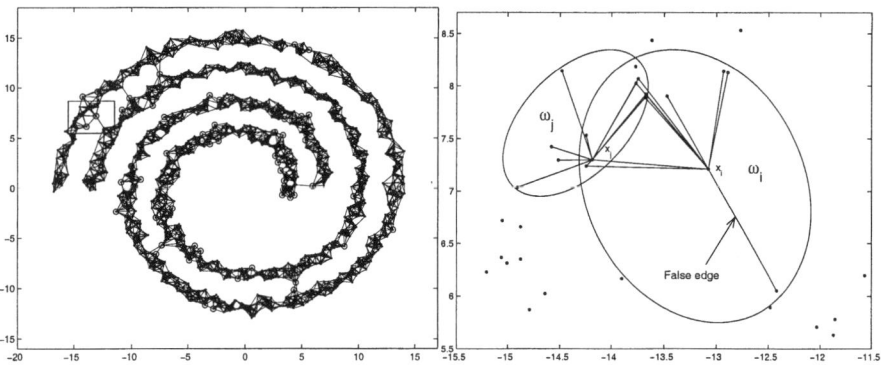

Fig. 1. Mutual neighborhood graph of a two-layer Swiss roll of 2000 points

Fig. 2. The rectangle area in Fig. 1

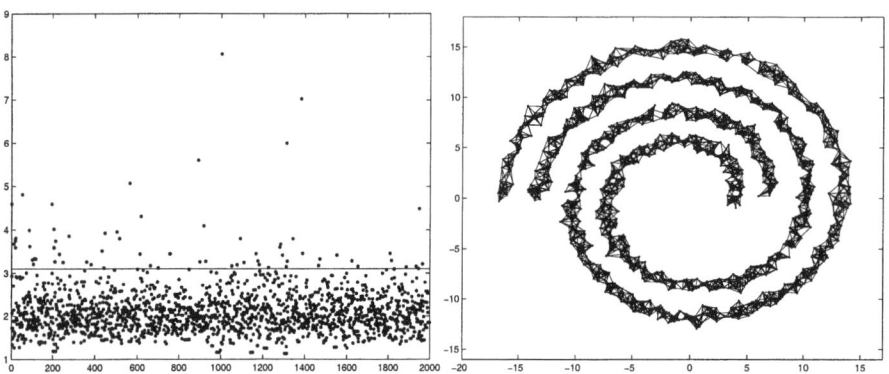

Fig. 3. Inadaptability of all points. The horizontal line is the threshold

Fig. 4. Mutual neighborhood graph after denoising of λ knowledge. $K = 10, P_{noise} = 8, P_{false} = 2$

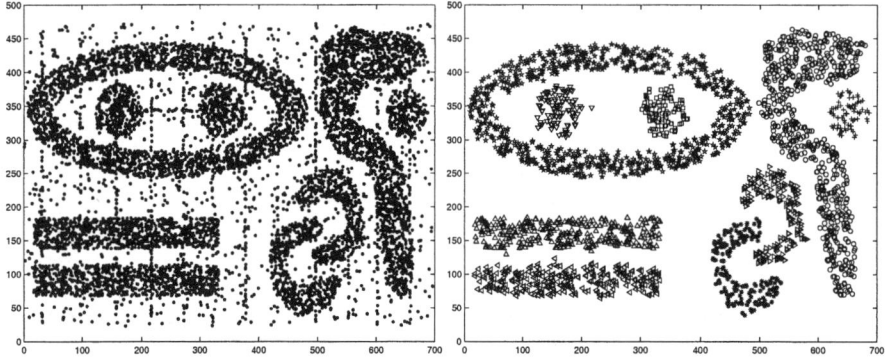

Fig. 5. A data set of 10000 points

Fig. 6. Clustering result of Fig. 5. $K = 11, P_{noise} = 0.8, P_{false} = 1$

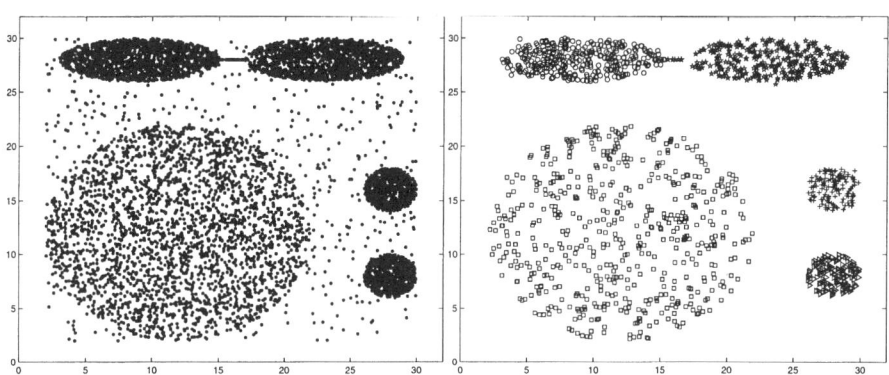

Fig. 7. A data set of 8000 points

Fig. 8. Clustering result of Fig. 7. $K = 6, P_{noise} = 1, P_{false} = 2$

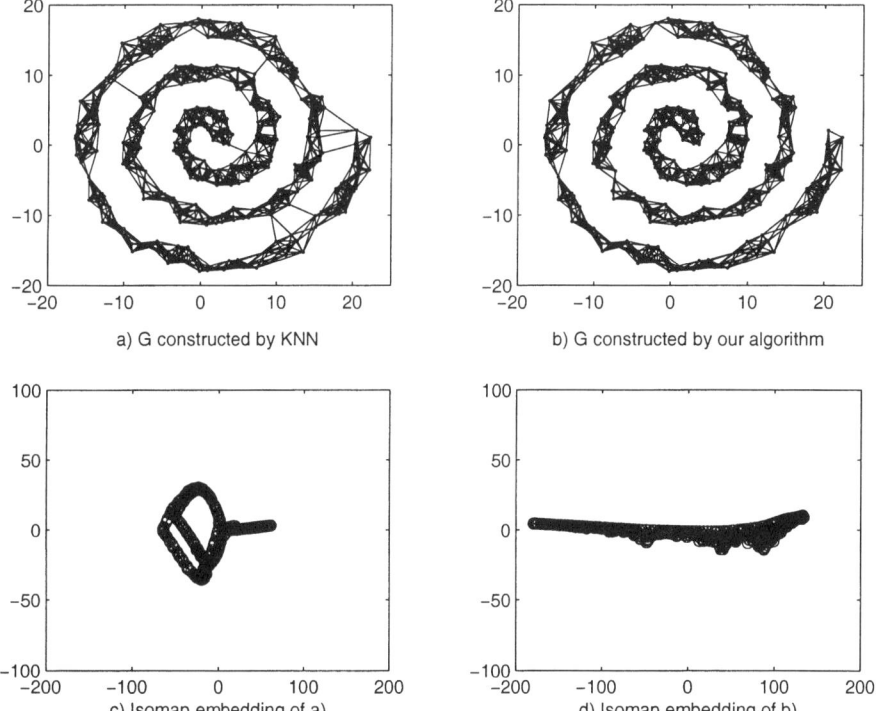

Fig. 9. Enhanced ISOMAP

4.3 Compare with DBSCAN

DBSCAN [4] is a well-known spatial clustering algorithm that has been shown to find clusters of arbitrary shapes. We have done some experiments to compare NK algorithm and DBSCAN.

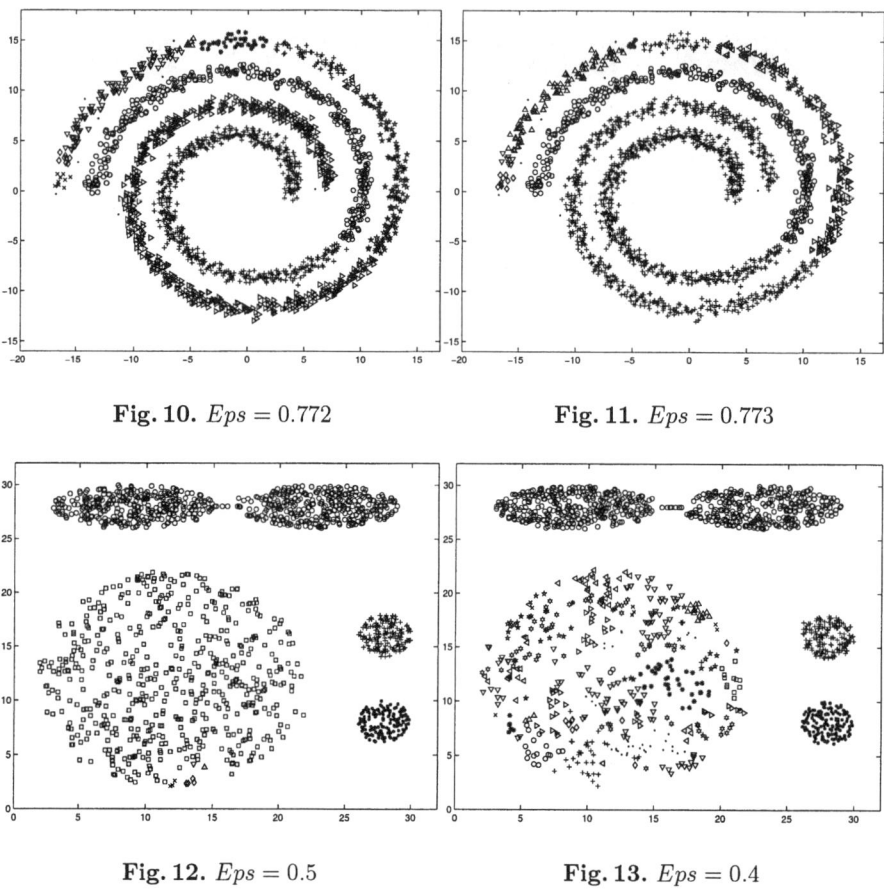

Fig. 10. $Eps = 0.772$

Fig. 11. $Eps = 0.773$

Fig. 12. $Eps = 0.5$

Fig. 13. $Eps = 0.4$

In most of our experiments, DBSCAN works very well, but it fails to perform well in some cases while NK algorithm can work well. Fig. 10-13 are some results of DBSACN. Following the recommendation of [4], the $MinPts$ was fixed to 4 and Eps was changed in these experiments. Fig. 10 is the best result of DBSCAN with $Eps = 0.772$ and there are 11 clusters. If Eps is increased to 0.773, some part of Swiss roll of different layers will be clustering into the same clustering, see Fig. 11. In Fig. 12 and Fig. 13 the data set contains clusters of different densities and the figures illustrate that DBSCAN cannot effectively find clusters of different densities [7, 19] while NK algorithm works well on the same data set. To keep the figure legible, only parts of the points are shown, and background noise is not shown.

4.4 Run-Time Analysis

The overall computational complexity of NK algorithm mainly depends on the amount of time it requires to compute nearest neighbors and compute eigenvalues of local covariance matrixes. The complexity of computing nearest neighbors is $O(dN^2)$ [9]. However, some other nearest neighbors computing algorithms such as K-D trees can be used to compute the neighbors in time $O(N \log N)$ [20]. Computing the eigenvalues of one local covariance matrix scales as $O(d^3)$ [9]. As a result, the overall complexity of NK algorithm is $O(dN^2 + d^3N)$. It will be greatly sped up if a faster neighbors computing algorithm is used.

We have implemented NK algorithm in MATLAB, running on a Pentium 4 2.0GHz processor. Table 2 gives the actual running times of the algorithm on different data sets of the same dimension of 2.

Table 2. Running time in seconds

Data Set	Size	Graph construction	Denoising	Overall
1	2000	2.4	0.8	3.2
2	4000	11.1	1.6	12.7
3	6000	27.5	2.5	30
4	8000	41	4	45

5 Discussion

Distance metrics are very important in many learning and data mining algorithms. MNN distance in knowledge embedding space is used as the new distance metric in NK algorithm. Here some explanation of how this distance metric is used for clustering will be given. If two points y_i and y_j are close under this distance metric, that is x_i is close to x_j and λ_i is close to λ_j, it means that in the input space, the coordinates of these two points are close and their local features are similar. In mutual neighborhood graph construction, each point is connected with its neighbors. This ensures that x_i is close to x_j if they are neighbors. Although, corresponding λ_i and λ_j are not always close since there are some false edges. So denoising is performed to remove false edges and after denoising, λ_i and λ_j become close. Because of this, in a denoised neighborhood graph, each pair of neighbors is close in knowledge embedded space. Note, the new distance metric is not used to measure the distance between each pair of points in the same cluster, but only the distance of neighbors.

There are three main parameters that are determined experimentally. The most important parameter is the number of neighbors K. The other two are P_{noise} and P_{false}. In practice, first decide P_{noise} and P_{false}, and then choose K. They can be chosen almost independently.

For data set without noise, P_{noise} should be a large number and easy to choose, such as 6 to 8 or even larger. If there is background noise, P_{noise} should be a small number, such as 0.1-1.5. We can set P_{noise} equal to 1 and then reduce it if not all the noise is removed or increase it if too many data points are removed. When choosing P_{noise}, the value of K is not important as long as it is not too small or too large. P_{false} is relative easy to choose. We can set $P_{false} = 2$ in most cases. If some points with false edges are not detected, then P_{false} should be smaller.

As we know, in neighborhood graph construction algorithm, K is difficult to choose, especially, when data set are complex. In our algorithm, K is easier to choose than many other algorithms profiting from the denoising trick. When false edges can't be removed, even if the points with false edges are detected, K should be smaller. When a data set is sparse or it is asymmetrical, sometimes a cluster will break where the data is very sparse. At this time, increasing K has some effect, but not a thorough solution. This is still a problem to be solved. Most of other clustering algorithm will still fail in the same environment. In our experiments, NK algorithm works much better than DBSCAN when the data set is sparse or it is asymmetrical.

6 Conclusion

This paper presents a new algorithm for clustering by knowledge embedding. Mutual neighborhood graphing is used for knowledge discovery and clustering. Eigenvalues of local covariance matrixes are used to represent local features. Denoising is needed because data sets are usually complex. The experiment results show that the algorithm can construct a quality neighborhood graph from a complex and noisy data set and it efficiently solves clustering problems.

Acknowledgements

We would like to thank Zhongbao Kou, Baibo Zhang, Shifeng Weng, Jun Wang, Tao Ban, and Jian'guo Li for a number of helpful discussions and suggestions.

References

1. Jain, A.K., Dubes, R.C.: Algorithms for Clustering Data. Prentice Hall (1988)
2. Kaufman, L., Rousseeuw, P.J.: Finding Groups in Data: an Introduction to Cluster Analysis. John Wiley & Sons (1990)
3. Ng, R., Han, J.: Efficient and effective clustering method for spatial data mining. In Proc. of the 20th VLDB Conference, Santiago, Chile (1994) 144-155
4. Martin Ester, Hans-Peter Kriegel, Jörg Sander, Xiaowei Xu: A Density-Based Algorithm for Discovering Clusters in Large Spatial Databases with Noise. KDD (1996) 226-231
5. Sudipto Guha, Rajeev Rastogi, Kyuseok Shim: CURE: An efficient clustering algorithm for large databases. In Proc. of 1998 ACM-SIGMOD Int. Conf. on Management of Data (1998)
6. Sudipto Guha, Rajeev Rastogi, Kyuseok Shim: ROCK: a robust clustering algorithm for categorical attributes. In Proc. of the 15th Intl Conf. on Data Eng. (1999)

7. Karypis, G., Han, E., Kumar, V.: CHAMELEON: A Hierarchical Clustering Algorithm Using Dynamic Modeling. IEEE Computer, 32, (1999) 68-75
8. Roweis, S.T., Saul, L.K.: Nonlinear dimensionality reduction by locally linear embedding. Science, Vol. 290 (2000) 2323-2326
9. Saul, L.K., Roweis, S.T.: An introduction to locally linear embedding. Tech. rep., AT&T Labs - Research (2001)
10. Fukunaga, K., Olsen, D.R.: An algorithm for finding intrinsic dimensionality of data. IEEE Transactions on Computers, Vol. 20 (1971) 176-183
11. Pettis, K., Bailey, I., Jain, T., Dubes, R.: An intrinsic dimensionality estimator from near-neighbor information. IEEE Transactions on Pattern Analysis and Machine Intelligence, Vol. 1 (1979) 25-37
12. Kambhatla, N., Leen, T.K.: Dimension reduction by local principal component analysis. Neural Computation, Vol. 9, num. 7 (1997) 1493-1516
13. Schölkopf, B., Smola, A.J., Müller, K.R.: Nonlinear Component Analysis as a Kernel Eigenvalue Problem. Neural Computation, 10 (1998) 1299-1319
14. Schölkopf, B., Mika, S., Burges, C.J.C., Knirsch, P., Müller, K.R., Raetsch, G., Smola, A.: Input Space vs. Feature Space in Kernel-Based Methods. IEEE Trans. on NN, Vol. 10, No. 5 (1999) 1000-1017
15. Schölkopf, B., Smola, A.J.: Learning with Kernels: Support Vector Machines, Regularization and Beyond. Cambridge, Massachusetts: MIT Press (2002)
16. Jain, A.K., Robert, P.W., Duin, Jianchang Mao: Statistical Pattern Recognition: A Review. IEEE Transactions on Pattern Analysis and Machine Intelligence (1999)
17. Harel, D., Koren, Y.: Clustering Spatial Data Using Random Walks. Proceedings of The 7th ACM Int. Conference on Knowledge Discovery and Data Mining (KDD'01). ACM press (2001) 281–286
18. Tenenbaum, J.B., Silvam, V.de., Langford J.C.: A global geometric framework for nonlinear dimensionality reduction. Science, Vol. 290 (2000) 2319-2323
19. Osmar, R., Zaïane, Andrew Foss, Chi-Hoon Lee, Weinan Wang: On Data Clustering Analysis: Scalability, Constraints and Validation, Sixth Pacific-Asia Conference on Knowledge Discovery and Data Mining (PAKDD'02), Taipei, Taiwan, May (2002)
20. Friedman, J.H., Bentley J.L., Finkel R.A.: An algorithm for finding best matches in logarithmic expected time. ACM Transactions on Mathematical Software, Vol. 3 (1997) 209-226

Ensembles of Multi-instance Learners

Zhi-Hua Zhou and Min-Ling Zhang

National Laboratory for Novel Software Technology,
Nanjing University, Nanjing 210093, China
zhouzh@nju.edu.cn
http://cs.nju.edu.cn/people/zhouzh/

Abstract. In multi-instance learning, the training set comprises labeled *bags* that are composed of unlabeled instances, and the task is to predict the labels of unseen bags. Through analyzing two famous multi-instance learning algorithms, this paper shows that many supervised learning algorithms can be adapted to multi-instance learning, as long as their focuses are shifted from the discrimination on the instances to the discrimination on the bags. Moreover, considering that ensemble learning paradigms can effectively enhance supervised learners, this paper proposes to build ensembles of multi-instance learners to solve multi-instance problems. Experiments on a real-world benchmark test show that ensemble learning paradigms can significantly enhance multi-instance learners, and the result achieved by EM-DD ensemble exceeds the best result on the benchmark test reported in literature.

1 Introduction

The term *multi-instance learning* was coined by Dietterich et al. [11] when they were investigating the problem of drug activity prediction. In this learning framework, the training set is composed of many *bags* each contains many instances. A bag is positively labeled if it contains at least one positive instance. Otherwise it is negatively labeled. The task is to learn some concept from the training bags for correctly labeling unseen bags. This task is very difficult because unlike supervised learning where all the training instances are labeled, here the labels of the individual instances are unknown. It has been shown that learning algorithms ignoring the characteristics of multi-instance learning could not work well in this scenario [11].

The PAC-learnability of multi-instance learning has been studied by many researchers [2][3][5][13], and some important results, such as 'if the instances in the bags are not independent then APR (Axis-Parallel Rectangle) learning [11] under the multi-instance learning framework is NP-hard' [3], have been obtained. At present, the most famous multi-instance learning algorithm is Diverse Density [14] which has been applied to several applications including stock prediction [14], natural scene classification [15], and content-based image retrieval [20]. There are also many other practical algorithms, such as Citation-kNN [18], Relic [17], ID3-MI [8], RIPPER-MI [8], EM-DD [21], BP-MIP [23], etc. Recently, multi-instance regression with real-valued outputs has begun to be studied [1][16]. It is worth noting that multi-instance learning has also attracted the attention of the ILP community. It has been suggested that multi-instance problems could be regarded as a bias on inductive logic programming, and the multi-instance paradigm could be the key between the propositional and relational representations, being more expressive than the former, and much easier to learn than the latter [9].

In this paper, two famous multi-instance learning algorithms, i.e. Diverse Density and Citation-kNN, are analyzed, which suggests that many supervised learning algorithms can be adapted to multi-instance learning as long as they attempt to discriminate the bags instead of the instances. Then, considering that ensemble learning paradigms that train multiple learners to solve a problem can effectively improve the generalization ability in supervised learning [10], this paper proposes to build multi-instance ensembles to solve multi-instance problems. Experiments on a real-world benchmark data set show that current multi-instance learners can be significantly enhanced by ensemble learning paradigms. Moreover, it is observed that the ensemble of a specific multi-instance learner, i.e. EM-DD, exhibits the best performance up to date on the benchmark test.

The rest of this paper is organized as follows. Section 2 analyzes the Diverse Density algorithm and the Citation-kNN algorithm. Section 3 proposes to build multi-instance ensembles. Section 4 presents the experimental results. Finally, Section 5 summarizes the contributions of this paper.

2 Adapt Supervised Algorithms to Multi-instance Learning

When proposing the notion of multi-instance learning, Dietterich et al. [11] raised an open problem, i.e. designing multiple instance modifications for popular machine learning algorithms. In fact, multi-instance versions of many machine learning algorithms have been developed in recent years [8][17][18][23]. However, there is no general rule indicating how to do such a modification.

Usually, the focus of a supervised learning algorithm is to discriminate the instances, which is feasible since all training instances are labeled in supervised scenario. But in multi-instance learning, it is infeasible to build a model through discriminating training instances because none of them is labeled. Moreover, if the label of a bag is simply regarded as the label of its instances, i.e. to believe that positive bag contains only positive instances and negative bag contains only negative instances, then the learning task may be very difficult although every training instance holds a label now. This is because the positive noise may be extremely high[1], as indicated by [11]. Therefore, whether it is possible to discriminate the training instances or not is the principal difference between supervised and multi-instance learning.

In this section we claim that many supervised learning algorithms can be adapted to multi-instance learning, as long as they shift their focuses from the

---

[1] Consider that a positive bag may contain hundreds or even thousands of negative instances but only one positive instance.

discrimination on the instances to the discrimination on the bags. We illustrate that two well-known multi-instance learning algorithms[2], i.e. Diverse Density and Citation-kNN, can be derived from standard Bayesian classifier and k-nearest neighbor algorithm according to our claim. These two algorithms are chosen to analyze because Diverse Density is the most famous multi-instance learning algorithm at present, and Citation-kNN had achieved the best result on the real-world multi-instance benchmark test [18] before EM-DD, a variant of Diverse Density, was proposed.

2.1 Diverse Density

The Diverse Density algorithm [14] regards each bag as a manifold, which is composed of many instances, i.e. feature vectors. If a new bag is positive then it is believed to intersect all positive feature-manifolds without intersecting any negative feature-manifolds. Intuitively, *diverse density* at a point in the feature space is defined to be a measure of how many different positive bags have instances near that point, and how far the negative instances are from that point. Thus, the task of multi-instance learning is transformed to search for a point in the feature space with the *maximum diverse density*.

It is evident that the key of the Diverse Density algorithm lies in the formal definition of the *maximum diverse density*, which is the objective to be optimized by the algorithm. Below we show that such a definition can be achieved through modifying standard Bayesian classifier according to the rule, i.e. shifting the focus from discriminating the instances to discriminating the bags.

Given data set D and a set of class labels, i.e. $C = \{c_1, c_2, \cdots, c_t\}$, to be predicted, the posterior probability of the class can be estimated according to the Bayes rule as shown in Eq. 1.

$$\Pr(C|D) = \frac{\Pr(D|C)\Pr(C)}{\Pr(D)} \quad (1)$$

What we want is the class label with the maximum posterior probability, as indicated in Eq. 2, where *Obj* denotes the objective.

$$\begin{aligned} \text{Obj} &= \arg\max_{1 \le k \le t} \Pr(c_k|D) \\ &= \arg\max_{1 \le k \le t} \frac{\Pr(D|c_k)\Pr(c_k)}{\Pr(D)} \end{aligned} \quad (2)$$

Considering that $\Pr(D)$ is a constant which can be dropped, and $\Pr(c_k)$ can also be dropped if we assume uniform prior, then Eq. 2 can be simplified as Eq. 3.

$$\text{Obj} = \arg\max_{1 \le k \le t} \Pr(D|c_k) \quad (3)$$

---

[2] Due to the limited paper length, the analyses of more multi-instance learning algorithms are left to be presented in a longer version of this paper.

Eq. 3 is enough when the goal is to discriminate the instances. But for discriminating the bags, it is helpful to consider $D = \{B_1^+, \cdots, B_m^+, B_1^-, \cdots, B_n^-\}$ where B_i^+ denotes the i-th positive bag while B_j^- denotes the j-th negative bag. Then, Eq. 3 can be re-written as Eq. 4 assuming that the bags are conditionally independent.

$$\mathrm{Obj} = \arg\max_{1 \le k \le t} \Pr\left(\{B_1^+, \cdots, B_m^+, B_1^-, \cdots, B_n^-\} | c_k\right)$$
$$= \arg\max_{1 \le k \le t} \prod_{1 \le i \le m} \Pr\left(B_i^+ | c_k\right) \prod_{1 \le j \le n} \Pr\left(B_j^- | c_k\right) \quad (4)$$

Now apply the Bayes rule to Eq. 4, we get Eq. 5.

$$\mathrm{Obj} = \arg\max_{1 \le k \le t} \prod_{1 \le i \le m} \frac{\Pr\left(c_k | B_i^+\right) \Pr\left(B_i^+\right)}{\Pr\left(c_k\right)} \prod_{1 \le j \le n} \frac{\Pr\left(c_k | B_j^-\right) \Pr\left(B_j^-\right)}{\Pr\left(c_k\right)} \quad (5)$$

Considering that $\prod_{1 \le i \le m} \Pr\left(B_i^+\right) \prod_{1 \le j \le n} \Pr\left(B_j^-\right)$ is a constant which can be dropped, and reminding that $\Pr\left(c_k\right)$ can be dropped as that has been done in Eq. 3 because we assume uniform prior, then Eq. 5 can be simplified as Eq. 6.

$$\mathrm{Obj} = \arg\max_{1 \le k \le t} \prod_{1 \le i \le m} \Pr\left(c_k | B_i^+\right) \prod_{1 \le j \le n} \Pr\left(c_k | B_j^-\right) \quad (6)$$

Eq. 6 is the general expression for the class label with the maximum posterior probability. Concretely, the class label for a specific point x in the feature space can be expressed as Eq. 7, where $(x = c_k)$ means the label of x is c_k.

$$\mathrm{Obj}^x = \arg\max_{1 \le k \le t} \prod_{1 \le i \le m} \Pr\left(x = c_k | B_i^+\right) \prod_{1 \le j \le n} \Pr\left(x = c_k | B_j^-\right) \quad (7)$$

If we want to find out a single point in the feature space where the maximum posterior probability of a specific class label, say c_h, is the biggest, then the point can be located according to Eq. 8.

$$\hat{x} = \arg\max_x \Pr\left(\mathrm{Obj}^x = c_h\right)$$
$$= \arg\max_x \prod_{1 \le i \le m} \Pr\left(x = c_h | B_i^+\right) \prod_{1 \le j \le n} \Pr\left(x = c_h | B_j^-\right) \quad (8)$$

It is interesting that Eq. 8 is neither more nor less than the formal definition of the *maximum diverse density* which is optimized by the Diverse Density algorithm [14]!

2.2 Citation-kNN

The Citation-kNN algorithm [18] is a nearest neighbor style algorithm, which borrows the notion of citation of scientific references in the way that a bag is labeled through analyzing not only its neighboring bags but also the bags that regard the concerned bag as a neighbor.

Nevertheless, it is evident that for any nearest neighbor style algorithm, the key lies in the definition of the distance metric which is utilized to measure the distance between different objects. Below we show that the key of Citation-kNN, i.e. the definition of the *minimal Hausdorff distance*, can be achieved through modifying standard k-nearest neighbor algorithm according to the rule, i.e. shifting the focus from discriminating the instances to discriminating the bags.

In standard k-nearest neighbor algorithm, each object, or instance, is regarded as a feature vector in the feature space. For two different feature vectors, i.e. a and b, the distance between them can be written as Eq. 9. Usually $\|a - b\|$ is realized as the Euclidean distance.

$$\text{Dist}(a, b) = \|a - b\| \qquad (9)$$

When the goal is to discriminate the instances, Eq. 9 is enough to be instantiated. But if the goal is to discriminate the bags, then Eq. 9 must be extended because now we should measure the distance between different bags.

Suppose we have two different bags, i.e. $A = \{a_1, a_2, \cdots, a_m\}$ and $B = \{b_1, b_2, \cdots, b_n\}$ where a_i $(1 \leq i \leq m)$ and b_j $(1 \leq j \leq n)$ are the instances. It is obvious that they can be regarded as two feature vector sets, where each a_i $(1 \leq i \leq m)$ or b_j $(1 \leq j \leq n)$ is a feature vector in the feature space. Therefore, the problem of measuring the distance between different bags is in fact the problem of measuring the distance between different feature vector sets.

Geometrically, a feature vector set can be viewed as a group of points enclosed in a contour in the feature space. Thus, an intuitive way to measure the distance between two feature vector sets is to define their distance as the distance between their nearest feature vectors, as illustrated in Fig. 1.

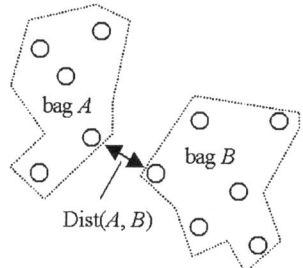

Fig. 1. An intuitive way to define the distance between bags

Formally, such a distance metric can be written as Eq. 10.

$$\begin{aligned}\text{Dist}(A, B) &= \min_{\substack{1 \leq i \leq m \\ 1 \leq j \leq n}} (\text{Dist}(a_i, b_j)) \\ &= \min_{a \in A} \min_{b \in B} \|a - b\|\end{aligned} \qquad (10)$$

It is interesting that Eq. 10 is neither more nor less than the formal definition of the *minimum Hausdorff distance*, which is employed by the Citation-kNN algorithm to measure the distance between different bags [18]!

Note that although Wang and Zucker admitted that using the *minimal Hausdorff distance* does allow k-nearest neighbor algorithm to be adapted to multi-instance learning, they also indicated that it is not sufficient [18]. This is is because the common prediction-generating scheme employed by k-nearest neighbor algorithms, i.e. *majority voting*, might be confused by false positive instances in positive bags in some cases. Therefore as mentioned before, the notion of citation and reference is introduced for obtaining the optimal performance.

However, it is evident that the utilization of the notion of citation and reference does not change the fact that the *minimal Hausdorff distance* is the key in adapting k-nearest neighbor algorithms to multi-instance learning. This is because the notion of citation and reference can also be introduced to improve the performance of k-nearest neighbor algorithms dealing with supervised learning tasks. More importantly, a k-nearest neighbor algorithm employing common distance metrics such as the Euclidean distance cannot work in multi-instance scenarios, even though it were facilitated with the notion of citation and reference; while a k-nearest neighbor algorithm employing the *minimal Hausdorff distance* can work in multi-instance scenarios, even though it does not take citation and reference into account.

In fact, through analyzing the experimental data presented in the Appendix of Wang and Zucker's paper [18], it could be found that when k is 3, the performance of the k-nearest neighbor algorithm employing the *minimal Hausdorff distance* without utilizing citation and reference is already comparable to or even better than that of some multi-instance learning algorithms such as Relic [17] and MULTINST [2] on *Musk1*, and RIPPER-MI [8] and GFS elim-count APR [11] on *Musk2*. Moreover, if the fact that the occurrence of positive bags is far smaller than that of negative bags has been considered so that a new bag is negatively labeled when ties appear in determining its label, the performance of the k-nearest neighbor algorithm employing the *minimal Hausdorff distance* without utilizing citation and reference would be 90.2% on *Musk1* and 82.4% on *Musk2*, respectively, when k is 2. It is interesting that this reaches the best performance of another multi-instance k-nearest neighbor algorithm, i.e. Bayesian-kNN, proposed by Wang and Zucker [18].

3 Multi-instance Ensemble

Ensemble learning paradigms train multiple versions of a base learner to solve a problem. Since ensembles are usually more accurate than single learners, one of the most active areas of research in supervised learning has been to study paradigms for constructing good ensembles [10].

Since we have shown in Section 2 that many supervised learning algorithms can be adapted to multi-instance learning, a consequent exciting idea is to see whether ensemble learning paradigms can be used to enhance multi-instance learners. Here we call ensemble of multi-instance learners as multi-instance ensemble.

During the past years, diverse ensemble learning algorithms have been developed, such as Bagging [6], Arc-x4 [7], AdaBoost [12], MultiBoost [19], GASEN [22], etc. In this section, we use a relatively simple algorithm, i.e. Bagging, to build the multi-instance ensembles.

Bagging employs bootstrap sampling to generate several training sets from the original training set and then trains component learners, i.e. multiple versions of the base learner, from each generated training set. The predictions of the component learners are combined via majority voting. The Bagging algorithm is shown in Table 1, where T bootstrap samples $S_1, S_2, \cdots, S_T$ are generated from the training set S and a component learner L_t is trained from each S_t, an ensemble L^* is built from $L_1, L_2, \cdots, L_T$ whose output is the class label receiving the most number of votes, x is the input feature vector, and Y is the set of class labels.

Table 1. The Bagging algorithm

Input: training set S, base learner L, trials of bootstrap sampling T
Output: ensemble L^*
Process:
    for $t = 1$ to T {
        $S_t =$ bootstrap sample from S
        $L_t = L(S_t)$
    }
    $L^*(x) = \arg\max_{y \in Y} \sum_{t:\, L_t(x)=y} 1$

We attempt to build multi-instance ensembles for four different base learners, i.e. Iterated-discrim APR [11], Diverse Density [14], Citation-kNN [18], and EM-DD [21]. The reason for choosing Diverse Density and Citation-kNN was discussed in Section 2. Here we briefly explain why the other two algorithms are chosen.

Iterated-discrim APR is the best Axis-Parallel Rectangle (abbreviated as APR) algorithm proposed by Dietterich et al. [11], which attempts to search for appropriate axis-parallel rectangles constructed by the conjunction of the features. Dietterich et al. [11] indicated that since the APR algorithms had been optimized to the *Musk* data, i.e. the only real-world multi-instance benchmark data until now, the performance of Iterated-discrim APR might be the upper bound of this benchmark test.

EM-DD [21] is a recent development in multi-instance learning, which combines the EM and Diverse Density algorithms. It converts the multi-instance problem to a single-instance setting by using EM to estimate the instance which is responsible for the label of the bag. The best performance on the real-world multi-instance benchmark test until now, i.e. predictive error rate as small as 3.2% on *Musk1* and 4.0% on *Musk2*, are achieved by this algorithm [21]. Note that the performance of EM-DD has already exceeded the upper bound of this benchmark test anticipated by Dietterich et al. [11].

4 Experiments

The experiments are performed on the *Musk* data, which is the only real-world benchmark test data for multi-instance learners at present.

The *Musk* data were generated in Dietterich et al.'s research on drug activity prediction [11]. Here each molecule is regarded as a bag, and its alternative low-energy shapes are regarded as the instances in the bag. A positive bag corresponds to a molecule qualified to make a certain drug, that is, at least one of its low-energy shapes could tightly bind to the target area of some larger protein molecules such as enzymes and cell-surface receptors. A negative bag corresponds to a molecule not qualified to make a certain drug, that is, none of its low-energy shapes could tightly bind to the target area.

In order to represent the shapes, a molecule is placed in a standard position and orientation and then a set of 162 rays emanating from the origin is constructed so that the molecular surface is sampled approximately uniformly. There are also four features that represented the position of an oxygen atom on the molecular surface. Therefore each instance in the bags is represented by 166 continuous attributes.

There are two data sets, i.e. *Musk1* and *Musk2*, both of which are publicly available from the UCI Machine Learning Repository [4]. *Musk1* contains 47 positive bags and 45 negative bags, and the number of instances contained in each bag ranges from 2 to 40. *Musk2* contains 39 positive bags and 63 negative bags, and the number of instances contained in each bag ranges from 1 to 1,044. Detailed information on the *Musk* data is tabulated in Table 2.

Table 2. The *Musk* data (72 molecules are shared in both data sets)

Data set	Dim.	Bags			Instances	Instances per bag		
		Total	Musk	Non-musk		Min	Max	Ave.
Musk1	166	92	47	45	476	2	40	5.17
Musk2	166	102	39	63	6,598	1	1,044	64.69

Ten-fold cross validation is performed on each *Musk* data set. In each fold, Bagging is employed to build an ensemble for each of the four base multi-instance learners, i.e. Iterated-discrim APR, Diverse Density, Citation-kNN, and EM-DD. Each ensemble comprises five versions of the base learner. The predictive error rates of the ensembles are shown in Table 3. For comparison, the best results of the single multi-instance learners reported in the literatures [11][14][18][21] are also included in Table 3.

Table 3. Predictive error rates (%) of single or ensembled multi-instance learners

Algorithm	Musk1		Musk2	
	Single	Ensemble	Single	Ensemble
Iterated-discrim APR	7.6	7.2	10.8	6.9
Diverse Density	11.1	8.2	17.5	11.0
Citation-kNN	7.6	5.2	13.7	12.9
EM-DD	3.2	3.1	4.0	3.0

Table 3 shows that Bagging can significantly improve the generalization ability of all the investigated multi-instance learners[3]. It is impressive that even the strongest multi-instance learner, i.e. EM-DD, can be enhanced by such a relatively simple ensemble learning algorithm. In fact, the EM-DD ensemble achieves the best performance up to date on both the *Musk* data sets, i.e. predictive error rate 3.1% on *Musk1* and 3.0% on *Musk2*.

Since the process of building ensemble of multi-instance learners has nothing being geared to any specific data, we believe that such a paradigm can be applied to any multi-instance problems. It is also reasonable to anticipate that such a paradigm may return more profit on difficult problems where no single multi-instance learners works very well. Moreover, the experiments reported in this section also suggest ensemble learning paradigms be investigated in more scenarios, not to be limited in supervised learning.

5 Conclusion

When formalizing the notion of multi-instance learning, Dietterich et al. [11] raised an open problem, i.e. designing multiple instance modifications for popular machine learning algorithms. Although multi-instance versions of many machine learning algorithms have been developed in recent years, there is no general rule indicating how to do such a modification until now.

This paper claims that many supervised learning algorithms can be adapted to multi-instance learning through shifting their focuses from the discrimination on instances to the discrimination on bags. Although the concrete shift process is dependent on the working mechanism of the supervised learning algorithm concerned, the rule for adaptation is feasible and general enough to be applied to diverse supervised learning algorithms. For example, this paper illustrates that how two famous multi-instance algorithms, i.e. Diverse Density and Citation-*k*NN, can be derived from standard Bayesian classifier and *k*-nearest neighbor algorithm, respectively, through shifting their focuses.

Designing multi-instance learning algorithms with strong generalization ability is always an important issue in this area. Considering that many supervised

---

[3] The results of the single multi-instance learners in Table 3 are the best results reported by their authors [11][14][18][21]. In our implementation, the performance of the single learners are slightly worse than these best results.

learning algorithms can be adapted to multi-instance learning, and ensemble learning paradigms can effectively enhance supervised learners, this paper claims to build multi-instance ensembles to solve multi-instance problems.

Experiments show that all the investigated multi-instance learners can be enhanced by a relatively simple ensemble learning algorithm, and the best result up to date on the real-world benchmark test of multi-instance learners is achieved by EM-DD ensemble. The experiments not only support our claim that building multi-instance ensembles is a good choice for solving multi-instance problems, but also suggest ensemble learning paradigms be investigated in more scenarios, not to be limited in supervised learning.

Acknowledgement

The comments and suggestions from the anonymous reviewers greatly improved this paper. This work was supported by the National Natural Science Foundation of China under the Grant No. 60105004, the Natural Science Foundation of Jiangsu Province under the Grant No. BK2001406, and the National 973 Fundamental Research Program of China under the Grant No. 2002CB312002.

References

1. Amar, R.A., Dooly, D.R., Goldman, S.A., Zhang, Q.: Multiple-instance learning of real-valued data. In: Proceedings of the 18th International Conference on Machine Learning, Williamstown, MA (2001) 3–10
2. Auer, P.: On learning from multi-instance examples: empirical evaluation of a theoretical approach. In: Proceedings of the 14th International Conference on Machine Learning, Nashville, TN (1997) 21–29
3. Auer, P., Long, P.M., Srinivasan, A.: Approximating hyper-rectangles: learning and pseudo-random sets. Journal of Computer and System Sciences **57** (1998) 376–388
4. Blake, C., Keogh, E., Merz, C.J.: UCI repository of machine learning databases [http://www.ics.uci.edu/~mlearn/MLRepository.html], Department of Information and Computer Science, University of California, Irvine, CA (1998)
5. Blum, A., Kalai, A.: A note on learning from multiple-instance examples. Machine Learning **30** (1998) 23–29
6. Breiman, L.: Bagging predictors. Machine Learning **24** (1996) 123–140
7. Breiman, L.: Bias, variance, and arcing classifiers. Technical Report 460, Statistics Department, University of California, Berkeley, CA (1996)
8. Chevaleyre, Y., Zucker, J.-D.: Solving multiple-instance and multiple-part learning problems with decision trees and rule sets. Application to the mutagenesis problem. In: Stroulia, E., Matwin, S. (eds.): Lecture Notes in Artificial Intelligence, Vol. 2056. Springer, Berlin (2001) 204–214
9. De Raedt, L.: Attribute-value learning versus inductive logic programming: the missing links. In: Page, D. (ed.): Lecture Notes in Artificial Intelligence, Vol. 1446. Springer, Berlin (1998) 1–8
10. Dietterich, T.G.: Machine learning research: four current directions. AI Magazine **18** (1997) 97–136

11. Dietterich, T.G., Lathrop, R.H., Lozano-Pérez, T.: Solving the multiple-instance problem with axis-parallel rectangles. Artificial Intelligence **89** (1997) 31–71
12. Freund, Y., Schapire, R.E.: A decision-theoretic generalization of on-line learning and an application to boosting. In: Proceedings of the 2nd European Conference on Computational Learning Theory, Barcelona, Spain (1995) 23–37
13. Long, P.M., Tan, L.: PAC learning axis-aligned rectangles with respect to product distributions from multiple-instance examples. Machine Learning **30** (1998) 7–21
14. Maron, O., Lozano-Pŕez, T.: A framework for multiple-instance learning. In: Jordan, M.I., Kearns, M.J., Solla, S.A. (eds.): Advances in Neural Information Processing Systems, Vol. 10. MIT Press, Cambridge, MA (1998) 570–576
15. Maron, O., Rantan, A.L.: Multiple-instance learning for natural scene classification. In: Proceedings of the 15th International Conference on Machine Learning, Williamstown, MA (2001) 341–349
16. Ray, S., Page, D.: Multiple instance regression. In: Proceedings of the 18th International Conference on Machine Learning, Williamstown, MA (2001) 425–432
17. Ruffo, G.: Learning single and multiple instance decision trees for computer security applications. PhD dissertation, Department of Computer Science, University of Turin, Torino, Italy (2000)
18. Wang, J., Zucker, J.-D.: Solving the multiple-instance problem: a lazy learning approach. In: Proceedings of the 17th International Conference on Machine Learning, San Francisco, CA (2000) 1119–1125
19. Webb, G.I.: MultiBoosting: a technique for combining Boosting and Wagging. Machine Learning **40** (2000) 159–196
20. Yang, C., Lozano-Pérez, T.: Image database retrieval with multiple-instance learning techniques. In: Proceedings of the 16th International Conference on Data Engineering, San Diego, CA (2000) 233–243
21. Zhang, Q., Goldman, S.A.: EM-DD: an improved multi-instance learning technique. In: Dietterich, T.G., Becker, S., Ghahramani, Z. (eds.): Advances in Neural Information Processing Systems, Vol. 14. MIT Press, Cambridge, MA (2002) 1073–1080
22. Zhou, Z.-H., Wu, J., Tang, W.: Ensembling neural networks: many could be better than all. Artificial Intelligence **137** (2002) 239–263
23. Zhou, Z.-H., Zhang, M.-L.: Neural networks for multi-instance learning. In: Proceedings of the International Conference on Intelligent Information Technology, Beijing, China (2002) 455–459

Author Index

Adriaans, Pieter   1

Bernard, Marc   169
Bohte, Sander M.   181
Bratko, Ivan   385
Brefeld, Ulf   23
Breiman, Leo   9
Buratto, Luciano   373

Campos, Pedro   35
Carbonell, Jaime   277
Chen, Chien Chin   47
Chen, Meng Chang   47
Chen, Yao-Tsung   47
Coste, François   60
Crook, Paul A.   72

Daelemans, Walter   84
d'Alché-Buc, Florence   265

Elkan, Charles   205
Elomaa, Tapio   193
Ernst, Damien   96

Faloutsos, Christos   10
Ferri, César   108, 121
Fischer, Jörg   133
Flach, Peter A.   121
Frank, Eibe   241, 468
Fredouille, Daniel   60
Fürnkranz, Johannes   145

Garcia, Pascal   157
Garg, Ashutosh   301
Geibel, Peter   23
Geurts, Pierre   96

Habrard, Amaury   169
Hall, Mark   241
Hayes, Gillian   72
Hernández-Orallo, José   108, 121
Heytens, Dries   421
Hoen, Pieter Jan 't   181

Hoste, Véronique   84
Huang, Thomas S.   301
Hüllermeier, Eyke   145

Jin, Rong   277

Kääriäinen, Matti   193
Kaski, Samuel   432
Kauchak, David   205
Kersting, Kristian   133
Khoussainov, Rinat   217
Koriche, Frédéric   229
Kushmerick, Nicholas   217

Landwehr, Niels   241
Langlois, Thibault   35
Lee, Jianguo   253
Lesot, Marie-Jeanne   265
Levy, Roger   397
Liu, Yan   277

Manderick, Bernard   421
Manning, Christopher D.   397, 409
Meulder, Fien De   84
Mitchell, Mark   409
Moriyama, Koichi   289

Naudts, Bart   84
Nowe, Ann   421
Numao, Masayuki   289

Peltonen, Jaakko   432
Pfahringer, Bernhard   468
Precup, Doina   313

Quinqueton, Joël   229

Rajaram, Shyamsundar   301
Ratitch, Bohdana   313
Rish, Irina   444
Robnik-Šikonja, Marko   325
Roma, Norbert   361
Rubin, Donald B.   16

Salido, Miguel Angel 108
Santana, Roberto 337
Sebban, Marc 169, 349
Shanahan, James G. 361
Sima'an, Khalil 373
Siolas, Georges 265
Šuc, Dorian 385
Suchier, Henri-Maxime 349
Sun, Yeali 47

Thompson, Cynthia A. 397
Toutanova, Kristina 409
Tuyls, Karl 421

Venna, Jarkko 432
Vilalta, Ricardo 444

Vinot, Romain 456

Wang, Jingdong 253
Wang, Shijun 480
Wehenkel, Louis 96
Weidmann, Nils 468
Wysotzki, Fritz 23

Yvon, François 456

Zhang, Changshui 253, 480
Zhang, Min-Ling 492
Zhang, Yungang 480
Zhou, Xiang Sean 301
Zhou, Zhi-Hua 492

Lecture Notes in Artificial Intelligence (LNAI)

Vol. 2636: E. Alonso, D, Kudenko, D. Kazakov (Eds.), Adaptive Agents and Multi-Agent Systems. XIV, 323 pages. 2003.

Vol. 2637: K.-Y. Whang, J. Jeon, K. Shim, J. Srivastava (Eds.), Advances in Knowledge Discovery and Data Mining. Proceedings, 2003. XVIII, 610 pages. 2003.

Vol. 2639: G. Wang, Q. Liu, Y. Yao, A. Skowron (Eds.), Rough Sets, Fuzzy Sets, Data Mining, and Granular Computing. Proceedings, 2003. XVII, 741 pages. 2003.

Vol. 2645: M.A. Wimmer (Ed.), Knowledge Management in Electronic Government. Proceedings, 2003. XI, 320 pages. 2003.

Vol. 2650: M.-P. Huget (Ed.), Communication in Multiagent Systems. VIII, 323 pages. 2003.

Vol. 2654: U. Schmid, Inductive Synthesis of Functional Programs. XXII, 398 pages. 2003.

Vol. 2662: H.-K. Kahng (Ed.), Information Networking. Proceedings, 2003. XVII, 1032 pages. 2003.

Vol. 2663: E. Menasalvas, J. Segovia, P.S. Szczepaniak (Eds.), Advances in Web Intelligence. Proceedings, 2003. XII, 350 pages. 2003.

Vol. 2671: Y. Xiang, B. Chaib-draa (Eds.), Advances in Artificial Intelligence. Proceedings, 2003. XIV, 642 pages. 2003.

Vol. 2680: P. Blackburn, C. Ghidini, R.M. Turner, F. Giunchiglia (Eds.), Modeling and Using Context. Proceedings, 2003. XII, 525 pages. 2003.

Vol. 2684: M.V. Butz, O. Sigaud, P. Gérard (Eds.), Anticipatory Behavior in Adaptive Learning Systems. X, 303 pages. 2003.

Vol. 2685: C. Freksa, W. Brauer, C. Habel, K.F. Wender (Eds.), Spatial Cognition III. X, 415 pages. 2003.

Vol. 2689: K.D. Ashley, D.G. Bridge (Eds.), Case-Based Reasoning Research and Development. Proceedings, 2003. XV, 734 pages. 2003.

Vol. 2691: V. Mařík, J. Müller, M. Pěchouček (Eds.), Multi-Agent Systems and Applications III. Proceedings, 2003. XIV, 660 pages. 2003.

Vol. 2699: M.G. Hinchey, J.L. Rash, W.F. Truszkowski, C. Rouff, D. Gordon-Spears (Eds.), Formal Approaches to Agent-Based Systems. Proceedings, 2002. IX, 297 pages. 2003.

Vol. 2700: M.T. Pazienza (Ed.), Information Extraction in the Web Era. XIII, 163 pages. 2003.

Vol. 2702: P. Brusilovsky, A. Corbett, F. de Rosis (Eds.), User Modeling 2003. Proceedings, 2003. XIV, 436 pages. 2003.

Vol. 2705: S. Renals, G. Grefenstette (Eds.), Text- and Speech-Triggered Information Access. Proceedings, 2000. VII, 197 pages. 2003.

Vol. 2711: T.D. Nielsen, N.L. Zhang (Eds.), Symbolic and Quantitative Approaches to Reasoning with Uncertainty. Proceedings, 2003. XII, 608 pages. 2003.

Vol. 2715: T. Bilgiç, B. De Baets, O. Kaynak (Eds.), Fuzzy Sets and Systems – IFSA 2003. Proceedings, 2003. XV, 735 pages. 2003.

Vol. 2718: P. W. H. Chung, C. Hinde, M. Ali (Eds.), Developments in Applied Artificial Intelligence. Proceedings, 2003. XIV, 817 pages. 2003.

Vol. 2721: N.J. Mamede, J. Baptista, I. Trancoso, M. das Graças Volpe Nunes (Eds.), Computational Processing of the Portuguese Language. Proceedings, 2003. XIV, 268 pages. 2003.

Vol. 2734: P. Perner, A. Rosenfeld (Eds.), Machine Learning and Data Mining in Pattern Recognition. Proceedings, 2003. XII, 440 pages. 2003.

Vol. 2741: F. Baader (Ed.), Automated Deduction – CADE-19. Proceedings, 2003. XII, 503 pages. 2003.

Vol. 2744: V. Mařík, D. McFarlane, P. Valckenaers (Eds.), Holonic and Multi-Agent Systems for Manufacturing. Proceedings, 2003. XI, 322 pages. 2003.

Vol. 2746: A. de Moor, W. Lex, B. Ganter (Eds.), Conceptual Structures for Knowledge Creation and Communication. Proceedings, 2003. XI, 405 pages. 2003.

Vol. 2752: G.A. Kaminka, P.U. Lima, R. Rojas (Eds.), RoboCup 2002: Robot Soccer World Cup VI. XVI, 498 pages. 2003.

Vol. 2773: V. Palade, R.J. Howlett, L. Jain (Eds.), Knowledge-Based Intelligent Information and Engineering Systems. Proceedings, Part I, 2003. LI, 1473 pages. 2003.

Vol. 2774: V. Palade, R.J. Howlett, L. Jain (Eds.), Knowledge-Based Intelligent Information and Engineering Systems. Proceedings, Part II, 2003. LI, 1443 pages. 2003.

Vol. 2777: B. Schölkopf, M.K. Warmuth (Eds.), Learning Theory and Kernel Machines. Proceedings, 2003. XIV, 746 pages. 2003.

Vol. 2782: M. Klusch, A. Omicini, S. Ossowski, H. Laamanen (Eds.), Cooperative Information Agents VII. Proceedings, 2003. XI, 345 pages. 2003.

Vol. 2792: T. Rist, R. Aylett, D. Ballin, J. Rickel (Eds.), Intelligent Virtual Agents. Proceedings, 2003. XV, 364 pages. 2003.

Vol. 2796: M. Cialdea Mayer, F. Pirri (Eds.), Automated Reasoning with Analytic Tableaux and Related Methods. Proceedings, 2003. X, 271 pages. 2003.

Vol. 2801: W. Banzhaf, T. Christaller, P. Dittrich, J.T. Kim, J. Ziegler (Eds.), Advances in Artificial Life. Proceedings, 2003. XVI, 905 pages. 2003.

Vol. 2807: V. Matoušek, P. Mautner (Eds.), Text, Speech and Dialogue. Proceedings, 2003. XIII, 426 pages. 2003.

Vol. 2821: A. Günter, R. Kruse, B. Neumann (Eds.), KI 2003: Advances in Artificial Intelligence. Proceedings, 2003. XII, 662 pages. 2003.

Vol. 2837: N. Lavrač, D. Gamberger, H. Blockeel, L. Todorovski (Eds.), Machine Learning: ECML 2003. Proceedings, 2003. XVI. 504 pages. 2003.

Vol. 2838: N. Lavrač, D. Gamberger, L. Todorovski, H. Blockeel (Eds.), Knowledge Discovery in Databases: PKDD 2003. Proceedings, 2003. XVI. 508 pages. 2003.

Lecture Notes in Computer Science

Vol. 2769: T. Koch, I. T. Sølvberg (Eds.), Research and Advanced Technology for Digital Libraries. Proceedings, 2003. XV, 536 pages. 2003.

Vol. 2773: V. Palade, R.J. Howlett, L. Jain (Eds.), Knowledge-Based Intelligent Information and Engineering Systems. Proceedings, Part I, 2003. LI, 1473 pages. 2003. (Subseries LNAI).

Vol. 2774: V. Palade, R.J. Howlett, L. Jain (Eds.), Knowledge-Based Intelligent Information and Engineering Systems. Proceedings, Part II, 2003. LI, 1443 pages. 2003. (Subseries LNAI).

Vol. 2776: V. Gorodetsky, L. Popyack, V. Skormin (Eds.), Computer Network Security. Proceedings, 2003. XIV, 470 pages. 2003.

Vol. 2777: B. Schölkopf, M.K. Warmuth (Eds.), Learning Theory and Kernel Machines. Proceedings, 2003. XIV, 746 pages. 2003. (Subseries LNAI).

Vol. 2778: P.Y.K. Cheung, G.A. Constantinides, J.T. de Sousa (Eds.), Field-Programmable Logic and Applications. Proceedings, 2003. XXVI, 1179 pages. 2003.

Vol. 2779: C.D. Walter, Ç.K. Koç, C. Paar (Eds.), Cryptographic Hardware and Embedded Systems – CHES 2003. Proceedings, 2003. XIII, 441 pages. 2003.

Vol. 2781: B. Michaelis, G. Krell (Eds.), Pattern Recognition. Proceedings, 2003. XVII, 621 pages. 2003.

Vol. 2782: M. Klusch, A. Omicini, S. Ossowski, H. Laamanen (Eds.), Cooperative Information Agents VII. Proceedings, 2003. XI, 345 pages. 2003. (Subseries LNAI).

Vol. 2783: W. Zhou, P. Nicholson, B. Corbitt, J. Fong (Eds.), Advances in Web-Based Learning – ICWL 2003. Proceedings, 2003. XV, 552 pages. 2003.

Vol. 2786: F. Oquendo (Ed.), Software Process Technology. Proceedings, 2003. X, 173 pages. 2003.

Vol. 2787: J. Timmis, P. Bentley, E. Hart (Eds.), Artificial Immune Systems. Proceedings, 2003. XI, 299 pages. 2003.

Vol. 2789: L. Böszörményi, P. Schojer (Eds.), Modular Programming Languages. Proceedings, 2003. XIII, 271 pages. 2003.

Vol. 2790: H. Kosch, L. Böszörményi, H. Hellwagner (Eds.), Euro-Par 2003 Parallel Processing. Proceedings, 2003. XXXV, 1320 pages. 2003.

Vol. 2792: T. Rist, R. Aylett, D. Ballin, J. Rickel (Eds.), Intelligent Virtual Agents. Proceedings, 2003. XV, 364 pages. 2003. (Subseries LNAI).

Vol. 2794: P. Kemper, W. H. Sanders (Eds.), Computer Performance Evaluation. Proceedings, 2003. X, 309 pages. 2003.

Vol. 2795: L. Chittaro (Ed.), Human-Computer Interaction with Mobile Devices and Services. Proceedings, 2003. XV, 494 pages. 2003.

Vol. 2796: M. Cialdea Mayer, F. Pirri (Eds.), Automated Reasoning with Analytic Tableaux and Related Methods. Proceedings, 2003. X, 271 pages. 2003. (Subseries LNAI).

Vol. 2798: L. Kalinichenko, R. Manthey, B. Thalheim, U. Wloka (Eds.), Advances in Databases and Information Systems. Proceedings, 2003. XIII, 431 pages. 2003.

Vol. 2799: J.J. Chico, E. Macii (Eds.), Integrated Circuit and System Design. Proceedings, 2003. XVII, 631 pages. 2003.

Vol. 2801: W. Banzhaf, T. Christaller, P. Dittrich, J.T. Kim, J. Ziegler (Eds.), Advances in Artificial Life. Proceedings, 2003. XVI, 905 pages. 2003. (Subseries LNAI).

Vol. 2803: M. Baaz, J.A. Makowsky (Eds.), Computer Science Logic. Proceedings, 2003. XII, 589 pages. 2003.

Vol. 2805: K. Araki, S. Gnesi, D. Mandrioli (Eds.), FME 2003: Formal Methods. Proceedings, 2003. XVII, 942 pages. 2003.

Vol. 2807: V. Matoušek, P. Mautner (Eds.), Text, Speech and Dialogue. Proceedings, 2003. XIII, 426 pages. 2003. (Subseries LNAI).

Vol. 2810: M.R. Berthold, H.-J. Lenz, E. Bradley, R. Kruse, C. Borgelt (Eds.), Advances in Intelligent Data Analysis V. Proceedings, 2003. XV, 624 pages. 2003.

Vol. 2812: G. Benson, R. Page (Eds.), Algorithms in Bioinformatics. Proceedings, 2003. X, 528 pages. 2003. (Subseries LNBI).

Vol. 2815: Y. Lindell, Composition of Secure Multi-Party Protocols. XVI, 192 pages. 2003.

Vol. 2817: D. Konstantas, M. Leonard, Y. Pigneur, S. Patel (Eds.), Object-Oriented Information Systems. Proceedings, 2003. XII, 426 pages. 2003.

Vol. 2818: H. Blanken, T. Grabs, H.-J. Schek, R. Schenkel, G. Weikum (Eds.), Intelligent Search on XML Data. XVII, 319 pages. 2003.

Vol. 2819: B. Benatallah, M.-C. Shan (Eds.), Technologies for E-Services. Proceedings, 2003. X, 203 pages. 2003.

Vol. 2820: G. Vigna, E. Jonsson, C. Kruegel (Eds.), Recent Advances in Intrusion Detection. Proceedings, 2003. X, 239 pages. 2003.

Vol. 2821: A. Günter, R. Kruse, B. Neumann (Eds.), KI 2003: Advances in Artificial Intelligence. Proceedings, 2003. XII, 662 pages. 2003. (Subseries LNAI).

Vol. 2832: G. Di Battista, U. Zwick (Eds.), Algorithms – ESA 2003. Proceedings, 2003. XIV, 790 pages. 2003.

Vol. 2834: X. Zhou, S. Jähnichen, M. Xu, J. Cao (Eds.), Advanced Parallel Processing Technologies. Proceedings, 2003. XIV, 679 pages. 2003.

Vol. 2837: N. Lavrač, D. Gamberger, H. Blockeel, L. Todorovski (Eds.), Machine Learning: ECML 2003. Proceedings, 2003. XVI, 504 pages. 2003. (Subseries LNAI).

Vol. 2838: N. Lavrač, D. Gamberger, L. Todorovski, H. Blockeel (Eds.), Knowledge Discovery in Databases: PKDD 2003. Proceedings, 2003. XVI, 508 pages. 2003. (Subseries LNAI).

Vol. 2839: A. Marshall, N. Agoulmine (Eds.), Management of Multimedia Networks and Services. Proceedings, 2003. XIV, 532 pages. 2003.